The Routledge Handbook of Heterodox Economics

T0384021

The Routledge Handbook of Heterodox Economics presents a comprehensive overview of the latest work on economic theory and policy from a 'pluralistic' heterodox perspective.

Contributions throughout the *Handbook* explore different theoretical perspectives including: Marxian–radical political economics; Post Keynesian–Sraffian economics; institutionalist–evolutionary economics; feminist economics; social economics; *Régulation* theory; the Social Structure of Accumulation approach; and ecological economics. They explain the structural properties and dynamics of capitalism, as well as propose economic and social policies for the benefit of the majority of the population. This book aims, firstly, to provide realistic and coherent theoretical frameworks to understand the capitalist economy in a constructive and forward-looking manner. Secondly, it delineates the future directions, as well as the current state, of heterodox economics, and then provides both 'heat and light' on controversial issues, drawing out the commonalities and differences among different heterodox economic approaches. The volume also envisions transformative economic and social policies for the majority of the population and explains why economics is, and should be treated as, a social science.

This *Handbook* will be of compelling interest to those, including students, who wish to learn about alternative economic theories and policies that are rarely found in conventional economics textbooks or discussed in the mainstream media, and to critical economists and other social scientists who are concerned with analyzing pressing socio-economic issues.

Tae-Hee Jo is Associate Professor in the Economics and Finance Department at The State University of New York–Buffalo State, USA, and a former Editor of the *Heterodox Economics Newsletter* (2009–13). He has been working on heterodox microeconomic theory from institutionalist, Marxian, and Post Keynesian perspectives.

Lynne Chester is Associate Professor in the University of Sydney's Department of Political Economy, Australia. She is recognized as a leading Australian scholar in the empirical application of *Régulation* theory. Her research focuses on a range of energy issues (affordability, security, markets, price formation, the environment) and the policy responses of capitalist economies through different institutional forms.

Carlo D'Ippoliti is Associate Professor of Economics at Sapienza University of Rome, Italy. He is the editor of *PSL Quarterly Review* and of *Moneta e Credito*, and his research focuses on the history of economic thought, feminist economics, and European political economy.

The Routledge Handbook of Heterodox Economics

Theorizing, Analyzing, and Transforming Capitalism

Edited by Tae-Hee Jo, Lynne Chester,
and Carlo D'Ippoliti

Routledge
Taylor & Francis Group

LONDON AND NEW YORK

First published 2018 by Routledge

2 Park Square, Milton Park, Abingdon, Oxfordshire OX14 4RN
52 Vanderbilt Avenue, New York, NY 10017

Routledge is an imprint of the Taylor & Francis Group, an informa business

First issued in paperback 2019

British Library Cataloguing-in-Publication Data
A catalogue record for this book is available from the British Library

Library of Congress Cataloging-in-Publication Data
Names: Jo, Tae-Hee, 1973– editor. | Chester, Lynne, editor. | D'Ippoliti, Carlo, editor.
Title: The Routledge handbook of heterodox economics / edited by Tae-Hee Jo,
    Lynne Chester, and Carlo D'Ippoliti.
Description: Abingdon, Oxon ; New York, NY : Routledge, 2017. |
    Includes bibliographical references and index.
Identifiers: LCCN 2017006638 | ISBN 9781138899940 (hardback) |
    ISBN 9781315707587 (ebook)
Subjects: LCSH: Economics. | Schools of economics.
Classification: LCC HB75 .R67476 2017 | DDC 330.15—dc23
LC record available at https://lccn.loc.gov/2017006638

ISBN: 978-1-138-89994-0 (hbk)
ISBN: 978-0-367-35682-8 (pbk)

Typeset in Bembo
by Apex CoVantage, LLC

Contents

Contents

Contents

Figures

Figures

Tables

Contributors

Siobhan Austen is Associate Professor in the School of Economics and Finance, and Director of Women in Social and Economic Research (WiSER) at Curtin University, Perth, Western Australia. She works on feminist and institutional economics, with a particular focus on the circumstances and experiences of women in labor markets.

Tuna Baskoy is Associate Professor in the Department of Politics and Public Administration at Ryerson University, Toronto, Canada. He is the author of *The Political Economy of European Union Competition Policy: A Case Study of the Telecommunications Industry* (Routledge, 2008) and director of the interdisciplinary PhD Program in Policy Studies at Ryerson University. He has been working on market governance and competition/antitrust policy in information and communication technology industries, and hazelnut market from institutionalist and Post Keynesian perspectives.

Jordan Brennan received his doctorate in political science from York University in Toronto, Canada. He works as an economist for Unifor, Canada's largest labor union in the private sector. In 2016–17, Jordan will be a visiting scholar at Harvard Law School. More information is available on his website: www.jordanbrennan.org.

Gabriel Brondino is Lecturer of Political Economy at The School of Social and Juridical Sciences of National University of Litoral, Argentina. He has been working on international trade, economic growth, and structural change from classical and Keynesian perspectives.

Scott Carter is Associate Professor of Economics at The University of Tulsa in Oklahoma, USA. His research interests concern comparative heterodox theories of value, distribution, and growth, and Sraffian and Marxian political economy, with emphasis on the unpublished papers of Piero Sraffa.

Lynne Chester is Associate Professor in the Department of Political Economy at The University of Sydney, Australia. Her research focuses on the application of *Régulation* theory to a range of energy issues (affordability, security, markets, price formation, the environment), and the policy responses of capitalist economies through different institutional forms.

Marcella Corsi is Full Professor of Economics at Sapienza University of Rome, Italy. Her research mainly focuses on issues related to social inclusion, social protection, and income distribution (often in a gender perspective). In these fields of study, she is the author of several articles published in English and Italian, and she has been one of the scientific coordinators of the European Network of Gender Equality Experts (www.enege.eu).

Andrew Cumbers is Professor of Regional Political Economy in the Adam Smith Business School at the University of Glasgow, Scotland. He is a Managing Editor of *Urban Studies* since 2005 and is author of *Reclaiming Public Ownership: Making Space for Economic Democracy* (Zed Books). He is currently working with Robert McMaster, Susan Cabaço, and Michael White on developing an index of economic democracy.

Carlo D'Ippoliti is Associate Professor of Economics at Sapienza University of Rome, Italy. He is the editor of *PSL Quarterly Review* and of *Moneta e Credito*. His research focuses on the history of economic thought, feminist economics, and European political economy.

Petra Dünhaupt is a research associate and a member of the Institute for International Political Economy (IPE) at the Berlin School of Economics and Law, Germany. Her research focuses on financialization and income distribution.

Anders Ekeland is senior advisor at Statistics Norway, member of the Management Committee of the Association for Heterodox Economics since 2011. He has been working on economic theory, innovation, and environmental policies from Marxian and Schumpeterian perspectives.

John Embery works at Leeds Beckett University, UK. He lectures on political economy and behavioral economics. He is currently working on a PhD in social economics. His research interests include heterodox approaches to shared agency, social networks, and time preference.

Víctor Ramiro Fernández is Full Professor of State Theory and Economic Geography at the School of Humanities and Sciences of the National University of Litoral, Argentina. He is Director of the Institute of Humanities and Social Sciences of Litoral (CONICET-UNL). His main work focuses on the state and its relation to development from a multidisciplinary perspective (historical materialism, critical geography, Latin American structuralism).

Claudius Gräbner is a Post-Doc researcher at the Institute for the Comprehensive Analysis of the Economy (ICAE) at Johannes Kepler University Linz, Austria. He obtained his PhD in economics at the Institute for Institutional and Innovation Economics at the University of Bremen, Germany. His research focuses on international and development economics, agent-based computational modeling, network analysis, and economic methodology from a complexity and evolutionary-institutional perspective.

Giulio Guarini is Assistant Professor of Economics at Tuscia University of Viterbo, Italy. He has been working on economic development, social inclusion, innovation, and sustainability from Post Keynesian and Capability Approach perspectives.

Eckhard Hein is Professor of Economics at the Berlin School of Economics and Law, Germany, a Co-Director of the Institute for International Political Economy (IPE), and managing co-editor of the *European Journal of Economics and Economic Policies: Intervention*. His research focuses on money, financial systems, distribution and growth, European economic policies, and Post Keynesian macroeconomics.

Contributors

John F. Henry is currently Senior Scholar at Levy Economics Institute, USA. Formerly, he served as Research Professor, University of Missouri-Kansas City, and is Professor Emeritus, California State University, Sacramento. His work centers on Marx, Veblen, institutionalism, and Post Keynesian theory. Henry is the 2017 Veblen-Commons Award recipient from the Association for Evolutionary Economics.

Elizabeth Hill is Senior Lecturer in the Department of Political Economy at The University of Sydney, Australia. Hill's research focuses on gender, work, and care in emerging and developed economies. She has published on women's work and collective action in the Indian informal economy, and work and care policy in Australia.

Tae-Hee Jo is Associate Professor in the Economics and Finance Department at The State University of New York–Buffalo State, USA and a former Editor of the *Heterodox Economics Newsletter* (2009–13). He has been working on heterodox microeconomic theory from institutionalist, Marxian, and Post Keynesian perspectives.

Jakob Kapeller is a philosopher and economist at Johannes Kepler University Linz, Austria. He is the Head of Department at the Institute for Comprehensive Analysis of the Economy (www.jku.at/icae) and serves as Editor of the *Heterodox Economics Newsletter*.

Anna Klimina is Associate Professor in the Economics Department at St. Thomas More College, University of Saskatchewan, Canada. Her primary research interests include economics of post-Soviet transition, seen through institutionalist and Post Keynesian perspectives, and history of Russian economic thought.

Agnès Labrousse is Associate Professor in Economics at the University of Picardie, France, and Associate Editor of *The Régulation Review*. She has been working on Eastern Germany, the pharmaceutical industry, and development issues from an institutionalist perspective.

Yan Liang is Associate Professor of Economics at Willamette University, USA. She is on the editorial board of *Journal of Economic Issues* and *The Chinese Economy*. She has been working on financial macroeconomics, economic development, and international finance from the Post Keynesian and institutionalist perspectives.

John Marangos is a Professor of Comparative Economic Systems at the Department of Balkan, Slavic and Oriental Studies at the University of Macedonia in Greece and former editor of the *Forum of Social Economics* (2006–11). Focal points of his research are the transition process, international development, and innovative methodologies for teaching economics.

John Marsh is a Senior Lecturer in Economics at Nottingham Trent University, UK. He is especially interested in the history of economic thought, Keynesian economics, and its influence on modern-day macroeconomics.

Wesley C. Marshall is a full professor-researcher at the UAM–Iztapalapa, Mexico. He is an associate editor of the *International Journal of Political Economy* and is a member of the editorial board of *Ola Financiera*. His interests are banking, the history of economic thought, and recent economic history.

Nuno Ornelas Martins is a Lecturer in Economics at the Católica Porto Business School, Universidade Católica Portuguesa, Portugal. He is also a researcher at Centro de Estudos de Gestão e Economia, and a member of the Cambridge Social Ontology Group.

Robert McMaster is Professor of Political Economy in the Adam Smith Business School at the University of Glasgow, Scotland. He has been a co-editor of the *Review of Social Economy* since 2005. He is currently working with Andrew Cumbers, Susan Cabaço, and Michael White on developing an index of economic democracy.

Sandrine Michel is Professor in Economics at the University of Montpellier, France. She investigates economic growth over the long-run in relation to structural change, notably the contribution of education and social services to the overcoming of crises, using quantitative and historical methods.

Jamie Morgan works at Leeds Beckett University, UK. He is the former coordinator of the Association for Heterodox Economics and edits *Real World Economics Review* with Edward Fullbrook. He has published widely in economics, political economy, sociology, philosophy, and area studies. He is currently working on problems of taxation of multinational corporations, as well as institutional iteration effects of financial stability.

Özgür Orhangazi is Associate Professor of Economics at Kadir Has University, Turkey. He is the author of *Financialization and the US Economy* (2008) and numerous articles and book chapters on financialization, financial crises, and alternative economic policies.

Bruce Philp is the Head of the Department of Strategy, Marketing and Economics at Birmingham City University, UK. He is interested in political economy and his research focuses on contemporary labor market issues, especially concerning the UK and EU economies.

Bent Arne Sæther is specialist director in the Norwegian Ministry of Climate and Environment, with more than two decades of experience from work on mainstream environmental economics, including critique from an ecological economics perspective.

Timothy Sharpe is Lecturer of Economics at the University of Newcastle, Australia, and Research Scholar at the Binzagr Institute for Sustainable Prosperity. His research is motivated by contemporary macroeconomic policy debates vis-à-vis the conduct of fiscal and monetary policy among advanced economies.

Ajit Sinha is Professor at Azim Premji University, Bangalore, India. He is the author of *Theories of Value from Adam Smith to Piero Sraffa* and *A Revolution in Economic Theory: The Economics of Piero Sraffa*. He has published extensively in the area of history of economic theory.

Lorraine Talbot is Professor of Company Law in Context at the University of York, UK. She is the Coordinating Lead Author of the International Panel for Social Progress based in Princeton University. Professor Talbot was awarded a Leverhulme Fellowship from 2015–17 to analyze the corporate form and to set out such reforms that will ensure the corporation meets social progress goals.

Contributors

Pavlina R. Tcherneva is Chair and Associate Professor of Economics, Bard College, USA and Research Scholar at the Levy Economics Institute. She is an early contributor to Modern Monetary Theory, with a focus on rethinking conventional macroeconomic stabilization policies.

Zdravka Todorova is Associate Professor in the Economics Department at Wright State University, USA. She has been working on heterodox economic theory combining a number of perspectives including institutionalist, Post Keynesian, and feminist.

Radha Upadhyaya is Research Fellow at the Institute for Development Studies, University of Nairobi, Kenya. Radha has over 12 years of teaching experience with particular focus on heterodox research methods, microeconomics, and finance and development. She has written on the Kenyan banking sector, banking regulation in East Africa, and African entrepreneurship.

Ramaa Vasudevan is Associate Professor in the Department of Economics at Colorado State University, USA and is on the Editorial Board of the *Review of Radical Political Economics*. She works on understanding capitalist dynamics from Marxian and Post Keynesian perspectives. She also works on the political economy of money and finance.

Matías Vernengo is Full Professor at Bucknell University, USA. He was formerly Senior Research Manager at the Central Bank of Argentina (BCRA), an external consultant to several United Nations organizations, and is the co-editor of the *Review of Keynesian Economics* and the editor in chief of The New Palgrave Dictionary Online. He specializes in macroeconomics, international political economy, and the history of economic ideas.

Marco Veronese Passarella is Lecturer in the Economics Division at the Leeds University Business School, UK. He has been working on monetary economics, macroeconomics, and history of economic thought, from Marxian and Post Keynesian perspectives.

Benjamin Wilhelm is Research Associate at the Institute for Sociology at the University of Gießen, Germany. His main research interests are shadow banking, financial regulation, and economic sociology.

Mary V. Wrenn is the Joan Robinson Research Fellow in Heterodox Economics at Girton College, University of Cambridge, UK. Mary's research interests include locating ontological concepts such as agency, identity, and fear within the historical framework of neoliberalism.

Part I
Introduction

The state of the art and challenges for heterodox economics

Tae-Hee Jo, Lynne Chester, and Carlo D'Ippoliti

The objectives and unique characteristics of this publication for heterodox economics

The Routledge Handbook of Heterodox Economics is a collection of essays written by authors representing a wide range of theoretical traditions within heterodox economics. It is a project that encapsulates past and current developments in heterodox economics for the purpose of 'analyzing, theorizing, and transforming capitalism.'

This has been an ambitious project. It is ambitious in terms of its multiple, challenging objectives that differentiate the present volume from other publications. The *Handbook* aims, first, to provide realistic and coherent theoretical frameworks—as an alternative to that provided by the mainstream (orthodox) perspective that dominates the teaching of economics and has informed many contemporary policies—to understand the capitalist economy in a constructive and forward-looking manner; second, to delineate the future directions, as well as the current state, of heterodox economics; third, to provide both 'heat and light' on persistent and controversial issues, drawing out the commonalities and differences between heterodox economic approaches; fourth, to envision transformative economic and social policies for the majority, not an elite group of the population; and, fifth, to explain why economics is, and should be treated as, a social science.

These objectives, and particularly the third, bears on the distinctive nature of this *Handbook*. All the chapters engage with more than one theoretical tradition in heterodox economics (see Table 1.1). This demonstrates the engagement of many heterodox economists with methodological pluralism compared to the monist methodology of mainstream economics. We, the three editors, consider that it is important to acknowledge and discuss the contributions that alternative theoretical frameworks can contribute to explaining the nature, dimensions, and dynamics of social reality. The *Handbook* is thus different from other handbooks and what may be considered companion volumes which explore a single heterodox school of economic thought. The *Handbook*'s engagement across different heterodox theoretical perspectives does not mean the uncritical acceptance of any or all approaches. On the contrary, the contributions throughout this *Handbook* provide constructive critiques of heterodox approaches. This contributes, in our view, to the ongoing development of different heterodox traditions and their applications.

Table 1.1 Theoretical orientations of each chapter

Part	Ch.	Title	CPE	Marx	Radical	PK-SR	OIE	SE	FE	ECOL	RT	SSA	Other
I	1	The state of art and challenges for heterodox economics	X	X	X	X	X	X	X	X	X	X	
II	2	Social provisioning process: a heterodox view of the economy	X	X		X	X	X	X	X			
	3	The social surplus approach: historical origins and present state	X	X		X							
	4	Accumulation regimes	X	X			X				X	X	
	5	Monetary theories of production	X	X		X							Circuitiste
	6	The principle of effective demand: Marx, Kalecki, Keynes, and beyond		X		X							
	7	Heterodox theories of value: a brief history	X	X		X							
	8	Theories of prices and alternative economic paradigms	X	X		X	X		X				Austrian
	9	Heterodox theories of distribution	X	X		X							
	10	The Micro–macro link in heterodox economics	X	X		X	X	X					Systemism, Schumpeterian, economic sociology
III	11	Society and its institutions	X	X		X	X	X	X				
	12	Heterodox economics and theories of interactive agency		X		X	X						
	13	Households in heterodox economic theory		X		X	X	X	X				
	14	A heterodox theory of the business enterprise	X	X		X	X						
	15	Heterodox theories of business competition and market governance		X		X							Austrian
	16	A Marxian understanding of the nature and form of dominant capitalist legal institutions		X	X		X						Legal, A. Berle, G. Means
	17	Money and monetary regimes				X							Chartalism, MMT
	18	Banks in developing countries				X	X	X					
	19	Shadow banking				X	X						Legal
	20	The informal economy in theory and policy: prospects for well-being						X	X				
	21	Inequality and poverty	X					X	X				A. Sen

	No.	Chapter title												School/approach
IV	22	The accumulation of capital: an analytical and historical overview		x	x	x							x	x	Structuralist
	23	A heterodox reconstruction of trade theory	x		x	x	x								
	24	Analyzing the organization of global production: thoughts from the periphery	x												Structuralist, World systems theory, global value chain
	25	Labor processes and outcomes: an institutional-heterodox framework					x								NIE (Ostrom)
	26	Heterodox theories of the business cycle		x	x	x									
	27	Heterodox theories of economic growth		x	x	x		x					x		Structuralist
	28	Financialization and the crises of capitalism		x	x	x		x						x	Structuralist
	29	Theories of international development: the Post Keynesian and Marxian alternatives		x		x	x								
	30	Energy, environment, and the economy		x	x	x			x						
V	31	An exit strategy from capitalism's ecological crisis							x	x					
	32	Restructuring financial systems with human advancement in mind			x	x				x					
	33	Rethinking the role of the state			x	x	x								
	34	The twenty-first century capitalist revolution: how the governance of large firms shapes prosperity and inequality		x	x	x	x								Capital as Power, A. Berle, G. Means
	35	Achieving full employment: history, theory, and policy		x	x	x	x								MMT
	36	Social welfare and social control		x	x	x	x	x							Dewey
VI	37	Heterodox economics as a living body of knowledge: community, (in)commensurability, critical engagement, and pluralism	x	x	x	x	x	x	x						Critical realism, pluralism

Notes: 'CPE' stands for classical political economy, 'Marx' for Marxian economics, 'Radical' for radical political economy (e.g., monopoly capital school and Monthly Review school), 'PK-SR' for Post Keynesian (including fundamentalist, Kaleckian) and Sraffian, 'OIE' for original institutionalist economics, 'SE' for social economics, 'FE' feminist economics, 'ECOL' for ecological economics, 'RT' for *Régulation* theory, 'SSA' for the Social Structure of Accumulation approach, 'MMT' for modern money theory, and 'NIE' for new institutional economics.

It is contestable whether it is possible (or desirable) to synthesize different heterodox economic traditions. It is possible to discern similarities and compatibility between heterodox traditions; likewise, there are differences and incompatibilities. Some heterodox economists have argued that synthesis, in varying degrees, is both possible and desirable (perhaps most strongly by Lee 2009: 200–202). The activities of heterodox associations and networks—such as the International Confederation of Associations for Pluralism in Economics (ICAPE), the Association for Heterodox Economics (AHE), the Society of Heterodox Economists (SHE), and the *Heterodox Economics Newsletter*—tacitly, if not overtly, promote pluralism and, on occasion, have explicitly supported a synthesis of heterodox approaches.[1] Others are more pessimistic about such prospects. For example, John King (2016: 10) notes that "[t]he difference within the various schools of heterodox economics—let alone between them—seem to me to be so substantial that any such intellectual Popular Front would prove to be a very unstable affair." The difference between these two positions lies in the emphasis on the degree of similarity or difference between heterodox approaches—"a glass half-empty of coherence vs. a glass half-full of coherence" (Lee 2009: 202). We do not advocate one or the other position although we do hope that this project may contribute to the endeavors of heterodox scholars to develop more coherent and comprehensive narratives of capitalism than can be illuminated from a single perspective.

The *Handbook* also has the following distinctive features. First, contributions are from a mix of established and emerging heterodox economists with an emphasis on the latter. A reviewer of our *Handbook* proposal remarked that "the major weakness of the book is the lack of well-known authors." We, however, think that this is a particular strength and unique feature of the *Handbook*. Fresh ideas and bold arguments are more often than not put forward by emerging scholars while established ones offer a somewhat more 'predictable' analysis given the period of time necessary to establish their careers and reputations. The evolution and development of the traditions within the heterodox economics community lie largely in, we believe, the work of emerging heterodox scholars. We hope that this *Handbook* provokes new directions for heterodox economics, which break from conventional understandings and practices of heterodoxy.

Another notable feature of the *Handbook* is that contributions are from scholars located in 16 different countries (see Table 1.2) and representing Marxian-radical political economy, Post Keynesian-Sraffian economics, institutionalist-evolutionary economics, feminist economics, social economics, *Régulation* theory, the Social Structure of Accumulation approach, ecological economics, and combinations of these traditions. This geographical and theoretical diversity portends well for the future of heterodoxy. Moreover, of the 44 contributors, nearly one-third are from women. This may not seem impressive and our aim was 50 percent of authors.[2] This gender imbalance is very indicative of the economics discipline generally, mainstream or heterodox. It also establishes a yardstick upon which future editions of the *Handbook* may seek to improve.

While these are ambitious objectives and unique features, the *Handbook* does not strive to cover all aspects of heterodox economics. Rather than a definitive volume (we doubt that such a volume(s) is possible), the *Handbook explores the theoretical and policy domains of heterodox economics*. Methodology, research methods, and the philosophy of heterodox economics do not form the focus of this *Handbook*, although these aspects are touched upon in the following sections of this Introduction as well as in some chapters (especially Chapter 39), if relevant to the discussion of a particular issue. This is not because those areas are less important than theory and policy, but because there are already significant publications which focus almost exclusively on these areas.[3] Moreover, many chapters in this volume attest explicitly or implicitly that heterodox economic theories and policies are firmly based on shared ontological foundations—for example, layered and structured reality, open systems of analysis, fundamental uncertainty, evolutionary-historical processes, and social relationships—that require multiple or mixed methods depending upon the research question at hand.

Table 1.2 The number of contributors by country

Country	Number
Argentina	2
Australia	4
Austria	1
Canada	3
France	2
Germany	4
Greece	1
India	1
Italy	3
Kenya	1
Mexico	1
Norway	2
Portugal	1
Turkey	1
United Kingdom	9
United States	8
16 countries	44 contributors

Note: Contributors are sorted into countries in which they are currently located.

With regard to theory and policy to which the *Handbook* explicitly speaks, there are some omissions. For example, while there is a chapter on the banking system in the context of developing countries, there is not a chapter discussing the banking system in developed countries. The latter could have discussed the roles played by banks in the context of instability, crisis, and accumulation. A chapter on the capitalist state may have been included as well. Shedding light on the roles of the state vis-à-vis other institutions and organizations is a *sine qua non* of most heterodox traditions. Rather than a separate chapter on the state, this issue is discussed within multiple chapters across three parts of the *Handbook*—'Society and its institutions,' 'Rethinking the role of the state,' and 'Social welfare and social control.' Apart from these two examples, readers might also consider there are other omissions which could form a goal for future editions.

A last distinctive feature of the *Handbook* is that it is not a diatribe criticizing mainstream economics. There is no doubt that criticism is an essential part of developing alternative perspectives. Past heterodox critiques of mainstream methodology, theory, and policy have led to significant progress in many traditions of heterodox economics. For this project, however, we asked contributors to focus their effort and space on discussing the capacity of more than one heterodox perspective to elucidate a topic, while limiting the critique of mainstream economics. Contributions to this volume are, therefore, not framed within mainstream logic, concepts, and frameworks—for example, the law of supply and demand or individual-rational-optimizing behavior. It is our intent to demonstrate the strengths of heterodox analysis and that the development of heterodox economic traditions can be independent of mainstream economics. Heterodox economics is not about complementing the mainstream or only standing in opposition. Moreover, while we support pluralism, theoretical eclecticism between heterodoxy and orthodoxy is not promoted in this *Handbook*. That is the subject of an existing discourse about the possible integration of heterodox approaches into many approaches within the monist methodology of mainstream economics—such as, experimental economics, behavioral economics, and evolutionary game theory (see, for example, Lee & Lavoie 2012).

Heterodox economics: methodology, theory, and community

What is heterodox economics? The answer to this question has been the subject of a long-standing debate by heterodox economists although no consensus has been reached. An attempt to answer this important question is necessary to the extent that this *Handbook* is *of* and *for* heterodox economics. In this section, we delineate a multi-layered meaning of heterodox economics, which underlies the heterodox economics community in recent decades around the world.

Heterodox economics is not a single unified school of thought. It is an umbrella term refer-ring to various schools of economic thought distinguished from mainstream economics in terms of theory, methodology, policy prescriptions, and community. This internal diversity at multiple levels is a major reason why a definition is difficult. If heterodox economics is to be defined, therefore, a broad (or minimalist) definition encapsulating core characteristics common to mul-tiple heterodox schools of economic thought would only be suitable. As we set out in the previ-ous section, this is the position adopted by the *Handbook* and requires some elaboration in order to understand the past development and current state of heterodox economics.

First of all, the label matters since naming is a social process of identifying and, thus, posi-tioning a particular paradigm vis-à-vis other paradigms in economics. Different labels des-ignating a dissident paradigm in economics have been deployed—for example, heterodox, non-mainstream, non-orthodox, unconventional, post-classical, progressive, and alternative. 'Heterodox' economics is most widely used in academia these days, although this is not neces-sarily the best term for various reasons. Notably, some scholars eschew this label because of its negative connotation. In fact, the etymology of 'heterodox' is twofold: 'another opinion, holding opinions other than the right' and 'of another or different opinion.' In the sense of the former, heterodox economics is conventionally perceived as being in opposition to the dominant position that is orthodox (in the intellectual sense) or mainstream economics (in the sociological sense). In other words, heterodox economics can be defined in terms of what it rejects, often implying erroneously that it does not have its own body of theory and policy. If this is what heterodox economics means, as Robert Prasch (2013: 20) points out, "[a]n unfor-tunate, if unintended consequence, is that it reaffirms the centrality of Neoclassical Econom-ics." Consequently, defining and practicing heterodox economics as in opposition can lead to a self-defeating outcome.[4]

Insofar as the development of heterodox economics is concerned, the oppositional defini-tion is more harmful than fruitful (this is, of course, not to suggest that the opposition to or criticism of mainstream economics is unnecessary or unimportant). There is no doubt that heterodox economists have developed their own theories and policies that are inextricably connected to the evolution of the capitalist economic system. That is, heterodox economics has and continues to develop with the evolution of the economic system as part of society; and the complexity and uncertain nature of this socio-historical evolution necessitates more than one economic perspective. As early as the 1930s, for example, institutionalists recognized their research program as 'heterodox' economics, which refers to "the study of economic institutions as an alternative substitute for the study of rational choice" (Ayres 1936: 234). Consider too the following statements: social economics is "a discipline studying the reciprocal relationship between economic science on the one hand and social philosophy, ethics and human dignity on the other" (Lutz 2009: 516); and "[f]eminist political economy is a counter-disciplinary approach to understanding the way in which GENDER has been culturally constructed and intertwined with the processes of CLASS formation, race and other forms of social identity to support women's disadvantaged social position" (Olson 1999: 327, original emphasis). In these respects, institutional, social, and feminist economics provide constructive research programs offering novel insights that are independent of—and not framed by—mainstream economics. P.A. O'Hara observes that the collective contribution of these insights provides a more comprehensive alternative to mainstream economics:

> [t]he main thing that social economists bring to the study [of heterodox economics] is an emphasis on ethics, morals and justice situated in an institutional setting. Institutionalists bring a pragmatic approach with a series of concepts of change and normative theory of progress, along with a commitment to policy. Marxists bring a set of theories of class and the economic surplus. Feminists bring a holistic account of the ongoing relationships between gender, class, and ethnicity in a context of difference. . . . And post-Keynesians contribute through an analysis of institutions set in real time, with the emphasis on effective demand, uncertainty and a monetary theory of production linked closely with policy recommendations.
>
> *O'Hara 2002: 611*

The existence of (and complementarity between) multiple heterodox traditions signals that heterodox economics exists independently of that to which it is opposed. Thus, a more positive definition of heterodox economics is (as the second etymology noted above indicates) that *it is a body of economic theory and policy developed and practiced independently of mainstream economics.*

Obviously, there are differences between the analytical concerns of different heterodox traditions. Such analytical differences, however, do not overshadow methodological commonalities; otherwise theoretical engagement and convergence are unlikely between different theoretical traditions. Lee (2012) observes theoretical engagement, during the first half of the twentieth century, between American institutionalists and Keynesians and Marxians, and subsequently between the latter and Post Keynesians. Engagement, integration, and synthesis across heterodox schools continued during the latter part of the twentieth century and into the new millennium. O'Hara (2007: 3) sets out in detail evidence of convergence between heterodox scholars vis-à-vis the principles of inquiry given the emphasis placed on "realism, holism, circular and/ or cumulative causation, institutions, and the role of values and social factors in economic life" by those who may be categorized as applying an institutional-evolutionary political economy approach. There is also historical evidence that the development of heterodox economics (and each tradition therein) has been fostered through professional organizations and social networks (see Lee 2009: 189–206). In other words, the development of heterodox economics is dependent to some extent upon the organization and continuation of the community of heterodox economists.

> This combination of professional and theoretical engagement has two important implications for heterodox economics. The first is that the community is distinct from the community of mainstream economists; and the second is that it generates the central value that underpins the community of heterodox economists: that is the value of pluralism—the right of different theoretical approaches to exist without qualification—and its corollary that engagement with the different approaches is a positive social value.
>
> *Lee 2009: 202*

Such an intellectual community (associations, journals, conferences, etc.), according to Lee (2011: 547), is built upon (and requires) the principle of 'intellectual or scientific pluralism'—that is, "tolerance for different theories, professional practices, and the existence of contested scientific inquiry"—which promotes theoretical engagements among members within the community.[5] From this community with pluralism view, we can derive a twofold sociological definition of heterodox economics: it is *a community of heterodox economists* that supports alternative theoretical frameworks and *a movement* aiming at developing theories and policies by means of developing an intellectual community or social network (Lee 2009: 1–20).

One essential aspect of heterodox economics is, however, not included in the above theoretical and sociological definitions—that is, philosophy and methodology. Lawson (2006: 485) contends that heterodox economics is "a rejection of a very specific form of methodological reductionism [that is, mathematical deductive modeling]."[6] The significance of this argument lies in its potential for constructively re-orienting and redefining heterodox economics:

> the various heterodox traditions can be identified as heterodox through a recognition of a fact that they advance claims or practices or orientations which are either concrete manifestations of, or presupposes for their legitimacy, a social ontology of the (seemingly coherent) sort set out above [that is, openness, process, and internal-relationship]. *In short, the set of projects currently collected together and systematized as heterodox economics is, in the first instance, an orientation in ontology.*
>
> *Lawson 2006: 498, original emphasis*

Lawson's ontological definition of heterodox economics is important because it illuminates the preconceptions and premises of economics to which mainstream economics pays no attention. However, a definition of heterodoxy *could* be extended to include the subject matter of heterodox perspective.

As noted earlier, it has been our objective for this *Handbook* to demonstrate actual and potential engagement among different traditions within heterodox economics. This engagement is possible, theoretically, methodologically, and through a general research agenda across heterodox traditions. As opposed to the mainstream's preoccupation with the optimal allocation of scarce resources arising from the purported rational choices of individuals, the concerns of heterodox economics can be broadly identified as focusing on a wide range of economic and social activities in a socio-historical context, including both market and non-market, paid and unpaid activities, undertaken by human beings and going concerns to ensure their survival and reproduction. This broadly defined heterodox research agenda is akin to the term 'social provisioning'—more commonly found in the lexicon of North American institutionalists than inherent to the wider heterodox community. Allan Gruchy (1987: 21) defines economics as the science of social provisioning, "the study of the ongoing economic process which provides the flow of goods and services required by society to meet the needs of those who participate in its activities" to which we may add Peterson's (1995: 570) more structural definition of social provisioning as being "how societies organize themselves to secure the material goods and services necessary to maintain and reproduce themselves." With this general subject matter, therefore, a definition of heterodox economics can also include *the study of the social provisioning process* which also reclaims the original meaning of 'political economy' or economics as a social science (Gruchy 1987: 21; Lee 2009: 8).

In sum, the contemporary meaning of heterodox economics can be delineated as multi-layered and multi-faceted. It has evolved from an initial quite strong predilection to concentrate around critiquing mainstream economics to a stage of developing its own coherent and logical theories and policies. Contributions throughout this volume are demonstrable evidence of this shift within heterodox economics.

Evolution of heterodox economics

It is beyond the scope of this introductory chapter to detail the intellectual and historical origins of all schools and approaches that comprise contemporary heterodox economics.[7] Instead, a brief overview of the origins and developments of heterodox economics is presented in order to situate this project.

Marxian economics, institutional-evolutionary economics, and other heterodox approaches rediscovering classical political economy took different paths in different contexts in the second half of the twentieth century. New approaches such as ecological and feminist economics emerged in the same period. While most heterodox schools implicitly or explicitly trace their intellectual lineage significantly earlier in time, to classical political economy (that is including, from a history of thought perspective, Marx among the classics),[8] we limit ourselves here to the mid and late twentieth century, when most heterodox traditions developed as self-evident communities of scholars.

As already stated, it has been an explicit objective for the chapters of this *Handbook* to integrate more than one theoretical perspective. Arguably, an integrative and pluralist approach is a constitutive method and a defining feature of heterodox economics, even though some heterodox economists are not necessarily open to other heterodox methods and approaches and/or do not endorse, practice, and promote pluralism (Lee 2009). Allowing for a certain idiosyncrasy in the collection of contributors to the *Handbook* and personal preferences, certain regularities emerge. Thus, as shown in the Table 1.1, in Europe the Sraffian school was historically associated with Post Keynesianism, whereas in the US Post Keynesians have developed stronger links with institutionalists; feminist economics and social economics often inform each other; and radical political economics has stronger links with the *Régulation* and the Social Structure of Accumulation approaches than other schools.

These links descend partially from the personal work of the founding figures of the respective schools (see, for example, Roncaglia 2005). Thus, institutionalism was historically dominant in the late nineteenth and early twentieth century in the US, where it became intertwined with a strong interest in evolutionary theory after key contributions especially by Veblen. Similarly, Cambridge in the United Kingdom provided the location for intellectual and personal connections between Keynes, Sraffa, and the 'Cambridge Circus,' after which Post Keynesianism developed in parallel with the Sraffian school. The interests of the leading figures of the 'Anglo-Italian school' led their followers to specialize in pure theory and/or history of economic thought, whereas in France Michel Aglietta and Robert Boyer, in particular, inspired a more historically informed analysis, closer in theory to Marxian economics and in method to institutionalism.

From these (and other) founding figures to the current development of heterodox economics, the path has been complex. As is well known, the rise of the marginalist approach was immediately met with opposition from, for example, exponents of the German historical school, institutionalists in the US and elsewhere, and from several points of view even by dissenters within the marginalist approach, such as Carl Menger. However, in most Western countries the marginalist approach reached prominence, if not dominance, until well after the First World War.

The Great Depression was a primary motivator of the work of Keynes and his followers, even though we would not advocate the search for mechanistic links between economic history and economic theory. On the one hand, for example, Sraffa commenced his critique of the Marshallian theory of the firm (and of market forms) before the Great Depression, and Keynes himself had published his main ideas on the crucial relevance of uncertainty (as opposed to calculable risk) in 1919. On the other hand, right after its publication the *General Theory* was interpreted and translated in the language of marginalism by Hicks and Modigliani, and thus subsumed into the mainstream. Thus, though being dominant, marginalism was never the only analytical perspective, and at the same time 'bastard Keynesianism' originated more or less contemporaneously with Post Keynesianism.

In these two forms, Keynesianism may be seen to dominate the economic policy debate during the Second World War, for the unavoidable necessity to finance war expenditure. Relevant exceptions are the countries that did not significantly take part in the war (such as several countries in the global South), and those that adopted a communist regime, where an extension of classical political economy with a Marxian strand could be discussed.

After the war, national experiences diverged again, and the claim (ascribed to Samuelson) that economists were "all Keynesians now" was surely exaggerated. Indeed, Continental Europe, at least in Germany, Italy, and Austria (and partly France and other Nazi-occupied countries), shares the experience of reconstruction of a 'democratic' academia after the pervasive political control of the previous dictatorships. In these countries, ordoliberal and even neoliberal economists gained prominence during the 1950s and 1960s (Pasinetti & Roncaglia 2006; Heise *et al.* 2017) within the universities, but also in the highest institutions, for example, with the appointment of Luigi Einaudi as President of the Italian Republic and Ludwig Erhard as Chancellor of the Federal Republic of Germany. Consequently, active predominant government involvement in the economy was perceived as a relic of authoritarianism, and liberalism was synonymized with civil and political liberty.

Thus, in Continental Europe mainstream economics was strongest during implementation of the Marshall Plan, and possibly least (though still in a majority position) during the stagflation of the late 1970s and 1980s. Thereafter mainstream economics reached its peak, whereas heterodox economics declined in the 1990s and 2000s (more on this below). Therefore, it is incorrect to associate the rise of monetarism and the 'new classical' reaction to new Keynesianism with a conservative turn in academic economics during and after the Thatcher–Reagan era.[9] Rather, the 1970s marked the beginning of a growing *polarization* in academic economics, at least in the US and Europe.

Both internal and external factors contributed to the growth of heterodox schools after the 1970s. Among the internal factors, there was the gradual return to their homeland (or the consolidation of their status in the host country) of several scholars who had fled autocratic regimes in Italy, Germany, Austria, and other countries. Often these scholars had studied in British and American universities where they met notable heterodox colleagues (often fellow compatriots who shared the same experience) such as Kalecki, Sraffa, Kaldor, Joan Robinson, and Richard Kahn, or eclectic and peculiar scholars such as John Hicks or Joseph Schumpeter. This migration flow before and during the Second World War facilitated further exchanges thereafter, on the basis of newly established funding grants and fellowships (Kregel 1988). Upon returning to their home country, the international networks and prestige of some of these scholars enabled them to communicate and compete with leading mainstream economists, mostly US trained, on a level playing field.[10]

With respect to the external factors contributing to the growth of heterodox economics in Europe in particular, mention should be made of the rapid growth of the higher education (university) system during the 1970s and 1980s, which created a steady demand for academic economists that in some national contexts opened new job opportunities for both less than outstanding mainstream economists and discriminated against heterodox economists (Heise *et al.* 2017).

These factors made significant growth possible, which allowed for the emergence and/or consolidation of new schools and paradigms of economics. Thus, in several countries, Marxism, which had mostly been expunged or almost never found its way into the 'legitimate' domain of mainstream economics, survived and developed in cognate disciplines such as history, geography, and sociology. Especially from the 1970s, interdisciplinary efforts brought about a reintroduction of Marxian political economy within academia. Around the same time, feminist studies increasingly found their applications within economics, often in the context of Marxian political economy. However, from the late 1980s a new consolidation of mainstream economics reduced this growth, or even compressed the space for heterodox economics. In response, heterodox economists established new associations and organizations during the 1980s and 1990s.

As Lee (2009: 59–65) recalls, initial debates were fierce even within heterodox associations, with tensions regarding, for instance, the membership of institutionalists within the Union for Radical Political Economics or Sraffians and Post Keynesians within the Conference of Socialist Economists. However, almost all heterodox economics associations now openly acknowledge economic pluralism as important to the teaching of economics and to the richness of the explanations provided by multiple perspectives. Indeed, the historical roots and developments briefly described here do not imply a predetermined future of heterodox economics. Rather, what is implied is that promising research programs are based largely on drawing from and connecting previously unrelated approaches or schools. This attitude and practice, arguably, develops in parallel to the growth of institutions and instruments that facilitate communication and exchange between communities and schools (and, as noted earlier, this has been an objective of this *Handbook*).

Economic pluralism offers the prospect of significantly improving our understanding of the economy and the possibilities to improve its functioning and outcomes. However, we do not envisage the future for heterodox economics through 'rose-colored glasses.' The pushback against heterodox economics that started in the 1980s has not slowed since the 2007–8 'great crisis' or the ensuing stagnation/depression. Rather, across the world and perhaps most noticeably in Europe, several consecutive years of austerity policies have placed significant pressures on publicly funded universities, and heterodox economists appear to suffer disproportionately from the shrinking of funding, resources, and academic positions (see, for example, AFEP 2009; Corsi *et al.* 2011; Heise *et al.* 2017). In a growing number of countries, the reduction of public resources is concealed under the 'banners' of efficiency and merit, with journal and university rankings simulating a supposedly competitive research market, and various citation metrics providing the semblance of neutrality and objectivity to the hiring and promotion processes of academics and the financing of research centers (Lee 2007).

Heterodox economists are responding to these challenges in several ways which may be termed the 'loyalty option,' the 'voice option,' and the 'exit option.' Concerning the 'loyalty' option, an increasing number of pluralist and heterodox journals are being added to the databases on which rankings are based (mainly, Scopus® by Elsevier, and Web of Science™ by Clarivate Analytics), thereby increasing the number of citations that other heterodox journals receive. Some scholars have proposed ways to navigate the system by modifying individual or collective behavior, including changes to scientific practices concerning publication and citation habits (Dobusch & Kapeller 2012).

There are also attempts at shaping a 'voice' option. Objections to the systematic undervaluation of heterodox economics within national research evaluation systems have occurred in Australia, France, Italy, and the UK, while in other countries, such as the Netherlands, the existing system has been perceived as less biased. Alternative metrics or rankings have been proposed by

Lee & Cronin (2010) and Corsi *et al.* (2011), and several heterodox associations continue to lobby for modifications and amendments to official national rankings.

Concerning the 'exit' option, in some countries there are attempts to lower the reliance on public financing of research and higher education by trying to attract private funds: either from local governments and student fees, as for example the newly funded Cusanus Hochschule in Germany, or from private foundations and social actors, such as the Greenwich Political Economy Research Centre in the UK.

Not all these activities are mutually exclusive; for example, some heterodox economists try to adapt in practice to new systems while also critiquing these systems; others increasingly seek private funding sources while also trying to maintain a good rating within the public system.[11] However, there has been no coordination, let alone discussion, among heterodox economists about a collective strategy to cope with that environment that is evolving in new hostile ways. There are crucial political as well as ethical issues concerning possible strategies under the 'loyalty' option. Authors, reviewers, editors, and organizations can strategically change their behavior, and the widespread scientific malpractice aimed at tilting the bibliometric game is probably growing within the heterodox community too, without a debate of these issues yet.

Conversely, the success of various tactics under the 'voice' and 'exit' options depends on external support for criticisms and protests against the current system and its bias in favor of the mainstream.[12] It falls on heterodox economists to both demonstrate their social usefulness and to help establish the conditions for it to be fully realized.

Structure and outline of this *Handbook*

This *Handbook* is structured in six parts. Part I (Chapter 1) provides a general introductory overview of the definition of heterodox economics, its origins, history, philosophy, methodology, and current state. This introductory chapter also explains the aims and objectives of the *Handbook*.

The theoretical cores of heterodox economics

Part II presents the core or fundamental theoretical frameworks that are shared by various traditions within heterodox economics—that is, Marxian-radical political economics, Post Keynesian-Sraffian economics, institutionalist-evolutionary economics, feminist economics, social economics, *Régulation* theory, the Social Structure of Accumulation approach, ecological economics, and combinations of these traditions. The chapters in Part II deal with 'fundamental' concepts in the sense that they are elements on which heterodox economic theories are based. The purpose of Part II is to distinguish the most distinctive, fundamental theoretical frameworks shared by heterodox economics traditions. Chapters in Part II not only encapsulate the historical development of theories (from classical political economy to present-day heterodox economic theories) but also demonstrate the relevance of these theories to advancing explanations of the workings and persistent problems of contemporary capitalism. Part II as a whole demonstrates that heterodox economics, through particular traditions or through integrated approaches, provides logically coherent alternatives to mainstream economics (including neoclassical economics); and the traditions of heterodox economics provide historically and socially grounded explanations of capitalism.

The opening chapter in Part II (Chapter 2) deals with the conceptualization of the social provisioning process. As discussed above, the study of the social provisioning process is one way to define (heterodox) economics. Tae-Hee Jo and Zdravka Todorova examine how the meaning of the economy and of economics changed from classical political economy to neoclassical economics; this comparison illustrates the latter's asocial and ahistorical view of the economy and of economics. The authors demonstrate that a broader definition of heterodox economics permits different theoretical explanations of the ways in which the social provisioning process can take place in different types of economies in different historical contexts.

The emphasis on the historicity of economic theories—that is, the evolutionary nature of economics—is examined in the following two chapters. In Chapter 3, Nuno Ornelas Martins investigates the concept of the social surplus and the historical origins of the social surplus approach. He shows that in classical political economy the concept of a social surplus was inextricably linked to the study of a circular process of production and distribution. When this approach was resurrected with the emergence of the Cambridge Keynesian tradition and the revival of Marx's original interpretation of classical political economy, the development of various heterodox traditions has tended to highlight differences between competing perspectives, rather than their common origins from the social surplus approach. However, according to Martins, consensus about the basic elements of a social surplus approach may constitute a promising route for the development of heterodox economics.

In the following chapter (Chapter 4), Agnès Labrousse and Sandrine Michel discuss the way in which the social surplus is distributed and, crucially, used—that is, accumulation regimes. Historical observation shows that accumulation—the process of adding productive capital to the previously invested amount of capital—undergoes long periods of stability, followed by periods of instability and crisis. Thus, especially *Régulation* theory and the Social Structure of Accumulation approach set out to study the dynamics of production, consumption and the distribution of income through institutional frameworks specific in time and location and which underpin macroeconomic regularities. In this way, Labrousse and Michel demonstrate that the evolutionary nature of the economy implies that economics should not assume a canonical accumulation regime but rather be concerned with a much broader variety of regimes.

The view of capitalism as a circular, surplus-oriented, sequence of interconnected monetary acts of production, distribution, and trade is further discussed in Chapter 5. Marco Veronese Passarella surveys the Post Keynesian, neochartalist, circuitist, and other heterodox monetary theories that focus on the process of creation, circulation, and destruction of monetary means in a world marked by class divide and social conflict.

In most heterodox traditions, monetary relations and the distributional conflict between social classes are intimately linked to the concept of effective demand, which is discussed in Chapter 6. In this chapter, Eckhard Hein surveys different strands of Post Keynesian economics (fundamentalists, Kaleckians, Sraffians, Kaldorians, institutionalists) and some strands of Neo-Marxian economics (the approaches focused on monopoly capitalism and under-consumption), showing how the principle of effective demand, and the claim of its validity for a monetary production economy, both in the short- and in the long-run, is at the core of heterodox macroeconomics. Thus, in the treatment of the basic pillars of heterodox economics, what the mainstream calls 'macroeconomic' concepts are often logically antecedent to 'microeconomic' ones. The rejection of the 'microfoundations of macroeconomics'—typical of mainstream economics—is analyzed from a logical and methodological perspective by Claudius Gräbner and Jakob Kapeller in the final chapter of Part II, Chapter 10.

Part II contains three other interrelated chapters. Ajit Sinha's Chapter 7 highlights the key differences between the classical and the marginalist (neoclassical and Austrian) approaches to the theory of value. Sinha stresses the distinction between the circular approach of classical political economy, built upon an objective approach to the theory of value, and the linear (subjective) approach of marginalism to value theory. Chapter 8, by Carlo D'Ippoliti, further investigates the different origins of these two approaches by tracing them back to the 'pre-analytical vision' of the functioning of the economy. While values and prices play completely different analytical roles in the two approaches (that is, an allocative and informative role versus a distributive one), theories of price formation hold analytical centrality in all economic paradigms, both heterodox and mainstream. For this reason, some economists refer to price theories as a demarcation line of what legitimately constitutes heterodox economics. Nevertheless, as D'Ippoliti suggests, there are still a number of contestable issues that should be analyzed.

Several heterodox traditions adopt pricing and income distribution models of simultaneous determination. However, as Scott Carter highlights in Chapter 9, this usually refers implicitly only to functional income distribution. Indeed, while personal income distribution is often studied by mainstream economists, heterodox economists more commonly focus on functional income distribution. However, as also argued by Corsi and Guarini in Chapter 21, it would be a mistake for heterodox economists to disregard the distribution of personal or household incomes. In sharing this view, Carter further surveys the main approaches that alternatively focus on wages or profits as 'system closures' and how these approaches have often collided within heterodox economics. Nevertheless, as exemplified by Sraffa, it is possible to develop formal models that encompass both possibilities, a fact that induces Carter's optimism for the future.

The anatomy of capitalism

The capitalist economy is a historically specific system of provisioning. Its specificity is character-ized by the relationship between agents, structures, and institutions. One manifestation of such a relationship is the production and distribution of the surplus, denominated in value terms, on which the capitalist economy is based. Heterodox economists hold that a theoretical discourse should be put into the socio–historical context so that a theory is fully understood and is modi-fied as the changes in the system transpire. With this rationale Part III scrutinizes the central constituents of the capitalist economy with a focus on the roles played by those constituents in a larger social context.

The opening chapter of Part III (Chapter 11) is John F. Henry's 'Society and its institutions.' Following a brief statement as to why mainstream economics cannot undertake an examina-tion of institutions as social constructs and accompanying ideology, this chapter explores the nature of institutions, highlights contributions to the analysis of institutions developed in several heterodox traditions, and critically evaluates weaknesses in these contributions, and proposes an approach that conjoins the various heterodox camps into a single effort that leads to a better understanding of such structures and the underlying ideology that supports these arrangements. The point of departure is Thorstein Veblen's (1909:626) definition of 'institutions' as "the settled habits of thought common to the generality of man." It is at once noted that Veblen's position entails an ideological component. But, for ideological appeals to have traction, they must speak to some underlying structure. Hence, a proper heterodox approach to institutions must examine both structure and the supporting ideological overlay as conjoined features of such organiza-tions or arrangements. In this examination, several prominent institutional forms, such as the state, money, and the household, are used as examples to demonstrate how institutionalists, social economists, Marxians, feminists, and Post Keynesians address the main issues surrounding this theme. Incorporated into this examination is a critical evaluation of the term 'society.' Too often society is employed in a casual, non-critical fashion as if there were a homogeneous, holistic unit within which all members of a specific social order are organized in a unified fashion. Henry contests such a line of argument. Henry also argues that the most prominent *social* institutions are, rather, *anti-social* in their organization and ideological support. To better understand the nature of institutions, then, requires an understanding of the make-up of the social order itself. This further requires an examination of the fundamental social relationships that constitute the core or foundation of the social order, thus, in the final analysis determining (or conditioning) the institutional fabric of that order. As a conclusion of this chapter, Henry proposes that heterodox economists should develop an analysis of institutions that draws on the strengths of the various heterodox approaches and, concurrently, minimizing (or eliminating) the weaknesses inherent in each line of attack.

If institutions are social arrangements and organizations, there must exist socially active agents who make and manage such institutions. In Chapter 12, 'Heterodox economics and theories of interactive agency,' Mary V. Wrenn examines agency, which is defined as the power to act, choose, imagine, understand, engage, and manipulate the biological and social environment. Obviously, this notion of agency is completely absent in mainstream economics; in place of interactive agency are asocial optimizing individuals disembedded from the society. Wrenn thus argues that interactive agency distinguishes heterodox economics—in particular, institutional, Marxian, and Post Keynesian economics—from the mainstream. While agency appears in different forms and often with varying degrees in different heterodox traditions, what is common to them is the interaction between agents and structures that shape the evolutionary path of the provisioning system. After carefully examining the concept and role of agency underpinning various heterodox approaches, Wrenn arrives at a conclusion that theories of interactive agency provide not only a powerful critique of mainstream economics but also a more socially relevant economic analysis.

The household is one indispensable and distinctive agent in the account of the system of provisioning and its evolution. However, the household is often subsumed in the heterodox discussion of the production of commodities and the reproduction of the economic system as a whole. In Chapter 13, Zdravka Todorova provides the theoretical grounds for developing a heterodox theory of the household that goes beyond the contributions (and limitations) of a single heterodox approach. With this goal in place, she examines various heterodox economic perspectives, such as feminist, Post Keynesian, Marxian, and social economics. This examination leads to the analytical categories of the household—that is, the household as a going concern, an institution, and an actor-participant (or socialized agent)—that shed light on the specificity and variations of household agency depending on the household's socio-economic position within the society; the inseparable connections to other agents and to surrounding institutions; and the production of non-commodities and non-market oriented activities such as care and recreation, which are often ignored by heterodox approaches. Consequently, Todorova concludes that the analysis of the household should be central in developing heterodox economics since the life process is maintained through the organization of household going concerns.

The following three chapters deal with the business enterprise, the dominant agent and organization that, in Thorstein Veblen's words, animate the "material framework of modern civilization in the industrial system" (Veblen 1904: 1). Drawing upon institutionalist, Marxian, and Post Keynesian economics, Tae-Hee Jo in Chapter 14 strives to build a heterodox theory of the business enterprise. The rationale behind this bold task is that while each heterodox economics tradition offers its own distinctive insights into the business enterprise that are alternative to the neoclassical-Marshallian theory of the firm, an integrative approach will offer a more comprehensive understanding of the business enterprise than each heterodox approach could do separately. The theory put forward in the chapter is institutional in that the business enterprise is conceptualized as a going concern whose primary goal is survival and reproduction by making strategic (as opposed to optimal) decisions; it is Marxian in that an array of business enterprise activities is formulated following Marx's circuit of capital schema; and it is Post Keynesian in that specific 'monetary' activities such as production, pricing, investment, financing, and competition are put in historical time (and fundamental uncertainty). Readers will find rich and radical implications as to how the business enterprise operates in corporate capitalism vis-à-vis the structure and dynamics of the provisioning process.

In Chapter 15, Tuna Baskoy argues that heterodox approaches in general conceptualize market competition as a dynamic-evolutionary process in which the power (or agency) of the business enterprise to control its environment in its own interests shapes market outcomes, rather than the structure of the market determines the enterprise decisions and market outcomes. The concept of power, as is found in Austrian, Marxian, and Post Keynesian economics, thus becomes important to the account of both competitive and cooperative enterprise activities in the market through market governance organizations (for example cartels and trade associations) and institutions (for example rules and regulations). An important implication of Baskoy's argument is the view that the market is a social creation and, hence, it is controlled, managed, and reproduced on a continual basis.

In Chapter 16, 'A Marxian understanding of the nature and form of dominant capitalist legal institutions,' Lorraine Talbot demonstrates how legal institutions reflect and enable particular stages of capitalist development. Utilizing Marx's analysis of credit and falling profit rates, and focusing on historic developments in the UK, Talbot discusses why the company form emerged as the dominant legal institution of capitalism from the late nineteenth century onwards. This chapter thus provides an explanation for the behavior of modern corporations and shows why they are increasingly driven to destructive short-termism rather than productive development and innovation. The chapter also examines moments in the current crisis, dubbed the 'Long Depression,' that are explicable through the Marxian lens. This chapter concludes by arguing that meaningful reform of the company from a socially progressive perspective begins with the removal of shareholder control rights.

As discussed in several chapters in Parts II and III, central to the theory of monetary production (à la Marxian, institutionalist, and Post Keynesian), along with the surplus approach and the theory of effective demand, is money as a social institution and a driver of real economic activities such as production, expenditure, and employment. Thus money and related systems of managing monetary resources are essential for us to understand key issues in heterodox economics. The following three chapters examine, respectively, the origins and nature of money, the banking system in developing countries, and the shadow banking system.

In Chapter 17 Pavlina R. Tcherneva defines money, following the chartalist-modern money approach, as a power relationship of a specific kind and a stratified social debt relationship measured in a unit of account determined by some authority. Thus, money emerges as a social mechanism of redistribution, usually by some authority of power (be it an ancient religious authority, a king, a colonial power, or a modern nation state). In other words, money is a 'creature of the state'—as opposed to a 'creature of the market' as in mainstream economics—which has played a key role in the transfer of real resources between parties and the redistribution of economic surplus. A notable implication of this chapter is that a historical understanding of the origins and evolving nature of money illuminates the economic possibilities under different institutional monetary arrangements in the modern world—that is, 'sovereign' and 'non-sovereign' monetary regimes (including freely floating currencies, currency pegs, currency boards, dollarized nations, and monetary unions).

In Chapter 18, Radha Upadhyaya critically examines contending approaches to the role of banking in the financial system of developing countries with a particular focus on sub-Saharan African countries and their development process. The conventional mainstream argument posits a positive long-term correlation between finance and economic growth, which requires the liberalization of the domestic financial system. Such an argument is based upon the assumption that growth is resource-constrained. However, most developing countries that went through financial liberalization in the 1980s and 1990s have not achieved the goal anticipated by the mainstream theory and policy. Upadhyaya argues that the focus on the relationship between finance and growth obscures more fundamental issues, such as the country-specific structural and institutional arrangement of the financial systems in sub-Saharan African countries. In the face of both the failure of the mainstream analysis and the lack of heterodox analysis, she suggests that the role of knowledge creation as a means to reduce uncertainty and the banking system as part of the larger social-institutional structure be taken into account in the analysis of financialization and its effects on growth.

The shadow banking system, which is located outside the regular banking system, has brought about scholarly and public debates after the financial crisis of 2007–8. Chapter 19 by Benjamin Wilhelm provides a heterodox and interdisciplinary understanding of the shadow banking system. Wilhelm proceeds his discussion as follows. First, he examines the institutional qualities of shadow banking. Second, he provides a legal perspective on the workings of shadow banking. And then he discusses the impact of regulation on the shadow banking system with regard to institutions, practices, and instability. In a nutshell, Wilhelm argues that the shadow banking system calls for a comprehensive analysis that touches upon the economic, social, legal, and political dimensions surrounding the system.

As many contributors of the *Handbook* point out, heterodox economists hold a broader view of the economy—that is, the process of social provisioning, including both market and non-market activities, paid and unpaid activities, and commodities and non-commodities. This heterodox view also implies that the so-called 'informal economy' should not be left out as it pertains to the accumulation of capital as well as the well-being of people. In Chapter 20, 'The informal economy in theory and policy: prospects for well-being,' Elizabeth Hill provides a thorough examination of the informal economy. Hill begins with the debate about the informal economy within the discourse of development economics and shows how theoretical and empirical understandings of economic informality have evolved and are now used to understand development, well-being, and insecurity/precarity around the world. As the informal sector grows, it has become 'normal' rather than aberrant. Hill finds that the shift in the theoretical understanding of informality has significant implications for how we conceptualize models of capital accumulation; how emerging economies build systems of social protection; and the patterns of growth and inequality. Other important issues analyzed in the chapter are the informal sector's role in providing employment and livelihood, limits on productivity, the prevailing policy regime, worker agency, the structure of the labor market, and impact of socio-economic organizations and institutions on livelihoods, well-being, and freedom. Apparently, the informal economy is a highly contested area of public policy. Hill's chapter will be a good starting point for further research on the informal economy from a heterodox perspective.

Chapter 21, the last chapter in Part III is an analysis of inequality and poverty, two pressing issues inherent to the capitalist economic system. Marcella Corsi and Giulio Guarini start the chapter with the discussion of income inequality, drawing upon a classical approach to distribution, and then explore the link between human development, social exclusion, and poverty. In the latter analysis, Corsi and Guarini find Sen's capability approach useful to the extent that poverty means the inability to live a minimally decent life, which is due largely to various forms of social exclusion, such as unemployment, financial exclusion, exclusion from the school system, that we observe in most capitalist economies. Thus the chapter pays particular attention to the process of social exclusion as it affects the most vulnerable individuals in the society by creating treacherous social traps. Corsi and Guarini's chapter thus makes a case that inability, poverty, and inequality are socially generated. If so, it is imperative to break this vicious spiral by establishing social institutions that provide vulnerable people with opportunities to get back into the social provisioning process, or to transform the way the system is organized.

The dynamics of the capitalist socio-economic structure

Understanding the components of agency, structure, and socio-economic institutions is necessary to understanding the dynamics of capitalism, which is the focus of Part IV. Many heterodox schools criticize the mainstream (and particularly, neoclassical economics) for its static method. Thus, with their focus on the dynamics of capitalism, the chapters in Part IV provide an overview of the scientifically fruitful alternatives to mainstream economics.

Ramaa Vasudevan opens Part IV of the *Handbook* (Chapter 22) with an analysis of capital accumulation—many heterodox schools recognize this as the engine of capitalist growth. Vasudevan compares classical-Marxian and Post Keynesian approaches to accumulation and growth with institutionalist, Social Structure of Accumulation, and *Régulation* approaches to discuss the institutional and structural changes integral to the process of capitalist accumulation particularly since the post-Second World War period.

Given the centrality of globalization in shaping growth and development patterns, the following two chapters deal with open-economy issues. In Chapter 23, Yan Liang examines the evolution of the terms of trade and the position of developing nations to provide a heterodox analysis of the causes of persistent unbalanced trade and its impacts on macroeconomic performance and long-run growth. Following Myrdal, Liang proposes the adoption of a 'double standard' by which beggar-thy-neighbor policies are still condemned but developing countries are permitted to protect their industries in pursuing a comprehensive development strategy.

In Chapter 24, Víctor Ramiro Fernández and Gabriel Brondino discuss the global value chains (GVC) approach to explain the main determinants of the industrial organization of international commodity production chains. They highlight how several works applying the GVC approach underestimate or ignore the role of power, the nation state, financialization, and geopolitics. Nonetheless, these concepts and players can be incorporated to provide a more realistic interpretation of the current features of global capital accumulation. This use of the GVC approach, according to the authors, is much more meaningful in shedding light on uneven development in 'peripheral' regions.

In Chapter 25, Siobhan Austen shifts the focus to theorizing labor situations, and identifies a number of similarities between Elinor Ostrom's Institutional Analysis and Design (IAD) theoretical framework and the approach adopted by the institutional economist, Bruce Kaufman. These similarities include a focus on actors, interactions, and, especially, the rules affecting particular labor situations. Austen concludes that these similarities create important opportunities for new heterodox analyses of labor and employment.

In Chapter 26, Matías Vernengo highlights that for heterodox theories the business cycle is endogenous, which means that shocks and propagation mechanisms are not central. Vernengo discusses the inherent instability of the capitalist system from Marxian and Post Keynesian perspectives. The former focuses on the rate of profit as the main variable through which to understand fluctuations; the latter emphasizes that not only the economic system is prone to crises, but also that it could settle at a stable and sub-optimal position in the long-run. Thus, growth is inherently cyclical and economic policy must be geared towards reducing the negative effects of the downward phase of the cycle and to stimulate a boom.

Özgür Orhangazi, in Chapter 27, focuses on Marxian (and Social Structure of Accumulation) and Post Keynesian approaches to economic growth, with a specific attention to growth in developing countries. Five main factors are identified that most heterodox schools recognize as critical to explaining economic growth: aggregate demand, distribution, instability, competition and technical change, and institutions.

However, heterodox theories generally are of the view that economic systems are prone to crises of reproduction and growth. Thus, in Chapter 28, Petra Dünhaupt surveys various strands of heterodox discourse on the financial and real explanations of crises, with a focus on financialization. While the topic has given rise to a burgeoning literature, Dünhaupt shows that heterodox traditions are not in agreement, with some heterodox traditions regarding financialization as a cause of crises and others treating it as a consequence of crises.

The final two chapters of Part IV deal respectively with economic development and the ecological crisis. In Chapter 29, John Marangos surveys alternative theories of international development based on Post Keynesian and Marxian perspectives of social provisioning. The similarities and differences of the different policy approaches to fiscal discipline, public expenditure priorities, tax reform, financial liberalization, exchange rates, trade liberalization, foreign direct investment, privatization, deregulation, property rights, and institution building are extracted.

In Chapter 30, for Anders Ekeland and Bent Arne Sæther ecological issues are the special interest of a minority of scholars. However, as humanity faces potentially devastating global warming, a rapid extinction of biodiversity and other serious environmental problems, theories and policies for full employment and a more equal distribution of resources can no longer be formulated without taking into consideration the ecological consequences. Focusing on ecological, Marxian, and Post Keynesian economics, Ekeland and Sæther show that while finding a solution is easier for mainstream economics—as it is based on the pervasive notion that the price mechanism can take care of all intended actions—drafting policy recommendations from a heterodox perspective requires an understanding of how the economy works, and how policies and strategies should be shaped.

Transforming the capitalist social provisioning process

The chapters in Part V extend the previous theoretical discussions into the policy arena—in particular, chapters in this part envision a more sustainable, egalitarian, equitable economic system that is consistent with and supported by heterodox economic theories. The six chapters of Part V focus on capitalism's ecological crisis, its financial systems, the role of the state, the relationship of the governance of large firms to prosperity and inequality, full employment, social welfare, and social control. All six chapters explain their respective ontological and methodological foundations, as well as the critical conceptualizations, which shape their proposed policy prescriptions.

The ecological crisis is the subject of Chapter 31 in which Lynne Chester contends that an effective exit strategy from the ecological crisis does not lie within the current options presented by the broad dichotomy of alternative policy prescriptions: those advocating the reform of capitalism using the same mechanisms which have embedded the ecological crisis (for example, ecological economics, steady-state economics); and, those proposing a new albeit highly unlikely socio-economic system (for example, ecological Marxism, socialist ecology). Chester argues that there must be a significant shift in our thinking to design a strategy that directly addresses the interdependencies between the spheres that constitute the social and economic organization of capitalism. This chapter contributes to this complex policy task with its analysis of the dialectical relationship between the ecological, energy, and economic spheres and proposes a new regime of capitalist accumulation in which the imperative of ecological preservation is compatible with capitalism's mode of production.

Chapter 32 moves the policy focus to the sphere of finance. Wesley C. Marshall argues that the 2007 global financial crisis not only occurred within the world's most powerful economic institutions in the geographical center of economic power, but the enormous sums of money involved also forced many to rethink the nature of money. Both the meteoric rise of the shadow banking system and its collapse and bailout point, according to Marshall, to the irrefutable observation that money is not scarce despite the global policy of propping up financial asset prices while restricting productive investment, employment, and production being neither economically nor politically sustainable. However, the alternative of abundant funding for full employment and production is also problematic, as simply producing more smoke and steel cannot be a way forward. This chapter proposes that a set of basic structures and principles can transform today's financialized global morass once the non-scarcity of money is openly recognized and understood because the many experiments and lessons learned in global finance mean that designing global, regional, national, and local financial structures is the easy part.

A vision of the state's role in a progressive transformation of the market economy is the focus for Chapter 33 authored by Anna Klimina. Policies to redistribute economic power receive particular attention. Large-scale companies, given the nature of technology and market uncertainties, are envisaged as remaining a key component of a market economy although these companies will require comprehensive restructuring to avoid fragmentation. State capitalism is viewed as a promising form of modern capitalism that can be re-imagined to acknowledge its inherent democratic promise. Through the lens of an institutionalist vision for democratic state control in market-based societies, the chapter discusses how, in state capitalist economies, the state as chief owner of society's productive property and principal controller of the social surplus can nurture institutions that promote effective economic democracy, thus becoming the agent of its own social control.

In Chapter 34, Jordan Brennan argues that the rise of the modern corporate form in early twentieth century helped spawn new schools of economic thought—institutionalism, Neo-Marxism, and Post Keynesianism being three examples—that began to use power (in its many incarnations) as an explanatory variable. Corporate power, according to Brennan, is the key to analyzing and explaining corporate governance. The chapter empirically substantiates this assertion by demonstrating that corporate concentration is strongly and inversely related to GDP growth and income equality, and that the concentration of assets and income among the 100 largest American-listed firms, in conjunction with resource redirection within these firms, has simultaneously depressed growth and exacerbated inequality. Consequently, it is argued, effective policies to alleviate secular stagnation and income inequality must address the corporate governance of large firms.

John Marsh, Timothy Sharpe, and Bruce Philp explore in Chapter 35 the concept of full employment in heterodox perspectives. The problem of unemployment is examined in historical context, alluding to the Great Depression, the 'Golden Age' of capitalism, stagflation, and supply-side policies (especially Thatcherism and Reaganomics). The concept of 'full employment' as a policy objective is explored in the context of Beveridge (1945), as well as post-war policy. These goals are set against theories in the heterodox tradition, which explain unemployment and offer policy prescriptions with regard to achieving full employment. Two heterodox approaches are considered: Marxian economics (in the context of the notion of the 'reserve army of the unemployed') and Post Keynesian aggregate demand management. The job guarantee is then presented as a full employment policy, with particular reference to how the program accommodates the issues raised by these heterodox schools of thought.

Part V concludes with Chapter 36, 'Social welfare and social control' authored by Andrew Cumbers and Robert McMaster. In this chapter, Cumbers and McMaster show how mainstream economics is founded on a utilitarian understanding of welfare, which has developed theoretically into revealed preferences, and so forth, and despite theoretical innovations the standard outlook is consequentialist, which renders all actions instrumental: the value of anything rests solely on its outcomes. Of course, according to the authors, this is also reflected by the mainstream predilection for exchange-value and commodification which means that social welfare is reduced to a series of calculations of a range of feasible (and expected) outcomes. Social control, on this understanding, is achieved through the market: the market represents freedom and dissipates power. Drawing from the extensive critique of both the consequentialist underpinnings of the mainstream and its adulation and conceptualization of the market, Cumbers and McMaster present an analysis that draws from the capabilities approach associated with the works of Amartya Sen and Martha Nussbaum, and apply this to argue about the need for economic democracy. The capabilities approach is based on the Aristotelian notion of human flourishing, and as such is resonant with aspects of Marx's analysis. It offers an alternative framework of the evaluation of well-being, impoverishment, and justice. An appealing aspect of the capabilities approach is that it invokes ontological realism in endeavoring to provide a framework of equality evaluation, despite the limitations of Sen's fairly modest framework in the context of neoliberalism. Cumbers and McMaster contend that capabilities are sensitive to institutional configurations, and that capabilities are more likely to be enhanced by deepening the processes of economic democracy. In doing so, they consider various models of economic democracy and their impact on ownership forms and production relations.

Conclusion

Chapter 37, by Jamie Morgan and John Embery, concludes the *Handbook* project in an effective manner by highlighting the prominent contributions within and reinforcing the objectives set out in this introductory chapter. Importantly, Morgan and Embery make their own case that heterodox economics is a pluralistic movement and a 'critical community' that restores the original meaning of economics as a social science, and hence that the success (in the sense of continuation and reproduction) of heterodox economics is independent of the innovation within mainstream economics; rather, it depends on the positive development of heterodox economic theory and policy, which are fostered by critical engagements among different heterodox traditions through the intellectual community of heterodox economists.

Notes

1 In the introductory chapter of *Future Directions for Heterodox Economics* (2008), a collection of essays presented at the 2003 ICAPE conference held at the University of Missouri-Kansas City, Robert Garnett (2008: 2, emphasis added) states that the book strives for "innovative new *connections* among formerly *separate* theoretical traditions (Marxian, Austrian, feminist, ecological, Sraffian, institutionalist, post-Keynesian)." (This aim reflects one of four goals of ICAPE, that is, "to promote a new spirit of pluralism in economics, involving critical conversation and tolerant communication among different approaches, within and across the barriers between the disciplines" (see ICAPE website, http://icape.org)). In the same volume, Sheila Dow (2008: 9) observes that "I have been increasingly aware that much of the interesting work among young scholars is synthetic in nature, exploring the middle ground between schools of thought and developing new ideas as a result of cross-fertilization. Indeed, arguably, the greatest developments in economics have been the result of new connections being made between formerly separate sets of ideas."
2 In *The Elgar Companion to Social Economics* (2015) 27 percent of contributors are women (14 out of 52) and in the *Oxford Handbook of Post-Keynesian Economics* (2013) 9 percent are women (5 of 56 contributors).
3 For research methods, we would refer readers to the *Handbook of Research Methods and Applications in Heterodox Economics*, edited by Frederic Lee and Bruce Cronin (Edward Elgar, 2016); and for methodology and philosophy, to the works of Tony Lawson such as *Reorienting Economics* (Routledge, 2003) and

Economics and Reality (Routledge, 1997), and *Applied Economics and the Critical Realist Critique*, edited by Paul Downward (Routledge, 2003). We would also recommend readers to see the list of readings on heterodox economics compiled by the *Heterodox Economics Newsletter*, http://heterodoxnews.com/hed/#entry-50.

4 Others do not favor the label 'heterodox' because the dualistic distinction between heterodoxy and orthodoxy-mainstream is considered to de-emphasize the variety and complexity within each, although it may be useful for the purpose of heuristic and analytical convenience (Dow 1990; Mearman 2012).

5 Whether this pluralism should be open to mainstream economics is another question (see Garnett 2011; Mearman 2011; Courvisanos 2016). Journal citation data show that heterodox economists tend to cite mainstream economists, but not *vice versa* (Kapeller 2010), although heterodox economists practice (or tolerate) pluralism to a greater or lesser degree than mainstream economists.

6 Most mainstream economists hold that their economics is the only legitimate paradigm. Regardless of the relevance or empirical validity, any theory that is not 'modeled' in mainstream language is not economics. Economics from the mainstream viewpoint is thus defined not "by its subject matter but by its way of thinking" (Coyle 2007: 232). Viewing economics in terms of methods is common to virtually all variants of mainstream-neoclassical economics, such as neoclassical-feminist economics, neoclassical-social economics (for example, Gary Becker), (evolutionary) game theory, and experimental economics. Some Harvard economics students, for instance, thought that their long-time professor, John Kenneth Galbraith, was not an economist, because "he wasn't a modeler" (Coyle 2007: 231). By the same token, most heterodox economists are not economists in the view of mainstream economists. Heterodox economists are not just the critics of mainstream economics but the 'enemies of economics' (Coleman 2002). Such a bizarre definition of economics is at odds with the nature of social science whose development is characterized by intellectual-scientific pluralism.

7 For the UK and the US, see Lee (2009); for France, see Facarello & Béraud (2000); for Italy, Garofalo & Graziani (2004); for Germany, Heise *et al.* (2017); for Austria, Klausinger (2016); for Spain, see Guerrero (2004).

8 This heritage, though, does not usually extend to topics of money and finance or ecology and natural resources. Perhaps for this reason, today Post Keynesians and ecological economists draw comparatively less from classical political economy.

9 Although of course in this period the teaching and practice of neoliberal economics was even violently enforced in some countries, such as Chile (see Valdés 1995).

10 Some of them obtained notable positions in academia. For example, Josef Steindl was conferred an honorary professorship at the University of Vienna, in spite of an initial cold reception (Guger & Walterskirchen 2012).

11 See, for example, the articles published in the 2010 special issue (Vol. 69, No. 5) of the *American Journal of Economics and Sociology*.

12 This includes financial as well as political support. In some countries, such as Germany, sources of support have so far been limited to trade unions and progressive parties' foundations, whereas in the US it is mostly non-partisan bodies that express a demand for non-mainstream economics. In other countries, such as France and Italy, there seems to be little, if any, social awareness of (and interest in) economic pluralism and the existence of heterodox economics.

References

Association Française d'Economie Politique (AFEP). 2009. Evolution of economics professors' recruitment since 2000 in France. Available from http://assoeconomiepolitique.org/wp-content/uploads/FAPE-State-of-pluralism-in-France-Final-Version.pdf [Accessed January 20, 2017]

Ayres, C.E. 1936. 'Fifty years' development in ideas of human nature and motivation.' *American Economic Review*, 26 (1, supplement): 224–236.

Beveridge, W. 1945. *Full Employment in a Free Society*. New York: Norton.

Coleman, W.O. 2002. *Economics and its Enemies*. New York: Palgrave Macmillan.

Corsi, M., D'Ippoliti, C., & Lucidi, F. 2011. 'On the evaluation of economic research: the case of Italy.' *Economia Política*, 28 (3): 369–402.

Courvisanos, J. 2016. 'In from the cold: from heterodoxy to a new mainstream pluralism,' *in*: J. Courvisanos, J. Doughney, & A. Millmow (eds.), *Reclaiming Pluralism in Economics*. London: Routledge, 303–316.

Coyle, D. 2007. *The Soulful Science: What Economists Really Do and Why It Matters*. Princeton, NJ: Princeton University Press.

Dobusch, L. & Kapeller, J. 2012. 'A guide to paradigmatic self-marginalization: lessons for Post-Keynesian economists.' *Review of Political Economy*, 24 (3): 469–487.

Dow, S.C. 1990. 'Beyond dualism.' *Cambridge Journal of Economics*, 12 (2): 143–157.

Dow, S.C. 2008. 'A future for schools of thought and pluralism in heterodox economics,' *in*: J.T. Harvey & R.F. Garnett (eds.), *Future Directions of Heterodox Economics*. Ann Arbor, MI: University of Michigan Press, 9–26.

Facarello, G. & Béraud, A. 2000. *Nouvelle histoire de la pensée économique: Des institutionnalistes à la période contemporaine*, tome 3, Paris: La Découverte.

Garnett, R.F. 2008. 'Introduction: pluralism and the future of heterodox economics,' *in*: J.T. Harvey & R.F. Garnett (eds.), *Future Directions of Heterodox Economics*. Ann Arbor, MI: University of Michigan Press, 1–6.

Garnett, R.F. 2011. 'Pluralism, academic freedom, and heterodox economics.' *Review of Radical Political Economics*, 43 (4): 562–572.

Garofalo, G. & Graziani, A. 2004. *La formazione degli economisti in Italia, 1950–1975*. Bologna: Il Mulino.

Gruchy, A. 1987. *The Reconstruction of Economics: An Analysis of the Fundamentals of Institutional Economics*. New York: Greenwood Press.

Guerrero, D. 2004. Historia del pensamiento económico heterodoxo. Available from http://www.eumed.net/cursecon/libreria [Accessed January 20, 2017]

Guger, A. & Walterskirchen, E. 2012. 'Josef Steindl's life and work in Austria.' *PSL Quarterly Review*, 65 (261): 135–149.

Heise, A., Sander, H., & Thieme, S. 2017. *Das Ende der Heterodoxie? Die Entwicklung der Wirtschaftswissenschaften in Deutschland*. Wiesbaden: Springer VS.

Kapeller, J. 2010. 'Some critical notes on citation metrics and heterodox economics.' *Review of Radical Political Economics*, 42 (3): 330–337.

King, J.E. 2016. 'Pluralist economics in my lifetime,' *in*: J. Courvisanos, J. Doughney, & A. Millmow (eds.), *Reclaiming Pluralism in Economics*. London: Routledge, 3–13.

Klausinger, H. 2016. 'The Nationalökonomische Gesellschaft (Austrian Economic Association) in the Interwar Period and beyond.' *Research in the History of Economic Thought and Methodology*, 34A: 9–43.

Kregel, J. 1988. *Recollections of Eminent Economists*. Basingstoke, UK: Macmillan.

Lawson, T. 2006. 'The nature of heterodox economics.' *Cambridge Journal of Economics*, 30 (4): 483–505.

Lee, F.S. 2007. 'The research assessment exercise, the state and the dominance of mainstream economics in British universities.' *Cambridge Journal of Economics*, 31 (2): 309–325.

Lee, F.S. 2009. *A History of Heterodox Economics: Challenging the Mainstream in the Twentieth Century*. London: Routledge.

Lee, F.S. 2011. 'The pluralism debate in heterodox economics.' *Review of Radical Political Economics*, 43 (4): 540–551.

Lee, F.S. 2012. 'Heterodox economics and its critics.' *Review of Political Economy*, 24 (2): 337–351.

Lee, F.S. & Cronin, B.C. 2010. 'Research quality rankings of heterodox economic journals in a contested discipline.' *American Journal of Economics and Sociology*, 69 (5): 1409–1452.

Lee, F.S. & Lavoie, M. (eds.) 2012. *In Defense of Post-Keynesian and Heterodox Economics*. London: Routledge.

Lutz, M.A. 2009. 'Social economics,' *in*: J. Peil & I. van Staveren (eds.), *Handbook of Economics and Ethics*. Cheltenham, UK: Edward Elgar, 516–522.

Mearman, A. 2011. 'Pluralism, heterodoxy, and the rhetoric of distinction.' *Review of Radical Political Economics*, 43 (4): 552–561.

Mearman, A. 2012. '"Heterodox economics" and the problems of classification.' *Journal of Economic Methodology*, 19 (4): 407–424.

O'Hara, P.A. 2002. 'The role of institutions and the current crises of capitalism: a reply to Howard Sherman and John Henry.' *Review of Social Economy*, 60 (4): 609–618.

O'Hara, P.A. 2007. 'Principles of institutional-evolutionary political economy: converging themes from the schools of heterodoxy.' *Journal of Economic Issues*, 41 (1): 1–42.

Olson, P. 1999. 'Feminist political economy: history and nature,' *in*: P.A. O'Hara (ed.), *Encyclopedia of Political Economy, Vol. 1*. London: Routledge, 327–331.

Pasinetti, L.L. & Roncaglia, A. 2006. 'Le scienze umane in Italia: il caso dell'economia politica.' *Rivista Italiana degli Economisti*, 11 (3): 463–475.

Peterson, J. 1995. 'For whom? Institutional economics and distributional issues in the economics classroom.' *Journal of Economic Issues*, 29 (2): 567–574.

Prasch, R.E. 2013. '100 words on heterodox economics,' *in*: T.-H. Jo (ed.), *Heterodox Economics Directory*, 5th edn. Available from http://heterodoxnews.com/directory/hed5.pdf [Accessed December 13, 2016]

Roncaglia, A. 2005. *The Wealth of Ideas: A History of Economic Thought*. Cambridge: Cambridge University Press.

Valdés, J.G. 1995. *Pinochet's Economists: The Chicago School in Chile*. Cambridge: Cambridge University Press.

Veblen, T. 1904. *The Theory of Business Enterprise*. New York: Charles Scribner's Sons.

Veblen, T. 1909. 'The limitations of marginal utility.' *Journal of Political Economy*, 17 (9): 620–636.

Part II
The theoretical cores of heterodox economics

2

Social provisioning process

A heterodox view of the economy

Tae-Hee Jo and Zdravka Todorova

Introduction

This chapter discusses the social provisioning process, a heterodox view of the economy and the subject matter of heterodox economic inquiry, which, we argue, provides theoretical and methodological grounds for developing heterodox economics as a historically emergent alternative to mainstream-neoclassical economics. Towards this end, we first examine how the meaning of the economy changed from classical political economy to neoclassical economics. The comparison between them manifests the latter's asocial and ahistorical view of the economy and economics. We also demonstrate that contemporary heterodox economics is the continuation and positive development of classical political economy that bears on the socially embedded view of the economy with a theoretical emphasis on production and distribution. In this respect, we argue that the social provisioning process is a felicitous concept of the economy in light of classical political economy as well as various persuasions in contemporary heterodox economics. The second section elaborates the social provisioning process and its implication for developing heterodox economics in a pluralistic manner. The last section concludes the chapter.

Classical political economy, neoclassical economics, and heterodox economics

The meaning of the economy, as found in Aristotle and ancient literature, is closely tied up with the management of the material basis of the household or the sovereign nation through non-economic institutions—politics, in particular. The term 'management' implies; firstly, the exercise of power of one or more social classes over others—that is, the class division with uneven distribution of social power is the social basis of the economy; secondly, the continuation and reproduction of the economy over time—that is, the economy involves instituted processes and going concerns; and thirdly, resources are made to be available as they go through the resource management process (production and reproduction). Initially, economics is thus defined as a science or art of managing the economy.

With this broad concept of the economy, classical political economy analyzed such activities as exchange, production, distribution, and consumption in the context of the social creation and accumulation of wealth. As discussed below, it was not until the emergence of neoclassical economics in the late nineteenth century that the economy was defined exclusively as market exchanges. The separation of the economy from the society is a deliberate break with the conventional meaning of the economy—that is, neoclassical economists' "basic strategy is to eliminate history and society from the subject and reduce it to a mathematical science—an optimization problem" (Steindl [1984] 1990: 243). This is a unique characteristic of mainstream-neoclassical economics. Apart from the neoclassical conception of the economy, heterodox economists, sociologists, anthropologists, among others, have not abandoned the view that the economy is part and parcel of society (Polanyi 1965, 1968; Granovetter 1985; Baranzini & Scazzieri 1986). In what follows the historical changes in the definition of economics is sketched from classical political economy to neoclassical economics.

From classical political economy to neoclassical economics

The management concept of the economy is epitomized in Adam Smith's definition of political economy. Smith declares that

> [p]olitical economy, considered a branch of the science of a statesman or legislator, proposes two distinct objects: first, to provide a plentiful revenue or subsistence for the people, or more properly to enable them to provide such a revenue or subsistence for themselves; and secondly, to supply the state or commonwealth with a revenue sufficient for the public services. It proposes to enrich both the people and the sovereign.
>
> *Smith [1776] 1994: 455*

For Smith, the nature of the economy lies in the provision of the material means of life so that the people and the nation as a whole continue their living. Accordingly, political economy is *an inquiry into the nature and causes of the wealth of nations*. Here readers should note the historical context from which Smith's definition emerges. For Smith and other classical political economists, it is inconceivable that the economy is separable from politics or society.

Other classical political economists held a similar view of political economy: "[t]o determine the laws which regulate this distribution [of rents, profits, and wages], is the principal problem in Political Economy" (Ricardo [1817] 1951: 5); "the science which treats of the production and distribution of wealth, so far as they depend upon the laws of human nature" (Mill 1836: 318). And for Karl Marx, political economy inquires into "the real relations of production in bourgeois society in contradistinction to vulgar economy, which deals with appearances only, ruminates without ceasing on the materials long since provided by scientific economy" (Marx 1867: 58). The 'real relations' or the underlying laws of the economy, from Marx's perspective, bear the capitalist class relationship that requires the exploitation of the working class by the capitalist class whose interest is accumulating capital that is rendered possible by generating the surplus in the capitalist mode of production.

Apparently, besides their political and ethical values, classical political economists address a common theoretical issue—that is, the creation and distribution of wealth or the surplus. Accordingly, the theoretical basis is the surplus approach in which wealth and its distribution is connected to the social structures and institutional arrangements of the time, and which is completely ignored by marginalist-neoclassical economics (Martins 2015: 226).

Economists after Ricardo and Marx, however, shifted their attention from the social to the individual. In the view of Nassau Senior, for example, political economy is the science of studying the behavior of an individual who "*desires to obtain additional wealth with as little sacrifice as possible*"

([1836] 1965: 138, italics in original). Carl Menger and Stanley Jevons, respectively, define that "[e]conomic theory is related to the practical activities of economizing men in much the same way that chemistry is related to the operations of the practical chemist" (Menger [1871] 2007: 48); economics is "a calculus of pleasure and pain; and the object of Economics is to maximize happiness by purchasing pleasure . . . at the lowest cost of pain" (Jevons [1871] 1965: 23).

What is noteworthy in these marginalist definitions of economics is that the relationship between individuals and resources, or between unlimited (and 'given') preferences and scarce (and 'given') resources, becomes the predominant subject matter of economics. At the same time, the theoretical concern with the relationship between human beings and society that governs the behavior of individuals therein, is eschewed. This shift in analytical focus calls for a new concept of scarcity. In the marginalist (and, later, neoclassical) thinking scarcity is invariably conceived as the paucity of available resources, rather than the difficulty of production (Baranzini & Scazzieri 1986: 21).

If rational or optimizing behavior taken out of the social context is the subject matter of economics, the appropriate method required to explain such behavior is to be mathematical and mechanical rather than historical and social. If a deductive-mathematical method is to be used, the starting point of economics is not the social reality found in the capitalist system, but the 'mental constructs' (or a set of hypothetical assumptions) that determine the practice of economics. Thus ensuing theories and models based on mental constructs "present this society as the natural or rational form of organization which, in one form or another, has existed universally" (Henry 2009: 28). In neoclassical theories and models, consequently, the "open, structured, processual, and highly internally related" nature of the social reality is replaced by a "closed atomistic reality" (Lawson 2005: 435–436). Theoretically, such a radical change in economists' thinking is also represented by the utility theory of value not only as an anti-thesis to the labor theory of value (Henry 1990: 238–244), but also as "a reaction against the criticism of the capitalist system by Marx and others" (Steindl [1984] 1990: 243), not to mention that the marginalist theory of price and distribution was designed to replace the classical surplus approach (Roncaglia 2005: 278–80). Furthermore, the neoclassical theory of production that is "a one-way avenue that leads from 'Factors of production' to 'Consumption goods'" objects to the classical approach to "the system of production and consumption as a circular process" (Sraffa 1960: 93). All these theoretical constructs reflecting the neoclassical view of capitalist economy led to the law of supply and demand, which is applied to economic activities as if there only exists competitive capitalism regardless of time and space (Henry 2009: 29–30). On this Alfred Marshall ([1890] 1947: viii) declares that "the general theory of the equilibrium of demand and supply is a Fundamental Idea running through the frames all the various parts of the central problem of Distribution and Exchange."

Consequently, the asocial, individualistic, and subjectivist view of economics is put in a nutshell by Lionel Robbins:

> The economist studies the disposal of scarce means. He is interested in the way different degrees of scarcity of different goods give rise to ratios of valuation between them, and he is interested in the way in which changes in conditions of scarcity, whether coming from changes in ends or changes in means—from the demand side or the supply side—affect these ratios. *Economics is the science which studies human behaviour as a relationship between ends and scarce means which have alternative uses.*
>
> *Robbins [1932] 1935: 16, italics added*

Robbins' definition has been received by virtually all neoclassical economists since then (Backhouse & Medema 2009a, b). Just to mention some notable examples echoing

Robbins: economics is "the study of principles governing the allocation of scarce means among competing ends when the objective of the allocation is to maximize the attainment of the ends" (Stigler 1942: 12); "An economic problem exists whenever *scarce* means are used to satisfy *alternative* ends" (Friedman 1962: 6, original italics); economics is about "[h]ow . . . we choose to use scarce resources with alternative uses, to meet prescribed ends" (Samuelson 1970: 13).

Obviously, the change in the definition of economics in the nineteenth and early twentieth centuries not only reflects the dominance of the capitalist class, but also requires a new set of theories and methods that are suitable for the asocial market-centered definition of economics. In other words, a definition of economics received by a group of economists is the representation of a particular standpoint that determines and legitimizes a set of theories and methods.

From classical political economy to heterodox economics

While the neoclassical view of the capitalist economy and economics is derived directly from individualism and marginalism, heterodox economics is deeply rooted in classical political economy's conceptualization of the economy that is an integral fabric of society. This socially embedded view of the economy is the entry point of both classical political economy and contemporary heterodox economics in terms of the scope, theory, and method. The scope of economics extends to non-market and unpaid activities enmeshed in a larger society. The method is not confined to the deductive-mathematical method. Such a vision of the economy and economics is most palpable in the works of Karl Marx, Thorstein Veblen, and John Maynard Keynes, the three notable precursors of heterodox economics, who continued Smith's political economy in one way or another (as opposed to the neoclassical interpretation of Smith). In stark contrast to hedonistic economics or neoclassical economics, Veblen and Keynes express their own vision of economics (that is in line with Marx's definition of scientific political economy as noted earlier):

> In so far as it is a science in the current sense of the term, any science, such as economics, which has to do with human conduct, becomes a generic inquiry into the human scheme of life; and where, as in economics, the subject of inquiry is the conduct of man in his dealings with the materials means of life, the science is necessarily an inquiry into the life-history of material civilization. . . . Not that the economist's inquiry isolates material civilization from all other phases and bearings of human culture, and so studies the motions of an abstractly conceived "economic man."
>
> *Veblen 1909: 627–628, original emphasis*

> He [a political economist] must be mathematician, historian, statesman, philosopher—to some degree. . . . He must study the present in the light of the past for the purpose of the future. No part of man's nature or his institutions must lie outside his regard.
>
> *Keynes 1972: 173–174*

> [A]gainst Robbins, economics is essentially a moral science and not a natural science. That is to say, it employs introspection and judgment of value.
>
> *Keynes 1973: 297*

In order to provide a dynamic explanation of the economic structure of society that governs the 'life-history of material civilization,' Marx, Veblen, and Keynes respectively developed a similar theoretical framework centered on the capitalist mode of production—that is, the way production is organized by capital (Marx), the business enterprise (Veblen), or entrepreneurs

(Keynes). It is not a coincidence that production is the central concern in their respective theoretical system. As noted earlier, in classical political economy the scarcity of resources at a given point in time is understood as a difficulty of production arising mainly from existing institutional arrangements, such as social, technical, legal, regulatory, and ideological setups. Furthermore, the neoclassical concept of scarcity becomes irrelevant and misleading if the economy is viewed from the historical-evolutionary perspective as in Marx, Veblen, and Keynes (Robinson [1977] 1980: 8; Henry 2011: 72–75).

In this production-oriented, production-based capitalist system, resources are reproduced in the technically interrelated process of production between capitals or industries—that is, the *circular production economy*, which is most rigorously and clearly formulated by Sraffa (1960). The circular production economy indicates that production is not only a complicated process that can hardly be represented by a simple neoclassical production function, but also a social process in which basic goods and surplus goods sectors are *technically* connected, and going concerns— households, the business enterprise, the state, and market governance organizations—are *socially* connected to each other through the structure of production and incomes. In this theoretical framework, the viability of the system as a whole (and of going concerns therein) becomes a fundamental question, as opposed to the feasibility of production based upon scarce resources and the efficient allocation of resources through the market mechanism (Walsh & Gram 1980: 397, 404–405; Baranzini & Scazzieri 1986: 34–35).

The viability of the system here means both economic and social reproduction that are intertwined in the process of production (Chiodi 2010: 324). Capitalists engage in the production of commodities with the expectation of generating the flow of monetary profits. With this expectation, the capitalists' and the state's decision to produce surplus goods—that is, *effective demand*— drives the production of basic goods, the employment of labor power, and the generation of profits in the circular production system. In this regard, the capitalist economy is also translated theoretically into the *surplus production economy* driven by effective demand (Lee & Jo 2011; Martins 2015). Furthermore, once the capitalist economy is seen through the lens of the theories of circular and surplus production, what matters most for the capitalist class is "the vendibility of output, its convertibility into money values, not its serviceability for the needs of mankind" (Veblen 1904: 51). The dominance of money-making activities over goods-making activities in the capitalist economy is also addressed by both Marx and Keynes: "the immediate purpose of capitalist production is not 'possession of other goods' but the appropriation of value, of money, of abstract wealth" (Marx 1969: 503); and "[a]n entrepreneur is interested not in the amount of product, but in the amount of *money* which will fall to his share" (Keynes 1979: 82, original italics). And this essential peculiarity of money or credit is captured in Marx's, Veblen's, and Keynes' view that capitalism is the *monetary production economy* (see Dillard 1980; Henry 2011).

The vendibility—that is, C'-M' in Marx's circuit of money capital—is the end of production (but not the end of capital). The means to achieve this end is the conversion of money capital into inputs (M-C) required in the process of production. In addition, there arises an inherent conflict of interests between the capitalist class and the working class (Marx) and between the vested interests and the underlying population (Veblen). Consequently, the livelihood of the working class (or the provisioning of use-value or goods and services represented by C-M-C') becomes subservient to the profit-oriented activities of the capitalist class—that is, M-C-M', the provisioning of exchange-value or monetary profits (Veblen 1904: 157–158).

In a nutshell, the heterodox economic framework following Marx, Veblen, and Keynes manifests that the historical development of capitalism centered on the production process is felicitously explained by the theories of circular, surplus, and monetary production. Heterodox economics equipped with these theories runs counter to the neoclassical framework centered on the market-exchange mechanism in which money plays no essential role. If the means of production are assumed to be scarce, either relatively or absolutely, the produced surplus goods have to be scarce as well. This logical consequence lacks empirical validity to the extent that in most advanced countries a pressing economic problem is not the 'scarcity' of inputs and outputs but the unequal distribution of 'abundant' surplus goods, and that in less developed countries it is not necessarily the scarcity of resources but the difficulty of production due to the lack of technology in utilizing given (but not scarce) resources or the lack of incomes earned by working-class households. It follows that the provisioning of goods and services is organized by those who make decisions to produce goods and services, and those who control the system of production and consumption, not by the hypothetical market price mechanism. Therefore, the viability of the capitalist system as a whole rests on incomes generated in the production process, as well as on outputs, relations, and activities located outside of socially organized markets. The material provisioning process encompassing a wide range of activities is in its nature social and historical. In the following section, we will further elaborate on the concept of the social provisioning process as a heterodox conception of the economy.

The social provisioning process

The principal implication of the preceding section is that heterodox economics is a body of historically contingent social theory with an analytical focus on real economic activities, as articulated by classical political economists and three precursors of heterodox economics. As a social science, economics explores constituents of society, which make up an organic whole of the social system. Such constituents include, but are not limited to, acting persons and organizations, their agency qua power to make strategic decisions, social structures and relationships, and social institutions. Essentially, individual units of economic activities are embedded in the economy, which is in turn embedded in and an integral part of the society.

Embeddedness bears the non-linear emergent relationship and interdependence between agents and structures. It is interactive agency through social institutions that renders individuals, organizations, and the whole society ongoing. It follows that an analytical reduction of the whole to the individual or the converse is neither possible nor sensible, since such an attempt removes the interrelationships between constituents that generate, constrain, or facilitate the dynamics of the social system. Furthermore, it is inconceivable that the economy can be reduced to a system of exchange coordinated by the market price mechanism.

In short, a heterodox view of the economy is "an instituted process of interaction between man and his environment, which results in a continuous supply of want-satisfying material means" (Polanyi 1968: 145). To our understanding (and as elaborated further below), this is a core vision of the economy received by economists of various heterodox persuasions. With this vision, economics may well be defined as "the study of the on-going process that provides the flow of goods and services required by society to meet the needs of those who participate in its activities. . . . [Economics is] the science of social provisioning" (Gruchy 1987: 21). In other words, "[economics] is really the study of the process whereby surpluses are created in economies, how they are extracted, who gets them and what they do with them" (Harcourt 1986: 5).

Heterodox economic theory and the social provisioning process

As of Gruchy's (1987) definition of economics, heterodox economists in different persuasions have accepted and expanded on it. Not only institutionalists but also Marxian, Post Keynesian, social, ecological, and feminist economists find that the concept of the social provisioning process is fitting with their own vision of the economy and economics (see, for example, Nelson 1993; Dugger 1996; Power 2004, 2015; Mellor 2006; Lee 2009; Jo 2011; Badeen 2015; Figart & Mutari 2015; Todorova 2015b). This favorable reception of Gruchy's definition has often led to an effort to synthesize heterodox approaches. Yet, such a synthesis, or openness to other heterodox approaches, is not always endorsed or exercised by heterodox economists. We leave open the question as to why heterodox economists are divided in the attitude towards an integrative approach. In what follows, instead, we make a case that the social provisioning process is a suitable (in a theoretical sense) and useful (in a sociological-communal sense) entry point to advance heterodox economics in a positive and constructive manner. Let us elaborate on the meaning of the social provisioning process.

Capitalist economy can be conceptualized and theorized in many different ways. The social provisioning process is one of them that lays emphasis on a social and processual-historical account as to how the economy is organized and reproduced. The social provisioning process is thus situated in the long intellectual tradition, which concerns the material basis of the society as an outcome of the open-ended interaction or struggle between human beings and nature, between social classes, and between agency and social structures (as discussed later).

Provisioning is a vast range of activities, including both market and non-market, paid and unpaid activities, undertaken by human agents and going-concern organizations for the sake of their survival and reproduction (Nelson 1993; Power 2004; Folbre 2009). Consider the provisioning of goods under capitalism. It is a course of action encompassing the use of resources, production, sales, and consumption. Its starting point is the business enterprise's decision to produce consumption (or surplus) goods given production technology that determines the use of particular resources produced by other sectors of the economy. Household consumption is thus dependent upon the for-market production decision to the extent that household wage incomes are earned as a reward for selling labor power to the business enterprise (or the capitalist class in general). That is, the business enterprise creates the demand for labor by creating jobs with specific labor skills, and the significant part of welfare of the working class is controlled by the business enterprise via controlling the wage rates and producing wage goods that are necessary for the working class (Veblen 1919: 160–163). The provisioning of commodities, therefore, is closely linked to the provisioning of technology, employment, income, and welfare, that are further rooted in the division of classes legitimizing the uneven distribution of socio-economic power qua agency and of distribution of income and wealth. In this regard, Kalecki (1943) observes that the capitalist class has a vested interest (and power) in maintaining less than full employment for both economic and political reasons. It follows that the provisioning of welfare for the majority of the society is not a result of market exchanges that are conditioned by the money-making activities of the business enterprise. In this respect, the Pareto efficient allocation of resources as a criterion for judging the state of welfare is irrelevant to the provisioning of welfare in the hierarchical class society. Instead, in light of the social provisioning process, material welfare is (to be) understood in the context of (re)production that is driven by capitalists' effective demand for surplus goods in the monetary-circular production economy whose structural-cyclical properties are formed by the set of social institutions.

Consider now the provisioning of resources. They come into use as they are needed to make goods and monetary profits. It is the production of goods and services combined with production technology currently in use that determines the volume and kind of resources to be utilized. That is to say, the processual causality runs from a production decision to resource provisioning, rather than given and scarce resources determine what and how much to produce. On this institutionalists argue that resources are not scarce, but 'they become' (De Gregori 1987) and they are socially generated, cultivated, and managed in the course of the provisioning of goods. It follows that if resources are not scarce, prices cannot be scarcity indexes. If there is no scarcity index, market activities cannot be coordinated by the price mechanism (Jo 2016). The concept of provisioning thus rejects the market price mechanism and, hence, requires an alternative theoretical framework that explains how activities are organized, "how resources are come into use, how wants arise, and what economic activities mean" (Dugger 1996: 32).

A social process of provisioning is also congruent with empirical and theoretical arguments that most prices of goods and services are determined outside the market in the sense that administrators of the business enterprise or of market governance organizations (such as cartels, trade associations, and price leadership) set prices by determining profit mark-ups over various costs of production. Product prices are thus administered and made to be stable so as the business enterprise to remain ongoing and to grow over time (Means [1933] 1992a, [1935] 1992b; Lee 2013), and wages are socially determined and administered (Figart *et al.* 2002: 211–212).

In the social provisioning process, agents make a living through going concerns whose basic and primary objective is continuation and growth, be it a household, a business enterprise, or the government. This objective is achieved by making strategic decisions, as opposed to optimal decisions, with the expectation of uncertain future outcomes as well as the consideration of existing institutional arrangements. It further implies that if we are concerned with a 'full economic analysis,' beyond 'pure theory,' both behaviors and institutions in a social context are to be taken into account, since they manifest a dynamic interrelationship between themselves in historical time (Bortis 1997: 103–108; Pasinetti 2005). In this regard, the social provisioning process calls for a 'full' or comprehensive economic analysis of the subject matter, as opposed to a partial, static, and pure one.

We find that the concept of the social provisioning process has the following analytical strengths. Firstly, a broadly defined provisioning concept enables a social analysis of economic activities. Consumption and production are, for example, explained in close connection to the underlying system of institutions, that are described as a mode of production, a social structure of accumulation, or accumulation regimes (see Chapter 4 by Labrousse & Michel in this volume). A going-concern household makes its living by engaging in the production and consumption of commodities (paid work) and non-commodities (unpaid work), such as birthing, raising, educating, and recreation, all of which are essential to the life process, as feminist economists point out. These production activities are intertwined with each other in that, for example, recreation and care activities require earned income, and to earn wage income labor power should be recreated or refreshed (Todorova 2015a: 109–110). In this regard, the process of social provisioning takes into account not only the circular production between industries (that is, input-output relations) but also the linkages between going-concern activities (that is, the connectivity between paid and unpaid, economic and social activities). Such an interrelationship can be extended to other constituents of society such as values, beliefs, institutions, technology, and environment, that are organized by the principles of reciprocity, redistribution, and exchange, as illustrated by a social fabric matrix (Hayden 1982, 2011). It thus becomes clear that once provisioning is reduced to market exchange, both non-market and unpaid activities are removed from economic analysis. Economics with the view of the social provisioning process unravels that, as feminist economists argue, choice and market exchange are not the central but secondary part of the provisioning process (Nelson 1993: 33) and "[c]entral to this [provisioning process] would be the idea of sufficiency and not the dynamics of the market or the profit-motive" (Mellor 2006: 146).

Secondly, the concept of the social provisioning process lends itself to a view that economic theory is a social and historical analysis of the subject matter assisted by diverse methods. As the social provisioning process in historical time is open-ended, an explanation of it is open to any analytical methods—quantitative, qualitative, or mixed—insofar as a selected method is suitable for the analysis of a particular subject matter in hand, as opposed to the idealized model world in which the actual social provisioning process has little or no meaning. This means that economics is not to be defined in terms of method or models, but to be defined in terms of its subject matter, which should not be confined to any particular method (Lee 2016). If economics is merely a set of analytical tools and methods that are designed to explain the relationship between individual behavior and scarce resources, historical changes and dynamics of the economy and its sub-systems are nothing but instantaneous and transient phenomena. An analysis of the social provisioning process, in contrast, takes into account underlying social relationships and social institutions, which give rise to structural and persistent change in society. An actual provisioning process may not be represented by a simple model that most economists wish to build. But the methodological position derived from the concept of the social provisioning process is that the simplicity of a model is not a sufficient condition for developing an economic theory, insofar as heterodox economics is concerned. What matters most in developing heterodox economic theory is the view that theory is a representation of the actual process of provisioning, and that theory explores how the provisioning process is organized and reproduced.

Conclusion

The social provisioning process is central in understanding and analyzing the economy as a system embedded within nature and society. Accordingly, heterodox economics may well be defined as the study of the social provisioning process. Such an expansive definition bears some theoretical, methodological, and sociological benefits.

At the theoretical level, if the economy is conceptualized as the social provisioning process, the primary analytical concern of economics lies in the provisioning of goods and services, resources, and welfare for the sake of reproduction of people and going-concern organizations in socio-historical context. That is, the entry point and basis of economic analysis is the society and its provisioning process. This is how classical political economy and heterodox economics have been practiced. Specifically, theories of circular, surplus, and monetary production offer an insight into how the capitalist economy is organized and controlled in the social context. The concept of the social provisioning process thus expands on the long tradition of economics as a social science, and promotes socio-economic changes in favor of the majority of the population by exploring the underlying institutions of the society.

At the level of methodology, the social provisioning process endorses a viewpoint that the economy is part and parcel of the society in which individuals and organizations make their living by engaging in a range of economic and non-economic, market and non-market, paid and unpaid activities. Thus the social provisioning process restores the original meaning of 'political economy,' as in Smith, Ricardo, Marx, Veblen, and Keynes, among others. It is also pointed out that an analysis of the social provisioning process is not confined to a particular method, since the social provisioning process is a view of the real world, not of the model world created by an abstract model.

Finally, an attempt to define heterodox economics as the science of the social provisioning process implies that the positive identity of heterodox economics can be established as heterodox economists expand on it with an emphasis on the commonalities between various traditions within heterodox economics. That is to say, current heterodox economics can be positioned in the wide spectrum of economics as an alternative to and independent of mainstream-neoclassical economics. Thus such an attempt is part of the deliberate and ongoing heterodox economics movement that goes beyond the opposition to mainstream-neoclassical economics.

Acknowledgments

This chapter is dedicated to Frederic S. Lee (1949–2014). He not only argued vigorously that the concept of the social provisioning process is a way to unite various heterodox traditions, but also showed in his theoretical work that a heterodox economic theory grounded in the social provisioning process is different from, independent of, and more relevant than the mainstream-neoclassical economics. He gladly took the task of writing this chapter for the *Handbook*, but, sadly, he died before writing it. We took over his task. We hope that we have addressed what he wanted to say, and that we have added value to his contribution to the analysis of the social provisioning process. We are grateful to John F. Henry, Nuno Ornelas Martins, Lynne Chester, and Carlo D'Ippoliti for their valuable comments.

References

Backhouse, R.E. & Medema, S.G. 2009a. 'Defining economics: the long road to acceptance of the Robbins definition.' *Economica*, 76 (Supplement): 805–820.
Backhouse, R.E. & Medema, S.G. 2009b. 'On the definition of economics.' *Journal of Economic Perspectives*, 23 (1): 221–233.
Badeen, D. 2015. 'An organicist critique of the ahistorical character of orthodox economics.' *Capital & Class*, 39 (1): 51–64.
Baranzini, M. & Scazzieri, R. 1986. 'Knowledge in economics: a framework,' in: M. Baranzini & R. Scazzieri (eds.), *Foundations of Economics: Structures of Inquiry and Economic Theory*. Oxford: Basil Blackwell, 1–88.
Bortis, H. 1997. *Institutions, Behaviour and Economic Theory*. Cambridge: Cambridge University Press.
Chiodi, G. 2010. 'The means of subsistence and the notion of 'viability' in Sraffa's surplus approach,' in: S. Zambelli (ed.), *Computable, Constructive and Behavioural Economic Dynamics: Essays in Honour of Kumaraswamy (Vela) Velupilla*. London: Routledge, 318–330.
De Gregori, T.R. 1987. 'Resources are not; they become: an institutional theory.' *Journal of Economic Issues*, 21 (3): 1241–1263.
Dillard, D. 1980. 'A monetary theory of production: Keynes and institutionalists.' *Journal of Economic Issues*, 14 (2): 255–273.
Dugger, W. 1996. 'Redefining economics: from market allocation to social provisioning,' in: C. Whalen (ed.), *Political Economy for the 21st Century*. Armonk, NY: M.E. Sharpe, 31–43.
Figart, D. & Mutari, E. 2015. 'Social provisioning through work,' in: J. Davis & W. Dolfsma (eds.), *The Elgar Companion to Social Economics*, 2nd edn. Cheltenham, UK: Edward Elgar, 314–330.
Figart, D., Mutari, E., & Power, M. 2002. *Living Wages, Equal Wages: Gender and Labor Market Policies in the United States*. London: Routledge.
Folbre, N. 2009. *Greed, Lust, and Gender: A History of Economic Ideas*. Oxford: Oxford University Press.
Friedman, M. 1962. *Price Theory: A Provisional Text*. Chicago: Aldine.
Granovetter, M. 1985. 'Economic action and social structure: the problem of embeddedness.' *American Journal of Sociology*, 91 (3): 481–510.
Gruchy, A. 1987. *The Reconstruction of Economics: An Analysis of the Fundamentals of Institutional Economics*. New York: Greenwood Press.
Harcourt, G.C. 1986. *Controversies in Political Economy*. New York: New York University Press.
Hayden, F.G. 1982. 'Social fabric matrix: from perspective to analytical tool.' *Journal of Economic Issues*, 16 (3): 637–662.
Hayden, F.G. 2011. 'Integrating the social structure of accumulation and social accounting matrix with the social fabric matrix.' *American Journal of Economics and Sociology*, 70 (5): 1208–1233.
Henry, J.F. 1990. *The Making of Neoclassical Economics*. Boston: Unwin Hyman.
Henry, J.F. 2009. 'The illusion of the epoch: neoclassical economics as a case study.' *Studi e Note di Economia*, 14 (1): 27–44.
Henry, J.F. 2011. 'Sismondi, Marx, and Veblen: precursors of Keynes,' in: J. Leclaire, T.-H. Jo, & J. Knodell (eds.), *Heterodox Analysis of Financial Crisis and Reform*. Cheltenham, UK: Edward Elgar, 72–83.
Jevons, W.S. [1871] 1965. *The Theory of Political Economy*. New York: Augustus M. Kelley.
Jo, T.-H. 2011. 'Social provisioning process and socio-economic modeling.' *American Journal of Economics and Sociology*, 70 (5): 1094–1116.

Jo, T.-H. 2016. 'What if there are no conventional price mechanisms?' *Journal of Economic Issues*, 50 (2): 327–344.

Kalecki, M. 1943. 'Political aspects of full employment.' *Political Quarterly*, 14 (4): 322–331.

Keynes, J.M. 1972. *Essays in Biography*. London: Macmillan.

Keynes, J.M. 1973. *The Collected Writings of John Maynard Keynes, Vol. XIV*. London: Macmillan.

Keynes, J.M. 1979. *The Collected Writings of John Maynard Keynes, Vol. XXIX*. London: Macmillan.

Lawson, T. 2005. 'The (confused) state of equilibrium analysis in modern economics: an explanation.' *Journal of Post Keynesian Economics*, 27 (3): 423–444.

Lee, F.S. 2009. *A History of Heterodox Economics: Challenging the Mainstream in the Twentieth Century*. London: Routledge.

Lee, F.S. 2013. 'Post-Keynesian price theory: from pricing to market governance to the economy as a whole,' *in*: G.C. Harcourt & P. Kriesler (eds.), *The Oxford Handbook of Post-Keynesian Economics, Vol. I*. Oxford: Oxford University Press, 467–484.

Lee, F.S. 2016. 'Modeling as a research method in heterodox economics,' *in*: F.S. Lee & B. Cronin (eds.), *Handbook of Research Methods and Applications in Heterodox Economics*. Cheltenham, UK: Edward Elgar, 272–285.

Lee, F.S. & Jo, T.-H. 2011. 'Social surplus approach and heterodox economics.' *Journal of Economic Issues*, 45 (4): 857–875.

Marshall, A. [1890] 1947. *Principles of Economics*, 8th edn. London: Macmillan.

Martins, N.O. 2015. 'Advancing heterodox economics in the tradition of the surplus approach,' *in*: T.-H. Jo & Z. Todorova (eds.), *Advancing the Frontiers of Heterodox Economics: Essays in Honor of Frederic S. Lee*. London: Routledge, 213–229.

Marx, K. 1867. *Capital, Vol. I*. Moscow: Progress Publishers.

Marx, K. 1969. *Theories of Surplus Value*. London: Lawrence and Wishart.

Means, G.C. [1933] 1992a. 'Theoretical chapters from proposed dissertation,' *in*: F.S. Lee & W.J. Samuels (eds.), *The Heterodox Economics of Gardiner C. Means: A Collection*. Armonk, NY: M.E. Sharpe, 6–31.

Means, G.C. [1935] 1992b. 'Industrial prices and their relative inflexibility,' *in*: F.S. Lee & W.J. Samuels (eds.), *The Heterodox Economics of Gardiner C. Means: A Collection*. Armonk, NY: M.E. Sharpe, 32–72.

Mellor, M. 2006. 'Ecofeminist political economy.' *International Journal of Green Economics*, 1 (1/2): 139–150.

Menger, C. [1871] 2007. *Principles of Economics*. Auburn, AL: The Ludwig von Mises Institute.

Mill, J.S. 1836. 'On the definition of political economy,' *in*: J.M. Robson (ed.), *Collected Works of John Stuart Mill, Vol. V*. Toronto: University of Toronto Press, 209–340.

Nelson, J. 1993. 'The study of choice or the study of provisioning? Gender and the definition of economics,' *in*: M. Ferber & J. Nelson (eds.), *Beyond Economic Man: Feminist Theory and Economics*. Chicago: University of Chicago Press, 23–36.

Pasinetti, L. 2005. 'From pure theory to full economic analysis–a place for the economic agent.' *Cahiers d'économie politique*, 2 (49): 211–216.

Polanyi, K. 1965. 'Aristotle discovers the economy,' *in*: K. Polanyi, C.M. Arensberg, & H.W. Pearson (eds.), *Trade and Market in the Early Empires: Economies in History and Theory*. Glencoe, IL: Free Press, 64–94.

Polanyi, K. 1968. 'The economy as instituted process,' *in*: G. Dalton (ed.), *Primitive, Archaic and Modern Economies: Essays of Karl Polanyi*. Garden City, NY: A Doubleday Anchor Original, 139–174.

Power, M. 2004. 'Social provisioning as a starting point for feminist economics.' *Feminist Economics*, 10 (3): 3–19.

Power, M. 2015. 'Social provisioning,' *in*: J.B. Davis & W. Dolfsma (eds.), *The Elgar Companion to Social Economics*, 2nd edn. Cheltenham, UK: Edward Elgar, 331–344.

Ricardo, D. [1817] 1951. *The Works and Correspondence of David Ricardo, Vol. I: Principle of Political Economy and Taxation*, edited by P. Sraffa. Cambridge: Cambridge University Press.

Robbins, L. [1932] 1935. *An Essay on the Nature and Significance of Economic Science*, 2nd edn. London: Macmillan.

Robinson, J. [1977] 1980. 'What are the questions?' *in*: *Collected Economic Papers, Vol. V*. Cambridge, MA: MIT Press, 1–31.

Roncaglia, A. 2005. *The Wealth of Ideas: A History of Economic Thought*. Cambridge: Cambridge University Press.

Samuelson, P.A 1970. *Economics*, 8th edn. New York: McGraw-Hill.

Senior, N. [1836] 1965. *An Outline of the Science of Political Economy*. New York: Augustus M. Kelley.

Smith, A. [1776] 1994. *An Inquiry into the Nature and Causes of the Wealth of Nations*. New York: The Modern Library.

Sraffa, P. 1960. *Production of Commodities by Means of Commodities*. Cambridge: Cambridge University Press.

Steindl, J. [1984] 1990. 'Reflections on the present state of economics,' in: *Economic Papers: 1941–88*. London: Macmillan, 241–252.

Stigler, G.J. 1942. *The Theory of Competitive Price*. New York: Macmillan.

Todorova, Z. 2015a. 'A further Veblenian articulation of a monetary production economy,' in: T.-H. Jo & F.S. Lee (eds.), *Marx, Veblen, and the Foundations of Heterodox Economics: Essays in Honor of John F. Henry*. London: Routledge, 102–122.

Todorova, Z. 2015b. 'Social provisioning within a culture–nature life process.' *Review of Political Economy*, 27 (3): 390–409.

Veblen, T. 1904. *The Theory of Business Enterprise*. New York: Charles Scribner's Sons.

Veblen, T. 1909. 'The limitations of marginal utility.' *Journal of Political Economy*, 17 (9): 620–636.

Veblen, T. 1919. *The Vested Interests and the Common Man*. New York: B.W. Huebsch.

Walsh, V. & Gram, H. 1980. *Classical and Neoclassical Theories of General Equilibrium*. Oxford: Oxford University Press.

3

The social surplus approach

Historical origins and present state

Nuno Ornelas Martins

Introduction

For classical political economists, the social surplus is the part of production that is not necessary for the reproduction of the existing social system. The surplus can either be re-invested in order to expand and transform the existing economic system, or wasted in luxury consumption, leading to economic decline. This depends on whether it is appropriated by a social class that re-invests it into productive activities, or uses it for luxury consumption. The distribution of the social surplus is thus an essential determinant of economic performance.

The ingredients for the development of a social surplus approach were first addressed by William Petty, and subsequently elaborated by Richard Cantillon. François Quesnay and the physiocrats provide the first systematic outline of a social surplus approach that conceptualizes a circular economic process of reproduction in which a surplus is produced. Adam Smith generalized Quesnay's social surplus approach, arguing that it is not just agriculture that contributes to the production of the social surplus emerges, as Quesnay and the physiocrats argue, but also other economic sectors.

David Ricardo elaborated Smith's perspective and defined the social surplus as the difference between total production and wages, measured in terms of embodied labor. Ricardo's theory was subsequently developed by Karl Marx, who defines the social surplus by subtracting from total production not only wages, but also the means of production, while measuring all these magnitudes in terms of the labor which is socially necessary for the reproduction of socio-economic activity.

Each of these authors provides significant advances to the social surplus approach, which becomes a dominant approach with Smith and Ricardo, within which what Marx called 'classical political economy,' a tradition of economic thinking ranging from Petty to Ricardo, and developed by Marx. After Ricardo, the social surplus approach is progressively abandoned, and is definitely rejected after the marginalist revolution undertaken by Stanley Jevons, Carl Menger, Léon Walras, and Alfred Marshall.

Unlike other marginalist authors, Marshall refers to a social surplus, which is defined in a radically different way, since it relies on subjective concepts. Marshall offered a re-interpretation of classical political economy in line with his own neoclassical contribution, contrarily to Marx's original interpretation. Arthur Cecil Pigou continued Marshall's contribution, leading to the early Cambridge economic tradition, shaped by Henry Sidgwick, Marshall, and Pigou.

John Maynard Keynes provided a critique of the Marshallian–Pigovian framework, leading to the separation of the Cambridge economic tradition into a Marshallian–Pigovian branch and a Keynesian branch. Keynes followed Marshall's interpretation of classical political economy, rather than Marx's original interpretation, and thus presented his work as a critique of the 'classical' school, which he did not distinguish from Marshall's and Pigou's neoclassical approach. Nevertheless, several authors associated with the Cambridge Keynesian tradition, such as Piero Sraffa, Michał Kalecki, and Joan Robinson, adopted and developed Marx's original interpretation of classical political economy instead, leading to a revival of the classical-Marxian surplus approach.

I shall here trace the historical development of the social surplus approach, starting with the classical political economists, while distinguishing between Marshall's development of a neoclassical social surplus approach, and the Cambridge Keynesians who developed the social surplus approach with an explicit reference to Marx's elaboration of the circular reproduction schemes of classical political economy. I shall argue that a development of the social surplus approach provides a promising route for the development of heterodox economics.

The classical social surplus approach

Karl Marx ([1867] 1999) dates the beginning of classical political economy to William Petty, who famously argued that land and labor are the mother and father of wealth, respectively. But Petty also notes that labor can be measured in terms of the quantity of land, which is necessary for sustaining the laborer throughout the quantity of time during which labor is performed. Rent, the surplus, is then obtained by subtracting the produce of land necessary to sustain the laborer from the total produce of the land (an example of this claim can be found in paragraph 13 of Chapter 4 of his 1662 book *Treatise on Taxes and Contributions*, on which see volume 1 of Petty 1899).

Richard Cantillon, drawing on Petty, also focused on land and labor, noting that land is the matter and labor is the form of wealth—for example, in the last paragraph (paragraph 12) of Chapter X (Part I) of his *Essai sur la Nature du Commerce en Général* (see Berg 2015). But again, Cantillon also argues in Chapter XI (Part I) of his *Essai* that we can measure labor in terms of the land necessary to sustain the laborer, while referring to Chapter IX of Petty's *Political Anatomy of Ireland* but noting, however, that Petty focused on effects and failed to understand causes.

François Quesnay, who in turn was influenced by Cantillon, also focuses on land as the origin of the surplus. Quesnay (see Kuczynski & Meek 1972) argues that agriculture is the only sector that produces more than what it needs to reproduce itself—that is, it is the only sector which produces a surplus, which can be found as rent. The surplus, for Quesnay, can be used in productive activities, leading to economic development, or in luxury and unproductive activities, leading to economic decline. Quesnay provides the first systematic conception of the economy as a circular process of reproduction where a surplus emerges.

Like Quesnay, Adam Smith argues that the surplus can be used in productive activities, leading to economic development, or in luxury and unproductive activities, leading to economic decline (Smith [1776] 1999: 357). Smith considers Quesnay's economic theory as the nearest approximation to truth ever published in political economy. But Smith ([1776] 1999: 387) criticizes Quesnay for considering artificers, manufacturers, and merchants as unproductive classes. Smith argues that although in his view farmers and country laborers employed in agriculture are more productive than artificers, manufacturers, and merchants, the latter also engage in productive activities, all of which contribute to the reproduction of the social surplus.

For Smith, value arises out of human labor. Since labor is performed in the various sectors of the economy, all these sectors contribute to the production of the social surplus. As Smith ([1776] 1999) argues in Chapter VI of Book I of the *Wealth of Nations*, in primitive societies commodities are produced mostly by labor, and so there is a more direct relation between the labor embodied in the production of a commodity and the value of the commodity in society. But with the development of the division of labor, each person cannot achieve all the necessities, conveniences, and amusements of life without others' labor. Thus, after the division of labor has reached some level of development, the measure of wealth becomes, according to Smith, the quantity of labor that a person can command.

The quantity of labor one can command gives a more precise measure of the power a person has in society. As Smith ([1776] 1999: 37) says, citing Thomas Hobbes, wealth is power, in this case the power to purchase or command the labor of others. While Petty, Cantillon, and Quesnay focus on wealth as such, and measure value in objective terms such as land and the corn it produces, Smith focuses more explicitly on the social power over others that wealth confers to an individual, by providing the power to purchase the labor of others. Smith ([1776] 1999: 40) notes that corn provides an approximate measure of value in the long-run but that labor commanded provides a more exact measure.

The distinction between labor commanded and labor embodied is at the root of the debate between Thomas Robert Malthus and David Ricardo. In his *Principles of Political Economy*, Malthus (1820) argues that supply and demand are the ultimate causes of value, which is measured in terms of the labor that can be commanded in market exchange. Ricardo, in contrast, argues that supply and demand cannot be the ultimate causes of value. Ricardo argues that if demand drives the price of a commodity above its ordinary value, determined by the cost of production (which includes wages, rents, and profits, as for Smith), and if labor is available for further production, the quantity of production will typically be increased as a response to the increase in demand, leading the price back to the cost of production.

Ricardo ([1817] 1821), like Smith ([1776] 1999), argues that supply and demand are merely accidental forces that drive the observed market price away from the underlying cost of production (Martins 2013). Ricardo also argues that the cost of production, which determines value in exchange, can be objectively measured in terms of the labor embodied in the process of production. In fact, since value in exchange is determined by the cost of production, the labor embodied in the process of production is not only an objective measure of value in exchange, but also the cause of value in exchange.

For Ricardo, the cost of production includes the social surplus, which he defines as the difference between total production and wages, where produced goods and wage goods are measured objectively in terms of embodied labor. Ricardo also notes that in agriculture, outputs produced can be used as inputs, so even if competition drives prices down, the reduction of output prices will lead also to a reduction in input prices while a surplus still exists. Competition between capitals in various sectors will ensure that other sectors have a surplus rate similar to the agricultural surplus rate. Agriculture plays a central role in Ricardo's analysis, as it did for Quesnay and the classical authors in general.

According to Ricardo, the social surplus is divided between profits and rents. Profits constitute the surplus obtained in the worst land, and rents constitute the differential surplus above profits provided by better lands. Ricardo also adopts Quesnay's and Smith's distinction between a productive and unproductive use of the surplus. For Ricardo, profits are typically used by capitalists for productive activities, and rents are typically wasted by landlords in luxury and unproductive activities.

The debate between Ricardo and Malthus is the starting point of the abandonment of the classical social surplus approach within the mainstream economic perspective, which is progressively reframed in terms of supply and demand forces, as Malthus argues it should be. Ricardo's argument that an increase in demand is offset by an increase in production presupposes the existence of labor available for further production, that is, surplus labor, or labor not fully employed. It is this presupposition that leads Ricardo, like Smith, to see demand and supply as mere accidental forces that drive the market price away from the ordinary or natural price, which is determined by the conditions of (re)production.

For Malthus, and for the subsequent dominant economic theory, supply and demand are the ultimate determinants of value, rather than mere accidental forces that drive market prices away from the cost of production. According to Marx ([1867] 1999), this leads to a shift from 'classical political economy' towards what he called 'vulgar political economy.' Whereas classical authors from Petty to Ricardo focus on the underlying conditions of the production and distribution of the surplus, 'vulgar political economy' focuses on superficial phenomena such as supply and demand.

In order to explain supply and demand, many influential economists after Ricardo drew upon subjectivist notions. Nassau William Senior argues that the first postulate of economics is that individuals desire to obtain wealth with as little sacrifice as possible. Senior's 'vulgar political economy' approach, according to Marx ([1867] 1999), is symptomatic of the inclusion within economic theory of subjective notions such as 'desire' and 'sacrifice,' which assume a key role in the explanation of demand and supply, respectively.

Subjective elements drawing upon such notions as 'sacrifice' or 'abstinence' are progressively introduced into the explanation of supply forces, by Nassau William Senior, John Stuart Mill, and John Elliot Cairnes. Subjective 'desires' are also introduced into the explanation of demand forces by Jules Dupuit and Hermann Heinrich Gossen. The marginalist revolution leads to the consolidation of a subjectivist approach where supply and demand forces play a key role, and value starts to be defined in terms of subjective desires such as utility, rather than in terms of the cost of production.

The neoclassical social surplus approach

Most marginalists were critical of classical political economy. But Marshall, unlike other marginalists, sees his perspective as a continuation of classical political economy, which he interprets in line with Malthus (while failing to note any significant difference between Malthus and Ricardo). Malthus had already interpreted Smith's theory of value in terms of his own analysis, where supply and demand play a systematic role in the explanation not only of the market price, but also of the natural price (Martins 2013). Thorstein Veblen (1900) saw Marshall's approach as the best work done within what he calls the 'neoclassical' school, which continues the classical approach, defined according to Marshall's conception, rather than Marx's original conception.

Marshall ([1890] 1920) uses supply and demand curves to define equilibrium prices and quantities, which are determined simultaneously at the intersection between supply and demand curves. Using supply and demand curves, Marshall identifies a consumer's surplus, and a producer's surplus, which together constitute the social surplus. The consumer's surplus is defined as the geometrical area below the demand curve, and above the horizontal line set by the equilibrium price. The producer's surplus is defined as the geometrical area above the supply curve, and below the horizontal line set by the equilibrium price.

Marshall claims to be in continuity with the classical approach of Smith and Ricardo, but his definition of the social surplus contrasts starkly to Ricardo's, who defines the social surplus as the numerical difference between the value of total production and the value of wages. Marshall, in contrast, relies upon subjective concepts such as utility and sacrifice, where utility explains demand curves, and sacrifice explains supply curves.

Marshall addresses the problem of distribution while taking marginal utility, rather than human labor, as the source of value. An important argument underlying Pigou's (1920) analysis, which draws upon Sidgwick and Marshall, is that since those with less income obtain a higher marginal utility from income than those with more income, the reduction of inequality must increase total utility for society as a whole. Pigou, like Marshall, also stressed the positive impacts of redistribution on the laboring capabilities of the poorest classes, with positive effects on productivity. For Marshall, the negative effects of inequality spring not only from its curtailment of the satisfaction of wants, but also through its effects on dwarfing human activity. And although Marshall thought both aspects are important for economics, he also thought that if one were to choose one of them as the most important for interpreting the history of mankind, that aspect would be human activities, rather than human wants.

The Marshallian–Pigovian framework continued to pay attention to problems of distribution, and led to the emergence of the field of welfare economics. But Lionel Robbins' (1938) critique of interpersonal comparisons of utility led to the relative neglect of this line of research, and the adoption of Pareto optimal conditions as a criterion of efficiency defined separately of issues pertaining to distribution. Robbins ([1932] 1935) also led to the redefinition of economics as the science that studies the allocation of scarce resources that have alternative uses. The distribution of the surplus is no longer a central concern within this mainstream scarcity approach.

The Marshallian–Pigovian explanation was criticized by John Maynard Keynes (1936) along different lines to Robbins. Keynes (1936) argues that the equilibrium between the demand for capital and the supply of capital cannot be explained using supply and demand curves in order to determine the price of capital (the interest rate), because those curves are constructed presupposing a given level of income. A change in either curve will entail a change in the level of income, and thus a change in the other curve. Thus, we cannot apply the Marshallian method of focusing on a given change while assuming that everything else remains constant. This also occurs with supply and demand curves for labor, since the changes in wages which those curves are meant to explain change also the level of income, and thus the curves which we are using as supposedly independent data in the first place, as Keynes (1936) notes.

Keynes' critique, many elements of which had been anticipated by Kalecki (1971) in articles originally written before Keynes' (1936) *General Theory*, led to the emergence of the Cambridge Keynesian tradition, which challenged the Marshallian–Pigovian framework. Piero Sraffa's critique of Marshallian supply and demand analysis also plays a significant role in the Cambridge Keynesian tradition. Sraffa (1926) argues that one cannot study changes in supply and demand curves while assuming everything else remains constant as Marshall does in his partial equilibrium analysis. Sraffa, like Keynes, argues that the economic system must be studied as a whole, rather than by focusing on isolated parts as Marshall does (Martins 2013).

The Cambridge controversies in the theory of capital

There are significant differences between Keynes, Kalecki, and Sraffa. Kalecki developed his approach independently of the Marshallian background. Keynes started from Marshall's approach and retained much including his interpretation of classical political economy although Keynes was critical of Pigou's development. Sraffa started from a critique of Marshall's approach. But Sraffa was led to a much more radical departure than Keynes, and to a revival of the classical surplus approach consistent with Marx's interpretation of classical political economy. If we consider the early debate between Malthus and Ricardo, Keynes would probably side with Malthus, and Sraffa would certainly side with Ricardo. There are, however, common elements that shaped the Cambridge Keynesian tradition. These appear more clearly in the Cambridge 'controversies' in the theory of capital. This debate was between Cambridge (United Kingdom) Keynesians such as Piero Sraffa, Joan Robinson, Luigi Pasinetti, and Pierangelo Garegnani, economists of Cambridge, Massachusetts in the United States (such as Paul Samuelson and Robert Solow), and other economists of Cambridge, UK (such as Frank Hahn and Christopher Bliss) (see Harcourt 1972).

As Avi Cohen & Geoffrey Harcourt (2003) note, we can identify several rounds in the Cambridge controversies in the theory of capital. In the first round the key issue at stake was the production function, and the possibility of establishing a monotonically decreasing relationship between the quantity of capital and its marginal productivity, which is seen as a determinant of the price of capital, that is, the rate of interest, while in an analogous way the marginal productivity of labor was seen as part of an explanation for the price of labor. Joan Robinson (1953–4) triggered the first round when she brought the critique of the production function to the public realm. The essential point raised by Sraffa and Robinson is that it is not possible to obtain an aggregate measure of capital before knowing the interest rate that enables us to aggregate capital from different time periods or different techniques at a point in time.

In the second round of the controversy, between 1956 and 1966, Robert Solow (1956, 1957), at the same time as Trevor Swan (1956), simply adopted a production function with only one capital good used in its own production, so that inconsistencies with aggregate capital are avoided. Paul Samuelson (1962) attempted to overcome the problems of the production function while making it a relevant concept in an economy with more than one good. As is well known, inconsistencies were again found in Samuelson's surrogate production function, leading Samuelson (1966) to concede defeat, while accepting that a monotonic relation between capital intensity and interest rate need not exist.

After conceding defeat the marginalist authors moved to a third round resorting to general equilibrium theory which, according to Christopher Bliss (1975) and Frank Hahn (1981), would avoid the inconsistencies found in the idea of aggregate capital and the idea of decreasing marginal productivity of capital (Cohen & Harcourt 2003). However, several problems with general equilibrium theory had already shown again that one cannot assume monotonically decreasing (excess) demand functions (see Cohen & Harcourt 2003; Martins 2013: 61–63) and inconsistencies arose again when attempting to describe the process of adjustment through time towards equilibrium through the mathematical analysis of supply and demand.

The Cambridge controversies in the theory of capital showed several inconsistencies in attempts to determine distribution endogenously through marginal productivity theory. Sraffa's (1960) contribution, in contrast, conceptualizes distribution as an exogenous aspect from the point of view of economic theory, meaning there is no consistent way of determining distribution mathematically through marginal productivity theory. As Garegnani (1984) explains, this leads back to the surplus approach of the classical political economists and Marx, where the distribution of the surplus is an exogenous aspect, determined by institutional and political factors. But Sraffa believed that this fact had deep political implications, since classical political economy "with its surplus to be arbitrarily divided leads straight to socialism" (cited in Garegnani 2005: 489).

As Cohen & Harcourt (2003: 210) note, Veblen's critique of John Bates Clark addressed the same problem. Clark (1891) explains the distribution between capital and labor in terms of marginal productivities, while Veblen (1908) stresses that the distribution of the social surplus depends upon social and political power. According to Cohen & Harcourt (2003: 208):

> Robinson argued—citing Veblen (1908) and raising the specter of Marx—that the meaning of capital lay in the property owned by the capitalist class, which confers on capitalists the legal right and economic authority to take a share of the surplus created by the production process.

After the consolidation of the Cambridge Keynesian tradition that took place as the Cambridge controversies in the theory of capital unfolded, two key approaches to the social surplus in the twentieth century can be identified, which remain until today: firstly, the neoclassical social surplus approach that draws upon Marshall's interpretation and development of classical political economy; and, secondly, the classical-Marxian surplus approach, elaborated by the Cambridge Keynesians who draw upon Marx's interpretation and development of classical political economy, such as Kalecki, Sraffa, and Robinson.

Inequality, welfare, and economic performance

Marginalism was developed without a clear political purpose, although Garegnani (2005: 489) suggests, based on Sraffa's unpublished writings, that Sraffa saw the political atmosphere as an 'environment of selection' that favors certain theories. But this need not mean that the theories that were selected and became dominant were developed with the intention to undermine attempts at redistribution, such as socialism. Walras, for one, was a socialist. And the developments of marginalism within the Cambridge tradition by Marshall and Pigou led to arguments for a more equal distribution.

Some examples are James Meade (1976) and Anthony Atkinson (1975), who can be seen as part of the Cambridge 'welfare' tradition started by Sidgwick, Marshall, and Pigou (Martins 2009). The impact of this tradition is still important, as can be seen not only in the continuing use of Marshall's notion of a social surplus in contemporary mainstream economics, but also in the debate surrounding contributions like Thomas Piketty's (2014), who was much influenced by Atkinson.

This concern with inequality is shared by authors connected to the Cambridge welfare tradition who do not adopt the neoclassical framework, such as Maurice Dobb and Amartya Sen. Dobb and Sen propose instead a return to classical-Marxian perspective. Sen's (1982) early contributions still draw upon the Marshallian–Pigovian framework to some extent, for example when advocating the possibility of partial interpersonal comparisons of utility, without assuming that exact and complete comparisons are always and everywhere possible. Sen, like Sidgwick, Marshall, and Pigou, all drawing upon John Stuart Mill, discerns different types of utility, such as happiness, desire, and satisfaction. Following Dobb's notion of 'rich description,' Sen advocates moving from a subjective utility-based approach towards a multi-dimensional approach to human well-being, centered on the notion of human 'capabilities,' or what human beings can objectively be or do (Sen 1982, 1992, 2005).

This more objective approach to human well-being is certainly more in line with the classical-Marxian approach, even if it is also present in Marshall's emphasis on human activities, rather than human wants, as a key aspect of economic analysis. Marshall ([1890] 1920) argues that greater equality is important not because it gives more income to those with a higher subjective marginal utility, but because it gives more income to those who will use it in order to satisfy more urgent (and objective) needs, rather than to those who will use it to satisfy less important (and more subjective) wants. Of course, the subsequent developments of the neoclassical approach went in a more subjectivist direction.

Sen's multi-dimensional approach to inequality raises several possibilities concerning the channels through which inequality influences not only human well-being, but also economic performance. Inequality reduces the access of a majority of the population to various goods and services which are important to the expansion of their capabilities, such as health, education, and culture. As Sen (1992) explains, human capabilities have an intrinsic value because of their impact on human well-being, and also an instrumental value in the sense that they foster socio-economic change (see also Martins 2009, 2013). Inequality has not only a direct impact on human well-being, but also an indirect impact on human well-being through its detrimental effect on economic performance, which was noted early on by Marshall ([1890] 1920) and Pigou (1920).

There are important connections between Sen's capability approach and the revival of the classical-Marxian framework undertaken by Cambridge Keynesians like Robinson, Sraffa, and Kalecki. Distribution, and the share of wages in particular, is a central determinant of various economic variables, such as prices (Sraffa 1960) and output (Kalecki 1971: 98–99). Wages are also determined by institutional factors. These institutional factors are reflected in Sen's notion of basic capabilities (that enable a certain standard of living), which can be incorporated into the classical-Marxian framework in order to define the level of wages that ensures the achievement of basic capabilities, as argued by Putnam & Walsh (2012) and Martins (2013).

If we want to achieve a better understanding of the consequences of inequality, studies of distribution cannot focus solely on the measurement of inequality. Rather, they must also look at the impact of the distribution of the surplus on the overall economic system not only through the supply side (connected to human capabilities and productivity), but also through the demand side. The demand-side channels are connected to the fact that those with a lower income have a higher marginal propensity to consume, as Keynes (1936) argues.

Keynes' approach to consumption is quite similar to Pigou's (1920) approach to human welfare. While Pigou argues that greater equality increases overall utility since more income is transferred to those who have a higher marginal utility (or to those who use income for satisfying more urgent and objective needs, as Marshall noted), Keynes argues that greater equality increases overall consumption since more income is transferred to those who have a higher marginal propensity to consume (see also Martins 2013: 105–107)

Pigou himself had applied this reasoning to consumption too. Pigou (1920) argues that the richer a person is, the smaller the proportion of their total income they will consume. Of course, Keynes (1936) provides a much more systematic development of his idea, which was also developed before by Kalecki (1971), who presupposes that workers consume all their income, while capitalists consume a share of their income. Keynes and Kalecki noted, unlike Pigou, that unless investment compensates the lack of consumption, the economy would systematically tend away from full employment.

One could think that luxury consumption compensates this lack of aggregate demand. But what happens is that luxury consumption is often financed by the stock of wealth, rather than by the flow of income, as Keynes (1936) notes, and so it refers to postponed consumption of a previous income. The flow of income is the key to understanding the long-term sustainability of consumption patterns, and those who receive a smaller income must spend a greater percentage of what they earn simply for achieving basic consumption needs. Those with higher incomes spend a smaller percentage even when luxury consumption is considered, while saving the remaining part of income. For this reason, consumption out of income will be reduced with the increase of income inequality.

In summary, while the Cambridge Keynesians discuss the influence of inequality on economic performance through demand-side channels, the Cambridge welfare tradition emphasizes essentially how inequality influences economic performance through supply-side channels. The supply-side effects of inequality on economic performance, stressed by Marshall and Pigou (and discussed more recently by Sen), must be seen together with the demand-side effects identified by Keynes and Kalecki, who studied the implications of inequality for effective demand and unemployment.

However, attempts to include distribution within the very analytical structure of economic theory occurred essentially within the Cambridge Keynesian tradition, and its revival of the classical-Marxian surplus approach, rather than within the Cambridge welfare tradition and the neoclassical surplus approach. Within contemporary neoclassical economics, Marshall's social surplus, constituted by the consumer's surplus and producer's surplus, is essentially a side product of the economic forces of supply and demand, represented by supply and demand curves. In the neoclassical framework distribution is thus determined by supply and demand forces, whereas Sen argues that distribution should be determined within an ethical and democratic framework.

The Kalecki–Keynes–Sraffa synthesis

Sraffa and Kalecki provide further important developments of the classical-Marxian social surplus approach, and of the impact of the distribution of the surplus on key economic variables such as prices and quantities. And even Keynes, who started from the Marshallian framework, ends up reaching similar results to those of Kalecki. Thus, Robinson ([1974] 1980: 48) argues that Keynes' *General Theory* has, like Kalecki's theory of employment and Sraffa's approach, "much more in common with the classical school of the first half of the nineteenth century than with the neoclassical doctrines in which Keynes himself was brought up."

The circular process of reproduction appears more clearly in the Kaleckian and Sraffian branches of Keynesianism, than in the neoclassical-Keynesian synthesis initiated by John Hicks (1937), and consolidated by Paul Samuelson (1947) (see Robinson 1975). As noted above, Keynes (1936) himself created much of the terminological confusion by designating the neoclassical approach as the 'classical' school, while criticizing it (see Martins 2013: 93–96).

The neoclassical synthesis addresses the determination of prices and quantities simultaneously and through the same framework, in terms of supply and demand curves. For this reason, it offers the appearance of greater coherence than the Cambridge Keynesian tradition. However, many of the apparent divergences within the Cambridge Keynesians spring from the fact that they study prices and quantities separately. In reality, their studies of prices and quantities draw upon the same classical-Marxian circular conception of production.

Sraffa (1960) focuses on a theory of value and distribution that provides the general conditions for the reproduction of the socio-economic process, while taking quantities as given. By defining the general conditions for the reproduction of the socio-economic process, Sraffa provides a framework that can be used for studying the more persistent elements of the economic system, such as the normal prices that enable the reproduction of the economic system (see Garegnani 1984, 2005).

While Sraffa provides a more abstract explanation of the prices that enable the reproduction of the economic system, Kalecki provides a more concrete explanation of why prices may remain relatively stable through time. Kalecki (1971: 43–49) notes the centrality of administrative prices in the economy, especially after the emergence of large corporations (see also, Lee 1998). The conventional price administered by the firm and its competitors not only persists over extended periods of time, but is also a central determinant of the price to be set in the following periods.

This conventional price is consistent with the natural or normal price as defined in classical political economy, which is simply the ordinary or average price based on the cost of production, that persists through time and multiple transactions, and appears in a more abstract formulation in Sraffa's (1960) system. This price enables acting persons and organizations to form expectations, which guide the reproduction of economic activities. Prices can be set within this objective approach through administrative procedures, which are part of a company's planning activities.

Nuno Ornelas Martins

As Kalecki (1987: 19–21) notes, it is not only the socialist economies of the past, but also the capitalist economies (past and present), that are largely coordinated by planning. Certainly there were many important differences between the capitalist and socialist economies throughout the twentieth century, but the more substantial differences must be found elsewhere than on the reliance on administrative planning *per se*. Even in sectors constituted by smaller firms or producers (including agriculture and extractive industries), the small firms and producers are part of a value chain where large companies set up prices for their commodities. Prices in those sectors are often demand–determined rather than administrative prices, but the mechanism of adjustment is often changes in quantities so as to conform to demand (including the destruction of what was produced) rather than changes in prices (Kalecki 1971: 43–49).

Quantities, in turn, can be seen as determined by the Kaleckian/Keynesian principle of effective demand. Robinson argues for a synthesis between Sraffa's theory of value and distribution, and the Kaleckian/Keynesian principle of effective demand, putting greater emphasis on a Sraffa–Kalecki synthesis on some occasions (Robinson [1974] 1980) and on a Sraffa–Keynes synthesis on other occasions (Robinson 1985). When attempting such a synthesis, one must also take into account the methodological differences between Sraffa, Kalecki, and Keynes. Sraffa focuses on the overall conditions for socio-economic reproduction, which can be seen as the theoretical correlates of elements that persist through time. But whatever elements persist through time are best seen as long-term averages and trends, within a turbulent process characterized by economic fluctuations, such as economic cycles. The latter have been a central concern of Kalecki, who notes that long-term phenomena are the result of cyclical fluctuations.

Sraffa is led to his methodological approach because he focuses on prices within a circular conception of the economy, while assuming that there are no changes in quantities. Keynes, in contrast, explains quantities in terms of effective demand, but without developing a circular conception that explains prices as an outcome of the process of reproduction. Can a synthesis be achieved, so that the Keynesian principle of effective demand is explained within a circular conception of reproduction such as the classical-Marxian one?

Such an approach was developed by Kalecki, who provided a circular conception of the economy, within which he explained prices in terms of cost of production, and quantities in terms of effective demand. It would seem that the synthesis between Sraffa and Keynes that Joan Robinson was looking for was already present, even if unintentionally, in the writings of Kalecki. Perhaps this explains Robinson's overall preference for the Kaleckian approach, to be further combined with Keynesian and Sraffian elements.

In Kalecki's approach, distribution is taken as an exogenous aspect, to be further explained in terms of what Kalecki (1971: 80–81) calls 'distribution factors,' which determine the distribution between wages and profits. Drawing upon the Kaleckian approach, we can see how distribution influences economic performance. Kalecki noted that increases in wages, leading to a more equal distribution of income, do not reduce profits. As Kalecki (1971) explains, the increase in wages of workers (who on average earn lower incomes than capitalists who receive profits) merely diverts profits from investment-goods industries and luxury-goods industries to wage-goods industries. In wage-goods industries, an increase in wages is spent in the goods produced, so it does not change the amount of profits in that industry. The profits which are reduced in industries connected to investment goods and luxury goods are spent by the wage earners of those industries in the wage-goods industries, and so profits remain the same for the economy as a whole, while output increases due to the increase in wages.

This means that greater equality in the distribution of the surplus will not lead to economic decline, but rather to greater economic prosperity. This conclusion, focusing on demand-side aspects, is similar to the conclusions reached within the Cambridge 'welfare' traditions of both the Marshallian–Pigovian neoclassical framework and Sen's development of the classical-Marxian framework. All of these authors focus on supply-side aspects such as the expansion of human capabilities, while also noting the positive implications of greater equality for human well-being. Greater equality, leading to the expansion of human capabilities, is not only an ethical goal, but also a means for improving economic performance, as Sen (1999) argues.

Much further work is still needed in order to provide a broader and clearer perspective of the implications of inequality in the distribution of the social surplus. But it seems that a more objective explanation of supply-side factors and demand-side factors, such as that undertaken in the classical-Marxian social surplus approach, provides a more solid ground for those studies, especially given the inconsistencies identified in the neoclassical framework during the Cambridge controversies in the theory of capital.

Concluding remarks

Inequality is a central concern for the classical political economists and Marx, for whom the central question of economic analysis is the study of the production and distribution of the economic surplus across various social classes. Inequality is also the central concern of the authors who pioneered the emergence of the modern approach to economics. This approach includes modern microeconomic analysis, which was greatly shaped by Marshall's and Walras's contribution, and modern macroeconomic analysis, which was to a great extent shaped by Keynes' contribution.

In fact, if we want to use the modern distinction between microeconomics and macroeconomics, we may say that the impact of inequality on economic performance through the demand-side channel was a central aspect of Keynes' (1936) macroeconomics, while the impact of inequality on human well-being and on economic performance through the supply-side channel was a central aspect of Marshall's ([1890] 1920) microeconomics. But as Sen (1999) notes, both aspects are connected, since unemployment, which is the result of macroeconomic forces connected to aggregate demand, has a detrimental effect on human capabilities, which are connected with aggregate supply, and human well-being in general.

John Kenneth Galbraith (1958, 1967) provides an integrated approach to this problem, while arguing that distribution is the central problem for contemporary affluent societies. Galbraith (1967) puts forward a theory that integrates the macroeconomic aspects with microeconomic aspects, noting the macroeconomic problem that those with higher income do not necessarily spend all of their income (as Kalecki and Keynes argue), while also providing a realistic microeconomic analysis of the modern corporation and the modern state, and its implications for the economy and society. The role of power in distribution has been progressively forgotten within mainstream economic theory and policy. A concern with the role of power in distribution continues within the heterodox economic traditions, where the central issue at stake is not the maximization of utility or profits, but rather the process of social provisioning, that is, the distribution of the surplus.

The emphasis of this chapter was on the traditions that attempt to establish an explicit connection to the classical surplus approach. But a surplus approach underpins many other heterodox contributions, as Frederic Lee & Tae-Hee Jo (2011) argue. Veblen is a case in point, as Robinson saw. Veblen provided the most influential non-Marxian perspective that draws upon (or at least presupposes) a social surplus approach in which the surplus is appropriated by a leisure class. Indeed, Veblen's critique of Clark anticipates many of the issues raised by Robinson and Sraffa in the Cambridge controversies in the theory of capital. An important conclusion of the latter controversies is that distribution is best seen as determined by institutional factors, rather than marginal productivities. Thus, contributions drawing on other heterodox traditions that address institutional aspects, even without explicitly referring to the classical-Marxian surplus approach, certainly have much to contribute to this topic.

The early neoclassical tradition of Marshall and Pigou had a great concern with distribution. But subjectivism made Pigou's approach an easy prey to Robbins' criticism of interpersonal comparisons of utility. Studies of distribution will not be of consequence unless the topic is addressed through a solid framework, which enables one to go beyond the mere measurement of inequality, towards a clearer understanding of the impact of distribution on economic performance and human well-being. The classical-Marxian surplus approach provides such a more objective approach, which has been rediscovered and developed after the critique of the Marshallian–Pigovian neoclassical approach undertaken by Keynes and Sraffa, as part of a conception in which social provisioning is aimed at the achievement of human development.

References

Atkinson, A. 1975. *The Economics of Inequality*. Oxford: Clarendon Press.

Berg, R. 2015. *Richard Cantillon Essay on the Nature of Trade in General: A Variorum Edition*. London: Routledge.

Bliss, C.J. 1975. *Capital Theory and the Distribution of Income*. Amsterdam: Elsevier North-Holland.

Clark, J.B. 1891. 'Distribution as determined by the law of rent.' *Quarterly Journal of Economics*, 5 (3): 289–318.

Cohen, A. & Harcourt, G.C. 2003. 'Whatever happened to the Cambridge capital theory controversies?' *Journal of Economic Perspectives*, 17 (1): 199–214.

Galbraith, J.K. 1958. *The Affluent Society*. Boston: Houghton Mifflin.

Galbraith, J.K. 1967. *The New Industrial State*. Boston: Houghton Mifflin.

Garegnani, P. 1984. 'Value and distribution in the classical economists and Marx.' *Oxford Economic Papers*, 36 (2): 291–325.

Garegnani, P. 2005. 'On a turning point in Sraffa's theoretical and interpretative position in the late 1920s.' *European Journal of the History of Economic Thought*, 12 (3): 453–492.

Hahn, F.H. 1981. 'General equilibrium theory,' *in*: D. Bell & I. Kristol (eds.), *The Crisis in Economic Theory*. New York: Basic Books, 123–138.

Harcourt, G.C. 1972. *Some Cambridge Controversies in the Theory of Capital*. Cambridge: Cambridge University Press.

Hicks, J.R. 1937. 'Mr. Keynes and the classics: a suggested interpretation.' *Econometrica*, 5 (2): 146–159.

Kalecki, M. 1971. *Selected Essays on the Dynamics of the Capitalist Economy*. Cambridge: Cambridge University Press.

Kalecki, M. 1987. *Selected Essays on Economic Planning*. Cambridge: Cambridge University Press.

Keynes, J. M. 1936. *The General Theory of Employment, Interest and Money*. London: Macmillan.

Kuczynski, M. & Meek, R.L. (eds.) 1972. *Quesnay's Tableau Économique*. London: Palgrave Macmillan.

Lee, F.S. 1998. *Post Keynesian Price Theory*. Cambridge: Cambridge University Press.

Lee, F.S. & Jo, T.-H. 2011. 'Social surplus approach and heterodox economics.' *Journal of Economic Issues*, 45 (4): 857–875.

Malthus, T.R. 1820. *Principles of Political Economy*. London: John Murray.

Marshall, A. [1890] 1920. *Principles of Economics*, 8th edn. London: Macmillan.

Martins, N. 2009. 'Sen's capability approach and Post Keynesianism: similarities, distinctions and the Cambridge tradition.' *Journal of Post Keynesian Economics*, 31 (4): 691–706.

Martins, N. 2013. *The Cambridge Revival of Political Economy*. London: Routledge.

Marx, K. [1867] 1999. *Capital, Vol. 1*. Oxford: Oxford University Press.

Meade, J. 1976. *The Just Economy*. London: Allen and Unwin.

Petty, W. 1899. *The Economic Writings of Sir William Petty*, vols 1–2, edited by C.H. Hull. Cambridge: Cambridge University Press.

Pigou, A.C. 1920. *The Economics of Welfare*. London: Macmillan.

Piketty, T. 2014. *Capital in the Twenty-First Century*. Cambridge, MA: The Belknap Press of Harvard University Press.

Putnam, H. & Walsh, V. (eds.) 2012. *The End of Value-Free Economics*. London: Routledge.

Ricardo, D. [1817] 1821. *Principles of Political Economy and Taxation*. London: John Murray.

Robbins, L. [1932] 1935. *An Essay on the Nature and Significance of Economic Science*. London: Macmillan.

Robbins, L. 1938. 'Interpersonal comparisons of utility: a comment.' *Economic Journal*, 48 (192): 635–641.

Robinson, J. 1953–4. 'The production function and the theory of capital.' *Review of Economic Studies*, 21 (2): 81–106.

Robinson, J. [1974] 1980. 'History versus equilibrium,' *in: Collected Economic Papers, Vol. 5*. Cambridge, MA: MIT Press, 48–58.

Robinson, J. 1975. 'What has become of the Keynesian revolution,' *in*: Milo Keynes (ed.), *Essays on John Maynard Keynes*. Cambridge: Cambridge University Press, 123–131.

Robinson, J. 1985. 'The theory of normal prices and the reconstruction of economic theory,' *in*: G. Feiwel (ed.), *Issues in Contemporary Macroeconomics and Distribution*. Albany, NY: SUNY Press, 157–165.

Samuelson, P.A. 1947. *Foundations of Economic Analysis*. Cambridge, MA: Harvard University Press.

Samuelson, P.A. 1962. 'Parable and realism in capital theory: the surrogate production function.' *Review of Economic Studies*, 29 (3): 193–206.

Samuelson, P.A. 1966. 'A summing up.' *Quarterly Journal of Economics*, 80 (4): 568–583.

Sen, A. 1982. *Choice, Welfare and Measurement*. Oxford: Blackwell.

Sen, A. 1992. *Inequality Reexamined*. Oxford: Oxford University Press.

Sen, A. 1999. *Development as Freedom*. Oxford: Oxford University Press.

Sen, A. 2005. 'Walsh on Sen after Putnam.' *Review of Political Economy*, 17 (1): 107–113.

Smith. A. [1776] 1999. *An Inquiry into the Nature and Causes of the Wealth of Nations*. Oxford: Oxford University Press.

Solow, R. 1956. 'A contribution to the theory of economic growth.' *Quarterly Journal of Economics*, 70 (1): 65–94.

Solow, R. 1957. 'Technical change and the aggregate production function.' *Review of Economics and Statistics*, 39 (3): 312–320.

Sraffa, P. 1926. 'The laws of returns under competitive conditions.' *Economic Journal*, 36 (144): 535–550.

Sraffa, P. 1960. *Production of Commodities by Means of Commodities*. Cambridge: Cambridge University Press.

Swan, T.W. 1956. 'Economic growth and capital accumulation.' *Economic Record*, 32 (2): 334–361.

Veblen, T. 1900. 'The preconceptions of economic science: III.' *Quarterly Journal of Economics*, 12 (4): 240–269.

Veblen, T. 1908. 'Professor Clark's economics.' *Quarterly Journal of Economics*, 22 (2): 147–195.

4

Accumulation regimes

Agnès Labrousse and Sandrine Michel

Introduction

Historical observation shows that accumulation undergoes long periods of stability, followed by long periods of instability and crisis, so the economist has to explain why an episode of growth, based on a seemingly 'virtuous' accumulation process, can enter into crisis. Accumulation regimes grasp the dynamic compatibility of production, income sharing, and demand dynamics: "the set of regularities that ensure the general and relatively coherent progress of capital accumulation, that is, which allow the resolution or postponement of the distortions and disequilibria to which the process continually gives rise" (Boyer & Saillard 2002: 334).

Two institutional theories, French *Régulation* theory (RT) and the American Social Structure of Accumulation (SSA) theory, are particularly relevant to the investigation of accumulation processes. According to both theories, capitalism operates within institutional frameworks that are specific to times and places and underpin macroeconomic regularities. Thus, accumulation regimes (or SSAs) are embedded in evolving institutional forms, including capital-labor relations, forms of competition, financial institutions, forms of the state, and international relations. Accordingly, there is no canonical accumulation regime but a variety of regimes.

In heterodox economics, analyzing the accumulation process goes hand in hand with a dynamic conception of the economy, relating economic regularities and fluctuations to mainly endogenous socio-economic developments, innovations, crises, irreversibility, and path-dependency effects. This is a departure from equilibrium thinking wherein economic fluctuations are seen as mere (mostly exogenous) perturbations and temporary deviations from a normal equilibrium state (Veblen 1899–1900).

Accumulation—the process of adding productive capital to the previously invested one—is closely linked to capitalism and its dynamics. The last three centuries have witnessed an extraordinary accumulation of capital: estimates indicate that capital multiplied 134 times between 1700 and 2008 (Bonneuil & Fressoz 2016). In the early stages of capitalism, classical economists underline investment-led growth but simultaneously express doubts regarding the possibility of accumulation as an endless process. However, with the exception of Thomas Malthus, they neglect the possibility of the lack of effective demand and its consequences for the accumulation process.

Two other traditions underline the instability and crisis-prone character of accumulation processes. Marxians, as well as German and American institutional economists (in the original tradition), demonstrate that the instability and the transformations of the accumulation process go hand in hand with the mutations of capitalism. Original institutional economists introduce the endogenous role of institutional and organizational arrangements to understand the accumulation process and its cycles. Thus, they initiate a long theoretical path towards the later notion of an 'accumulation regime.' This notion was developed from the 1970s onward by RT, which displays many commonalities with SSA theory. These theories develop comparable theoretical building blocks to study past and present accumulation regimes and to uncover their sheer diversity in time and space.

Accumulation before the notion of accumulation regime

The classical economists and Marx consider capital accumulation as the central characteristic of industrial economies. The original institutional economists integrate institutions to analyze endogenous accumulation dynamics.

Accumulation and the classics: beyond the steady state?

The classical economists attribute the increasing wealth of nations to a virtuous accumulation circle: capital accumulation enables an increase in the number of productive workers and enhances the division of labor, leading to an increase in production and productivity and thus profits. Parsimony is a cardinal capitalist virtue for Smith (1776), as profits are translated into savings that are then used to finance further investments. This investment-driven growth model makes sense in early industrial capitalism, as entrepreneurs, heading small-scale family companies, re-invest their profits.

However for most classical economists the long-run exhaustion of accumulation, captured by the concept of the steady state, is inescapable. Population growth triggers allegedly diminishing returns in agriculture and impacts the whole economy, as higher corn prices increase subsistence wages, thus decreasing profits and slowing down accumulation. Ricardo (1817) considers international trade to be a transient back-up growth engine, and focuses his explanation of accumulation dynamics on the supply side.

Yet, far from a steady growth preceding the steady state, crises occurred from the very beginning of capitalism (Sismondi [1827] 1971; Malthus 1836). According to Malthus (1836), crises originate in under-consumption, making capital accumulation unsustainable. This demand-side explanation contrasts with exogenous explanations (for example, J.-B. Say ([1803] 1872) and the incompetence of government).

Marxian accumulation: instability and crisis

For Marx (1867), the expansion of capitalism combines the pursuit of accumulation with exploitation of the labor force. To inform this dynamic, he first analyzes the origin of profit in production by introducing the theory of surplus value. Second, he studies the circulation of capital in all its phases and focuses on the transformations of capital from one state to another. With the 'falling rate of profit and its countervailing tendencies,' he introduces contradictions between the requirements of the production of surplus value and the circulation of capital. These contradictions are permanent, and are first expressed in a low but manageable intensity. But, in the longer term, contradictions spin out of control and society as a whole goes into crisis.

Thus, the capitalists' permanent pursuit of profit faces the risk of over-accumulation. Like Sismondi ([1827] 1971) and Malthus (1836), Marx associates over-accumulation, defined as an excess of capital, with a large range of ill-effects. He also shares their understanding of counteracting processes, and develops the concept of devaluation as a means to purge the excess of capital (Marx 1867: 30, 1894: 605–609). The devaluation of capital appears as a way of producing a non-value necessary to achieve capital valorization. Over-accumulation and devaluation are two sides of the same coin.

Referring to Marx, Harvey (1982: 190–203) classifies devaluation into two categories. The first and 'gentle one' belongs to the inner logic of capitalism. It represents the constant devaluation of existing capital. It delays the falling rate of profit. It focuses mainly on maintaining the dynamics of the labor-capital relation according to the leading force of profit. Marx analyzes the devaluation of labor power as a general tendency of accumulation. The increase in labor productivity has the capacity to cheapen goods and consequently wages, that is, the value of the workforce (Marx 1867: 220). Because of competition, this depreciation is soon generalized through commodity prices to all sellers aspiring to recover surplus value. The issue is: who supports this depreciation? For Marx, the burden falls on workers. Indeed, the increase of labor productivity (meaning, exploitation) constitutes a robust means for capitalists to secure the surplus value (Marx 1867: 418). Accordingly, to augment the profit share in global value, capitalists have to contain wages and employment, and keeping labor-power 'devalued' in order to maintain future accumulation.

The second devaluation category is more dramatic. It occurs during crises. In this case, devaluation has to support the elimination of the capital that is in excess, under three main forms featured by their effect on the rate of profit (Marx 1894: 173). First, it may be done in a radical way when it takes the form of a destruction of productive capital and labor power. Second, devaluation can take the form of a negative rate of profit. However, the excess capital can be kept as an economic value losing all entitlement to be remunerated by profit (zero profit rate). Third, it can be kept as capital but will be valued at a lower rate than the average (the genesis of share ownership). The depth of the devaluation depends on the extent of over-accumulation. In this type of devaluation the reproduction of the economic dynamic can lead to irreversible structural changes. The association of crisis devaluations with economic change is the core of economic instability.

The generalization of capital devaluation during economic crises impacts social relations because this process constitutes a threat to the reproduction of class relations. Social bonds come into tension and lines of social conflict emerge over who has to bear the burden of capital destruction. These conflicts oppose capitalists against capitalists and capitalists against workers. In Marx's (1894: 175) view, a devaluation process through an accumulation crisis can renew its course on a new basis.

The inheritance of Marx is neither clear nor unanimous. Issues raised by his closest followers are often contradictory for the interpretation of globalization. For example, Luxemburg (1913) analyzes imperialism as a painless devaluation process of capital in a context of a structural accumulation crisis in developed countries, whereas Hilferding ([1910] 1981) puts forward the concentration of capital and the increasing role of banks in exporting capital to achieve an extra-profit. They also differ in their appraisal of the end of capitalism, as some support revolutionary lines (Luxemburg 1913; Lenin 1918), while others envision a democratic path (Hilferding [1910] 1981; Kautsky 1927).

Accumulation in old institutional approaches: measuring and theorizing context-dependent capitalist dynamics

From the second half of the nineteenth century, a historical and institutional form of political economy developed in the German historical school and the American original institutional economics. These economists depart from both the nascent marginalist equilibrium thinking and Marxian determinism. Like Marx, they underline the innovative but conflictual and crisis-prone character of capitalism. However, they are more aware of the diversity of capitalist dynamics and questioned the very idea of universal laws of economic development. They provide important methods and results to conceptualize the processes of capital accumulation.

From a methodological perspective, their theory is grounded in careful empirical research and participates in the ongoing improvement of techniques to organize and analyze time-series data. Economic fluctuations are decomposed into trend, cyclical, seasonal, and irregular components. For them, "the explanation of cycles . . . belongs to the group of endogenous doctrine, which on the basis of meticulous documentation and decomposition of the process seeks to identify its causes from within" (Spiethoff [1923] 1925:69). They typify these fluctuations according to their duration and cause. Different kinds of cycles are highlighted, from the business cycle, conceived as the basic movement (Mitchell 1927), to the long cycle, epitomizing the structural movement of the economy (Schumpeter 1939). They both stress recurrences and crises as components of cycles.

Integrating an international comparative perspective, and drawing on relationships between local and global dynamics, they insist on the historical and institutional context in which production, investment, unemployment, innovation, relative prices, or money are embedded (Schmoller 1901; Sombart 1927; Simiand 1933). The observed variations in the timing and depth of economic fluctuations are ingrained in these diverse historical backgrounds, rather than being expressed as pre-defined schemes (Burns & Mitchell 1946). Even if national economies display similar features (such as the development of monetary exchange and capital accumulation, and profit as a growth engine), and thus comparable economic movements, various path-dependent development trajectories do persist (Veblen 1915). Crises also take various forms depending on the evolving economic structure, such as the over-production of consumption or production goods, and financial crises accompanying the development of fictitious capital (Veblen 1915). The features of these developments can be traced back to socially embedded institutional sets and policies that are partly idiosyncratic.

These efforts are part of a vast theoretical project to unravel the endogenous dynamics of economic systems, their structural variety in time and space, and to link them to evolving techniques and lifestyles, organizations and institutions (Schmoller 1901). Notably, the latest generation of the German historicists feature the historical diversity of capitalism(s). Both Sombart (1927) and Weber (1984–2016) investigate the unique emergence of capitalist accumulation, highlighting a complex web of religious, (geo)political, and economic factors. Far from being an inherent trait of human nature, the desire for gain, Sombart (1927) argues, is a capitalist social and political construct. Implementing the capitalist wage-labor organization requires an artificial and 'violent' disciplining of labor. The significant savings necessary for accumulation in early capitalism were enabled by the extremely uneven distribution of wealth, and by the henceforth prevalent interest in accumulating—the latter being the paradoxical by-product of the protestant ethos, as Weber (1904–5, in 1984–2016: I-18) asserted.

From nascent to advanced capitalism, different types of accumulation and demand evolved. Sombart (1927) distinguishes two sources of capitalist demand. Exogenous demand (outside capitalism) was prevalent in the 'early capitalism.' The output of production was sold mainly to people who were neither business entrepreneurs nor their employees, including landed proprietors, high finance (brokers and speculators), governments, and populations outside Western Europe. With the development of capitalist relations, endogenous demand has played a growing role, as it embraced both the purchase of consumer goods by capitalist entrepreneurs and their employees, and the purchase of production goods by firms. Sombart (1927) uses British, French, and American statistics to show that real wages doubled within the period of advanced capitalism. It fueled a demand for its own products by innovating and changing its methods.

As business organizations became more intensive, speeding up operations, rationalizing the use of materials, equipment and personnel, labor productivity doubled. 'Late capitalism,' according to Sombart (1927), goes with new waves of mutations after World War I, including the incursion of normative ideas into business practice, the disestablishment of profit-seeking as the sole guide of economic activity, declining flexibility, a steadier course of evolution, the substitution of agreements and planning for free competition, the standardizing of industrial organization, and the growing share and control by the state over the economy (the rise of 'regulated capitalism' and of socialism). Capitalism according to Sombart is multi-faceted and compatible with a bewildering array of organizational forms and 'economic styles.' The rise of large business is not synonymous with the sweeping concentration of business control forecasted by Marx. Corporate organizations co-exist with small businesses, cooperatives, and communal enterprises.

These points have much in common with the historical account of accumulation regimes highlighted by RT many decades later. Like the German historical school, RT belongs to historical institutionalism. However, the genesis of RT does not exhibit any direct affiliation with its German predecessors.

Accumulation regimes: contemporary theoretical approaches

RT and SSA are institutional approaches that emerged in France and the US in the 1970s, at a pivotal time in their post-war economic trajectories. These approaches conceptualize capitalism as an open system embedded within social, political, and cultural institutions affecting its dynamics, notably the accumulation process.

The genesis of Régulation theory and SSA: strong commonalities

Régulation theory is inspired by Marxian insights into the contradictory dynamics of capitalism, Kaleckian and Keynesian macroeconomics, and the Annales historical school (Boyer [1986] 1990). Its purpose is to explain the period of relatively high and stable growth of the post-war 'Golden Age' followed by slow growth and macroeconomic disequilibria in the advanced industrialized economies, particularly arising from the 1970s economic crisis. Vintage RT investigates the long-term transformations of capitalism, starting with case studies of the US (Aglietta [1976] 2000) and France (CEPREMAP-CORDES 1977). It characterizes the Golden Age as a Fordist accumulation regime embedded in a complex of institutional forms. Comparative studies reveal that there were several forms of Fordism, as well as non-Fordist dynamics (Boyer & Mistral 1986).

The origin of SSA is strikingly similar. Reich (1993) identifies the original theoretical perspective as emerging from Marxian views concerning class conflicts, and from Marxian and Keynesian macroeconomics. It developed "to understand the origin of the exceptional growth of the post-Second World War period, and to analyze the mechanisms and consequences of the structural crisis that struck the US in the late 1960s" (Coban 2002: 299). These similarities enabled some common work (Bowles & Boyer 1988). Fundamentally, RT and SSA explain the move from growth to crisis by a shared set of hypotheses. Let us scrutinize this further.

Accumulation regimes: the building blocks

According to Boyer & Saillard (2002: 38):

> régulation theory describes the social and economic patterns that enable accumulation to occur in the long term between two structural crises. These regular patterns as a whole are

summarized by the notion of an accumulation regime. Identifying regular patterns does not require the exclusion of crises: the description of accumulation regimes includes their evolution and potential crises. . . . Where neoclassical and post-Keynesian theory look for a general, invariable model, régulationists recognize a variety of accumulation regimes . . . that are transformed over the long term and vary in both time and space.[1]

An accumulation regime refers to "the set of regularities that ensure the general and relatively coherent evolution of capital accumulation, that is, which allow the resolution or postponement of the distortions and disequilibria to which the process continually gives rise" (Boyer 2002b: 335). These patterns relate to five key characteristics.

The first characteristic is the evolution of the *organization of production* and of *labor's relationship to the means of production*. The implementation of the Fordist productivist work organization was associated with in-house careers, long-term commitment, and employment stability, whereas the contemporary finance-dominated regime promotes flexibility of commitment and labor-shedding strategies.

The second characteristic is the *time horizon for the valorization of capital*, translating into *management principles*. The Fordist accumulation regime—with its *ex ante* sharing of productivity gains, the stabilizing role of the state, and its 'patient capital'—enhanced the foreseeability of economic activities and lengthened the time horizon of firms (Boyer 2004: 57–58), as it is translated into long-term planning and investment, and a high level of in-house production. The contemporary finance-dominated accumulation regime fell back on short-termism (the volatility of speculative finance, a high degree of uncertainty), as it is translated into the financialization of management standards (Aglietta [1976] 2000) including shareholder value, benchmarking, and outsourcing.

The third characteristic is a *distribution of value* that enables the dynamic reproduction of the dominant social bloc (Amable 2003). In Fordism, the wage-earning class became an essential political force as a compromise emerged between the managers of firms and industry workers against rentiers, resulting in the productivity indexation of wages and lower wage disparity. In the contemporary finance-dominated regime a polarization of income and wealth distribution has developed, leading to a decrease of the wage-share, emergence of sky-high wages for a tiny 'elite,' and the comeback of the rentier thanks to a management-stakeholder compromise.

The fourth characteristic is a *composition of social demand* matching the *tendencies in the development of productive capacity*. In the Fordist regime, the regular development of direct and indirect wages enabled a dynamic fit of mass consumption with a steadily increasing mass production. In the finance-dominated regime, for workers the wealth effect is at best limited, public and private debt or export are considered back-up engines of growth, and there is a strong tendency to overcapacity.

The fifth characteristic is an *articulation with non-capitalist economic forms*, when significant in the investigated socio-economic configuration. This point is highly relevant for developing countries but also for advanced capitalist ones. For instance, many Fordist countries experienced a large increase in higher education enrolments, primarily funded through public expenditure. In the finance-dominated regime, this model more or less persisted until the 1990s. Subsequently structural changes have been implemented. Higher education is moving towards private funding by individuals, as meritocratic selection is progressively replaced by pecuniary selection, embedded in a more competitive and hierarchical organization (Carpentier 2015).

Both RT and SSA propose formal models in support of their analyses. They started in a similar way, building linear macroeconomic models to test the stability of the determinants of economic dynamics. The SSA's models estimate the determinants of profits in the US context after World War II and examine how public policies failed to restore the previous dynamics of profit in the Reagan era (Bowles *et al.* 1983; Gordon 1991). Early *Régulationist* models focus mainly on the Gross Domestic Product (GDP) growth rate based on labor productivity and overall final demand. Variations in the model's specifications generate several regimes and scenarios (Boyer 1988; Billaudot 2002). These models were subsequently enriched by focusing on regime changes rather than invariances, introducing more refined econometric techniques (Boyer & Juillard 1994). Furthermore, some SSA contributors develop evolutionary game models to formalize individual preferences while abandoning the self-interest axiom (Bowles 2004). Later *Régulationist* models strive to capture a higher level of complexity. Lordon (1991) formulates bold propositions to move towards endogenous non-linear dynamics. He formalizes the dynamic instability proper to 'minor crises.' Using bifurcations models, he explores the structural instability specific to major crises. He then formalizes a truly endogenous process of structural change in which the repetition of a conjuncture over the long-run produces structural deformations. He calls this *Régulationist*-specific change 'endometabolism' (Lordon 1993, 1997). For both RT and SSA, the ongoing challenge is to formalize the 'recomposition' processes through which new institutional forms emerge.

The embeddedness of accumulation regimes in a conjunction of institutional forms

Following the Annales school historian Ernest Labrousse, the crucial message of RT is that every society displays the economic evolution and crises that correspond to its structure (Boyer 2002a: 14). This structure is an amalgam of institutional forms or, in SSA nomenclature, the social structure of accumulation is a "coherent set of economic, political and cultural/ideological institutions that provides a structure for capitalist economic activity" (Kotz 2003: 263). In *Régulationist* parlance, institutional forms result from struggles, conflicts, and power relationships crystallized in institutionalized compromises. Political coalitions are thus at the heart of institutionalized compromises which create sets of rules, rights, and obligations. Thus, they frame the strategies and behaviors of the groups and individuals involved (André 2002). Institutional forms are situated in time and space. Therefore, institutional forms do not express pre-existing economic laws. Conversely, institutions create localized regularities that are contingent on a given social configuration.

Here again, RT and SSA develop comparable institutional matrixes to investigate historically situated economies:

1   The *wage-labor nexus* (RT) and *capital-labor relations* (SSA), including the organization of work, labor–management relations, and sources of labor supply.
2   *Forms of competition* (RT) and *capital-capital relations* (SSA), including forms of competition and corporate governance.
3   The *financial/monetary regime* (RT) and *financial institutions* (SSA).
4   The *state-economy relationship* (RT) and the *government's role* (SSA).
5   The *insertion in the international regime* (RT) and *international relations and institutions* (SSA).

SSA theory integrated initially a sixth crucial element: the *dominant political coalition*. A new SSA emerges only after a realignment of political coalitions. This concept was initially implicit in RT, but later *Régulationists* directly tackled this political issue. Lordon (1999), drawing on Bourdieu, explores the role of symbolic power in the construction of economic ideas and policies. Amable (2003: 66) introduces the Gramsci-inspired notion of *dominant social bloc*:

the institutional configuration of an economy depends on the formation of a stable dominant social bloc coalescing different socio-political groups prone to support a coalition with
a certain political strategy. Implementing this strategy will lead to institutional change in a
direction that is beneficial to the dominant social bloc. However, the social bloc itself is a
coalition of different and sometimes diverging interests; the institutional structure that will
result from the political strategy that it supports will therefore be a compromise, which may
be more or less explicit.

These interdependent institutional forms are hierarchically ordered. The *Régulationist* notion
of *institutional hierarchy* grasps the dominance of one institutional form over others. It hinges on
power relations and political coalitions, as some collective actors are able to restructure institutional compromises beyond their direct sphere of influence. For example, the post-World War II
arrangements reflected the need for compromise with the wage-earning class. The 1990s saw
the rise to power of internationalized financial capital, imposing its logic and rhetoric on the
state (in search of credibility), the wage-labor nexus (subject to the flexibility imperative), and the
monetary regime (in charge of financial stability) (Boyer 2002b: 331).

Institutional forms co-evolve and even cohere. As Amable (2003: 6) suggests, "economic 'models' should not be considered just as a collection of institutional forms, but also as a set of complementarity relations between these institutions, which form the basis of the coherence between
the specific institutional forms of each model." This notion of *institutional complementarity* refers
to the contingent compatibility of institutional forms that may emerge in some economies after

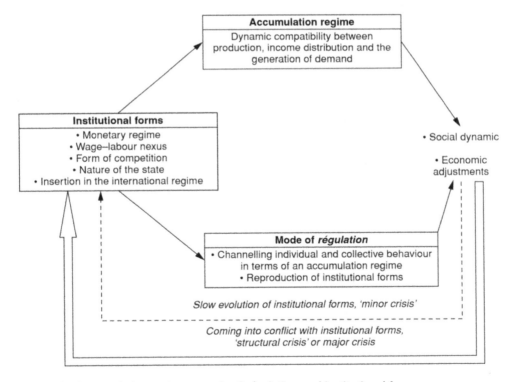

Figure 4.1 Accumulation regimes, mode of *régulation*, and institutional forms
Source: Boyer & Saillard (2002: 44).

mutual adjustment processes. One example of this complementarity is the Fordist conjunction of the contract-based nominal wage with a credit economy in which the national money supply is endogenous with limited constraints imposed by the international system (Boyer 2002b: 330).

The reproduction of institutional forms over time enables the emergence of stabilized patterns of behaviors that define a *régulation mode* (see Figure 4.1). It does not mean identical reproduction, but rather historical representation, as "unforeseen events arise, cycles follow one another, institutional forms gradually change and there emerges the possibility of evolutions so contradictory that they become explosive" (Boyer & Saillard 2002: 42). All accumulation regimes and *régulation* modes are finite, as they are affected by serial disequilibria and conflicts that eventually destabilize them. Similarly, every SSA is subject to both exogenous shocks and endogenously created tensions. These frictions eventually erode the SSA, compromising its ability to promote returns, investments, and growth. RT distinguishes between *minor crises* that are accommodated via adjustments of existing institutions, and *structural crises* leading to a profound restructuring of institutional forms.

It should be stressed that RT is explicitly a *non-functionalist approach*. It scrutinizes the dynamic viability of a set of institutionalized compromises when there is no *a priori* reason why they should define a stable or virtuous accumulation regime (Boyer 2002a: 2). It refutes the idea that more efficient accumulation regimes drive out less efficient ones. Notably, the conceptualization of (post-)Fordism is not the core of RT; rather, it is a local outcome of RT's theoretical framework. RT investigates an extensive variety of evolving socio-historic configurations. It is a historicized theory working as a general investigation matrix to analyze localized arrangements.

Evolution and diversity of accumulation regimes

RT identifies a broad range of accumulation regimes. This diversity in time and space relates to capitalist, emerging, semi-peripheral, and socialist economies. Delineating a situated dominant accumulation mode like Fordism or finance-dominated accumulation should never blind us to the existence of a variety of compossible regimes.

Diachronic diversity in long-standing capitalist economies: a highly stylized history

Extensive accumulation with competitive Régulation mode: the Great nineteenth century

During the nineteenth century, agriculture-based accumulation (and crises) progressively moved towards an extensive accumulation regime relying on a massive mobilization of labor and capital, with weak growth in productivity and wage purchasing power. Capitalist development conquered new spheres of activity and globalized. Wage labor was developing but remained marginal. Workers' consumption played a minor part in the macroeconomic loop, and accumulation relied mainly on the profits of entrepreneurs, rentiers, and farmers, as well as public spending and external demand. Wage earners were in a weak position, as wages were both low and synchronized with the business cycle. Employment and wages rose with economic activity, then plummeted with the downturn. It is a regime of cyclical growth with recurrent crises, embedded in a competitive *régulation* mode.

Intensive accumulation without mass consumption: the inter-war period

The period around the turn of the twentieth century witnessed the increasing development of finance, the emergence of large capitalist enterprises, and the progression of wage labor, particularly in the US. This laid the groundwork for the emergence of an intensive accumulation regime in the inter-war period in which the conditions of production are transformed to increase productivity, raising the capital stock per worker. The rationalization of production techniques enabled increasing economies of scale and the rise of mass production. With the development of wage labor, wages became an essential component of demand. However, wage formation remained competitive, curbing their progression and leading to wage stagnation. Despite significant productivity gains, over-production emerged and led to the Great Depression. Meanwhile, collective wage bargaining progressed together with the implementation of indirect wage elements, prefiguring the next regime.

Golden Age Fordism: intensive accumulation with mass consumption

Fordism was dominant in many developed countries during the Golden Age of capitalism, linking intensive accumulation with mass consumption. It co-existed with mixed or alternative accumulation regimes in various economies. Fordism can be stylized as an accumulation regime defined by three characteristics (Boyer 2002b).

The first characteristic is a system of *work organization* striving for continuous growth in productivity. Building on the 'scientific management' techniques of Taylorism, Fordism promotes the division of labor, the mechanization of production processes, and the separation of conception and production. The assembly line epitomizes this form of industrial engineering, which tends to diffuse into many sectors.

However, this work organization is not enough. The second characteristic of the Fordist growth mode is an *institutionalized share of productivity gains* for workers. The US collective bargaining agreements of the 1960s (Aglietta [1976] 2000) and the French policy of 'sharing the dividends of progress' (Boyer 1979) are examples of institutionalized social compromises allowing for the regular growth of wage income fueling demand. These two characteristics define the Fordist wage-labor nexus and enable a virtuous circle between mass production, mass consumption, and high growth.

Third, this combination is embedded in mutually enforcing *institutional forms*. These include the centrality of the wage-labor nexus associated with worker–manager balance, oligopolistic forms of competition, credit-based monetary regimes allied with the taming of speculative finance, embedded state-economy relationships based on Keynesian counter-cyclical policies, high levels of public spending and taxation, and major welfare state developments (Delorme & André 1983). The adjustment of production and demand occurred primarily within each country, for this is an inward-looking intensive accumulation regime governed by internal consumption.

Growing internationalization thus destabilized this institutional architecture and after a period of internal adjustments, the Fordist accumulation regime went into a major crisis during the 1970s. This crisis saw the erosion of productivity gains and profits, the fragmentation of previous compromises linked with internationalization and the expansion of the service sector, and the end of the Bretton Woods agreements. SSA researchers obtain similar results for the US (Coban 2002: 303).

The intrinsic fragility of the finance-dominated accumulation regime

The *régulation* mode was deeply transformed by neoliberal reforms, including deregulation and re-regulation, privatizations, financialization, and a deepening of internationalization. A diversity of accumulation regimes emerged from previous ones, translated into distinct national and regional trajectories. Yet some common trends in Organization for Economic Cooperation and Development (OECD) countries are noticeable, notably a shift in the hierarchy of institutional forms. All institutional forms became largely affected by finance, including the redefinition of the state-economy relationship, competition forms, and insertion in the international regime. While the Golden Age was dominated by the wage-labor nexus, wages reverted to an adjustment variable in the finance-dominated regime. A decisive shift in power relations at the expense of labor took place, reflected in the fall of wage shares across OECD economies and widening inequalities. SSA contributions highlight that in the US during the 1970s and 1980s, income inequalities rose as a result of efforts to maintain the profit share. Kotz (2015: 11) argues that wage stagnation, supported by powerful forces driving 'disequalization,' is now at the heart of neoliberal capitalism.

In a nutshell, the pattern and pace of contemporary accumulation in OECD countries is increasingly shaped by financialization, to varying degrees and modalities, and typically characterized by *slow* and *fragile* accumulation (Stockhammer 2009). In major economies the investment/profit ratio shows a declining trend. With the dominance of shareholder value (Lordon 1999), there is a shift in management behavior from 'retain and reinvest' to 'downsize and distribute' (Lazonick & O'Sullivan 2000). Financialization may accompany stagnation or increasingly volatile growth that, in some cases, has emerged in the form of temporary consumer credit-led growth. Wages' flexibilization, growing unemployment, and acute international competition have exerted downward pressure on domestic demand, leading to strategies that are either not viable in the long-run or not generalizable. Some countries like the US exhibit a credit-fueled consumption-driven growth model with large current account deficits, while others like Germany and Japan demonstrate an export-driven growth model with low consumption growth and large current account surpluses (Stockhammer 2009).

This regime displays poor performance in terms of economic, environmental, and social outcomes, and is ultimately unsustainable. Unregulated financial markets are prone to endogenous instability (Orléan [2011] 2014), and macroeconomic shocks from the financial sector have become more severe and frequent, expressing the growing contradictions of this regime. The Global Financial Crisis (GFC) of 2007–2008 signals the opening of a major crisis of this regime, the overcoming of which is radically uncertain (Boyer 2009). SSA contributors emphasize the necessity of engaging in more social contestation (Reich 2009). Boyer (2015) highlights the prominent role of political factors both in the institutional lock-in of financial hegemony and in finding a way out of the crisis. Other *Régulationists* emphasize a conflict of *régulation*. In the field of the wage-labor nexus, this conflict expresses the inability to retain previous Fordist compromises, represented by the decrease of the labor share of income. It also reveals an inability to adapt to emerging tendencies—like social spending as an increasing factor of economic growth—to build new compromises (Michel 2013).

Synchronic diversity in capitalist systems and beyond

Multi-level diversity within Golden Age capitalism

In the Golden Age, the national level was the determinant. There was a broad diversity of trajectories linked to idiosyncratic national configurations of institutional forms. For instance, Germany's diversified quality production model (Streeck 1995) and the versatility and professionalism of German workers contrasted with Fordist standardization. Contrastingly, Japan exhibited certain Fordist elements without the wage compromise, including parallel growth in the capital goods and consumption goods sectors, a virtuous cycle in mass production and mass consumption.

Wages were influenced by business cycles and not indexed to productivity, and investment was pulled by profit rather than demand (Inoue & Yamada 2002). The micro- or meso-corporatism of large Japanese companies and Toyotism were also distinctive features.

At the meso level, there were non-Fordist sector-based dynamics even in Fordist accumulation regimes like Golden Age France. An interesting case is the construction sector, as it experienced strong capital returns together with weak labor productivity. Because of the heavy demand from leading manufacturing sectors to the construction sector, a transfer of productivity gains took place. Construction also played a key role in spreading Fordist consumption and production norms throughout the French economy, thereby supporting the establishment of an intensive accumulation regime (Du Tertre 2002: 205). Overall, there is a vast diversity of sector dynamics governed by specific rules and technical constraints.

It should be stressed that RT is a multi-level institutional theory, rather than merely a macroeconomic theory. Disaggregated analysis is also possible at the product level—for example, agricultural goods such as wine, poultry, and vegetables (Bartoli & Boulet 1990). As Saillard (2002: 186) identifies:

> At this level the main aim of the analysis is to explain the social definition of an accumulation base. Enormous diversity in configurations is possible and obviously it is more complicated to trace them back to macroeconomics. On the other hand, this type of 'micro-institutional' approach broadens the analysis of micro-patterns, the advance of crisis and potential elements of change.

Diversity in developing economies and beyond capitalism

There is a wealth of studies investigating accumulation and *régulation* paths around the world. However, Africa is the least-analyzed continent. Latin America exhibits a huge diversity of regimes and institutional forms, with the common feature that accumulation regimes are dominated by the mode of insertion into the international regime (Boyer 2012; Régulation Review 2012). North-East Asia (Japan, South Korea, China) is also a fruitful ground for *Régulationist* studies (Boyer *et al.* 2011) and, more recently, South-East Asia (Régulation Review 2013, 2014). The rise of China's accumulation centers redistributes industrial powers and impacts on other Asian accumulation regimes, triggering institutional changes even in more developed countries. China tends towards over-accumulation and faces difficulties developing new drivers of growth besides investment and export, despite recent wage increases. Social and territorial inequalities and environmental conflicts also polarize Chinese society.

The *Régulationist* framework has also been applied to centrally planned economies (Chavance 1987). These economies were initially characterized by an extensive accumulation regime performing accelerated industrialization, over-investment, and drastic consumption curbing. *Régulation* through shortage dominated—ubiquitous chronic shortages of the labor force, inputs, and production and consumption goods leading to a discontinuous work process ('arrhythmic Taylorism'), labor hoarding, incremental process innovation rather than disruptive technical change, and severe consumption rationing. This resource-constrained accumulation regime contrasts with the canonical capitalist over-production tendency. In the 1970s, because of these systemic constraints, these economies failed to switch to an intensive accumulation regime incorporating radical innovations and diversified production and consumption patterns. This resulted in a sharp downward trend of growth and a structural crisis, followed by a systemic collapse. Although homogenizing, the Soviet system was characterized by specific, historically grounded trajectories that shaped partially its transformation from the 1990s onward.

Agnès Labrousse, Sandrine Michel

Some avenues of research: ecologies of accumulation

Both the *Régulationist* 'Sectors and Territories Network' and the SSA spatialization school place special emphasis on the manner in which accumulation regimes produce differential results at differing spatial scales. There are synchronic complementarities between dissimilar but inter-related accumulation regimes. In a context of increasing transnationalization, it is particularly important to investigate the *complex ecology of accumulation regimes*, in terms of the "co-existence, structural coupling, mutual conditioning, and co-evolution of different, but compossible accumulation regimes and modes of regulation" (Sum 2015). Let us think of 'Chinamerica' or, within Europe, how German mercantilism feeds on Eastern Europe dependent industries and the debt-driven accumulation of Southern European countries. Dominant countries are able to impose costs on other spaces or future generations. This ecology of accumulation regimes has to be coupled with ecological prospects.

From the early developments of capitalism to its contemporary forms, the *ecological dimension of accumulation regimes* is a highly pressing issue. Sombart (1927: 1137–1155) shows that capitalism flourished by robbing the soil, felling the forests, and drawing on irreplaceable mineral resources. The greater part of capital goods, he argues, represents not annual income but the consumption of man's natural patrimony. The acceleration of accumulation in capitalist centers went hand in hand with the great acceleration of the environmental destruction that typifies the so-called Anthropocene. Recent works demonstrate that unequal ecological exchange is a crucial factor in accumulation, from imperial Great Britain to the Pax Americana (Bonneuil & Fressoz 2016). Dominant accumulation centers are able to fuel their accumulation with artificially cheap resources from the periphery of developing countries, and largely externalize the ecological costs and constraints while improving the ecological quality of their territories. Despite the early *Régulationist* work by Lipietz (2002) on the society-environment relation, and significant advances more recently (Rousseau & Zuindeau 2007; Boyer 2015), this relationship is not systematically integrated into *Régulationist* studies. This should change, as there is increasing evidence that the Anthropocene is foremost a Capitalocene (Bonneuil & Fressoz 2016).

Note

1 Notwithstanding, Post Keynesians and *Régulationists* engage in fruitful collaborations (Régulation Review 2011).

References

Aglietta, M. [1976] 2000. *A Theory of Capitalist Regulation: The US Experience*. London: Verso Classics.
Amable, B. 2003. *The Diversity of Modern Capitalism*. Oxford: Oxford University Press.
André, C. 2002. 'The welfare state and the institutional compromises: from origins to contemporary crisis,' *in*: R. Boyer & Y. Saillard (eds.), *Régulation Theory: The State of the Art*. London: Routledge, 94–100.
Bartoli, P. & Boulet, D. 1990. 'Conditions d'une approche en termes de régulation sectorielle. Le cas de la sphère viticole.' *Cahiers d'économie et sociologie rurales*, 17: 7–38.
Billaudot, B. 2002. 'Short- and medium-term macroeconomic dynamics,' *in*: R. Boyer & Y. Saillard (eds.), *Régulation Theory: The State of the Art*. London: Routledge, 144–152.
Bonneuil, C. & Fressoz, J.-B. 2016. *The Shock of the Anthropocene: The Earth, History and Us*. London: Verso Books.
Bowles, S. 2004. *Microeconomics: Behavior, Institutions, and Evolution*. Princeton, NJ: Princeton University Press.
Bowles, S. & Boyer, R. 1988. 'Labor discipline and aggregate demand: a macroeconomic model.' *American Economic Review*, 78 (2): 395–400.
Bowles, S., Gordon, D.M., & Weisskopf, T.E. 1983. 'Long swings and the non-reproductive cycle.' *American Economic Review*, 73 (2): 152–157.

Boyer, R. 1979. 'Wage formation in historical perspective: the French experience.' *Cambridge Journal of Economics*, 3 (2): 99–118.

Boyer, R. [1986] 1990. *The Régulation School: A Critical Introduction.* New York: Columbia University Press.

Boyer, R. 1988. 'Formalizing growth regimes,' *in*: G. Dosi, C. Freeman, R. Nelson, G. Silverberg, & L. Soete (eds.), *Technical Change and Economic Theory.* London: Pinter, 608–622.

Boyer, R. 2002a. 'The origins of *régulation* theory,' *in*: R. Boyer & Y. Saillard (eds.), *Régulation Theory: The State of the Art.* London: Routledge, 13–20.

Boyer, R. 2002b. 'Is *régulation* theory an original theory of economic institutions?' *in*: R. Boyer & Y. Saillard (eds.), *Régulation Theory: The State of the Art.* London: Routledge, 320–333.

Boyer, R. 2004. *Théorie de la régulation, 1. Les fondamentaux.* Paris: La Découverte.

Boyer, R. 2009. 'Feu le régime d'accumulation tiré par la finance.' *Revue de la régulation*, 5. Available from http://regulation.revues.org/7367 [Accessed March 2, 2016]

Boyer, R. 2012. 'Diversité et évolution des capitalismes en Amérique latine.' *Revue de la régulation*, 11. Available from http://regulation.revues.org/9720 [Accessed March 2, 2016]

Boyer, R. 2015. *Economie politique des capitalismes: Théorie de la régulation et des crises.* Paris: La Découverte, Grands Repères.

Boyer, R. & Juillard, M. 1994. *Analyse de la croissance séculaire américaine: un modèle de croissance à plusieurs régimes.* Commissariat Général au Plan, Paris: Cepremap.

Boyer, R. & Mistral, J. (eds.) 1986. *Capitalismes fin de siècle.* Paris: PUF.

Boyer, R. & Saillard, Y. (eds.) 2002. *Régulation Theory: The State of the Art.* London: Routledge.

Boyer, R., Uemura, H., & Isogai, A. (eds.) 2011. *Diversity and Transformation of Asian Capitalisms.* London: Routledge.

Burns, A.F. & Mitchell, W.C. 1946. *Measuring Business Cycles.* Cambridge, MA: NBER.

Carpentier, V. 2015. Political economy of higher education and socio-economic crises: global and national perspectives. Paper presented at the conference on 'The Theory of Regulation in Times of Crisis,' Paris, 9–12 June. Available from http://theorie-regulation.org/colloques/colloque-rr-2015/programme-rr2015/ [Accessed March 2, 2016]

CEPREMAP-CORDES. 1977. Approches de l'inflation: l'exemple français. Report of the Research Convention for the Commissariat Général au Plan, 22/176, December.

Chavance, B. (ed.) 1987. *Régulation, cycles et crises dans les économies socialistes.* Paris: EHESS.

Coban, A. 2002. '*Régulation* and the American radical school,' *in*: R. Boyer & Y. Saillard (eds.), *Régulation Theory: The State of the Art.* London: Routledge, 299–305.

Delorme, R. & André, C. 1983. *L'Etat et l'économie: Un essai d'explication de l'évolution des dépenses publiques en France (1870–1980).* Paris: Seuil.

Du Tertre, C. 2002. 'Sector-based dimensions of *régulation* and the wage–labour nexus,' *in*: R. Boyer & Y. Saillard (eds.), *Régulation Theory: The State of the Art.* London: Routledge, 204–213.

Gordon, D.M. 1991. 'Kaldor's macro system: too much cumulation, too few contradictions,' *in*: E.J. Nell & W. Semmler (eds.), *Nicholas Kaldor and Mainstream Economics.* London: Macmillan, 518–548.

Harvey, D. 1982. *The Limits to Capital.* Oxford: Blackwell.

Hilferding, R. [1910] 1981. *Finance Capital. A Study of the Latest Phase of Capitalist Development.* London: Routledge. Available from: https://www.marxists.org/archive/hilferding/1910/finkap/ [Accessed March 2, 2016]

Inoue, Y. & Yamada, T. 2002. 'Japan: demythologising regulation,' *in*: R. Boyer & Y. Saillard (eds.), *Régulation Theory: The State of the Art.* London: Routledge, 260–266.

Kautsky, K. 1927. *The Materialist Conception of History.* London: Yale University Press. Available from: https://www.marxists.org/archive/kautsky/1927/abstract/mch-abs.htm [Accessed April 12, 2016]

Kotz, D.M. 2003. 'Neoliberalism and the social structure of accumulation theory of long-run capital accumulation.' *Review of Radical Political Economics*, 35 (3): 263–270.

Kotz, D.M. 2015. 'Explaining rising inequality: capitalism in general or social structure of accumulation?' Paper presented at the conference on 'The Theory of Regulation in Times of Crisis,' Paris, 9–12 June. Available from http://theorie-regulation.org/colloques/colloque-rr-2015/programme-rr2015/ [Accessed March 2, 2016]

Lazonick, W. & O'Sullivan, M. 2000. 'Maximising shareholder value: a new ideology for corporate governance.' *Economy and Society*, 29 (1): 13–35.

Lenin, V.I. 1918. *The State and Revolution*, Marxists Internet Archive. Available from https://www.marxists.org/archive/lenin/works/1917/staterev/ [Accessed April 12, 2016]

Lipietz, A. 2002. 'Régulationist political ecology or environmental economics?' *in*: R. Boyer & Y. Saillard (eds.), *Régulation Theory: The State of the Art.* London: Routledge, 223–227.

Lordon, F. 1991. 'Théorie de la croissance: quelques développements récents.' *Observations et diagnostics économiques*, 37 (juillet): 193–243.

Lordon, F. 1993. Irrégularités des trajectoires de croissance, évolutions et dynamique non-linéaire. Vers une schématisation de l'endométabolisme. PhD dissertation. École des hautes études en sciences sociales (EHESS), France.

Lordon, F. 1997. 'Endogenous structural change and crisis in a multiple time-scales growth model.' *Journal of Evolutionary Economics*, 7 (1): 1–21.

Lordon, F. 1999. 'Vers une théorie régulationniste de la politique. Croyances économiques et pouvoir symbolique.' *L'année de la régulation*, 3: 169–207.

Luxemburg, R. 1913. *The Accumulation of Capital: A Contribution to an Economic Explanation to Imperialism.* Marxists Internet Archive. Available from https://www.marxists.org/archive/luxemburg/1913/accumulation-capital/ [Accessed April 12, 2016]

Malthus, T. R. 1836. *Principles of Political Economy*, 2nd edn. London: W. Pickering. Available from http://lf-oll.s3.amazonaws.com/titles/2188/Malthus_1462_EBk_v6.0.pdf [Accessed April 12, 2016]

Marx, K. 1867. *Capital, Volume I.* Marxists Internet Archive. Available from https://www.marxists.org/archive/marx/works/dowload/pdf/Capital-Volume-I.pdf [Accessed April 12, 2016]

Marx, K. 1894. *Capital, Volume III.* Marxists Internet Archive. Available from https://www.marxists.org/archive/marx/works/download/pdf/Capital-Volume-III.pdf [Accessed April 12, 2016]

Michel, S. 2013. Wage–labour nexus and social spending over the long period: the emergence of a conflict of *Régulation*. Paper presented at the 15th AHE conference, London, 4–6 July.

Mitchell, W.C. 1927. *Business Cycles: The Problem and Its Setting.* Cambridge, MA: NBER.

Orléan, A. [2011] 2014. *The Empire of Value.* Cambridge, MA: MIT Press.

Régulation Review. 2011. 'Post-Keynesianism and Régulation theory: common perspectives.' *Régulation Review*, 10 (2). Available from http://regulation.revues.org/9527 [Accessed April 12, 2016]

Régulation Review. 2012. 'Editorial: capitalisms in Latin America.' *Régulation Review*, 11 (1). Available from http://regulation.revues.org/10026 [Accessed April 12, 2016]

Régulation Review. 2013. 'Editorial: political economy of contemporary Asia (1).' *Régulation Review*, 13 (1). Available from http://regulation.revues.org/10275 [Accessed April 12, 2016]

Régulation Review. 2014. 'Editorial: political economy of contemporary Asia (2).' *Régulation Review*, 15 (1). Available from http://regulation.revues.org/10810 [Accessed April 12, 2016]

Reich, M. 1993. 'Radical economics in historical perspective.' *Review of Radical Political Economics*, 25 (3): 43–50.

Reich, M. 2009. The crisis of contemporary capitalism: the social structure of accumulation (SSA) perspective. Paper presented at the 21st SASE Annual Meeting, Paris, 16–18 July.

Ricardo, D. 1817. *On the Principles of Political Economy and Taxation.* Library of Economics and Liberty. Available from http://www.econlib.org/library/Ricardo/ricP.html [Accessed April 12, 2016]

Rousseau, S. & Zuindeau, B. 2007. 'Théorie de la régulation et développement durable.' *Régulation Review*, 1. Available from http://regulation.revues.org/1298 [Accessed April 12, 2016]

Saillard, Y. 2002. 'Globalisation, localisation and sector-based specialisation: what is the future of national *régulation*?' in: R. Boyer & Y. Saillard (eds.), *Régulation Theory: The State of the Art.* London: Routledge, 183–189.

Say, J.-B. [1803] 1972. *Traité d'économie politique.* Paris: Calmann-Lévy.

Schmoller, G. 1901. *Grundriss der Allgemeinen Volkswirtschaftslehre.* Leipzig: Duncker und Humblot.

Schumpeter, J.A. 1939. *Business Cycles: A Theoretical, Historical and Statistical Analysis of the Capitalist Process.* New York: McGraw-Hill.

Simiand, F. 1933. *Les fluctuations économiques en longue période et la crise mondiale.* Paris: PUF.

Sismondi, J. [1827] 1971. *Nouveaux principes d'Economie Politique*, 2ème edition. Paris: Calmann-Lévy.

Smith, A. 1776. *An Inquiry into the Nature and the Causes of the Wealth Of Nations.* Library of Economics and Liberty. Available from http://www.econlib.org/library/Smith/smWN.html [Accessed April 12, 2016]

Sombart, W. 1927. *Der Moderne Kapitalismus.* München: Duncker and Humblot.

Spiethoff, A. [1923] 1925. 'Krisen.' *Handwörterbuch der Staatswissenschaften*, 6: 8–91.

Stockhammer, E. 2009. 'The finance-dominated accumulation regime, income distribution and the present crisis.' *Papeles de Europa*, 19: 58–81.

Streeck, W. 1995. German capitalism: does it exist? Can it survive? Max-Planck-Institut für Gesellschaftsforschung. Discussion Paper 95/5, November.

Sum, N.-L. 2015. Integrating variegated capitalism into Régulationist work on China: semantic, institutional and spatial fixes/imaginaries. Paper presented at the conference on 'The Theory of Regulation in Times of Crisis,' Paris, 9–12 June.

Veblen, T. 1899–1900. 'The preconceptions of economic science.' *The Quarterly Journal of Economics*, 3 (2): 121–150; 13 (4): 396–426; 14 (2): 240–269.

Veblen, T. 1915. *Imperial Germany and the Industrial Revolution*. New York: Macmillan.

Weber, M. 1984–2016. *Max-Weber-Gesamtausgabe [Collected Works]*. *In*: H. Baier, R. Lepsius, & W.J. Mommsen (eds.), 41 Volumes. Tübingen: Mohr-Siebeck.

5

Monetary theories of production

Marco Veronese Passarella

Introduction

The view of capitalism as a circular and surplus-oriented sequence of interconnected (monetary) relationships of production, distribution, and trade has ancient roots. These can be traced back to the theory of the *avances* developed by French physiocrats in the eighteenth century. The pioneering physiocrat studies provided the ground for the 'wage fund' doctrine elaborated by David Ricardo (along with John R. McCulloch) in the nineteenth century. As stressed by Graziani (1989, 2003), Ricardo's insights led to two opposing views of economy and society. On the one hand, the Ricardian take was seen to support the idea that an already accumulated 'fund' (be it corn or money) is necessary in order to undertake productive investment. As such, Ricardo's approach laid the foundations for the neoclassical (or marginalist) theory of price and distribution, based on the concept of the (partial or general simultaneous) natural equilibrium and the loanable funds theory. This neoclassical interpretation of Ricardo prevails in current mainstream economics and the economic policy debate, underpinned by the microeconomic causality from saving to investment. On the other hand, a different rendition of the Ricardian theory was proposed in the twentieth century. This alternative view stresses the division of capitalist society into different and rival social classes, whose monetary interactions give rise to a sequential process of production, distribution, and trade. This conflictual, monetary, and macroeconomic interpretation of Ricardo was pioneered by Marx, particularly in the first four chapters of the second volume of *Capital* ([1885] 1978).

Although initially ignored by the academic world, Marx's view of capitalism as a surplus-driven monetary production economy exhibits a striking resemblance to the work of some 'dissenting' economists of the twentieth century. In the first draft of what subsequently became the *General Theory* (1936), entitled *A Monetary Theory of Production* (1932), John Maynard Keynes explicitly referred to the Marxian analysis of the capitalist form of circulation. Keynes describes a monetary production economy as an economic system

> in which expectations of the future influence decisions taken today; or, one in which money is a subtle device for linking the present and future; or one in which production begins with money on the expectation of ending with more money later.
>
> *Wray 1999: 1*

The link between the Marxian analysis of the 'inner laws of movement' of capitalism and the Keynesian 'methodology of aggregates' was not developed by Keynes himself. Rather, it was the subsequent generations of heterodox economists who explicitly engaged with the task of developing a critical theory of capitalist economies. In this regard, two main groups of economists should be mentioned: first, the members of the broadly defined Cambridge school of economics; and, second, the proponents of what may be termed the 'modern endogenous theories of money.' The first group is rather heterogeneous but its members share two common features. First, they reject the neoclassical theory and second, they focus mainly on economic growth and income distribution. This group includes both the strictly defined Post Keynesians, meaning the direct pupils of Keynes and Michał Kalecki,[1] and the proponents of the surplus approach pioneered by Piero Sraffa.[2] The second group appears as heterogeneous as the first one. However, its proponents share a well-defined theoretical feature. They usually focus on the role played by money and finance, that is, on the endogenous process of creation, circulation, and destruction of monetary means within a capitalist economy. This group includes the 'American' Post Keynesians,[3] the modern money theory (or neochartalist approach),[4] and the Franco-Italian theory of monetary circuit.[5]

This chapter focuses primarily on the second line of research. Its chief purpose is to outline the main features of modern monetary theories of production, particularly the original circuit approach and the current literature about stock–flow consistent models. Weaknesses, strengths, and recent developments are covered as well. The chapter is organized as follows. The second section provides a thorough description of the monetary circuit view. It is shown that circuit economists, along with other heterodox monetary economists, committed to set up a systematic analysis of the inner working of a monetary economy of production. The third section compares the circuit view with both the dominant approach in macroeconomics and with other heterodox lines of research, including the 'old' Cambridge school of economics. The fourth section addresses current developments in the monetary theories of production. The fifth section discusses both the limitations of the original circuit approach and the new possibilities offered by stock–flow consistent models. The final section offers some concluding remarks and suggests that stock–flow consistent models are renewing and strengthening the tradition of the monetary theories of production.

Capitalism as a monetary circuit

As mentioned in the first section, the view of capitalism as a circuit of interconnected acts of production, distribution, and trade has ancient roots. While the French physiocrats (and, at least to some extent, Ricardo) used to focus on the process of creation, circulation, and consumption of the *produit net* of the agricultural sector, defined in real terms, Marx shifted the attention to the process of creation, circulation, and destruction of the monetary surplus within a capitalist system. Such a macro-monetary view of capitalism shows a considerable degree of affinity with a set of heterodox monetary theories of the twentieth century—notably, with the 'hidden' line of research that stretches from Knut Wicksell's *Interest and Prices* (1898) to Joseph Schumpeter's *The Theory of Economic Development* ([1911] 1934), and then to Keynes' *Treatise on Money* (1930) and the works of Kalecki (1971). The theory of monetary circuit can be regarded as a synthesis and refinement of the above line of research. It was mainly developed by French and Italian authors between the mid-1970s and the early 1990s and its essential analytical skeleton lies beneath other monetary theories of production.[6] This is the reason the circuit approach can be used as the benchmark model.

The simplest circuit accounting model refers to a closed economy, comprised of three macro-sectors: the banking sector (including clearing or commercial banks); the corporate sector (including non-financial or production firms); and the household sector (including workers or wage earners). Other financial intermediaries (notably, saving and investment banks, and non-bank financial institutions) are usually assumed away, but the role of financial markets and assets is explicitly accounted for. The intervention of the state is generally neglected, at least to a first approximation (the rationale is pointed out below). Irrespective of the level of institutional sophistication, capitalist dynamics are always triggered by the decision of firms to start the production process. That decision is based on expected demand for products (this is the way the principle of 'effective demand' is included in the circuit theory). From a microeconomic perspective, each firm needs a certain amount of monetary means to purchase the factors of production. In other words, each firm has to cover all of its current costs, including both the labor cost and the cost of capital or intermediate goods (such as buildings, machinery, raw materials, and inventories). From a macroeconomic or social perspective, the trade of intermediate goods should be better regarded as an exchange that is 'internal' to the corporate sector. In other words, if we consider firms as one integrated and consolidated sector, the only 'external' purchase they have to make is to hire workers. Consequently, their only cost or payment concerns the wage bill (Moore 1983; Graziani 2003). Whatever the perspective chosen, entrepreneurs (or managers) need to borrow from banks. Money and labor are the only 'things' that the corporate sector cannot (directly) reproduce on its own. The amount of credit granted by the clearing banks to firms at this initial stage of the circuit is usually termed the 'initial finance.' Such an act of monetary creation is the spark that triggers the overall capitalist process of production, distribution, and trade. Given the target interest rate steered by the central bank, negotiations between commercial banks and firms determine the amount of credit (that is, the initial finance) and/or the actual nominal interest rate on loans. It is assumed that only firms are admitted to bank credit in the initial stage of the circuit, to cover production costs and start the production process. Once this initial step of the circuit has been taken, households and financial intermediaries can also access the credit market (for example, to finance extra consumption and/or financial investments). The reason is that the class divide is not just an instrumental hypothesis. It is a theoretical, ontological, and methodological pillar of the circuit approach. In other words, there is a twofold relation between class identity and access to credit money.[7]

Accordingly, decisions about the amount and the composition of output are made autonomously by the capitalist class, meaning firms and banks. Both the employment rate and the types of jobs available are determined in this stage. This means that bargaining between firms and trade unions within the labor market only determines the nominal wage rate, rather than the real compensation of workers or the employment level. Consumer preferences can only have an indirect effect on production structure and job creation, through their possible impact on sales expectations of firms. As a result, consumer sovereignty is replaced by producer sovereignty within this model. Working-class households can only make decisions on how to distribute their money incomes between consumption expenditure, additional cash balances (bank deposits), or purchase of financial assets (bonds, shares, or other securities).[8] In the simplest model, the government sector is assumed away. Financial assets other than bank deposits can only be issued by firms. Consequently, the initial liquidity flows back to firms whatever the kind of expenditure made by households (be it consumption or purchase of financial assets). This 'final finance' is what enables firms to repay their debt towards clearing banks. To the extent that this happens, an equal amount of money is destroyed. However, households can also decide to save a portion of their income in the form of bank deposits. In this case, the greater the liquid balances held by households, the greater the losses suffered by the corporate sector. From an accounting viewpoint, an equal amount of money remains in existence in the form of corporate debt (and household credit) towards the banking system (Graziani 2003). The standard representation of the circuit of monetary transactions and flows within a closed capitalist economy, with bank money only, is provided by Figure 5.1. As stressed by neochartalist authors, in the real world the circuit of bank money is coupled with the circuit of *fiat* money (legal tender or reserves) created by the state (Wray 1998).[9] When the government spends, the central bank debits the account of the Treasury, while crediting the accounts of (private) clearing banks by the same amount. These newly created reserves flow into the economy as the government sector buys goods and services from the private sector. Plainly, taxation and sales of sovereign bonds have the opposite effect. They allow the

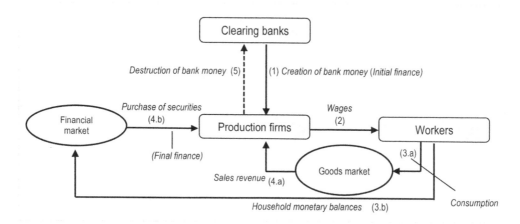

Figure 5.1 The circuit of bank money in a monetary production economy
Note: For the sake of simplicity, government, central bank, and foreign sector are neglected.

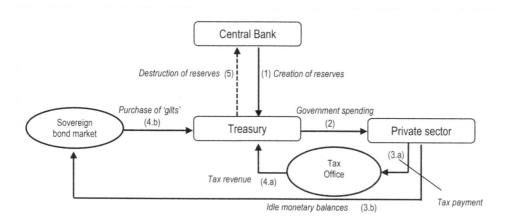

Figure 5.2 The circuit of fiat money in a monetary production economy
Notes: For the sake of simplicity, the foreign sector is neglected. In addition, clearing banks, firms, and households are consolidated in the "private sector."

government to absorb liquidity from the system (that is, to destroy a part of the reserves created), thereby affecting the term structure of interest rates. This second circuit is sketched by Figure 5.2.

A comparison with other approaches

The chief aim of the circuit approach has been claimed to account for the process of creation and destruction of money (both viewed as endogenous phenomena) under a capitalist system during 'normal times.' As a result, both the precautionary and the speculative motives for holding money are usually ruled out of the picture, and so is the investigation of the determinants of liquidity preference. Similarly, the government and the foreign sector are generally neglected in the first stage of the analysis. This feature differentiates the monetary circuit approach from the one adopted by Keynes (1936) in the *General Theory* (but not in the *Treatise* of 1930 and post-1937 writings) and from other monetary theories of production. The simplified accounting nature of the circuit framework is a strength when outlining the key features of a pure bank-money capitalist economy. It allows its proponents to develop a macro-monetary analysis regardless of hypotheses on the behavior of economic agents. In addition, it enables them to argue for a multiplicity of possible 'equilibria' of the economy, and for the irrelevance of 'wealth effects' as spontaneous adjusting mechanisms, due to the endogeneity of money (Graziani 1994; Sawyer & Veronese Passarella 2015).[10] Finally, the very basic circuit framework sheds light on the long-lasting controversy about the origin of social surplus value. It suggests that capital valorization, for capitalists taken as a social class (namely, for the corporate sector regarded as a fully aggregate and consolidated industry), can only derive from exchanges they make outside their own social class. However, the only possible 'external exchange' for them is the purchase of labor power from the working class. Therefore, it is only to the extent that capitalists or firms 'use' labor power within the production process, and appropriate a share of output, that they can realize the social surplus in the form of profit. Accordingly, profits earned by firms can only arise from the difference between the total living labor spent by workers in the production sphere and the quantity of labor that the working class gets back in the form of wages (Graziani 1997a, 1997b). Thus, although this aspect is usually neglected by other heterodox monetary economists, including most *circuitistes*, the circuit approach can possibly offer a sound macro-monetary explanation about the origin of the social surplus from surplus labor. In this sense, it could be regarded as a Marxian rendition of the Keynesian methodology of aggregates.[11]

As it is argued in the fourth section, the circuit framework still provides the monetary core of (current) Post Keynesian or structuralist models. Since its inception, it has offered a harsh critique of the mainstream theories of the 1970–80s,[12] while providing an alternative foundation for macroeconomics. The explicit recognition of the endogenous nature of money, along with the multiplicity, non-optimality, and path-dependency of economic equilibria, was in stark contrast to the general equilibrium model (be it static and deterministic, or dynamic and stochastic) and the connected theory of loanable funds. From this perspective, the recent rise and academic success of the New Keynesian approach may well be regarded as a recognition (implicit, late, and only partial though it is) of both the theoretical soundness and the empirical relevance of endogenous money approaches, including the theory of monetary circuit. While the neoclassical principle of the 'long-run neutrality of money' is usually not questioned by the New Keynesians, money supply targeting is rejected in favor of money being a residual of inflation targeting by central banks via short-term interest rate smoothing. To put it differently, the supply of money is regarded as an endogenous variable of a model in which the LM curve is replaced by a central banking rule. Consequently, from an endogenous money perspective, the current mainstream in macroeconomics represents a step forward, at least compared to the previous neoclassical models.

By contrast, the emphasis of current models (including the New Keynesian one) on natural output and unemployment, along with rational-expectation microfoundations, is in stark contrast to the macroeconomic or social nature of the monetary theories of production. The point is that the behavior of individuals and social groups cannot but be 'procedural,' while current levels of output and employment depend on the specific path that led to those levels. In other words, there is no such thing as an exogenously given optimal equilibrium of the economic system, let alone a free market mechanism assuring the maximization of both economic efficiency and individual well-being in the long-run. Within a financially sophisticated capitalist economy, continuous intervention by the government sector and the central bank is necessary. This should be coupled with an active industrial policy by the government, aiming to redefine the qualitative composition of output. For such a coordinated intervention creates those 'ceilings and floors'—as Hyman Minsky used to term them—that smooth and constrain the instability of the system.[13]

While the emphasis on the struggle between labor and capital, and between industrial capital and financial capital, resembles the conflictual view of the Sraffian surplus approach, the stress on the monetary nature of social relations distances the circuit view from the surplus one. However, the two lines of research are not necessarily incompatible (see, for example, Lavoie 2006, 2014; Cesaratto & Mongiovi 2015). Since the mid-2000s, attempts have been made to embed the Sraffian theory of price and distribution in a monetary circuit framework (Brancaccio 2008). Analogous considerations could be made for most 'orthodox' Marxian approaches to political economy, whereas it has been already argued that there is a clear affinity between the circuit approach and recent monetary renditions of Marx (Bellofiore 1989; Bellofiore *et al.* 2000). The resemblance of the circuit theory (and other current monetary theories of production) to Post Keynesian models of growth and distribution is similarly apparent.[14] The historical link between different branches of the monetary theory of production is sketched in Figure 5.3 (which is a re-elaboration of Figure 1.1 in Lavoie 2006: 3). Recent theoretical developments are discussed further in the next section.

Recent theoretical developments

It was mentioned earlier that the emphasis on the creation, circulation, and destruction of money explains why the analytical tool chosen by early *circuitistes* to support their theory was a one-period accounting analysis of a pure bank-money closed economy with no public sector. Clearly, this simplification turns out to be a limitation when a more detailed analysis concerning cross-sector relations and variegated institutional settings is to be undertaken. For the same reason, the basic circuit framework is unsuitable for econometric and other empirical applications. While many dynamic models have been developed by Post Keynesians and other heterodox monetary economists since the 1980s, a general benchmark model, underpinning a unified theory of monetary production, was still missing in the mid-1990s. Such a theoretical and methodological gap has been progressively bridged thanks to the rise of the stock-flow consistent approach to macroeconomics (SFCA hereafter). The SFCA is not a brand-new macroeconomic theory. Rather, it is a modeling method deeply grounded in the Post Keynesian or structuralist paradigm in economics. It was pioneered by James Tobin (1982) and has subsequently been developed by Wynne Godley, Marc Lavoie, and other heterodox monetary economists.[15] SFCA economists base their models on sound social matrixes or accounting frameworks that integrate financial flows of funds with cross-sector balance sheets. These frameworks allow SFCA economists to point out the analytical skeleton of their models. In addition, they provide a consistency check mechanism for their hypotheses, while reducing the degrees of freedom of theory. Finally, such a rigorous social accounting allows SFCA modelers to shed light on the relations between economic sectors and within social groups (Dos Santos 2006). Against this methodological background, several

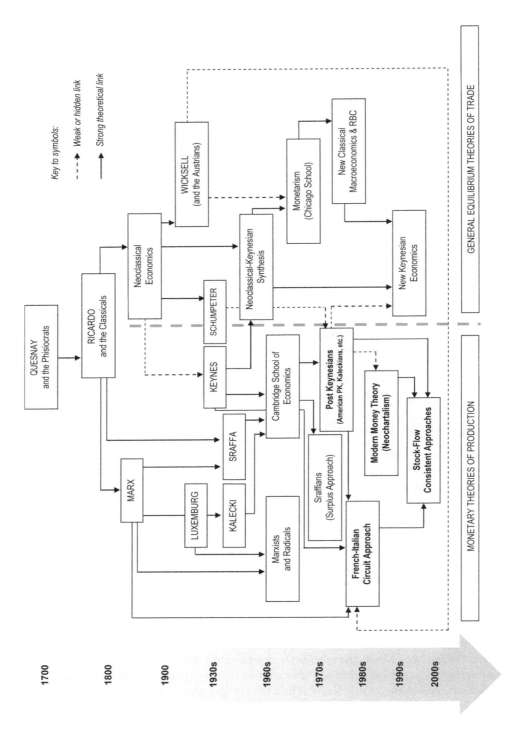

Figure 5.3 The evolutionary tree of monetary macroeconomics from physiocrats to current monetary theories of production

dynamic models have been developed since the early 2000s, in which economic variables move 'forward non-ergodically in historic time' (Godley & Lavoie 2007: 9). In short, the method adopted by SFCA modelers is made up by three steps: "(1) do the (SFC) accounting; (2) establish the relevant behavioural relationships; and (3) perform 'comparative dynamics' exercises (generally with the help of computer simulations) to see how the model behaves" (Dos Santos 2005: 713). In other words, SFCA modelers set up a dynamic 'artificial economy' grounded on stylized facts. They then use this analytical device (consisting of a set of difference or differential equations) to derive some system-wide logical implications. They focus, in particular, on the twofold relation between flows and stocks. Sectoral budget constraints are carefully modeled as well. As has been mentioned, this allows SFCA theorists to make their assumptions explicit and to limit the number of hypotheses on behavior. The last step in SFCA methodology is to perform some comparative experiments to check the sensitivity of the model to changes in key exogenous variables and parameter values.

Notice that, in principle, the above method could be used to model different economic theories, be they mainstream or heterodox. At the same time, it logically leads to question the concept of 'natural equilibrium.' It allows modeling of the transition from one dynamic time position to another, thereby recognizing that "the conditions under which this transition occurs may affect the final position of equilibrium" (Lavoie 2006: 15). Accordingly, the SFCA turns out to be particularly fruitful when pinpointing structural macro-monetary models. In other words, it allows extending the basic (one-period or pure-flow) circuit scheme to a dynamic financially and institutionally augmented monetary production economy. In fact, the strict link between the circuit approach and the SFCA has been stressed explicitly by both circuit and SFCA economists.[16] The social accounting nature of the SFCA helps one "to understand how production is being financed . . . at the beginning of the production period" (Godley & Lavoie 2007: 47). More precisely, the first step of the monetary circuit with private money can be represented by means of a reduced transactions-flow matrix based on a quadruple-entry bookkeeping. Under a monetary production economy, with no legal tender, money is created as non-financial firms borrow from clearing banks. As is shown in the gray area of Table 5.1, both new bank loans and a corresponding amount of newly created bank deposits are initially held by the corporate sector. Clearing banks create private money *ex nihilo* in the form of deposits that are credited to the account of firms before the production takes place. However, this is just a transitory situation as firms instantaneously transfer these bank deposits to workers in exchange for labor power (see dotted arrow in Table 5.1). Notice that the "moment these funds are transferred, they constitute households' income. Before a single unit is spent on consumer goods, the entire amount of the bank deposits constitutes savings by households, and these are equal to the new loans granted to production firms" (Godley & Lavoie 2007: 49). This is the second logical step of the monetary circuit, and it is shown by other entries in Table 5.1.[17] Eventually, workers spend their income by purchasing consumption goods and/or newly issued securities, thereby allowing firms to recover their money balances and pay back their debt to clearing banks. In other words, bank money is destroyed as households use their monetary balances to buy something from firms. This final step of monetary transactions is the one shown in Table 5.2.[18]

Financialization and other open issues

The SFCA *inter alia* addresses the four most important questions raised by the original circuit approach. The first question relates to the particular price setting adopted by circuit authors. The second question is tied with the first one and concerns the effectiveness of active fiscal policies within a monetary circuit scheme. The third question is about the so-called 'paradox of profit.'

Table 5.1 Initial steps of the monetary circuit

	Households	Production firms		Clearing banks		Σ
		Current	Capital	Current	Capital	
Consumption						−
Investment		$+I$	$-I$			0
Wages	$+WB$	$-WB$				0
Change in loans			$+\Delta L_f$		$-\Delta L$	0
Change in deposits	$-\Delta M_h$		$[-\Delta M_f]$		$+\Delta M$	0
Σ	0	0	0	−	0	0

Note: A "+" before a magnitude denotes an asset, whereas "−" denotes a liability.

Table 5.2 The final step of the monetary circuit: the transactions-flow matrix

	Households	Production firms		Clearing banks		Σ
		Current	Capital	Current	Capital	
Consumption	$-C$	$+C$				0
Investment		$+I$	$-I$			0
Wages	$+WB$	$-WB$				0
Profits of firms	$+FD_f$	$-F_f$	$+FU_f$			0
Profits of banks	$+FD_b$			$-F_b$	$+FU_b$	0
Interests on loans		$-r_{1(-1)} L_{f(-1)}$		$+r_{1(-1)} L_{(-1)}$		0
Interests on deposits	$+r_{m(-1)} M_{h(-1)}$			$-r_{m(-1)} M_{(-1)}$		0
Interests on securities	$+r_{b(-1)} B_{h(-1)}$	$-r_{b(-1)} B_{(-1)}$				0
Change in loans			$+\Delta L_f$		$-\Delta L$	0
Change in deposits	$-\Delta M_h$				$+\Delta M$	0
Change in securities	$-\Delta B_h$		$+\Delta B$			0
Σ	0	0	0	0	0	0

Notes: A "+" before a magnitude denotes a receipt or a source of funds, whereas "−" denotes a payment or a use of funds. For the sake of simplicity, both the government and the central bank are neglected. Securities can include bonds, shares, and other financial assets. Notice that *FD* stands for distributed profits, whereas *FU* stands for retained profits. Finally, r_b, r_m, and r_l are the rates of return on securities, deposits, and loans, respectively.

The fourth question is about the evolution of the financial system in the past three decades, changes associated with the term 'financialization.'

The first two questions relate to price setting and the effectiveness of active fiscal policies. In the basic (one-period) circuit model, the unit price of output is usually derived in such a way that there is never excess or lack of demand. When household consumption (and saving) decisions do not match the composition of output chosen by firms, the costing margin adjusts to clear the market. For instance, if the consumption demand is greater than the production of consumer goods, their unit price will rise correspondingly. This suggests that investment is always *ex post* covered by savings, be they voluntary or 'forced.' In other words, household savings never constrain corporate investment plans (as claimed by the proponents of loanable fund theories). In addition, this approach enables the questioning and replacement of the concept of consumer sovereignty with that of producer sovereignty, as it makes it clear that household preferences can only have an indirect effect on production plans. However, for the same reason, any increase in aggregate demand components will lead to a corresponding rise in costing margin and unit price of output, with no effect on employment and real output. This corollary is potentially at odds with the Post Keynesian advocacy for an active fiscal policy to support and stabilize the economy (Seccareccia 2015). Furthermore, when a plurality of industries is taken into consideration, the above pricing turns out to be inconsistent with the hypothesis of long-run equalization of profit rates across sectors advocated by Marxian and Sraffian economists (for example, Lunghini & Bianchi 2004). By contrast, the SFCA demonstrates that decisions about composition of output are eventually made by firms via cost-plus pricing (as advocated by the *circuitistes*), while recognizing that the economy is demand-led both in the short-run and in the long-run (as traditionally advocated by the Post Keynesians). This restores the effectiveness of fiscal policy, while clarifying that the controversy around the circuit pricing is just a consequence of the simplified structure— particularly of the 'one-period' horizon—of the benchmark framework.[19]

As mentioned, a third question concerns what is usually termed the 'paradox of profit,' that is, the impossibility for capitalists as a whole to obtain from the market more (inside) money than they invested in each single period. This paradox was historically raised by some Marxians, in particular, Rosa Luxemburg (see Bellofiore & Veronese Passarella 2009, among others) and the debate has never been resolved.[20] In modern terms, the point is that "in a credit economy, in a single period, the revenues of firms can at most equal the initial finance received for production costs and they do not cover interest payment" (Caverzasi & Godin 2015: 13). While many interesting solutions and interpretations have been proposed in recent decades, the SFCA positions the debate within a sound accounting framework (Lavoie 2004; Zezza 2012).

The last question raised by the original circuit approach is its fitness for the analysis of financialization. More precisely, it has been argued that the circuit approach would only sketch a manufacturing-oriented system in which banks play the major role in financing production and investment, while financial markets have a passive role in channeling household saving to firms. Since the end of the 1970s, however, financial markets and intermediaries have begun to occupy a central position in many Western economies. The traditional link between non-financial firms and banks has been largely severed, whereas the bank-financial market axis "has taken center stage" (Seccareccia 2012: 284). Consequently, it has been argued that the original circuit scheme should be amended (Veronese Passarella 2014) or even abandoned (Lysandrou 2014) in light of recent structural and institutional developments. While it is debatable whether the basic circuit scheme would only describe a specific historical configuration of capitalism,[21] the dynamic structure of SFCA social matrixes and models is certainly more suitable for the analysis of complex, financially sophisticated economies. In principle, there is no limit to the number of financial markets, intermediaries, assets, and relations, which can be modeled.[22] In other words, the SFCA provides a more flexible analytical tool, thereby enabling its proponents to examine different historical configurations of capitalism, while remaining soundly grounded in the tradition of the monetary theories of production.

Final remarks

The purpose of this chapter is to present the view of capitalism as a circular and surplus-oriented sequence of interconnected monetary acts of production, distribution, and trade. This view has ancient roots, which can be traced back to the pioneering insights of French physiocrats, and then to the works of David Ricardo, Karl Marx, Knut Wicksell, John Maynard Keynes, and other dissenting monetary economists of the twentieth century. Modern monetary theories of production aim to recover and develop the above 'heretical' line of research, focusing mainly on the process of creation, circulation, and destruction of money in a world marked by class divide and social conflict. Among different heterodox monetary approaches, the so-called theory of monetary circuit represents a major attempt to set up a comprehensive social (or macroeconomic) accounting skeleton of capitalist relationships. This, in turn, was meant to establish the ground for both a critique of mainstream economics and a new critical theory, fully engaged with the monetary nature of capitalism. Path-breaking though it was, the original circuit approach has been shown to suffer from some limitations, due to the oversimplified structure of the basic framework. Its 'one period' horizon does not allow for an accurate analysis of capitalist dynamics, let alone of the process of financialization. The stock-flow consistent approach developed by Wynne Godley and other heterodox economists since the late 1990s provides a flexible analytical tool to bridge the above gaps, while renewing and strengthening the tradition of the monetary theories of production. Unlike mainstream approaches to economics, stock-flow consistent models explicitly account for the multiple, path-dependent, and transient nature of economic equilibria, resulting from the monetary and conflictual nature of capitalist economies and societies. For non-apologetic, or real world, macroeconomics "has to put at the heart of its discourse not the 'imperfections' of the market, but rather the 'normality' of power and conflict, not only between labor and capital, but also between fractions of capital, and between capitalisms" (Bellofiore 2013: 430).

Notes

1 Notably, Richard Kahn, Nicholas Kaldor, and Joan Robinson.
2 Pierangelo Garegnani, Luigi Pasinetti, and Ian Steedman, among others.
3 Notably, Paul Davidson, Hyman Minsky, and Basil Moore. The latter is sometimes regarded as the founding father of the 'horizontalist' theory of money creation. Notice that the horizontalist approach deeply influenced circuit authors. Alfred Eichner, Joseph Steindl, and Sidney Weintraub must be mentioned as well.
4 Whose main advocates are Stephanie Kelton, Bill Mitchell, Warren Mosler, and Randall Wray.
5 Notably, Alain Barrère, Augusto Graziani, Alain Parguez, and Frédéric Poulon. A similar (but not identical) theory, usually labeled the 'quantum theory of money emissions,' has been developed by the French economist Bernard Schmitt since the 1960s. Finally, notice that another French economist, Jaques Le Bourva, is sometimes regarded as a forerunner of the circuit approach.
6 On the one hand, Post Keynesian economists usually recognize the strict link between their take and the circuit one (Lavoie 2006). Some of them explicitly refer to the monetary circuit approach as the 'Post Keynesian circuit approach' or the 'French and Italian Post Keynesian school' (Godley & Lavoie 2007: 47). On the other hand, the modern money theory can be regarded as the circuit theory of the creation, circulation, and destruction of legal tender (Wray 1998).
7 Notice that, from an accounting viewpoint, there must be correspondence between the wage bill paid to workers and the cost of produced goods. Therefore, the initial finance can be measured both by the wage bill and by the value of inventories (Godley & Cripps 1981; Graziani 2003; Godley & Lavoie 2007). The former refers to the bank exposure of firms in a single instant of time. The latter refers to the corporate demand for credit in the initial stage of the circuit. See also note 18.
8 Workers can hold financial assets. However, they are minority shareholders by definition, with no power on corporate decisions. In this sense, the only difference between bonds and shares is the way returns are paid, for example, whether as interest payments or as dividends.
9 Notice that this additional flow of liquidity, along with the one deriving from net export (when a single national economy is considered), allows firms to realize profits in monetary form. In other words, it allows overcoming the 'paradox of profit.' The latter is discussed in the fifth section.
10 As has been pointed out, this approach "challenges the basic assumptions of orthodox theory by rejecting the initial definition of the economic and social world as being populated by identical individuals,

where consumers are sovereign, technology is exogenous and money is neutral. Large social or 'macro' groups matter, and corporate power is essential in a world of permanent imbalances and conflicts" (Bellofiore 2013: 426).

11 The link between the Marxian labor theory of value and the Keynesian macroeconomics has been recognized by other heterodox monetarist economists (for example, Dillard 1984; Wray 1999).

12 These mainstream theories include the neoclassical-Keynesian synthesis, which dominated economics until the early 1970s, and what may be termed the monetarist approaches (including early Chicago school monetarism, the new classical macroeconomics based on rational expectations, and the real business cycle school).

13 Notice that the intervention of the government is explicitly admitted in New Keynesian models. However, it usually takes the form of monetary policies. Fiscal intervention is admitted as well, but mainly in the form of automatic stabilizers. By contrast, discretionary fiscal policies should be just exceptional and temporary. All of the above measures are only effective in the short-run, due to price stickiness or other temporary frictions. For the economy is assumed to return to its natural equilibrium (path) in the medium- to long-run.

14 The reference is to the models pioneered by Nicholas Kaldor, Joan Robinson, and Luigi Pasinetti in the period between the mid-1950s and the early 1960s, and further developed (and amended) by Kaleckian economists in the 1980–90s (see Lavoie 2014 for a thorough survey).

15 See, among others, Godley & Cripps (1983), Godley (1999), Lavoie & Godley (2001), Taylor (2004), Dos Santos (2006), Dos Santos & Zezza (2008). The fundamental reference for SFCA modelers is *Monetary Economics* by Godley & Lavoie (2007). See Caverzasi & Godin (2015) for a recent survey.

16 See, for instance, Graziani (2003), Godley (2004), Lavoie (2004), Godley & Lavoie (2007), Zezza (2012), Veronese Passarella (2014), and Sawyer & Veronese Passarella (2015).

17 At this stage of the circuit, "output has been produced but not yet sold. The unsold production constitutes an increase in inventories [that] is accounted as investment in working capital." Looking at the current account of firms in Table 5.1, "inventories must necessarily rise by an amount exactly equal to the production costs, the wages paid WB." Looking at the "capital account, it is clear that the value of this investment in inventories must be financed by the new loans initially obtained" (Godley & Lavoie 2007: 49–50). As a result, the following equality holds: $I = WB = \Delta L_f = \Delta M_h$, where I stands for inventories (or other circulating capital), WB stands for wage bill, ΔL_f is new bank loans to firms, and ΔM_h is new bank deposits held by workers.

18 In fact, the very comparison between Table 5.1 with Table 5.2 "helps us understand the distinction between initial and final finance which has been underlined by the circuitistes" (Godley & Lavoie 2007: 50).

19 In the circuit one-period model, the price of output is derived from the market clearing condition: $p \cdot N \cdot a = N \cdot w \cdot (1 - s) + b \cdot p \cdot N \cdot a$, where N is the employment level, a is the labor productivity, w is the nominal wage rate, s is the average propensity to save out of wages, and b is the share of output devoted to investment. Accordingly, $N \cdot a$ is the real supply of goods, $N \cdot w (1 - s)$ is the nominal consumption of wage earners, and $b \cdot p \cdot N \cdot a$ is the nominal investment (for example, Graziani 2003). Solving for the unit price of output, one gets: $p = (w/a) (1 - b)$. Circuit theorists assume that the scale of production (that is, N) is chosen by the corporate sector, along with the composition of output (via the propensity to invest, b). Household consumption-saving decisions only affect the costing margin (defined as $r = (b - s)/(1 - b)$) and hence the unit price of output, which is the endogenous variable of the model. The rationale of these assumptions is linked with the twofold aim of the circuit approach: first, to analyze money creation and destruction during 'normal times' (that is, abstracting from liquidity trap, credit rationing, and lack of demand); second, to question the principle of consumer sovereignty (for example, Sawyer & Veronese Passarella 2015).

20 Incidentally, Luxemburg can be considered the 'bridge' between Marx and Kalecki in the evolutionary tree of monetary theories of production.

21 The circuit approach "should not be considered a mere 'empirical' description of the 'old' Fordist manufacturing system . . . Rather, [it] must be regarded as . . . a logical meta-model such as the *Tableau économique* of François Quesnay's and the Marxian reproduction schemes. Its function is to define the conditions of macro-monetary reproducibility of the system (that is, the solvency requirements for the corporate sector and hence for the economy as a whole), regardless of any individual behavioral function. In other words, [it] defines the *necessary* monetary relationships between sectors (corresponding to well-defined social classes) and markets" (Veronese Passarella 2014: 17–18).

22 See, among others, Lavoie (2008), van Treeck (2009), Hein & van Treeck (2010), Michell & Toporowski (2012), Reyes & Mazier (2014), and Sawyer & Veronese Passarella (2015).

References

Bellofiore, R. 1989. 'A monetary labor theory of value.' *Review of Radical Political Economics*, 21 (1–2): 1–25.

Bellofiore, R. 2013. 'A heterodox structural Keynesian: honouring Augusto Graziani.' *Review of Keynesian Economics*, 1 (4): 425–430.

Bellofiore, R. & Veronese Passarella, M. 2009. 'Finance and the realization problem in Rosa Luxemburg: a 'circuitist' reappraisal,' *in*: J. Ponsot & S. Rossi (eds.), *The Political Economy of Monetary Circuits: Tradition and Change in Post-Keynesian Economics*. Basingstoke, UK: Palgrave Macmillan, 98–115.

Bellofiore, R., Davanzati, G.F., & Realfonzo, R. 2000. 'Marx inside the circuit: discipline device, wage bargaining and unemployment in a sequential monetary economy.' *Review of Political Economy*, 12 (4): 403–417.

Brancaccio, E. 2008. 'Solvency and labour effort in a monetary theory of reproduction.' *European Journal of Economic and Social Systems*, 21 (2): 195–211.

Caverzasi, E. & Godin, A. 2015. 'Post-Keynesian stock-flow-consistent modelling: a survey.' *Cambridge Journal of Economics*, 39 (1): 157–187.

Cesaratto, S. & Mongiovi, G. 2015. 'Pierangelo Garegnani, the classical surplus approach and demand-led growth: introduction to the symposium.' *Review of Political Economy*, 27 (2): 103–110.

Dillard, D. 1984. 'Keynes and Marx: a centennial appraisal.' *Journal of Post Keynesian Economics*, 6 (3): 421–432.

Dos Santos, C.H. 2005. 'A stock-flow consistent general framework for formal Minskyan analyses of closed economies.' *Journal of Post Keynesian Economics*, 27 (4): 711–735.

Dos Santos, C.H. 2006. 'Keynesian theorising during hard times: stock-flow consistent models as an unexplored 'frontier' of Keynesian macroeconomics.' *Cambridge Journal of Economics*, 30 (4): 541–565.

Dos Santos, C.H. & Zezza, G. 2008. 'A simplified, 'benchmark,' stock-flow consistent Post-Keynesian growth model.' *Metroeconomica*, 59 (3): 441–478.

Godley, W. 1999. 'Money and credit in a Keynesian model of income determination.' *Cambridge Journal of Economics*, 23 (4): 393–411.

Godley, W. 2004. 'Weaving cloth from Graziani's thread: endogenous money in a simple (but complete) Keynesian model,' *in*: R. Arena & N. Salvadori (eds.), *Money, Credit and the Role of the State: Essay in Honour of Augusto Graziani*. London: Ashgate, 127–135.

Godley, W. & Cripps, F. 1983. *Macroeconomics*. London: Fontana.

Godley, W. & Lavoie, M. 2007. *Monetary Economics: An Integrated Approach to Credit, Money, Income, Production and Wealth*. Basingstoke, UK: Palgrave Macmillan.

Graziani, A. 1989. 'The theory of the monetary circuit.' *Thames Papers in Political Economy*, 1 (Spring): 1–26.

Graziani, A. 1994. 'Real wages and the loans-deposits controversy.' *Economie Appliquée*, 47 (1): 31–46.

Graziani, A. 1997a. 'Let's rehabilitate the theory of value.' *International Journal of Political Economy*, 27 (2): 21–25.

Graziani, A. 1997b. 'The Marxist theory of money.' *International Journal of Political Economy*, 27 (2): 26–50.

Graziani, A. 2003. *The Monetary Theory of Production*. Cambridge: Cambridge University Press.

Hein, E. & van Treeck, T. 2010. 'Financialisation and rising shareholder power in Kaleckian/ Post-Kaleckian models of distribution and growth.' *Review of Political Economy*, 22 (2): 205–233.

Kalecki, M. 1971. *Selected Essays on the Dynamics of the Capitalist Economy, 1933–1970*. Cambridge: Cambridge University Press.

Keynes, J.M. 1930. *A Treatise on Money*. London: Macmillan.

Keynes, J.M. [1936] 1973. *The General Theory of Employment, Interest and Money*. London: Macmillan.

Lavoie, M. 2004. 'Circuit and coherent stock-flow accounting,' *in*: R. Arena & N. Salvadori (eds.), *Money, Credit, and the Role of the State: Essays in Honour of Augusto Graziani*. Aldershot: Ashgate, 136–151.

Lavoie, M. 2006. *Introduction to Post-Keynesian Economics*. Basingstoke, UK: Palgrave Macmillan.

Lavoie, M. 2008. 'Financialisation issues in a Post-Keynesian stock-flow consistent model.' *Intervention: European Journal of Economics and Economic Policies*, 5 (2): 331–356.

Lavoie, M. 2014. *Post-Keynesian Economics: New Foundations*. Cheltenham, UK: Edward Elgar.

Lavoie, M. and Godley, W. 2001. 'Kaleckian models of growth in a coherent stock-flow monetary framework: a Kaldorian view.' *Journal of Post Keynesian Economics*, 24 (2): 277–311.

Lunghini, G. & Bianchi, C. 2004. 'The monetary circuit and income distribution: bankers as landlords?' *in*: R. Arena & N. Salvadori (eds.), *Money, Credit and the Role of the State: Essays in Honour of Augusto Graziani*. Aldershot: Ashgate, 152–174.

Lysandrou, P. 2014. Financialisation and the limits of circuit theory. Paper presented at the 24th Annual Workshop. School of African and Oriental Studies, University of London.

Marx, K. [1885] 1978. *Capital: A Critique of Political Economy, Volume II*. London: Penguin Books.

Michell, J. & Toporowski, J. 2011. 'The stock-flow consistent approach with active financial markets,' *in*: D.B. Papadimitriou & G. Zezza (eds.), *Contributions to Stock-Flow Modelling: Essays in Honor of Wynne Godley*. Basingstoke, UK: Palgrave Macmillan, 173–196.

Moore, B.J. 1983. 'Unpacking the post Keynesian black box: bank lending and the money supply.' *Journal of Post Keynesian Economics*, 5 (4): 537–556.

Reyes, L. & Mazier, J. 2014. 'Financialized growth regime: lessons from Stock Flow Consistent models.' *Revue de la régulation. Capitalisme, institutions, pouvoirs*, 16. Published online. Available from https://regulation.revues.org/11021 [Accessed February 16, 2016]

Sawyer, M. & Veronese Passarella, M. 2015. 'The monetary circuit in the age of financialisation.' *Metroeconomica*, 68 (2): 321–353.

Schumpeter, J.A. [1911] 1934. *The Theory of Economic Development*. Cambridge, MA: Harvard University Press.

Seccareccia, M. 2012. 'Financialization and the transformation of commercial banking: understanding the recent Canadian experience before and during the international financial crisis.' *Journal of Post Keynesian Economics*, 35 (2): 277–300.

Seccareccia, M. 2015. Augusto Graziani and Hyman P. Minsky on aggregate price formation: how appropriate are their views to an understanding of the macroeconomic impact of fiscal policy? A critical appraisial. Paper presented at *A day in honour of Augusto Graziani* workshop. Jean Monnet Université, Paris, January 20.

Taylor, L. 2004. 'Exchange rate indeterminacy in portfolio balance, Mundell-Fleming and uncovered interest rate parity models.' *Cambridge Journal of Economics*, 28 (2): 205–227.

Tobin, J. 1982. 'Money and finance in the macroeconomic process.' *Journal of Money, Credit and Banking*, 14 (2): 171–204.

van Treeck, T. 2009. 'A synthetic, stock-flow consistent macroeconomic model of 'financialisation'.' *Cambridge Journal of Economics*, 33 (3): 467–493.

Veronese Passarella, M. 2014. 'Financialization and the monetary circuit: a macro-accounting approach.' *Review of Political Economy*, 26 (1): 128–148.

Wicksell, K. 1898. *Interest and Prices (Geldzins and Güterpreise): A Study of the Causes Regulating the Value of Money*. Translated from the German by R.F. Kahn. London: Macmillan.

Wray, L.R. 1998. *Understanding Modern Money: The Key to Full Employment and Price Stability*. Cheltenham, UK: Edward Elgar.

Wray, L.R. 1999. Theories of value and the monetary theory of production. Levy Economics Institute Working Paper No. 261. The Jerome Levy Economics Institute of Bard College.

Zezza, G. 2012. 'Godley and Graziani: stock-flow consistent monetary circuits,' *in*: D.B. Papadimitriou & G. Zezza (eds.), *Contributions in Stock-Flow Modeling: Essays in Honor of Wynne Godley*. Basingstoke, UK: Palgrave Macmillan, 154–172.

6

The principle of effective demand
Marx, Kalecki, Keynes, and beyond

Eckhard Hein

Introduction

The rejection of Say's law, and the associated notion that there are no long run limits to output and growth besides those given by productive capacities, unites several strands of heterodox macroeconomic theory. As Keynes (1979) makes clear in the drafts leading to the *General Theory* (1936), Say's law can only be assumed to hold in a barter economy where aggregate demand and aggregate supply cannot deviate; in a real-wage or cooperative economy where money is only used as a means of exchange but not as a store of value; or in a neutral economy where there is a market mechanism, such as the real or commodity rate of interest in the neoclassical capital market, which ensures that the part of income saved and hence not spent by households for consumption purposes is spent by firms for investment purposes. However, in a monetary or entrepreneur economy, and hence 'in the world in which we live,' there may be leakages from the circuit of income (saving) which are not exactly compensated for by injections (investment) of the same amount, and aggregate demand may systematically deviate from aggregate supply. Therefore, output and growth are determined by aggregate demand, and thus adjust towards the latter, in the short and in the long period.

The principle of effective demand, and the related claim that economic activity in a monetary production economy is demand-determined, is the core of heterodox macroeconomics. This includes all the different strands of Post Keynesian economics, encompassing the fundamentalists, the Kaleckians, the Sraffians, the Kaldorians, and the institutionalists (Lavoie 2014: 30–47), as well as some strands of Neo-Marxian economics, particularly in the monopoly capitalism and under-consumptionist school (Foster 2014). The foundations of the principle of effective demand cannot only draw on Keynes' contributions, but can already be found in Marx's and Kalecki's work, in particular, where they are closely linked with the notion of distributional conflict between classes or social groups. The second section of this chapter outlines the foundations of the principle of effective demand and its relationship with the respective notion of a capitalist or a monetary production economy in the works of Marx, Kalecki, and Keynes. The third section provides a simple short run macroeconomic model, which is built on the principle of effective demand, as well as on the distributional conflict between different social groups (or classes): rentiers, managers, and workers. This section develops a kind of 'workhorse model' with which many heterodox macroeconomists might agree. In the fourth section we move to the long run and review the integration of the principle of effective demand into heterodox, particularly Post Keynesian, approaches to distribution and growth. The fifth and final section briefly summarizes and concludes the chapter.

The rejection of Say's law and the principle of effective demand in Marx, Kalecki, and Keynes

The rejection of Say's law and its replacement with the principle of effective demand in the works of Marx, Kalecki, and Keynes is based on their respective views of capitalist economies as monetary production economies. Following Schumpeter's (1954: 277–278) distinction, all three contributions can be classified as following monetary analysis, as opposed to real analysis. Whereas in the former, money and monetary variables are essential for the determination of the real variables of the system, both in the short and in the long run, in the latter money is a veil, which has no long run effects on the real economy.

Karl Marx[1]

In *Capital, Volume I*, Karl Marx (1867: 97–144) discusses three principal roles of money—money as a standard of value, money as a means of circulation, and 'money as money,' including money as a store of value, as a means of payment, and as universal money. Money as a medium of circulation means that the succession of sales (C-M) and purchases (M-C) in the circuit C-M-C (commodity–money–commodity) of simple commodity production is interrupted. This function of money provides Marx with the first argument to explicitly reject Ricardo's version of Say's law in his *Theories of Surplus Value* and it constitutes Marx's 'possibility theory of crisis' (Marx 1861–63: 499–508).[2] In this 'possibility theory of crisis' the existence and use of money is the reason why a general crisis of over-production *may* occur; it is not yet an explanation why an actual crisis *will* occur.[3] Since 'money as money' includes its potential function as a store of value (hoarding), an increase in the willingness to hoard causes a lack of aggregate demand for the economy as a whole and may therefore trigger a general crisis. Of course, this will only hold true if the demand for holding money does not constitute a demand for production and output. If money were a produced commodity, an increase in the demand for money would not generate a deficiency of aggregate demand. Therefore, money cannot be a reproducible commodity—a conclusion Marx did not seem to be aware of, because he built his theory of money on the assumption of a money-commodity—that is, gold.

Marx's second argument against Say's law derives from the function of money as a means of payment, when the sale of a commodity and the realization of its price are separated (Marx 1861–63: 511). The seller becomes a creditor, the buyer a debtor, and money is the standard and the subject of a creditor-debtor contract. In such a system, on the one hand, the demand for commodities is no longer limited by income created in production. On the other hand, money as a means of payment increases the vulnerability and fragility of the system. Capitalists not only have to find appropriate demand for their produced commodities, but have to find it within a certain period of time in order to be able to meet their payment obligations. If there are unanticipated changes in market prices for final products between the purchase of a commodity as an input for production and the sale of the final product, capitalists may be unable to meet their payment commitments. The default of individual units of capital may interrupt credit chains and trigger a general crisis.[4]

The rejection of Say's law and its necessary replacement with a theory of effective demand, as well as the need for endogenous money for the expansion of capitalist economies, become clear in Marx's discussion of simple and expanded reproduction in *Capital, Volume II* (Marx 1885: 396–527). In the schemes of reproduction Marx analyzes the conditions for capitalist reproduction in a two-sector model without foreign trade or economic activity by the state. Sector 1 produces means of production and Sector 2 produces means of consumption. The supply price of each sector is given by constant capital costs expended in production (K_c), wage costs (W) and normal profits (Π), either determined by the rate of surplus value, if relative prices are determined by labor values, or by the general rate of profit for the economy as a whole, if relative prices are determined by prices of production. The demand for output of Sector 1 consists of gross investment (I^g) in constant capital for both sectors, while the demand for output of Sector 2 consists of consumption demand out of profits (C_Π) and out of wages (C_w). For the values of aggregate demand and aggregate supply we therefore have:

$$K_{c1} + W_1 + \Pi_1 + K_{c2} + W_2 + \Pi_2 = I_1^g + I_2^g + C_{w1} + C_{w2} + C_{\Pi1} + C_{\Pi2} \tag{6.1}$$

Assuming that wages for the workers' class as a whole are completely spent on consumption goods, and hence $W_1 + W_2 = C_{w1} + C_{w2}$, we get:

$$\Pi_1 + \Pi_2 = I_1 + I_2 + C_{\Pi1} + C_{\Pi2} \tag{6.2}$$

where $I = I^g - K_c$ denotes net investment. From this, Kalecki's (1968) interpretation of Marx's schemes of reproduction arises. As capitalists cannot determine their sales and profits, but can only decide about their expenditures on investment and consumption goods, these expenditures have to ensure that *produced* profits will become *realized* profits. Therefore, net investment determines saving (S) in Marx's schemes of reproduction:

$$S = S_1 + S_2 = \Pi_1 - C_{\Pi1} + \Pi_2 - C_{\Pi2} = I_1 + I_2 = I \tag{6.3}$$

The capitalists' investment and consumption thus determine their aggregate profits—it is the capitalists who have to advance the required amount of money in order to realize their produced and expected profits. A realization failure, the inability to sell commodities at predetermined prices, may occur if there is insufficient investment or consumption demand by capitalists. Aggregate supply will then exceed aggregate demand and the economy will suffer from unused productive capacity and unemployment, and hence from a crisis.

Whether Marx's principle of effective demand provides the conditions for an under-employment equilibrium, or a state of rest, is a matter of debate. Whereas Sardoni (2011) argues that Marx's microeconomics only allows for dynamic disequilibrium processes, we suggest that Marx's contributions are, in principle, consistent with an under-employment equilibrium or state of rest of the Post Keynesian/Kaleckian type (Hein 2006), which we discuss below.

Michał Kalecki[5]

Michał Kalecki did not elaborate on the monetary and financial system of a capitalist economy in any systematic way (Sawyer 2001). But his "laconic" (Sawyer 2001: 487) writings on the subject are perfectly compatible with Post Keynesian endogenous money and credit theory, as several authors claim (Sawyer 1985: 88–107, 2001; Dymski 1996). In two early papers, Kalecki (1932, 1969: 26–33) supposes that an economic expansion requires the simultaneous expansion of the volume of credit as a precondition to allow for financing of increasing production and investment, independently of prior saving. The volume of credit is determined by credit demand, and the banking sector is capable of supplying the required amount of credit at a given rate of interest. Therefore, Kalecki follows the Post Keynesian causality in monetary theory—credit demand determines credit supply, generating deposits with the commercial banks and making credit money an endogenous variable which is determined by credit creation and repayment. The rate of interest is a monetary category exogenous to the income generating process, which is mainly under the control of the monetary authorities and the banking sector.

Based on these monetary foundations and Kalecki's determination of functional income distribution by mark-up pricing on roughly constant unit variable costs up to full capacity output (Kalecki 1954: 11–41; Hein 2014: 183–192), we can outline Kalecki's theory of effective demand following the elaborations in Kalecki (1954: 45–52). Assuming a closed economy without government activity, production takes place in three departments of the economy. Department 1 produces investment goods, Department 2 consumption goods for capitalists, and Department 3 consumption goods for workers. Each department is vertically integrated, and hence produces all required raw materials and intermediate products within the department. Total national income (Y) is divided between workers and capitalists. Workers receive wages (W) and capitalists receive profits (Π), including retained earnings, dividends, interest, and rent. Since the national product is equal to the sum of investment expenditures (I), consumption out of profits (C_{Π}), and consumption out of wages (C_W), it follows that:

$$Y = W + \Pi = C_w + C_{\Pi} + I \tag{6.4}$$

The respective price levels for consumption goods and investment goods, and the weighted average price level for aggregate output are determined by mark-up pricing in incompletely competitive goods markets. Marginal and average variable costs marked up by firms are constant up to full capacity output, and hence prices are constant as long as the sectors of the economy operate below full capacity utilization. Subtracting wages from both sides of Equation (6.4), we obtain:

$$\Pi = C_{\Pi} + I - S_w \tag{6.5}$$

Profits are thus equal to consumption out of profits plus investment minus saving out of wages ($S_w = W - C_w$). If workers do not save and rather spend their income entirely on consumption goods ($W = C_w$), Equations (6.4) and (6.5) become:

$$\Pi = C_{\Pi} + I \tag{6.6}$$

Profits are thus equal to consumption out of profits plus investment in capital stock. Kalecki (1954: 46) reads the causality of this equation from right to left:

> Now, it is clear that capitalists may decide to consume or to invest more in a given period than in the preceding one, but they cannot decide to earn more. It is, therefore, their investment and consumption decisions which determine profits, and not vice versa.

With given prices, workers' expenditures determine the output of Department 3, which produces consumption goods for workers, whereas capitalists' expenditures determine the outputs of Departments 1 and 2, which produce investment goods and consumption goods for capitalists, respectively. The value of the output of Department 3 is equal to the sum of wages, and the value of the output of Departments 1 and 2 is equal to total profits in the economy. It should not come as a surprise that Kalecki's results so far do not diverge from those of Marx,

Eckhard Hein

because Kalecki's considerations are based on Marx's schemes of reproduction in *Capital, Volume II* (Marx 1885: 396–527).

We can further elaborate on Kalecki's approach (1954: 45–52), assuming that capitalists' consumption expenditures are proportional to profits and ignoring the stable or autonomous part included in Kalecki's reasoning as well as any time lags. Therefore, we obtain the following simple function for consumption out of profits, with c_Π representing the constant marginal and hence average propensity to consume out of profits:

$$C_\Pi = c_\Pi \Pi, \quad 0 \le c_\Pi < 1 \tag{6.7}$$

Inserting Equation (6.7) into Equation (6.6) yields the following determination of the equilibrium level of profits in the economy as a whole:

$$\Pi = \frac{I}{1 - c_\Pi} = \frac{I}{s_\Pi}, \quad 0 \le c_\Pi < 1, 0 < s_\Pi \le 1 \tag{6.8}$$

Profits are thus determined by capitalists' investment in capital stock and by the propensity to consume or the propensity to save out of profits ($s_\Pi = 1 - c_\Pi$). As Equation (6.8) shows, we arrive at a first Kaleckian multiplier, which contains the sum of profits realized by the firms as a multiple of their investment expenditures. Since income distribution and hence the share of profits in national income is mainly determined by the mark-up in firms' price setting, the change in profits takes place through a change of aggregate production, thus the degree of utilization of the capital stock, and in national income. Taking into account that the share of gross profits in national income is defined as $h = \Pi / Y$, Equation (6.8) becomes:

$$Y = \frac{I}{(1 - c_\Pi)h} = \frac{I}{s_\Pi h}, \quad 0 \le c_\Pi < 1, 0 < s_\Pi \le 1 \tag{6.9}$$

Equation (6.9) displays a second Kaleckian multiplier, linking capitalists' investment expenditures with GDP or national income. The multiplier effect of exogenous investment expenditures depends inversely on the propensity to save out of profits and the profit share in national income. Therefore, the Kaleckian approach contains both a paradox of saving—that is, an increase in the propensity to save lowers profits and national income, and a paradox of costs—that is, a higher profit share and a lower wage share are detrimental to national income without affecting the sum of profits.

John Maynard Keynes[6]

John Maynard Keynes' research program of a monetary theory of production is at the very root of his principle of effective demand. In particular, the drafts preceding the *General Theory* (Keynes 1979), but less so the *General Theory* itself (Keynes 1936), aim at providing a monetary theory of production, which Keynes (1933: 408–409, italics in the original) outlines as follows:

> In my opinion the main reason why the problem of crises is unsolved . . . is to be found in the lack of what might be termed a *monetary theory of production*. . . . The theory which I desiderate would deal . . . with an economy in which money plays a part of its own and affects motives and decisions and is, in short, one of the operative factors in the situation, so that the course of events cannot be predicted, either in the long period or in the short, without a knowledge of the behaviour of money between the first state and the last.

In the drafts of the *General Theory*, Keynes distinguishes a monetary economy from a barter economy, a real-wage or cooperative economy, and a neutral economy (Keynes 1979: 76–101). In the barter economy there cannot be any deviation of aggregate demand from aggregate supply, because in real exchange nobody can sell without buying simultaneously and hence demand is always equal to supply by definition. In the real-wage or cooperative economy, economic agents use money, but only as means of exchange in order to facilitate trade and the allocation of the social product. Therefore, there are no leakages from the monetary circuit and aggregate demand always equals aggregate supply. In the neutral economy, money may additionally be used as a store of value and there may be leakages from the monetary circuit. However, these leakages are exactly offset by injections of the same amount through an endogenous economic process, and aggregate demand therefore corresponds to aggregate supply.[7] In a monetary or entrepreneur economy, however, there may be leakages from the monetary circuit, which are not exactly compensated for by injections; aggregate demand may therefore deviate from aggregate supply, and the latter will have to adjust to the former. Say's law will therefore not hold, mainly for two reasons, and has to be replaced by the principle of effective demand.

First, income may be used by households for other purposes than direct spending on consumption goods. It is the specific nature of money, which may cause leakages from the monetary circuit and create insufficient aggregate demand. Money can neither be fully substituted nor can it be reproduced by means of employing factors of production (Keynes 1979: 86).

Second, monetary injections may not automatically offset monetary leakages from the circuit of incomes as they are independent of current income in a modern credit economy. In particular, firms' production and investment decisions are geared towards monetary profits, and firms' spending for investment purposes may therefore be insufficient to make aggregate demand equal to aggregate supply at the level of full employment (Keynes 1979: 81–82).

In Chapter 3 of the *General Theory*, Keynes (1936: 23–34) explains the principle of effective demand by distinguishing the aggregate supply function $[Z = Z(N)]$ and the aggregate demand function $[D = D(N)]$. The Z-function represents the aggregate supply price of output as a function of employment (N). The supply price per unit of output (p) consists of unit production costs plus unit normal profits, and aggregate supply is then given by the level of employment and labor productivity ($y = Y^r / N$), real output (Y^r) per unit of labor employed, in the following way:

$$Z = Nyp \tag{6.10}$$

The Z-function will therefore be shaped by the productivity of labor, determined by the technology of production, and output prices, which are affected by the price-setting behavior of firms. With constant marginal and hence average labor productivity, constant nominal wage rates and thus constant unit labor costs, as well as constant mark-ups and therefore constant output prices, the Z-function will be linear, as in Figure 6.1.

The D-function presents the proceeds expected by the entrepreneurs, also as a function of employment. In an economy in which Say's law holds, the Z- and D-functions coincide, and the level of employment can then be determined by the neoclassical full employment labor market equilibrium based on utility-maximizing labor supply of households and profit-maximizing labor demand of firms (Keynes 1936: 26). In a monetary production economy, however, aggregate demand may diverge from aggregate supply, as explained above, and the D-function will thus be different from the Z-function, and this will give rise to the principle of effective demand.

Eckhard Hein

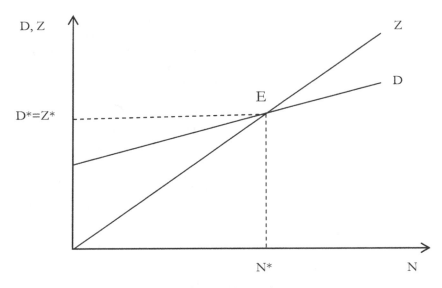

Figure 6.1 Keynes' (1936) principle of effective demand
Source: Author's presentation.

With Keynes (1936: 28–32) we can distinguish two components of the D-function: the first is affected by income—that is, income-dependent consumption (C); the second is independent of income—that is, autonomous or exogenous investment (I). For the first component, we can assume a constant marginal propensity to consume out of income (c) for the economy as a whole, which is positive but below unity. Total nominal income (Y) is given by employment, labor productivity, and the price level ($Y = Y^r p = Nyp$), and aggregate demand is hence:

$$D = c(Nyp) + I, \quad 0 < c < 1 \tag{6.11}$$

The point of intersection (E) of the Z- and D-curves in Figure 6.1 is "the effective demand" (Keynes 1936: 25). Aggregate demand at this level of employment is exactly equal to aggregate supply, and firms can sell the level of output associated with this level of employment at the expected or required prices. For this equilibrium level of employment (N^*) we have:

$$Z(N^*) = D(N^*) \tag{6.12}$$

and hence:

$$N^* = \frac{I}{(1-c)yp} \tag{6.13}$$

An increase in investment (or any other autonomous demand aggregate, like income-independent consumption, government expenditures, or exports) will raise the equilibrium level of employment. The same is true for an increase in the propensity to consume out of income—and we have the paradox of saving again.

As can easily be seen, our derivation of equilibrium employment in the D-Z-model can be translated into equilibrium income from the textbook income-expenditure model, because from Equation (6.13) we also get:

$$Y^* = \left(Nyp\right)^* = \frac{I}{\left(1-c\right)} \tag{6.14}$$

with Y^* as equilibrium income and $\left(1/\left(1-c\right)\right)$ as the income multiplier for investment.

The volume of employment determined by the point of effective demand in Figure 6.1 and by Equation (6.13) may well deviate from full employment in the labor market. However any response in the labor market, that is any change in nominal wages affecting output prices, real wages, and/or income distribution, will only have an impact on employment through aggregate demand and aggregate supply in the goods market. For a closer examination of the features and determinants of the goods market equilibrium, we will therefore outline a simple short run macroeconomic model in the following section.

A simple Post Keynesian/Kaleckian short run macroeconomic model based on the principle of effective demand

The Post Keynesian/Kaleckian short run macroeconomic model to be outlined in this section provides an endogenous determination of investment, income, and profits. It includes some monetary and financial variables—that is, a stock of debt and a monetary rate of interest, which seems to be required for a model driven by effective demand, and it explicitly considers functional income distribution.

Let us assume, for the sake of simplicity, that in a closed economy without a government, a homogeneous output is produced with a fixed coefficient production technology, using labor and a non-depreciating capital stock as inputs. Workers receive wages which they entirely consume and firms receive profits. These profits are partly retained in the firms, and hence saved, and partly distributed to rentiers in the form of interest payments. Rentiers consume part of their income and save the rest. Long-term finance of the capital stock consists of accumulated retained earnings of the firms, on the one hand, and external finance in terms of long-term credit granted by rentiers, on the other hand. The capital stock, as well as the stock of debt and the stock of accumulated retained earnings, are treated as constants in our short run macroeconomic model—for an analysis of the long run dynamics of these variables in distribution and growth models based on similar foundations, see for example Hein (2008: 100–123, 2014: 337–374).

Firms have some price setting power and they determine prices in the goods market by applying a mark-up (m) to unit labor costs, the ratio of the nominal wage rate, and labor productivity, which are assumed to be constant up to full capacity output:

$$p = \left[1 + m\left(i\right)\right]\frac{w}{y}, \, m \geq 0, \frac{\partial m}{\partial i} \geq 0 \tag{6.15}$$

The mark-up is affected by the degree of competition in the goods market and the bargaining power of workers in the labor market, which each constrain the price setting power of the individual firm (Kalecki 1954: 11–27; Hein 2014: 183–192). Furthermore, apart from profits, the mark-up has to cover overhead costs and is thus potentially affected by changes in interest costs. With the stock of debt of the firms given in the short run, a change in the rate of interest will induce an upwards pressure on the mark-up, in particular if it is associated with weakened bargaining power of workers and/or a lower degree of competition in the goods market. The rate of interest in our model is a monetary category, with the short-term rate determined by central bank policies and the long-term rate also affected by liquidity and risk assessments of financial wealth holders (Lavoie 2014: 182–274). The relevant rate of interest in our model is the long-term rate of interest corrected for inflation, which we will call the real rate of interest (i).

The mark-up determines the profit share in national income, which is therefore affected by any changes in the determinants of the mark-up, including a change in the real rate of interest:

$$h = \frac{\Pi}{Y} = \frac{m(i)}{1 + m(i)} \tag{6.16}$$

Savings consist of retained earnings of firms, the difference between total profits and rentiers' income (R), and saving out of rentiers' income (S_R):

$$S = \Pi - R + S_R = hY - (1 - s_R)iB, \quad 1 \geq s_R > 0 \tag{6.17}$$

Rentiers' income is determined by the rate of interest and the stock of debt (B), and the propensity to save out of rentiers' income (s_R) is assumed to be positive and constant.

In a monetary production economy, investment of firms is independent of any prior saving in the economy, because firms have access to finance generated endogenously by the financial sector.[8] The investment function proposed here contains Keynesian and Kaleckian features. First, following Keynes (1936), we assume that investment decisions of firms are determined by long-term expectations and by animal spirits—that is, the "spontaneous urge to action rather than inaction" (Keynes 1936: 161), which are represented by a shift parameter I_a in Equation (6.18). Second, investment is affected by (expected) sales and hence income, represented by the accelerator term βY. And third, we have included a negative effect of the rate of interest and interest payments on investment, represented by $-\theta iB$. Although a negative effect of the rate of interest on investment decisions is in line with Keynes' theory of investment based on the marginal efficiency of capital and the rate of interest, here we rely more on Kalecki's (1937) concept of the 'principle of increasing risk.' Higher interest payments have a negative effect on investment, because they reduce the firms' own means of finance, which are important because access to external means in imperfect financial markets is constrained. The amount of own means of finance of the firm is usually a criterion for creditworthiness and thus impacts the amount of external finance a firm can raise. Furthermore, a drain of internal means of finance increases the risk of illiquidity of the firm relying on external finance and thus dampens the willingness to invest in the capital stock. Given these considerations, we arrive at the following investment function:

$$I = I_a + \beta Y - \theta iB, \quad I_a, \beta, \theta \geq 0 \tag{6.18}$$

Equation (6.19) presents the goods market equilibrium condition, the equality of investment and saving, and in Equation (6.20) we have the Keynesian stability condition:

$$I = S \tag{6.19}$$

$$\frac{\partial S}{\partial Y} > \frac{\partial I}{\partial Y} \Rightarrow h - \beta > 0 \tag{6.20}$$

The goods market equilibrium values for income, investment (as well as saving) and profits can be found in Equations (6.21), (6.22), and (6.23):

$$Y^* = \frac{I_a + (1 - s_R - \theta)iB}{h - \beta} \tag{6.21}$$

$$I^* = S^* = \frac{I_a h + [\beta(1 - s_R) - \theta h]iB}{h - \beta} \tag{6.22}$$

$$\Pi^* = \frac{h\left[I_a + \left(1 - s_R - \theta\right)iB\right]}{h - \beta} \qquad (6.23)$$

As summarized in Table 6.1, an increase in long-term expectations and animal spirits—or in autonomous deficit-financed expenditures by the government or an external sector in a more elaborated model—will have expansionary effects on all endogenous variables. An increase in the propensity to save out of rentiers' income reduces equilibrium income, investment, and profits; the paradox of saving is thus valid with respect to all three endogenous variables. A rise in the profit share will have negative effects on equilibrium income, investment, and profits. This is the 'paradox of costs' (Rowthorn 1981), whereby lowering the real wage rate and the wage share, and thus increasing the profit share is detrimental to aggregate profits. Finally, a change in the real interest rate has ambiguous effects on the equilibrium values of the model, as can be seen in Equations (6.21a), (6.22a), and (6.23a):

$$\frac{\partial Y^*}{\partial i} = \frac{\left(1 - s_R - \theta\right) - Y^* \dfrac{\partial h}{\partial i}}{h - \beta} \qquad (6.21a)$$

$$\frac{\partial I^*}{\partial i} = \frac{\left[\beta\left(1 - s_R\right) - \theta h\right]B - \beta Y^* \dfrac{\partial h}{\partial i}}{h - \beta} \qquad (6.22a)$$

$$\frac{\partial \Pi^*}{\partial i} = \frac{\left(1 - s_R - \theta\right)hB - \dfrac{\beta}{h - \beta}\dfrac{\partial h}{\partial i}}{h - \beta} \qquad (6.23a)$$

If the mark-up is interest-inelastic and the propensity to consume out of rentiers' income exceeds the marginal effect of internal funds on investment $(1 - s_R - \theta > 0)$, a higher interest rate will trigger higher equilibrium values for income and profits. A positive effect on equilibrium investment would also require a strong accelerator effect of income on investment decisions. This constellation is known as the 'puzzling case' (Lavoie 1995). Even when a change in the interest rate has only a mild impact on the mark-up and the profit share, which has dampening effects on equilibrium income, investment, and profits, the puzzling case effects may persist, in particular for equilibrium income and profits. With strong effects of a change in the interest rate on the profit share, the impact of a higher rate of interest on equilibrium income, investment, and profits may

Table 6.1 Responses of equilibrium output/income (Y*), investment/saving (I*=S*) and profits (Π*) toward changes in exogenous variables and parameters

	Y*	I* = S*	Π*
I_a	+	+	+
s_R	−	−	−
h	−	−	−
i	?	?	?

turn negative. And if the 'normal case' (Lavoie 1995) conditions prevail, which means that the propensity to consume out of rentiers' income falls short of the marginal effect of internal funds on investment $(1 - s_R - \theta < 0)$, a higher interest rate will trigger lower equilibrium values for income, profits, and investment at any rate, irrespective of an interest-elastic or inelastic profit share.

These are the principal features of the income generation process in a short run macroeconomic model based on the principle of effective demand in a monetary production economy. They should also be at the core of more elaborated heterodox macroeconomic models, furthermore including the inflation generating process, and featuring the discussion of macroeconomic policies, that is monetary, fiscal, and wage/incomes policies and their coordination, as shown for example in Hein & Stockhammer (2011).

The long run principle of effective demand in heterodox distribution and growth models

As is well known, several Cambridge Post Keynesians were mainly concerned with extending Keynes' and Kalecki's principle of effective demand from the short period, with given productive capacities, to the long period applying it to distribution and growth issues (Harcourt 2006). Joan Robinson (1962: 82–83) famously summarizes the credo of Post Keynesian growth theories as follows:

> The Keynesian models (including our own) are designed to project into the long period the central thesis of the *General Theory*, that firms are free, within wide limits, to accumulate as they please, and that the rate of saving of the economy as a whole accommodates itself to the rate of investment that they decree.

Pasinetti (2001) also claims that the principle of effective demand, and hence the notion that macroeconomic activity is demand-determined, is of long run nature and should also include changes in technology and the composition of demand. He further argues that the validity of the principle is independent of any specific institutions and market structures.

Basically, we can distinguish two approaches applying the principle of effective demand to long run growth and distribution.[9] There are the first generation Post Keynesian distribution and growth models by Nicholas Kaldor (1955–56, 1957) and Joan Robinson (1956, 1962) relying on flexible prices in the goods market and full utilization of productive capacities given by the capital stock in the long run, or even also on full employment (Kaldor). In these models, in the long run, saving adjusts to investment through changes in income distribution and the profit share becomes endogenous with respect to capital accumulation. Alternatively, the second generation Post Keynesian models (Rowthorn 1981; Dutt 1984; Bhaduri & Marglin 1990; Kurz 1990), based on the works of Michał Kalecki (1954) and Josef Steindl (1952), contain cost-determined prices, which are inelastic with respect to demand, and variable rates of capacity utilization (and employment). Also in the long run, saving adjusts to investment through changes in output growth and utilization of growing productive capacities.

Starting from our model economy in the previous section, and ignoring the details on investment finance,[10] the principal differences between the two approaches can be explained as follows. By definition, the rate of profit (r) is given by the profit share, the rate of capacity utilization (u), and the capital-potential output ratio (v):

$$r = \frac{\Pi}{K} = \frac{\Pi}{Y} \frac{Y^r}{Y^p} \frac{Y^p}{K^r} = hu\frac{1}{v} \tag{6.24}$$

with K for the nominal capital stock, K^r for the real capital stock, Y for nominal output, Y^r for real output, and Y^p for potential output.

With a fixed coefficient production technology (or with Harrod neutral technical change) the capital-potential output ratio is a constant:

$$v = \bar{v} \tag{6.25}$$

Assuming the propensity to save out of wages to be zero, saving only draws on profits and we obtain for the saving-capital ratio or the saving rate (σ):

$$\sigma = \frac{S}{K} = s_\Pi \frac{\Pi}{K} = s_\Pi h u \frac{1}{v}, \qquad 1 \geq s_\Pi > 0 \tag{6.26}$$

The saving rate is thus determined by the propensity to save out of profits and the profit rate, or its components. Generally, the rate of capital accumulation (g) depends on long-term expectation and 'animal spirits' (α) and on the (expected) rate of profit, and hence on its constituting elements:

$$g = \frac{I}{K} = g(\alpha, r) = g(\alpha, h, u, v), \qquad \frac{\partial g}{\partial \alpha} > 0, \frac{\partial g}{\partial r} > 0, \frac{\partial g}{\partial h} > 0, \frac{\partial g}{\partial u} > 0, \frac{\partial g}{\partial v} < 0 \tag{6.27}$$

For the growth equilibrium in our demand-led growth model, we have:

$$g = \sigma \tag{6.28}$$

and for the stability condition it follows:

$$\frac{\partial \sigma}{\partial r} - \frac{\partial g}{\partial r} > 0 \tag{6.29}$$

The closure of the first generation Post Keynesian models by Kaldor and Robinson assumes that in the long run growth equilibrium firms utilize their productive capacities provided by the capital stock at some exogenously given normal or target rate (u_n):

$$u = u_n \tag{6.30}$$

so that the profit share becomes the accommodating variable. The equilibrium rates of capital accumulation and of profit are then determined endogenously through a variable profit share:

$$r^* = \frac{g^*}{s_\Pi} \tag{6.31}$$

$$h^* = \frac{g^*}{s_\Pi u_n \frac{1}{v}} \tag{6.32}$$

Figure 6.2 displays the Kaldorian/Robinsonian Post Keynesian demand-led growth model. The g-σ equilibrium includes the determination of the equilibrium accumulation rate, saving rate, profit rate, and hence profit share. An improvement in animal spirits, that is a shift of the g-function to the right, or a fall in the propensity to save out of profits, that is a counter clockwise rotation of the σ-function, as shown in Figure 6.2, will raise the equilibrium accumulation and growth rate as well as the profit rate and the profit share. Therefore, we have a long run version of the paradox of saving in this model. However, the paradox of costs from the short run model of the previous section has disappeared. Functional income distribution is not a parameter but an endogenous variable, and the wage share is now inversely related to equilibrium accumulation and growth rates. A higher equilibrium accumulation and growth rate generates and requires a higher profit share and thus a lower wage share in national income.

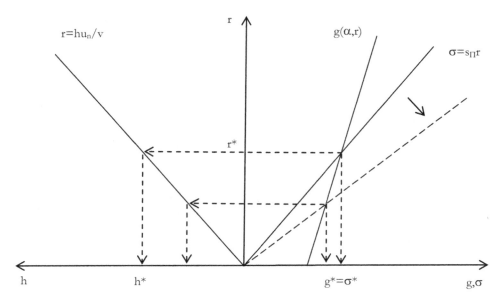

Figure 6.2 The Kaldorian/Robinsonian Post Keynesian distribution and growth model
Note: The rotation of the σ-curve shows the effect of a rise in the propensity to save out of profits.
Source: Author's presentation.

The closure of the second generation Post Keynesian distribution and growth models, the Kaleckian/Steindlian models, assumes that also in the long run, functional income distribution and hence the profit share are mainly determined by mark-up pricing of firms in the goods market, with the mark-up being affected by those variables outlined in the previous section:

$$h = h(m) \tag{6.33}$$

This means that the rate of capacity utilization becomes an endogenous variable. The equilibrium rates of capital accumulation and of profit are again endogenously determined, but now via a variable rate of capacity utilization:

$$r^* = \frac{g^*}{s_\Pi} \tag{6.34}$$

$$u^* = \frac{g^*}{s_\Pi h \dfrac{1}{v}} \tag{6.35}$$

Figure 6.3 shows the Kaleckian/Steindlian variant of the Post Keynesian demand-led growth model. Here the g-σ equilibrium includes the determination of the equilibrium saving rate, accumulation rate, profit rate, and rate of capacity utilization. Again, a positive shift in animal spirits and a reduction in the propensity to save out of profits are expansionary and increase the equilibrium accumulation and growth rate, as well as the profit rate and the rate of capacity utilization. On top of the paradox of saving, the Kaleckian/Steindlian model also allows for the paradox of costs in long run growth. A lower profit share, and thus a higher wage share, cause a counter clockwise rotation of the r-function in the left part of Figure 6.3, which will generate a higher equilibrium

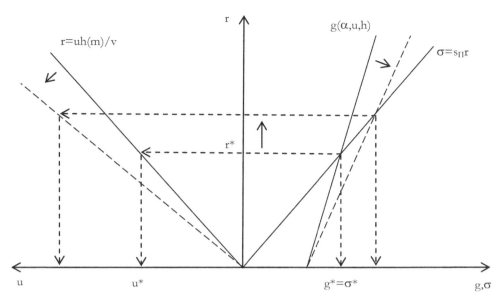

Figure 6.3 The Kaleckian/Steindlian Post Keynesian distribution and growth model
Note: The rotations of the r-curve and the σ-curve show the effect of a fall in the profit share.
Source: Author's presentation.

rate of capacity utilization associated with the g-σ equilibrium in the right part. However, that is not where the story ends, because the Kaleckians explicitly include the components of the profit rate into their investment functions. The neo-Kaleckian variant, proposed by Rowthorn (1981) and Dutt (1984) in particular, includes a strong effect of the rate of capacity utilization and neglects a direct effect of the profit share on investment decisions. Therefore any fall in the profit share will rotate the g-function clockwise, as shown in Figure 6.3, because each profit rate will then be associated with a higher rate of capacity utilization. As an overall result of a lower profit share, we get a higher rate of accumulation and growth, a higher rate of profit, and a higher rate of capacity utilization in the new equilibrium. The paradox of costs is fully valid, and demand (capacity utilization) and growth (capital accumulation) are unambiguously wage-led. In the post-Kaleckian model, suggested by Bhaduri & Marglin (1990) and Kurz (1990), however, these results may change, because the profit share is included as a further determinant into the investment function. This will dampen the redistribution-induced rotation of the g-function and may even reverse it. Therefore, different regimes may be derived, depending on the relative importance of capacity utilization and profitability in the investment function, and on the propensity to save out of profit: wage-led demand and wage-led growth; wage-led demand and profit-led growth; and profit-led demand and profit-led growth (Hein 2014: 258–267).

The Kaleckian treatment of the rate of capacity as an endogenous variable in long run growth models, which may deviate from the normal or target rate of utilization of firms, has been criticized by several Harrodian and Marxian authors, like Duménil & Lévy (1999), Shaikh (2009), and Skott (2010).[11] Including an exogenous normal or target rate of utilization into the Kaleckian models makes them prone to cumulative Harrodian instability, which then has to be contained by other mechanisms in the model, like an endogenous shift in income distribution and the respective change in the average propensity to save, or an endogenous change in animal spirits and thus in the inducement to invest. As a result, the paradox of costs completely disappears from the long run equilibrium, and in several approaches even the paradox of saving vanishes, and thus the validity of the principle of effective demand. Hein *et al.* (2012) discuss several Kaleckian responses to the critiques. The first type of responses questions the uniqueness of a target rate of capacity utilization, as well as the ability of firms to realize utilization targets when they are faced with other contradicting targets. The second type of responses provides several mechanisms by means of which utilization targets may become endogenous to actual capacity utilization, and thereby retains the paradox of saving and a potential paradox of costs.

The determinations of capital accumulation, growth, and the rate of profit by the principle of effective demand, as outlined in this section, provide the foundations for more elaborated demand-driven distribution and growth models. Several areas deserve mention:[12] the inclusion of an external sector generating export-led growth models (Kaldor 1970); the consideration of a balance-of-payments constraint to growth (Thirlwall 1979; Blecker 2013); the endogenous determination of technological progress and productivity growth (Kaldor 1957; Rowthorn 1981); the explicit integration and discussion of money, interest, and credit (Dutt 1995; Lavoie 1995; Hein 2008); and recent elaborations on finance-dominated capitalism in the context of demand-led growth models (Hein 2012).

Conclusion

This chapter reviewed the principle of effective demand from different angles. The second section demonstrated that the principle of effective demand can be found in, and based on, the contributions of Karl Marx, Michał Kalecki, and John Maynard Keynes. Based on these works can be argued that viewing modern capitalist economies as monetary production economies necessarily implies the validity and importance of the principle of effective demand. The third section outlined a simple short run macroeconomic model based on the principle of effective demand. The model provides an endogenous determination of investment, income, and profits; it explicitly includes some monetary and financial variables, that is, a stock of debt and a monetary rate of interest, and it considers functional income distribution. Within the context of this model we could derive the paradox of saving and the paradox of costs. The fourth section considered the long run importance of the principle of effective demand in heterodox distribution and growth models. We distinguished two main strands of Post Keynesian demand-driven growth models, the Kaldorian/Robinsonian strand and the Kaleckian/Steindlian variant. Whereas the latter is able to retain both the paradox of saving and, depending on the precise accumulation function, the paradox of costs, the former only preserves the paradox of saving in the long run, whereas the paradox of costs disappears. Finally, we addressed some issues around, and extensions of, demand-driven growth models.

Acknowledgments

For helpful comments I am most grateful to Daniel Detzer, Achim Truger, and the editors of this *Handbook*. And for editing assistance I have to thank Luisa Bunescu and James Masterson. The remaining errors are mine, of course.

Notes

1 This section draws on Hein (2008: 16–29).
2 Ricardo's version of Say's law differs from the neoclassical version, because it is neither associated with full employment of labor nor is there an economic mechanism equating saving and investment. It simply implies that saving and investment are identical (Garegnani 1978, 1979).

3 On Marx's rejection of Say's law see more explicitly Kenway (1980) and Sardoni (2011: 11–23).
4 The role of credit in economic crises is explored in more detail by Marx in *Capital, Volume III* (Marx 1894: 476–519).
5 This section partly draws on Hein (2014: 192–199).
6 This section partly draws on Hein (2008: 30–43).
7 In a neoclassical model this endogenous mechanism is the real rate of interest in the capital market which is supposed to equilibrate real saving and real investment.
8 See Hein (2008: Chapter 10) for a more detailed discussion distinguishing initial finance and final finance, or finance and funding, based on a monetary circuit approach in the tradition of Graziani (1989), Seccareccia (1996), and others.
9 For a detailed presentation and discussion of Post Keynesian distribution and growth models, see Hein (2014).
10 For the integration of money, interest and finance into different versions of Post Keynesian distribution and growth models, see Hein (2008, 2014: Chapter 9).
11 See Hein *et al.* (2012), Hein (2014: 441–471) and Lavoie (2014: 387–405) for detailed discussions.
12 More extensive literature reviews and model discussions on each of these areas can be found in Hein (2014).

References

Bhaduri, A. & Marglin, S. 1990. 'Unemployment and the real wage: the economic basis for contesting political ideologies.' *Cambridge Journal of Economics*, 14 (4): 375–393.

Blecker, R.A. 2013. 'Long-run growth in open economies: export-led cumulative causation or a balance-of-payments constraint?' *in*: G.C. Harcourt & P. Kriesler (eds.), *The Oxford Handbook of Post-Keynesian Economics, Vol. I*. Oxford: Oxford University Press, 390–414.

Duménil, G. & Lévy, D. 1999. 'Being Keynesian in the short term and classical in the long term: the traverse to classical long-term equilibrium.' *The Manchester School*, 67 (6): 684–716.

Dutt, A.K. 1984. 'Stagnation, income distribution and monopoly power.' *Cambridge Journal of Economics*, 8 (1): 25–40.

Dutt, A.K. 1995. 'Internal finance and monopoly power in capitalist economies: a reformulation of Steindl's growth model.' *Metroeconomica*, 46 (1): 16–34.

Dymski, G.A. 1996. 'Kalecki's monetary economics,' *in*: J.E. King (ed.), *An Alternative Macroeconomic Theory: The Kaleckian Model and Post-Keynesian Economics*. Boston: Kluwer, 115–140.

Foster, J.B. 2014. *The Theory of Monopoly Capitalism: An Elaboration of Marxian Political Economy*. New York: Monthly Review Press.

Garegnani, P. 1978. 'Notes on consumption, investment and effective demand, Part I.' *Cambridge Journal of Economics*, 2 (4): 335–353.

Garegnani, P. 1979. 'Notes on consumption, investment and effective demand, Part II.' *Cambridge Journal of Economics*, 3 (1): 63–82.

Graziani, A. 1989. 'The theory of the monetary circuit.' *Thames Papers in Political Economy*, Spring: 1–26.

Harcourt, G.C. 2006. *The Structure of Post-Keynesian Economics: The Core Contributions of the Pioneers*. Cambridge, UK: Cambridge University Press.

Hein, E. 2006. 'Money, interest and capital accumulation in Karl Marx's economics: a monetary interpretation and some similarities to post-Keynesian approaches.' *European Journal of the History of Economic Thought*, 13 (1): 113–140.

Hein, E. 2008. *Money, Distribution Conflict and Capital Accumulation: Contributions to 'Monetary Analysis.'* Basingstoke, UK: Palgrave Macmillan.

Hein, E. 2012. *The Macroeconomics of Finance-dominated Capitalism—and its Crisis*. Cheltenham, UK: Edward Elgar.

Hein, E. 2014. *Distribution and Growth after Keynes: A Post-Keynesian Guide*. Cheltenham, UK: Edward Elgar.

Hein, E., Lavoie, M., & van Treeck, T. 2012. 'Harrodian instability and the 'normal rate' of capacity utilization in Kaleckian models of distribution and growth—a survey.' *Metroeconomica*, 63 (1): 139–169.

Hein, E. & Stockhammer, E. 2011. 'A post-Keynesian macroeconomic model of inflation, distribution and employment,' *in*: E. Hein & E. Stockhammer (eds.), *A Modern Guide to Keynesian Macroeconomics and Economic Policies*. Cheltenham, UK: Edward Elgar, 112–136.

Kaldor, N. 1955–56. 'Alternative theories of distribution.' *Review of Economic Studies*, 23 (2): 83–100.

Kaldor, N. 1957. 'A model of economic growth.' *The Economic Journal*, 67 (268): 591–624.

Kaldor, N. 1970. 'The case for regional policies.' *Scottish Journal of Political Economy*, 17 (3): 337–348.

Kalecki, M. [1932] 1990. 'The business cycle and inflation,' in: J. Osiatynski (ed.), *Collected Works of Michał Kalecki, Vol. I.* Oxford: Clarendon Press, 147–155.

Kalecki, M. [1936] 1982. 'Some remarks on Keynes' theory (Pare uwag o teorii Keynesa).' *Ekonomista*, 3: 18–26; 'Kalecki's review of Keynes' *General Theory*,' translated by F. Targetti & B. Kinda-Hass. *Australian Economic Papers*, 21 (39): 245–253.

Kalecki, M. 1937. 'The principle of increasing risk.' *Economica*, 4 (16): 440–447.

Kalecki, M. 1954. *Theory of Economic Dynamics.* London: George Allen and Unwin.

Kalecki, M. 1968. 'The Marxian equations of reproduction and modern economics.' *Social Science Information*, 7 (6): 73–79.

Kalecki, M. 1969. *Studies in the Theory of Business Cycles, 1933–1939.* London: Basil Blackwell.

Kenway, P. 1980. 'Marx, Keynes and the possibility theory of crisis.' *Cambridge Journal of Economics*, 4 (1): 23–36.

Keynes, J.M. [1933] 1987. 'A monetary theory of production,' in: *The Collected Writings of John Maynard Keynes, Vol. XIII.* London: Macmillan, 408–411.

Keynes, J.M. [1936] 1973. *The General Theory of Employment, Interest and Money*, in: *The Collected Writings of John Maynard Keynes, Vol. VII.* London: Macmillan.

Keynes, J.M. 1979. *The General Theory and After. A Supplement*, in: *The Collected Writings of John Maynard Keynes, Vol. XXIX.* London: Macmillan.

Kurz, H.D. 1990. 'Technical change, growth and distribution: a steady-state approach to "unsteady" growth,' in: H.D. Kurz, *Capital, Distribution and Effective Demand.* Cambridge, UK: Polity Press, 210–239.

Lavoie, M. 1995. 'Interest rates in post-Keynesian models of growth and distribution.' *Metroeconomica*, 46 (2): 146–177.

Lavoie, M. 2014. *Post-Keynesian Economics: New Foundations.* Cheltenham, UK: Edward Elgar.

Marx, K. [1861–63] 1967. *Theorien über den Mehrwert. Zweiter Teil, Marx-Engels-Werke.* Bd. 26.2, Berlin: Dietz Verlag.

Marx, K. [1867] 1967. *Capital: A Critique of Political Economy.* Volume I: *The Process of Capitalist Production.* New York: International Publishers.

Marx, K. [1885] 1967. *Capital: A Critique of Political Economy.* Volume II: *The Process of Circulation of Capital.* New York: International Publishers.

Marx, K. [1894] 1967. *Capital: A Critique of Political Economy.* Volume III: *The Process of Capitalist Production as a Whole.* New York: International Publishers.

Pasinetti, L.L. 2001. 'The principle of effective demand and its relevance in the long run.' *Journal of Post Keynesian Economics*, 23 (3): 383–390.

Robinson, J. 1956. *The Accumulation of Capital.* London: Macmillan.

Robinson, J. 1962. *Essays in the Theory of Economic Growth.* London: Macmillan.

Rowthorn, R.E. 1981. 'Demand, real wages and economic growth.' *Thames Papers in Political Economy*, Autumn: 1–39.

Sardoni, C. 2011. *Unemployment, Recession and Effective Demand: The Contributions of Marx, Keynes and Kalecki.* Cheltenham, UK: Edward Elgar.

Sawyer, M. 1985. *The Economics of Michał Kalecki.* Armonk, NY: M.E. Sharpe.

Sawyer, M. 2001. 'Kalecki on money and finance.' *European Journal of the History of Economic Thought*, 8 (4): 487–508.

Schumpeter, J.A. 1954. *History of Economic Analysis.* New York: Oxford University Press.

Seccareccia, M. 1996. 'Post Keynesian fundism and monetary circulation,' in: G. Deleplace & E. Nell (eds.), *Money in Motion.* London: Macmillan, 400–416.

Shaikh, A. 2009. 'Economic policy in a growth context: a classical synthesis of Keynes and Harrod.' *Metroeconomica*, 60 (3): 455–494.

Skott, P. 2010. 'Growth, instability and cycles: Harrodian and Kaleckian models of accumulation and income distribution,' in: M. Setterfield (ed.), *Handbook of Alternative Theories of Economic Growth.* Cheltenham, UK: Edward Elgar, 108–131.

Steindl, J. [1952] 1976. *Maturity and Stagnation in American Capitalism.* 2nd edn. Oxford: Blackwell.

Thirlwall, A. P. 1979. 'The balance of payments constraint as an explanation of international growth differences.' *Banca Nazionale del Lavoro Quarterly Review*, 32 (128): 45–53.

7

Heterodox theories of value
A brief history

Ajit Sinha

Introduction

An object or an activity is an 'economic entity' only if it has power to attract something in exchange. Thus it is fundamental for economics to understand how an object or an activity acquires exchange-value. The theories of value of heterodox economic traditions are rooted in classical political economy, which takes up this problem only with respect to commodities that are reproducible as they considered only those to be important in understanding an economic system. The classical economists were fundamentally interested in finding out the *essential cause* that gives rise to the exchange-value of commodities. The problem of exchange-value, however, also immediately raises the question of the scale by which it can be measured. As we shall see, the problem of the ultimate cause of value in the classical tradition gets entangled with the question of the scale of its measure—the cause must explain the *change* in value but at the same time must not affect the scale by which the change is measured. In this chapter we discuss three major developments in the history of value theory in heterodox economic traditions. First we discuss the problem as set up by Adam Smith, then criticized and developed by Ricardo and Marx and subsequently reconstructed by Sraffa, whose reconstruction removes the notion of equilibrium from the theory of value, which makes it most compatible with all hues of heterodox economics.

Adam Smith

In the *Wealth of Nations* Adam Smith ([1776] 1981) devotes three short chapters (V, VI, and VII of Book I) to his theory of value, which set the ground for the classical theory of value and distribution. After establishing that the true wealth of a nation does not lie in the quantity of money-commodity a nation has accumulated but rather in the quantity of goods and services available per capita, Smith points out that the increase in the true wealth of a nation lies in two things: (i) improvements in the productivity of labor and (ii) the investment of savings in the employment of productive labor not unproductive labor, of which the former is by far the more important. Smith then goes on to argue that improvements in the productivity of labor largely depend on the extent of the division of labor applied in the production of any specific good, which in turn depends on the extent of its market. When the market for a good becomes very large, Smith argues, an opportunity arises for different aspects of the production of a commodity, which were earlier performed within a household or a factory, to be divided into independent trades and thus the division of labor at the level of a household or a factory grows into a social division of labor. It is the existence of the social division of labor that brings to the fore the question of commodity exchange.

However, instead of immediately posing the question of the principle that regulates the exchange ratios of commodities in an economy characterized by the social division of labor, Smith begins by raising the problem of the *measurement* of a commodity's value or a nation's wealth. Of course, if the problem is only to determine the exchange ratios of commodities then any commodity could serve the purpose of measuring the values of other commodities and thus the prevalent money-commodity, say gold or silver, would very well foot the bill. Thus it is clear that the theoretical problem posited by Smith is a different one. The problem is not of a *measure* of value at a point of time but rather of the measure of a *change* in value. For example, if the wealth of a nation is the availability of all goods and services at a point of time then their aggregate value in terms of money can be treated as a surrogate for the measurement of the wealth of a nation. But could the rise and fall in the total money-value of wealth be taken as a surrogate for measuring the rise and fall in a nation's real wealth as the mercantilists had purportedly argued? Smith's argument against such reasoning is that the value of money-commodity itself fluctuates independently of the aggregate of goods and services like the price of any other commodity. Therefore it cannot be a correct measure for measuring the *changes* in the wealth of a nation or the value of any other commodity over time.

This brings Adam Smith to the problem of the *essential* or the *ultimate cause* of value. What is it that causes a commodity to be valuable in the first place—that is, to command money or some other commodity in exchange? If one could find the ultimate cause that confers this property on a commodity then one would *ipso facto* know the measure to use for determining the changes in the *real* value of a commodity over time. Here we find that the question of a *measure* of value is intricately linked with the question of the *essential* or *ultimate cause* of value.

This takes Adam Smith deep into human history—that is, the 'early and rude state of society.' The basic idea is that primitive man must have had to wrest his subsistence from nature by working against nature with his bare hands. Thus production can be reduced to an *exchange* between man and nature. Adam Smith thought that this primitive exchange can also explain the exchange between man and man. Since the price paid for subsistence is the 'toil and trouble' of a certain period, possession of the subsistence produced can command or exchange for a certain period of toil and trouble of any other man. Thus the *real* measure of value is the 'subsistence' that buys the 'toil and trouble' or labor, which is the ultimate source of the value of a commodity.

Smith realizes that in a capitalist economy the 'subsistence' that a worker receives for his 'toil and trouble' fluctuates over time. He maintains that such fluctuations in the values of the commodities that constitute the 'subsistence basket' as the 'toil and trouble'—or the *sacrifice* made by the worker to receive the 'subsistence basket'—remains the same and it is the sacrifice of the worker that measures the *real* cost of acquiring the commodity. This, of course, does not resolve the matter. The 'toil and trouble' represents the subjective notion of 'sacrifice' on the part of the worker which may not be measurable. But Smith insists that it can be measured by the 'objective' measure of hours of labor spent by the worker in the production process.

Adam Smith argues that in the 'early and rude state of society' laborers own their means of production or they produce the means of production from scratch. In this society Smith maintains that it would be natural for laborers to exchange their products in accordance with the total labor-time required to produce the respective commodities. In this case, the amount of labor that takes to produce a commodity is equal to the amount of labor that commodity can command of somebody else's labor embodied in the other commodity. Thus the problem of the determination of the relative value of commodities coincides with the problem of the measure of value. According to Adam Smith, this coincidence, however, breaks down once the means of production becomes the private property of a class other than the laborers. Once a class of capitalists, who advance the means of production and the subsistence of the laborers during the production process, arrives on the scene and demands a share in the net product, it immediately creates a discrepancy between a commodity's power to command the amount of labor-time and the amount of labor-time that is taken to produce that commodity—obviously the commodity's command of labor must be higher than the labor-time it takes to produce the commodity if the capitalists' share in the net output is to be positive. Thus, once the net output is distributed among two or more classes of people, Adam Smith argues, the principle of exchange of commodities (according to the total labor-time required to produce the respective commodities) no longer holds.

The alternative theory of value determination that Adam Smith proposes when net output is distributed to various classes is fundamentally a theory based on accounting. Smith argues that the size of the net output must be equal to the sum of total wages plus profits plus rents if the net output is divided into only three income categories. Similarly, the value of capital can in turn be broken down to wages, profits, and rents by going back into the chain of production. Thus adding up all the direct and indirect wages, profits, and rents will measure the total value of gross output. From this it follows that the price of a commodity is constituted by adding the aliquot parts of direct and indirect wages, profits, and rents that the production of that commodity generates.

Subsequently Smith argues that for any given economy at any given point in time there exists, as known data, a 'natural' rate of profits, wages, and rents. From the aggregation of these natural rates one can determine the 'natural price' or value of any commodity. These 'natural' rates are not the 'actual' rates that must exist at that moment however. They are the rates around which actual rates are at any given moment fluctuating—they can be thought of as averages of the past several years of actual rates although they are not just a statistical notion. These natural rates are those that specify the general equilibrium of the system—that is, if the 'actual' rates are equal to the 'natural' rates then the economy will be at rest. In other words, there will be no internal tendency for the economy to move from that position On the other hand, if the 'actual' rates are not equal to the 'natural' rates then there will be an inherent tendency—due to free competition in the economy—for the 'actual' rates to move toward the 'natural rates.' Hence the 'natural' rates generate a gravitational force that pulls towards the 'actual' rates.

Ricardo

Ricardo ([1821] 1951) criticizes Adam Smith for both his choice of the wage-unit as the 'invariable' measure of value as well as his so-called 'additive' theory of value. First of all, Ricardo points out that real wages do fluctuate over time and, hence, there is nothing inherent in wage-units, compared to any arbitrary commodity, to be claimed as an 'invariable' measure of value. As we have seen, Adam Smith had of course recognized that wages do fluctuate over time which he defends from the standpoint of the laborer. Smith argues that if we compare eight hours of work by a laborer over two time periods, the 'sacrifice' or hardship that the laborer endures in both time periods remain the same and that is the *real* price the laborer pays in exchange for his or her subsistence. Now, if the subsistence basket contains more or less of commodities then—as far as the laborer is concerned—it is the value of those commodities that are falling or rising because the laborer is buying more or less for the same amount of payment she makes for acquiring the subsistence. This 'measure' may be sensible for measuring the changes in the wealth of a nation on the grounds of welfare. Given that the class of laborers constitutes the majority of population, a measure of a rise or fall in the wealth of a nation must represent the improvement or worsening of the conditions of its working force. Yet, it is not a 'scientific' measure that would ensure that when a change in the value of a commodity is measured against this yardstick it always measures the changes that have occurred in the commodity and not in the yardstick itself. That was Ricardo's main objection to it.

With respect to Adam Smith's 'additive' theory of value, Ricardo argues that it was logically flawed—if the net output of an economy is distributed or divided among three classes then it cannot be claimed that its size is determined by adding up independently determined wages, profits, and rents. Since if wages and profits are given from outside then rents have to be the residual and cannot also be from outside. In other words, according to Ricardo, Adam Smith fails to recognize that there is a constraint binding the size of the total income. Elsewhere (Sinha 2010a, b) I have argued that this is not a justified criticism of Adam Smith as he does acknowledge the constraint binding net output and determined rent as the residual.

In Ricardo's opinion, however, Adam Smith errs to think that his labor theory of value was only valid for the 'early and rude state of society.' Ricardo argues that the labor theory of value remains a 'correct' theory for value determination even in a capitalist society where the net output is distributed between two or three classes. Let us suppose that there are no landlords but a class of capitalists exists who advance the subsistence and implements to workers who produce two commodities and demand a rate of profit on their capital investment. Ricardo shows that, as long as the ratio of labor-time taken to produce the implements used (that is, indirect labor) and the direct labor-time to produce the two commodities remains the same, it does not matter what rate of profits (which must be uniform in a competitive economy) the respective capitalists receive. The exchange ratio between the two commodities will not be affected—that is, they would still exchange in the ratio of the total labor-time needed to produce the respective commodities. Ricardo also argues that the rent of land is determined by a principle that makes it irrelevant for the determination of relative values of commodities. Thus, Ricardo contends that Adam Smith was wrong in thinking that the labor theory of value is invalidated once an income category other than wages emerges.

Ricardo, however, acknowledges that when the ratios of direct to indirect labor-time in various industries are not equal then the competitive condition of a uniform rate of profits across industries comes into contradiction with the principle of the labor theory of value. When wages are reduced from their full share of net output, the various industries release income in proportion to the number of workers they directly employ. Now if the ratio of direct to indirect labor of various industries is not equal then industry-wide release or transfer of income from their wage bills will give lower rate of profits for industries that are relatively 'capital intensive' and *vice versa*. Thus the competitive condition of equalization of the rate of profits across industries must result in modifying the exchange ratios of commodities from their original labor-time ratios.

How much must the labor theory of value be 'modified' in the face of heterogeneous ratios of direct to indirect labor-time across industries? Ricardo offers no answer. Adam Smith set the problem in terms of measuring the *changes* in the wealth of a nation over periods of time, Ricardo also set the problem of measuring the *changes* in the distribution of income over periods of time. In this context, Ricardo argues that with population growth more food must be produced. Given diminishing returns on land, it takes more labor-time to produce the same wage basket, which amounts to proportionately more labor-time devoted to producing wages on the marginal land and proportionately less labor-time devoted to producing what amounts to profits. Therefore, this should lead to a fall in the rate of profits. The idea was to show that the *changes* in the relative distribution of income over time can be explained exclusively through changes in the labor-time needed to produce the commodities, which Ricardo also considers to be the *ultimate cause* of value.

Yet again Ricardo faces the problem that changes in wages or the rate of profits modifies the relative values of commodities. Therefore the measure of changes in value—in terms of any arbitrary commodity—may nullify or reverse the effect caused by the changes in the labor-time used to produce the commodities. This led Ricardo to search for a commodity that would remain 'invariant' in the face of changes in the rate of profits. He did not find or theoretically construct any commodity that would fulfill such a requirement. All he did is to assume that (i) his money-commodity 'gold' was always produced by the same amount of labor-time and that (ii) the composition of its direct and indirect labor-time was somewhere near the middle of most of the commodities produced. Thus the effect of changes in the rate of profits on the values of most commodities, when measured against gold, remained small enough to be ignored. Sraffa (1951) argues that Ricardo was searching for an 'average' commodity as a yardstick such that the price changes (due to changes in the rate of profits) would be such that the total value of the net output will remain constant before and after the change in the rate of profits—that is, the size of the pie remains constant when it is cut in different proportions.

Elsewhere (Sinha 2010a, c) I have argued that Ricardo's 'invariable measure of value' was designed to show that changes in the rate of profits have no effect on the values of commodities when measured against this particular yardstick. Thus it could be established that labor-time is the sole or ultimate cause of the change in values and the distribution of income, and that the apparent changes in value due to changes in the rate of profits is solely due to the arbitrary nature of the money-commodity that we have to choose as a measuring yardstick for changes in values. This idea is, however, illogical as changes in the rate of profits affect relative values of commodities and therefore there cannot be any commodity either in reality or theory against which relative values of commodities would not change. Ricardo finally comes to this realization, as six days before his untimely death he wrote to James Mill:

> I have been thinking a good deal on this subject lately but without much improvement—I see the same difficulties as before and am more confirmed than ever that strictly speaking there is not in nature any correct measure of value nor can any ingenuity suggest one, for what constitutes a correct measure for some things is a reason why it cannot be a correct one for other.
>
> *Ricardo [1823] 1952: 372, dated Sept. 5, 1823*

Marx

Marx ([1905–10] 1963) criticizes Ricardo for getting bogged down by a 'secondary' problem of searching for an 'invariable measure of value.' Marx argues that classical economists such as Adam Smith and David Ricardo are unable to solve the problem of value because they are unable to understand the nature of profit in the capitalist system. Marx's central criticism of classical economics is that it is unable to penetrate through the appearances to get to the essence of capitalism. Marx ([1867] 1977) argues that the wealth of a capitalist nation appears as an immense collection of commodities, which in his opinion is akin to a 'cell' of a living organism and therefore an understanding of this living organism must begin with an analysis of its 'cell,' meaning a commodity in singular. In its appearance a commodity has two characteristics: (i) it has some use to someone in society—that is, it has *use-value*, and (ii) it always stands in a relation of exchange with some other commodity (the money-commodity)—that is, it has *exchange-value*. Marx argues that though use-value is necessary for a commodity to have an exchange-value, it is not something that explains the quantitative relation that exchange-value represents, since use-values of two commodities cannot be quantitatively compared.

The next step in Marx's argument is that an exchange relation between two commodities represents a relation of equality, that is, something equal in quantity changes hands. He further argues the *only* thing that is common to both the commodities is that they are both products of labor. At this stage Marx argues that labor itself has two aspects: (i) concrete labor and (ii) abstract labor. Concrete labor represents the actual laboring process that ends up in the production of a particular use-value such as the laboring activity of an ironsmith that produces a sword. Abstract labor, on the other hand, represents the expenditure of energy by the ironsmith in the laboring process. In this case there is no qualitative distinction between the labor of an ironsmith or a goldsmith. It is the pure expenditure of human energy and can be quantitatively compared irrespective of the form in which it is spent.

Marx argues that what changes hands in equal quantity, in an exchange relation, is the abstract labor that is embodied in the two commodities. Here Marx makes a distinction between (a) the value and (b) the exchange-value of a commodity. The amount of abstract labor embodied in a commodity is called the value of a commodity, which is an *absolute* category—it exists in a singular commodity. Marx's contention is that the value of a commodity manifests itself only in relation to an exchange with another commodity. Thus exchange-value is an outward appearance of the essence of a commodity, which is its value.

Marx then poses the question: if exchange-value represents the exchange of equal values then where does profit come from? In a capitalist system, a capitalist begins with a certain amount of money capital with which she buys raw materials, machines, etc. and also hires workers for a wage to produce a commodity which she sells in the market to recoup her money. Now, if the quantity of money the capitalist ends up with equals the quantity of money she started with (that is, M–C–M) then the whole process would be irrational from the point of view of the capitalist. Thus for this system to be meaningful the capitalist must end up with more money than she started with (that is, M–C–M', where M' > M). But the problem is: if the exchange involved represents an exchange of equal values then where does more money come from?

Marx's answer is this. When the capitalist pays wages to the worker this *appears* to be a price paid for the laboring activity that the worker performs in the production process and so all costs are fully paid. But *actually* what the worker exchanges with the capitalist for a wage is not laboring activity but the worker's *capacity to work*, which Marx calls 'labor-power' in contradistinction to 'labor' as such. The value of labor-power is also determined by the same principle as the value of any other commodity—that is, its value is determined by the amount of abstract labor-time needed to produce and reproduce the worker's capacity to work at any given socio-historical moment. Thus given the wage basket, the value of labor-power is derived by reducing the wage-basket to the total abstract labor-time embodied in those commodities.

Marx contends that capitalism as a mode of production survives only because the value of labor-power turns out to be less than the labor-time that workers expend in the production process. This is the part of laboring activity that turns into profits for the capitalists. Thus the value of a commodity can be analyzed first into two distinct parts and then into three distinct parts: first, the value of a commodity is made up of the abstract labor-time embodied in all the raw materials, machines, etc. used up in producing the commodity—the indirect labor-time of the classical economists, which Marx called 'constant capital' (c), plus the direct laboring activity performed by the worker in producing the commodity—the classical economists' direct labor-time.

It is Marx's contention that though the classical economists analyzed the process of production in these two separate parts in the context of their labor theory of value, they failed to take the decisive step of analyzing the laboring activity itself in its two component parts: (i) the value of labor-power, which Marx called 'variable capital' (v), and (ii) the remaining laboring activity, which Marx called 'surplus labor' or 'surplus value' (s). Thus the value of a commodity is made up of $c + v + s$, where $c + v$ represents the value of capital investment by the capitalist for producing the commodity and $[s/(c + v)]$ the rate of profit received by the capitalist on the sale of the commodity, which explains M' > M of the circuit of capital.

Let us suppose that a commodity's value is given by λ_i, then $\lambda_i = c_i + v_i + s_i$ and therefore the rate of profits in terms of the value produced in this industry is given by $s_i/(c_i + v_i)$. This can be written as $(s_i/v_i)/(c_i/v_i + 1)$. Similarly for other commodities, such as j, k, etc., the value of their rate of profits can be written as $(s_j/v_j)/(c_j/v_j + 1)$, $(s_k/v_k)/(c_k/v_k + 1)$, etc. The ratio s_i/v_i is called the 'rate of surplus value' or the rate of exploitation—it is the ratio in which the total direct labor-time is divided between what goes to the capitalists and what goes to the workers. In general one assumes that this ratio should be uniform across industries as the length of a working day is generally fixed conventionally or by law, and wages are determined at the level of the whole economy and not at an individual industry level. The ratio c_i/v_i is the ratio of the value of the total capital invested between its non-human (raw materials, machines, etc.) and human components. This ratio is a Marxian surrogate for the classical indirect to direct labor ratio and there is no reason to think that it should be uniform across industries as it represents specific techniques of producing different use-values.

Now, if s_i/v_i, s_j/v_j, s_k/v_k are equal and c_i/v_i, c_j/v_j, c_k/v_k are not equal, then their respective value rate of profits, say r_i, r_j, r_k, would not be equal either. If equal values change hands in exchange, then it is clear that the rate of profits received in various industries will not be equal. But Marx, following Adam Smith and other classical economists, maintains that in a competitive capitalist economy the rate of profits must be equal across sectors in a state of equilibrium. The problem is one of how to reconcile this contradiction.

Marx's ([1894] 1991) proposed solution is as follows: at the level of value analysis we know it is the surplus value that is appropriated by the capitalists. So we add up all the surplus values produced by all industries, which gives us the total value appropriated by the capitalist class as a whole. If we divide this total surplus value produced in the economic system, say S, by the total constant plus variable capital of the system, say $(C + V)$, then the ratio $S/(C + V)$ gives us the average rate of profit of the economic system, which is the rate of profits that must be received by all industries. Mathematically, Marx's argument can be presented thus:

$$(c_1 + v_1) [1 + S/(C + V)] = P_1$$
$$(c_2 + v_2) [1 + S/(C + V)] = P_2$$
$$\ldots$$
$$(c_n + v_n) [1 + S/(C + V)] = P_n$$

In other words, the competitive mechanism of the capitalist system amounts to an exercise of pooling all the surplus value produced in the economic system into one pond and then redistributing it equally to all individual industries in proportion to their relative capital investment. This process takes place by establishing the exchange ratios of commodities such that all industries end up receiving an equal rate of profit. Thus the exchange-values do not represent an exchange of equal values. As a matter of fact, the industries whose rates of profits are higher must exchange more values against less value from the industries with lower value rates of profits—that is, P_i/P_j is not equal to λ_i/λ_j. However, $\Sigma P_i = \Sigma \lambda_i$ and $\Sigma r_i (c_i + v_i) = S$, that is, the total prices of production are equal to total value, and total profits are equal to total surplus value. Thus value is the 'stuff' of capitalism which circulates, gets exchanged, and divided between classes but the competitive mechanism of capitalism creates an appearance of this 'stuff' in such a way that its true nature is obscured.

There are two fundamental problems with Marx's analysis. Böhm-Bawerk ([1896] 1949) argues that Marx's conclusion contradicts his premise. Recall that Marx argues that the exchange of two commodities represents the change of hands of something equal. This was the premise from which he derives that it was an equal amount of abstract labor-time embodied in the two commodities that changed hands in the process of exchanging commodities. But in conclusion Marx claims that actually equal abstract labor-time does not change hands in an exchange relation, which contradicts the premise. The only way to overcome this criticism is to scrap the premise as unnecessary. One could simply claim that the total labor-time in terms of human energy expenditure represented by simple unskilled homogeneous labor-time embodied in a commodity, say λ, can be analyzed into three component parts, $c + v + s$. On the basis of this one can determine the rate of profits and the exchange ratios of the economic system in equilibrium.

Bortkiewicz ([1907] 1949), however, raises a more serious problem with Marx's transformation of values to the prices of production. Bortkiewicz argues that Marx makes a mistake in measuring capital. If the production prices of commodities are not equal to their values then the relevant measure of capital must also be in terms of the prices of production and not in terms of values. Thus the average rate of profits derived by Marx is not the correct average rate of profits and so the measure of those prices of production are also incorrect. What it amounts to is that Marx's system of equations is not well defined.

Once we allow the prices of production to appear on the left-hand side of the equations as well, then we return to Ricardo's world and Marx's analysis of a singular commodity as value loses all analytical significance—we are in the world of relative values and profits to begin with. Once values are replaced by unknown prices of production on the left-hand side of the equations, it becomes clear that Marx's system of equations is underdetermined because it has more unknowns to solve than it has independent equations. In this system an extra equation for the *numéraire*—the measuring yardstick—can be added from outside the system and then the equations can be solved for an equal rate of profits and relative prices. If one puts the condition that the total prices of production must equal total values in the system, which satisfies Marx's yardstick of maintaining all deviations of prices of production from value to be zero, then there is no reason to assume that the total profits in the system would be equal to total surplus value (see Seton 1957). So Marx's value analysis of a commodity no longer appears to reveal the *essence* of exchange-values and profits.

Marx was aware that his method of deriving the rate of profits and prices of production had some problems and that he needed to replace values with the unknown prices of production on the left-hand side of the equations as well (see Marx [1894] 1991: 264–265). In this case, he came to the conclusion that he can only make a much weaker claim that the rate of profits would be positive if and only if the rate of surplus value is positive—a proposition that is valid and was later christened as 'fundamental Marxian Theorem' by Morishima (1973). But, as Samuelson (1974) shows, after Sraffa (1960) we know that prices and the rate of profits can be directly determined from the physical input-output data without going through value determination. In that case it can be shown that positive surplus value exists if and only if there is a positive rate of profits. In other words, the arrow of causation can go both ways, which amounts to saying that no arrow of causation can be drawn.

Sraffa

For Sraffa (1960) one major distinction between the classical theory of value and the orthodox one lies in their attitude to the measurability of the variables on which the theory depends. Sraffa thinks that a scientific theory must be based only on objectively observable and measurable variables. Thus, he was of the view that classical and Marxian economics include only those variables that can be objectively and directly measured on some scale, whereas orthodox theory bases itself on the subjectivities of agents, which cannot be directly measured. On this basis Sraffa develops a theory of value that is based on only objectively given physical input and output data. However, he rejected the classical idea of finding the essential or ultimate cause of value. Instead, he developed a geometrical theory, which establishes exact relations that must prevail between the theoretical variables at any given moment and not the discovery of the cause of their existence. Sraffa's commitment to basing his theory solely on observed data at any given moment also led him to reject the classical idea of the center of gravitation or equilibrium, since such notions are *ideal* and not observable at any given moment. Functional relations of orthodox economics that generate causal forces for variables to move in certain prescribed directions are also rejected on the grounds that, at any given moment, functions do not exist; at best, only a point exists.

Sraffa's approach to the problem of value follows Adam Smith's general approach of looking at it as an accounting problem. If we start with an economic system with workers and wages as the only income category (as in Adam Smith's 'early and rude state of society') then total net income must be appropriated by workers as wages. The assumption that uniform labor receives uniform wages leads to a solution of exchange-values as relative values must be equal to relative total labor-time embodied in respective commodities. If wages are reduced then some net output will be released. If this net output must be appropriated by a class of capitalists such that every capitalist receives a uniform rate of profits on capital invested then the question is: what exchange-values must prevail that would account for the values of industrial capital investments and the values of their net outputs such that the ratios of their net output values to capital investments are equal and the value of total net output released by reducing wages is accounted for as total profits in the system? Sraffa showed that the system needs no additional information (for example, demand) to solve for a set of relative values and a uniform rate of profits that would account for the net output released as profits.

We have seen that Adam Smith claims the 'natural' rates of wages, profits, and rents are given independently of values and that prices only account for those given rates at any moment. In Sraffa's opinion another major line of demarcation between classical theory and orthodox theory is that the distribution of income in terms of the rates of wages, profits, and rents is determined independently of the determination of exchange-values, whereas the orthodox theory determines simultaneously these distributional variables with exchange-values. In Sraffa's theory of value determination described above, the rate of profits is simultaneously determined with prices. So the question is: how does it rehabilitate the classical theory? The answer to this lies in the fact that the above description of Sraffa's price theory is not yet complete.

Sraffa goes on to show that there exists one and only one set of multipliers (which can be discovered from the observed actual system of production) that would convert it into a system such that the physical composition of its net output and total capital is the same. Sraffa calls it the standard system. In this case, the ratio of the net output to total capital or the maximum rate of profits of the system (R) can be determined by the physical system independently of exchange-values. If the net output of the standard system, which he called the Standard commodity, is used as the measuring yardstick to measure given wages and values then it can be shown that in the observed actual system there exists a relationship between the rate of wages (w), the rate of profits (r), and the maximum rate of profits (R) given by $r = R(1 - w)$, which holds for all the values of w. Since R is independent of both r and w as well as the values of commodities and w is taken to be given from outside the system of equations, it follows that r can be determined independently of exchange-values. This establishes the classical and Marxian position that the theory of distribution can be separated from the theory of value.

The last point in this context is the condition of the equal rate of profits in Sraffa's equations. As we know in the classical tradition this is used as the condition of equilibrium (that is, an *ideal*) of the system. But Sraffa's system of equations represents an observed actual system of inputs and outputs at any moment. So how can one reconcile the empirical system with the ideal position? One way is to assume constant returns to scale for all industries but Sraffa emphatically denies making any such assumption. It is my contention (see Sinha 2010a, 2012, 2016) that no reconciliation is needed. Sraffa's standard system reveals the average rate of profits of the observed empirical system as a 'non-price phenomenon.' It is the mathematical property of the 'average' that leads to the conclusion that whatever is leftover of the net output after the payment of wages in terms of the Standard commodity must be distributed according to a uniform rate of profits—this is not a condition of equilibrium of the economic system however. Thus we have for the first time a theory of value that does not rely on the notion of equilibrium.

Conclusion

In this chapter we have traced out three major theoretical developments in the theory of value, beginning with Adam Smith and then to Ricardo and Marx and finally the reconstruction of this tradition by Sraffa. Two theoretical problems have been highlighted: (i) the question of the scale by which the value of a commodity can be measured and (ii) what causes a commodity to acquire value to begin with. Adam Smith poses the question of the *measure* of value prior to the question of the *cause* of value. This was because the problem of value was posed in the context of *change* in the value of a commodity over time. The question was: what scale is to be used to measure the change? It was the search for this scale that led Adam Smith to the question of the *ultimate cause* of value.

Adam Smith argues that the ultimate cause of value lies in the primordial productive activity when man works against nature directly. There are two aspects to this primary exchange between man and nature: (i) it is a laboring activity where man sacrifices his ease and comfort and (ii) it results in the appropriation of income. How these two elements of the primordial exchange between man and nature relate to the value of a commodity is the source of most of the confusion and controversies in the classical tradition of value. Adam Smith argues that in the primordial state the two aspects of the exchange are united in the same individual, which results in a simple rule of exchange for commodities; but once appropriation gets disconnected from the laboring activity, no such simple rule of exchange holds any longer. Smith emphasizes the relation of the appropriation of income with value and develops a theory of value which is mainly a problem of accounting for income *given its rule of distribution from outside*.

Ricardo, in opposition to Adam Smith, emphasizes the relation of laboring activity with value. He argues that even though, in general, it cannot be established that the laboring activity *per se* determines the value of a commodity at a point of time, one could argue that *changes* in value of a commodity can be directly related to *changes* in laboring activity. It was in this context that Ricardo faces the problem of the scale or the 'invariable measure' of value—a problem that he was not able to resolve.

Marx goes a step further than Ricardo and argues that one can establish a direct relation between the exchange-values of commodities at a point of time with the laboring activity. Marx argues that the classical economists, particularly Ricardo, could not solve the problem of the determination of exchange-values of commodities on the basis of the data on laboring activity alone because they did not ask the question: where do profits come from? His answer in terms of surplus labor or the surplus value, however, failed to solve the problem as he left the question of the scale unresolved.

Sraffa reconstructs the classical paradigm by going back to Adam Smith in the sense of formulating the problem of value in terms of accounting for a *given* net output and its distribution in terms of wages, profits, and rents. In this context Sraffa showed that income distribution can be taken as given from outside independently of the exchange ratios of commodities and it can be shown that the exchange ratios of commodities are completely determined once income distribution is specified. In this context Sraffa needed a scale of measure that would not be affected by changes in distribution, which he discovered in the Standard commodity.

References

Böhm-Bawerk, E. von. [1896] 1949. *Karl Marx and the Close of his System*. New York: Augustus M. Kelley.

Bortkiewicz, L. von. [1907] 1949. 'On the correction of Marx's fundamental theoretical construction in the third volume of *Capital*,' in: P.M. Sweezy (ed.), *Karl Marx and the Close of his System*, 199–221.

Marx, K. [1867] 1977. *Capital, Vol. I*. New York: Vintage.

Marx, K. [1894] 1991. *Capital, Vol. III*. London: Penguin Classics.

Marx, K. [1905–10] 1963. *Theories of Surplus Value*. Part II. Moscow: Progress Publishers.

Morishima, M. 1973. *Marx's Economics: A Dual Theory of Value and Growth*. Cambridge: Cambridge University Press.

Ricardo, D. [1821] 1951. *The Works and Correspondence of David Ricardo, Vol. I*, edited by P. Sraffa. Cambridge: Cambridge University Press.

Ricardo, D. [1823] 1952. *The Works and Correspondence of David Ricardo, Vol. IX*, edited by P. Sraffa. Cambridge: Cambridge University Press.

Samuelson, P.A. 1974. 'Insight and detour in the theory of exploitation: a reply to Baumol.' *Journal of Economic Literature*, 12 (1): 62–70.

Seton, F. 1957. 'The "Transformation Problem".' *The Review of Economic Studies*, 24 (3): 149–160.

Sinha, A. 2010a. *Theories of Value from Adam Smith to Piero Sraffa*. London: Routledge.

Sinha, A. 2010b. 'In defence of Adam Smith's theory of value.' *European Journal of the History of Economic Thought*, 17 (1): 29–48.

Sinha, A. 2010c. 'A note on Ricardo's invariable measure of value.' *Cahiers d'économie politique*, 58: 133–144.

Sinha, A. 2012. 'Listen to Sraffa's silences: a new interpretation of Sraffa's *Production of Commodities*.' *Cambridge Journal of Economics*, 36 (6): 1323–1339.

Sinha, A. 2016. *A Revolution in Economic Theory: The Economics of Piero Sraffa*. London: Palgrave Macmillan.

Smith, A. [1776] 1981. *An Inquiry Into the Nature and Causes of the Wealth of Nations*, Vol. I. Indianapolis, IN: Library Fund.

Sraffa, P. 1951. 'Introduction,' in: *Works and Correspondence of David Ricardo, Vol. I*. Cambridge: Cambridge University Press.

Sraffa, P. 1960. *Production of Commodities by Means of Commodities*. Cambridge: Cambridge University Press.

8

Theories of prices and alternative economic paradigms

Carlo D'Ippoliti

In a state of society, however, in which the industrial system is entirely founded on purchase and sale . . . the question of Value is fundamental. Almost every speculation respecting the economical interests of a society thus constituted implies some theory of Value: the smallest error on that subject infects with corresponding error all our other conclusions; and anything vague or misty in our conception of it creates confusion and uncertainty in everything else.

Mill [1848] 1871: 456

Introduction

For some heterodox economics schools values are different from prices, while others regard such distinction as metaphysical. This difference of approach is related to different opinions on what function(s) the price system takes on in a capitalist economy. By discussing these different functions (allocative, distributive, and informative), this chapter shows that price and value theory holds analytical centrality in all economic paradigms, both heterodox and mainstream, to the point of defining contemporary heterodox (and thus orthodox) economics.

Indeed, the concepts of price and value, and thus price theory, directly descend from an economist's general picture of the working of the economy as a whole. To use Schumpeter's (1954) terminology, I refer here to the 'pre-analytical vision,' that is the first, ideologically inspired step of economic theorization. While not yet articulated in concepts and variables, a vision contains some elements (and significantly, not others) and preliminary implicit hypotheses on the causal links between these elements—it thus crucially shapes the subsequent phases of theorization. Since price theory descends from the pre-analytical vision of the working of the economy as a whole, it inherits its analytical centrality from the general character of this vision.

The literature on the theory of value and prices is vast and ever expanding, and no attempt is made here to provide a comprehensive review of it.[1] Rather, I will focus on the two main visions of the working of the economy that, with alternate fortunes, have developed throughout the history of economic thought, which I shall call the 'marketplace vision' and the 'market-system vision.' In turn, these are related to two main approaches to price theory: the subjective and the objective approach, respectively. I argue that all heterodox traditions hold some variant of the market-system vision of the economy and the objective approach to prices (with the exception of Austrian economics and some strands of ecological and evolutionary economics).

It appears that sharing the same pre-analytical vision, thus the same or compatible theories of value, are necessary conditions to assess the compatibility between schools of economic thought, if not the potential for their integration (D'Ippoliti & Roncaglia 2015). This may appear surprising to some, given that heterodox economics seem to reflect mainstream economics' bipartition of a mathematically sophisticated 'high theory,' where prices and values are explicitly considered, and applications of 'lowbrow theory,' which often even make recourse to marginalist supply-and-demand mechanisms.

Thus, it seems necessary to investigate the possibility for a wide-tent pluralist approach within the boundaries of the market-system view of the economy and the associated objective concept of prices. This will be the object of the present chapter.

Value and price

In part, difficulties in the debate on value and price theories derive from the adoption of the same terms with different meanings or conceptual underpinnings. Thus, it is first of all necessary to clarify the terminology used in this chapter. This terminology does not reflect the one adopted by any single school, but it appears as necessary in order to compare different, occasionally incommensurable approaches.[2]

For our purposes, we can use the terms object, good, commodity, and service as interchangeable, unless explicitly noted. Since the Middle Ages, scholars recognize two different aspects of an object's ability to meet some human desire: one, a property of the object; and the other, an idiosyncratic feeling of the individual. With respect to both, we shall refer to this ability as the object's *value in use*. As is well known, mainstream economics assumes that such property is quantifiable through a cardinal or ordinal utility function. In turn, value in use is assumed to directly or indirectly determine a second sort of value, referred to as *value in exchange*. Such exchange-value is the degree to which a commodity performs a second function, that is, it can be given or taken in exchange for something else. The notion that value in use measures or causes value in exchange will be referred to here as the *subjective approach* to value, because it postulates that value derives from introspection.

By contrast, the British classical political economists, and most heterodox economists after them, consider the existence of some value in use as a simple precondition for the object to have some value in exchange. But value in use is not generally considered a measure of value in exchange and/or it does not exert a quantifiable influence on it. The cause or measure of value in exchange must be sought elsewhere, in variables external to the individual; thus, this approach will be referred to here as the *objective approach* to value. This term descends from the history of economic thought on this subject, which is mostly concerned with variables that may be objectively determined, pertaining to the technology, distribution of income, and institutions of a certain society.

Indeed, at least since Petty, we have a distinct view that the difficulty to supply must be the real determinant of the value in exchange of a commodity, its 'natural price.' Since at the time money itself was either a commodity, such as gold and silver, or its value was directly proportional to the quantity of a commodity, it was obvious that money was not an adequate unit of measurement because its own value was subject to change. Petty put forward a theory of natural prices based on production costs (often simplified as a labor theory of value or, according to some historians of thought, a land-and-labor theory of value). After Petty, Cantillon proposed a land theory of value. Later, the British classical political economists almost unanimously employed a labor theory of value, alternatively based on the notions of labor commanded or labor employed. The evolution of the theory of value in classical political economy as well as its more recent reconstruction by Piero Sraffa are recounted in Chapter 7 (by Sinha) in this volume. Subsequent developments, as is well known, see neoclassical economists rescuing the earlier subjective approach in a new, mathematically sophisticated way. In contrast, within contemporary heterodoxy, different schools have developed different concepts and analyses of prices and values, while most heterodox schools agree on employing some form of the objective approach.

In the subjective approach, an object's value in exchange is its *price*. Each agent has a reservation price, that is the maximum value that a buyer is willing to pay in order to obtain it, or the minimum value that a seller is willing to accept in order to part with it. The *market price* is the equilibrium value that does not induce any buyer or seller to change her behavior (see next section for a more detailed definition).

In the objective approach, several different positions have been put forward. As will be discussed in the next sections, some economists did not (and do not) think that the price at which each transaction takes place is liable to theorization. Others do not object to the theorization of market prices, but see them as very volatile or anyway not the only relevant quantity. In both cases, economists following the objective approach refer to different concepts—that is, *value* (as opposed to market price), *natural price*, *normal price*, *long-run price*, *production price*, or several other concepts, depending on the specific theory. What all these concepts have in common is that they represent the abstract, social characteristics of an object's value in exchange, as opposed to the vagaries of the turbulent capitalist economy that affect its volatile—possibly random—market price. Thus, these terms denote different notions of *regulating prices*, that is, values that are relevant for the analysis at hand. For example, theories in which the accumulation of capital is a fundamental driver of economic activity, will have regulating prices as the values that firms use when making investment decisions; or theories in which free entry and exit from an industry are key concepts will exhibit regulating values as those that are assumed to prevail under competitive conditions (these may or may not coincide with the former example).

Thus, in the rest of this chapter 'value' and 'price,' in the specific sense of regulating price, will be used as synonymous, when it is not relevant to making a distinction between approaches in which a specific notion of regulating price is being adopted. In any case, both value and (regulating) price will be assumed to be different from market prices, which may or may not qualify as theoretical variables.

Adopting this terminology, price theory encompasses both value theory (that is, the analysis of the determinants of regulating prices) and the analysis of the relation between values and market prices.

Pre-analytical visions of the economy and the role of prices

Many social thinkers tend to think of the market as a *marketplace*, a distinct point in space and time in which one-shot exchanges take place. Archetypal images of this vision may be the stock exchange, a flea market, or a street market. From this perspective, each individual comes to the marketplace already endowed with money, goods, and/or the ability to work (we do not ask where this endowment comes from), engages in one or more transactions, and leaves the marketplace. If we further assume that goods are perishable (for example, fish), suppliers will not leave the market until their endowments are exhausted, thus the idea of equilibrium as 'market clearing' emerges. In such a setup, the value in exchange, or the market price of a particular good is determined by the interplay of the exogenously given quantity brought to the market and buyers' preferences. Adding the assumption of the law of one price, as a consequence of competition among buyers and among sellers separately, and the assumption that no transaction takes place at a price different from the equilibrium one, we get a theory of price explained by supply and demand.

Today, among the heterodox schools only Austrian economics and some strands of ecological and evolutionary economics start from this pre-analytical vision; as a consequence, Austrians consistently stick to a subjective theory of value (though not necessarily the marginalist theory, as shown for example by Menger), while the ecological and evolutionary schools exhibit some internal variation, as hinted to below.

Contrary to the view of the market as a marketplace, others conceptualize the market as a *social system* of recurring exchanges, in a society based on the division of labor and social stratification. Archetypal images of this vision are Cantillon's description of the mutual dependence of town and countryside, the nationalist ideal of an autarchic economy, or the asymmetric relations of the global North and South in the contemporary world economy. For the sake of simplicity, at least at the pre-analytical stage of theorizing it is pictured that productive units produce only one or a few kinds of commodities, and thus everybody needs to continuously carry out a number of transactions in order to obtain the vast assortment of goods and services that they need. Notably, such transactions include firms, which need to buy their means of production in the market. Thus, according to this vision the production and distribution of commodities are intertwined, and the crucial analytical problem is how such a decentralized society can survive and even grow (in a sustainable manner, if we adopt an ecological point of view). While in the marketplace vision the given data are initial endowments and fixed preferences, in the market-as-a-social-system vision the main givens are technology and the social organization of production. If we assume competition (but the assumption can be modified, as discussed further below), prices are determined in the process of production in which a unit's product is another one's means of production. Thus a system of prices has to be such that no productive unit buys its means of production at too high a cost (thus incurring losses) or too low (thus benefiting of exceptional profits). Otherwise, competition between capitalists would lead some firms out of business (in the former case), or would attract more firms in the industry (in the latter).

The difference in the respective focuses on the sphere of exchange in the marketplace view and the sphere of production in the market-system view, led some authors to denote this as the defining feature of the two main economic paradigms of mainstream and heterodox economics. However, it must be stressed that the differences are pervasive and concern the pre-analytical vision, conceptualization, and formalization of the functioning of the economy, and are not limited to the greater or lesser focus on some aspects of it. For this reason, most heterodox economists object to a research program that seeks compatibility between mainstream economics and specific heterodox theories.

In the marketplace view, prices play a crucial *allocative role*. While the 'equilibrium' price depends on the equality of supply and demand, each quantity in turn depends on prices, positively (the quantity supplied) and negatively (the quantity demanded). The problem of simultaneous interdependence is solved through the conceptualization of price equations, and the bulk of the mainstream literature on 'general equilibrium' theory is devoted to showing that a solution to a system of equations representing market clearing in all markets exists (although such a solution may lack crucial desired characteristics such as uniqueness and stability). Under these conditions, prices' allocative role consists in inducing firms and consumers to change their demand and supply in response to discrepancies between prices and the agents' subjective assessment of the value of each good. Although prices are surreptitiously equalized across individuals with the assumption of a no-arbitrage condition (Mirowski 1989: 236), prices are defined at the individual level, as a measure of her desires (or 'preferences') in relation to scarce means. At the aggregate level, prices are thus indexes of the overall scarcity of a good or service (given its best production technology) relative to the market demand for it; and aggregates such as an economy's total value added are a measure of an economy's capacity to satisfy (unlimited) human wants.

In mainstream economics, such a subjective evaluation is expressed by firms' marginal costs and consumers' marginal utility. However, since the very beginning of the so-called marginal-ist revolution, many were aware that individual desires are incommensurable and probably not even liable to precise quantification: this was for example Menger's position. Moreover, historical evidence suggests that even in market societies and even abstracting from non-market provision of goods and services, prices do not necessarily play an allocative role: more often than not, it is quantities that adjust to accommodate demand and supply shocks, with prices kept fixed by regulation, convenience, or convention (Braudel 1967). Thus, a branch of 'neo-Austrian' eco-nomics emerged, based on the notion of out-of-equilibrium dynamics, in which prices are fixed for a meaningful time interval. Finally, while not immediately apparent at the time, the 'socialist calculation debate' in the 1930s highlighted the political relevance of understanding prices as the carriers of diffused information that is not available to any single market participant (Hayek 1948). These and possibly other causes of dissent from mainstream economics led to a differ-ent concept of prices and their role within Austrian economics, that is the role of transferring information processed by markets.[3]

This different notion of prices is one of the main reasons why some Austrian economists identify themselves as 'heterodox.' However, the Austrians' adherence to a marketplace view and its associated notion of prices as determined by the equilibrium of supply and demand are the reasons why other heterodox economists consider Austrian economics a variant of mainstream economics (D'Ippoliti & Roncaglia 2015).

It is noteworthy that the recent 'information revolution' within mainstream economics gave centrality to the notions of markets as information processors and prices as information carriers. This is made evident by the increasing relevance of the notion of informational efficiency (espe-cially, of financial markets, following the works by Eugene Fama) and its complicated relation with allocative efficiency (Stiglitz & Grossman 1980).[4] Consequently, a slow convergence of the price concept may be taking place among the schools that start from a marketplace vision, and the mainstream approach may become increasingly similar to the Austrian.

In the market-system view, the notion of market clearing is absent and prices play a com-pletely different role—that is, coordinating capitalist production by distributing the resources necessary for the continuation of production and the surplus among industries and between social classes. Here, the schematic idea is that production in a capitalist society requires the prior expenditure of money to buy the means of production and to pay for workers' wages (constituting 'capital'); capitalists advance money capital with the view of gaining it back with a profit through sales (the 'realization' of capital). Prices determine the aggregate value of the means of production and the revenues, and the purchasing power of wages, profits, and rents. Since both exchanges among productive units (and between workers and firms) and exchanges of final consumption goods take place in markets, any transfer of purchasing power must take place through exchange-values.[5]

In this approach too, even if exchange-values are by definition relative, it makes sense to compute aggregate values of capital, profit, or the economic surplus. These quantities represent a collection of heterogeneous commodities and services, aggregated by weighting them for their price. In intuitive terms, the price here is an index of difficulty of production in a society with particular technology and social institutions that determine the functional distribution of income.[6]

Open issues in the objective approach

All heterodox traditions hold some variant of the market-system vision of the economy and the objective approach to prices; as explained above, those that do not should probably not be defined as heterodox, from a theoretical point of view. However, the peculiar position of (American) institutional economics should be singled out. As Jo (2016) summarizes, early institutionalists and Veblen himself occasionally recur to simple supply and demand reasoning, perhaps because of its hegemonic role in US academic economics. Truly, basic pillars of institutional thought, such as socially constructed preferences and artificially created scarcity, highlight the role of the agency of dominant elites and going concerns that are obviously alternative to the mechanistic and impersonal price mechanism posited by marginalist economics. But subjective factors play a significant role in some institutional analyses of prices, leading to questions as to these authors' adherence to the objective paradigm. This is true, for example, of the influences of 'ceremonial efficiency' on prices and wages, or the strong role attributed to habits and conventions.

These factors are not totally absent in other objective approaches—most heterodox economists agree that, for example, the determination of the socially necessary labor to produce a commodity and the level of the subsistence wage are historically contingent, and affected by institutional factors. However, the issue is methodological insofar as the assumption of *general* mechanisms of economic processes "is not the way institutionalists explain economic activities. There is no universally ordained institutional economics. All institutional theories are (to be) historically contingent due to the specificity of social institutions and the heterogeneity of agency therein" (Jo 2016: 338). If one views that the institutional approach should have a distinct theory for each historical case, then it is not possible to enlist institutionalists in either the subjective or the objective camp. If instead we define (varieties of) capitalism as a sufficiently specific spectrum of validity for a certain theory—that is, for the identification of a general mechanism—then it should be possible to develop an institutional theory of prices. Jo (2016) makes such an attempt, but as a matter of fact he ends up delineating an institutional theory of pricing, rather than a price theory.

Apart from these methodological issues, four main conceptual issues seem to be most relevant in assessing the potential for mutual compatibility between heterodox theories of value: (i) the relation between values in exchange and relative prices, with the associated concepts of natural, production, and market prices; (ii) the role and scope of the labor theory of value; (iii) the definition and inclusion in the analysis of what counts as 'labor'; and (iv) the mutual relation between the determination of quantities and prices.

Natural prices, production prices, and market prices

The first systematic treatments of value as determined only by objective forces may be traced back to Petty, Cantillon, and later the physiocrats and the British classicals. The fact that they often held different conceptual views may be a source of continuing differences between contemporary approaches.

Petty wrote at a time when a strong quantitative turn was pervading natural sciences, with the early developments of classical mechanics. He notoriously set himself to only talk "in Terms of Number, Weight, or Measure," expressly leaving aside the subjective variables "that depend upon the mutable Minds, Opinions, Appetites and Passions" (quoted in Roncaglia 2005: 56). This drive for quantification led Petty to first inquire into adequate subjects of quantitative analysis. In his 'Dialogue of Diamonds,' Petty sketches the procedure through which an imaginary diamond dealer traces back each specific diamond—with its size, weight, color, etc.—to an ideal diamond, by means of correction coefficients. In turn, there will be an ideal market for the ideal diamond, in which the law of one price prevails. Therefore commodities and markets, thus *market prices*, are but abstractions, useful to establish a link between the seemingly disconnected exchanges in a given society. Each transaction is affected by a myriad of erratic elements (for example, bargaining power) and it would be impossible to develop a quantitative theory of what may be considered a random collection of disconnected facts.

Most classical political economists shared the idea that this conceptualization of the market price is not liable to precise quantitative theorization. Such a concept of the market price begs a question: what then is systematic or permanent and thus liable for quantitative theorization in market exchanges? Many later writers interpret Adam Smith's analogy of gravitation as implying that market prices turbulently and erratically move over time, but always exhibit a long-run tendency to approach the respective *natural prices*. Smith defined natural prices differently from Petty (as well as from Cantillon and the physiocrats), but their analytical role is the same with all these authors—that is, regulating capitalist economic activity in a society.

In contemporary analyses, the 'econophysics' literature and some heterodox economists take up this conceptualization of the market price and argue for the use of a stochastic approach to account for its randomness. Significantly, though, this way the market price again becomes a variable liable to precise quantification. Nonetheless, the use of statistical distributions does not necessarily imply that the notion of *regulating prices* is useless (see, for example, Shaikh 2016). Ultimately, natural or production prices, or labor values—all instances of prices that regulate capitalist activity in a given society—may still be relevant in this approach, since they are the reference point for capitalists or other agents who make decisions.

According to Marshall's interpretation of Smith, natural prices regulate the long-run tendencies of production, in that natural prices correspond to the sum of wages, profits, and rents paid at their natural rate (with some ambiguities and risks of circular reasoning). This long-run equilibrium is reached because competition between capitalists equalizes profit rates across industries (as competition between workers and rentiers equalizes wage and rent rates). Contrary to this interpretation, Andrews (2015: 266) brings up J.S. Mill's interpretation of natural prices as logical requirements: they are the prices that allow production to continue unchanged. Not only market prices need not gravitate around them, but also production may actually not continue, and indeed it is very unlikely for it to remain unchanged in the face of capital accumulation, technological innovations, and social developments.

There is bidirectional causality between conceptual analyses of contemporary price theories and historical investigations. For example, Adam Smith's and the other classical political economists' views on natural prices have often been re-interpreted (or clarified, depending on the point of view) and debated within the Sraffian school. At the same time, Sraffian and other historical analyses help clarify the conceptual foundations of contemporary approaches to prices. This example is especially pertinent because there is a clear connection between the concept of natural prices and Sraffa's (1960) *production prices*. Some Sraffians (for example, Garegnani, Pasinetti, and Schefold) interpret production prices as long-run end positions of a gravitation process driven by the competition among capitalists, while others (for example, Roncaglia, Sen, and Arena) hold a 'snapshot interpretation,' according to which production prices express the instantaneous conditions of reproduction of a capitalist system at a specific moment. The former conceptualization of production prices is in obvious continuity with Marshall's (and possibly Ricardo's) interpretation of Smith's natural prices, whereas the latter is in continuity with Mill's.

This conceptual divergence has relevance for the potential complementarity between the Sraffian approach and other heterodox approaches (see Aspromourgos 2004; Lavoie 2011). Some claim—but this is a subject of ongoing controversy—that the assumption that production prices represent long-run equilibrium positions implies an assumption of constant returns to scale. This latter assumption is in turn incompatible with the conceptualization of production by several other heterodox schools, which typically posit increasing returns. The snapshot interpretation seems more able to conceptually accommodate not only increasing returns to scale, but also—at least in principle—radical uncertainty (which has always been connected to profits in the economic literature), which is crucial from a Post Keynesian perspective. Conversely, the notion of production prices as long-run end positions is historically closer to the Marxian approach. In Marxian treatment, however, labor values are more important than prices, and thus the debate on the compatibility of Sraffa's approach with the Marxian one has rather revolved around the relation between labor values and production prices, the so-called transformation problem, which is dealt with in the next section.

Thus, while the debate around the compatibility of various price theories usually revolves around the mathematical properties of formal models (such as the high number of exogenous variables in Sraffa's systems, or their degrees of freedom), the conceptual underpinnings of these models seem equally, if not more, important.

The value of labor

Piero Sraffa's 1960 *Production of Commodities by Means of Commodities* sparked successive rounds of debate on the relation and compatibility between his analysis and Marx's. Towards the end of the 1970s, the majority view seems to have been that Marx's labor values may be given a consistent treatment that is not incompatible with Sraffa's analysis; however, production prices are independent of Marx's labor values and the latter are possibly not even needed to discuss class struggle (see Steedman 1977). These results may be a cause for the subsequent independence of Sraffian economics from Marxian economics, 'the no-communication monologues' (Bellofiore 2012). Recent archival work on both Marx's and Sraffa's papers is igniting new debates, shifting focus from the 'transformation problem' to the similarity and potential filiation of Sraffa's system with Marx's reproduction schemes (and from Quesnay's *Tableau Économique*). Part of the reason for this shift is that, as informed by the 'new interpretation' of Marx's theory, many Marxists now hold the labor theory of value only at the macroeconomic level.[7]

However, here too conceptual differences could be more relevant than formal compatibility. For example, in a simple Sraffa system the labor embodied may be computed through a 'reduction to dated quantities of labor.' However, even ignoring the existence of a commodity residual, whose size depends on the rate of profits, this procedure only shows how much labor would have been necessary to produce a certain commodity, had the current technology been used since the very beginning of production—that is, the production of the commodities' means of production, and the means of production of the commodities' means of production, and so on. This is not just different from what Marx was interested in, but it is indeed a very un-Marxian hypothesis, far away from his evolutionary approach (Mirowski 1989: 182).

On conceptual grounds, there is a more obvious sense in which the Marxian theory of value is complementary to, but has not been substituted by, Sraffa's systems. As was made clear within the Cambridge capital controversies, 'capital' (and surplus, and thus profits) has two meanings: a heterogeneous collection of commodities and a homogeneous monetary value (Cohen & Harcourt 2003). In the latter sense, reference to an absolute value such as labor embodied has a clear conceptual sense, independent of relative prices.

Moreover, Marxian economists consider living labor (and the difference between labor and labor power) to explain the 'cause' of surplus value—that is, surplus labor; it consists of all labor activities exerted for a time over and above what is necessary to produce the goods used for workers' consumption. Even in some Sraffian treatments, labor is considered to be the only ultimate source of exchange-value and thus it retains a conceptual significance independently of production prices (see, for example, Pasinetti 1981).

The issue of the (degree of) compatibility between the Sraffian system and Marxian economics concerns formal models as well. For example, a relevant issue comes up when trying to determine which distributive variable is taken as exogenously given in Sraffa's equations. The approach closest to Marx's (and the classics') treatment is to assume the wage as given. It is usually assumed to be at the level of reproduction of the workforce, implying that the given wage is not necessarily the minimum necessary for subsistence but what is socially necessary in a certain society at a certain time. Such focus on the reproduction of workers has been considered as an obvious potential link with feminist literature (Picchio 1992). An approach closer to Post Keynesian economics, inspired by Sraffa's (1960) own treatment, is to take the profit rate as given, possibly determined by the interest rate and thus highlighting the relevance of financialization in contemporary capitalism. A third hypothesis, embraced for example by Sylos Labini, is that either of the given variables is itself variable; whether it is given or variable depends on the historical specificity of the society we wish to analyze. This last approach is obviously the closest to institutional economics.

Finally, the exogenous givens of Sraffa's systems, be they explicit or implicit, concern not only distribution but also technology. This point is especially relevant to the extent that the definition of industries, outputs, and input coefficients implicitly define 'productive' and 'unproductive' labor, as will be discussed in the next section.

The price of omissions

As with 'natural,' the adjective 'productive' has not been a value-free term in the history of economic thought. Smith's critique of the physiocrats' assumption that only agricultural labor is productive is well known. Yet, Smith too struggled with the concept of productive labor. Until today, it is fair to say that contemporary heterodox schools do not have a shared understanding of what 'productive' means. From the point of view of price theory one definition is that only the labor that contributes to the production of surplus value should be considered as productive. This may or may not encompass all labor exerted in society, depending on one's conceptualization of some aspects that are often at the margins of the pre-analytical vision of the market system, even though they involve growing shares of the population. Thus, from a Marxian perspective all wage labor involved in capitalist production (though possibly not in the sphere of circulation) should be considered productive. Evidently, this may exclude non-wage labor or employment in non-capitalist sectors of the economy.

From a Sraffian perspective, even though it obviously depends on production coefficients and output levels, each industry's productivity can only be computed given the distributive variables and production prices (because the means of production and outputs are heterogeneous quantities). That is to say, every industry's productivity depends on that of other industries. In this perspective, more relevant concepts are the viability and/or self-reproducibility of an industry, and thus all labor that contributes to the economic system's reproduction and accumulation should be considered as productive. A further complication in both the Marxian and the Sraffian approaches is that, as explained in the previous section, natural and production prices are *regulating* prices—that is, they are not the selling prices of every firm in an industry and not even necessarily of any firm. Rather, regulating prices connote what is 'socially necessary'—that is, the values taken as a reference point by the capitalists for their new investments. Thus, even in capitalist production there is 'waste,' bearing unproductive work to the extent that not all firms adopt the socially necessary technique of production at all times. Waste is all the more relevant under non-competitive market conditions, when capitalist firms incur non-socially necessary expenditures such as the costs of marketing, advertising, etc. (Sylos Labini [1956] 1962; Baran & Sweezy 1966).

Exceptions or variants of the above definition of productive labor are found in both mainstream and heterodox economic literature. Austrians, adopting a marketplace vision of the economy, consider all employed labor as productive, because all labor produces *value in use*. Post Keynesians define productivity on the basis of value added rather than surplus labor, even though many Post Keynesians consider finance as 'unproductive.'

Ultimately, all models (and even non-formalized theories) must include an infinite number of *ceteris paribus* clauses, since no one-to-one theoretical mapping of reality is possible. What is kept out of the analysis is an indication of which factors are considered to be of secondary or no relevance to the determination of a certain phenomenon. Thus, the industries or sectors that are ignored by price theory imply that certain kinds of work are deemed of secondary relevance to the production of surplus value and/or the reproduction of the economy—they are implicitly assumed to be unproductive work. From this point of view, at least three elements that are usually excluded (or only included in the *ceteris paribus* clauses) seem to deserve a closer investigation than has so far been done in extant literature on price theory.

A first element is the public sector. Its usual exclusion from price theory may be due to implicit hypotheses of 'first approximation' in formal models. But at the conceptual level it confirms the prejudice that publicly provided goods and services are deemed to be irrelevant for the production of surplus value, the accumulation of capital, and the reproduction of society (contra, see Corsi & D'Ippoliti 2013).

A second element is the financial sector. Its characteristic exclusion from the analysis of prices cannot be considered as an acceptable approximation, because the financial sector necessarily affects the interest rate and possibly the profit rate (and the wage rate), therefore the value of the surplus. Employment in the financial sector may be considered unproductive if finance is considered to belong to the circulation or the consumption sphere (Barba & de Vivo 2012). Some assume a 'banking sector' that earns the same rate of profit as all other industries, which then determines an interest rate that is conceptualized as the price of banks' output (Shaikh 2016). Further complications arise from the consideration of who pays and who receives interest payments, with interest alternatively considered as a deduction from the pool of profits or an internal transfer among capitalists. Indeed, recent research shows that in a Sraffian system the impact of bank lending on the distribution of income can be non-trivial (Panico *et al.* 2012).

Finally, a third crucial element is unpaid labor, especially housework and unpaid care labor. The issue has obviously been raised by feminist economists. It should be noted again that the definition of productive and unproductive labor has systemic consequences for the definition and value of the product and of the surplus product, as well as for their distribution; thus this issue should be of general interest for all economists and cannot be ignored even on first approximation (Picchio 1992). If households are considered as productive because they are necessary for the reproduction of the system, several conceptual issues emerge, which have not yet found a definitive solution. According to Todorova (2009), it is possible to conceptualize unpaid work in terms of capitalist firms' payment to workers of a wage bill smaller than that which would grant the reproduction of the labor force, that is Todorova's 'warranted wage bill.' However, the attribution of a value to unpaid work (that is, the difference between the actual wage bill and the warranted wage bill) assumes that there is a common unit of measurement—that is, given the current heterodox approaches to price theory, a market value for unpaid work. The problem of comparability between paid and unpaid labor is solved within marginalist economics by tracing back both kinds of labor to their subjective value in use (disutility). But in the heterodox economic approaches, value, though defined differently by each school, is generally not a matter of individual appreciation: its definition is inherently related to the capitalist mode of production (be it labor values, prices of production, etc.). Thus, the introduction of a non-capitalist mode of production in the theoretical system calls for yet another redefinition of an appropriate concept and a measure of value, through which heterogeneous quantities pertaining to the different parts of the system (the capitalist and the non-capitalist) could be compared straightforwardly.

Folbre (1982) finds such a common unit of measurement in the 'labor embodied' measure of value, on the grounds that the concept of 'socially necessary labor' may apply to both paid and unpaid work equally. Folbre's claim is that Marx considered the labor theory of value as only applicable to capitalist production because in that case competition eliminates inefficient producers; however, it can be assumed that other social forces may induce households to produce efficiently too. Thus in her view establishing a clear meaning of 'socially necessary household labor' is required. Besides the acceptance of this specific approach, it is noteworthy here that this procedure drastically modifies the very *concepts* of 'labor embodied' and 'value.'

Prices and quantities

One last open issue is the relationship between prices and quantities. This is perhaps the most complicated and controversial of the four issues considered here. It is virtually impossible to adequately summarize the vast number of positions and related issues in a single chapter, since the issue at stake spans from economic methodology to the history of economic thought, to formal models. Indeed, heterodox economists' views vary on the level at which the link (if any) between prices and quantities should be sought.

At the macroeconomic level, new interpretations of Marxian economics take quantities into account in the determination of labor values (Bellofiore 2012). Similarly, in the Sraffian literature, Pasinetti developed his model of structural dynamics, which considers the interplay of effective demand and production prices, before the publication of Sraffa (1960) and later further developed it in Pasinetti (1981). Conversely, Roncaglia & Tonveronachi (2014) are skeptical about the search for an all-encompassing formal model of the whole economy; rather they argue for the usefulness of Keynes' 'short causal chains' in economic modeling, and the opportunity to limit the search for compatibility between models at the conceptual level.

The approach looking for (and requiring) conceptual compatibility without a necessary formal compatibility inevitably produces less elegant and comprehensive models, but it allows room for (conceptual) integration of several disparate approaches.[8] However, many heterodox economists maintain that seeking theoretical integration at the formal modeling level (as for example attempted by Lee & Jo 2011) is necessary to establish a consistent theoretical alternative to the mainstream.

With regard to Marshallian 'partial equilibrium,' two main issues arise. The first is the role of demand and the associated issue of economies of scale, obviously relevant in Post Keynesian literature, for example. In general, classical political economists did not ignore the role of demand. Not only did they consider demand variations as a cause of continuous, transitory market perturbations, as in Adam Smith's gravitation metaphor, but they also perceived a systematic nexus between prices and demand. For example J.-B. Say noticed that as the price of a commodity increases, the number of consumers who can afford to buy it falls (Chapter 21, by Corsi & Guarini in this volume). Similarly J. S. Mill, incorrectly accused of having 'corrupted' the classical theory of value, highlighted that if firms buy their means of production in advance of production and sales, and if they face a financial constraint, then as the price of a means of production increases, firms will demand less of it (without implying substitutability between various means of production; see D'Ippoliti 2011). These insights are a long shot from a demand-and-supply theory of the determination of market prices, which is founded on a completely different pre-analytical vision and a formal model of market clearing based on supply and demand *curves*.

The second issue that arises at the industry and/or firm level is the relation between values, or natural or production prices, and firms' *pricing* procedures. For historical reasons, in the literature the need to establish a clear connection between the two has been explicitly linked to the reciprocal relation of Sraffian and Post Keynesian economics (Lavoie 2011). But the connection is relevant for Marxian economics and other approaches as well. For example, Post Keynesian economists tend to consider prices as determined by a mark-up on costs (Lee 1998). This is only compatible with Sraffa's production prices—when interpreted as long-run positions—if by costs we imply the 'normal costs' that are associated with the best technology in the industry and a 'normal' degree of capacity utilization, and if the mark-up comprises a competitively determined 'pure remuneration of capital' that cannot be fixed independently by the firms but has to relate to the economic system as a whole (Aspromourgos 2004).

More research on these analytical constraints is surely warranted, but once again it seems appropriate to draw attention to the need for mutual conceptual compatibility. For example, Sylos Labini ([1956] 1962) and in the Marxian tradition Baran & Sweezy (1966) raised the issue that all-pervading oligopolistic or monopolistic market forms are not just a partial equilibrium issue: they have pervasive systemic consequences (for example on the pace and diffusion of technological progress). This view is patently at odds with the long-run conception of production prices, based on the notion of free entry and exit from an industry. The degree to which the two conceptions can be reconciled, for example with the addiction of an exogenously determined 'extra-profit' vector that is dependent on firms' market power, is still a matter of controversy.

In short, the link between theories of prices and theories of output levels directly calls into question how best to conceptualize the general pre-analytical vision described above. Thus, issues such as whether and how the same vision can represent different historical varieties of capitalism—for example, the competitive, oligopolistic, and money-manager stages of capitalism—become crucial.

Recent developments in the objective approach

By way of conclusion, it seems fitting to briefly describe a recent stream of literature spinning off from the debates on price theory. For several reasons, mainstream economics has increasingly become a field of applied statistics with increasingly less attention to economic concepts. By the same token we observe an empirical turn in heterodox studies on price theory. Institutional constraints such as journal and department rankings or hiring and promotion procedures may explain this trend. But possibly new computational possibilities and theoretical reasons are relevant factors too. As is well known, the Cambridge capital controversies address the theoretical inconsistency of marginalist economic theory. Immediately thereafter, mainstream economists ignored the results of that debate often on the grounds of lack of empirical evidence (or even empirical relevance, from the mainstream viewpoint; see Cohen & Harcourt 2003). Thus, some Marxian and Sraffian economists may deem it necessary to continue their critique on this new level.

In the new empirical turn, at least two strands of literature should be distinguished. One may be labeled a positivist research program, looking at the data in order to falsify and/or compare theories. Thus, statistical investigations of the empirical relevance of paradoxes in the marginalist capital theory increasingly make use of input-output tables (for a review see Schefold 2016).[9] Similarly, the transformation problem has been investigated by trying to measure how much prices diverge from labor values (for example, Shaikh 2016). Perhaps the most copious branch of this literature is devoted to the empirical investigation of Marx's laws of tendency of capitalism, in particular that of the falling rate of profit (see Basu 2015). The other strand of literature tries to apply the theory in search of a quantification of the main variables involved and/or a refinement of the theory itself by means of induction from the data (see, for example, Mariolis & Tsoulfidis 2015).

In all these exercises, a crucial difficulty is finding an acceptable empirical quantity with which to measure, or at least approximate, the theoretical variables. For example, Basu (2015) describes how 'Marxian national accounts' have to be produced before empirical analyses of Marxian theory can be carried out. Similarly, as Shaikh (2016) notes, the use of time-series data may be tricky because the notion of reproduction of the system is instantaneous—that is, the surplus (and thus profits) should be measured using both input and output prices of the same period, whereas firms (and national accounts) measure profits on the basis of historic costs.

Most efforts are usually made to correct national accounting aggregates, for example transforming value added into surplus value by deducting workers' necessary expenses. However, crucial difficulties lie in the quantification of prices and/or values too. For example, since Phillips (1966) it is obvious that waste (in the sense of non-socially necessary expenditure) should be deducted too. Moreover, since different theoretical approaches embrace different concepts of regulating prices, they need different empirical methods. For example, the straightforward use of observed input-output matrixes proposed as if they represented Sraffian systems is highly problematic, because it implies the assumption that the average technology used in each industry is the best technology given prices and income distribution, as well as several other assumptions concerning fixed capital and capacity utilization. Evidently, acceptance of these assumptions depends on one's opinion on the concept of long-run positions and of the convergence process, and those Sraffians who withhold the snapshot view will consider empirical testing of the theory virtually impossible.

In conclusion, the burgeoning empirical literature on price theory is showing great potential for cross-fertilization and even integration across several heterodox approaches. But as is the case of the methodological and theoretical literatures, conceptual, analytical, and empirical hurdles still remain. Given these cognitive costs and the obviously lower professional rewards, if marginalism was correct, all (utility-maximizing) economists would prefer to be mainstream.

Acknowledgments

I am grateful to Scott Carter, Lynne Chester, Massimo Cingolani, Tae-Hee Jo, Maria Cristina Marcuzzo, Alessandro Roncaglia, and Bertram Schefold for comments and criticisms on previous drafts of this chapter. All remaining errors are mine.

Notes

1 Recent surveys on the topic may be found, for example, in the June 2015 Symposium of the *Review of Radical Political Economics*; the 2012 Special Issue, Vol. 47, No. 2, of the *Cambridge Journal of Economics*; or the three volumes edited by Levrero, Palumbo, and Stirati (Levrero *et al.* 2013).
2 Most of the terms and conceptualization used in this chapter are drawn from Roncaglia (2005). However, in several cases historians of economic thought have not yet found a definitive agreement on the interpretation of the thought of several scholars cited here, and even heterodox scholars may disagree with some of the interpretations put forward in what follows.

3 This conceptualization of price best applies to Hayek. The early Austrians (such as Böhm-Bawerk) and later Hicks were rather concerned with the role of prices in establishing the necessary link between economic activities through time. The emphasis on the methodological and analytical role of time is fully pertinent to the theory of value, and recognized as such by many heterodox approaches (see Cohen & Harcourt 2003).

4 Similarly, prices increasingly play an overall different, purely methodological role in mainstream microeconomics, most clearly highlighted by the 'Chicago price theory' (Weyl 2015) and its burgeoning empirical applications. Here prices are a mere mathematical formulation with no specific conceptual meaning: they descend from the conceptualization of any social issue as an optimization problem, in which a market price or a shadow price is mathematically the adjustment variable leading to equilibrium. Accordingly, there can be 'implicit' prices for anything, irrespective of the assumption of actual or potential exchanges.

5 From this point of view, Mirowski (1989) defines the objective approach as a 'substance' theory of value since it conceptualizes value as a property of the commodities (and labor power) exchanged. This view best fits the Marxian approach, while several Sraffian economists would object to it and, instead, conceptualize exchange-value as a property of the whole system of production.

6 However, even if prices are measures of *relative* value in exchange, their changes affect the *absolute* size of aggregate values because they denote changes in the technology and/or in the distribution of income (Shaikh 2016).

7 It thus retains relevance for the quantification, for example, of the surplus. However, its role as a theory of prices is lost.

8 For example, Pasinetti (1981) is bound to take a more restrictive approach, founding his analysis on the view that not only production prices but also the distributive variables are 'natural' in the sense that they are independent of social institutions and can be determined at the level of pure logic: a position that obviously runs counter to institutionalist insights.

9 These exercises typically find few examples of capital paradoxes, and gave birth to a literature dedicated to the explanation of the supposed limited empirical relevance of the Cambridge critique of the marginalist theory of value. However, to some extent these results are driven by the very data chosen since, as shown by Bharadwaj (1970), the maximum number of switching points between two hypothetical systems is equal to the number of different basic commodities (without double counting).

References

Andrews, D. 2015. 'Natural price and the long run: Alfred Marshall's misreading of Adam Smith.' *Cambridge Journal of Economics*, 39 (1): 265–279.

Aspromourgos, T. 2004. 'Sraffian research programmes and unorthodox economics.' *Review of Political Economy*, 16 (2): 179–206.

Baran, P.A. & Sweezy, P. 1966. *Monopoly Capital: An Essay on the American Economic and Social Order.* New York: Monthly Review Press.

Barba, A. & de Vivo, G. 2012. 'An 'unproductive labour' view of finance.' *Cambridge Journal of Economics*, 36 (6): 1479–1496.

Basu, D. 2015. A selective review of recent quantitative empirical research in Marxist political economy. University of Massachusetts Amherst, Department of Economics Working Paper 2015–05. Available from https://www.umass.edu/economics/publications/2015-05.pdf [Accessed August 30, 2016]

Bharadwaj, K. 1970. 'On the maximum number of switches between two production systems.' *Schweizerische Zeitschrift für Volkwirthschaft und Statistik*, 106 (4): 409–429.

Bellofiore, R. 2012. 'The 'tiresome objector' and Old Moor: a renewal of the debate on Marx after Sraffa based on the unpublished material at the Wren Library.' *Cambridge Journal of Economics*, 36 (6): 1385–1399.

Braudel, F. 1967. *Civilisation matérielle, économie et capitalisme, XVe–XVIIIe siècle. Vol. 1: Les structures du quotidien.* Paris: Colin.

Cohen, A.J. & Harcourt, G.C. 2003. 'Retrospectives: whatever happened to the Cambridge capital theory controversies?' *The Journal of Economic Perspectives*, 17 (1): 199–214.

Corsi, M. & D'Ippoliti, C. 2013. 'The productivity of the public sector: a classical view.' *PSL Quarterly Review*, 66 (267): 403–434.

D'Ippoliti, C. 2011. *Economics and Diversity.* London and New York: Routledge.

D'Ippoliti, C. & Roncaglia, A. 2015. 'Heterodox economics and the history of economic thought,' *in*: T.-H. Jo & Z. Todorova (eds.), *Advancing the Frontiers of Heterodox Economics: Essays in Honor of Frederic S. Lee.* London: Routledge, 21–38.

Folbre, N. 1982. 'Exploitation comes home: a critique of the Marxian theory of family labour.' *Cambridge Journal of Economics*, 6 (4): 317–329.

Hayek, F.A. 1948. 'The meaning of competition,' *in*: *Individualism and Economic Order.* Chicago: University of Chicago Press, 92–106.

Jo, T.-H. 2016. 'What if there are no conventional price mechanisms?' *Journal of Economic Issues*, 50 (2): 327–344.

Lavoie, M. 2011. 'Should Sraffian economics be dropped out of the Post-Keynesian school?' *Économies et Sociétés*, 44 (7): 1027–1059.

Lee, F.S. 1998. *Post Keynesian Price Theory.* Cambridge: Cambridge University Press.

Lee, F.S. & Jo, T.-H. 2011. 'Social surplus approach and heterodox economics.' *Journal of Economic Issues*, 45 (4): 857–875.

Levrero, E.S., Palumbo, A., & Stirati, A. 2013. *Sraffa and the Reconstruction of Economic Theory: Volume One.* Basingstoke, UK: Palgrave Macmillan.

Mariolis, T. & Tsoulfidis, L. 2015. Capital theory 'paradoxes' and paradoxical results: resolved or continued? MPRA Working Paper 68214. Available from https://mpra.ub.uni-muenchen.de/68214/ [Accessed August 30, 2016]

Mill, J.S. [1848] 1871. *Principles of Political Economy, With Some of Their Applications to Social Philosophy.* London: Parker.

Mirowski, P. 1989. *More Heat than Light: Economics as Social Physics, Physics as Nature's Economics.* Cambridge: Cambridge University Press.

Panico, C., Pinto, A., & Anyul, M. P. 2012. 'Income distribution and the size of the financial sector: a Sraffian analysis.' *Cambridge Journal of Economics*, 36 (6): 1455–1477.

Pasinetti, L.L. 1981. *Structural Change and Economic Growth: A Theoretical Essay on the Dynamics of the Wealth of Nations.* Cambridge: Cambridge University Press.

Phillips, J.D. 1966. 'Appendix: estimating the economic surplus,' *in*: P.A. Baran & P. Sweezy (eds.), *Monopoly Capital: An Essay on the American Economic and Social Order.* New York: Monthly Review Press, 369–391.

Picchio, A. 1992. *Social Reproduction: The Political Economy of the Labour Market.* Cambridge: Cambridge University Press.

Roncaglia, A. 2005. *The Wealth of Ideas: A History of Economic Thought.* Cambridge: Cambridge University Press.

Roncaglia, A. & Tonveronachi, M. 2014. 'Post-Keynesian, post-Sraffian economics: an outline,' *in*: D.B. Papadimitriou (ed.), *Contributions to Economic Theory, Policy, Development and Finance: Essays in Honor of Jan A. Kregel.* Basingstoke, UK: Palgrave Macmillan.

Schefold, B. 2016. Marx, the production function and the old neoclassical equilibrium: workable under the same assumptions? With an appendix on the likelihood of reswitching and of Wicksell effects. Centro Sraffa Working Paper 19. Available from http://www.centrosraffa.org/public/6c384fc3-ba7a-4b1d-858c-75db58468eec.pdf [Accessed August 30, 2016]

Schumpeter, J.A. 1954. *History of Economic Analysis*, edited by E. Boody Schumpeter. New York: Oxford University Press.

Shaikh, A. 2016. *Capitalism: Competition, Conflict, Crises.* New York: Oxford University Press.

Sraffa, P. 1960. *Production of Commodities by Means of Commodities.* Cambridge: Cambridge University Press.

Steedman, I. 1977. *Marx after Sraffa.* London: NLB.

Stiglitz, J. & Grossman, S. 1980. 'On the impossibility of informationally efficient markets.' *American Economic Review*, 70 (3): 393–408.

Sylos Labini, P. [1956] 1962. *Oligopoly and Technical Progress.* Cambridge, MA: Harvard University Press.

Todorova, Z. 2009. *Money and Households in a Capitalist Economy.* Cheltenham, UK: Edward Elgar.

Weyl, E.G. 2015. 'Price theory.' *Journal of Economic Literature*, forthcoming. Available from http://ssrn.com/abstract=2444233 [Accessed August 30, 2016]

9

Heterodox theories of distribution

Scott Carter

Introduction

Economists measure the distribution of income in two ways: the functional distribution of revenue or the size of the distribution of earnings. Functional distribution is older in economic theorizing as it appears in the classical notion of income shares to different economic classes.[1] Within the general framework of the classical model, classes are broadly defined by their private property relations in the production process of capitalist market economies. Workers own their laboring capacity and receive wages (W), landlords own non-produced and non-reproducible ('land') inputs and receive rent (R), and capitalists own the produced means of production and receive profits (Z); more advanced models include in the profit relation the interest rate and the role of finance generally. In aggregate, the sum of these distributed revenues is equal to the total national income:

National income (Y) = Wages (W) + Rents (R) + [Profits (Z) + Interest (*i*)]

The importance of the mechanisms (or 'laws') that determine distribution in classical theory is made explicit by David Ricardo in the first edition of *Principles of Political Economy* (1817), where he calls it the "principal problem in Political Economy" (Sraffa 1951: 5). This importance attached to income distribution received less attention from those at the forefront of the marginalist revolution, with perhaps Walras being the more thorough in developing the distributional aspects of the new marginal calculus (Sandmo 2014). With the development of marginal productivity theory in the 1890s, based on the same marginal principle as to utility demonstrated 20 years earlier, authors such as J.B. Clark, Knut Wicksell, and Philip Wicksteed among others were able to wed the diminishing margin of cultivation in Ricardian theory to the newly found theoretical apparatus (Sandmo 2014: 21–27). They developed a purported general theory of the determination of factor income shares by combining theories of productivity, value, and distribution under one theoretical rubric and methodology.

The shape of the size income distribution first appears with the work of Pareto in the 1890s (Persky 1992). Here the (ostensibly) same aggregate income considered in the analysis of functional distribution is now subject to a different conceptualization. Instead of the aggregate shares of various revenue streams to different classes, 'size distribution' considers the income stream that accrues to a set of individual units such as households, families, and individual people.

Pareto posited a 'law of distribution' that was fundamentally skewed. This means that equal portions of individuals receive different incomes, with 'less people' receiving 'more income,' and *vice versa*. Pareto drew this relation in terms of a linear downward sloping double logarithmic curve, which has been henceforth called the Pareto distribution (Persky 1992; Sandmo 2014). Pareto held that the skewed distribution was an empirical fact evident across diverse ranges of societies and peoples, and hence dependent on 'human nature,' which led to the view that any attempt to alter this otherwise naturally skewed distribution would result in failure and indeed backfire. Economists of the day who were critical of the view of policy ineffectiveness in altering the skewed income distribution (and the dangerous bedfellows politically that this brought to the surface) included Lorenz, Pigou, and Gini (Persky 1992: 187–188). Ever since, the relationship between functional and size distribution has remained a subject of controversy.

This chapter considers heterodox approaches to the problem of distribution and is organized into three sections. The section that follows this introduction discusses three heterodox theories of distribution: (i) classical and Marxian approaches, (ii) the Cambridge theories in both their 'physicalist' and 'monetary' expressions, and (iii) recent Neo-Kaleckian approaches. The section after considers theoretical resonances and connections between functional and size distribution which have recently become a cutting edge area of research in heterodox approaches, including advancements in econo-physics. The final section concludes.

Recent developments in heterodox theories

This section focuses on three mainstay heterodox theories of distribution. They are (i) the classical and Marxian theory, inclusive of significant Sraffian elements; (ii) the Cambridge theory, inclusive of the 'physicalist' natural rate of growth theory of profits as well as the rate of interest-infused monetary theory of profits; and (iii) the Neo-Kaleckian theory that develops the relationship between income distribution and aggregate demand and productive capacity. Broadly speaking the latter two theories are 'Post Keynesian' in the sense that the distribution parameter is closed from the output account side of the ledger, although this is less unequivocal in Neo-Kaleckian approaches as labor market struggle can play a role in the determination of the mark-up, leading to a certain degree of closure coming from the wage bargain (hence income account). Modern classical theories including Marxian primarily consider the wage bargain and/or the 'subsistence wage' to be the determining factors as regards systemic 'net' closure.

Classical and Marxian theory

One of the features of the classical model is the conception of 'normal' conditions that are assumed to govern systems characterized by free competition. Two illustrative (though not exhaustive) approaches along these lines are: (i) the surplus approach to value and distribution of the so-called 'Sraffian' school, developed for example by Garegnani (1984, 1987) and given analytical treatment in Kurz & Salvadori (1995); and (ii) the theory of regulating capital in Anwar Shaikh's (2016) development of the Marxian framework. In both approaches, classical causality is maintained and the closure of the system via the wage relation (specified differently in the different frameworks) runs *from* the profit rate *to* the rates of accumulation of capital and the investment of profit, with the nexus linking the two being the propensity to save and to accumulate profits.

The hallmark of the Sraffian approach is the 'long-period position,' where wages are determined (via various mechanisms) to some 'normal' level which in turn gives rise to 'normal' profits, the 'normal' prices of production, and the 'normal' utilization of capacity. This is termed the *fully adjusted situation* where the above 'normal' categories are adjusted to effective demand (Panico 2011: 168). It is important to emphasize that 'normality' does not necessitate full employment. The conditions that determine the normality tend also to ascribe uniformity in the rates of wages and profits under conditions of 'free competition' (Kurz & Salvadori 1995: 1–15).

Shaikh's (2016: 14–15, 259–326) approach to conditions of 'normality' conceives of the notion of 'regulating conditions' and the theory of 'real competition,' the latter conceived not as a game as in neoclassical perfect and imperfect competition but rather warfare as profit-seeking capitals adjust to the highest sustainable rate of return, termed the *regulating conditions*. The determination of the regulating conditions occurs from a complex mosaic of competitive processes at both the intra- and inter-industrial level. The basic mechanism is that within industries best-practice techniques—that are generally socially reproducible—determine the regulating capital of that industry, and these regulating conditions once identified become subject to competition across industries (Shaikh 1978, 1980, 2016; Botwinick 1993).

Classical closure of the distribution parameter from the wage-side means that wages are 'given' and profits a residual. The notion of a 'given' wage rate has a long history in political economy, going as far back at least to Quesnay and the Physiocratic school. The argument is basically that certain physiological, social, historical, and/or demographic conditions exist such that systemic social reproduction includes and ensures an 'efficient laboring class' (Levrero 2013: 92). The definition of what constitutes an 'efficient laboring class' is often a matter of interpretation, as is the necessary bundle of wage goods that brings this about. At one end of the theoretical spectrum is the iron-law of wages where the wage bundle is limited by the bare physiological existence of the workers, which is enforced by means of Malthusian–Ricardian demographic equilibrium of death and birth rates—a notion that Marx himself vehemently rejected (Baumol 1983; Levrero 2013; Shaikh 2016). At the other end of the spectrum there are sociological and historical theories that posit a relatively 'given' wage bundle that is above the bare minimum. And although the mechanisms and assumptions by which the 'given bundle' are proposed are physiological or socio-historical, what is common to both is the idea that the subsistence wage is determined by the price of the 'given'—that is non-market determined—bundle of wage goods (Levine 1988; Roncaglia 1988; Green 1991; Chiodi 2010; Bellofiore 2012, 2014; Levrero 2013; Giovannoni 2014; Shaikh 2016).

That the 'subsistence wage' is generally acknowledged to not refer to a biological minimum means that 'subsistence' is defined broadly to include the socio-historical conditions in the reproduction of the working class, and even here class struggle can play a role in influencing those broad conditions. Levrero (2013) discusses many disparate conditions affecting the level of real wages (see especially the figure on p. 101 and related discussion). He develops the thesis that the minimum wage is a function of the 'wage inherited from the past' and argues that workers' bargaining power determines whether the actual wage will be greater than this minimum wage. Workers' bargaining power is described as a function of the conditions in the labor market (often proxied by the unemployment rate), the level of worker organization, and the general social and political climate, where

> all . . . have some degree of autonomy in determining the strength of the workers in the wage bargain, and thus in determining if the wage rate will be higher or equal to the subsistence wage – the wage inherited from the past, and which forms a minimum floor in wage-bargaining.
>
> *Levrero 2013: 101*

A recent approach to the specification of the wage in terms of classical closure is given in Shaikh (2016: 638–676). The socio-historical minimum is assumed to be some constant portion (α)

of the productivity of labor, leaving the remainder $(1 - \alpha)$ as the maximal surplus wage equal to the productivity of labor (y^*). The surplus wage is a different constant proportion α' between the minimal subsistence wage and labor productivity (the subscript 't' refers to time):

$$w_t^* = \left[(\alpha_t) + \alpha_t'(1 - \alpha_t) \right] \cdot y_t^* \qquad (9.1)$$

The bracketed term is the class struggle parameter. It consists of the 'subsistence' portion (α) out of total productivity (y), which represents the 'given bundle' determined by the social and historical conditions necessary for the reproduction of the working class, and a portion, $\alpha'(1 - \alpha)$, that represents the surplus wage or share out of net product above the minimum wage. This is depicted in the 'truncated' version of the wage share distribution schedule shown in Figure 9.1. The parameters of class struggle include the length and intensity of the working day, the level of working-class organization in making effective changes, and the disciplining mechanism of the unemployment rate (Bellofiore 2014; Petri 2014; Shaikh 2016).

Various forces influence each of the share values on the vertical axis. The lower limit of the subsistence wage itself can vary, as can the relationship with the surplus wage.

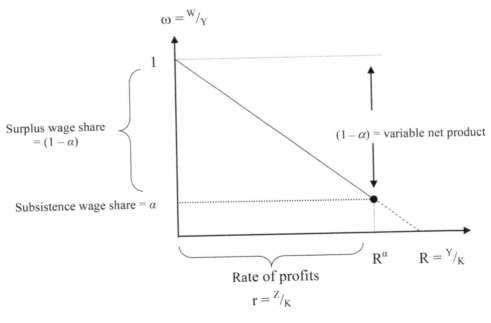

Where: $\omega = {}^W/_Y$ = wage share in national income
$(1 - \alpha)$ = Surplus portion of wage share (variable)
α = Subsistence portion of wage share (floor)
$r = {}^Z/_K$ = Range of actual profit rate
R^α = Maximum profit rate at subsistence wage share
$R = {}^Y/_K$ = net output-capital ratio = maximum possible rate of profit.

Figure 9.1 Wage share distribution schedule for subsistence and surplus wages

The disciplining effect of the unemployment rate, or Marx's reserve army of labor, is generally a feature of Marxian-inspired models beginning with Goodwin's (1967) famous article (Rowthorn 1981, 1999; Levine 1988; Bhaduri & Marglin 1990; Green 1991; Glyn 1995, 2009; Levrero 2013; Shaikh 2016). The specification regarding the unemployment rate is the basis of the classical wage curve (Blanchflower & Oswald 1990; Card 1995; Shaikh 2016: 648–650) where the wage rate exhibits an inverse relation to the rate of unemployment.

This determination of income distribution for classical closure on the wage-side relates to the Marxian reserve army of labor story in a two-stage process. In the first instance, social conditions, norms, and class struggle help to shape the particular value of the class struggle parameter, which establishes the share of wages in productivity (Green 1991). This establishes the overall regime of distribution which following Marx's reserve army idea will be associated with a (dynamic-stable) regime of distribution where 'short-run' changes in the wage share are cyclically associated with changes in the unemployment rate. When the labor market is 'tight' the actual rate of unemployment is less than the critical rate and the wage share rises, and when the labor market is 'loose' the actual rate of unemployment is greater than the critical rate and the wage share falls. Leftward or backward shifts in the classical wage curve and/or counter-clockwise rotating shifts indicate decreased worker strength. In this case, a new regime and hence a new wage curve has occurred (Shaikh 2016: 667). There has been a growing interest in Goodwin-type models, including extensions of the model to consider investments and aggregate demand (Skott 1989b), empirical tests across OEDC countries (Harvie 2000), and issues in labor market conflict (Rezai 2011; Palley 2012).

Cambridge theory

One of the core tenets of Cambridge theory is the causality running *to* distributional relations (such as profitability, the profit rate, the wage share, and/or wage rate) *from* some other source. Within this tradition there have been two distinct approaches as to what constitutes that source. The first approach is the 'physicalist' growth-theoretic approach and the vast literature and rich discussion around the Cambridge equation where the rate of profit is determined by the so-called 'natural rate of growth' or investment-capital ratio divided by the propensity to save out of profit-type revenue (s_z). The second approach is the 'monetary' interest rate-theoretic approach that is built on the cryptic statement made by Piero Sraffa (1960: 33) in §44 of his *Production of Commodities by Means of Commodities*, that the money rate of interest determines the profit rate. It is important to emphasize that in both approaches the profit rate is the dependent variable in terms of how the system closes. Once the profit rate is determined from outside of the revenue account it then acts upon the wage element, and (surplus) wages become a residual.

The growth-theoretic approach accepts the causality proposed by Keynes' widow's cruse theory of profits (see Kurz & Salvadori 1995; Pasinetti 2000) introduced in the *Treatise on Money*. The basic idea is that the investment behavior of the capitalist class determines profitability, hence output account relations determine those of the income account. By reversing classical causality, Cambridge theory introduced the role of aggregate and/or effective demand in the determinants of income distribution.

Kaldor (1956) and Pasinetti (1962) developed the basic framework for this approach initially within conditions of full employment and later in models that fully adjusted in the presence of unemployment. Setting the propensities to save out of wage-type and profit-type revenue as

s_w and s_z respectively, and assuming that $0 < s_w < s_z < 1$, the standard derivation of the profit share and profit rate is as follows:

$$\text{Profit share: } (1 - \omega) = \frac{Z}{Y} = \frac{1}{s_z - s_w}\left(\frac{I}{Y}\right) - \frac{s_w}{s_z - s_w} \tag{9.2}$$

$$\text{Profit rate: } r = \frac{Z}{K} = \frac{1}{s_z - s_w}\left(\frac{I}{K}\right) - \frac{s_w}{s_z - s_w}\left(\frac{Y}{K}\right) \tag{9.3}$$

where ω is the wage share, Y aggregate income, Z aggregate profits, I aggregate investments, and K the value of the capital stock. For both the profit share and the profit rate, the investment relation is the determining force; for the profit share it is the investment-output ratio $\left(\frac{I}{Y}\right)$, and for the profit rate it is the rate of capital accumulation $\left(\frac{I}{K}\right)$ (called the natural rate of growth) under the assumption of a constant output-capital ratio ($\rho = \frac{Y}{K}$, equal to the maximum rate of profit).

The determination of the profit share constitutes the model's 'theory' of distribution, such that the profit share is endogenous and in line with the level of investment spending. Equation (9.2) is the Cambridge equation when workers save; when workers do not save then $s_w = 0$ and Equation (9.2) reduces to the famous form in which the Cambridge equation is mostly known:

$$\text{Cambridge equation: } r = \frac{Z}{K} = \frac{1}{s_z}\left(\frac{I}{K}\right) = \frac{g_K}{s_z} \tag{9.4}$$

In Baranzini & Mari's (2009) exhaustive survey of Cambridge models, the Cambridge equation is shown to be robust in a variety of different scenarios in which different conditions are relaxed and/or introduced. Perhaps the most important is the relaxation of the full employment assumption in lieu of the possibly less than full employment 'fully adjusted situation' associated with normal prices and quantities (Pasinetti 1981: 44). Also important is the development of steady-state growth models compatible with those of both full employment and fully adjusted growth (Bortis 1993).

Among the extensions to the Cambridge theory, one is the inclusion of differentiated interest rates on the wealth of different classes. The upshot is that two rates of return manifest: (i) the rate of profit, which is the rate of return of capitalists' saving; and (ii) the rate of interest by which "is meant the rate at which the workers place their savings into the hands of capitalists" (Baranzini & Mari 2009: 6). Inclusion of the monetary sector here is expressed in terms of portfolio choice where workers' savings take the form of bonds issued by firms (Palley 1996, 2002). Park (2006) extends this framework by relaxing the assumption that workers' consumption is limited by the wage bill and accordingly introduces a credit-money system.

Another extension made to the Cambridge model is the introduction of the analysis of the public sector with respect to the aggregate propensities to consume, save, accumulate, and run budget deficits or surpluses. The works by Steedman (1972) and Fleck & Domenghino (1987) incorporate government spending and direct and indirect taxation and thereby arrive "at a more generalised version of the Cambridge equation according to which the workers' propensity to save determines . . . the steady state of income distribution" (Baranzini & Mari 2009: 13). There has also been recent literature that relaxes the assumption of exogenous savings propensities of the various classes (Baranzini & Mari 2009: 22–23). Here a differentiated accumulation structure is posited, where workers or wage earners generally accumulate wealth accrued over the life-cycle and capitalists or profit earners adopt a bequest motive approach and accumulate wealth inter-generationally (Wolff 1988; Teixeira *et al.* 1998; Palley 2010).

Monetary approaches develop the cryptic comment in §44 of Sraffa (1960) that the money rates of interest determine the profit rate in monetary theories of distribution (Garegnani 1979; Panico 1980, 1985, 1988a, b; Pivetti 1985, 1991; Panico *et al.* 2012; Bellofiore 2014; Deleplace 2014; Biermann 2015). Here the interest rate is the independent variable, which determines the profit rate and accordingly closes the distribution parameter. The mechanisms that determine the interest rate range from monetary authorities' interventions (Garegnani 1979; Pivetti 1991) to the presence of financial instruments (Panico 1985, 1988a, b). Recently Deleplace (2014) and Biermann (2015) have advanced a thesis similar to Lawlor & Horn (1992) that the rate of interest which determines the profit rate in Sraffa are the commodity own-rates of interest measured in money.

Neo-Kaleckian theory

In the Neo-Kaleckian branch of Post Keynesian economics the influence of distribution on aggregate and effective demand emerges as the paramount issue (Bhaduri & Marglin 1990; Taylor 2004; Barbosa-Filho & Taylor 2006; Nikoforos & Foley 2012). Neo-Kaleckian theory generally posits imperfect competition in the product market and conflict in the labor market, and the two are thought to interact in the expression of the mark-up (Lavioe 2014; Palley 2016), with simple versions the mark-up is written directly as a function of the profit share.[2]

The Neo-Kaleckian school is known for its usage of the Bhaduri-Marglin (1990) (B&M) model although earlier variants of the original model do abound (Rowthorn 1981; Dutt 1990). The B&M model is robust in conceptualizing the growth and distribution process, and provides explanation for a variety of different demand, productivity, and distributive regimes. The key relationship regarding the role of demand and distribution has to do with the slope of the steady-state effective demand IS curve and its intersection with the 'distributive curve' drawn in the profit share-capacity utilization space (Taylor 2004; Barbosa-Fihlo & Taylor 2006; Nikoforos & Foley 2012).

The IS schedule is the relationship between distributive shares and capacity on the 'demand' side. The schedule is derived under the assumption that an excess of investment over saving increases the level of capacity, the latter defined as the ratio of actual to potential output $\left(u = \dfrac{Y_{actual}}{Y_{potential}} \right)$. This means that the change in capacity is equal to the change in the investment-saving balance. Saving and investment are written as functions of the wage share ω and capacity utilization rate (u): $I = I(\omega; u)$ and $S = S(\omega; u)$. The IS curve is expressed as the change in capacity with respect to the change in income distribution, as follows:

$$\frac{du}{d\omega} = -\frac{I_\omega - S_\omega}{I_u - S_u} \tag{9.5}$$

where the subscripts denote partial derivatives.

The denominator in Equation (9.5) is negative "under the . . . *Keynesian stability condition* . . . that saving is more responsive than investment to a change in output" (Nikoforos & Foley 2012: 203, emphasis in original), meaning that the sign of the numerator becomes of interest. If saving reacts more than investment to a change in the wage share, the numerator is positive, meaning that as the wage share rises the amount of capacity utilization also rises, thereby increasing output and aggregate demand. Here the demand regime is *wage-led*. The opposite happens in a *profit-led* demand regime, when the numerator is negative. Here redistribution to wages decreases the capacity utilization rate thereby decreasing output and aggregate demand; or alternatively expressed in terms of the profit share, the distribution towards profits leads to higher capacity, output, and demand. In terms of the schedule, a wage-led demand regime will have an upward sloping IS curve in the wage share-capacity space and a profit-led demand regime will have a downward sloping IS curve in that same space (Taylor 2004; Barbosa-Fihlo & Taylor 2006; Nikoforos & Foley 2012; Lavoie 2014).

The distributive curve considers the relationship between distributive shares and capacity on the utilization or 'production' side. It can also have a positive or negative slope, and in fact Nikoforos & Foley (2012) show evidence of non-linearity in a u-shaped distributive curve, such that it has both slopes at different levels of capacity. The distributive curve expresses the change in the wage share given a change in capacity utilization as the ratio of the difference in the rates of real wage and productivity growth:

$$\frac{d\omega}{du} = -\frac{\hat{w}_u - \hat{y}_u}{\hat{w}_u - \hat{y}_u} \tag{9.6}$$

where $\hat{w}_j$ is the rate of change of real wages given a change in j, $\hat{y}_j$ is the rate of change of productivity given a change in j, and $j = u, \omega$.

A positive distributive schedule indicates that the wage share increases with increases in capacity utilization and this scenario relates to wage-inflation and the profit squeeze. A negative distributive schedule is the case of price inflation and forced saving. Combining the IS demand schedule with the distributive curve yields the Neo-Kaleckian equilibrium situation.

The strength of the B&M model is the ability to handle a variety of different scenarios under the same analytical setting, as positive and negative slopes of both the IS and the distributive schedules in the ω-u space are possible. Neo-Kaleckian growth and distribution theory has garnered much use from the B&M model as there has been an explosion of studies that are both theoretical and empirical in exploring the robustness and verifiability of the wage-led and profit-led demand thesis. The main result includes the possibility of an economy to be in either wage-led or profit-led growth regimes, and the regime which dominates an economy is mostly an empirical and historical question.

Wage-led demand growth holds when increases in the wage share lead to increases in the capacity utilization rate, thereby increasing output and aggregate demand, and profit-led demand growth is said to hold when the wage share increases lead to a decrease in those indicators (Barbosa-Filho & Taylor 2006; Hein & Vogel 2008; Stockhammer *et al.* 2009). To these wage- and profit-led demand effects Lavoie & Stockhammer (2012) add supply-side productivity effects. Wage-led productivity growth is defined as increases in productivity growth when there is an increase in wage growth.[3] Profit-led productivity growth is the opposite case, when the growth in wages causes productivity growth to slow down (Lavoie & Stockhammer 2012: 16). The empirical literature inspired by tests of the B&M model has been quite fruitful. Lavoie & Stockhammer (2012: 18–20) report summary results for 12 studies[4] from 1995 to 2012 that have tested the B&M model for a total of seven advanced economies.[5] The results reported by the majority of studies find domestic wage-led demand regimes with increasingly profit-led demand once international trade is included.

The functional-size distribution nexus

Heterodox economics in the classical, Marxian, and Post Keynesian traditions at the theoretical level has mostly focused on functional distribution, although the personal distribution of income is becoming a growing area of interest for heterodox economists. A recent empirical study extending the Neo-Kaleckian framework to personal distribution is Carvahlo & Rezai (2016). They begin with the observation of a shift in functional distribution from wage to profit revenue over the past 20 years, and this had been associated with redistribution towards high-income earners in the size distribution of the wage component. In this framework, size distribution affects functional distribution and, through the latter, also regimes of demand according to Neo-Kaleckian theory. The question becomes one of determining the influence on aggregate demand of increased inequality in wage income. Size distribution is incorporated into the B&M model where aggregate income is determined by independent investment and saving decisions. The investment function depends positively on capacity utilization, the profit rate, as well as an autonomous component of 'animal spirits.' It is the savings function that Carvahlo & Rezai (2016) make dependent on size distribution and the focus here is on the wage portion of income broadly defined (Bowles & Boyer 1995; Taylor 2004; Barbosa-Filho & Taylor 2006; Tavani & Vasudevan 2014). The distribution of revenue among wage earners influences the propensity to save out of wages, with a decrease in the wage share (increase in the profit share) as the causal mechanism for the increased inequality across the spectrum of wage earners (Carvahlo & Rezai 2016: 495).

Different sectors and different classes

Galbraith (1998, 2011), Lavoie (2009), and Palley (2005, 2014, 2016) develop theoretical relationships between functional and size distribution. In Galbraith, for example, the personal dimension in functional distribution turns on the dichotomy of the macroeconomy in terms of different sectors—the consumption sector, the service sector, and the knowledge sector. So sub-aggregating the macroeconomy allows for analysis of the income distribution within each sector according to its specific economic, competitive, structural, etc. conditions. This leads Galbraith (2011: 38–39) to conclude that "we thus have a macroeconomic theory of the evolution of personal income distribution, according to which inequality varies with the movements of aggregate demand, differentiated by sector."

Lavoie (2009, 2014) and Palley (2005, 2014, 2016) consider the personal-functional relationship to be related to the 'overhead work' and income streams consisting of wage-type and profit-type revenues accrued to a third economic class in the system. The possibility of income consisting of both wage-type and profit-type revenues has been discussed ever since Pasinetti's (1962) extension of Kaldor's Keynesian growth and distribution model. Palley (2005, 2014, 2016) develops the B&M model to include a measure of income inequality defined as the ratio of capitalists' to workers' income, each of whom are able to garner both wage- and profit-type revenues. Key to this relationship is the structure of ownership in the accrual of the respective income streams, denoted in the present context as θ_{ij}, read as the ownership share of individual agent i in the income stream of type j, where i = workers and capitalists and j = wage-type and profit-type revenue. It is important—with the extension from the functional to the personal—to keep the individual agents (workers versus capitalists) distinct from the revenue-flows (wages versus profits) so that mapping their interaction is as transparent as possible.

Scott Carter

Income to laborers (Y_L) and income to capitalists (Y_K) are the sums of their respective profit-type (Z) and wage-type (W) income:

Capitalists' income: $Y_K = \theta_{KW} W + \theta_{KZ} Z$ (9.7a)

Workers' income: $Y_L = \theta_{LW} W + \theta_{LZ} Z$ (9.7b)

Dividing each of the income streams by total income (Y) yields the shares of worker and capitalist incomes in the total national income, which Palley (2016: 6) reduces to a function of the ownership structure and distributive shares:

Capitalists' income share: $\gamma_K = \dfrac{Y_K}{Y} = \theta_{KW} \dfrac{W}{Y} + \theta_{KZ} \dfrac{Z}{Y} = \theta_{KW} \omega + \theta_{KZ}(1-\omega)$ (9.8a)

Workers' income share: $\gamma_L = \dfrac{Y_L}{Y} = \theta_{LW} \dfrac{W}{Y} + \theta_{LZ} \dfrac{Z}{Y} = \theta_{LW} \omega + \theta_{LZ}(1-\omega)$ (9.8b)

where the measure of inequality, ψ, is equal to the ratio of capitalist to worker income:

$$\psi = \frac{\gamma_K}{\gamma_L} = \frac{\theta_{KW}\omega + \theta_{KZ}(1-\omega)}{\theta_{LW}\omega + \theta_{LZ}(1-\omega)}$$ (9.9)

From this relation Palley (2016: 6) concludes that "income inequality depends on the functional distribution of income, the division of the wage bill, and the ownership distribution of the capital stock." This seems to be a fruitful way to move forward in developing specific relationships, accounting or otherwise, in mapping functional to size distribution and *vice versa*.

These developments can be interwoven with a graphical exposition adapted from the neo-classical approach of Atkinson & Bourguignon (2000) in the development of the structural relationship between functional and size distribution. Here we find that, although neoclassically oriented, their approach once modified provides a broad way to conceive of the functional-size nexus. As with the classical model, it is assumed here that there is uniformity in both the wage and profit rates. The functional distribution of (macro) revenue is by revenue type and size distribution of (micro) earnings by income recipient, the latter designated as the household (HH). The macro revenue type is given by the sum of the wage bill (W) and gross profits (Z), where:

$$Y = W + Z = (w^* L) + (r^* p^* K)$$ (9.10)

The wage bill is a monetary magnitude determined by the product of the uniform 'normal' money wage rate (w^*) and the aggregate quantity of labor (L). Gross profits are also a monetary magnitude determined by the product of the uniform 'normal' rate profit (r^*), the money prices-of-production of aggregate capital inputs (p^*), and the quantity of such inputs (K).

At the level of the micro-earning recipient, consider the case when the total number of households (HH) are equal to worker-households (HH^W) receiving wage-type revenue plus capitalist households (HH^Z) receiving profit-type revenue. In a purely egalitarian society, the ownership across both earned and unearned revenue accrual will be exactly the same.[6] However, equitable distribution in income is not only the result of complete social equity in ownership shares across individuals, and a purely class-based society too could equitably distribute revenues and incomes as well, so long as the overall class division of individuals is equal to the wage share of income. The *wage share of perfect equality* (ω^{PE}) in a pure class system is therefore the share of wages in national income when equal to the aggregate breakdown of individual wage and profit earning streams. To make matters simple we will consider the individual unit to be the 'household' which in the two-class society will be divided into worker and capitalist households (HH^W and HH^Z, respectively).

$$\omega^{PE} = \frac{HH^W}{HH} = hh^W$$

where hh^W is the portion of household wage-type income stream recipients out of total; hh is the cumulative aggregate total income stream of all individuals, that is, $hh^W + hh^Z = 1$.

We can now relate functional to size distribution. To do so the functional income distribution in Equation (9.10) is transformed into the wage-share variant by dividing both sides by total value-added Y:

$$1 = \omega + \frac{r^*}{R} \tag{9.11}$$

Solving for r^* yields the well-known equation for the uniform rate of profit written as the product of the profit share and the output-capital ratio *qua* maximum rate of profit (Sraffa 1960; Kurz & Salvadori 1995; Foley & Michl 1999):

$$r^* = (1 - \omega)R \tag{9.12}$$

where R = output-capital ratio = maximum rate of profit.

A two-quadrant graph that links functional distribution in quadrant I to size distribution in quadrant II can be drawn. Functional distribution is the sum of the wage bill and gross profits, whereas the streams of earnings accrue to the different households. Assumed is the limiting case of workers consumption being equal to their wage bill, hence workers do not save. This reduces both the realism as well as the complexity of the exposition, but does provide an

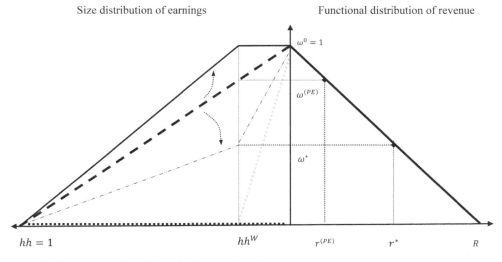

Figure 9.2 Functional and size distribution interface

indication of the nature of the functional-size interface under such limiting conditions. The wage share of perfect equality corresponds to a one-to-one ratio between the income received and the income recipient. If wages were to increase beyond perfect equality, admittedly a very unlikely scenario, then profit earners receive less revenue resulting in overall inequality in the system. Inequality here is driven by the share of wage revenue exceeding the proportion in wage-recipients. In the more likely scenario of wages decreasing below the threshold of perfect equality, profit earners receive proportionally more revenue. Inequality here is driven by profit revenues accruing in excess proportion to the number of profit earning income recipients. The absolute lower limit to the distribution parameter corresponds to a wage share of zero, although most heterodox theories posit a lower limit to the wage set by the historical and social conditions of society.

Atkinson & Bourguignon (2000: 8) show a graph similar to that of quadrant II shown in Figure 9.2, except they do not posit the case of a wage share of unity (hence no trapezoid). Based on this simple two-class economy they show that the measure of profit-driven inequality is determined by the Gini coefficient calculated as the proportion of wage-earning households minus the share of wages in national income:

$$\text{Gini} = hh_{\Sigma}^{W} - \omega^{*}$$

The overall distribution of income of course does not fit this nice two-class schema, and incorporation of different income types has always presented issues for heterodox and neoclassical theorizing alike. Instead, the above is only meant to provide an overall broad picture to the functional dimension in the size distribution nexus.

Econo-physics and the 'two-class theory of income distribution'

One of the most relevant results from empirical studies of the size distribution of earnings at an analytical level shows that the upper tail of the income distribution is of a different character than that of the remaining portion of the income distribution. Shown in various studies (Drăgulescu & Yakovenko 2000, 2001a, b; Silva et al. 2002; Aoyama et al. 2003; Fujiwara et al. 2003; Silva & Yakavenko 2005; Wright 2005, 2011; Shaikh et al. 2014; Shaikh 2016), the income of the 'rich' is subject to a Pareto-type power distribution that allows greater intensity of concentration, and the income of the 'non-rich' is subject to an exponential distribution with a lessened intensity of concentration. Terming the former 'superthermal' and the latter 'thermal' income classes, Silva & Yakavenko (2005: 1) characterize this as follows:

> We show that the US economy has a well-defined two-class structure. The majority of the population . . . belongs to the lower class and has a very stable in time exponential ('thermal') distribution of income. The upper class . . . has a power-law ('superthermal') distribution, whose parameters significantly change with the rise and fall of the stock market.

Wright (2011: 19) develops the results described above in terms of an analytical framework and simulation much in line with the precepts of classical and Marxian political economy. His simulation model is called the 'dynamic computational model of the social relations of production' or SR model for short. This model develops all sorts of dynamic properties consistent with real capitalist economic systems and reproduces with simulations many of the empirical patterns and results that have emerged from empirical studies, two of which stand out for our purposes: (i) that the "class of capitalists is numerically small, whereas the class of workers, that is those actors who predominantly rely on wage income for their subsistence, constitute the vast majority of the population" (Wright 2011: 11); and (ii) that the "empirical distribution is characterised by a highly unequal distribution of income, in which a very small number of households receive a disproportionate amount of the total" (Wright 2011: 19). Wright develops these results in terms of an analytical framework in line with the precepts of classical and Marxian political economy and concludes that

> the higher, property income, regime of income distribution can be fitted to a Pareto (or power) distribution whereas the lower, or wage-income, regime, which represents the vast majority of the population, is normally fitted to a lognormal distribution, but recently researchers report that an exponential (Boltzmann-Gibbs) distribution better describes the empirical data.
>
> *Wright 2011: 19*

Shaikh (2016: 751–755) calls this evidence the "econo-physics two-class theory of income distribution" or EPTC. In relating this to increased income inequality evidenced since 1979–1980, Shaikh (2016: 755, original emphasis) draws the following conclusions:

> If labor income is exponentially distributed . . . a rise in the Gini of overall income distribution must come from a rise in property income relative to labor income. Indeed, the EPTC group explicitly links the rise in property income with the rise in stock market prices . . . [as] the overall Gini depends on the proportion of property income to total income. It follows that the overall degree of income inequality ultimately rests on the ratio of profits to wages, that is, *on the basic division of value added.* This is a fundamentally classical result.

Conclusion

In this chapter the distribution of income has been considered in terms of three different heterodox theories of distribution: classical/Marxian theory, Cambridge theory, and Neo-Kaleckian theory. Each of the theories was considered in terms of its closure and the basic mechanisms underlying and interacting within each model as well as the functional-size distribution nexus and the implications for various heterodox theories. Finally, the chapter explored the frontiers with other disciplines such as that of econo-physics.

For the classical-Marxian model, fully adjusted normal and/or regulating conditions were posited as the centers-of-gravitation for the system. Classical-Marxian theory closes the system from the wage-side of the ledger and causality runs from profitability to the accumulation of capital and growth. Differences in the mechanisms that determine closure are wages as a 'given' and constant bundle of commodities versus wages conceived as a share of net productivity. Important extensions of the model include incorporation of disciplining effects on labor such as the unemployment rate which constitutes a proxy of labor market conditions, and further research could consider the impact of labor market institutions such as union concentration.

Cambridge theory closes the system from rates of accumulation and growth to profitability and income distribution. The Cambridge equation was shown to be robust and susceptible to various implementations and applications, and the research agenda outlined in Baranzini & Mari (2009) is very fruitful including theoretical applications of the functional-size nexus, the introduction of financial variables, and the consideration of other socio-economic classes. The Cambridge theory was also shown to have two variants: the physicalist natural rate of growth or accumulation perspective; and the interest rate monetary sector perspective. Common to both perspectives is the profit rate as the dependent variable as regards aggregate systemic closure, and the rate of capital accumulation as the independent variable as regards income distribution. The latter means that in terms of the distribution parameter it is the profit rate that determines the level of relative wages, exactly the opposite of the classical traditions.

Neo-Kaleckian theory was shown to be a robust way to conceive of the role of income distribution in terms of regimes of demand as well as productivity. The generality of the framework and its applicability across a variety of scenarios makes the model very useful in terms of both theory and policy. The importance of the latter is highlighted by the fact that economic policy can be framed in terms of equitable ways in which the economy can recover and sustain itself, expressed in terms of regimes of wage-led growth. Here economic analysis becomes less of a description of the workings of market forces and more of an application of directing the economy towards ways in which economic activity works for all members of the economy, not just the capital-owning class.

Heterodox theories of distribution have the marked distinction to harken back to the dictum Ricardo made in his Preface that distribution is the 'principal problem' of our science. This stands in contrast with orthodox-neoclassical theories where 'distribution' is often relegated to the ghetto of being normative rather than positive in its essential form theoretically, and highly problematic when implemented as policy. Many heterodox economists consider this dismissal of the conceptual and practical merit of distribution as apologetics for the capitalist order and status quo. It is to the credit of heterodox approaches to place emphasis on the role of distribution as both a theoretical-category and a policy-target, and this broadens the scope of economic inquiry generally for all theories, orthodox and heterodox.

Notes

1 For recent retrospective on the theory of distribution from a history of thought standpoint see: also Atkinson & Bourguignon (2000), Atkinson (2009), and Glyn (2009); other important surveys on income distribution can be found in Marchal & Ducros (1968), Bronfenbrenner (1971), Pen (1971), Ranadive (1978), Sahota (1978), and the entries in Asimakopulos (1988); see also the *New Palgrave Dictionary* entries for the various schools of thought: neoclassical (Bliss 1987), classical (Pivetti 1987), Keynesian (Baranzini 1987), and Marxian (Gordon 1987).
2 Post Keynesian theories of the mark-up include various mechanisms, some of them being monopoly power, degree of concentration, risk of new entry, and worker resistance (Eichner & Kregel 1975; Skott 1989a; Lee 1998; Shapiro 2000), target return rates that finance a firm's desired growth rate (Godley & Lavoie 2007; Lavoie 2014), and forward-looking strategic behavior (Shapiro & Sawyer 2003).
3 Lavoie & Stockhammer (2012: 15) and Lavoie (2014: 320) call this the 'Webb-Effect' after Sidney Webb and note that this has resonance with the mainstream efficiency wage thesis.
4 These studies are: Bowles & Boyer (1995); Stockhammer & Onaran (2004); Barbosa-Filho & Taylor (2006); Naastepad & Storm (2006–07); Ederer & Stockhammer (2007); Hein & Vogel (2008); Stockhammer et al. (2009); Stockhammer et al. (2011); Stockhammer & Stehrer (2011), and Onaran et al. (2012).
5 The countries are the Euro area, Germany, France, the Netherlands, Austria, the United Kingdom, Japan, and the United States.
6 One Editor of the *Handbook* pointed out that the scenario posited assumes the wage rate and the profit rate are uniform, and that such proviso is untenable if we wish to talk about the real world. To reiterate, the present exercise is to show in a simple diagram the connections between the functional and size distribution in such a limiting case. The criticism generally against uniformity in the wage and profit rates is an important matter beyond the scope of this chapter.

References

Aoyama, H., Souma, W., & Fujiwara, Y. 2003. 'Growth and fluctuations of personal and company's income.' *Physica A*, 324: 352–358.
Asimakopulos, A. (ed.) 1988. *Theories of Income Distribution*. Boston: Kluwer Academic Press.

Atkinson, A. 2009. 'Factor shares: the principal problem of political economy?' *Oxford Review of Economic Policy*, 25 (1): 3–16.

Atkinson, A. & Bourguignon, F. 2000. 'Introduction: income distribution and economics,' *in* A. Atkinson & F. Bourguignon (eds.), *Handbook of Income Distribution*. Geneva: Elsevier Science, 1–88.

Baranzini, M. 1987. 'Distribution: Keynesian,' in: J. Eatwell, M. Milgate, & P. Newman (eds.), *The New Palgrave Dictionary of Economics*. Basingstoke, UK: Palgrave Macmillan, 876–8.

Baranzini, M. & Mari, C. 2009. The Cantabrigiensis–Italian school of income distribution. Unpublished Manuscript.

Barbosa-Filho, N. & Taylor, L. 2006. 'Distributive and demand cycles in the US economy – a structuralist Goodwin model.' *Metroeconomica*, 57 (3): 389–411.

Baumol, W. 1983. 'Marx and the Iron Law of wages.' *American Economic Review*, 73 (2): 303–308.

Bellofiore, R. 2012. 'The "tiresome objector" and old moor: a renewal of the debate on Marx after Sraffa based on the unpublished material at the Wren Library.' *Cambridge Journal of Economics*, 36 (6): 1385–1399.

Bellofiore, R. 2014. 'The loneliness of the long distance thinker: Sraffa, Marx and the critique of political economy,' in: R. Bellofiore & S. Carter (eds.), *Towards a New Understanding of Sraffa: Insights into Archival Research*. Basingstoke, UK: Palgrave Macmillan, 198–240.

Bhaduri, A. & Marglin, S. 1990. 'Unemployment and the real wage: the economic basis for contesting political ideologies.' *Cambridge Journal of Economics*, 14 (4): 375–393.

Biermann, A. 2015. Money, interest, and profit in the theory of distribution: a Sraffian approach. Unpublished Manuscript, the University Frankfurt. Available from http://www.boeckler.de/pdf/v_2015_10_23_biermann.pdf [Accessed April 1, 2016]

Blanchflower, D.G. & Oswald, A.J. 1990. *The Wage Curve*. Cambridge, MA: The MIT Press.

Bliss, C. 1987. 'Distribution: neoclassical,' in: J. Eatwell, M. Milgate, & P. Newman. *The New Palgrave Dictionary of Economics*. Basingstoke, UK: Palgrave Macmillan, 883–886.

Bortis, H. 1993. 'Notes on the Cambridge equation.' *Journal of Post Keynesian Economics*, 16 (1): 105–126.

Botwinick, H. 1993. *Persistent Inequalities: Wage Disparity under Capitalist Competition*. Princeton, NJ: Princeton University Press.

Bowles, S. & Boyer, R. 1995. 'Wages, aggregate demand, and employment in an open economy: an empirical investigation,' in: G. Epstein & H. Gintis (eds.), *Macroeconomic Policy after the Conservative Era: Studies in Investment, Saving and Finance*. Cambridge: Cambridge University Press, 143–171.

Bronfenbrenner, M. 1971. *Income Distribution Theory*. New York: Aldine.

Card, D. 1995. 'The wage curve: a review.' *Journal of Economic Literature*, 33 (2): 785–799.

Carvahlo, L. & Rezai, A. 2016. 'Personal income inequality and aggregate demand.' *Cambridge Journal of Economics*, 40 (2): 491–505.

Chiodi, G. 2010. 'The means of subsistence and the notion of 'viability' in Sraffa's surplus approach,' in: S. Zambelli (ed.), *Computable, Constructive and Behavioural Economic Dynamics: Essays in Honour of Kumaraswamy (Vela) Velupillai*. London: Routledge, 318–330.

Deleplace, G. 2014. 'The essentiality of money on the Sraffa Papers,' in: R. Bellofiore & S. Carter (eds.), *Towards a New Understanding of Sraffa: Insights into Archival Research*. Basingstoke, UK: Palgrave Macmillan, 139–166.

Drăgulescu, A.A. & Yakovenko, V.M. 2000. 'Statistical mechanics of money.' *The European Physical Journal B*, 17: 723–729.

Drăgulescu, A.A. & Yakovenko, V.M. 2001a. 'Evidence for the exponential distribution of income in the USA.' *The European Physical Journal B*, 20: 585–589.

Drăgulescu, A.A. & Yakovenko, V.M. 2001b. 'Exponential and power-law probability distributions of wealth and income in the United Kingdom and the United States.' *Physica A*, 299: 213–221.

Dutt, A. 1990. *Growth, Distribution, and Uneven Development*. Cambridge: Cambridge University Press.

Ederer, S. & Stockhammer, E. 2007. 'Wages and aggregate demand in France: an empirical investigation,' in: E. Hein & A. Truger (eds.), *Money, Distribution, and Economic Policy – Alternatives to Orthodox Macroeconomics*. Cheltenham, UK: Edward Elgar, 119–138.

Eichner, A. & Kregel, J. 1975. 'An essay on Post-Keynesian theory: a new paradigm in economics.' *Journal of Economic Literature*, 13 (4): 1293–1314.

Fleck, F. & Domenghino, C.-M. 1987. 'Cambridge (UK) versus Cambridge (Mass): a Keynesian solution of "Pasinetti's Paradox".' *Journal of Post Keynesian Economics*, 19 (1): 22–36.

Foley, D. & Michl, T. 1999. *Growth and Distribution*. Cambridge, MA: Harvard University Press.

Fujiwara, Y., Souma, W., Aoyama, H., Kaizoji, T., & Aoki, M. 2003. 'Growth and fluctuations of personal income.' *Physica A*, 321: 598–604.

Scott Carter

Galbraith, J.K. 1998. *Created Unequal: The Crisis in American Pay.* Chicago: University of Chicago Press.
Galbraith, J.K. 2011. 'Income distribution,' in: R. Holt & S. Pressman (eds.), *A New Guide to Post Keynesian Economics.* New York: Routledge, 32–41.
Garegnani, P. 1979. 'Notes on consumption, investment and effective demand.' *Cambridge Journal of Economics*, 3 (1): 83–89.
Garegnani, P. 1984. 'Value and distribution in the classical economists and Marx.' *Oxford Economics Papers*, 36 (2): 291–325.
Garegnani, P. 1987. 'Surplus approach to value and distribution,' in: J. Eatwell, M. Milgate, & P. Newman (eds.), *The New Palgrave Dictionary of Economics.* Basingstoke, UK: Palgrave Macmillan, 560–574.
Giovannoni, O. 2014. What do we know about the labor share and the profit share? Part I: Theories. University of Texas Inequality Project Working Paper No. 65. Available from http://utip.lbj.utexas.edu/papers/UTIP%2064.pdf [Accessed April 1, 2016]
Glyn, A. 1995. 'Unemployment and inequality.' *Oxford Review of Economic Policy*, 11 (1): 196–213.
Glyn, A. 2009. 'Functional distribution and inequality,' in: W. Salverda, B. Nolan, & T.M. Smeeding (eds.), *Oxford Handbook of Economic Inequality.* Oxford: Oxford University Press, 99–124.
Godley, W. & Lavoie, M. 2007. *Monetary Economics: An Integrated Approach to Credit, Money, Income, Production, and Wealth.* Basingstoke, UK: Palgrave Macmillan.
Goodwin, R. 1967. 'A growth cycle,' in: C. Feinstein (ed.), *Socialism, Capitalism, and Economic Growth.* Cambridge: Cambridge University Press, 54–58.
Gordon, D. 1987. 'Distribution: Marxian,' in: J. Eatwell, M. Milgate, & P. Newman (eds.), *The New Palgrave Dictionary of Economics.* Basingstoke, UK: Palgrave Macmillan, 878–883.
Green, F. 1991. 'The relationship of wages to the value of labour-power in Marx's labour market.' *Cambridge Journal of Economics*, 15 (2): 199–213.
Harvie, D. 2000. 'Testing Goodwin: growth cycles in ten OECD countries.' *Cambridge Journal of Economics*, 24 (3): 349–376.
Hein, E. & Vogel, L. 2008. 'Distribution and growth reconsidered – empirical results for six OECD countries.' *Cambridge Journal of Economics*, 32 (3): 479–511.
Kaldor, N. 1956. 'Alternative theories of distribution.' *Review of Economic Studies*, 23 (2): 83–100.
Kurz, H. & Salvadori, N. 1995. *Theory of Production: A Long Period Analysis.* Cambridge: Cambridge University Press.
Lavoie, M. 2009. 'Cadrisme within a Post-Keynesian model of growth and distribution.' *Review of Political Economy*, 21 (3): 369–391.
Lavoie, M. 2014. *Post-Keynesian Economics: New Foundations.* Northampton, MA: Edward Elgar.
Lavoie, M. & Stockhammer, E. 2012. *Wage-led Growth: An Equitable Strategy for Economic Recovery.* Basingstoke, UK: Palgrave Macmillan.
Lawlor, M.S. & Horn, B. 1992. 'Notes on the Sraffa–Hayek exchange.' *Review of Political Economy*, 4 (3): 317–340.
Lee, F.S. 1998. *Post Keynesian Price Theory.* Cambridge: Cambridge University Press.
Levine, D. 1988. 'Marx's theory of income distribution,' in: A. Asimakopulos (ed.), *Theories of Income Distribution.* Boston: Kluwer Academic, 19–74.
Levrero, E.S. 2013. 'Marx on absolute and relative wages and the modern theory of distribution.' *Review of Political Economy*, 25 (1): 91–116.
Marchal, J. & Ducros, B. (eds.) 1968. *The Distribution of National Income.* London: Macmillan.
Naastepad, C.W.M. & Storm, S. 2006–07. 'OECD demand regimes (1960–2000).' *Journal of Post Keynesian Economics*, 29 (2): 213–248.
Nikiforos, M. & Foley, D. 2012. 'Distribution and capacity utilization: conceptual issues and empirical evidence.' *Metroeconomica*, 63 (1): 200–229.
Onaran, Ö., Stockhammer, E., & Grafl, L. 2012. 'The finance-dominated growth regime, distribution, and aggregate demand in the US.' *Cambridge Journal of Economics*, 35 (4): 637–661.
Palley, T. 1996. 'Inside debt, aggregate demand, and the Cambridge theory of distribution.' *Cambridge Journal of Economics*, 20 (4): 465–474.
Palley, T. 2002. 'Financial institutions and the Cambridge theory of distribution.' *Cambridge Journal of Economics*, 26 (2): 275–277.
Palley, T. 2005. 'Class conflict and the Cambridge theory of distribution,' in: B. Gibson (ed.), *The Economics of Joan Robinson: A Centennial Celebration.* Cheltenham, UK: Edward Elgar, 203–224.
Palley, T. 2010. 'The relative permanent income theory of consumption: a synthetic Keynes–Duesenberry–Friedman Model.' *Review of Political Economy*, 22 (1): 41–56.

Palley, T. 2012. A Neo-Kaleckian–Goodwin model of capitalistic economic growth: monopoly power, managerial pay, labor market conflict, and endogenous technical progress. Institut für Makroökonomie und Konjunkturforschung Working Paper 105. Available from http://www.boeckler.de/pdf/p_imk_wp_105_2012.pdf [Accessed April 1, 2016]

Palley, T. 2014. 'Wealth and wealth distribution in the Neo-Kaleckian growth model.' *Journal of Post Keynesian Economics*, 34 (3): 453–474.

Palley, T. 2016. Inequality and growth in Neo-Kaleckian and Cambridge growth theory. Political Economy Research Institute Working Paper No. 417. Available from http://www.peri.umass.edu/fileadmin/pdf/working_papers/working_papers_401-450/WP417.pdf [Accessed June 1, 2016]

Panico, C. 1980. 'Marx's analysis of the relationship between the rate of interest and the rate of profits.' *Cambridge Journal of Economics*, 4 (4): 363–378.

Panico, C. 1985. 'Market forces and the relation between the rates of interest and profits.' *Contributions to Political Economy*, 4 (1): 37–60.

Panico, C. 1988a. 'Sraffa on money and banking.' *Cambridge Journal of Economics*, 12 (1): 2–28.

Panico, C. 1988b. *Interest and Profit in the Theories of Value and Distribution*. London: Macmillan.

Panico, C. 2011. 'Monetary influences on distribution: a comparison of Post Keynesian theories,' *in:* R. Ciccone, C. Gehrke, & G. Mongiovi (eds.), *Sraffa and Modern Economics, Volume II*. New York: Routledge, 168–185.

Panico, C., Pinto, A., & Anyul, M. P. 2012. 'Income distribution and the size of the financial sector: a Sraffian analysis.' *Cambridge Journal of Economics*, 36 (6): 1455–1478.

Park, M.-S. 2006. 'The financial system and the Pasinetti theorem.' *Cambridge Journal of Economics*, 30 (2): 201–217.

Pasinetti, L. 1962. 'Rate of profit and income distribution in relation to the rate of economic growth.' *Review of Economic Studies*, 29 (4): 267–279.

Pasinetti, L. 1981. *Structural Change and Economic Growth: A Theoretical Essay on the Dynamics of the Wealth of Nations*. Cambridge: Cambridge University Press.

Pasinetti, L. 2000. 'Critique of the neoclassical theory of growth and distribution.' *Banca Nazionale del Lavoro Quarterly Review*, 23 (3): 383–390.

Pen, J. 1971. *Income Distribution: Facts, Theories, Policies*. New York: Praeger.

Persky, J. 1992. 'Pareto's Law.' *Journal of Economic Perspectives*, 6 (2): 181–190.

Petri, D. 2014. 'On the Neoricardian criticism of irrelevance,' *in:* R. Bellofiore & S. Carter (eds.), *Towards a New Understanding of Sraffa: Insights into Archival Research*. Basingstoke, UK: Palgrave Macmillan, 25–46.

Pivetti, M. 1985. 'On the monetary explanation of distribution.' *Political Economy: Studies in the Surplus Approach*, 1 (2): 73–104.

Pivetti, M. 1987. 'Distribution: classical,' *in:* J. Eatwell, M. Milgate, & P. Newman (eds.), *The New Palgrave Dictionary of Economics*. Basingstoke, UK: Palgrave Macmillan, 873–876.

Pivetti, M. 1991. *An Essay on Money and Distribution*. London: Macmillan.

Ranadive, K.R. 1978. *Income Distribution: The Unsolved Puzzle*. Bombay: Oxford University Press.

Rezai, A. 2011. Goodwin cycles, distributional conflict, and productivity growth. The New School for Social Research Department of Economics Working Paper 10/2011. Available from http://www.economicpolicyresearch.org/econ/2011/NSSR_WP_102011.pdf [Accessed April 1, 2016]

Roncaglia, A. 1988. 'The neo-Ricardian approach and the distribution of income,' *in:* A. Asimakopulos (ed.), *Theories of Income Distribution*. Boston: Kluwer Academic, 159–180.

Rowthorn, R. 1981. 'Demand, real wages and economic growth.' *Thames Papers in Political Economy*, Autumn: 1–39.

Rowthorn, R. 1999. 'Unemployment, wage-bargaining and capital–labour substitution.' *Cambridge Journal of Economics*, 23 (4): 413–425.

Sahota, G. S. 1978. 'Theories of personal distribution: a survey.' *Journal of Economic Literature*, 16 (1): 1–55.

Sandmo, A. 2014. 'The principal problem in political economy: income distribution in the history of economic thought,' *in:* A. Atkinson & F. Bourguignon (eds.), *Handbook of Income Distribution, SET vols. 2A*. Amsterdam: Elsevier, 3–66.

Shaikh, A. 1978. 'Political economy and capitalism: notes on Dobb's theory of crisis.' *Cambridge Journal of Economics*, 2 (2): 233–251.

Shaikh, A. 1980. 'Marxian competition versus perfect competition: further comments on the so-called 'choice of technique'.' *Cambridge Journal of Economics*, 4 (1): 75–83.

Shaikh, A. 2016. *Capitalism: Competition, Conflict, Crises*. New York: Oxford University Press.

Shaikh, A., Papanikolaou, N., & Wiener, N. 2014. 'Race, gender, and the econophysics of income distribution.' *Physica A*, 414: 54–60.

Shapiro, N. & Sawyer, M. 2003. 'Post Keynesian price theory.' *Journal of Post Keynesian Economics*, 25 (3): 355–365.

Shapiro, N. 2000. 'Review of *Post Keynesian Price Theory* by Frederic S. Lee.' *Journal of Economic Issues*, 34 (4): 990–992.

Silva, A. C. & Yakovenko, V. M. 2005. 'Temporal evolution of the 'thermal' and 'superthermal' income classes in the USA during 1983–2001.' *Europhysics Letters*, 69: 304–310.

Silva, J., Slud, E., & Takamoto, T. 2002. 'Statistical equilibrium wealth distributions in an exchange economy with stochastic preferences.' *Journal of Economic Theory*, 106 (2): 417–435.

Skott, P. 1989a. *Conflict and Effective Demand in Economic Growth*. Cambridge: Cambridge University Press.

Skott, P. 1989b. 'Effective demand, class struggle and cyclical growth.' *International Economic Review*, 30 (1): 231–247.

Sraffa, P. (ed.) 1951. *The Works and Correspondence of David Ricardo, Vol. I*. Cambridge: Cambridge University Press.

Sraffa, P. 1960. *Production of Commodities by Means of Commodities: Prelude to a Critique of Economic Theory*. Cambridge: Cambridge University Press.

Steedman, I. 1972. 'The state and outcome of the Pasinetti Process.' *The Economic Journal*, 82 (328): 1387–1395.

Stockhammer, E. & Onaran, O. 2004. 'Accumulation, distribution and employment: a structural VAR approach to a Kaleckian macro-model.' *Structural Change and Economic Dynamics*, 15 (4): 421–447.

Stockhammer, E. & Stehrer, R. 2011. 'Goodwin or Kalecki in demand? Functional income distribution and aggregate demand in the short run.' *Review of Radical Political Economics*, 43 (4): 506–522.

Stockhammer, E., Hein, E., & Grafl, L. 2011. 'Globalization and the effects of changes in functional income distribution on aggregate demand in Germany.' *International Review of Applied Economics*, 25 (1): 1–23.

Stockhammer, E., Onaran, O., & Ederer, S. 2009. 'Functional income distribution and aggregate demand in the Euro area.' *Cambridge Journal of Economics*, 33 (1): 139–159.

Tavani, D. & Vasudevan, R. 2014. 'Capitalists, workers, and managers: wage inequality and effective demand.' *Structural Change and Economic Dynamics*, 30 (September): 120–131.

Taylor, L. 2004. *Reconstructing Macroeconomics: Structuralist Proposals and Critiques of the Mainstream*. Cambridge, MA: Harvard University Press.

Teixeira, J. R., Sugahara, R., & Baranzini, M. 1998. 'On micro-foundations for the Kaldor-Pasinetti growth model with taxation and bequest.' *Anais do XXVI Encontro Nacional de Economia*, 1: 505–518.

Wolff, E. N. 1988. 'Life-cycle savings and the individual distribution of wealth by class,' *in*: D. Kessler & A. Masson (eds.), *Modelling the Accumulation and Distribution of Wealth*. Oxford: Oxford University Press, 261–280.

Wright, I. 2005. 'The social architecture of capitalism.' *Physica A*, 346: 589–620.

Wright, I. 2011. Classical macrodynamics and the labor theory of value. The Open University Discussion Papers in Economics No. 76. Available from http://www.open.ac.uk/socialsciences/main/__assets/lqd8gqeaxeewkdpjof.pdf [Accessed April 1, 2016]

10

The micro–macro link in heterodox economics

Claudius Gräbner and Jakob Kapeller

Introduction

Any discussion of the micro–macro link in heterodox economics entails two main questions. The first question is relevant for social sciences in general and asks for the correct or adequate treatment of aggregates and aggregation in social theory. Any answer to this general question incorporates a series of diverse philosophical viewpoints, including: ontological claims, for example, whether social and economic aggregates exist; epistemological questions, for example, regarding the role played by aggregates and aggregation in economic theory; and methodological aspects, for example, how to adequately model processes of aggregation. Given that economics faces myriad problems of aggregation—as in the case of market interaction, macroeconomic aggregates, or interpersonal coordination and contracting—the quest to provide suitable theoretical tools to adequately address aggregates and aggregation is of special interest to economists of different persuasions.

The second major question is more specific and asks for similarities and differences in the treatment of aggregates and aggregation among heterodox economists. From a traditional viewpoint one might question the idea that there is something like a consistent vision of the micro–macro link in heterodoxy, since different interpretations of the micro–macro link have been attributed to various strands of heterodox research. While some heterodox economists may prioritize either micro- or macro-level analysis, others emphasize the meso level as a decisive intermediate layer between the more traditional approaches focusing on either microeconomic or macroeconomic aspects.

Against this backdrop, this chapter introduces a unifying heterodox approach to the micro–macro link in economics. The first section emphasizes the analytical problems that may arise from popular misunderstandings about the relationship of individual and aggregate levels. This discussion illustrates why a thorough understanding of aggregation and aggregates in science is necessary. In the second section we show that the different heterodox approaches to the micro–macro link in economics are not only consistent, but complementary to each other and allow for a concise treatment of the micro–macro link in economics based on a set of shared fundamental principles. The third section embeds the heterodox economic view on aggregation in a 'systemist' framework and demonstrates that heterodox economic theory and research practice can be

Claudius Gräbner, Jakob Kapeller

substantiated and summarized by a more general, philosophical perspective on aggregates and aggregation in science. We argue that such a general philosophical framework opens possibilities for advancing heterodox theory, because it allows scholars from different heterodox starting points to relate their theories to each other via a consistent meta-language. The last section offers some concluding thoughts.

Aggregates and aggregation in science: an illustration of compositional fallacies

Scientific endeavor often deals with the relation between aggregate entities, like a family, a nation or a firm, and their individual constituents—family members, citizens, or employees. In disentangling this relationship between the 'whole' and its 'parts,' errors may occur, which can be understood as compositional fallacies. Such compositional fallacies arise from either a wrong treatment of aggregation or a wrong treatment of aggregates, and may lead to a deficient understanding of the whole as well as its parts. This section provides illustrations of four typical compositional fallacies and their conceptual sources, in order to develop a basic understanding of the problems usually associated with the micro–macro link in the social sciences. For a more complete exposition of the particular fallacies, see Kapeller (2015).

One typical error related to aggregation is underestimating the role of relations across individuals. Aggregates contain not only individual entities but also a corresponding set of relations, which tie their individual nodes together and create a certain structure. Taking these relations into account is crucial for an adequate understanding of the constitution of the aggregate entity. For example, a central concern in feminist economics is to take individuals and their mutual relations instead of households as the starting point for economic analysis. Otherwise the important 'aggregation procedure' from individual to household preferences and the underlying relational structure among individuals that explains the often detrimental position of women would be neglected (Drèze & Sen 1989). Taking the household as a fundamental economic actor, therefore, contributes to the exclusion of gender issues from economic analysis. This example illustrates that aggregation problems are central to economic analysis and can appear in rather early stages of theorizing as the behavior of some aggregate social system, like a family or a nation, strongly depends on its internal structure, that is, its relational setup.

Most standard economic models, both mainstream and heterodox, ignore relational setups entirely and determine aggregate behavior by some simple procedure of summing up across individual entities. The 'simplistic fallacy' is thereby based on a deficient understanding of aggregation, which views the 'whole' as no different from the 'sum of its parts.' Such a view conflicts with two basic observations. First, aggregates may develop properties that no individual part possesses, such as a firm's success. Second, individuals may acquire certain properties precisely because they are part of some whole, for example, a country's citizen. In both cases we find that 'more is different' (Anderson 1972), as these newly acquired attributes may be conceived as 'emergent properties,' meaning novel features that arise because an aggregate is constituted or sustained. For the case of families such novel properties include the possibilities of raising offspring, lending mutual support, and creating collective identities and a shared organization of common rights and duties, which may leave some family members in a dependent and potentially deprived situation compared with others. These aspects are often neglected, for instance, if households with multiple members are represented by a single utility function.

Another fallacy regarding the micro–macro link in economics is the assumption that causality across different levels only runs from individual elements to aggregate properties ('bottom-up'), which we label the 'hierarchical fallacy.' Current mainstream economics follows such a routine

146

by imposing a general "hierarchical stipulation that macro-theories require a microeconomic foundation to obtain full validity" (Rothschild 1988: 14). The economic mainstream thereby emphasizes the necessity of reductionist strategies, which explain aggregate phenomena by 'summing up' the behavior and properties of the parts (for example, Robbins 1932; Lucas 1976). By contrast, heterodox economists of different persuasions advocate for a multi-level approach to economic theorizing (for example, Dopfer *et al.* 2004; Lee 2011; King 2012), emphasizing the changing conditions and constraints for economic action on different levels and the mutual co-existence of top-down and bottom-up mechanisms.

One reason why such a 'hierarchical stipulation' creates more problems than it solves when theorizing about economic phenomena is that emergent properties not only arise permanently, but also feed back on their constituents, which cannot be assessed within a unidirectional framework. Consider, for example, innovation in market environments and the associated forces of 'creative destruction' (Schumpeter 1942) and 'path-dependency' (David 1985); or the continuous evolution of social routines (Hodgson & Knudsen 2004) and consumer preferences (Witt 2001). In these contexts, where the relationship between individual action and aggregate outcomes is manifold and complex, the epistemological presupposition of a 'hierarchical stipulation' of micro over macro acts as a dual barrier to clear understanding. First, it leads to the 'static fallacy' which asserts that aggregate properties can always be reduced to lower-level entities, thereby underestimating the dynamics and complexity of social interactions, and overlooking the unexpected. Second, it gives rise to the related 'dogmatic fallacy,' comprising the methodological claims that aggregate properties *should* always be reduced to (current) micro-knowledge and that higher-level mechanisms are mere residuals of individual behavior and therefore negligible. Consequentially, emergent aggregate properties are not accorded any meaningful explanatory role.[1]

In contrast, causally relevant top-down relationships in economics can be found in various contexts. We can think of the influence of social norms and regulation on business practices or the social mediation of consumption preferences within a certain community. In the case of the family, traditions, power, and hierarchy are of vital importance for understanding women's deprivation (Drèze & Sen 1989). The importance of such top-down mechanisms in economics has long been emphasized by heterodox economists, some of whom would even claim to inverse the 'hierarchical stipulation' inherent in mainstream economics and, conversely, demand a 'macroeconomic foundation' for microeconomics (for example, King 2012).

One natural example of a heterodox research strategy following this tradition is stock-flow consistent macroeconomics (Godley & Lavoie 2007). Here, one starts with accounting identities and other stylized macroeconomic facts to study macroeconomic dynamics, rather than starting with speculative assumptions about the behavior of a 'representative household' (see Kirman 1992), as it is common in dynamic stochastic general equilibrium models. While such a 'macro-founded' approach provides an important alternative perspective on macroeconomic dynamics, it is not to be seen as superior to a micro-founded approach *per se*. Rather its contribution is to make macroeconomic constraints explicit in modeling, which serves as an important heuristic even when the model is eventually based on microeconomic relationships and assumptions as in so-called 'agent-based stock-flow consistent models,' which study the economy as a complex system with both bottom-up and top-down effects (for example, Caiani *et al.* 2016). Hence, the merit of taking different levels of analysis into account often lies in the enriching of perspectives on economic phenomena, which aligns well with heterodox economists' practice of pluralist engagement.

Table 10.1 summarizes the conceptual and methodological pitfalls collected in this section and illustrates the relation between these four fallacies. In what follows, we first examine the principles that heterodox economists have developed to deal with aggregates and aggregation

Table 10.1 Compositional fallacies: an overview

	Main error	Fallacious routine	Underlying misconception
The simplistic fallacy	Ignoring relations, i.e. underestimating the complexity of aggregation	Simply summing up individual properties	Wrong treatment of aggregation: "the whole is nothing more than the sum of its parts."
The static fallacy	Ignoring the possibility of unexplainable novelties / irreducible properties	Any aggregate property can be reduced	
The dogmatic fallacy	Ignoring that higher-level mechanisms can be studied on their own	Always aim at providing bottom-up explanations	Treatment of aggregates: "wholes cannot be explanatory—they do not carry mechanisms."
The hierarchical fallacy	Ignoring the possibility of downward causation	Never provide top-down explanations	

in economics, before developing a general philosophical foundation suitable for summarizing heterodox approaches.

A heterodox perspective on the micro–macro link: why the whole is more than the sum of its parts

One overarching theme in heterodox economic theorizing is that the consideration of social wholes is important for understanding socio-economic processes and outcomes. This view implies that wholes are more than a mere sum of their parts, since they exhibit non-trivial properties and carry effects of various sorts which cannot be gleaned from looking solely to their constituent parts. However, this idea has also been subject to different interpretations and applications within heterodox economics, leading to a series of distinct vantage points on the role of aggregates and aggregation in economics. Some scholars focus on the explanatory role of top-down mechanisms, while others try to escape the simplistic fallacy by building particularly sophisticated micro-founded models. They are united in treating the micro–macro link as a complex relationship that deserves theoretical attention, because social and economic aggregates may constitute novel objects or, at least, come with novel features, which may have specific real world consequences. We now turn to four fundamental perspectives that have played a decisive role in heterodox treatments of the micro–macro link.

The whole is more than the sum of its parts

One main implication of the idea that wholes do make a difference is to consider the spatial and temporal variance of social configurations in order to identify distinct realms of economic activity. Such distinctions may refer to historical differences (for example, 'medieval feudalism' versus 'twentieth century welfare state capitalism'), spatial variations (for example, 'core' and 'periphery') or distinct spheres of economic activities (for example, 'competitive market societies' versus 'subsistence communities'). These distinctions are deemed important since the course and effects of economic activities depend on their social and historical circumstances.

Such differentiations are often found in classical political economy. Consider, for instance, John Stuart Mill's distinction between the sphere of production and the sphere of distribution. For Mill, the decisive difference between these two economic realms is that while the former is constrained by nature, the latter is solely shaped by human institutions (Mill 1848: II.1.1–2). Consequently, different laws and assumptions apply in these contexts.

In Mill's account, humankind is clearly subject to 'macrofoundations' in the form of environmental, historical, and societal forces, as they largely define the constraints and modes of economic activity. In this regard many heterodox economists argue that holistic factors, like culture or institutions, are important for explaining social phenomena and allow for top-down effects or downward causation within their economic theorizing. In a bold and overarching interpretation, this view may extend to the claim that social and economic conditions completely determine actions, fate, and feelings of individuals. Such a view of socio-economic determinism is often associated with Marx's concept of 'historical materialism,' although such an interpretation does not do justice to the original Marxian account.[2] A more accurate account would probably compare the heterodox approach to that of a physicist studying the behavior of a single element (for example, the behavior of a comet entering the solar system or the pressure in some gas-container in a lab) by taking full account of the surrounding system (for example, the composition of the solar system or the size of the container) to correctly anticipate the impact of the latter (Andersen *et al.* 2000). This more modest attitude is key to understanding a variety of heterodox ideas, from ecological economists' emphasis on absolute constraints (Georgescu-Roegen 1971) to Keynes' definition of economics as "the art of choosing models which are relevant to the contemporary world" (Keynes ([1938] 1973: 296).

Relations matter

A second application of the general idea that social wholes make a difference focuses on the interrelatedness of individuals. Attention is devoted to the relations between individuals, and the corresponding impact of other people's attitudes and behavior on an individual's economic thought and action.

Interactions among agents as well as between structure and agency are of prime interest to heterodox economists, including: the analysis of interactions and relations across individual agents and of preference formation in the context of social emulation (following Marx or Veblen); the emergence of routines in organizations (Nelson & Winter 1982); and questions of social identity and the evolution of cooperation (Axelrod 1984; Bowles & Gintis 2011). Such a perspective naturally takes relations seriously and allows for agents of different influence and power, thereby serving as a guide for theorizing about self-reinforcing effects (Merton 1968), path-dependency (David 1985; Arthur 1989), wealth concentration, power structures, and elites (Rothschild 1971) as well as other forms of cumulative advantage (Myrdal 1957). One important implication of this reasoning is the conceptualization of an economy as a circular flow, where one person's expenditure adds to another person's income. This circular flow views monetary transactions as fundamental interactions, which constitute mutual interdependencies among single economic actors. The consequences of these interdependencies are a major theme in heterodox economics.

This focus on the role of relations avoids the simplistic fallacy by understanding social wholes as constituted by a set of individual nodes and their corresponding relational setup. Social relations play a twofold role. First, they serve as a transmission belt for cultural norms, institutional conventions, established hierarchies, shared goals, and aspirations within a social whole. Second, relations serve as a means for understanding how individual actions might influence social wholes and, hence, provide a lens for assessing social change and novelty.

The role of social relations as a transmission belt features prominently in heterodox economic thought and can be traced back to Karl Marx and Friedrich Engels ([1845] 2004: 122), who speak of individuals as an "ensemble of the social relations"; Thorstein Veblen (1899), who emphasized the social formation of consumer preferences; or Karl Polanyi (1944), who coined the term 'embeddedness' to highlight how individual economic action is always embedded in a certain socio-historical context. From a dynamic perspective this view can also be used to analyze questions of social mobility, where relational structures serve as a means for preserving social hierarchies as in Bowles & Gintis (1975) or Bourdieu (1998), who studied the role of educational systems for stratification in the US and France.

The second major feature of social relations, which allows active agents to influence aggregate properties, also has a prominent role in heterodox thinking and is exemplified by conceptions such as Schumpeter's entrepreneur (1934) and Keynes' animal spirits (1936). Both emphasize that some individual decisions are of great impact for future developments. Against this backdrop it comes as no surprise that active agency plays an important role in heterodox approaches to economic cooperation and trust, path creation and path dependence, and institutional design (for example, Hirschmann 1970).

This dual character of social relations allows for top-down as well as bottom-up effects and thereby captures the fact that individual agents and social structure are mutually interdependent. This point was most explicitly taken up by Mark Granovetter (1985), who refined the concept of embeddedness. Granovetter distinguished between over-socialized and under-socialized conceptions of individuals, attributing the latter to neoclassical and new institutional economics, while the former can be found in holistic approaches to social and economic analysis.

Both conceptions eventually posit an atomistic conception of individuals devoid of any relational embedding. For the over-socialized individuals, action has already been completely determined by social forces as a whole and quite independently of any specific relational setup, while under-socialized individuals do not have any significant relations to others. Granovetter (1985: 487) sees the embeddedness perspective as a conceptual alternative, wherein

[a]ctors do not behave or decide as atoms outside a social context, nor do they adhere slavishly to a script written for them by the particular intersection of social categories that they happen to occupy. Their attempts at purposive action are instead embedded in concrete, ongoing systems of social relations.

In this view, issues of trust and sympathy affect all interpersonal relations, even those, which are constituted as pure economic relations of exchange. The economic implications of this reasoning are non-trivial, as they concern industrial structure, trust levels and bargaining processes as well as the level of economic performance. A classic example is given by the high-tech sector, where clusters of coordination and cooperation are particularly common. These clusters are characterized by regular interactions among the involved suppliers, developers, and customers, which lead to a quasi-integration of different steps throughout the supply chain, although theses steps are carried out by formally independent organizations. The longer such relations exist, the more do they 'outgrow' the market and become insensitive to market signals such as 'prices' (Elsner et al. 2015).

However, Granovetter (1985) stresses that social embeddedness is not only a source of trust, stability, and cooperation, but can also lead to exploitation, disorder, and conflict. Hence,

Granovetter's approach does not allow for general predictions aside from the claim that "network structures matter," since outcomes eventually depend on the overall network structure. For example, determining whether a system is vulnerable to particular interest groups who work against general interests, thereby depleting stability and trust, depends on the concrete case at hand.

In mainstream economic accounts such structural properties largely remain implicit; for instance, most Walrasian general equilibrium models do not account for networks explicitly, but implicitly assume the system to be structured as a bipartite star network, as illustrated in Figure 10.1(a). In this setup agents are not directly related to each other, but rather connected indirectly via a central auctioneer who has direct relationships with all agents and, hence, resides in the network's center. A change of the network structure has non-trivial effects. An otherwise identical model economy characterized by a ring network, depicted in Figure 10.1(b), exhibits very different distributional characteristics and price patterns to the star network, implicit in the conventional Arrow–Debreu economy (Albin & Foley 1992).

Real networks are, of course, neither rings nor stars. Network analysis has made impressive progress since the 1990s and found that most empirical networks look in some ways similar to Figure 10.1(c). There are few nodes with many connections, and many nodes with few connections. Furthermore, nodes are organized into different clusters.[3] The economic implications of this structure is an important avenue for future research.

But can we make reasonable predictions about the meso or macro level of the economy, given a precise description of the micro components as well as their relations? Notwithstanding the obvious merits of such an approach, the next section explains why a general affirmative answer to this question cannot be provided.

There is real novelty

Another aspect of a heterodox perspective on the micro–macro link, which is strongly intertwined with incorporating relations into social and economic analysis, is the notion that novel objects or properties constantly arise in the course of social interaction. This specific aspect of social wholes—the fact they are carriers and transmitters of genuine novelty—is at the heart of this subsection.

Economic systems regularly produce novel features that are not predictable from past data. The emergence of novelty can be most intuitively illustrated for the case of innovation, which was a key element in the work of Joseph Schumpeter. Schumpeter ([1934] 2011: 66) distinguishes

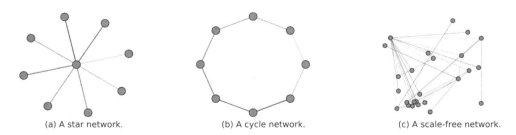

| (a) A star network. | (b) A cycle network. | (c) A scale-free network. |

Figure 10.1   Three different social networks

Notes: (a) represents the theoretical Arrow–Debreu Economy with the Walrasian auctioneer in the center; (b) is a ring, capturing dense neighborhood structures; (c) shows a scale free network.

Source: Author's own illustration.

between five types of innovation, such as the development of a new good, the introduction of products of higher quality, or alternative methods of production.

All these innovations may represent or bring forth novelties that were not existent in an economic system before. They may carry new mechanisms that fundamentally change the functioning of the economic system as a whole. For example, the advent of contemporary globalization not only came with cheaper import goods, but also introduced a new mechanism—the race for national competitiveness—which puts different countries in a competition for serving the interests of powerful transnational corporations. The invention of digital computers led to new markets, new goods, and new lifestyles, which continue to influence our society via novel mechanisms in various ways. While innovations are often a creative recombination of existing ideas, neither the exact way of recombination nor its consequences for society are a priori predictable.

This fact motivates heterodox economists to further investigate the micro–macro link to gain a deeper understanding of this non-predictability. One main pillar in this context is the development of arguments on fundamental uncertainty in economic action, which focuses on the role of crucial decisions in investment whose effects are very hard or impossible to anticipate. These circumstances give scope to alternative economic motives beyond conventional utility maximization such as routines and rules, individual vision and passion (as in Schumpeter's entrepreneur), or inherited instincts (as exemplified by Veblen's 'instinct of workmanship').

Another venue of work in this context aims for a refined conception of 'meso' in economic analysis (Dopfer et al. 2004; Elsner & Schwardt 2014). Proponents argue for a 'micro–meso–macro' framework as a substitute for the conventional micro–macro dichotomy. In such a framework the economic agents represent the micro level of the economy and are heterogeneous as they carry different rules. A rule and all its actualizations constitute a meso unit, which is seen as a key element in evolutionary economic investigation, since the interaction of rules is understood as a main driver of economic change on the macro level. Assume, for instance, that creditors and debtors in a given economy mutually adapt their crediting and borrowing behavior to each other. In such a setup increased risk taking on the side of creditors, who are prone to forget or ignore past turbulences, would be mirrored by increased borrowing by debtors leading to potentially unsustainable levels of debt. Hence, we can reach the classic Minskyan result that stability breeds instability (Minsky 1986) by employing a simple model of rule convergence on credit markets.

The obvious advantage of such an analytical framework is that it facilitates a focus on economic change and thus greater understanding of the source of the unpredictability of real novelty within the economy. One more specific expression of this rather general claim is provided by the theory of path dependence, originating from the seminal papers on technological lock-in by David (1985) and Arthur (1989). We can disentangle path-dependent processes into three different phases (Sydow et al. 2009; Dobusch & Kapeller 2013).

The first phase, path creation, characterizes a situation of contingency. Events happening at this stage are usually "outside the ex-ante knowledge of the observer" (Arthur 1989: 118). They are nevertheless important because these events characterize the initial conditions for the second phase, where an ergodic dynamic process, characterized by positive feedback effects and subsequent, causally linked events, leads to the dominance of one particular standard. The positive feedback may stem from different forms of network effects based on increasing returns, preferential attachment, learning and coordination effects, complementarity, or the convergence of expectations. The last phase, the resulting lock-in, reflects the resilience of the dominating standard against change. Thus, while it is almost impossible to predict the diffusion process *ex ante*, it only becomes possible to identify the dominant technology after one has entered the second phase of the path-dependent process.

Hence, path-dependency theory focuses on the mechanisms underlying the introduction of novelties and the creation and persistence of social standards of different forms, including social norms, organizational rules, business practices, and technological requirements. It provides a theoretical rationale for the emergence of novelties and explicates the difficulties in predicting such novelties. At the same time path-dependency theory is silent on the effects brought forth by such novelties, which often represent controversial questions in heterodox economics. A prime example is given by the effect of the adoption and diffusion of new innovations on the level of employment; while some innovations indeed function as labor-saving devices (as in the standard Keynesian approach), others may increase employment due to the creation of additional demand induced by novel products or improvements in product-quality and versatility (as in the Schumpeterian approach, see Witt 2001). Which effect eventually dominates in the face of general technological progress or a specific innovation is, hence, a question which can be hardly answered *ex ante*.

These arguments imply that *ex ante* predictions are often difficult or impossible, since the emergence and effects of novelties can hardly be fully anticipated. Nevertheless, the relevant trajectory can of course be explained *ex post*, as we can trace how a specific successful innovation diffused into society and how it affects their members.

Aggregation and welfare

Finally, our fourth perspective on social wholes and their role in economic theorizing relates to the normative question of economic welfare in the context of aggregation. Mandeville ([1714] 1962) advanced the view that 'private vice' in the form of egocentric instrumental rationality leads to 'public benefits,' that is, the maximization of social welfare. This view is deeply inscribed in modern mainstream economics, especially in the two fundamental theorems of welfare economics. While many heterodox economists could surely accept that the Mandeville case is a *possible* state of affairs, they also tend to critically examine the necessary conditions for such a result. Classical examples in this context include rationality traps—for example, if I can improve my view in the theater by standing up, will there also be a collective improvement if everyone follows this rationale?—and the 'tragedy of the commons' which describes the unsustainable usage a public good in the absence of a suitable mode of social coordination (Ostrom 1990). More formally, such cases can be expressed in the form of a prisoner's dilemma, which illustrates the core property of rationality traps and tragedies of the commons, namely that myopic individually rational actions will lead to the worst possible aggregate outcome. This relationship is the main reason why some heterodox economists consider a prisoner's dilemma as one archetype for heterodox economic modeling (Elsner *et al.* 2015). Since the welfare aspects of social organization are a general *topos* of heterodox economic theorizing, we find variants of this argument in several heterodox traditions: ecological economists' emphasis on collective good problems (such as climate change); Marxian perspectives on power and conflict; and evolutionary and institutional economists' focus on the role of social norms, conventions, and law in resolving social dilemmas.

Systemism as a general framework

Systemism and heterodoxy

While the label 'systemism' might seem new, one can be assured that the practice of systemism is far from something completely novel. We introduce systemism to provide a full-fledged philosophical concept, which encompasses the basic heterodox arguments on the micro–macro link in economics. The development of systemism owes mainly to the works of Mario Bunge, philosopher and polymath, who aimed to transgress the traditional dichotomy between individualism and holism, which he perceived as an outdated hindrance to social research and epistemological debate.

Bunge cites a variety of examples for what he conceives as a 'systemist' social research. Interestingly, within these passages the names of heterodox economists come in definitely non-random abundance. Among others, Bunge mentions John Maynard Keynes and Wassily Leontief (Bunge 2004: 187), Max Weber, Joseph A. Schumpeter, Thorstein B. Veblen, or K. William Kapp (Bunge 1999: 92–93). More recent examples of heterodox approaches compatible with a systemist perspective include understanding economics as the study of the social provisioning process (Jo 2011) and evolutionary economists' focus on the meso level of economic activity (Dopfer *et al.* 2004). In sum, these observations suggest that heterodox economic approaches are salient candidates for illustrating a systemist approach to social and economic issues and, conversely, systemism serves as a natural candidate for substantiating established practices in heterodox economic research from an epistemological viewpoint.

Systemism: key ideas and concepts

Systemism is built upon the fundamental twin concept of systems and mechanisms, where the latter are situated within or between the former. Thereby any object or entity in systemist analysis is considered either as a system itself or as a component of a system (Bunge 1996).

A system is composed by a set of nodes or components (its *composition*) with a particular relational setup (a system's *structure* or *organization*) situated within a certain *environment*. The interrelatedness of agents not only contributes to the constitution of a specific system, but gives rise to a variety of 'ontological novelties': that is, some features that the whole possesses, but its components lack (*global properties*, like a nation's culture or a firm's success); or some features that components acquire precisely because they are part of some system (*relational properties*, like being a creditor, a wife, or an employee; see Bunge 1996). The concept of a system can therefore be applied on several levels. For example, a family is a system consisting of different members with particular relations to each other; at the same time, it is part of a community system within which it has several relations to other components of the community. The resulting levels take the form of a hierarchy of sub- and super-systems, which serve as a basic ontological framework. Such a hierarchical understanding of reality has been insinuated by several heterodox approaches, in particular in the work of Herbert Simon (1962), who provides an evolutionary explanation for the predominance of hierarchy in complex social systems.

The second fundamental aspect in systemism is a focus on *mechanisms*, meaning law-like relationships, and the attempt to provide mechanism-based explanations of social phenomena (Bunge 1997). Mechanisms work within or across social systems and lead to continuous changes and stabilization of a given system. This is why we conceive of them "as a process (or sequence of states) in a concrete system, natural or social," (Bunge 2004: 186). Thereby three rough types of mechanisms can be distinguished. First, within-level mechanisms operate within social systems, but address only one ontological layer; for example, a reduction in hourly income may induce a household to increase working hours. Second, bridging mechanisms also work within a certain social system but can take the form of agency-structure relations (a bottom–up mechanism or upward causation) or structure-agency relations (top-down mechanisms or downward causation). The former provide a theoretical alternative for the aggregation of individual behavior, going beyond a mere 'summing up' of individual properties by employing theoretical mechanisms for means of aggregation. Examples of such 'bridging mechanisms' are bandwagon effects, where final outcomes depend on the sequence of individual moves; positive feedback effects, which may lead to path-dependent properties of social systems; or emulation effects, where individual behavior conforms to or is constrained by the behavior of others as in the case of rationality traps. Finally, there are mechanisms operating between a system and its environment (overlapping and surrounding systems), such as the imitation of technologies or competition among firms. One example of a truly systemist heterodox approach integrating all these relevant processes is the agent-based stock-flow consistent models, which aim to transcend both purely individualist and holist approaches.

This focus on concrete mechanisms in systemist epistemology aims to refine the standard model of scientific explanation, by uncovering the generative mechanisms *underlying* empirical relationships instead of simply collecting and applying these relationships. To explain the death of a person with their property of being human, and the fact that all humans eventually die, is not very insightful; rather we should try to identify the concrete mechanisms that have led to the state of affairs to eventually arrive at more general theories (Bunge 1997: 425).[4]

Note that systemism is not a theory, but rather an ontological and epistemological heuristic, like "a viewpoint, or a strategy for designing research projects whose aim is to discover some of the features of systems of a particular kind" (Bunge 2004: 191). Considering this fact and the fundamental aspects of systemist models, we suggest that systemism is a well-suited philosophical framework to structure heterodox theorizing on the micro–macro link as outlined above. Based on these considerations, the next section explores the relation between heterodox economic arguments and the systemic framework.

Heterodox economics in a systemist framework

Bunge's concept of systemism does not only provide a suitable philosophical framework for heterodox theorizing on the micro–macro link, but also offers an intuitive way to express and conceptualize theoretical considerations on micro–macro interactions. The following examples illustrate this aspect from a practical perspective.

The first illustration is provided by Bowles & Park (2005), who use the Veblenian concept of social emulation to explain the allegedly counterintuitive relationship between rising inequality and increasing working hours (Figure 10.2). Due to social emulation of preferences, a higher

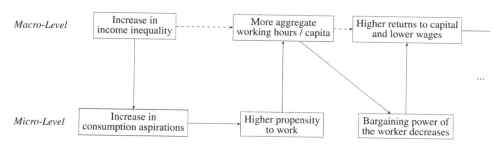

Figure 10.2   Income inequality, labor supply, and economic development in a systemist framework drawing on Bowles & Park (2005)
Source: Author's own illustration, based on Bowles & Park (2005).

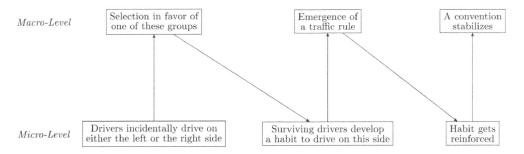

Figure 10.3 The evolution of a traffic convention based on Hodgson & Knudsen (2004) in a systemist framework
Source: Author's own illustration, based on Hodgson & Knudsen (2004).

level of income inequality induces an increase in consumption aspirations across households. In order to live up to these aspirations, a (sizable) subset of these households may increase their working effort, which leads to an increase of average working hours. A possible extension of this argument is that this increase in the supply of labor reduces the bargaining power of workers, leading to lower wages and further increasing income inequality, resulting in a path-dependent downward spiral.

Our second illustration considers the emergence and evolution of social conventions. Hodgson & Knudsen (2004) discuss an agent-based model where drivers are forced to decide whether to drive on the left or on the right side of a street. They study the conditions required to guarantee the emergence of a stable convention. While their major finding is that habit-formation is a probable vantage point for the emergence of conventions, the illustration in Figure 10.3 extends the underlying argument by illustrating the emergence of conventions in a systemist framework considering both bottom-up and top-down effects.

These examples show that Bunge's concept of systemism is far away from a methodological straight-jacket. On the contrary, the schematic approach utilized in these examples aims at illustrating how this approach can be employed to facilitate conceptual thinking and the crafting of ontologically sensible theoretical frameworks on the basis of a solid epistemological foundation. It further provides a useful meta-language that enables the effective comparison of different approaches towards the micro–macro link in heterodox economics and to exploit the potential complementarities among these different approaches (see also Dobusch & Kapeller 2012).

Conclusion

The complex relationship between different ontological levels has received considerable attention in heterodox theorizing. This has led to a number of important independent contributions on the role of aggregates and the issue of aggregation in social research, which often allow heterodox economists to circumvent typical fallacies of aggregation identified in the second section of this chapter.

In this chapter we demonstrate that the central pillars of different heterodox conceptions of the micro–macro link are not only complementary, but can also be subsumed under a common philosophical umbrella labeled 'systemism.' This umbrella is a useful device helping to explore the commonalities and differences in various approaches to the micro–macro link in heterodox economics. In many cases such comparisons will facilitate 'heterodox convergence,' as in the case of evolutionary-institutional and social economics (Elsner 2014), while in other cases the relationship may take the form of productive disagreement. Such an endeavor requires a common denominator for the different approaches enabling mutual communication and comparability. We argue this missing component is exactly what systemism can supply.

Acknowledgments

We would like to thank Alessandro Caiani, Wolfram Elsner, Volker Gadenne, Iciar Dominguez Lacasa, and the editors for their valuable comments on earlier drafts of this chapter. All remaining errors are our own.

Notes

1 The proposition that any aggregate property can be reduced is objectionable on two levels. First, one could argue that such an undertaking is often principally infeasible, because the relevant initial data is never completely known and the associated set of calculations might lack a determinable solution. Sometimes it is even asserted that some specific higher-level activities like human consciousness (Chalmers 2006) or conscious agents (Popper 1979: 292) bear no direct mechanistic relationships with lower-level activities. Second, one could argue that such an undertaking would be practically infeasible since issues become too complicated given the limitation of our current empirical and theoretical knowledge (see Simon 1962).
2 Consider Marx's claim that "men make their own history, but they do not make it as they please; they do not make it under circumstances chosen by themselves, but under circumstances directly encountered, given and transmitted from the past" (Marx 1852: 15).
3 One should be more precise than the space of this book chapter allows. See Newman (2003) for an introduction considering most recent advances in the literature.
4 Note that Bunge (1997) uses this argument not only to question the conventional covering law model, but also to criticize other concepts, like hermeneutics or Occam's razor, which neglect the main task to bring forth new and testable hypotheses.

References

Albin, P. & Foley, D. 1992. 'Decentralized, dispersed exchange without an auctioneer.' *Journal of Economic Behavior & Organization*, 18 (1): 27–51.
Andersen, P.B., Emmeche, C., Finnemann, N.O., & Christiansen, P.V. (eds.) 2000. *Downward Causation*. Aarhus, DK: Aarhus University Press.
Anderson, P.W. 1972. 'More is different.' *Science*, 177 (4047): 393–396.
Arthur, B. 1989. 'Competing technologies, increasing returns, and lock-in by historical events.' *The Economic Journal*, 99 (394): 116–131.
Axelrod, R. 1984. *The Evolution of Cooperation*. New York: Basic Books.
Bourdieu, P. 1998. *Practical Reason: On the Theory of Action*. Stanford, CA: Stanford University Press.
Bowles, S. & Gintis, H. 1975. *Schooling in Capitalist America*. New York: Basic Books.
Bowles, S. & Gintis, H. 2011. *A Cooperative Species*. Princeton, NJ: Princeton University Press.
Bowles, S. & Park, Y. 2005. 'Emulation, inequality, and work hours: was Thorsten Veblen right?' *The Economic Journal*, 115 (507): F397–F412.
Bunge, M. 1996. *Finding Philosophy in Social Science*. New Haven, CT: Yale University Press.
Bunge, M. 1997. 'Mechanism and explanation.' *Philosophy of the Social Sciences*, 27 (4): 410–465.
Bunge, M. [1998] 1999. *Social Science under Debate*. Toronto: University of Toronto Press.
Bunge, M. 2004. 'How does it work: the search for explanatory mechanisms.' *Philosophy of the Social Sciences*, 34 (2): 182–210.
Caiani, A., Godin, A., Caverzasi, E., Gallegati, M., Kinsella, S., & Stiglitz, J. 2016. 'Agent based-stock flow consistent macroeconomics: Towards a benchmark model.' *Journal of Economic Dynamics & Control*, 69: 375–408.
Chalmers, D.J. 2006. 'Strong and weak emergence,' *in*: P. Clayton & P. Davies (eds.), *The Re-emergence of Emergence*. Cambridge, UK: Cambridge University Press, 244–254.

Claudius Gräbner, Jakob Kapeller

David, P.A. 1985. 'Clio and the economics of QWERTY.' *American Economic Review*, 75 (2): 332–337.

Dobusch, L. & Kapeller, J. 2012. 'Heterodox united vs. mainstream city? Sketching a framework for interested pluralism in economics.' *Journal of Economic Issues*, 46 (4): 1035–1057.

Dobusch, L. & Kapeller, J. 2013. 'Breaking new paths: theory and method in path dependence research.' *Schmalenbach Business Review*, 65 (3): 288–311.

Dopfer, K., Foster, J., & Potts, J. 2004. 'Micro–meso–macro.' *Journal of Evolutionary Economics*, 14 (3): 263–279.

Drèze, J. & Sen, A. 1989. *Hunger and Public Action*. Oxford: Clarendon Press.

Elsner, W. 2014. 'Social economics and evolutionary institutionalism today.' *Forum for Social Economics*, published online. Available from http://dx.doi.org/10.1080/07360932.2014.964744 [Accessed February 29, 2016]

Elsner, W. & Schwardt, H. 2014. 'Trust and arena size: expectations, institutions, and general trust, and critical population and group sizes.' *Journal of Institutional Economics*, 10 (1): 107–134.

Elsner, W., Heinrich, T., & Schwardt, H. 2015. *The Microeconomics of Complex Economies*. Amsterdam: Academic Press.

Georgescu-Roegen, N. 1971. *The Entropy Law and the Economic Process*. Cambridge, MA: Harvard University Press.

Godley, W. & Lavoie, M. 2007. *Monetary Economics*. New York: Palgrave Macmillan.

Granovetter, M. 1985. 'Economic action and social structure: the problem of embeddedness.' *American Journal of Sociology*, 91 (3): 481–510.

Hirschmann, A.O. 1970. *Exit, Voice, and Loyalty: Responses to Decline in Firms, Organizations, and States*. Cambridge, MA: Harvard University Press.

Hodgson, G.M. & Knudsen, T. 2004. 'The complex evolution of a simple traffic convention: the functions and implications of habit.' *Journal of Economic Behavior & Organization*, 54 (1): 19–47.

Jo, T.-H. 2011. 'Social provisioning process and socio-economic modeling.' *American Journal of Economics and Sociology*, 70 (5): 1094–1116.

Kapeller, J. 2015. 'Beyond foundations: systemism in economic thinking.' in: T.-H. Jo & Z. Todorova (eds.), *Advancing the Frontiers in Heterodox Economics: Essays in Honor of Frederic S. Lee*. London: Routledge, 115–134.

Keynes, J.M. [1936] 2007. *The General Theory of Employment, Interest and Money*. London: Macmillan.

Keynes, J.M. [1938] 1973. 'Letter to Roy Harrod,' in: *Collected Works of J.M. Keynes, Volume XIV*. London: Macmillan, 295–300.

King, J.E. 2012. *The Microfoundations Delusion: Metaphor and Dogma in the History of Macroeconomics*. Cheltenham, UK: Edward Elgar.

Kirman, A. 1992. 'What or whom does the representative individual represent?' *Journal of Economic Perspectives* 6(2): 117–136.

Lee, F.S. 2011. 'Heterodox microeconomics and the foundation of heterodox macroeconomics.' *Economia Informa*, 367: 6–20.

Lucas, R.E. 1976. 'Econometric policy evaluation: a critique.' *Carnegie–Rochester Conference Series on Public Policy*, 1 (1): 19–46.

Mandeville, B. [1714] 1962. *The Fable of the Bees or Private Vices, Publick Benefits*. New York: Capricorn Books.

Marx, K. [1852] 2008. *The Eighteenth Brumaire of Louis Napoleon*. Rockville, MD: Wildside Press.

Marx, K. & Engels, F. [1845] 2004. 'Theses on Feuerbach,' in: *The German Ideology*. New York: International Publishers, 121–123.

Merton, R.K. 1968. 'The Matthew effect in science.' *Science*, 159 (3810): 56–63.

Mill, J.S. [1848] 1909. *Principles of Political Economy with Some of Their Applications to Social Philosophy*. London: Longmans, Green and Co.

Minsky, H.P. 1986. *Stabilizing an Unstable Economy*. New Haven, CT: Yale University Press.

Myrdal, G. 1957. *Economic Theory and Underdeveloped Regions*. London: Gerald Duckworth.

Nelson, R.R. & Winter, S.G. [1982] 1996. *An Evolutionary Theory of Economic Change*. Cambridge, MA: Belknap Press.

Newman, M.E.J. 2003. 'The structure and function of complex networks.' *SIAMReview*, 45 (2): 167–256.

Ostrom, E. 1990. *Governing the Commons: The Evolution of Institutions for Collective Action*. Cambridge, UK: Cambridge University Press.

Polanyi, K. [1944] 2001. *The Great Transformation: The Political and Economic Origins of Our Time*. Beacon Press.

Popper, K.R. 1979. *Objective Knowledge: An Evolutionary Approach*. Oxford: Clarendon Press.

Robbins, L. 1932. *An Essay on the Nature and Significance of Economic Science*. London: Macmillan.

Rothschild, K.W. 1971. *Power in Economics*. Harmondsworth, UK: Penguin.

Rothschild, K.W. 1988. 'Micro-foundations, ad hocery, and Keynesian theory.' *Atlantic Economic Journal*, 16 (2): 12–21.

Schelling, T.C. 1978. *Micromotives and Macrobehavior*. New York: Norton and Company.

Schumpeter, J.A. [1934] 2011. *The Theory of Economic Development*, 2nd edn. New Brunswick: Transaction Publishers.

Schumpeter, J.A. [1942] 1975. *Capitalism, Socialism and Democracy*. New York: Harper and Row.

Simon, H.A. 1962. 'The architecture of complexity.' *Proceedings of the American Philosophical Society*, 106 (6): 467–482.

Sydow, J., Schreyögg, G., & Koch, J. 2009. 'Organizational path dependence: opening the black box.' *Academy of Management Review*, 34 (4): 689–709.

Witt, U. 2001. 'Learning to consume—a theory of wants and the growth of demand.' *Journal of Evolutionary Economics*, 11 (1): 23–36.

Veblen, T.B. [1899] 1979. *The Theory of the Leisure Class*. London: Allen & Unwin.

Part III
The anatomy of capitalism

11

Society and its institutions

John F. Henry

Introduction

Unlike neoclassical (or mainstream) economists, heterodox economists are necessarily interested in the examination of institutions—though those entering from different theoretical vantage points display different levels of interest and different approaches. One fundamental reason why we observe a difference between mainstream and heterodox theorists in this regard lies in their respective foundations. All heterodox economists, regardless of specific theoretical orientation, approach the analysis of the economy from some version of an 'embedded' methodology (Polanyi 1944). That is, the economy is seen in a social context. 'Society' incontrovertibly necessitates various arrangements or organizations in order to function—or even exist—and such arrangements require supporting concepts to allow sufficient cohesion among participants, or these would dissolve in some anarchical fashion. Such arrangements and organizations are 'institutions.'

Neoclassical theory, in contrast, starts its analysis from the vantage point of a non-social, hypothetical individual. Consider the words of Frank Knight (1960: 71), one of the most critically minded twentieth-century theorists: "I do not see how we can talk sense about economics without considering the economic behavior of the isolated individual. Only in that way can we expect to get rid by abstraction of all the social relationships." First, economic theory based on the hypothetical Robinson Crusoe is driven as far as it can be on the foundation of rational, utility-maximizing individuals in search of equilibrium. Only then the various complications posed by the various social relations into which people enter, as captured in institutions, can be introduced. And these institutions are likely to pose 'frictions' that disturb the economic narrative, but not in such a way as to irrevocably damage it. Hence, institutions are not of primary or even significant concern—except in that they may, and probably will, interfere with the workings of an 'ideal,' perfectly competitive, laissez-faire model that, left to its internal workings, generates optimal outcomes.

Some might object that the new institutionalists have superseded this methodological individualist approach. Such an objection is not correct. While there certainly is the appearance that a significant alteration has taken place, the substance of the argument has not changed. Consider the position taken by Oliver Williamson (1975: 1): "[t]he new institutional economists both draw on microtheory and, for the most part, regard what they are doing as complementary to, rather than a substitute for, conventional analysis." Further, "[t]ransaction cost economics is akin to orthodoxy in its insistence that economizing is central to economic organization" (Williamson 1987: xii). As a leading (original) institutionalist has pointed out, even the work of Elinor Ostrom "assumes that the world is made up of and directed by individuals who are rational calculators" (Hayden 2011: 468).

As a last word on the neoclassical framework and approach, Diane Coyle in a recent work designed to counter the typical heterodox (mainly institutionalist) complaints directed toward orthodoxy, argues that neoclassicism has changed its stripes. To be sure, *circa* 1970, such protests may have been appropriate, as conventional theory was mechanical and sterile. But, matters have changed. However, after reviewing various developments within this framework that ostensibly have changed the substance of the argument, she concludes that the *core* of the theory has not changed. Rational choice (and utility maximization), self-interested (non-social) behavior, and (the search for) equilibrium still form the core of conventional theory. From a hypothetical, ideal entry point, one can then add asymmetric information, non-competitive market forms, and so on, and it is these modifications that ostensibly make neoclassical economics the vibrant theoretical system it is today (Coyle 2007: 251–254). Coyle (2007: 252) quotes Paul Lazear as one authority: "We may permit imperfect information, transaction costs and other intervening variables to muddy the waters, but we do not model behavior as being determined by forces beyond the control of the individual." In other words, nothing fundamental has changed; neoclassical theory's point of departure is still the same individualist foundation as expressed by Frank Knight and earlier economists going back to at least Jeremy Bentham ([1780] 1969: 87) who forthrightly stated, "[t]he community is a fictitious body, composed of the individual persons who are considered as constituting its members." (I note that in Coyle's account there is no mention of money. The significance of this omission will be apparent below.)

A heterodox approach to institutions

In what follows, a general argument is developed that addresses what I consider to be strengths and shortcomings in the heterodox approaches to institutions, and I suggest a strategy that might assist in bringing the various heterodox camps into a unified—or, at least closely aligned—program, based on their respective strengths, to develop a better, more cogent analysis than that offered by conventional economics. Before that, a caveat: I do not consider Austrian economists to be heterodox as they rest on the same individualist (classical liberal) foundation as neoclassical theorists. Hence, they do not figure in my account. Additionally, I usually subsume the Sraffian contribution under the more general school of classical political economy given its close affinity to the works of Adam Smith, David Ricardo, and Karl Marx.

A useful point of departure is Thorstein Veblen's (1909: 626) definition of institutions as "the settled habits of thought common to the generality of man." Why invoke Veblen? I suggest that Veblen serves as something of a standard by which the state of heterodoxy can be evaluated. Initially, Veblen developed an articulate, forceful criticism of neoclassical theory. And this is important in any program to establish a heterodox—that is, non-neoclassical—theory. Further, in his many works, Veblen has spoken to institutionalism, and is claimed to be one of this perspective's founders, and he has spoken to Post Keynesianism (Wray 2007), to Marxian economics (Mouhammed 1994), and to feminism (Gilman 1999). As well, Veblen addresses issues of social valuation, and is thus sympathetic to the work of social economists (Tool 1977).

In his definition, it is at once noted that Veblen's position entails an ideological component. But, for ideological appeals to have traction, they must speak to some underlying structure. Hence, a proper heterodox approach to institutions must examine both structure (or organization) and the supporting ideological overlay as conjoined features of such organizations or arrangements: structure requires ideological support, and ideology reinforces structure.

Let us reflect on the terms 'freedom' and 'democracy.' The 'settled habits of thought' have it that western society upholds and promotes such conceptions. And, there are institutional arrangements that underlie both, in particular some form of representative government that extolls the personal worth of the individual. The first question raised in a heterodox approach to this issue is (or should be) just what does 'freedom' or 'democracy' mean? This is an ideological issue. The second question is (or should be) just what is the social nature of government? Thus, government, as an institution, must be brought under examination. There is a strong tendency among heterodox economists to view government—at least those forms current in modern capitalist nations—as (potentially) providing various solutions to problems created by the market. But when government activity exacerbates such problems or does not address problems in a way suggested by heterodox policy proposals, the institutional nature and character of government is not (or is rarely) called into question. However, calls are put forward for the selection of a different cast of politicians to seize the helm of government and set things right. I shall address this issue more fully below. The initial point is that institutions must be subjected to critical scrutiny at both the ideological and structural level. What does such an examination require?

It is accepted by heterodox economists of whatever persuasion that institutions are fundamentally 'social.' That is, they are created in a social environment, by and through social organizations to achieve social ends. Hence, in order to better understand and critically evaluate institutions, the point of departure must be an examination of that social context, namely, society. This presents the first difficulty given the current state of heterodoxy.

Specifying what is meant by society is necessary and problematic. Clearly, those of a heterodox persuasion do not develop their argument on a methodological individualist foundation, as do neoclassical theorists. Individuals are claimed to be social, so an investigation of society is mandated. Further, for institutionalists and social economists in particular, the claim is made that culture, a creation of society, is of great significance, so culture must be taken into account. However, what is meant by society? What is meant by culture? In order to better articulate the issues at stake, I turn to Frank Knight's 1939 article, 'Ethics of economic reform.'

Admitting that man is a social animal, Knight then objects to what he terms 'groupism,' any theory that originates in society. The central tenet of groupism is that society is real and is "the real repository of value, and the real choosing subject or moral agent" (Knight [1939] 1982: 92). According to Knight, there are two problems with such a conception. First, society—as a unit of analysis—must be identified, and this is impossible without the introduction of a political state (Knight [1939] 1982: 97–99). The state is claimed to represent the whole of society (as in Hegel), but this requires that the state embody the general will (as in Rousseau).[1]

In reality, however, there are only individual wills, and unless the state uses its political power to impose a supposed general will, no consensus can be formed. That is, the state must use dictatorial power, in whatever form, to create and affirm cohesion (more on this below). Groupism, therefore, is anti-freedom (in the classical liberal, individualist sense).

I suggest that Knight has a point. Too often institutionalists, social economists, and even Marxian scholars refer to society as if it were an organic whole. (Post Keynesians and feminists are not at the center of this specific critique.) Thus, there are social (or societal) interests in which all individual members somehow have the same interests as those of society. Granted, there may be frictions among sections of the population, but these can be appeased through some sort of democratic process (see below). This speaks to the issue of general will. Rousseau eventually settled on God as representing and imposing the general will, and if any entity has dictatorial power it is God. The classical economists (including Marx) were better in this regard as they divided society into economic classes, each with its own interests that were not necessarily (and usually not) in accord with other classes. The state, then, usually cannot represent all of society. For Smith, for example, the state's main function was to protect the interests of property owners. Even in this respect, however, there are problems as not all workers, say, have the same working-class interests, and there are different interests represented by different sets of property owners. The analyses surrounding the objectives of industrial and financial capitalists found in Marx, Veblen, and Keynes, among others is indicative of such differences.

This issue returns us to Veblen who writes against the notion of (capitalist) society as an organic whole. Rather, it was a fractious, antagonistic organization in which 'absentee owners' and the 'underlying population' had fundamentally different interests in which the former were interested in pecuniary gain and the latter, social provisioning. And these objectives were (usually) in conflict. The state, then could not advance the interests of all classes of the population in some harmonious fashion. Rather, the state was designed to represent vested interests—those who placed pecuniary gain as primary.

> [M]odern politics is business politics. . . . This is true both of foreign and domestic policy. Legislation, police surveillance, the administration of justice, the military and diplomatic service, all are chiefly concerned with business relations, pecuniary interests, and they have little more than an incidental bearing on other human interests.
>
> *Veblen [1904] 1975: 286, 269*

At the same time, a pretense of cohesion, of social solidarity had to be put forward in order to minimize conflict and permit the extant economic organization to function. For Veblen, the main ideological force through which this is accomplished is patriotism (or nationalism), and patriotism was always associated with competition and best promoted in wartime.

> Patriotism may be defined as a sense of partisan solidarity in respect of prestige. . . . The patriotic spirit is a spirit of emulation, evidently, at the same time that it is emulation shot through with a sense of solidarity. It belongs under the general caption of sportsmanship, rather than of workmanship. Now, any enterprise in sportsmanship is bent on an invidious success, which must involve as its major purpose the defeat and humiliation of some competitor. . . . Its aim is a differential gain . . . and the emulative spirit that comes under the head of patriotism . . . seeks this differential advantage by injury of the rival rather than by an increase of home-bred well-being.
>
> *Veblen 1917: 31, 33*

Thus, rather than an understanding of society as some organic whole, the underlying arrangements of capitalist (and other) societies promoted cleavages, cleavages that required some governing process or mechanism to conceal those cleavages and prevent societal disorder. Institutions, in particular patriotism, were created to generate the illusion that the state was representative of all. I contend that this position escapes Knight's criticism, and can serve as something of a starting point for a more critical understanding of society.

The second consideration is Knight's position on the early-twentieth-century inclusion of information arising from early anthropologists' investigations into primitive cultures in which *homo economicus* was not found—at least not in a fully developed sense. Indeed, such investigations found their way into the conventional economic journals of the day such as the *Journal of Political Economy* (see Pearson 2000). In 1941, Knight wrote a critical essay on this trend, directed at the then recent work of Melville Herskovitz's (1940), *The Economic Life of Primitive Peoples*. Essentially, economists had to maintain their core assumption of individual rationality in the neoclassical sense; otherwise, confusion would reign and economists would not be able to say anything useful. Moreover, economists should not seek an understanding of primitive peoples as such peoples were creatures of their specific cultures.

> He would then avoid any appearance of teaching anthropology as such, unless he uses, in its entirety, some actual and full report of a particular society at a particular date by and anthropologist accept in his own profession as reliable.
>
> *Knight 1941: 261*

That is, as people's behaviors differed based on different cultures, there was no universal behavioral assumption that would serve as the underlying foundation from which to construct economic theory. *Homo economicus*, while surely stylized, permits the development of a powerful theoretical system.

This is the challenge, and it goes back to the *Methodenstreit* of the nineteenth century: can a position on the nature of society and its accompanying culture be established that the respective camps of heterodoxy agree upon and which serves as something of a foundation upon which to build a heterodox general theory? *Homo economicus*, as Knight states, has well-served neoclassicism; it is a very powerful ideological concept and appeals to the notion of freedom as articulated in classical liberalism—a notion resting on the individual.

One essential component of such a foundation must be that society consists of social relationships among its members. Otherwise, the term society would be meaningless. Bentham ([1780] 1969) would have been right: the community (society) was a fiction. Hence, the examination of *social* institutions requires an examination of the social relationships underlying such structures and accompanying ideology. In other words, institutions, at their foundation, *are social relationships*, and social relationships must then be articulated and shown to constitute the core of any examination of institutions.

On government and the state

In the heterodox literature, the prevailing tendency is to equate government and the state, or, at least to use the terms interchangeably. Another tendency is to juxtapose the state and the market. A third tendency is to understand the state as an institution capable of achieving objectives in the larger public interest. (These tendencies are well-referenced in Chapter 33 by Anna Klimina in this volume.) These inclinations create problems in examining the nature of institutions and the relations among institutions and the creation of an organization promoting the process of social provisioning (see below).

The first issue is the equating of the state and government. To be sure, in modern organizations, there is clearly a relationship between these institutional structures. But, such a relationship has not always existed, nor is the relationship one of equivalence. There has always been some form of governmental setup, no matter how minimal. This is not true for state institutions. In primitive society, for example, governments existed in the form of either elected officials (chiefs, sachems), or the convening of the clan/tribal population as a whole. Government was a non-coercive arrangement and attempted to advance the mutual interests of the population as agreed upon by those populations. The state, on the other hand, represents coercion: policing mechanisms, legal systems that require courts independent of the population, prisons, and the like. Indeed, there is a large literature on the development of the state that clearly demonstrates the difference between non-state organizations—which did display government—and state societies (see, for example, Yoffee 2005).

The perspective in which government and the state are seen as equivalent represents two weaknesses in heterodox theories. In these approaches, there is insufficient attention paid to comparative analysis, a weakness specifically noted in the Post Keynesian literature except for those of a 'Chartalist' orientation. In particular, to properly understand institutions in the modern, mainly capitalist context, there must be reference points to those organizations in which the modern institutions did not exist. Otherwise, we fall into a neoclassical 'trap' in which a universalist position is put forward arguing some sort of naturalist approach to institutions—again, running counter to Veblen's position on neoclassical theorizing: rather than institutions as social relationships requiring analysis as to their origins and development, these are seen to arise in response to a natural, necessary requirement to facilitate a solution to a universal economic problem—often the search for efficiency. In conventional theory, for example, money arises to overcome the inefficiencies associated with barter. In primitive societies/economies, we do not see laws, standing courts, prisons, standing armies, policing mechanisms, and the like. (Nor do we see money.) These are characteristic of the state. So, the questions should be: why do such institutions exist, what is their purpose, and whom do they serve? If we accept that institutions are social relationships in their structural/ideological expressions, then such an inquiry should be seen as necessary in order to better understand these institutions in a historic/social context. That is, the heterodox approach to institutions must be developed on the basis of a comparative methodology in which history is taken seriously and is incorporated into the analysis. But, for the most part, this is not an aspect of the heterodox agenda, though we do see lip-service paid to history (see Hodgson 2001). Consider the implications. Governments have existed in both early, egalitarian societies as well as the more recent inegalitarian class societies of slavery, feudalism, and capitalism but states have existed only in the latter. What then is the function of the state? Is it to assist in the development and preservation of inequality? To be sure, there is overlap between government and the state in that, for example, laws are the creation of government. But the state is not the government as we do not observe such an equivalence throughout history.

This raises the next point, which speaks to institutions directly. If the state is designed to promote and preserve inequality, then many institutions must not be seen as social, but rather as anti-social—a much more evocative term. Various segregationist arrangements—for example, 'Jim Crow' in the United States,[2] and apartheid in South Africa—are certainly institutions, and the accompanying ideology is that of racial inferiority as a natural foundation for such institutions. These are arrangements developed to promote inequality. As such, they damage the interests of significant portions of the general population, weaken the social provisioning process, and, thus, I argue, are anti-social. I suggest that greater attention should be paid to these anti-social institutions as analysis of these arrangements will cast much light on the nature of contemporary society. These arrangements must not be seen as aberrant or misguided, but integral to the social relations that constitute institutions. Otherwise, why would they exist?

This leads to the second weakness. There is great emphasis among heterodox economists that the state (read government) should do the right thing in advancing the interests of the general population. This approach leads to a reformist position, and the success of reformism must be based on an underlying understanding of society ordered in such a way that economic matters can be satisfactorily resolved within that very society. That is, in the final analysis, there is a common interest that can be served through appropriate institutional adjustments. Indicative of this is the work of J. Fagg Foster, a noted and influential institutionalist theorist. Foster's theory of institutional adjustment places great reliance on government to implement change.[3] The locus or origin of change is recognized interdependence, the understanding that any change requires the participation—willingly or not—of those affected by such change. And, any institutional change must adhere to the principle of minimal dislocation (see Tool 2000 for a good, sympathetic account). If one adheres to Foster's position, it appears that a progressive agenda can be developed—and all heterodox economists desire this—*if* some democratic form of government exists, *if* participation of all those affected occurs, and *if* the proposed change is minimally disruptive.

That is, Foster's theory is constrained by existing arrangements on the assumption that there is a possible harmonious outcome within those arrangements. Whether this is correct or not depends upon a critical evaluation of just those arrangements, those institutions. In short, one reads complaints by heterodox economists that governments (states) are not advancing the interests of the (vast) majority, but, rather, serving the interests of those who benefit at the expense of that majority. Perhaps this is precisely what they have been created to do. But, this issue requires a more thorough examination than current heterodoxy has engaged in. Again, return to Veblen for an alternative position:

> In the long run, so soon as the privation and chronic derangement which follows from this application of business principles has grown unduly irksome and becomes intolerable, there is due to come a sentimental revulsion and a muttering protest that "something will have to be done about it". . . Thoughtful persons will then devise remedial measures . . . In a community which is addicted to business principles, the remedial measures which are brought under advisement in such a case by responsible citizens and officials are bound to be of a businesslike nature; designed in all reason to safeguard the accomplished facts of absentee ownership.
>
> *Veblen [1923] 1964: 424*

The last issue in this regard is that of the nature of markets and the relation of the state and the market. There are two areas of concern. In addition to the state being ill-defined, we also find this true of the market. Heterodox economists tend to employ the term market as a singular expression and, thus, barren of heterodox content. Excursions into economic history and comparative analysis will demonstrate that there is no singular, that is, universal market. Peasant markets in the feudal period, for example, are not those of the modern, capitalist period. This is a point made by John Maynard Keynes in his general critique of neoclassical theory when he contrasted the 'entrepreneur' economy and that of the medieval, 'co-operative' economy (Keynes [1933] 1979: 81).

Supplementing the above point, it is noted that much heterodox literature continues to employ supply-demand analysis—however implicit. Yet, since—at least—Sraffa's 1960 *Production of Commodities by Means of Commodities*, it is known that such an approach is misguided (at best). We can develop a theory of prices independently of the neoclassical perspective. Yet, we do not see this incorporated in most of the heterodox literature (see Aspromourgos 2013).

The inattention to specifying the institutional essentials of capitalist markets poses a theoretical problem. If the capitalist market is not properly specified, and the term markets is incorporated in any heterodox account without such specification, we then see implicit conformity with the universalist, naturalist position of neoclassicism: all markets are the same (in a fundamental sense), and we have always experienced market exchange. Essentially, is the market simply the institution within which goods (and labor) are exchanged—the neoclassical perspective? Or is the market the institution through which debt is cleared—a Post Keynesian perspective? The difference in these two positions is significant, as the Post Keynesian perspective casts a much more illuminating light on the nature of a capitalist social order as it speaks directly to the understanding of money and a 'monetary production economy.'

The second concern is that of the juxtaposition of 'state' and 'market.' Most heterodox theory does recognize, following Karl Polanyi and others, that markets are creatures of the state. As

Polanyi ([1944] 2001: 147) puts it: "While laissez-faire economy was the product of deliberate state action, subsequent restrictions on laissez-faire started in a spontaneous way. Laissez-faire [or the market] was planned; planning was not".

Now, if Polanyi's position is considered correct, then there should be no fundamental conflict or antagonism of market and state. Yet, in calling for institutional change to further the provisioning process—a process that market relations are claimed to impair—there is a tendency to invoke the state (read, government) to rectify the problem. When the state fails to act accordingly, it is chastised. To be sure, the state (government) may alter or introduce institutions that do ameliorate the perceived problem(s), but these will always be undertaken within the economic structure that triggered the problem initially—as Veblen argued. A classic illustration of this is the set of reforms undertaken by the Roosevelt Administration (in the USA) in the 1930s. At no point did these touch the underlying, fundamental social relations of a capitalist order. For example, the much-touted Glass–Steagall Banking Act of 1933, separating commercial and investment banking, did not affect the institutional *substance* of the financial sector. Rather, the financial sector was saved to live another day—only to create more harm in the present period.

The above critique is akin to the positions taken by Thorstein Veblen in these matters. While my standard may not be that of other heterodox economists, Veblen can serve as at least a point of departure for discussion and evaluation of a potential heterodox program that seeks to bring the various heterodox camps into closer alignment.

Some specific illustrations: money and the household

Money

Money is an institution. Indeed, it is the most important institution contained within the prevailing capitalist form of organization as capitalism is a 'monetary production economy' (Dillard 1987, see as well his 1980 essay focusing on Keynes and institutionalism). As this form of economic organization is structured around the business enterprise and its pursuit of monetary profit, the understanding of money as the central institution around which the system revolves is pivotal to unraveling the core relations and processes constituting its essential nature and characteristics. It should be noted that Dillard (1980) traces his 'money as an institution' account from Marx ('the first institutionalist') through Hyman Minsky, incorporating Veblen, Keynes, Wesley Clair Mitchell, and Morris Copeland. (John R. Commons could have been brought into his essay as well.) That is, this position on money is (or should be) fundamental to the Marxian, Keynesian/ Post Keynesian, and institutionalist perspectives—a heterodox foundation.

In her chapter, "Money and Monetary Regimes" (Chapter 17, this volume), Pavlina Tcherneva begins by stating that: "[a] historical journey through the origins of money indicates that money is first and foremost a social relationship. More precisely, it is a *power* credit-debt relationship" (238). This sentence incorporates a significant set of propositions. Money—an institution—is a social relationship. More specifically, it is a *power* relationship. Power is integral to understanding money. Money, then, is a social arrangement applicable to inegalitarian or class societies: we do not see money in the earlier, egalitarian form of society. This raises the issue of the state. To develop and preserve power, a set of institutions must be developed in support of those in a superior position—creditors—to safeguard them from those in an inferior position—debtors. This, then, requires an examination of the institutions of law, including but not limited to bankruptcy law, policing agencies, prisons (as in debtors' prison), and so on. Again, as above, the state only exists in such inegalitarian societies.

Further, to fully understand money, a historical (or comparative) approach must be developed. This must draw on work emanating from anthropology, archaeology, and history (as normally understood)—a pluralist method. Two recent such works are referenced here: David Graeber (2001), *Debt: The First 5000 Years*; Christine Desan (2014), *Making Money*. (I note that Desan is a professor of law. That is, the legal aspects of money, historically considered, are essential in the understanding of money.) Heterodox economists tend to give such aspects of institutions short shrift, focusing on purely economic matters. This was not always the case. An examination of the work of John R. Commons, for example, demonstrates a keen appreciation for the significance of law in framing and solidifying institutions (see his 1924 *Legal Foundations of Capitalism*, see also Atkinson & Paschall 2016).

The last thing to note is that the neoclassical story (and its Austrian variant), resting on money as a mere medium of exchange to reduce (eliminate) the inefficiencies of barter, is ruled out as a compelling theoretical account: history negates it. This partially explains why in Coyle's (2007) account above, money is not referenced as one of the supposed advances of modern, mainstream economics compared to the 'sterile' neoclassicism of the 1970s (and before). In the neoclassical, mainstream, and Austrian stories, money simply is not of importance. The implication of this point is that heterodoxy is not just some reaction to neoclassicism—something of a contrarian position. Rather, it is a theoretical position(s), buttressed by historical fact that attempts to explain institutions on their own social foundations.

If one moves beyond Tcherneva's account mentioned above, one also sees a role for social economics. Social economists place great emphasis on values, on ethics, on moral standards. Money, and its related social aspects, does require the promotion of an ethical standard, a standard that can (and, I would suggest, must) be challenged. The best heterodox economists in a position both to explicate the standard usually proffered as well as to challenge that standard are those in the social economics camp. Neoclassical theorists ostensibly eschew social values and value judgments. (This stated position is, of course, invalid as values are implicitly contained in the very foundations of the theory.) Heterodox economists should overtly incorporate their ethical position in their own accounts because such a position addresses policy.

What is a so-called good policy? Why is it so? Consider: most (all?) neoclassical economists are averse to minimum wage laws. Why? Such laws violate good market analysis and disturb/disrupt labor market equilibrium conditions. As a consequence, people will suffer. That is, markets are good and attempts to override or circumvent markets are bad. Heterodox economists support minimum wage laws: I know of no exceptions. And, they not only support such laws, but recommend fairly healthy minimum wages. Why? There is, of course, the standard, Keynesian position that such wages increase incomes and thus, consumer spending, thus, increases in aggregate demand. But, beyond this 'economistic' argument, we also see arguments based on 'labor' as consisting of human beings, not mere factors of production (see, for example, Prasch 2004). As human beings and members of larger society, laborers should be (note the word, should) treated with respect. This is a value judgment, one based on an ethical standard. In this, one should not neglect the work of Piero Sraffa. Granted, his *Production of Commodities by Means of Commodities* (1960) is a quite technical account. Beneath the technical argument, however, lies an ethical standard in that the viability of a system is not merely economic reproduction, but *social* reproduction. For Sraffa, viability means "*survival of the system as a whole*—a characteristically *holistic* goal to be pursued by *any* human community" (Chiodi 2010: 324, italics in original). Economic surplus, that output which allows an economy to grow, is "a *social* construction, an ultimate reflection of *ethical, religious, and political values* existing in the system and shaping . . . the relationships among people" (Chiodi 2010: 324, italics in original).

The household

What about the household? In the above, the Marxian, Post Keynesian, social economist, institutionalist perspectives were integrated—at least to some extent; however, there was no reference to the heterodox feminist account. But, it is in the analysis of the household—as an institution—that the feminist perspective can be most illuminating. This might be expected, as feminists focus on the role, place, and status of women. There are, I suggest, two areas where more work needs to be undertaken.

The modern capitalist society (standard) household is not natural or universal. To hold this position would be consistent, again, with the neoclassical approach. To better specify the modern household as an institution with an explicit structure and ideological aspects, history and comparative analysis must be better incorporated into current accounts. In this, scholarship originating in anthropology is obviously significant. However, to incorporate such studies and accompanying theoretical arguments, one must be mindful that there is no singular position in this discipline. Anthropology, as all social sciences, displays the same divisions found in economics: there are (the equivalent of) neoclassical and heterodox anthropologies, and heterodoxy is further segmented in different camps. I contend that in many respects, earlier (nineteenth century) anthropology was superior to much of current work. Lewis Henry Morgan, for example, was less influenced by concerns surrounding the sanctity of the 'nuclear' (or capitalist) family than those who followed him. When he demonstrated, relying on then-current research, including his own, that the modern family did not always exist, that capitalist relations did not always exist, that our ancestors lived in communist or communal arrangements, a reaction set in to rescue then-current institutions from such heresy—in particular, the family.[4]

The other area which needs to be developed is the position of the household—or family—within a monetary production economy. Work on such a project has already begun. I suggest that Zdravka Todorova's (2009), *Money and Households in a Capitalist Economy* is an excellent foundation from which to develop this undertaking as it incorporates Post Keynesian, institutionalist, and feminist theory (see also her contribution to this volume, Chapter 13). If it is accepted that money is the key institution in a monetary production economy, a well-developed theory of the household that places this institution squarely within such an economy as an integral, monetary social relationship will greatly facilitate a better understanding of the household itself. And, what is true for the household is true for all institutions. I cannot envision any institution that is not in some fashion affected by the economy, and this means that all institutions are interrelated with monetary production. Environmental concerns, race, gender beyond the household, war—all (and more) such issues must be brought into account.

What is to be done? A proposal

It is recognized that there are long-standing divisions among heterodox practitioners. The various camps all developed well before thought was given to the possibility of unifying these orientations into a heterodox community. Moreover, within each camp there are divisions. Simply put, there is no single Post Keynesian, Marxian, institutionalist, social economist 'general theory.' And these divisions can be rancorous. It would appear that any proposal suggesting the possibility of the formation of a heterodox community with a shared vision directed toward a common objective (or end) would be met with reservation—at a minimum.[5]

At the same time, even though there are differences among and within each camp, the various factions *can* and do meet, discuss, argue, and publish in their respective journals. Further, there are periodic movements to attempt greater integration among the different camps. A promising development is that of the conjoining of the Post Keynesian and institutionalist versions of heterodoxy. Post Keynesian Institutionalism (or PKI) argues that there is enough commonality and cross-fertilization among adherents of both approaches to allow a unified approach to the examination of institutions as well as the larger economic—and social—order (for a brief overview, see Whalen 2012). An objection might be raised that such a development has been percolating since at least the 1980s—and I would date the beginnings earlier—with no general consensus as to what PKI entails. Hence, this is offered as further proof that the construction of *a* single heterodox theory is wishful thinking.

Beyond the attempt to integrate institutionalism and Post Keynesianism, one can point to the formations of the Association for Heterodox Economics, l'Association Française d'Économie Politique, the International Initiative for Promoting Political Economy, the International Confederation of Associations for Pluralism in Economics, among others. The question regarding organizations such as these is: while they are serious attempts to bring the various heterodox streams together, why haven't they succeeded in generating a single heterodox theory? A partial—and unsatisfactory answer—is that such organizations are relatively new, and it does take time for *a* theoretical perspective to achieve sufficient mass to be acknowledged.

The main problem, I contend, is that there is no agreement as to what the foundation of *a* single heterodox theory should be. Observe that there are factions within the neoclassical community. Debate, sometimes quite fractious, does take place, but only at the periphery of the theory. There is agreement as to the *core*, the heart of this perspective—as specified in Coyle's (2007) account. No such heterodox equivalent has been created, and, thus, no *effective* single alternative to the conventional theory has developed.

Could the work of Thorstein Veblen provide such a foundation? I argue, yes. This does not mean that Veblen should be followed uncritically—obviously. Further, Veblen wrote at the turn of the previous century and there have been immense institutional changes since his time. But, as discussed above, his work does speak to *all* the various branches of heterodoxy, and *does* provide an articulate, well-reasoned, and forceful rejoinder to neoclassicism. Clearly, the work of others must be brought into the search for foundations, Marx and Keynes in particular. (I would not disregard Adam Smith in such a catalogue. Smith did 'set the table,' and a goodly amount of heterodox argument is traceable to Smith. Smith, along with Ricardo, is certainly represented by one branch of the Sraffians.) And, it is distinctly possible that the issue around which a foundation could be established is the nature of institutions.[6] This would drive the development of *a* theoretical perspective into every facet of capitalist (and non-capitalist) society(ies). Further, a clear statement must be developed as to what the overriding objective of such a program would be. Should it be to enhance the social provisioning process? This would be one possibility. What would this entail?

Clearly, not all those associated with specific heterodox approaches will be congenial to such a call. So be it. There must be recognition that existing arrangements—institutions—have not achieved what has been a long-standing objective of heterodoxy—replacing neoclassicism as the reigning theoretical perspective. The university, academic journals, and think tanks have all been hostile to any significant attempt to breach the neoclassical fortress. Recent evidence of this is that, following the 2007–8 financial debacle, nothing in conventional theory has changed. Many in the heterodox community believed that a window had indeed opened and the conventional representatives of the economics discipline would be open to a more critical, non-orthodox perspective. (I was not one of these optimists.) It is obvious that such optimism was not warranted—existing institutions augured against such an outcome. And this should have been recognized—had Veblen been taken seriously.

Beyond this, and more importantly, heterodoxy has failed the larger population. All heterodox economists are so-called progressives. They all want to see the implementation of policy and accompanying institutional arrangements that improve the lives of the majority. Would anyone argue that this has been the case over the last 40 years—at least in western democracies?

It is time to take stock, recognize deficiencies in theory, seek to correct these, and attempt to organize the various heterodox camps into a single heterodox theoretical approach. In this, the respective positions of each camp must be respected, but no specific theoretical component can be honored: everything is up for discussion. In all this, attention must be scrupulously paid to any introduction of neoclassical theory. This theory goes well beyond its formal aspects. It is a general theory of social order. This must be understood, and it must be answered. The only operative answer is based on a well-formulated anti-neoclassical account that rests on firm and realistic foundations. If there is to be a *heterodox* program, there must be a *heterodox* theory.

Notes

1 Note that Knight ([1939] 1982) does not reference Hegel or Rousseau.
2 The 'Jim Crow' or segregationist system was instituted in the post-Civil War period, mainly in the South—the bastion of slavery. Specifically, it separated black and white populations through legal, social, and political demarcations, including restrictions on voting rights. While usually seen as 'just' anti-black, it also affected the well-being of most whites, in particular, poor whites. See, Woodward (1955) for an authoritative account.
3 Fagg Foster left no written paper in which his theory of institutional adjustment is fully articulated. Most of what is known of his work is the result of notes taken by students in his graduate courses at the University of Denver and now-published conference papers in a special issue of the *Journal of Economic Issues*, Vol. 15, No. 4, 1981. For Foster's sketch of his theory, see Foster (1981).
4 See Morgan (1877). For a criticism of the anti-Morgan anthropology, see Briffault ([1933] 1969). For a recent illustration of a neoclassical version of anthropology—*published in a heterodox journal*—see Caldararo (2009).
5 Daniel Rodgers' *Age of Fracture* (2011) speaks to this issue. In the 1960s and early 1970s, it appeared that various 'progressive' political programs were uniting around a common theme. And that theme was anti-capitalism. However, no central, unifying element was developed. Hence, the anti-war, civil rights, environmentalist, feminist, etc. movements split into their separate divisions. And, within each division, there were subdivisions. I suggest that Rodgers' argument addresses exactly the same set of issues regarding heterodoxy.
6 In the above, while there has been no reference to either *Régulation* Theory or the approach of those working in the Social Structure of Accumulation (SSA) tradition, both of these perspectives do have a focus on institutions. I am not convinced, however, that these approaches investigate and analyze institutions themselves. Rather, they—in particular the proponents of SSA—look backward and posit the existence of specific institutions that promote or retard the accumulation process. Thus, if there is a successful accumulation process under examination, institutions prevalent during such a period are asserted to be accommodating of accumulation. If a sluggish economy prevails, then a set of different institutions are said to prevail. However, I do agree that the *Régulationists* seem to present a better argument than those associated with the SSA approach.

References

Aspromourgos, T. 2013. 'Sraffa's system in relation to some main currents in unorthodox economics," *in*: E.S. Levrero, A. Palumbo, & A. Stirati (eds.), *Sraffa and the Reconstruction of Economic Theory, Volume 3*. New York: Palgrave Macmillan, 15–33.
Atkinson, G. & Paschall, S. 2016. *Law and Economics from an Evolutionary Perspective*. Cheltenham, UK: Edward Elgar.
Bentham, J. [1780] 1969. 'An introduction to the principles of morals and legislation,' *in*: M. Mack (ed.), *A Benthamite Reader*. New York: Pegasus, 78–167.
Briffault, R. [1933] 1969. 'Recent anthropology,' *in*: *Reasons for Anger*. Freeport, NY: Books for Libraries Press.
Caldararo, N. 2009. 'Primitive and modern economics: derivatives, liquidity, value, panic and crises, a uniformitarian view.' *Forum for Social Economics*, 38 (1): 31–51.

Chiodi, G. 2010. 'The means of subsistence and the notion of 'viability' in Sraffa's surplus approach,' *in*: S. Zambelli (ed.), *Computable, Constructive and Behavioural Economic Dynamics: Essays in Honour of Kumaraswamy (Vela) Velupilla.* London: Routledge, 318–330.

Coyle, D. 2007. *The Soulful Science: What Economists Really Do and Why It Matters.* Princeton, NJ: Princeton University Press.

Desan, C. 2014. *Making Money: Coins, Currency, and the Coming of Capitalism.* Oxford: Oxford University Press.

Dillard, D. 1980. 'A monetary theory of production: Keynes and the institutionalists.' *Journal of Economic Issues*, 14 (2): 255–273.

Dillard, D. 1987. 'Money as an institution of capitalism.' *Journal of Economic Issues*, 21 (4): 1623–1647.

Foster, J. 1981. 'The theory of institutional adjustment.' *Journal of Economic Issues*, 15 (4): 923–928.

Gilman, N. 1999. 'Thorstein Veblen's neglected feminism.' *Journal of Economic Issues*, 33 (3): 689–711.

Graeber, D. 2001. *Debt: The First 5000 Years.* Brooklyn, NY: Melville House.

Hayden, F.G. 2011. 'Usefulness to original institutional economics (OIE) of normative criteria theory in the frameworks of Elinor Ostrom's institutional analysis and development (IAD) and Paul A. Sabatier's advocacy coalition framework (ACF).' *Journal of Economic Issues*, 45 (2): 465–474.

Herskovitz, M. 1940. *The Economic Life of Primitive People.* New York: Alfred A. Knopf.

Hodgson, G. 2001. *How Economics Forgot History.* New York: Routledge.

Keynes, J.M. [1933] 1979. 'The General Theory and after: a supplement,' *in*: D. Moggridge (ed.), *The Collected Writings of John Maynard Keynes, Vol. XXIX.* London: Macmillan.

Knight, F. [1939] 1982. 'Ethics of economic reform,' *in: Freedom and Reform.* Indianapolis, IN: Liberty Press, 55–153.

Knight, F. 1941. 'Anthropology and economics.' *Journal of Political Economy*, 49 (2): 247–268.

Knight, F. 1960. *Intelligence and Democratic Action.* Cambridge, MA: Harvard University Press.

Morgan, L.H. 1877. *Ancient Society.* New York: Henry Holt.

Mouhammed, A. 1994. 'Veblen and the business cycle: a Marxist perspective.' *Review of Radical Political Economics*, 26 (1): 134–148.

Pearson, H. 2000. 'Homo economicus goes native, 1859–1945: the rise and fall of primitive economics.' *History of Political Economy*, 32 (4): 933–989.

Polanyi, K. [1944] 2001. *The Great Transformation.* Boston: The Beacon Press.

Prasch, R. 2004. 'How is labor distinct from broccoli,' *in*: J. Knoedler & D. Champlin (eds.), *The Institutionalist Tradition in Labor Economics.* Armonk, NY: M.E. Sharpe, 146–158.

Rodgers, D. 2011. *Age of Fracture.* Cambridge, MA: Harvard University Press.

Todorova, Z. 2009. *Money and Households in a Capitalist Economy: A Gendered Post Keynesian–Institutional Approach.* Northampton, MA: Edward Elgar.

Tool, M. 1977. 'A social value theory in neoinstitutional economics.' *Journal of Economic Issues*, 11 (4): 832–846.

Tool, M. 2000. *Value Theory and Economic Progress: The Institutional Economics of J. Fagg Foster.* Boston: Kluwer Academic Publishers.

Veblen, T. [1904] 1975. *The Theory of Business Enterprise.* New York: Augustus M. Kelly.

Veblen, T. 1909. 'The limitations of marginal utility.' *Journal of Political Economy*, 17 (9): 620–636.

Veblen, T. 1917. *An Inquiry into the Nature of Peace and the Terms of its Perpetuation.* New York: B.W. Huebsch.

Veblen, T. [1923] 1964. *Absentee Ownership and Business Enterprise in Recent Times: The Case of America.* New York: Augustus M. Kelley.

Whalen, C. 2012. Post-Keynesian institutionalism after the great recession. Levy Economics Institute Working Paper No. 724, May. Available from http://www.levyinstitute.org/pubs/wp_724.pdf [Accessed January 31, 2016]

Williamson, O.E. 1975. *Markets and Hierarchies: Analysis and Antitrust Implications.* New York: Free Press.

Williamson, O.E. 1987. *The Economic Institutions of Capitalism.* New York: Free Press.

Woodward, C. 1955. *The Strange Career of Jim Crow.* New York: Oxford University Press.

Wray, L.R. 2007. 'Veblen's theory of business enterprise and Keynes's monetary theory of production.' *Journal of Economic Issues*, 61 (2): 617–623.

Yoffee, N. 2005. *Myths of the Archaic State.* Cambridge: Cambridge University Press.

12

Heterodox economics and theories of interactive agency[1]

Mary V. Wrenn

Introduction

Agency is power—the power to act and the power to choose, the power to imagine, and the power to understand, engage, and manipulate the surrounding biological and social environment. Mainstream economics defines agency in terms of methodological individualism and the individual agent by an optimizing, rational economic man. Agency within the mainstream framework is endowed without discretion to all individuals who independently choose to act based on the weight of 'objective' costs and benefits (Davis 2003; Lavoie 2006). One of the justifications for this simplified depiction of the acting individual is that such behavior is observable in the animal world; indeed 'optimization' may be found at the microscopic level (Hodgson 2004). The explanation of behavior in a Petri dish, however, does not provide a satisfactory or meaningful explanation in the crucible of the real world, with intelligent, creative, and socially situated human beings—at least not to heterodox economists.

The argument set forth here is that heterodox economics is distinguished from mainstream economics by the way in which it conceptualizes and deploys individual agency and consequently, interactive agency. The procedure is straightforward. In the first section, the theory of the individual in heterodox economics is discussed by outlining the conceptualization and internal evolution of the economic agent and her agency, and how that theoretical construct fits within the research programs of three heterodox schools of thought: original institutional economics (OIE), Marxian economics, and Post Keynesianism. The second section explores the ways in which these three heterodox schools theorize that an individual's agency changes in response to external forces, both structural sources and mechanisms of mediation between structure and the individual. The third section builds upon the discussion laid out in the previous two sections by detailing the concept of interactive agency, again exploring the similarities and differences between the three heterodox schools. The final section concludes that the similarities which unite these heterodox schools offer a much more complex, nuanced, and ultimately more useful theory of interactive agency and that such complementarity need not require a sacrifice of diversity or pluralism more broadly.

Heterodox theories of the individual

To the heterodox economist, agency cannot be captured or analyzed by a simple, one-dimensional rendering of the individual as is presented by mainstream economics. Agency must instead be examined by its own internal development and responses to external forces; agency must be described not only in terms of how much an individual possesses, but also in terms of how it came to be and how it evolves. The individual, economic agent has antecedents and consequences that give shape to her perceptions of the world and form the individual's mental models. The individual is a totality of her mental models, including models that not only shape perception but that also influence the choice of relevant models to select, apply, filter, and interpret data. An individual's agency is the product of her mental models; in other words, the individual's mental models directly influence the degree of agency the individual is able to exercise in the decision-making process.

All individuals engage and exercise agency during their decision-making processes; agency and its underlying mental models constitute the mechanism of discretion, and agency is the impetus of action (Smith 2010). The thought process involved in decision-making and action can therefore only be understood in terms of the individual's agency and mental models (Pratten 1993). Indeed, agency is crucial in decision theory. Decision theory itself is not only useful in terms of noting what choices individuals make in which context, but in understanding the processes of how individuals choose. A well-developed decision theoretical framework containing a dynamic and interactive interpretation of the individual is thus imperative in understanding the individual and, by extension, in the construction of socially operational, productive, and relevant economic policy (Simon 1978; Lee 2010).

Two sorts of costs emerge when policy makers in government (as well as operation-management policy makers within firms) ignore individual behavior and the fundamental importance of agency in constructing efficacious policy. The first is fairly transparent, and simply entails ignoring the basic constitution of the individual in terms of motivation and norms, and thereby essentially missing the objective mark in terms of creating instrumental policy. The second involves the undermining of initially situated norms through the introduction of policy, which is able to reach its intent but does so in a manner that reconstitutes the individual by reshaping her priorities or incentives. Policy maneuvers might reach the desired effect, but do so by stripping away norms already in place, and are inefficient in cost terms. Both 'costs' might emerge in government policy directives meant to direct incentives. For instance, assuming that unemployed individuals are 'lazy' and structuring policy to tighten restrictions on unemployment benefits makes presumptions about the incentives internal to the individual. As well, such policy directives may change the structure of norms. Attempting to direct incentives when there is a gap in demand for employment could create a culture among the unemployed, instituting new norms and destroying the very incentive such policy intends to direct (Hargreaves Heap 2001). In this instance, ignoring agency and ignoring the fundamental ontological make-up of individuals may not only lead to inefficacious policy making but dangerous neglect as well.

The OIE maintains a long-standing tradition of rebellion against the methodological individualism of conventional economics. Indeed, the clear goal of Thorstein Veblen was to develop a theory of agency to replace the unsatisfactory theory of the optimizing rational economic man—the "hedonistic . . . lightening calculator"—of neoclassical economics (Veblen 1898b: 389). In the development of an alternative theory of agency, the OIE of the early twentieth century placed primacy on the development of a more complete ontology of the individual, paying close attention to the cultural mechanisms, which shaped and channeled the individual's mental models.

For the OIE, the individual is born with certain instincts that have evolved since the emergence of human beings, such as the capacity for language. Humans must have an innate sense of how to communicate in order to physically manipulate the body—lips, tongue, vocal cords, lungs—to produce sound. Once a human is able to communicate, interaction with the surrounding structural context, including intersubjective relationships with other individuals, builds up the range of language, including dialect and culturally specific rhetoric (Hodgson 2004). The incorporation of instincts into the theory of the individual does not, however, imply universality of ontology or static conceptions of behavior. Evolution may work to change instinct through natural selection: workmanship naturally evolved as an instinctual trait as evidenced by the very survival of the human race (Hodgson 2004). Instinct, habit, and patterns of behavior form the building blocks of the individual's mental models.

Marxian thought addresses agency very specifically in terms of the agent-structure relationship under the capitalist rubric, as Marx's historical materialism insists that a single element or individual cannot be studied apart from the totality in which it is situated. Indeed, much of the work in Marxian thought has focused on the individual as part of a collective set within the more general context of society. The insistence of Marxian scholars to examine structural forces is born of this philosophy; that it is impossible to understand the totality from the perspective of the individual as the individual is a product of the totality. The individual is not autonomous but neither is she completely structurally determined.

Individuals are born with base human instincts for survival and in meeting the fundamental physiological needs for survival the individual must manipulate the surrounding environment. This manipulation, set within a community of individuals, becomes organized into a productive process, the development of which is determined by the materials and tools at the disposal of the individuals, and which results in the creation of a social structure that is subject to its own evolutionary inertia and to the further manipulation of individuals. Individuals, however, do not remain unaffected by the changing means of survival and production:

> [Men] begin to distinguish themselves from animals as soon as they begin to produce their means of subsistence, a step which is conditioned by their physical organization. By producing their means of subsistence, men are indirectly producing their actual material life . . . . The nature of individuals thus depends on the material conditions determining their production.
>
> *Marx & Engels 1995: 42*

The individual thus transforms nature into an object for use through the application of labor. The individual is also transformed by the very act of creating that object and its newly created use; what was once imagined becomes a necessity, and further imagination results in the individual again manipulating the surrounding environment to adapt to these newly formed mental models (Gould 1978). "Hunger is hunger, but the hunger gratified by cooked meat eaten with a knife and fork is different from a hunger from that which bolts down raw meat with the aid of hand, nail and tooth" (Marx & Engels 1995: 132).

Despite, or perhaps because of the diversity within Post Keynesian thought, the concept of agency from a distinctly Post Keynesian perspective is "an area of work that is still in development" (McKenna & Zannoni 2012: 1). An examination of some of the core concepts which inform the Post Keynesian theory of the individual, however, provides insight into the direction and development of the unfolding progress on this school's conceptualization of agency. The Post Keynesian treatment of uncertainty provides the most obvious and well-developed entry point.

Post Keynesians challenge the idea that individuals can foresee the future and rationally understand the consequences of enumerated future events in order to develop a 'well-behaved' preference ordering. It is clear that Post Keynesian fundamental uncertainty is different from the uncertainty found in mainstream economics, for fundamental uncertainty is not based on known and stable probability distributions. Uncertainty takes the form of fundamental uncertainty, which is essentially non-ergodic and reflects the temporally non-syncopated nature of institutional and individual evolution (Dunn 2001; Lavoie 2006). By contrast, risk in mainstream economics relies on epistemological distinctions to account for heterogeneity in individuals. Greater access to information in the mainstream framework allows for Bayesian updating of subjective probabilities thereby allowing the individual to approach objective risk through a learning process (Hodgson 1998; Rosser 2001). The theory of fundamental uncertainty is characterized by ontologically non-determined and diverse individuals with heterogeneous mental models. Variations in the ontological *and* epistemological nature of individuals open the door to innumerable and unforeseeable—fundamentally unknowable—future possibilities (Dunn 2001; Lavoie 2006).

Structure and mechanisms of mediation

Mental models and agency are informed but not determined by the surrounding structural context. Structure broadly defined consists of enduring patterns of social relations (Barone 1998). The individual is situated within a historically specific structural context. While sustained, structure is not permanent nor inherently stable (Pratten 1993). Socially and temporally resilient structures may become institutionalized and as such represent "deeply layered," dynamic social complexes (Giddens 1979: 64–65). Institutions therefore differ from structure by virtue of establishment within society and greater ability to influence agency (what Hodgson (2002) refers to as 'reconstitutive downward causation'). The key to the semantic difference is simply that institutions, as a subset of structure, wield greater influence and more directly 'reconstitute' the mental models of agents (Hodgson 2002). For the sake of semantic simplicity, and in order to expose causation rather than obscure focus by differentiating in terms of depth of causation, the remainder of this chapter refers to structures and institutions synonymously.

Structure, which manifests via the persistent, often tacit, contextual relations within and through which individuals act, partially shapes the individual's agency through various social mechanisms such as power relations, resource allocation, and both formal and informal constraints and obligations. The influence, however, of structure and institutions on agency consists of much more than a mere constraining mechanism (Wrenn 2015). Legal infrastructure, norms, and customs of behavior may all act as constraints but those norms and customs which instead change the mental model of the agent, so that she chooses behavior based on preferences not fear of retribution or promise of reward, has changed (that is, reconstituted) her agency as well. Preferences, therefore, may be changed endogenously as a result of structural pressures. Furthermore, the institutionalization of enduring structures may occur either in objective reality, or as interpretively and subjectively represented in the individual's mental models (Hodgson 2004). As such, the broadly acknowledged systematic guidelines or norms of institutions are incorporated selectively into the mental models of agents and represent mechanisms by which changes in mental models and agency might be mediated.

According to the OIE's theoretical framework, humans at their base have instinctual drives but the working out of these instincts, the behavior through and in which these instincts present themselves, is determined by the cultural milieu to which the individual has been exposed (Hamilton 1953). Habits, which are initiated and reinforced by the structural complex, thus work to modify and develop previously inherited instinctual behavior (Veblen 1898a). This is not to say that the OIE denies or reduces the internal development of agency of the individual or to suggest that 'magical' social forces act to form the individual's mental models, but rather to emphasize that structure changes an individual's mental models, thus changing the very personality, the fundamental essence, of the individual (Hodgson 2004).

Habits and instincts are part of the cognitive framework, in other words, part of an individual's mental models and are at least partially informed by institutions and structure. Habits, routines, competency base, and skills are not static, but evolve with the changing structure and the changing individual (Davis 2003). Causation, however, does not run one-way from structure through habit to change instincts and behavior in a unidirectional fashion. Indeed, behavioral patterns are the combined result, in subjectively determined portions, of genetic composition, habituation, inertia, enculturation, path dependence, and cumulative causation. Habituation is a stabilizing and creative force in terms of institutional formation and evolution, as well as stabilized and channeled into change by the surrounding structural context (Hodgson 1998).

Institutions and more broadly, structure, are more than just a backdrop; more than just the scaffolding on which to hang human action or a foundation off which to build. Institutions, according to the OIE, are structures, which develop organically, shaping the mental models of individuals and in turn are shaped by humans in all their fallibility. Likewise, individuals carry forward mental models inherited and shaped from past patterns of behavior but are capable of creativity and innovation (Mayhew 2001).

The concept of identity plays a key role in the ontological description of the individual in Marxian theory. In opposition to the highly individualized and self-determined ideologies that buttress the mechanisms of capitalism, Marxian thought focuses on the structural forces that shape the identity of the individual. Class is a social construct yet constitutes the core of identity; class is the lens through which the individual sees herself, the world, and her place in it. Individuals inherit social and class roles and are structurally conditioned from birth to occupy their proper roles through the socialization process and the enculturation of conformity (Barone 1998). The individual does not exist apart from her class identity and the horizontal relationships therein, and agency is therefore defined at the level of class. Class membership defines, informs, embodies, and is the locus of agency (Parenti 1994; Davis 2003).

Marxian scholars, such as Ebert (2005), stress that a 'productive' concept of agency should be framed in terms of class structure and avoid the secondary structural forces of identity politics that coincide with lifestyle and demographic distinctions, such as race, religion, and gender. This is not to deny structural influences on agency outside of class structure, but rather to see secondary structure in terms and as the result of a historically class-based society: "'Difference' is acquired in identity politics by essentially culturalizing the social divisions of labor" (Ebert 2005: 37–38). As such, agency conceived outside of class identity veils the origins of social structure that evolved as a result of class divisions. Class structure is phenomenon; the secondary structure of identity politics is epiphenomenon. To not place class at the center of inquiry is to deny the driving force behind agency and secondary structure (Bowles & Gintis 1986; Ebert 2005).

Secondary structure as driven by class structure works to shape identity. Lifestyle and demographics as part of the secondary structure create cross-class or 'fractured identities.' Culture, family, and education constitute the central structures in the socialization process and the means by which social and class roles are rationalized as either inherent or meritocratic (Barone 1998: 16–17). According to Ebert (2005), however, identity politics represents a means by which the managerial class might distinguish itself from the working class without resorting to class distinctions and thereby threatening the existing social order. Focusing on secondary structurally determined identity thus obscures and perpetuates the socially structured inequality of class-based society.

Structure created by productive relations in turn creates and shapes the remaining structural forms, such as intersubjective relationships and identity. The roles that individuals play, the opportunities presented to them, the perceptions they hold of the world—their mental models—are conscripted by social structure (Pratten 1993). Exploitation of the working class could not persist without an underlying social structure, which shapes the mental models of individuals and makes the relations of production palatable and without which the irrationality of the system might be exposed, leaving it vulnerable to resistance, sabotage, or revolution. Moreover, the persistence of social and ultimately class structures, Barone (1998) argues, cannot be understood in any meaningful way without understanding and studying the culture which perpetuates it. Marxian scholars, such as Gramsci ([1948] 1995), argue that structures outside of class influence individual self-perception, preferences, and which norms would be internalized (Hodgson 2004): "Our capacity to think and act on the world is dependent on other people who are themselves both subjects and objects of history" (Gramsci [1948] 1995: 660). Objective structures and institutions require mental models to sustain both the collective level of socially shared mental models and the individual level to rationalize and sustain (Barone 1998).

The Post Keynesians also recognize the role of the collective (although not necessarily defined in terms of class, as in Marxian economics) in the shaping of an individual's mental models and consequently her agency. In contrast to the strict rationality of mainstream economics, individuals within the Post Keynesian framework at times are driven to action by what Keynes referred to as 'animal spirits' when confronted with uncertainty. As such, individuals rely upon their mental models—described as 'gut instinct'—or act in response to emotional impulses. Individuals might also make intersubjective comparisons, rely on intuition, adopt behavior that conforms to commonly held beliefs, or get swept up in mob mentalities as coping mechanisms and as decision-making guides under uncertainty. Such decision-making devices also serve the purpose of allowing individuals to deflect blame for 'bad' decisions. Under these non-routinized scenarios, uncertainty is fundamentally non-quantifiable and hence, essentially non-ergodic (Rosser 2001).

In non-crucial or routine decisions individuals often rely on conventions to make decisions (Rosser 2001). Conventions inform mental models by acting as heuristic devices, helping to imbue data with meaning as well as form the foundation of social interaction—all of which allow individuals to make decisions under uncertainty. The construction and evolution of mental models is determined in part by the surrounding structural milieu and intersubjective relationships. Likewise, the formation and evolution of institutions will differ according to the mental models of the proximate individuals (McKenna & Zannoni 2012).

Theories of interactive agency

Recognition of the ability of structure to change and influence an individual's mental model should not be stretched to the point of determinism. Agency depicted through the socially embedded conceptualization of the individual is not true agency if the individual is not imbued with the power to influence the surrounding structure in a truly interactive fashion. Furthermore, that individual must possess the power of self-reference while recognizing, regardless of accuracy, social influences and her power to act and react to them (Davis 2003). While methodological individualism ignores structural influence on agency, methodological collectivism (or methodological holism) casts the individual as the passive recipient of structural information and pressure (Tauheed 2013). In order to avoid the reductionism of methodological individualism *and* the overly socialized individual of methodological collectivism—"to reject the grandiose delusion of being puppet-masters but also to resist the supine conclusion that [individuals] are mere marionettes" (Archer 1995: 65)—care must be taken to link agency and structure as opposed to subsuming one into the other. Ontologically speaking, agent and structure must be analyzed as separate social strata.

In order not to subsume an agent into structure or structure into an agent, the interdependence of agent and structure must be acknowledged while also recognizing the simultaneous independence of each—the autonomous and internal forces—that propel agent and structure down their respective evolutionary paths (Tauheed 2013). Structures and agency exist independently and evolve in non-syncopated historical time. The only meaningful way to examine the interplay between agent and structure without submitting one to the evolutional force of the other is to examine the relationship between the two over time (Archer 1995). Thus, structure and agency are approached as simultaneously sensitive to the workings of one another while also consisting, and evolving independently, of independent inertia (Lawson 1997). These theories of interactive agency allow for mutual causation between institutions and agent and simultaneously recognize the interdependence and independence of agent and institutions (Davis 2003). Such respect for the dichotomous forces, which inform the development of agent and structure leads not only to understanding each more clearly but also serves as an important consideration in the development of economic policy. Structural economic policy changes that do not consider or anticipate the interaction between a structural shift and the effected individuals are not likely to succeed. One needs only to turn to the application of shock therapy in Eastern Europe for a striking example of such failure, where political and economic institutions were transformed quickly from centralized planned economies to market economies, leaving individuals confused being unaccustomed to these new institutions (see Taylor & Wrenn 2003; Taylor 2006).

The interaction between agency and structure provides heterodox economists with a richer, fuller ontological description and explanation of the diverse range of human behavior than that of the calculative individual in mainstream economics. Mainstream economics makes *a priori* assumptions about the composition and constitution—the ontology—of the individual and therefore her agency, by assuming uniformity in the antecedent, historical context and imagined consequences across all individuals, in effect homogenizing the process by which information is perceived.

Mainstream economics furthermore attempts to differentiate between individuals on epistemological grounds via models, which incorporate imperfect knowledge in an effort to address the diversity between economic agents. To recognize ontological differences between individuals is to recognize the full diversity of mental models that individuals hold and the contextual framework within which those mental models evolved and continue to evolve. Likewise, to respect ontological diversity means to remove wildly independent self-determination and appreciate the variation in individual agency. The interactive agency framework, which simultaneously recognizes the interdependence and independence of agent and structure is "so general to accommodate a variety of more specific theories" (Davis 2003: 127–128). This is evident in the examination of the theories of interactive agency for OIE, Marxian economics, and Post Keynesianism.

Interactive agency is a defining theory in the project of the OIE. Individuals inform the composition and functioning of institutions and structure directly and through their intersubjective relationships with one another, and institutions inform the composition and functioning of an individual's mental models by reinforcing habits and informing the individual's cognitive process. As such, institutions and individuals maintain their independence—they are not ontologically equivalent—while simultaneously being interdependent (Hodgson 1998).

As a matter of practicality, structure is more enduring and longer-lived, especially once institutionalized, than agent or agency. As a result, the future expectations of the individual are at least partially informed by the current and expected future environment through structural influence on understanding, cognition, and cultural norms. Knowledge as such is embodied not only in the individual but within structure and represents communally held (mostly tacit) knowledge. The individual learns—and adapts her mental models—from the communal stock of knowledge shared through intersubjective relations, from the structural repository of knowledge and from her own experience (Hodgson 2004).

Hodgson (2004) argues that in his development of the concept of interactive agency, Veblen recognized the mutual dependence between agent and structure as well as the irreducibility of one into the other. By recognizing that agent and structure are also independent entities, the internal integrity of both is acknowledged as well as the temporally asymmetric evolution of each—the antecedents and consequents. Agent and structure evolve partially due to mutual though non-equivalent influence and partially due to internal, independent inertia. Agent and structure are thus mutually causative but not mutually constitutive (Hodgson 2004). The OIE acknowledges the ontological differences in individuals and their mental models as well as the organic evolution of institutions, and, moreover, recognizes the interdependence and independence of each. Agent and structure are both creators and created; are independent and interdependent; mutually causative but not mutually constitutive—in other words, interactive.

Regardless of the debate within Marxian thought as to whether structure outside of class should be studied in terms of conditioning agency, it is apparent that the relationship between agency and structure is the centerpiece of the Marxian theory of the individual. The collective identity formulation of agency is clearly important in Marxian economics but is not at odds with interactive agency and the internal evolution of the individual. Indeed, the collective is considered a structure and the shared intentions of the collective's members are influenced by the constituency of the collective, thereby allowing for agent-structure interaction within the collective as well as in the more general social structure framework. There is no contradiction between the two: the collective conceptualization of Marxian economics simply adds another layer to the agency-structure relationship (Davis 2003).

Social totality thus consists of three levels: the macro level of institutions; the meso level of collective groups; and, the micro level of the individual. The agency-structure relationship functions through all three levels (Barone 1998). Within the social totality, institutionalized structure and the labor process transform individuals and social groups who, in turn, singly and collectively transform the social structure and totality. Agency and structure evolve according to non-syncopated, independent timetables, yet are simultaneously subject to the pressures and influences of the other's evolutionary path. The interdependence between agency and structure is thus tightly interwoven: agency and structure are interdependent yet maintain their own internal logic and temporally distinct evolutionary progressions (Gould 1978). Agents are not passive recipients of structure—agency and identity are the driving forces behind structural reproduction (whether secondary or primary), persistence, and hysteresis (Barone 1998).

Marx and Marxian scholars possess a heightened sensitivity to social injustice. Social injustice does not exist in ideologies, which emphasize self-determination and wildly independent agency. Such ideologies serve to justify existing power structures and sustain the mechanisms of what Marxian scholars perceive to be a dehumanizing system of production (Parenti 1994). Marxian thought emphasizes the relationship between structure and agency in order to address the systemic social injustice inherent in the capitalist system. But Marx and Marxian thought also recognize and respect the individual and the individual's ability to manipulate the surrounding structural environment. The over-socialized or overly structured depiction of the individual and agency, listing too heavily towards methodological collectivism, does not accurately characterize the Marxian treatment of the individual. Indeed, Marx himself was writing against the highly individualized writings of the classical economists, and about a system he found noxious and ultimately debilitating in terms of the human spirit and creative impulse (O'Boyle 2013). Marx, however, recognized the essential and intrinsic agency of the individual, the possibilities imbued in the courses of action chosen by the individual, and warned against reifying society and the social structures therein. The individual was not stripped of her agency: agency was cast in light of the structural constraints imposed by the relations of production. Marx viewed the agent-structure relationship as both independent and interdependent (Gould 1978).

> Individuals have always built on themselves, but naturally on themselves within their histori-
> cal conditions and relationships, not on the 'pure' individual in the sense of the ideologists.
> But . . . there appears a division within the life of each individual, insofar as it is personal and
> insofar as it is determined by some branch of labour and the conditions pertaining to it . . . .
> We do not mean it to be understood from this that . . . [individuals] cease to be persons; but
> their personality is conditioned and determined by quite definite class relationships.
>
> *Marx & Engels 1995: 83–84*

Regardless of the means of subjugation or dominance, Marx always maintains that the agent remains an agent, never becoming solely an object nor to be understood only in terms of inter-subjective relationships (Gould 1978). Indeed, for Marx and in the current Marxian tradition, the agent-structure relationship is interactive—influence runs both ways. To the Marxian economist, however, the social structure of inequality endemic to capitalism and the resulting unnecessary misery imposed on the majority of humankind with its humiliating and crippling effect on the psyche of the individual is of primary focus and concern.

The Cartesian conception of the purely intellectually constructed mental model found in the mainstream's rational economic man is deliberately avoided under the Post Keynesian rubric. The social structure, more than acting as a constraint on choice, partly informs the agent's belief system, while choices made by individuals, in turn, inform the social structure. The individual does, however, maintain internal integrity and autonomy—structure is not deterministic and individuals are still capable of free will. Indeed, both structure and agent maintain independence while remaining interactive. The Post Keynesian conceptualization of agency therefore eschews both methodological individualism and methodological collectivism in favor of interactive agency whereby the individual agent makes choices within a cultural context and the choices influence the very social structure wherein the original choice was. Such dynamism need not indicate social instability. The stability of any social structure, or in larger review social system, is insured over the long-run by the very influence of social structure on its constituents; in other words, by conventions, rules, and norms. Stability does not intimate, however, ergodicity (Todorova 2005; McKenna & Zannoni 2012).

Although—until relatively recently—largely implicit, Post Keynesian thought addresses and frames agency in interactive terms with "dynamic interaction between agent and structure" (McKenna & Zannoni 2012: 2). Through fundamental uncertainty and by refuting rational expectations and ergodic uncertainty, however, Post Keynesians have consistently underscored the evolution of mental models within a structural context and the interactive communication and affectation between agent and structure. Moreover, as Post Keynesianism evolves, it is clear that a more well-defined conceptualization of interactive agency continues to coalesce. Lee (2010), in building on the work of Alfred Eichner, explicitly employs interactive agency in order to construct a heterodox macro-micro theory of value. In Lee's (2010) theory interactive agency acts as the critical linchpin which connects individuals and the wider social structure of accumulation and production.

Closing remarks

Through the discussion of mental models, structure, agency, and their respective evolutions, the three heterodox schools examined herein are able to provide ontological detail about the individual that addresses the range of human behavior and reaches beyond epistemological constraints and maximizing motivations. The three heterodox schools conceptualize the individual and explore the interaction between agent and structure from different theoretical frameworks.

Their theoretical constructions of the economic individual are congruous and their constructions of the interactive agency are theoretically compatible. Theories of interactive agency are necessary but not sufficient for heterodox economic thought. What distinguishes heterodox economic thought is the constant, temporally asymmetric, back-and-forth affectation between agent and structure, which augments and shapes, but does not entirely determine the nature, composition, and evolutionary paths of each. Complementary theoretical threads running through the frameworks of each of these three schools of heterodox economic thought include elements of non-ergodic and subjective uncertainty, ontological (as opposed to strictly epistemological) distinctions between individuals, temporally non-syncopated evolution of individuals and institutions, and the interdependence and independence of agent and structure—in other words, interactive agency.

The OIE and Marxian scholars maintain the strongest and most developed conceptualization of the individual and interactive agency, perhaps because the respective progenitors of each tradition recognized the incumbency in avoiding the self-determined individualism of their historically respective orthodoxies: Marx and classical political economics, Veblen and neoclassical economics. Marx specifically aimed to warn of the debilitating and dehumanizing effects of the structure of the capitalist mode of production on the agency and identity of the individual leading ultimately to her alienation. Likewise, Veblen sought to replace the neoclassical reductivist image of the individual and call attention to the sway of market power and emulative psychosis impinged on the mental models and agency of individuals through consumer-driven society. While within Post Keynesianism, the conceptualization of agency is still an evolving theoretical construct, Post Keynesian thinkers undoubtedly incorporate agency through fundamental uncertainty and the construction of the Post Keynesian macro-micro model of value thereby demonstrating ontological differentiations between individuals as well as interactivity between structure and agent.

The purpose of this chapter has not been to suggest that these diverse heterodox schools should consolidate or homogenize the economic individual and the discretion and power she is able to exercise in the decision-making process. Such an attempt would run counter to the idea of pluralism embodied in the prefix 'hetero.' Rather, the purpose of this chapter is to suggest that theories of interactive agency present a defining characteristic of heterodox economics and a common base from which heterodox economists might develop not just a critique of mainstream's 'isolated, definitive human datum' but also open the door to a more pluralist economics discipline and greater collegial cross-school discourse. Such a widening of the discipline to a pluralism of thought perhaps will construct more socially relevant thought and innovation, which might then provide socially relevant measures of reform.

> Heterodox economics may have a more promising future than most imagine. If the elements of an alternative conception of the individual described here coalesce around an increasingly resonant set of concerns regarding individual life in today's socially complex world, the better intuitions that heterodox economists have about institutions and social structures could place them in a position to speak with greater authority about society's concern over the increasing vulnerability of individuals.
>
> *Davis 2003: 191*

While some may object to either too broad a spectrum of possibilities as provided by pluralism and others to the dangers in what might be considered consolidating or homogenizing economic thought, the assurance offered by genuine scientific inquiry in economics should satisfy both. Common ground does not suggest common outcomes or common goals. Common, or at the least contributory, ground does, however, provide a base from which to start economic inquiry and integration as well as democratic policy changes. In as much, scientific inquiry and the democratic process are parallel in quest and process: the objective of both is not to simply reach consensus but instead to provide a process by which inquiry and reasoned discourse create an economics that is a self-correcting social science focused on the resolution of social anxieties charged with the task of social reform (Tilman 1987).

Note

1 This chapter is based upon and draws substantially from previously published work (Wrenn 2007). Since that time, Wrenn's work on agency has shifted out of the heterodox methodological context to the historical contextualization of neoliberalism (see Wrenn 2015) as part of her broader research on ontology and neoliberalism.

References

Archer, M.S. 1995. *Realist Social Theory: The Morphogenetic Approach*. Cambridge: Cambridge University Press.

Barone, C. 1998. 'Political economy of classism: towards a more integrated multilevel view.' *Review of Radical Political Economics*, 30 (2): 1–30.

Bowles, S. & Gintis, H. 1986. *Democracy and Capitalism: Property, Community, and the Contradictions of Modern Social Thought*. New York: Basic Books.

Davis, J.B. 2003. *The Theory of the Individual in Economics: Identity and Value*. London: Routledge.

Dunn, S. P. 2001. 'Bounded rationality is not fundamental uncertainty: a Post Keynesian perspective.' *Journal of Post Keynesian Economics*, 23 (4): 567–587.

Ebert, T.L. 2005. 'Rematerializing feminism.' *Science and Society*, 69 (1): 33–55.

Giddens, A. 1979. *Central Problems in Social Theory: Action, Structure and Contradiction in Social Analysis*. Berkeley, CA: University of California Press.

Gould, C.C. 1978. *Marx's Social Ontology: Individuality and Community in Marx's Theory of Social Reality*. Cambridge, MA: MIT Press.

Gramsci, A. [1948] 1995. *Antonio Gramsci: Further Selections from the Prison Notebooks*, edited by D. Boothman. New York: New York University Press.

Hamilton, D.B. 1953. *Newtonian Classicism and Darwinian Institutionalism: A Study of Change in Economic Theory*. Albuquerque, NM: The University of New Mexico Press.

Hargreaves Heap, S. P. 2001. 'Expressive rationality: is self-worth just another kind of preference?' in: U. Mäki (ed.), *The Economic World View: Studies in the Ontology of Economics*. Cambridge: Cambridge University Press, 98–113.

Hodgson, G.M. 1998. 'The approach of institutional economics.' *Journal of Economic Literature*, 36 (1): 166–192.

Hodgson, G.M. 2002. 'Reconstitutive downward causation: social structure and the development of individual agency,' in: E. Fullbrook (ed.), *Intersubjectivity in Economics: Agents and Structures*. London: Routledge, 159–180.

Hodgson, G.M. 2004. *The Evolution of Institutional Economics: Agency, Structure, and Darwinism in American Institutionalism*. London: Routledge.

Lavoie, M. 2006. 'Do heterodox theories have anything in common? A post-Keynesian point of view.' *European Journal of Economics and Economic Policies: Intervention*, 3 (1): 87–112.

Lawson, T. 1997. *Economics and Reality*. London: Routledge.

Lee, F.S. 2010. 'Alfred Eichner's missing "complete model": a heterodox micro–macro model of a monetary production economy,' in: M. Lavoie, L.-P. Rochon, & M. Seccareccia (eds.), *Money and Macrodynamics: Alfred Eichner and Post-Keynesian Economics*. London: Routledge, 22–42.

Marx, K. & Engels, F. 1995. *The German Ideology*. New York: International Publishers.

Mayhew, A. 2001. 'Human agency, cumulative causation, and the state.' *Journal of Economic Issues*, 35 (2): 239–250.

McKenna, E.J. & Zannoni, D.C. 2012. 'Agency,' in: J.E. King (ed.), *The Elgar Companion to Post Keynesian Economics*, 2nd edn. Cheltenham, UK: Edward Elgar, 1–5.

O'Boyle, B. 2013. 'Reproducing the social structure: a Marxist critique of Anthony Giddens's structuration methodology.' *Cambridge Journal of Economics*, 37 (5): 1019–1033.

Parenti, M. 1994. *Land of Idols: Political Mythology in America*. New York: St. Martin's Press.

Pratten, S. 1993. 'Structure, agency and Marx's analysis of the labour process.' *Review of Political Economy*, 5 (4): 403–426.

Rosser, J.B. 2001. 'Alternative Keynesian and Post Keynesian perspectives on uncertainty and expectations.' *Journal of Post Keynesian Economics*, 23 (4): 545–566.

Simon, H.A. 1978. 'Rational decision-making in business organizations: Nobel memorial lecture,' *in*: A. Lindbeck (ed.), *Economic Sciences*. Singapore: World Scientific Publishing, 343–371.

Smith, C. 2010. *What is a Person? Rethinking Humanity, Social Life, and the Moral Good from the Person Up.* Chicago: The University of Chicago Press.

Tauheed, L.F. 2013. 'A critical institutionalist reconciliation of "contradictory" institutionalist institutions: institutions and social provisioning.' *Journal of Economic Issues*, 47 (4): 827–853.

Taylor, L.J. 2006. The role of informal institutions in the transition: how households in Krasnodar, Russia are coping with change. PhD Dissertation. Colorado State University.

Taylor, L.J. & Wrenn, M.V. 2003. 'Forging new relationships: social capital in the transition.' *Forum for Social Economics*, 33 (1): 1–11.

Tilman, R. 1987. 'The neoinstrumental theory of democracy.' *Journal of Economic Issues*, 21 (3): 1379–1401.

Todorova, Z. 2005. 'Habits of thought, agency, and transformation: An institutional approach to feminist ecological economics.' *Feminist Economics*, 11 (3): 126–132.

Veblen, T. 1898a. 'The instinct of workmanship and the irksomeness of labor.' *The American Journal of Sociology*, 4 (2): 187–201.

Veblen, T. 1898b. 'Why is economics not an evolutionary science?' *The Quarterly Journal of Economics*, 12 (4): 373–397.

Wrenn, M.V. 2007. 'Searching for common ground: interactive agency in heterodox economics.' *European Journal of Economics and Economic Policies: Intervention*, 4 (2): 247–269.

Wrenn, M.V. 2015. 'Agency and neoliberalism.' *Cambridge Journal of Economics*, 39 (5): 1231–1243.

13

Households in heterodox economic theory

Zdravka Todorova

Introduction

Within heterodox economics, the household has been conceptualized as an expenditure and financial unit; as a part of production and monetary circuits; as the relations of the reproduction of labor power; as a source of macroeconomic growth, stability, and instability; as a site of exploitation; as a through-time producer; as an entity understood and formed through colonial relations; as the site of and an actor in global production and financial remittances; and a combination of these scopes (O'Hara 1995; Elson 1998; Hanmer & Akram-Lodhi 1998; Peterson 2003; Charusheela & Danby 2006; Fraad *et al.* 2009; Todorova 2009; Safri & Graham 2010; Hewitson 2013). Both inter- and intra-household relations have received attention at the empirical and conceptual levels, especially within feminist and Marxian-feminist economics (Robeyns 2005; Fraad *et al.* 2009).

The present chapter builds on various heterodox approaches to economics to explore a direction towards analyzing households within a broader heterodox economic theory of social provisioning. The first section delineates the theoretical foundations of households within heterodox economic perspectives. The second section discusses the analytical categories of the household as a going concern, the household as an institution, and the household as an actor-participant within a system of provisioning processes. Finally, the chapter offers suggestions for future developments.

Theoretical foundations of households within heterodox economic perspectives

There have been considerable attempts to meld together heterodox economic approaches (Lee 2012: 123). This is a development in the right direction if heterodox economists are concerned with a systemic understanding of economic problems. Various heterodox approaches have focused on different aspects or levels of economic reality. Conceptualizing households within heterodox economics will thus mean bringing together developments and insights from various approaches. In this section I delineate theoretical elements that to my understanding represent the most fundamental developments of heterodox economic thought that will enrich heterodox theorizing of households.

Below the surface of exchange and beyond monetary production: social provisioning

A fundamental distinctive element of any heterodox economic approach is a theoretical framework that is able to see below the surface of exchange. Heterodox frameworks in general analyze production as a money-making activity and the distribution of income and resources as socially governed and determined. In heterodox economics these two key aspects of the capitalist economy are not conflated with market exchange. Instead, socially produced and distributed surpluses, the creation of resources, together with the agency and structure of classes play a central role in analyzing the capitalist economy (Lee & Jo 2011; Philp & Trigg 2015). This premise is evident in Marxian-radical, original institutionalist, Post Keynesian (including Kaleckian and Sraffian), structuralist, circuitist, Social Structures of Accumulation, *Régulation*, some feminist approaches, and various combinations of these (see Lee 2012: 116). Diving below the surface of exchange has brought into question the market mechanism as an explanation of production and distribution, and has led heterodox economists to explore their social and historical organizations.

However, in this endeavor some heterodox economists, particularly feminists, argue that production is broader than the monetary production of commodities for market exchange (see, for example, Elson 1998; Peterson 2003; Charushela & Danby 2006; Todorova 2009; Safri & Graham 2010). In this respect, the analysis of households from a heterodox economics perspective should be based on distinguishing the production of commodities from the production of non-commodities, and on the articulation of the distinct logics, motives, and valuations that govern market and non-market oriented activities that are nonetheless part of a system of provisioning (Todorova 2015a). Consequently, the concept of *social provisioning* provides a broader meaning of the economy, as wells as a starting point for theorizing households within heterodox economics (Dugger 1996; Power 2004; Todorova 2015b; Jo & Todorova's chapter in this volume).

Multi-faceted humans with living bodies and social provisioning within ecosystems

An understanding of the economy as a social provisioning process is empowered by a notion of multi-faceted humans and their multi-faceted interactions, motives, and values. This means conceiving of humans as living beings, with social lives and identities beyond their economic positions as consumers and material providers. Continuation of life should thus be paramount in the conceptualization of households, given that the processes of social provisioning are part of ecosystems and have ecological bases and consequences. People and households ought to be theorized from the outset as both biological and social beings. Heterodox economics is well-suited to the conceptualization of this sociality outside of market interactions.

Multi-faceted and living humans are important for heterodox theorizing of households. First, such a conception of human beings helps develop a broader formulation of household economic activities including care and recreation (Todorova 2015c). Second, it supports a more comprehensive understanding of vulnerabilities as well as capabilities of people within households. Third, it enables an evolutionary (as opposed to static and non-living) and context-specific (as opposed to universalizing) analysis of households and their relations, motivations, and agencies that impacts and is impacted by social and natural processes. Finally, the conception of multi-faceted and living humans is an understanding that humans have various experiences, goals, and identities resulting in diverse households. Such analyses are strengthened by the conception of a system of processes as described below.

Individuality and diversity

Having diversity within theoretical foundations enables the evolutionary analysis of the household organizations, such as the emergence of the single parent, global migrant worker, and dual-career commuter households, which are connected theoretically to changes in social provisioning and more generally to the evolution of culture-nature processes (Hardill 2002; Peterson 2003). The evolution of the household organization is a subset of institutional change and the evolution of the economic system. The diversity of household arrangements is connected to various positions, experiences, and historical developments in terms of social class, gender, race/ethnicity, citizenship/residency processes, as well as to the evolution of social provisioning within geopolitical and environmental contexts. Consequently, households should not be an analytical category that subsumes the existence of individuals and their diverse experiences. These are essential, rather than tangential, for the heterodox economic analysis of social provisioning.

Classes, power, and capabilities

Within heterodox economics, diversity among and within households cannot be conceived without engaging in explicit analyses of power, hierarchical relations, and social and economic classes; and without connecting these analyses to agency and social structures (Power 2004; Lee 2011). Household choice, decision-making, perceptions, identities, and agency cannot be understood outside of social and economic classes, hierarchical relations, and collective power to create and pursue vested interests and capabilities. That hierarchies within households and among households' socio-economic positions need to be conceived together with desires and actions to change those positions and social arrangements of distribution means that heterodox analyses should allow for the multi-dimensionality of power. This further means that in addition to oppression and invidious distinction, the analysis of power needs to capture the creation of capabilities (Robeyns 2005), and the differences among households in developing and exercising those.

Households and their agencies

In conceiving of households' agency, it is important to connect the differences among and within households to a notion of levels and types of agency. That is, questions about agency are linked to classes, power, and hierarchies. However, individuals and going concerns cannot be subsumed into aggregate categories, if agency is to be taken into account (Jo 2015). The notion of agency presumes a developed and socialized individuality (Davis 2003: 11). Social structures are not mere outcomes of an aggregate individual's will, and the socialization of the individual does not mean a complete determination of the self (for an elaborate exposition see Archer 2000: 253–282). Consequently, with respect to intra-household relations there must be a conceptualization of diverse selves that are not entirely explained by social norms and the structure of the household as a going concern. Analytically, this allows for the emergence of various forms of household going concerns, as well as for actions towards altering household positions and structural arrangements.

Based on the above theoretical points, below I discuss three fundamental categories that are necessary for theorizing households—going concerns, institutions, and processes, and that are consistent with developments in heterodox economics. I will explain the importance of distinguishing between the household as an institution and as a going concern that participates and contributes to the emergence of an evolving system of nature-culture-provisioning processes.

Households as going concerns

Social activities are organized and carried out by going concerns. Going concerns engage in continuous, relatively stable social activities through which they exercise certain agencies. Households are going concerns that take various forms of organization. Place(s) and spaces of residence are part of the household going concern. Analyses of kinship and familial ties may be part of the household as a going concern, but do not necessarily overlap with them.

If we understand the household as a going concern, rather than a static unit, the focus of inquiry shifts to *how people live over time.* The concept of a going concern enables evolutionary analyses that allow complexities over time and space, and transcend unitary, fixed, and universalizing notions of 'the household,' and captures the diversity among households with respect to their geographical characteristics, methods of obtaining a livelihood, and marriage and co-habitation arrangements. For example, migrant workers are engaged in maintaining a household of members who do not reside together continuously. This is done through financial remittances as well as emotional relations and support. Those households may also be part of another household, as in the case of domestic work and care or the co-habitation of workers. Similarly, dual-career households with members holding jobs in different regions and living in separate dwellings are engaged in maintaining a household as a going concern. Furthermore, a household as a going concern is a broader concept than a financial unit of cash (out)flows and financial obligations.

In heterodox economics, particularly grounded in institutional economics, the concept of the going concern has been developed with respect to the business enterprise (see Veblen [1904] 2005; Commons [1924] 1995; Jo & Henry 2015). What distinguishes households as going concerns from other forms of going concerns needs further articulation. For example, the going concern of the business enterprise continues as the expectation for future profits continues. A liquidated or near bankrupt business enterprise ceases to be a going concern. However, a household continues to be a going concern after the depletion of assets and income flows (although as a result of that it could disintegrate through death, or transform through divorce, migration, etc.).

Identifying activities are not sufficient to distinguish households from other institutions (Hendon 1996: 46), given that consumption, recreation, even care activities take place within other going concerns too, such as the business enterprise; and, moreover, that production takes place within households. Motivation and valuation are also not exclusively designated to a particular going concern. For example, care as paid employment can be motivated by both money and caring (Zelizer 2010; England *et al.* 2013); and predatory and invidious motivation could in fact underline some household activities (Todorova 2015a).

An application of the concept of the going concern to the household should reflect the conceptualization of the economy as a social provisioning process beyond production for market exchange. As stressed by feminist economists, households engage in paid and unpaid activities that are central to social provisioning and communities (Power 2004). Unpaid activities include household work, care, recreational, and consumption activities. Such unpaid activities are part of the reproduction and maintenance of the labor force through birthing, bringing-up children, caring, socializing, and other daily support care activities. These activities support capital accumulation and, generally, the social provisioning process. Informal employment blurs the lines between paid and unpaid work (Charusheela & Danby 2006). Households and home-based paid work, as well as unpaid work and care, are part of global commodity chains and economies (Peterson 2003; Collins 2014; Ramamurthy 2014). The growth of commodity production means that households are part of debtor–creditor relations and vulnerable to entrepreneurial expectations and to neoliberal policies such as privatization (see, for example, LeBaron 2010; LeBaron & Roberts 2013). Unpaid household work and care can only partially offset a worsened household's financial position and livelihood, because households must obtain money through participation in the market process to purchase goods and services, and to service debts and pay taxes. Structural changes such as precarious employment, rising medical debts, and the costs of education cannot be fully circumvented by engaging in non-market oriented production and more generally non-market household and community activities. Yet, financial responsibility and costs are shifted onto households (Resnick & Wolff 2006).

This is amplified by distinctions among households based on income and wealth (Wolff & Zacharias 2013). Such distinctions can be understood not only as individual household characteristics, but also as social-class relations embedded in the ways that household incomes are earned and spent, and established and perpetuated via institutions, such as the educational system. Household going concerns interact with institutions differently based on those differentiated social-class relations (Lareau & Cox 2011; Lareau & Calarco 2012; Miller & Sperry 2012; Stephens et al. 2012).

The household as an institution

Households as going concerns, together with particular emergent working rules, procedures, social beliefs, symbols, discourse, and conventional wisdom regarding their organization and operation, as well as related emerging personal attitudes, constitute *the institution of the household*. All of these are analytical categories or elements of social processes.

A particular evolution of those elements results in specific habits of thought, such as the 'breadwinner household.' The term 'habits of thought' refers to the institutionalized patterns of practices and ideas that can serve as an ideal for aspiration, and as a criterion for value judgment. As in the case of the breadwinner model of the household, for example, a particular idea or habit can have a normative effect on policy and influences judgments of success and worthiness, even if the model is dwindling or unachievable by most (Peterson & Peterson 1994; Rose 2000).

The analytical distinction between the household as a going concern and the household as an institution enables us to conceptualize not only the variations of households, but also their common institutional position in the economic structure. The household as an institution occupies a passive position within the hierarchy of money, and with respect to the determination of effective demand, output, and employment (Bell 2001; Todorova 2009). In a capitalist economy the overall monetary wealth and income of households is determined by the activities of business enterprises and the state, both of which determine the level and composition of income, employment, and effective demand, and thus the ability of households to repay their debt obligations. Those are limitations of the household as an institution. However, there are different household going concerns, including capitalist and working-class households, which engage in the social provisioning process in different manners. That is to say, all households must navigate surrounding environment and address problems that arise outside their realm of influence in order for them to remain as going concerns, but household going concerns located in different social strata encounter different types or degrees of limitations. Thus, there are variations in agency among households with respect to their interactions with institutions, their ability to engage in social provisioning activities in order to support their lives and lifestyles; and with respect to their ability to direct other households' lives.

Cardwell & Todorova (2016) note that it is useful to think of some household going concerns as operating through the institution of the household; and others operating also through other institutions. They argue, for example, that under money-manager capitalism a concentrated financial sector inhibits the agency of household going concerns who act only through the institution of the household, while providing opportunities for political and economic agency of household going concerns that transcend their institution and/or that are able to exercise agency as going concerns through financial institutions.[1] They also argue that differences in agency among household going concerns (due to economic class and the ability to operate as agents outside the household institution) are indeed amplified by the limitations of the household institution in the capitalist economy.

The implication of such variations in household agency for heterodox economic theory is that households cannot be theorized as merely passive or choice-making individual entities. Understanding specificities and variations of households and their experiences is enhanced by an understanding of the structural positions of households as institutions. That some households are able to take advantage of particular institutions in their own interests indicates distinctions and hierarchies among household going concerns, which are consistent with different patterns of household behavior. To better explain such variations in household agency in the social context, economic analyses ought to be able to conceptualize social processes and to investigate developments in their elements—symbols, discourse, social beliefs, conventional wisdom, personal attitudes and perceptions, working rules, procedures, and rituals (Todorova 2014, 2015a, b).

Households and processes

'Processes' is a term used in different theoretical frameworks. For example, building on and broadening Marxian theory Fraad et al. (2009) and Resnick & Wolff (2009) look at the internal household structure by conceptualizing 'class processes' within the household. They see the appropriation and distribution of a surplus as a fundamental class process, and argue for envisioning the class process also within the household. First, their notion of the class process is specific to an analysis based on the labor theory of value, and, second, this analysis is extended to households to argue that exploitation as conceptualized by Marx also occurs within the household. Some feminist economists have also pointed out the usefulness of refocusing analyses on processes (Nelson 1993; Power 2004).

Elsewhere I have suggested a way to develop the notion of a process. A process pertains to structures that precede individual and collective actions through going concerns that contribute to the evolution of structural arrangements. The emergence and transformation of the elements of social processes (such as conventions and discourse) is the result of the agency of all sorts of going concerns. Thus, the concept of a process encompasses the analysis of agency and structure and hence micro–macro theory in an integrative manner. The appendix shows a suggested typology of interconnected evolving processes of nature, culture, and provisioning, discussed by Todorova (2014, 2015a, b, c).

The offered typology has the following implications with respect to household theory. First, a process need not be analytically confined to a realm of the household or to any other single institution. For example, the emergence and representation of femininity and masculinity can be defined as a 'gender process' that can emerge and interact with any other process, and be a part of the activities and practices of any going concern. The particular context and investigation will determine the actual relations. Therefore households are not designated as separate units in respective social and cultural realms.

Second, rather than just focusing on households' demographic characteristics, the suggested system of processes enables the investigation of systemic relations of race/ethnicity, gender, etc. This is the point of column 3 in the appendix. Those are not just personal characteristics or variables, but social processes as defined above. There is value in making a distinction between processes that are directly governed by or associated with a particular going concern (citizenship and residency via the state), and those that are not (but nonetheless affected by going concerns, such as language).

Household going concerns are part of the whole system of processes. For example, while the state governs the social process of citizenship and residency, households are very much part of that process, as evidenced by global chains of migrant care workers (see Safri & Graham 2010; Collins 2014). In this example, it is easy to see that households participating in labor and care processes of social provisioning are also part of supervision, surveillance, and direction processes. Again, specific connections between these processes will be determined by specific investigations. To do so one needs further details in the specification of the analytical categories of social process. Thus, what are the conventions (procedures and working rules) for state surveillance of migrant care providers, and how do they evolve? How do they intersect with social beliefs about household organization, gender roles, work, care, race and ethnicity, and citizenship, for example? What are emerging habits of thought? An example is a global household of a migrant care-giver who relies on somebody's unpaid family labor to care for her own household (see Safri & Graham 2010; Yeates 2014).

Finally, theorizing of households should not be secondary to the main narrative of a heterodox economic approach. For example, if we look at commodity chains, we can see a myriad of social provisioning processes. The feminist literature on world systems and commodity chains has shown how global production is built on decentralized home-based production intertwined with reproductive activities and gender norms (Collins 2014; Dunaway 2014). Home-based production and the putting-out system have been a part of the early development of capitalism and continue to be central in the modern global commodity chain and capital accumulation (Kessler-Harris [1982] 2003; Ross 2014). That is, the blurring of the boundaries between home and work (Hardill 2002) is not just an aspect of the early stage of capitalism; it is in fact central to contemporary business cost-cutting techniques, as well as the neoliberal discourse and practices of 'entrepreneurial self' (Mirowski 2013) addressing household 'strategies' for survival. Of course, theorizing households is important for a better understanding of commodity chains. Moreover, it is important since human life is maintained through the organizing and sustaining of household going concerns—this should be central in developing heterodox economics. The system of processes is useful in opening the vast fields of inquiry in this direction.

Conclusions and future directions

My concern in this chapter has been the development of a theory of the household beyond a particular stream of heterodox economics. While useful for specific purposes, a Post Keynesian theory of the household, for example, is a limited project; so is a Marxian or feminist approach. A project of building bridges among heterodox streams may eventually lead to a broader heterodox theory (see, for example, Todorova 2009). Here I have delineated a set of starting points for such a theory with respect to households in the social provisioning process.

There is no doubt that each heterodox tradition has its own contribution to the analysis of households under capitalism. Post Keynesians, for example, specify and emphasize the limited financial position of households in the monetary production economy. Post Keynesian analyses are in general at the level of households as institutions as explained above. Feminist economists point to the centrality of non-commodity production, gendered capabilities, and intra-household relations. Marxian-feminists point to the role of households in capital accumulation. Those approaches go deeper into the household going concern and explore its connections to the elements of social processes and structures. Ecological economists and institutionalists have pointed out the centrality of living human beings within ecosystems and complex social provisioning systems. The Social Structure of Accumulation approach provides an analysis of the changes in institutional arrangements and accumulation regimes with particular regard to their systemic effects.

Individual heterodox approaches have paid attention to different aspects (with different scopes) of social provisioning. Given that more heterodox economists cross boundaries, it would be a worthwhile effort if each tradition engages in theory development within heterodox economics as broadly defined. This is my hope in delineating the theoretical entry points and basic analytical categories. Following are some general directions for future development in the heterodox theory of the household.

First, I have argued for the usefulness of the notion of the going concern applied to households. This concept should be further developed specifically regarding households, since application has been primarily with respect to the business enterprise. Particularly, how are households distinguished from other going concerns? How and why do household going concerns differ in terms of their organization, operation, background, and agency?

Second, given the recognition of institutional commonality among households, what are the mechanisms through which some households transcend their limitations as institutions, and how do they operate through other institutions to exercise a different type of agency than other household going concerns who remain more limited in their action?

Third, how are collective actions of households enabled and restrained within social provisioning, and how do households contribute to the evolution of social and natural processes? Within given contexts, what are the specific connections among household going concerns, other going concerns, and processes? What are the roles of households in the emergence of specific habits of thought? The proposed system of processes opens ways to bring in the centrality of households into social provisioning and heterodox economics. In combination with developed heterodox methods, it offers a way to think about and to research households within a broadly heterodox economic theory.

Appendix: a system of processes

(1) Biological and geographical processes	(2) Processes formulated on the basis of a social provisioning activity	(3) Processes not formulated on the basis of a social provisioning activity	
		(3a) Affected by, but not operating through, specific going concerns	(3b) Identified with going concerns
Biospheric processes	Care	Gender	Citizenship and legal residency (state, international institutions)
Production of biomass	Labor	Social class	Economic class
Information sourcing	Recreation	Race and ethnicity	(business enterprise, state, international institutions)
Habitat	Consumption	Language	Ownership
Bodies	Mobility and residence		(business enterprise, state, international institutions, courts, military)
Birth	Communication, expression, and persuasion		Contracts and justice
Lactation	Cultivation and transmission of knowledge, memories, tools		(courts, state, international institutions)
Cognition and emotions	Undertaking (investing; organizing; mobilization)		Worship
Development	Resource creation and usage		(temples, religious establishments)
Spirituality	Machine process (production; mechanization of activities)		Kinship
Sexuality	Supervision, surveillance, and direction		(households, tribes)
Illness	Threat and punishment		
Impairment	Distribution		
Aging	Deprivation		
Death	WasteExchange, trade, speculation/ gift		
Information sourcing	Debt–credit/gift		
Physical space	Violence		
Landscapes			
Localities/places			
Buildings/architecture			
Infrastructure			

Source: This is an updated and modified version of tables published in Todorova (2014, 2015b).

Note

1 Undertaking political actions and creating other going concerns, such as unions and consumer cooperatives, and mobilization, are also important for theorizing, especially considering the discussed multi-
faceted agent. These also represent the possibility to act through other institutions.

References

Archer, M. 2000. *Being Human: The Problem of Agency*. New York: Routledge.
Bell, S. 2001. 'The role of the state and the hierarchy of money.' *Cambridge Journal of Economics*, 25 (2): 149–165.
Cardwell, L. & Todorova, Z. 2016. 'Evolution of U.S. household agency over stages of capitalism.' *Journal of Economic Issues*, 50 (2): 542–548.
Charusheela, S. & Danby, C. 2006. 'A through-time framework for producer households.' *Review of Political Economy*, 18 (1): 29–49.
Collins, J. 2014. 'A feminist approach to overcoming the closed boxes of the commodity chain,' in: W. Dunaway (ed.), *Gendered Commodity Chains: Seeing Women's Work and Households in Global Production*. Stanford, CA: Stanford University Press, 27–38.
Commons, J. [1924] 1995. *Legal Foundations of Capitalism*. New Brunswick, NJ: Transactions Publishers.
Davis, J. 2003. *The Theory of the Individual in Economics: Identity and Value*. New York: Routledge.
Dugger, W. 1996. 'Redefining economics: from market allocation to social provisioning,' in: C. Whalen (ed.), *Political Economy for the 21st Century*. Armonk, NY: M.E. Sharpe, 31–43.
Dunaway, W. 2014. 'Through the portal of the household: conceptualizing women's subsidies to commodity chains,' in: W. Dunaway (ed.), *Gendered Commodity Chains: Seeing Women's Work and Households in Global Production*. Stanford, CA: Stanford University Press, 55–72.
Elson, D. 1998. 'The economic, the political and the domestic: businesses, states and households in the organisation of production.' *New Political Economy*, 3 (2): 189–208.
England, P., Folbre, N., & Leana, C. 2013. 'Motivating care,' in: N. Folbre (ed.), *For Love and Money: Care Provision in the United States*. New York: Russell Sage Foundation, 21–40.
Fraad, H., Resnick, S., & Wolff, R. 2009. 'For every knight in shining armour, there's a castle waiting to be cleaned: a Marxist-Feminist analysis of the household,' in: G. Cassano (ed.), *Class Struggle on the Home Front: Work, Conflict, and Exploitation in the Household*. New York: Palgrave Macmillan, 19–71.
Hanmer, L. & Akram-Lodhi, A.H. 1998. 'In the "house of the spirits": toward a Post Keynesian theory of the household.' *Journal of Post Keynesian Economics*, 20 (3): 415–433.
Hardill, I. 2002. *Gender, Migration and the Dual Career Household*. New York: Routledge.
Hendon, J. 1996. 'Archaeological approaches to the organization of domestic labor: household practice and domestic relations.' *Annual Review of Anthropology*, 25 (1): 45–61.
Hewitson, G. 2013. 'Economics and the family: a Postcolonial perspective." *Cambridge Journal of Economics*, 37 (1): 91–111.
Jo, T.-H. 2015. 'Heterodox microeconomics and heterodox microfoundations,' in: T.-H. Jo & Z. Todorova (eds.), *Advancing the Frontiers of Heterodox Economics: Essays in Honor of Frederic S. Lee*. London: Routledge, 97–114.
Jo, T.-H. & Henry, J.F. 2015. 'The business enterprise in the age of money manager capitalism.' *Journal of Economic Issues*, 49 (1): 23–46.
Kessler-Harris, A. [1982] 2003. 'From household manufactures to wage work,' in: *Out to Work: A History of Wage-Earning Women, in the United States*. New York: Oxford University Press, 20–44.
Lareau, A. & Cox, A. 2011. 'Social class and the transition to adulthood; differences in parents' interactions with institutions,' in: M.J. Carlson & P. England (eds.), *Social Class and Changing Families in an Unequal America*. Stanford, CA: Stanford University Press, 134–164.
Lareau, A. & Calarco, J. 2012. 'Class, cultural capital, and institutions: the case of families and schools,' in: S.T. Fiske & H.R. Markus (eds.), *Facing Social Class: How Societal Rank Influences Interaction*. New York: Russell Sage Foundation, 61–86.
LeBaron, G. 2010. 'The political economy of the household: neoliberal restructuring, enclosures, and daily life.' *Review of International Political Economy*, 17 (5): 889–912.
LeBaron, G. & Roberts, A. 2013. 'Toward a feminist political economy of capitalism and carcerality.' *Signs*, 36 (1): 19–44.
Lee, F.S. 2011. 'Modeling the economy as a whole: an integrative approach.' *The American Journal of Economics and Sociology*, 70 (5): 1282–1314.

Lee, F.S. 2012. 'Heterodox economics and its critics,' *in*: F.S. Lee & M. Lavoie (eds.), *In Defense of Post-Keynesian and Heterodox Economics*. London: Routledge, 104–132.

Lee, F.S. & Jo, T.-H. 2011. 'Social surplus approach and heterodox economics.' *Journal of Economic Issues*, 45 (4): 857–875.

Miller, P.J. & Sperry, D.E. 2012. 'Déjà vu: the continuing misrecognition of low-income children's verbal abilities,' *in*: S.T. Fiske & H.R. Markus (eds.), *Facing Social Class: How Societal Rank Influences Interaction*. New York: Russell Sage Foundation, 109–130.

Mirowski, P. 2013. *Never Let a Serious Crisis Go to Waste*. London: Verso.

Nelson, J. 1993. 'The study of choice or the study of provisioning? Gender and the definition of economics,' *in*: M. Ferber & J. Nelson (eds.), *Beyond Economic Man: Feminist Theory and Economics*. Chicago: University of Chicago Press, 23–37.

O'Hara. P.A. 1995. 'Household labor, the family, and macroeconomic instability in the United States: 1940s–1990s.' *Review of Social Economy*, 53 (1): 89–120.

Peterson, J. & Peterson, C. 1994. 'Single mother families and the dual welfare state.' *Review of Social Economy*, 52 (3): 314–338.

Peterson, S. 2003. *A Critical Rewriting of Global Political Economy: Integrating Reproductive, Productive and Virtual Economies*. New York: Routledge.

Philp, B. & Trigg, A. 2015. 'Heterodox economics, distribution and the class struggle,' *in*: T.-H. Jo & Z. Todorova (eds.), *Advancing the Frontiers of Heterodox Economics: Essays in Honor of Frederic S. Lee*. New York: Routledge.

Power, M. 2004. 'Social provisioning as a starting point for feminist economics.' *Feminist Economics*, 10 (3): 3–21.

Ramamurthy, P. 2014. 'Feminist commodity chain analysis: a framework to conceptualize value and interpret perplexity,' *in*: W. Dunaway (ed.), *Gendered Commodity Chains: Seeing Women's Work and Households in Global Production*. Stanford, CA: Stanford University Press, 38–52.

Resnick, S. & Wolff, R. 2006. 'The Reagan–Bush strategy: shifting crises from enterprises to households,' *in*: S. Resnick & R. Wolff (eds.), *New Departures in Marxian Theory*. New York: Routledge, 309–353.

Resnick, S. & Wolff, R. 2009. 'The class analysis of households extended: children, fathers, and family budgets,' *in*: G. Cassano (ed.), *Class Struggle on the Home Front: Work, Conflict, and Exploitation in the Household*. New York: Palgrave Macmillan, 86–116.

Robeyns, I. 2005. 'The capability approach: a theoretical survey.' *Journal of Human Development*, 6 (1): 93–117.

Rose, N. 2000. 'Scapegoating poor women: an analysis of welfare reform.' *Journal of Economic Issues*, 34 (2): 143–157.

Ross, R. 2014. 'In chains at the bottom of the pyramid: gender, the informal economy, and sweated labor in global apparel production,' *in*: W. Dunaway (ed.), *Gendered Commodity Chains: Seeing Women's Work and Households in Global Production*. Stanford, CA: Stanford University Press, 91–105.

Safri, M. & Graham, J. 2010. 'The global household: toward a feminist postcapitalist international political economy.' *Signs*, 36 (1): 99–125.

Stephens, N.M., Fryberg, S.A., & Markus, H.R. 2012. 'It's your choice: how middle-class model of independence disadvantages working-class Americans,' *in*: S.T. Fiske & H.R. Markus (eds.), *Facing Social Class: How Societal Rank Influences Interaction*. New York: Russell Sage Foundation, 87–106.

Todorova, Z. 2009. *Money and Households in a Capitalist Economy: A Gendered Post Keynesian–Institutional Analysis*. Northampton, MA: Edward Elgar.

Todorova, Z. 2014. 'Consumption as a social process.' *Journal of Economic Issues*, 48 (3): 663–679.

Todorova, Z. 2015a. 'A further Veblenian articulation of a monetary theory of production,' *in*: T.-H. Jo & F.S. Lee (eds.), *Marx, Veblen, and the Foundations of Heterodox Economics: Essays in Honor of John F. Henry*. London: Routledge, 102–123.

Todorova, Z. 2015b. 'Social provisioning within a culture-culture life-process.' *Review of Political Economy*, 27 (3): 390–409.

Todorova, Z. 2015c. 'Economic and social class in theorizing unpaid household activities under capitalism.' *Journal of Economic Issues*, 49 (2): 425–433.

Veblen, T. [1904] 2005. *The Theory of Business Enterprise*. New York: Cosimo Classics.

Wolff, E. & Zacharias, A. 2013. 'Class structure and economic inequality. *Cambridge Journal of Economics*, 37 (6): 1381–1406.

Yeates, N. 2014. 'Global care chains: bringing in transnational reproductive laborer households,' *in*: W. Dunaway (ed.), *Gendered Commodity Chains: Seeing Women's Work and Households in Global Production*. Stanford, CA: Stanford University Press, 175–189.

Zelizer, V. 2010. 'Caring everywhere,' *in*: E. Boris & R. Salazar Parrenas (eds.), *Intimate Labors: Cultures, Technologies and the Politics of Care*. Stanford, CA: Stanford University Press, 267–279.

14

A heterodox theory of the business enterprise

Tae-Hee Jo

Introduction

This chapter is an attempt to develop a heterodox theory of the business enterprise incorporating contributions made by various theoretical traditions in heterodox economics, in particular Marxian, Post Keynesian, and institutionalist economics. The rationale behind this task is that while each heterodox economics tradition offers its own distinctive insights into the business enterprise that are alternative to the neoclassical theory of the firm, an integrative approach will offer a more comprehensive understanding of the business enterprise than each heterodox approach could do separately.

Heterodox economics concerns the structure and dynamics of the provisioning process that pertains to the livelihood of people in the social-historical context (see Chapter 2 by Jo & Todorova in this volume). From this view of heterodox economics, a heterodox theory of the business enterprise addresses itself to how business enterprise activities are organized vis-à-vis the structure and dynamics of the social provisioning process, rather than exploring how the representative firm maximizes its profits following the market price mechanism. Thus a heterodox theory of the business enterprise is a constructive approach that is independent of the neoclassical theory of the firm. A preliminary step to develop the former would be a clear understanding of the latter, in particular its underlying premises and scope.

The standard neoclassical theory of the firm is predicated on the ahistorical view of the business enterprise. The fundamental neoclassical doctrine is that the Marshallian representative firm engages in production, exchange, investment, and employment on the marginalist principle. In this theoretical configuration the neoclassical firm is squarely defined as a profit-maximizing rational individual whose activities follow the rule of the market that is assumed to be universal and normal (and hence ahistorical). That is, "in the beginning there were markets" (Williamson 1975: 20) and there emerged firms in order to economize the use of scarce resources. Such an unquestioned neoclassical premise is theological rather than historical.

Major controversies in economics in the twentieth century, such as the 'empty boxes' debate (1920s), the marginalist controversy (1940s–50s), the administered price controversy (1930s, 1960s–70s), and the capital controversy (1950s–70s) challenged the conventional explanation of capital accumulation, production, exchange, and distribution. These issues are related to the question as to how the business enterprise carries out productive activities under capitalism. The controversies, taken as a whole, suggest that not only is the neoclassical firm theory flawed, but also the entire neoclassical framework based upon the market price mechanism is problematic as the former is a core theoretical constituent of the latter. More specifically, heterodox economists argue on the theoretical ground that production does not take place, if a firm's technology displays non-diminishing marginal returns. That is to say, the upward sloping supply curve or the firm itself can only exist under the perfectly competitive market structure in which the law of supply and demand works, and in which a firm is nothing but a 'mediator' or 'empty box' between (the owners of) inputs and (the consumers of) outputs. This means that the standard supply curve and the production function remove both the production process and other decision-making processes within the business enterprise and the inter-industrial connections ('circular' production) among business enterprises (Sraffa 1926, 1960; Robertson *et al.* 1930; Harcourt 1972; Shapiro 1976). Furthermore, on the empirical ground that the real world business enterprises do not follow the marginalist principle in setting their prices and producing goods and services; and the law–like supply-demand mechanism is not found in most real world markets (Lester 1946; Means 1962, 1972; Lee 1981, 1990–91; Jo 2016). These devastating critiques of the neoclassical theory of the firm suggest that the Marshallian firm theory be rejected (Sraffa 1930: 93) and, instead, develop an alternative theory that is internally coherent and historically grounded.

Notwithstanding all the controversies, neoclassical defenders have preserved their approach to the firm with minor modifications, such as imperfect competition, incomplete information, bounded rationality, transaction costs, price rigidity, and the like. The gist of the Marshallian firm has remained dominant in economics textbooks since the late nineteenth century (see Lee 2010 for the survey of 112 economics textbooks from 1899 to 2002). Yet, these 'more realistic' or *ad hoc* assumptions derived from selected reality have never questioned the root problem of the neoclassical theory of the firm.

Arguably, the above claim implies that the current neoclassical theory of the firm refers to the Marshallian theory as well as all the variants incorporating those modified assumptions, but still subscribing to core neoclassical premises—*inter alia*, resource scarcity, optimizing firm behavior, and the supply-demand framework. Those variants, insofar as the theory of the firm is concerned, include, but are not limited to, new institutional-transaction cost theory (Coase 1937; Williamson 1975, 1987), evolutionary theory (Nelson & Winter 1982), principal-agent theory (Jensen & Meckling 1976), and the contractual approach (Alchian & Demsetz 1972). It is quite obvious that the latter two theories are fully in line with neoclassical economics. The first two are often welcomed by some heterodox economists, because they are 'more realistic' than the standard neoclassical theory of the firm. However, it should be noted that these theories remain faithful to the above-mentioned neoclassical premises. For example, Williamson (1987: xii) notes that "[t]ransaction cost economics is akin to orthodoxy in its insistence that economizing is central to economic organization." And Nelson & Winter (1982: 18–19, original emphasis) remark that

[t]he models in this book are of "industries" . . . in a market context characterized by product demand and input supply curves. In modeling these situations we often find it convenient to assume that "temporary equilibrium" is achieved. . . . Together with market supply and demand conditions that are exogenous to the firms in question, these firm decisions determine market prices of inputs and outputs.

The point is that common to these neoclassical theories of the firm is the conviction that the market price mechanism ensures the efficient allocation of scarce resources, given that markets are competitive and individuals are rational. It follows that the firm, either in the form of the 'nexus of contracts' or a 'hierarchical organization,' is secondary to the market mechanism. This position is, as argued and articulated in this chapter, incompatible with a heterodox theory of the business enterprise, which is grounded in the view that the business enterprise is a going concern exercising its agency through strategic decisions in the context of the monetary production economy.

There is no doubt that significant development in heterodox approaches to the business enterprise has been made. But still further development, articulation, and clarification are required due not only to the changes in the way the capitalist economy works, but also to the continuing acceptance of the neoclassical firm by heterodox economists. If heterodox economics means an independent and alternative approach to mainstream-neoclassical economics, as the present author understands, the current state is certainly unsatisfactory. With this concern in mind, this chapter aims to make a positive contribution to the heterodox approach to the business enterprise. By positive it is meant that compatible (but not all inclusive) heterodox accounts of the business enterprise are integrated in order to rejuvenate its radical insights into the evolving capitalist provisioning process, and to offer a more comprehensive analysis of the business enterprise than a single heterodox approach would do. Critiques of the neoclassical theory of the firm will be kept to a minimum in this chapter, since substantive critiques have already been addressed from various heterodox perspectives (see, for example, Shapiro 1976; Dugger 1976; Eichner 1976; Lee 1981; Spread 2016).

This chapter is structured as follows. The first section begins with the monetary theory of production that is germane to the analysis of corporate capitalism whose reproduction is driven mainly by business enterprise's production activities. In this context, the business enterprise is to be conceptualized as a going concern, as opposed to an optimizing firm. The second section explores business enterprise's strategic decisions and actions in historical time. In particular, such key decisions and actions as a quantity decision, financing, investment, cost-accounting, pricing, production, sales, and competition are delineated in detail. The final section concludes the chapter.

The theoretical underpinning of the business enterprise

The monetary theory of production

Corporate capitalism as a system of provision is qualitatively and quantitatively distinct from the previous stage of capitalism. Most neoclassical economists have paid little or no attention to this particular stage of capitalism insofar as their theory is concerned. The neoclassical theory of the firm remains in the era of a 'money economy' (à la Veblen), 'trading economy' (à la Means), or 'cooperative economy' (à la Keynes) in which the production of commodities is undertaken for the sake of making more commodities through, allegedly, the unfettered market system. Heterodox thinkers, however, place the corporate enterprise in the context of a 'credit economy' (Veblen), 'engineering economy' (Means), or 'entrepreneur economy' (Keynes) in which the production of commodities is undertaken for the sake of making more money, and in which corporate business enterprises control not only market exchanges in terms of price and quantity but also the entire society in terms of the rules of conduct and prevailing culture (Veblen 1904: 50–51, 150–151; Means [1933] 1992: 10–15; Keynes 1979: 81–83).

The monetary theory of production developed by Marxian, institutionalist, and Post Keynesian economists concerns how the capitalist system reproduces itself over historical time. The engine of a monetary production economy is a range of productive activities conducted by the business enterprise, while other going concerns, such as the state, households, market governance organizations, and trade unions contribute to the reproduction of the system in a direct or indirect way.

In order for the economy as the monetized social provisioning process to continue, an array of basic goods (the means of production) and surplus goods (the means of consumption) needs to be produced and distributed on a continuous basis. The means of production are used in the production of surplus goods; and surplus goods are distributed among social classes. Thus the enterprise's strategic decision to produce surplus goods (that is, effective demand for surplus goods) induces the production of basic goods, the employment of labor power, and other required means of production, and, consequently, the generation of income streams including wage incomes that are used to purchase surplus goods. Thus the analytical building blocks of the monetary theory of production are the surplus approach (à la classical-Marxian, Sraffian-Post Keynesian, institutionalist) and the theory of effective demand (à la Keynes and Kaleckian-Post Keynesian). In this framework, the reproduction of the system as a whole is tied up with the reproduction of business enterprises through the production of the surplus goods. Of course, the reproduction of the system and of participating agents in historical time (or under fundamental uncertainty) is not guaranteed or predetermined. A necessary, but not sufficient, condition for reproduction is agency qua the capability of making goal-oriented strategic decisions *and* of controlling the business enterprise itself and other going concerns in a larger social context. Therefore, the monetary theory of production should be historically-socially grounded by incorporating strategic decisions at the enterprise level, which is absent in a conventional macro, aggregate, or structural account of the monetary production economy (Dillard 1980; Lee & Jo 2011; Spread 2016).

The business enterprise as a going concern

An appropriate concept of the business enterprise in the context of the monetary production is a going concern. As articulated initially by institutionalists and also received widely in practice (for example, accounting practices), the going concern means that the business enterprise is established and structured with the expectation of continuing its business over long time horizons (Veblen 1904: 137; Commons [1924] 1974: 145; Sterling 1968; Jo & Henry 2015: 28–29). This concept pertains in particular to strategic decisions in socio-historical contexts. By a strategic decision it is meant that the going concern strives to achieve a specific goal depending upon the list of priorities at a point in time. For example, survival would be the highest priority during a recession or crisis, while expansion is preferred to other goals in prosperity. With regard to the latter, increasing investment with the expectation of expanding market sales may result in the bankruptcy of the going concern. Not that such a decision is made poorly, but the economy we find in the real world is full of paradoxes (Kalecki 1937: 96) or of uncertainties (Keynes 1936). If decisions and actions are understood in the historical context (or 'radical uncertainty' as in Post Keynesianism or the 'evolutionary process' as in institutionalism), they cannot be optimal or rational (in the neoclassical sense). Therefore, a going concern does not maximize profits or minimize costs, but strives to earn profits, reduce costs, or remain ongoing (Moss 1981: 199; Lee 1990–91: 259–260).[1] This is clearly an alternative view of the business enterprise, which is incompatible with Alfred Marshall's dictum that "the general theory of the equilibrium of demand and supply is a Fundamental Idea running through the frames of all the various parts of the central problem of Distribution and Exchange" ([1890] 1947, viii).

With a going concern as a real acting organization, the analytical focus is placed on administration or control. To remain ongoing its sequential activities embedded in the historical process of provisioning must be administered. Prices and quantity produced, for instance, are administered by going concerns individually or collectively. In particular, as shall be examined in detail later, administered prices do not clear markets, but contribute to the continuation of a going concern by generating the flow of profits.

With regard to administration, an essential analytical feature of a going concern is its division into a going plant and a going business. A going plant refers to production activities ranging from the procurement of inputs to the production of outputs taking place at the plant level, while a going business involves a wide range of administrative, decision-making processes both at the plant and enterprise levels. That is, within a going concern, production is organized by administration through internal working rules, such as costing, accounting, and pricing practices, while market exchanges are organized by market governance organizations along with external rules of regulation set by the state (Veblen 1904: 157–158; Commons [1924] 1974: 160; Lee 2013: 468).

Whether it is small or big, therefore, a business enterprise is a going concern insofar as it is structured and managed in order to achieve its goals in a systematic manner. The continuation of the business enterprise enables it to be valued based upon its physical assets as well as intangible assets, 'goodwill,' or 'putative earning capacity' (Veblen 1904: 138–139, 155; Commons [1924] 1974: 160; Lee 1990–91: 256–257). The increasing importance of goodwill over physical assets has increasingly become an essential characteristic of modern corporate enterprises (see Serfati 2008). The capitalization and valuation of a going concern based upon goodwill implies that the business enterprise cannot be separated from its surrounding social environment. A going enterprise is thus an 'embedded' agent, and the administration of a going concern itself is not sufficient for it to continue over extended periods of time. What is required, among other things, is the control over other going concerns in the course of production, competition, and exchange.

In a nutshell, the distinguishing mark of the going concern is its continuation and reproduction through production and management. The going concern is thus a suitable concept of the business enterprise, which is an alternative to the neoclassical firm—a rational, optimizing, representative, and equilibrium firm operating in the asocial-ahistorical model world. The following section explores strategic going-concern activities that constitute a heterodox theory of the business enterprise.

Strategic enterprise decisions and actions in the monetary production economy

The schema of enterprise activities

The entry point of a heterodox theory of the business enterprise is the socio-historical context in which the capitalist business enterprise finds its motivation and mode of production. The business enterprise engages in production activities in order for its reproduction. Production process thus requires the transformation of money capital into commodity capital, and the realization of commodity capital into monetary profits. Such essential characteristics are illustrated most sharply by Marx in his schema of the circuit of capital at the level of the economic system as a whole (Marx 1990: 111).

$$M - C \ldots P \ldots C' - M' \tag{Schema 14.1}$$

where M denotes money capital, C commodities (inputs), P production, C' commodities (outputs), and M' money income (profits). Its abstract and structural form, however, does not explain a range of enterprise decisions and actions that are necessary to understand the business enterprise.

For the sake of explaining strategic decisions and actions of the business enterprise implied in Marx's 'structural' schema, let us assume that the manufacturing going enterprise produces a single good or a product line at the plant with multiple plant segments therein. A single production period is the real time required to produce a certain amount of goods. The duration of the production period depends upon production and managerial techniques as well as the intensity or pace of labor employed (Levine 1978: 264–271). An accounting period (normally, one calendar year) includes multiple production periods. With this time-oriented production structure of a going concern, we are able to delineate sequential productive activities as follows.

$$\underbrace{M_{t-1} \underset{[M_{t-1}+B_t]}{\overset{s_1}{\rightarrow}} M_t \underset{[DC+OC]}{\overset{s_2}{\rightarrow}} ETC_b \underset{[p=EATC_b(1+\gamma)]}{\overset{s_3}{\rightarrow}} P \underset{[\mathbf{A}\oplus\mathbf{L}:\mathbf{K}\rightarrow q_b]}{\overset{s_4}{\rightarrow}} TR_b \underset{[pq_b]}{\overset{s_5}{\rightarrow}} TR_a \underset{[TR_a-ETC_b-T-D-B_t']}{\overset{s_6}{\rightarrow}} M_t'}_{\text{Accounting Period}}$$

(Schema 14.2)

where M_{t-1} is retained earnings from the previous accounting period; B_t bank loans; M_t money capital in the current accounting period; DC direct costs; OC overhead costs; ETC_b enterprise total costs at the budgeted output level (q_b); $EATC_b$ enterprise average total costs at q_b; p the administered price; γ a profit mark-up; P production; $\mathbf{A}$ an array of material or intermediate inputs that are combined ($\oplus$) to $\mathbf{L}$, an array of labor inputs; $\mathbf{K}$ an array of fixed investment goods; ':' denotes 'given' for an accounting period; $TR_b = pq_b$ total expected revenue; $TR_a = pq_a$ total actual revenue at the actual quantity demanded q_a; M_t' retained earnings of the current accounting period after paying the corporate income tax (T), dividends (D), and debts ($B_t' = (1+i)B_t$), if $B_t > 0$ and i is a rate of interest on bank loans.

As illustrated above each stage in the circuit of capital is connected through arrows which indicate sequential actions over calendar time—that is, financing and investment (s_1), cost-accounting (s_2), pricing (s_3), production (s_4), sales and competition (s_5), and saving (s_6). These actions incur bank loans (B_t), cost items (DC and OC), price (p), budgeted output (q_b), actual quantity sold (q_a), dividends (D), corporate tax (T), debt payments (B_t'), and retained earnings (M_t'). Marx's circuit of capital thus becomes concretized when it is represented by the schema of enterprise activities consisting of technologically specific structures (that is, ETC_b, P, TR_b, M_t, M_t'), as well as institutionally specific causal mechanisms (s_1 through s_6) along with internal and external working rules set by enterprise administrators and market regulators. While both schemata demonstrate that a going economy (Schema 14.1) or a going enterprise (Schema 14.2) is centered on the production of commodities in a continuous and sequential manner, Schema 14.2 displays more clearly that production requires a range of supporting administrative activities and capitalist agency represented by causal mechanisms. Schema 14.2 thus indicates that going-concern activities are structured and enduring, as well as open-ended due to agency represented by and embedded in causal mechanisms. For example, a product price is determined and administered by the business enterprise following its costing and pricing rules so that the enterprise remains ongoing, rather than the determination of the product price resting on market supply and demand schedules in the neoclassical exchange economy. Let me elaborate on essential enterprise decisions.

Quantity decision

A going enterprise in the monetary production economy engages in production activities with the expectation of expanding capital ($TR_b - ETC_b > 0$) or, at least, of surviving and continuing its business ($TR_b = ETC_b$). A quantity decision should be made *before* the enterprise goes through the production process. It is obvious that the expected is seldom equal to the actual—that is, the total actual revenue (TR_a) is determined by actual market sales that fluctuate along the business cycles. Due to radical uncertainty in the actual sales and revenue the going enterprise has to set the budgeted output level (q_b) that becomes the reference point in the course of financing/ investment (s_1), costing (s_2), pricing (s_3), and production (s_4). Specifically, q_b corresponding to expected sales is determined, given the array of productive capacity embodying currently available production techniques (or the number of plants and plant segments employing $\mathbf{K}$ in s_4). Thus the quantity decision is central to the entire schema of enterprise activities to the extent that it is the basis of other decisions. That q_b is normally less than full productive capacity implies that the adjustment of quantity produced to market sales is done by opening up or closing down plant segments already installed. While the quantity adjustment occurs over production periods, a change in productive capacity through investment takes more than one accounting period (Lee 1998: 202–203, 2013: 470). It should also be noticed from the above schema that the quantity decision is separated from a price decision (the latter will be discussed below).

Financing and investment

Investment demand for $\mathbf{K}$ across accounting periods is made possible by using money capital financed internally and externally. There is a body of empirical evidence supporting the importance of internal finance over external finance. Essentially, retained earnings are directly bound up with the administered stability of a going enterprise under inherently unstable capitalism (Andrews 1949: 229–250; Eichner 1976: 189–223; Harcourt & Kenyon 1976; Moss 1981: 32–37; Jo 2015). Empirical studies show that internal finance is a safer and cheaper means of investment, while external finance is mainly used to invest in financial assets (Gezici 2007; Kliman & Williams 2015). These findings are also consistent with macro-level data that non-financial corporations in advanced economies rely chiefly on retained earnings in financing fixed investment (see, for example, Corbett & Jenkinson 1997). The upshot is that the main source of fixed investment is the strategically generated internal means of finance, which enables a going concern to continue and/or expand its business over time. Moreover, investment decisions are not much affected by the changes in the rates of interest; instead, what the management of a going enterprise concerns most is earnings from investments.[2] This position is at odds with widely received theoretical accounts. Neoclassical economists posit that the 'efficient' financial market determines the optimal amount of loanable funds. Keynes and most Post Keynesian macroeconomists lay emphasis on external financing on the ground that the level of investment is determined by the supply and demand prices of capital goods (see, for example, Keynes 1936: 248; Minsky 1986: 171–198). Common to both neoclassical and Post Keynesian accounts is the replacement of the going concern's capability of making strategic decisions with the Marshallian supply-demand framework in which resource scarcity and diminishing marginal returns are assumed (Jo 2015). Deliberate investment decisions of the going enterprise suggest that the Marshallian supply-demand framework and the Marshallian firm therein be dropped (Jo 2016).

Cost-accounting and pricing

With available money capital (M_i) advanced, an array of inputs required to produce the predetermined budgeted level of output (q_b) is to be purchased. In order to make purchasing decisions in a systematic and continuous fashion, a range of costs items are identified and reckoned following cost-accounting procedures qua rules adopted by the going concern. Since a going concern continues, all the earnings and expenses have to be accurately calculated at the end of each accounting period. Corresponding to the organizational structure of a going concern (that is, a going plant and a going business), the division of enterprise total costs (ETC) into direct costs

(DC) and overhead costs (OC) is necessary. OC are further divided into shop expenses (SE) and enterprise expenses (EE), where SE refer to the costs of supervising the production, managing, and running the enterprise (for example, salaries of foremen, supporting staff, and supervisors, costs of materials needed to maintain those staffs and supervisors, depreciation costs), and EE refer to the costs of running multiple plant segments and the costs of sales and advertisement, and the like. Typically, SE and EE are allocated equally over multiple production periods. The structure of enterprise total costs at q_b is represented by the following equation (Lee & Jo 2010).

$$ETC_b = DC_b + SE + EE \qquad\qquad (s_2)$$

where DC_b consist of labor input costs and material input costs. Consequently, enterprise average total costs (or unit costs) are:

$$EATC_b = \frac{ETC_b}{q_b} = ADC_b + ASE + AEE \qquad\qquad (s_2')$$

Once all the cost items identified and calculated, a going concern is able to set the product price following a pricing procedure. It is widely observed that real world business enterprises utilize various pricing procedures—that is, the mark-up-oriented and costing-oriented pricing procedures, and their variants depending upon the way budgeted costs or mark-ups are determined by a going concern (Andrews 1949: 157–161; Kalecki 1954: 11–27; Eichner 1976: 55–107; Lee 1998; Gu & Lee 2012; Lavoie 2014: 156–175). The basic idea of pricing is represented by the following equation.

$$p = EATC_b(1 + \gamma) \qquad\qquad (s_3)$$

where a profit mark-up (γ) set by the pricing administrator in order to ensure a profit margin earned when a unit of output is sold. This cost-plus pricing principle takes slightly different forms depending upon the way a mark-up is determined or costs are accounted. Variants of pricing procedures can be summarized into the following:

Direct cost pricing: $p = ADC_b(1 + \theta)$

Total cost pricing: $p = EATC_b(1 + \gamma)$ or $ADC_b(1 + \beta)(1 + \rho)(1 + \gamma)$

Target rate of return pricing: $p = EATC_b\left(1 + \dfrac{\lambda\Phi}{q_b \times EATC_b}\right)$

where θ is a mark-up for overhead costs and profits; β and ρ are, respectively, mark-ups for SE and EE; and λ is a target rate of return on the value of enterprise's capital assets (Φ). The first two pricing procedures are costing-oriented in the sense that given a customarily determined mark-up, a particular costing procedure is selected. The last is mark-up-oriented in the sense that a particular mark-up is determined given a costing procedure. The difference between the two groups lies in customary working rules and a particular objective to be achieved by a going concern. For example, the target rate of return pricing becomes the primary procedure to set the price if the business enterprise aims to generate retained earnings that are required to implement a planned investment project.

All the empirically grounded pricing procedures demonstrate that product prices are strategically determined and administered before outputs are produced and traded in the market, that prices vary as different cost-accounting systems, pricing procedures, and/or mark-ups are chosen by the price administrator, that prices are stable for multiple production periods irrespective of changes in actual costs and market demand, and that prices do not clear markets but are designed to reproduce business enterprises (Means [1933] 1992; Andrews 1949; Eichner 1976; Lee 1998). It comes as no surprise that a substantial body of empirical evidence lends support to the above argument that prices are administered and made to be stable for the sake of reproducing the business enterprise over historical time (see, for example, Fabiani *et al.* 2007).

Production process

One significant implication of the schema of enterprise activities running from s_2 to s_3 is that price decisions are separated from quantity decisions. There is thus no structural relationship between price and quantity, no law of demand and supply, and no profit-maximizing firm. Administered prices rely mainly upon production-managerial techniques, administrative conventions or rules, and organizational structures of a going concern. The amount of quantity produced is set at the budgeted level and remains fixed for multiple production periods or for the entire accounting period (see Melmies 2010). Then the question comes down to how production is undertaken by the business enterprise.

Like other activities, production is conceptualized as a sequential process in calendar time—that is, an accounting period consisting of f production periods. What is also required is the specification of the unit of production. Insofar as a manufacturing enterprise is concerned, the unit of production is the going plant in which multiple plant segments (PS) are installed along with an array of fixed investment goods ($\mathbf{K}$), of employed skilled labor ($\mathbf{L}$), and of material inputs ($\mathbf{A}$). At the plant segment level for a single production period, the schema of production corresponding to the cost structure of the going enterprise can be delineated like below:

$$\text{PS} : \mathbf{a}_d \oplus \frac{1}{f}\mathbf{a}_s \oplus \frac{1}{f}\mathbf{a}_e \oplus \mathbf{l}_d \oplus \frac{1}{f}\mathbf{l}_s \oplus \frac{1}{f}\mathbf{l}_e : \mathbf{k}_d, \mathbf{k}_s, \mathbf{k}_e \rightarrow q \tag{s_4'}$$

where $\mathbf{a}_d = \mathbf{A}_d/q$ is a vector of direct intermediate input production coefficients for a production period, and its i-th element a_{di} is the amount of i-th direct intermediate input ($\mathbf{A}_d$) used to produce one unit of output q per production period; $\mathbf{a}_s = \mathbf{A}_s/q$ and $\mathbf{a}_e = \mathbf{A}_e/q$ vectors of shop and enterprise intermediate input production coefficients that are equally divided into f production periods; $\mathbf{l}_d = \mathbf{L}_d/q$ a vector of direct labor input production coefficients; $\mathbf{l}_s = \mathbf{L}_s/q$ and $\mathbf{l}_e = \mathbf{L}_e/q$, vectors of shop and enterprise labor input production coefficients that are equally divided into f production periods; $\mathbf{k}_d$, $\mathbf{k}_s$, and $\mathbf{k}_e$ vectors of fixed investment goods associated with production, shop, and enterprise activities. To simplify the production at the plant segment level:

$$\text{PS} : \mathbf{a} \oplus \mathbf{l} : \mathbf{k} \rightarrow q \tag{s_4''}$$

where $\mathbf{a}, \mathbf{l}$, and $\mathbf{k}$ include all types of differentiated inputs and fixed investment goods at the plant segment level. Assuming that the total number of plant segments is m, the plant's maximum level of output produced per production period is q_{max}. Thus production at the plant level can be formulated like below:

$$\text{Plant: } \sum_{i=1}^{m}\mathbf{a}_i \oplus \mathbf{l}_i : \mathbf{k}_i \rightarrow \sum_{i=1}^{m}q_i = q_{max} \tag{s_4^*}$$

Or to generalize the production schema at the enterprise level for an accounting period with the budgeted output (q_b) strategically chosen by the management $(q \leq q_b < f \times q_{max})$, we get the schema of production as part of the schema of enterprise activities.

$$\mathbf{A} \oplus \mathbf{L}: \mathbf{K} \rightarrow q_b \qquad (s_4)$$

This rather complicated (but not as complex as reality) production schema delineates that production is a sequential process taking place at the plant level, given technical conditions in terms of the use of differentiated inputs and fixed investment goods, organizational structures, and working rules adopted by the going enterprise. All types of differentiated inputs are socially created (in particular, the joint stock of knowledge and skills), technically connected to each other, and jointly utilized in the process of production. Each plant segment, plant, and going enterprise is distinctive in terms of production technique, that is the way employed inputs are transformed into outputs. This particular property implies that the linear aggregation of inputs and outputs into a single homogeneous variable should be avoided. Furthermore, the strategically chosen budgeted output level, q_b, is less than full production capacity (that is, $f \times q_{max} - q_b > 0$). That is, the going enterprise holds reserved capacity in the form of unused plant segments. Indeed, q_b is subject to change across production periods in response to the observed or expected changes in market sales. To increase (or decrease) quantity produced, unused plant segments are opened up (or closed down). The quantity adjustment occurs while the administered price remains unchanged. This means that the enterprise activities do not generate the upward sloping continuous supply curve, and that profit maximization or cost minimization is not possible. Without optimizing behavior, such concepts as relatively scarce resources, marginal products, and production functions with variable input proportions have no meaning. In a nutshell, the account of production from the heterodox perspective is incompatible with the neoclassical production theory (Means [1933] 1992; 1962; Andrews 1949; Eichner 1976; Robinson 1980; Lee 1998, 2013).

Sales, competition, and reproduction

Foregoing discussions on the enterprise decision-making processes with regard to investment, finance, cost, price, and production indicate that strategic decisions are necessary, but not sufficient, for the reproduction of the going enterprise. What is also required for the stability and reproduction of the going enterprise is the control of the market. A range of the means of control is put into practice to ensure that the market for a product exists and generates profits on a continuous basis. The market is in this regard created and controlled by the business enterprise by way of both creating a good or service and administering price, quantity, sales, and competition at the market level, rather than the business enterprise takes the market structure and mechanism as given (Galbraith 1967; Fligstein 1990).

The heterodox theory of the business enterprise delineated here thus extends to market exchanges and competition. In Schema 14.2 illustrated above s_5 is a process in which the actual revenue (pq_a) is realized at the predetermined administered price. The actual revenue is thus partly controlled through enterprise price administration. And it is also partly controlled, as noted earlier, through sales promotion and, more importantly, establishing goodwill that involves sellers and buyers. But the impact of goodwill on the actual revenue depends upon, among others, price differentials. Obviously, without goodwill or social networks in general, it is not likely that enterprises in the market set the same price because each enterprise goes through a unique decision-making process with differentiated production and managerial techniques that are embodied in costing, pricing, and production processes. The reality is that a stable 'common' price within a narrow range is found in most product markets. To put it another way, the price of a product is made to be stable not only because individual enterprises set the price following a particular pricing procedure, but also because going enterprises in the market view the stable market price as mutually beneficial to the extent that ruinous price wars are avoided and the variations in cash flows are reduced. The latter necessitates such market governance organizations as trade associations, cartels, and price leadership. In other words, collective market control is not contradictory to market competition. Rather control and competition are two sides of enterprise activities that lend support to the survival and reproduction over time (Veblen 1923; Means [1933] 1992; Pribram 1935; Meyer 1986). This approach to competition capturing the importance of deliberate 'association' between business enterprises breaks with the conventional view that economic activities are organized only by the principles of 'separation' in the market and 'command' within the enterprise (Lopes & Caldas 2015), or that the degree of market concentration determines market prices through profit mark-ups (Lee 2012).

At the final stage of the schema of enterprise activities for an accounting period is the disbursement of gross profits to the government (T), to shareholders (D), to lenders (B_t'), and to the enterprise itself (M_t'). How each amount or ratio out of gross profits is determined is also important for the continuation and expansion of the going enterprise. Debt payments are directly linked to the amount of funds externally financed and the rate of interest. As discussed earlier, external financing is supplementary to (not a substitute for) internal financing. Corporate income tax rates are determined by the government. What remains is dividend payouts and retained earnings that *prima facie* bear an inverse relationship between them.

Conventionally, it has been widely received that either the division between retained earnings and dividend payments is unimportant with regard to the market value of the corporation; or an optimal capital structure is achieved since shareholders and management optimize their respective behavior through efficient markets (Modigliani & Miller 1958). Empirical evidence runs counter to this position. As pointed out earlier, retained earnings have been dominant as a means of financing investment as they are critical to the survival of the enterprise under fundamental uncertainty. Moreover, the supply-demand framework can hardly be applied to real world enterprise investment (Andrews 1949; Eichner 1976; Jo 2015). As for dividend payments, data indicates that corporate managers tend to stabilize the dividend payout ratio in response to a range of variability in terms of shareholders' liquidity preference and tax position, stock prices, and the like. Thus a particular dividend policy is selected strategically by the corporation (Wood 1975: 40–52). A notable change observed in recent decades is that the dividend payout ratio is increasing along with the increase in stock buybacks. Consequently, the financialization thesis endorsed by many heterodox economists suggests that the portion of retained earnings used for fixed investment declines since dividends and stock buybacks are internally financed (Orhangazi 2008; Dallery 2009; Fung 2010; Lazonick 2013). This is a dilemma of the going enterprise—that is, neoliberal financialization has been driven by a mutual interest of both financial and non-financial business enterprises in the pursuit of ever-increasing monetary gains by replacing goods-making activities with money-making activities. As a result the very foundation of capitalism and of the going concern has become weakened as evidenced by increasing instability of financialized economies (Crotty 2003; Jo & Henry 2015).

Conclusion

This chapter has shown that it is possible to develop a heterodox theory of the business enterprise that is an alternative to and independent of the neoclassical firm theory. It is rendered possible by, firstly, understanding the business enterprise in the context of the monetary production economy articulated by Marxian, Post Keynesian, and institutional economics; secondly, conceptualizing the business enterprise as a going concern consisting of a going plant and a going business following the institutionalist account; and thirdly, explaining key decision-making processes taking place in historical time. Consequently, it is demonstrated that the going concern exercises its goal-oriented agency in the course of making strategic decisions, given (but not fixed) technical conditions, organizational structures, and working rules in order to continue its business over historical time. The schema of enterprise activities examined in this chapter also indicates that the going enterprise is not confined by the presumed rule of the market, but deliberately strives to control the market by means of administering price and quantity, creating goods and services, and/or making mutually rewarding social relationships (that is, goodwill) between going enterprises. Therefore, the heterodox theory of the business enterprise proposed in this chapter offers quite different, radical implications as to how the business enterprise operates in corporate capitalism.

An attempt to build such an integrative heterodox theory could be either promising or insufficient. Promising in that, once done successfully, it would offer more comprehensive insights into the business enterprise as we find in the real world than a single heterodox approach would do. This is what I aimed for in writing this chapter. At the same time, it should be admitted that a judgment as to whether this has been done successfully or not lies in the eyes of the shrewd reader. One might rightly argue that the present attempt is insufficient to the extent that it neglects some important aspects specific to a particular strand in heterodox economics— for example, theories of value and distribution that are integral parts of classical-Marxian, Post Keynesian, and institutional analyses of the monetary production economy. Perhaps a better and more comprehensive work could be done in the future, incorporating those theoretical issues as well as contributions made by other heterodox approaches, such as social, feminist, and ecological economics, that are not examined in this chapter.

Notes

1 Optimization is a theoretical construct that bears no resemblance to real world actions. It should be made clear that optimization does not leave room for strategic decisions since actors should follow the market rule (that is, marginal revenue = marginal cost) set by the structure of the market. Optimization is, therefore, incompatible with a going concern that pursues multiple goals by undertaking strategic decisions in historical time. If we are concerned with the actual historical process, such logically connected neoclassical concepts as scarcity, optimization, equilibrium, and market clearing should be discarded. However, many heterodox economists of past and present, including J.M. Keynes, Joan Robinson, and Michał Kalecki (in their early works), rely on profit maximization in their account of the enterprise behavior (Chilosi 1989; Marcuzzo & Sanfilippo 2007; Lavoie 2014: 124). If we are concerned with building an alternative to the Marshallian firm, a better starting point should be, among others, T.B. Veblen, G.C. Means, D.H. MacGregor, and P.W.S. Andrews (Lee 1981).

2 It should not be inferred here that interest rates have no impact on investment-financing decisions. The long-term interest rate is, on the one hand, taken into account in making investment decisions on **K**. Yet, it is rather stable over time. Thus it could be assumed fixed and, hence, has little to do with the variability in investment. On the other hand, the short-term interest rate affects investment for temporary or urgent purposes and short-term finance is readily available as long as the stability of the business is secured. All this implies that interest rates are not the main factor of investment; nor are they the "regulator of the capitalism economy" (Andrews 1949: 235–240; see also, Kalecki 1990: 366).

References

Alchian, A.A. & Demsetz, H. 1972. 'Production, information costs, and economic organization.' *American Economic Review*, 62 (5): 777–795.

Andrews, P.W.S. 1949. *Manufacturing Business*. London: Macmillan.

Chilosi, A. 1989. 'Kalecki's quest for the microeconomic foundations of his macroeconomic theory,' in: M. Sebastiani (ed.), *Kalecki's Relevance Today*. London: Macmillan, 101–120.

Coase, R.H. 1937. 'The nature of the firm.' *Economica*, 4 (16): 386–405.

Commons, J.R. [1924] 1974. *Legal Foundations of Capitalism*. New York: Augustus M. Kelley.

Corbett, J. & Jenkinson, T. 1997. 'How is investment financed? A study of Germany, Japan, the United Kingdom and the United States.' *The Manchester School of Economic and Social Studies*, 65 (Supplement 1): 69–93.

Crotty, J.R. 2003. 'The neoliberal paradox: the impact of destructive product market competition and impatient finance on nonfinancial corporations in the neoliberal era.' *Review of Radical Political Economics*, 35 (3): 271–279.

Dallery, T. 2009. 'Post-Keynesian theories of the firm under financialization.' *Review of Radical Political Economics*, 41 (4): 492–515.

Dillard, D. 1980. 'A monetary theory of production: Keynes and Institutionalists.' *Journal of Economic Issues*, 14 (2): 255–273.

Dugger, W.M. 1976. 'Ideological and scientific functions of the neoclassical theory of the firm.' *Journal of Economic Issues*, 10 (2): 313–324.

Eichner, A.S. 1976. *The Megacorp and Oligopoly: Micro Foundations of Macro Dynamics*. Cambridge: Cambridge University Press.

Fabiani, S., Gattulli, A., & Sabbatini, R. 2007. 'The pricing behavior of Italian firms: new survey evidence on price stickiness,' in: S. Fabiani, C. Loupias, F. Martins, & R. Sabbatini (eds.), *Pricing Decisions in the Euro Area: How Firms Set Prices and Why*. Oxford: Oxford University Press, 110–123.

Fligstein, N. 1990. *The Transformation of Corporate Control*. Cambridge, MA: Harvard University Press.

Fung, M. 2010. 'The megacorp in a global economy,' in: M. Lavoie, L.-P. Rochon, & M. Seccareccia (eds.), *Money and Macrodynamics: Alfred Eichner and Post-Keynesian Economics*. Armonk, NY: M.E. Sharpe, 96–115.

Galbraith, J.K. 1967. *The New Industrial State*. Boston: Houghton Mifflin.

Gezici, A. 2007. Investment under financial liberalization: channels of liquidity and uncertainty. PhD dissertation. University of Massachusetts, Amherst, USA.

Gu, G.C. & Lee, F.S. 2012. 'Pricing and prices,' in: J.E. King (ed.), *Elgar Companion to Post Keynesian Economics*, 2nd edn. Cheltenham, UK: Edward Elgar, 456–462.

Harcourt, G.C. 1972. *Some Cambridge Controversies in the Theory of Capital*. Cambridge: Cambridge University Press.

Harcourt, G.C. & Kenyon, P. 1976. 'Pricing and the investment decision.' *Kyklos*, 29 (3): 449–477.

Jensen, M.C. & Meckling, W.H. 1976. 'Theory of the firm: managerial behavior, agency costs, and capital structure.' *Journal of Financial Economics*, 3 (4): 305–360.

Jo, T.-H. 2015. 'Financing investment under fundamental uncertainty and instability: a heterodox microeconomic view.' *Bulletin of Political Economy*, 9 (1): 33–54.

Jo, T.-H. 2016. 'What if there are no conventional price mechanisms?' *Journal of Economic Issues*, 50 (2): 327–344.

Jo, T.-H. & Henry, J.F. 2015. 'The business enterprise in the age of money manager capitalism.' *Journal of Economic Issues*, 49 (1): 23–46.

Kalecki, M. 1937. 'A theory of the business cycle.' *Review of Economic Studies*, 4 (2): 77–97.

Kalecki, M. 1954. *Theory of Economic Dynamics*. London: George Allen and Unwin.

Kalecki, M. 1990. 'Three ways to full-employment,' in: J. Osiatyński (ed.), *Collected Works of Michał Kalecki, Vol. I*. Oxford: Oxford University Press, 357–376.

Keynes, J.M. 1936. *The General Theory of Employment, Interest and Money*. London: Macmillan.

Keynes, J.M. 1979. *The Collected Writings of John Maynard Keynes, Vol. XXIX*. London: Macmillan.

Kliman, A. & Williams, S.D. 2015. 'Why "financialization" hasn't depressed US productive investment.' *Cambridge Journal of Economics*, 39 (1): 67–92.

Lavoie, M. 2014. *Post-Keynesian Economics: New Foundations*. Cheltenham, UK: Edward Elgar.

Lazonick, W. 2013. 'Financialization of the U.S. corporation: what has been lost, and how it can be regained.' *Seattle University Law Review*, 36 (2): 857–910.

Lee, F.S. 1981. 'The Oxford challenge to Marshallian supply and demand: the history of the Oxford Economists' Research Group.' *Oxford Economic Papers*, 33 (3): 339–351.

Lee, F.S. 1990–91. 'Marginalist controversy and Post Keynesian price theory.' *Journal of Post Keynesian Economics*, 13 (2): 252–263.

Lee, F.S. 1998. *Post Keynesian Price Theory*. Cambridge: Cambridge University Press.

Lee, F.S. 2010. 'A heterodox teaching of neoclassical microeconomic theory.' *International Journal of Pluralism and Economics Education*, 1 (3): 203–235.

Lee, F.S. 2012. 'Competition, going enterprise, and economic activity,' in: J.K. Moudud, C. Bina, & P.L. Mason (eds.), *Alternative Theories of Competition: Challenges to the Orthodoxy*. London: Routledge, 160–173.

Lee, F.S. 2013. 'Post-Keynesian price theory: from pricing to market governance to the economy as a whole,' *in*: G.C. Harcourt & P. Kriesler (eds.), *The Oxford Handbook of Post-Keynesian Economics, Vol. I*. Oxford: Oxford University Press, 467–484.

Lee, F.S. & Jo, T.-H. 2010. Heterodox production and cost theory of the business enterprise. MPRA Working Paper 27635. Available from http://mpra.ub.uni-muenchen.de/27635 [Accessed August 16, 2015]

Lee, F.S. & Jo, T.-H. 2011. 'Social surplus approach and heterodox economics.' *Journal of Economic Issues*, 45 (4): 857–875.

Lester, R.A. 1946. 'Shortcomings of marginal analysis for wage-employment problems.' *American Economic Review*, 36 (1): 63–82.

Levine, D.P. 1978. *Economic Theory, Volume I: The Elementary Relations of Economic Life*. London: Routledge & Kegan Paul.

Lopes, H. & Caldas, J.C. 2015. 'The cement of the firm: command, separation or association?' *in*: J.B. Davis & W. Dolfsma (eds.), *The Elgar Companion to Social Economics*, 2nd edn. Cheltenham, UK: Edward Elgar, 349–363.

Marcuzzo, M.C. & Sanfilippo, E. 2007. 'Profit maximization in the Cambridge tradition of economics,' *in*: M. Forstater, G. Mongiovi, & S. Pressman (eds.), *Post-Keynesian Macroeconomics: Essays in Honour of Ingrid Rima*. London: Routledge, 77–86.

Marshall, A. [1890] 1947. *Principles of Economics*, 8th edn. London: Macmillan.

Marx, K. 1990. *Capital, Vol. II*. New York: Penguin Books.

Means, G.C. [1933] 1992. 'Theoretical chapters from proposed dissertation,' *in*: F.S. Lee & W.J. Samuels (eds.), *The Heterodox Economics of Gardiner C. Means: A Collection*. Armonk, NY: M.E. Sharpe, 6–31.

Means, G.C. 1962. *The Corporate Revolution in America: Economic Reality vs. Economic Theory*. New York: Crowell-Collier Press.

Means, G.C. 1972. 'The administered-price thesis reconfirmed.' *American Economic Review*, 62 (3): 292–306.

Melmies, J. 2010. 'New-Keynesians versus post-Keynesians on the theory of prices.' *Journal of Post Keynesian Economics*, 32 (3): 445–466.

Meyer, P.B. 1986. 'The corporate person and social control: responding to deregulation.' *Review of Radical Political Economics*, 18 (3): 65–84.

Minsky, H.P. 1986. *Stabilizing an Unstable Economy*. New Haven, CT: Yale University Press.

Modigliani, F. & Miller, M.H. 1958. 'The cost of capital, corporate finance and the theory of investment.' *American Economic Review*, 48 (3): 161–197.

Moss, S. 1981. *An Economic Theory of Business Strategy: An Essay in Dynamics Without Equilibrium*. New York: John Wiley and Sons.

Nelson, R.R. & Winter, S.G. 1982. *An Evolutionary Theory of Economic Change*. Cambridge, MA: Harvard University Press.

Orhangazi, Ö. 2008. *Financialization and the US Economy*. Cheltenham, UK: Edward Elgar.

Pribram, K. 1935. 'Controlled competition and the organization of American industry.' *Quarterly Journal of Economics*, 49 (3): 371–393.

Robertson, D.H., Sraffa, P., & Shove, F.G. 1930. 'Increasing returns and the representative firm: a symposium.' *The Economic Journal*, 40 (157): 79–116.

Robinson, J. 1980. 'The production function and the theory of capital,' *in*: *Collected Economic Papers, Vol. II*. Cambridge, MA: MIT Press, 114–131.

Serfati, C. 2008. 'Financial dimensions of transnational corporations, global value chain and technical innovation.' *Journal of Innovation Economics*, 2: 35–61.

Shapiro, N. 1976. 'The neoclassical theory of the firm.' *Review of Radical Political Economics*, 8 (4): 17–29.

Spread, P. 2016. 'Companies and markets: economic theories of the firm and a concept of companies as bargaining agencies.' *Cambridge Journal of Economics*, 40 (3): 727–753.

Sraffa, P. 1926. 'The laws of returns under competitive conditions.' *The Economic Journal*, 36 (144): 535–550.

Sraffa, P. 1930. 'A criticism and rejoinder.' *The Economic Journal*, 40 (157): 89–93.

Sraffa, P. 1960. *Production of Commodities by Means of Commodities*. Cambridge: Cambridge University Press.

Sterling, R.R. 1968. 'The going concern: an examination.' *Accounting Review*, 43 (3): 481–502.

Veblen, T.B. 1904. *The Theory of Business Enterprise*. New York: Charles Scribner's Sons.

Veblen, T.B. 1923. *Absentee Ownership and Business Enterprise in Recent Times: The Case of America*. New York: Sentry Press.

Williamson, O.E. 1975. *Markets and Hierarchies: Analysis and Antitrust Implications*. New York: Free Press.

Williamson, O.E. 1987. *The Economic Institutions of Capitalism*. New York: Free Press.

Wood, A. 1975. *A Theory of Profits*. Cambridge: Cambridge University Press.

15

Heterodox theories of business competition and market governance

Tuna Baskoy

Introduction

Business competition, which refers to a particular type of relationship between business enterprises, is at the heart of the capitalist market economy. At first glance, it may seem a simple and straightforward concept. It is, however, a complex phenomenon with systemic reverberations. As Malcolm Sawyer (1989: 141) notes, various theoretical approaches to competition have a significant impact on the analysis of market dynamics and outcomes, and hence, the desirability of capitalism as an economic system. The pivotal factor for understanding the origins of differences between the major theoretical approaches is the notion of market power, which can be defined as the ability of business enterprises to control their environment to some extent in their own interests (Monvoisin & Rochon 2006: 21–22).

Mainstream theories of perfect competition and contestable markets prefer private market governance in the absence of market power. The theory of perfect competition offers a static understanding of competition by emphasizing the stylized structural properties of the market such as identical products, perfect knowledge, many producers and sellers, and free entry and exit (Nicholson 1997: 218). Likewise, the theory of contestable markets acknowledges market power by relaxing the assumption of the requisite number of business enterprises for competition to be effective in allocating resources. Yet, as long as market entry and exit are absolutely free and costless, the market power of oligopolies and monopolies is ephemeral and temporary (Baumol 1982: 3). In any case, market power that is portrayed as a property belonging to an individual business enterprise either does not exist in the theory of perfect competition at all or is temporary in the theory of contestable markets at best. Market governance is ensured through the independent practices of individual business enterprises alone (Williamson 2005: 1–18).

The following question is still unanswered: How can one explain the evolution of markets over time, which bears on the persistence of market power and market governance? It is argued in this chapter that while various heterodox economic theories—in particular, Austrian, Marxian, and Post Keynesian—conceptualize competition as a dynamic and historical process where power is influential in shaping market outcomes, the Post Keynesian approach captures the issue of governance in a more effective and realistic manner than the Austrian and Marxian views.

Tuna Baskoy

The strength of the Post Keynesian approach is derived from its emphasis on the positive role of the state in taming market power to stabilize otherwise unstable capitalist markets as part of pro-social policy. The following sections are structured as follows. The second section examines the key concepts as market and market governance. The third section assesses the Austrian approach to competition and market governance, which is followed by Marxian theory in the fourth section. The fifth section evaluates the Post Keynesian approach. The final section discusses and recapitulates the key findings.

Definitions: market and governance

Without a clear definition of the market, a standard macroeconomics textbook goes directly to an analysis of goods or financial markets (see, for example, Blanchard & Melino 1999). This is possibly because the primary focus of orthodox (mainstream) microeconomics is the market. However this does not mean that there is a clear and universal definition of the market. Mainstream economists take location or place as a reference point to delineate markets (Lyons 2004: 21; Arnold 2008: 54). For heterodox economists, the market means more than a place. "In its more general and abstract usage, *market* refers to a set of sellers and buyers whose activities affect the price at which a *particular commodity* is sold" (Baumol *et al.* 2009: 209, original italics). Players and the outcomes of their actions in terms of the price for a particular commodity are the two crucial factors in defining this concept. Similarly, Thorstein Veblen (1923: 392) emphasizes "the volume of effective demand" and commodity prices thereby underlining the activities of buyers and sellers and their impact on price. Lee (2010: 31), on the other hand, takes all the transactions of a specific product as the basis for defining the market. Acknowledging these viewpoints, this chapter adopts Fernandez-Huerga's (2013: 366–371) market definition which can be articulated as a special type of social structure interwoven by and with a series of informal and formal institutions that structure and facilitate the exchange of things for money to satisfy demand. Formal and informal institutions draw the boundaries where exchange takes place and at the same time these institutions shape the role played by business enterprises, consumers, the state, and non-state actors in market governance.

In a similar vein, governance derives ultimately from the Greek verb *kubernáo*, meaning to *steer* (Peters 2012: 7). 'Steering' suggests that governance is as much about manner or way as *it is about* process. Yet, mainstream economists offer a structuralist perception of governance as "the institutional framework in which contracts are initiated, negotiated, monitored, adapted, enforced, and terminated" (Palay 1984: 265). In reality, the institutional framework is not considered and the chief concern is the role of private contracts and other similar arrangements in facilitating exchange between business enterprises (Van Hoi *et al.* 2009: 381).

From the Post Keynesian perspective, Baskoy (2012: 387) defines governance as "the process of crafting and implementing laws and regulations to reduce instability and decrease uncertainty in the market." Jo (2013: 456) distinguishes between market governance and market regulation, arguing that whereas the business enterprise manages market governance, the state is responsible for regulating the market. Lee (2013a: 476), however, includes the state, business enterprises, and non-state organizations in his view of market governance. Common to these definitions is the notion that market governance is a process as well as a way of steering markets in defining the relations of competition, cooperation, and market-specific definitions (Fligstein 1996: 658). This notion may appear in formal laws and regulations as well as in informal rules, norms, and practices. Just as formal and informal structures, rules and institutions for coordinating collective activity are part and parcel of governance, so too are public, private, and non-state organizations, and all decisions related to the market (Boscheck 2008: 8). With these concepts of market and governance in mind, let us turn to different heterodox approaches to see how each analyzes business competition and market governance.

The Austrian view

Unlike the neoclassical conception of competition, which emphasizes the number of players and price as two crucial factors, scholars of the Austrian economics tradition portray business competition "as a dynamic and faltering human process of rivalry and bargaining" (Endres 1997: 145). It is a dynamic process of discovery in time, not as a state of static timeless equilibrium (O'Driscoll & Rizzo 2015: 139). For Carl Menger, competition is bound with the behavior of business enterprises (Mantzavinos 1999: 685–686). By taking a subjectivist and individualist starting point, Friedrich Hayek (1978: 179) describes competition as much a conflict over price as over non-price elements. Both producers and buyers learn the best available production techniques, products, prices, etc. through the process of competition (Hayek 1948: 95–96).

In contrast to Menger and Hayek, Joseph Schumpeter is more objectivist and combines individualism with holism (Arena 2015: 77–90; Janberg 2015: 91–105). At the same time, Schumpeter maintains that competition is best understood as a process and variables such as a new type of business organization, a new type of commodity, new production techniques and technologies, and a new source of supply are the major sources of power in the process of competition. Business enterprises compete with one another not only for profit margins but for challenging the very foundations and lives of their competitors (Schumpeter 1950: 84). Expressed differently, competition is a "perennial gale of creative destruction" (Littlechild 1978: 33). New commodities, new technologies, and new types of organization, among others, are the strengths of business enterprises in the process of competition. In short, competition is a historical process with evolutionary dynamics (Metcalfe 2013: 124).

In the Austrian tradition, market power stems from new technology, new products, new organization, new sources of raw materials, new markets, the size of business enterprises, and their collective action in the forms of cartels, and the like. In particular, size is a major strength in that bigness induces business enterprises to discover and exploit opportunities to reduce costs and introduce new products with adequate resources (Littlechild 1978: 37). The Austrian school jettisons the idea of a positive relationship between the number of competitors and the intensity of competition—that is, healthy competition does not necessarily require many players. Besides, oligopolies and cartels are seen as "an important means of securing profit opportunities by facilitating planning and reducing the risks of business enterprise in a world of uncertainty" (Endres 1997: 132). Market power is essential for individual business enterprises to control and stabilize otherwise turbulent and unstable markets where the constant pressure of competition is assumed and the behavior of business enterprises remains the center of attention.

There is also an emphasis on private market governance in the Austrian tradition, like its neoclassical counterparts, in that the effectiveness of competition is the key to preventing inefficiency more quickly than public policy. Entrepreneurs have much more expertise in identifying inefficiencies in the market than economists, judges or legislators in the presence of free market entry (Kirzner 1985: 142). Moreover, entrepreneurs bear financial responsibility for their decisions, not the regulators (High 1984: 31). Abolishing restrictions imposed by the state is presented as one of the best ways to increase competition. There is heavy reliance on private market actors in market governance instead of the state ensuring the public good.

In sum, the theoretical innovation of the Austrian tradition is twofold: first, the portrayal of competition as a dynamic and evolutionary process; and, second, the shift in the unit of analysis specifically to entrepreneurs and their behavior with a strong emphasis on the significance of non-price forms of competition (Endres 1997: 5). The Austrian school points to the existence and necessity of market power, its various sources, and the role of technology in business competition. Nonetheless, it falls short of explaining the persistence of market power for governance, the role of the financial sector, or the changing organizational forms of business enterprises. The state's role is limited also to keeping markets open with a number of softening caveats like efficiency, which, in turn, makes the state literally unnecessary and hence under-theorized.

The Marxian view

What distinguishes the Marxian perspective from the Austrian view is its insistence on the permanent and augmenting nature of market power because of the perception of the business enterprise as a self-expanding value and its impact on the state's involvement in market governance in addition to its emphasis on the cyclical evolution of competition and market concentration (Shapiro 1976). Essentially, business competition is 'striving' between economic units; it is a process through which production, realization, and distribution of surplus value is carried out (Marx 1973: 751). Competition is not peaceful, but warlike—the coercive "action of capital upon capital" (Marx 1968: 30). Strictly speaking, competition between capital coerces individual business enterprises to develop new products, new technologies, new production processes, or to find new geographic markets and new ways of managing relations with their competitors and the state (Marx 1967: 316).

Marx considers interactions not only between business enterprises of different sizes, but also between different sectors (finance, industry, and agriculture) and between business enterprises and the state (Marx 1976: 534–535). In analyzing the relationship between financial and industrial sectors, joint stock companies serve as a bridge and Marx draws three conclusions concerning business competition. First, the joint stock company, as a new form of production organization, makes it possible to produce commodities on large scales and at a lower cost. Second, the joint stock company's shares are owned by many, which brings about the socialization of capital. Finally, managers, not shareholders, run day-to-day operations of the joint stock company, which results in the separation of ownership from management with the following reverberations:

> [I]t produces a new financial aristocracy, a new kind of parasite in the guise of company promoters, speculators and merely nominal directors; an entire system of swindling and cheating with respect to the promotion of companies, issue of shares and share dealings. It is private production unchecked by private ownership.
>
> *Marx 1976: 569*

The emergence of the joint stock company changes the mode of business competition markedly, as powerful competitors vigorously compete for market share to benefit from economies of scale.

For Marx, competition is cyclical and its intensity changes over the business cycle with fluctuations in profitability. Basically, an increase in competition for market share triggers a temporary rise in wages and, thus, a sharper decline in the rate of profit (Marx 1976: 565). Competition also fosters the creation of new technology and introduction of new machinery by business enterprises to reduce production costs (Marx 1973: 776). Every new production technique makes commodities cheaper initially. Those capitalists who apply new techniques first earn more profit. Nonetheless, competition equalizes profit rates in relative terms by universalizing new production techniques within an industry through accelerating the speed of the diffusion of technology (Marx 1973: 373). Business enterprises also tend to expand geographically, and consequently intensify competition within as well as between countries (Marx 1952: 39, 1976: 1014).

Production in large quantities by many business enterprises leads to a market glut and, thus, a problem of profit realization via sales, even after geographic market expansion. A price hike in inputs and a sharp decline in commodity prices reduces profit margins drastically, which does not immediately impact on the reckless expansion in industrial investment and productive capacity because of speculations and 'dirty' tricks—that is, inflating profits while hiding losses in order to attract more capital (Marx 1976: 567). The credit system serves as a basis for speculative activities in the market with its ability to enable the acts of buying and selling to be spread out over time (Marx 1976: 567). When it becomes clear to the financial sector that 'promised' profits cannot be realized, it stops lending abruptly to the industrial sector that is now in urgent need, thereby accelerating bankruptcies, acquisitions, hostile takeovers, mergers, and hence market concentration which may not be as unilinear as it may sound (Marx 1952: 44, 1976: 331–332, 572).

Marxian scholars emphasize a shift from price to non-price competition with the concentration and centralization of capital. For instance, Rudolf Hilferding (1981: 189–193) points to the existence of major obstacles for the downward movement of prices. Cartels, restrictive practices, combinations, fusions, amalgamations, advertising, and other selling efforts are a few market practices that business enterprises deploy to prevent declining profits, however transient they may be. Similarly, Vladimir Lenin (1963: 40) maintains that market concentration does not mean the disappearance of competition altogether, but the emergence of something new, which is "a mixture of free competition and monopoly." Lenin also maintains that restrictive practices and cartels become the foremost tactics in competition. Some of these practices are the cessation of raw material supplies and labor, cutting off deliveries, the closing of trade outlets, cartel agreements, price cuts, the stopping of credit, and boycotts both at national and, especially, international levels (Lenin 1963: 26). In short, the joint stock company means that competition acquires a new face.

Marx clarifies how the power of business enterprises influences public policies and, therefore, state-economy relations. In *The Communist Manifesto*, Marx and Engels (Marx 1994: 161) reveal their vision of the modern state: "The executive of the modern State is but a committee for managing the common affairs of the whole bourgeoisie." The bourgeoisie, which owns the means of production, establishes itself in the modern representative state. Certainly, public power is nothing but "merely the organized power of one class for oppressing another" (Marx 1994: 176). In *The German Ideology*, Marx (1994: 154) contends that the state is principally an institutional form within which a double process of integration of the entire civil society and an assertion of the common interests of individual capitalists takes place. In one way or another, the state serves the interests of the dominant class with its active involvement in market governance.

To sum up, the Marxian view theorizes competition as a dynamic and evolutionary process between business enterprises. Essential in this process is the role of joint stock companies and their relations with the financial sector and the state in the context of market governance. Accruing from size, new technology, new commodities, new organizational structures, and relations with competitors and the state, market power is a factor that shapes the governance of markets by affecting the process of competition directly as well as affecting political decisions. Attributing to the state an active economic role broadens the concept of market governance. Nevertheless, representing the state as an institution that serves the interests of the capitalists directly or indirectly is problematic in that it eliminates the possibility of the state being autonomous in making and implementing policies that may be against the interests of the capitalist class from time to time.

The Post Keynesian view

Post Keynesian economics shares some of the core assumptions of heterodox economics including realism, organicism, reasonable rationality, production, disequilibria, and instability. Its distinct features are the principle of effective demand, investment as the driving force behind saving, the monetary theory of production, historical and irreversible time, fundamental uncertainty, anti-reductionist microfoundations, and the importance of institutions and power relations (Lavoie 2014: 33–34). For Post Keynesians, the economic system proceeds along a long-term secular growth path with short-term cyclical movements (Langlois 1993: 87). Economic processes take place in real time and contractual relations are required to reduce fundamental uncertainty and an unpredictable future in a monetary or capitalist economy. Contracts for the payment of money are written in calendar time. Historical time means that decisions are irreversible—that is, once a decision is made and put into practice it is hard to reverse without incurring any significant cost (Henry 2012: 530). Market power is a major means in the hands of business enterprises to reduce, if not fully eliminate, uncertainty in and outside the market (Monvoisin & Rochon 2006: 21–22).

The modern big corporation is a typical market player in Post Keynesian economics. Alfred Eichner (1985: 30–31) calls it a 'megacorp,' which operates several plants in each of the industries to which it belongs and usually opens up or shuts down plant segments over the business cycle. Following the institutionalist view of the business enterprise, Lee (2013b: 166), and Jo & Henry (2015: 28–29) label the business enterprise a 'going concern,' which has an indefinite life span and engages in continuous economic activity with its two organizational parts of 'going plant' (productive capabilities) and 'going business' (managerial capabilities). The primary objective of the business enterprise is to survive competition, which is only possible with a profitable business (Lee 2002: 122). Despite significant differences in their ability to maintain price when demand varies, business enterprises strive for market power to have control over pricing decisions (Minsky 1986: 157).

Technical progress, which is endogenous to "the normal functioning of the capitalist system," requires more capital and thereby encourages industry concentration (Kalecki 1941:179, 1962: 147). It is not unusual to see a few big business enterprises with price-setting ability surrounded by a multitude of small enterprises offering slightly different products and adjusting their cost margins to stay competitive (Lavoie 2001: 22). Capital-intensive industries are more concentrated to fulfill the wishes of both investors and bankers who look for some guarantee that price competition will not happen, especially in manufacturing and utility industries (Minsky 1986: 167). Thus, oligopolistic markets make up a significant portion of economic structures in industrialized countries (Eichner 1976). As a corollary of this, cost-plus pricing, which may appear in different forms, is the common business enterprise practice to ensure its survival among other objectives (Lee 1998).

With an emphasis on a specific type of market form, it may be wrong to infer that Post Keynesians advocate a structuralist approach to business competition. On the contrary, Post Keynesian economics is "rooted in a dynamic process" and concerned with "the analysis of the economy in disequilibrium" (Eichner & Kregel 1975: 1294–1296). Competition is not perceived as an end-state; rather it is a dynamic process that takes place through investment and capital accumulation in a capitalist market economy (Kenyon 1979: 40). Whereas the overall state of the economy determines the totality of cash flows, competition distributes them among business enterprises (Minsky 1986: 142–143).

Business enterprises compete with each other on the basis of price and non-price elements to remain profitable (Sawyer 1994: 10). Having more or less similar cost structures and size, the bigger ones do not often use their power to compete on the basis of price as a way of avoiding its destructive and inconclusive outcomes (Lee 1998). Instead, price leadership develops in such markets (Shapiro & Mott 1995: 43). There is more of a role for non-price competition such as research and development, investment, discretionary expenditures and product differentiation, than price competition (Eichner & Kregel 1975: 5; Eichner 1983: 138–148). Price competition is not ruled out completely. It is acknowledged, but can be very rare and yet bloody, whenever it happens (Lavoie 2001: 27).

In line with Lavoie's description of the oligopolistic market and Kalecki's view on the impact of innovations on competition, Joseph Steindl (1987: 11) argues that there is no one type of business enterprise that plays a leading role and disrupting the order in industry. Accordingly, Steindl makes an analytical distinction between the 'defensive (weaker) or aggressive (stronger)' and 'conservative or innovative' business enterprise. Facing intense competition, even medium or fairly big business enterprises may be reduced to the level of normal profits, whenever their innovative competitors achieve sufficiently large cost differentials. In other words, normal profits are not necessarily the sole characteristic of small business enterprises. Big business enterprises can be marginalized in an industry as well as in the face of strong competitive pressure. The only difference to be noted is the duration that it takes. A longer time is required for progressive business enterprises to exert serious pressure on their bigger 'marginal' counterparts (Steindl 1952: 53).

With respect to the anatomy and internal dynamics of competition, Post Keynesians identify stagnation, upturn, downturn, and crisis as four phases of a typical business cycle (Alves et al. 2008: 413). Intensity of competition depends on demand and hence profit opportunities, and fluctuates over a full business cycle. Stagnation is a stage during which competition is subdued with low demand, which triggers reduced supply in the market. Demand picks up gradually at the beginning of an upturn. Instead of having a uniform price, business enterprises develop a price structure that corresponds to the different qualities and types of the product (Steindl 1952: 40). Progressive business enterprises have greater gross profit margins, and therefore higher net profit margins compared to their marginal counterparts thanks to cost-reducing technical innovations. They adopt new technical methods to decrease their costs and improve their profit margins, which may not be the case for smaller competitors. If progressive business enterprises expand faster than the growth of the industry, the absolute market share of other business enterprises necessarily declines, thereby facilitating absolute concentration in the concerned industry, especially after a few competitors are eliminated from the market (Steindl 1952: 42).

There is a financial dimension to competition as well. According to Hyman Minsky (1986: 178): "[d]uring periods of tranquil expansion, profit-seeking financial institutions invent and reinvent 'new' forms of money, substitutes for money in portfolios, and financing techniques for various types of activity: financial innovation is a characteristic of our economy in good times." In other words, banks are willing to help industrialists to expand when they see profit opportunities in times of growing demand which itself fuels economic growth. They create new credit opportunities for investors as a way of boosting their own profitability.

Business enterprises use their market power to raise their mark-up during business upswings (Atesoglu 1997: 646). Occasionally, prices may increase with excess demand especially when small innovative business enterprises have difficulty in adding new productive capacity to offer new products during business upswings. In such markets, business enterprises raise their prices to deal with their inability to meet the immediate excess demand, which may not last very long. High profit margins attract new competitors, obviously. When the growth in demand for industry products becomes stable, business enterprises correct the deviation of actual price from its long-run level by reducing their mark-ups in the next period (Sen & Vaidya 1995: 42). In explaining when business enterprises cut or raise prices, Nai-Pew Ong (1981: 103–105) emphasizes the existence of defensive as well as offensive pricing in a stratified industry during upturns and downturns. Whereas the objective of defensive pricing is to protect market share by blocking the expansion of the marginal business enterprises progressively, offensive target pricing aims at eliminating the marginal business enterprises by bankrupting and driving them out of the market.

An increase in the industry's profit margin leads to an increasing rate of internal accumulation, a driving force behind further investment and increasing output. If the growth rate of output is greater than the expansion of the industry's growth rate in terms of demand, competition between business enterprises becomes intense (Steindl 1952: 45). Progressive business enterprises step up their selling efforts, which results in an actual loss of sales on the part of their peers. In response to this strategy, other business enterprises either cut their prices or increase costs by quality competition or product differentiation and more extensive advertisement (Steindl 1952: 43). The latter is the most-widely used practice, which appears as product differentiation and selling efforts to segment the market.

Knowing that competition is harmful and that markets are unstable, competitors form cartels, trusts, and alliances in order to mitigate the effects of price competition during the downturns, in addition to mergers, acquisitions, and takeovers. Nonetheless, such agreements are often violated after competitors reduce their mark-up to increase market share. Moreover, the existence of a strong belief that the agreement will soon be violated in such an uncertain environment anyway is itself another factor behind the fact that cartels are not stable. Another tactic that small business enterprises particularly deploy is adulterating their products and using 'dirty tricks' to sabotage their competitors' business (Eichner 1969: 14, 58).

The financial sector has a role to play in this process as well: "Strong and unregulated competition in the markets of products produced by capital-intensive processes is incompatible with the uncertainty attenuation required by financiers and bankers before they hazard substantial funds in the financing of such processes" (Minsky 1986: 170). Immediate reaction from the financial sector is to restrict the flow of funds into the industry, which, in turn, amplifies the financial difficulties of the business enterprises that expanded quickly during the upturn. Technologically innovative as well as high-cost competitors with difficulties in borrowing from the financial sector might disappear through bankruptcies, mergers, and acquisitions, thereby escalating market concentration. In turn, the average profit margin in the industry rises again in proportion to costs. Whenever this increase is above a certain level that leads to more internal accumulation in the industry, business enterprises can use the surplus for the purpose of expansion of the industry as a whole. Then a new competitive struggle sets in again, but under the leadership of few bigger competitors this time (Steindl 1952: 43). The state plays a role in market governance through regulatory commissions and policies such as antitrust/competition law to regulate business competition (Lee 2013a: 476, 2013b).

It is obvious that market power is a comprehensive concept in Post Keynesian economics. Certainly, the size of the business enterprise is important, but it is not the only source, as in the neoclassical theories of perfect competition and contestable markets. Innovations, new products, product differentiation, technology, organization, sales efforts, relations with other business enterprises as well as state regulations can be the sources of market power. In a way, having more information than others, whether it is information about technology, organization, competitors, or the state, is the quintessential source of power. Similar to the Austrian view, market power can reduce uncertainty by enabling business enterprises to control their environment, but does not eliminate it fully (Monvoisin & Rochon 2006: 22–23). Business enterprises use their power to manage competition and ensure orderly governance to cope with instability and fundamental uncertainty.

What differentiates the Post Keynesian view from the Austrian and the Marxian approaches is that the former is also concerned with the uncertainty that the power of business enterprises creates for the public at large (Pressman 2007: 26). Exerting power on the state has a boomerang effect in that a reduction in real wages and tax revenues creates uncertainty for business enterprises by decreasing demand from workers and the state. Business enterprises become reluctant to invest in productive capacity. This fuels unemployment and hence poverty. Despite some controversy over the nature of the state in Post Keynesian economics, the state is perceived to be an institution that helps mitigate uncertainty through public policies such as antitrust/competition policy to regulate business competition, fiscal policy to soften business cycles, and social policy to lessen the uncertainty of future incomes, unlike the Marxian or the Austrian views (Pressman 2006: 4–8). For Post Keynesians, the public good reflects the interests of the broader society, not just those of the capitalist class which may be adversely affected from public policies that aim to occasionally achieve the public good.

Discussion and conclusions

It is clear from the preceding discussion that the way market governance is conceived depends on the vantage points each theoretical framework takes with respect to the vision of business competition and market power. The mainstream theories of perfect competition and contestable markets are concerned exclusively with the structural properties of the market and hence offer a static understanding of competition. Market power is non-existent or ephemeral and short-lived. By contrast, the Austrian, Marxian, and Post Keynesian approaches perceive it as a dynamic, evolutionary, and historical process. This is the similarity between all three perspectives.

A major difference between the Austrian and the other two heterodox perspectives originates from this fact: the former is interested in the behavior of business enterprises while taking their organizational structure and the pressure of competition as a given; the Marxian and Post Keynesian perspectives emphasize the changing organizational structure of business enterprises with the emergence of the joint stock company and the megacorp, fluctuations in the intensity of competition depending on demand, profit opportunities, and the availability of credit. The upshot of these differences among these three heterodox approaches is the nature of market power, which the Austrian School, in contrast to the Marxian and Post Keynesian traditions, recognizes as transient and temporary.

Both the Marxian and Post Keynesian perspectives underline the permanent and self-augmenting nature of market power. In contrast to equating market power with the number and size of business enterprises and their ability to increase market prices as in the mainstream theories of perfect competition and contestable markets, the Austrian, Marxian, and Post Keynesian approaches broaden the scope of the variables by emphasizing competition on the basis of new products, production technologies, organizational structure, raw material sources, markets, in addition to forming cartels, merging, and acquiring competitors to gain power. However, market power is temporary in the Austrian approach, as opposed to the Marxian and Post Keynesian traditions, which underline the permanent and augmented character of market power together with its reverberations for market governance. Post Keynesians contend that market power is essential for business firms to exert control over their environment and reduce uncertainty (Dunn 2008: 178).

When it comes to market governance, there is a heavy reliance on business enterprises in both the neoclassical theories of perfect competition and contestable markets and Austrian economics. The key public policy message they deliver is that the market should be 'left alone.' Business enterprises and consumers are the best ones to know their own interests. Their approach to market governance is limited to the market level and supply conditions. Private market actors and their behavior is the subject of market governance. Yet, there is an image of the market operating in a vacuum, rather than part of an evolving broader social, political, and cultural context. The state is pictured as an external actor that creates a level playing field to keep the market open at best. Moreover, there is resistance against the state's involvement in the market because politicians and public administrators may not make the best decisions on behalf of the market. Public policy failure has wider adverse consequences than those of market failure.

For Marxians and Post Keynesians, market governance is a broader concept that includes both private sector players, state actors, and non-profit organizations. They locate the market as part of the whole economy and emphasize the role of the financial sector in the process of competition depending on demand and hence profit opportunities in historical time. Not surprisingly, the state is an active player in market governance along with private, public, and non-profit organizations. Mergers, acquisitions, joint ventures, cartels, and all forms of explicit and tacit coalitions and agreements that aim to manage quantity, quality, and price are some of the practices conducted by business enterprises. To deal with them, the state engages in market governance through its marketing boards or regulatory agencies in both the Marxian and Post Keynesian traditions. By and large, the Post Keynesian view is more comprehensive and balanced in studying the role of the state and the significance of the public good in market governance, rather than seeing any public policy in the interest of the capitalist class and hence equating the public good with that of the dominant classes.

The Post Keynesian view is comparatively new in theorizing business competition and the state, compared to the Marxian approach. The former may incorporate how competition as a cyclical process works in such a way that it acts both as a mechanism to pressure business enterprises to innovate or disappear and the attempts of business enterprises to redefine the parameters of competition for their advantage at the same time. Linking the macro and micro levels will be useful to understand how some business enterprises are successful in meeting and thwarting competitive pressures with innovative responses, while others take their place in the dustbins of history. Another lesson Post Keynesian economics may take from the Marxian thought is to unpack the state and theorize it comprehensively, rather than generally treating it as a black box that strives to achieve the public interest under any condition. This will definitely enrich the future Post Keynesian agenda for public policy and governance.

Acknowledgments

The author thanks the editors of the *Handbook* for their very valuable comments, along with Joseph Fantauzzi who helped with proof-reading and organizing the bibliography. The usual disclaimer applies.

References

Alves Jr., A.J., Dymski, G.A., & De Paula, L.-F. 2008. 'Banking strategy and credit expansion: a post-Keynesian approach.' *Cambridge Journal of Economics*, 32 (3): 395–420.
Arena, R. 2015. 'On the intellectual foundations of Hayek's and Schumpeter's economics: an appraisal.' *Journal of Evolutionary Economics*, 25 (1): 77–90.
Arnold, R.A. 2008. *Economics*, 9th edn. Mason, OH: South-Western Cengage Learning.
Atesoglu, S.H. 1997. 'A post Keynesian explanation of U.S. inflation?' *Journal of Post Keynesian Economics*, 19 (5): 639–649.
Baskoy, T. 2012. 'Market governance,' *in*: J.E. King (ed.), *The Elgar Companion to Post Keynesian Economics*, 2nd edn. Cheltenham, UK: Edward Elgar, 387–392.

Baumol, W. 1982. 'Contestable markets: an uprising in the theory of industry structure.' *American Economic Review*, 72 (1): 1–15.

Baumol, W.J., Binder, A.S., Lavoie, M., & Seccareccia, M. 2009. *Microeconomics: Principles and Policy*, 1st Canadian edn. Toronto: Nelson.

Blanchard, O. & Melino, A. 1999. *Macroeconomics*, 1st Canadian edn. Scarborough, ON: Prentice Hall.

Bork, R.H. 1967. 'The goals of antitrust policy.' *American Economic Review*, 57 (2): 242–253.

Boscheck, R. 2008. 'Strategies, markets and governance,' *in*: R. Boscheck, C. Batruch, S. Hamilton, J.-P. Lehmann, C. Pfeiffer, U. Steger, & M. Yaziji. *Strategies, Markets and Governance: Exploring Commercial and Regulatory Agendas*. Cambridge, UK: Cambridge University Press, 3–32.

Dunn, S.P. 2008. *The 'Uncertain' Foundations of Post Keynesian Economics: Essays in Exploration*. London: Routledge.

Eichner, A.S. 1969. *The Emergency of Oligopoly: Sugar Refining as a Case Study*. Baltimore, MD: John's Hopkins Press.

Eichner, A.S. 1976. *The Megacorp and Oligopoly: Micro Foundations of Macro Dynamics*. Cambridge, UK: Cambridge University Press.

Eichner, A.S. 1983. 'The micro foundations of the corporate economy.' *Managerial and Decision Economics*, 4 (3): 136–152.

Eichner, A.S. 1985. *Toward a New Economy: Essays in Post-Keynesian and Institutionalist Theory*. Armonk, NY: M.E. Sharpe.

Eichner, A.S. & Kregel, J.A. 1975. 'An essay on post-Keynesian theory: a new paradigm in economics.' *Journal of Economic Literature*, 13 (4): 1293–1314.

Endres, A.M. 1997. *Neoclassical Microeconomic Theory: The Founding Austrian Version*. London: Routledge.

Fernandez-Huerga, E. 2013. 'The market concept: a characterization from institutional and Post-Keynesian economics.' *American Journal of Economics and Sociology*, 72 (2): 361–385.

Fligstein, N. 1996. 'Markets as politics: a political-cultural approach to market institutions.' *American Sociological Review*, 61 (4): 656–673.

Hayek, F.A. 1948. *Individualism and Economic Order*. Chicago: University of Chicago Press.

Hayek, F.A. 1978. *New Studies in Philosophy, Politics, Economics and the History of Ideas*. Chicago: Chicago University Press.

Henry, J.F. 2012. 'Time in economic history,' *in*: J.E. King (ed.), *The Elgar Companion to Post Keynesian Economics*, 2nd edn. Cheltenham, UK: Edward Elgar, 528–533.

High, J. 1984. 'Bork's paradox: static vs. dynamic efficiency in antitrust analysis.' *Contemporary Policy Issues*, 3 (2): 21–32.

Hilferding, H. 1981. *Finance Capital: A Study of the Latest Phase of Capitalist Development*. London: Routledge.

Janberg, V. 2015. 'Schumpeter and Mises as 'Austrian Economists.' *Journal of Evolutionary Economics*, 25 (1): 91–105.

Jo, T.-H. 2013. 'Saving private business enterprises: a heterodox microeconomic approach to market governance and market regulation.' *American Journal of Economics and Sociology*, 72 (2): 447–467.

Jo, T.-H. & Henry, J.F. 2015. 'The business enterprise in the age of money manager capitalism.' *Journal of Economic Issues*, 49 (1): 23–46.

Kalecki, M. 1941. 'A theorem on technical progress.' *Review of Economic Studies*, 8 (3): 178–184.

Kalecki, M. 1962. 'Observations on the theory of growth.' *Economic Journal*, 72 (285): 134–153.

Kenyon, P. 1979. 'Pricing,' *in*: A.S. Eichner (ed.), *A Guide to Post-Keynesian Economics*. White Plains, NY: M.E. Sharpe, 34–45.

Kirzner, I.M. 1985. *Discovery and the Capitalist Process*. Chicago: University of Chicago Press.

Langlois, C.C. 1993. 'Monopoly price determination in the operational unit period.' *Journal of Post Keynesian Economics*, 16 (1): 81–103.

Lavoie, M. 2001. 'Pricing,' *in*: R. P.F Holt & S. Pressman (eds.), *A New Guide to Post Keynesian Economics*. London: Routledge, 21–31.

Lavoie, M. 2014. *Post-Keynesian Economics: New Foundations*. Cheltenham, UK: Edward Elgar.

Lee, F.S. 1998. *Post Keynesian Price Theory*. Cambridge: Cambridge University Press.

Lee, F.S. 2002. 'Post Keynesian economics (1930–2000): an emerging heterodox economic theory of capitalism,' *in*: D. Dowd (ed.), *Understanding Capitalism: Critical Analysis from Karl Marx to Amartya Sen*. London: Pluto Press, 108–131.

Lee, F.S. 2010. 'Alfred Eichner's missing 'complete model': a heterodox micro-macro model of monetary production economy,' *in*: M. Lavoie, L.-P. Rochon, & M. Seccareccia (eds.), *Money and Macrodynamics: Alfred Eichner and Post-Keynesian Economics*. Armonk, NY: M.E. Sharpe, 22–42.

Lee, F.S. 2013a. 'Post-Keynesian price theory: from pricing to market governance to the economy as a whole,' *in*: G.C. Harcourt & P. Kriesler (eds.), *The Oxford Handbook of Post-Keynesian Economics, Vol. 1: Theory and Origins*. Oxford: Oxford University Press, 467–484.

Lee, F.S. 2013b. 'Competition, going enterprise, and economic activity,' *in*: J.K. Mouded, C. Bina, & P.L. Mason (eds.), *Alternative Theories of Competition: Challenges to the Orthodoxy*. London: Routledge, 160–173.

Lenin, V.I. 1963. *Imperialism: The Highest Stage of Capitalism, A Popular Outline*. New York: International Publishers.

Littlechild, S.C. 1978. *Fallacy of the Mixed Economy: An Austrian Critique of Conventional Mainstream Economics and of British Economic Policy*. London: Institute of Economic Affairs.

Lyons, B. 2004. *Canadian Microeconomics: Problems and Policies*, 7th edn. Toronto: Pearson Education.

Marx, K. 1952. *Wage Labor and Capital*. Moscow: Progressive Publishers.

Marx, K. 1967. *Capital: A Critique of Political Economy, Vol. 1*. New York: International Publishers.

Marx, K. 1968. *Theories of Surplus-Value*, Volume IV of *Capital*, Part II. Moscow: Progress Publishers.

Marx, K. 1973. *Grundrisse: Foundations of the Critique of Political Economy*. Middlesex, UK: Penguin Books.

Marx, K. 1976. *Capital: A Critique of Political Economy, Vol. 3*. London: Penguin Books.

Marx, K. 1994. *Selected Writings*, L.H. Simon (ed.), Indianapolis, IN: Hackett Publishing Company.

Mantzavinos, C. 1999. 'Carl Menger and the theory of competition.' *Journal of Economics and Statistics*, 219 (5/6): 685–686.

Metcalfe, J.S. 2013. 'Schumpeterian competition,' *in*: J.K. Moudud, C. Bina, & P.L. Mason (eds.), *Alternative Theories of Competition: Challenges to the Orthodoxy*. London: Routledge, 111–126.

Minsky, H.P. 1986. *Stabilizing an Unstable Economy*. New Haven, CT: Yale University Press.

Monvoisin, V. & Rochon, L.-P. 2006. 'Economic power and the real world: a post-Keynesian analysis of power.' *International Journal of Political Economy*, 35 (4): 5–30.

Nicholson, W.E. 1997. *Intermediate Microeconomics and its Application*, 7th edn. Fort Worth, TX: Dryden Press.

O'Driscoll, G.P. & Rizzo, M.J. 2015. *Austrian Economics Re-Examined: The Economics of Time and Ignorance*. London: Routledge.

Ong, N.-P. 1981. 'Target pricing, competition, and growth.' *Journal of Post Keynesian Economics*, 4 (1): 101–116.

Palay, T.M. 1984. 'Comparative institutional economics: the governance of rail freight contracting.' *Journal of Legal Studies*, 13 (2): 265–287.

Peters, G. 2012. 'Is governance for everybody? The use and abuse of governance,' *in*: A.M. Bissessar (ed.), *Governance: Is it for Everyone?* New York: Nova Science Publishers, 1–12

Pressman, S. 2006. 'Alternative views of the state,' *in*: S. Pressman (ed.), *Alternative Theories of the State*. Basingstoke, UK: Palgrave Macmillan, 113–138.

Pressman, S. 2007. 'What can Post Keynesian economics teach us about poverty?' *in*: R. P.F. Holt & S. Pressman (eds.), *Empirical Post Keynesian Economics: Looking at the Real World*. Armonk, NY: M.E. Sharpe, 21–43.

Sawyer, M.C. 1989. *The Challenge of Radical Political Economy: An Introduction to the Alternatives to Neo-Classical Economics*. Savage, MD: Barnes & Noble Books.

Sawyer, M.C. 1994. 'Post-Keynesian and Marxian notions of competition,' *in*: M. Glick (ed.), *Competition, Technology and Money: Classical and Post-Keynesian Perspectives*. Aldershot, UK: Edward Elgar, 3–23.

Schumpeter, J.A. 1950. *Capitalism, Socialism and Democracy*, 3rd edn. New York: Harper and Row.

Scott, A. 2000. 'Economic geography: the great half-century.' *Cambridge Journal of Economics*, 24 (4): 483–504.

Sen, K. & Vaidya, R.R. 1995. 'The determination of industrial prices in India: a Post Keynesian approach.' *Journal of Post Keynesian Economics*, 18 (1): 29–52.

Shapiro, N. 1976. 'The neoclassical theory of the firm.' *Review of Radical Political Economics*, 8 (4): 17–29.

Shapiro, N. & Mott, T. 1995. 'Firm-determined prices: the post-Keynesian conception,' *in*: P. Wells (ed.), *Post-Keynesian Economic Theory*. Boston: Kluwer Academic Publishers, 35–48.

Steindl, J. 1952. *Maturity and Stagnation in American Capitalism*. Oxford: Basil Blackwell.

Steindl, J. 1987. 'Kalecki's theory of pricing: notes on the margin,' *in*: G. Fink, G. Poll, & M. Riese (eds.), *Economic Theory, Political Power and Social Justice: Festschrift Kazimierz Laski*. New York: Springer-Verlag, 1–18.

Van Hoi, P., Mol, A. P.J., & Oosterveer, P.J.M. 2009. 'Market governance for safe food in developing countries: the case of low-pesticide vegetables in Vietnam.' *Journal of Environmental Management*, 91 (2): 380–388.

Veblen, T. 1923. *Absentee Ownership and Business Enterprise in Recent Times: The Case of America*. New York: B.W. Huebsch.

Williamson, O.E. 2005. 'The economics of governance.' *American Economic Review*, 95 (2): 1–18.

16

A Marxian understanding of the nature and form of dominant capitalist legal institutions

Lorraine Talbot

Introduction

Capitalism is the organization of production around the systematic extraction of value from labor. Unlike other economic systems it does so through market exchange rather than overt coercion and it relies upon the illusion of free and equal exchange. In the exchange between labor and capital, labor power becomes a property form that is exchanged for a wage. As a Marxian legal theorist Pashukanis notes, social relations of production "assume a reified form in that the products of labor are related to each other as values" (Pashukanis [1929] 1987: 111). In the exchange of values—wage for labor—labor power is not fully compensated and the uncompensated part is captured by capital as profit.

Legally, the relationship between capital and labor is encapsulated in the employment contract. The emergence of the bilateral contract as ubiquitous to the market is important because it obfuscates the inequality between labor and capital. The contract form constructs both parties as the market actors of neoclassical theory. In entering the labor contract, the worker becomes a self-serving market actor making free use of his or her property—not an exploited worker.

The labor contract is, therefore, the primary legal institution of capitalism. It is necessary for market exchange but additionally it constructs labor as a legal subject, possessing legal rights, legal equality and capable of entering into legally binding arrangements for the exchange of values. As the bearer of labor power, the worker acquires the "capacity to become a legal subject and a bearer of rights" (Pashukanis [1929] 1987: 112). Indeed, for exchange to take place, the worker must be able to exercise rights as an autonomous legal subject. So contract law, and specifically the labor contract, encompasses the myth and fetishization of equivalent exchange that underpins the relationship between labor and capital and the exchange of labor for wage.

The relationship between labor and capital is exercised within legal organizations in which production takes place. The dominant organizational forms have changed in accordance with developments in capitalism itself. In the UK, from the late eighteenth century and well into the nineteenth century, capitalism in its early entrepreneurial period existed mainly in the legal form of the partnership. The partnership, whose legal norms were later codified in the Partnership Act 1890, made partners prima facie equals in respect of managing, owning, and extracting profits from the business. It also made them equally and personally liable for the debts of the business.

Any recourse to investment outside the individual partners was treated as debts, which prima facie gave no legal claims on the business. However, outside investment was rarely required as the surpluses captured from its workers were so high in this period that much could be ploughed back into the business. The early decades of capitalist production were labor intensive with low fixed capital requirements and so business had little recourse to outside investors. The high proportion of labor to fixed capital expenditure, goes some way to explaining the average real rate of return on fixed capital in this period calculated as 39.8 percent in the period of 1855–1874 (Maito 2014: 5). The Marxian theorization of this outcome is discussed in the first and second sections.

As high profits were generally assured in early capitalism, the risk of unlimited liability was minimal. Thus, although limited liability was available to businesses from 1855, if registered as limited liability companies, few established business chose to do so (Shannon 1932). The partnership provided all the legal structures necessary to enable distribution of profit, entitlement to manage and allocation of liabilities. The business was owned and controlled by the same people, a small group of insiders profiting from high levels of labor exploitation. High profits were not hampered by state policy as the state did little to moderate the exploitation of labor. No legislation existed to protect the safety, working hours, pay, or liberty of labor. In response, many groups of workers set up their own legal institutions. Friendly societies were established at the end of the eighteenth century followed by mutual building societies. These organizations were funded by contributions from small groups of workers. Friendly societies provided funds for members injured at work or for members' bereaved families. Building societies enabled members to buy land or property in which to live and to escape the tyranny of landlords. Through building societies, workers claimed some personal independence through private property ownership (Talbot 2010). These two (social or hybrid) institutional forms arose as a direct result of the economic imperatives of the time. Labor-intensive production depended on landless wage labor working for as long as possible for as little as possible.

The emergence of these hybrid forms is an example of Polanyi's 'double movement' (Polanyi [1944] 2001). According to Polanyi, the expansion of the capitalist market disembeds labor from the prevailing social context. In Britain's case, capitalism disembeds a previously agricultural labor force from its long-standing social systems of support (and oppression). Labor becomes individual vendors of their own labor power in a newly industrializing economy. As Polanyi showed, the disembedding effect of the market results in a 'double movement.' Society reacts against the market's conflict with understood social and cultural norms. The double movement is an attempt to re-embed the market within activities and institutions, which reflect and reassert long-standing social and cultural norms. Thus, the exploitation of labor by capital through one legal form is countered by others designed to increase labor independence from capital and recreate social relations of support. The dehumanizing effect of capitalist work conditions are met by the humanizing intention of the worker-led social institutions.

These hybrid forms and their contemporary counterparts are of great interest to modern progressives. However, for brevity and focus they will not be further examined in this chapter. The remainder of the chapter will consider capitalism from the late nineteenth century onwards. Stated briefly, this period was characterized by the rise of joint stock limited liability companies and reduced profit rates. This combination occurred because the 'organic composition of capital' has changed during this period, reducing that element which creates value, labor (Marx [1867] 1954: 623). Joint stock companies were already available with unlimited liability from 1844,[1] and with limited liability from 1855 in the UK, but, as noted above this particular institutional form only became popular with industrial capitalists at the end of the nineteenth century when the return on capital investment dropped sharply. The company form provides huge advantages for its investors as shareholders. Their returns can be maximized while their liability for the company's debts is limited to the unpaid portion of their shares, or if fully paid up, as was the norm by the end of the nineteenth century, no liability at all. Shareholders enjoy profits for the full duration of the company's existence without any participation in its day-to-day management. The attributes of the company have made it the legal institution par excellence for the delivery of value to capital in the modern period of capitalism, characterized by reduced profit rates and frequent crises.

From the twentieth century and particularly since globalization, the separate corporate personality possessed by a company[2] has allowed capital to increase value extraction and to further reduce shareholders exposure to risk. For example, because companies are able to own shares and to claim the protections available to shareholders, they can form vast national and global corporate networks by forming new companies and owning the shares (and thus the control rights) in them. These 'subsidiary' companies can then perform activities required by the group, which are more likely to harm the environment or people, than the activities undertaken by the well-capitalized parent company. Any liabilities that arise as a result of this are the responsibility of the subsidiaries because the parent is protected by the limited liability enjoyed by all shareholders.

Separate corporate personality has also enabled companies to transfer valuable properties to subsidiaries based in low tax areas so to reduce the overall tax paid by the group. Today, companies are legally allowed to repurchase their own shares with retained profits or borrowed money so as to enhance the value of the remaining shares. This use of company funds entirely bypasses the productive entity itself, avoiding investments in production, research, and development, or efforts to train and retain employees. How and why the company is driven to behave in this 'psychopathic' way is examined in the proceeding section using Marx's theories of value, profit rates falls, credit, and the joint stock company.

Marx's theory of value and the tendency of the rate of profit to fall

In developing a theory on the origins of value, Marx asks why commodities sold at the end of the production process command a greater value than the sum of their inputs if those inputs have been purchased at market value. Marx identifies labor as the input that produces more value than it is paid because unlike other elements in the production process, which are bought at market price, labor's ultimate value is not yet complete or realized. Labor is bought for a period of time to be utilized in the production process as the employer requires. Labor is a living thing, flexible and bound only by the hours worked each day. The amount of unpaid labor-time that may be extracted, and thus the amount of the surplus that is available for distribution, depends on levels of industrial organization, technical development, the ability of management to organize labor, and labor's own competency.

Marx ([1867] 1954: 623) further argues that the value of a commodity derives from the labor embodied in it so that commodities exchange according to the average 'socially necessary' labor-time used to produce them. That average will change over time as capitalists strive to make labor more productive. Businesses that produce commodities with more labor-time than the average will fail whereas those who produce with less labor-time will enjoy high profits. At every particular stage of capitalist development, there is a level of labor-time required to reproduce labor's own existence; this is affected by such issues as the level of labor rights and the cost of the commodities which labor requires to reproduce its own existence. Labor then works beyond those hours.

Because of the flexible and uncertain nature of the values labor can produce in a working day, Marx identifies labor in the productive process as 'variable capital.' As the values of other elements of the productive process are complete, Marx refers to them as 'constant capital.' The combination of variable and constant capital Marx terms the 'organic composition of capital.' As production develops, labor uses more constant capital in a working day. This leads to either a reduction in the labor force or a general increase in the size and output of the productive organization. Either way, "the proportion of variable capital decreases in relation to constant capital" (Marx [1867] 1954: 623). Marx estimates that in the eighteenth century the organic composition of capital in the spinning industry was about 50 percent constant capital to 50 percent variable capital, but at the time of writing *Capital I* in 1867, the composition was 87.5 percent constant capital and 12.5 percent variable capital (Marx [1867] 1954: 623). Competition in capitalism pushes productive organizations to make labor more productive thereby reducing, as a proportion of total capital, the element of production that produces value, variable capital. (Marx [1867] 1954: 623). This means that the average amount of labor-time required to make a particular commodity decreases. With it the proportion of surplus value to investment decreases. Although the amount of products produced increases, ultimately their price falls.

This is counteracted by the reduction in labor-time required to produce other elements of the productive process, such as tools. It may also be adjusted by the lower wages capital is able to pay once labor is reduced in the workplace and an impoverished 'reserve army of labor' is created and "kept in misery in order to be always at the disposal of capital" (Marx [1894] 1962: 486). One of the paradoxes of capitalism is that the more successful it becomes at social production the more it negatively impacts on the social world of the non-capitalist class. Capitalism "turns every economical progress into a social calamity" (Marx [1894] 1962: 486–487).

The drive to make labor more productive eventually changes the legal institutions that capitalists adopt. Competition leads to many smaller capitalists being put out of business by the larger, who ultimately come to operate under the legal framework of the (joint stock) company. Moreover, the high constant capital levels of the remaining industries create a barrier against new competitors. In Marx's ([1867] 1954: 626) words:

> The battle of competition is fought by cheapening of commodities. The cheapness of commodities depends, *ceteris paribus*, on the productiveness of labour, and this again on the scale of production. Therefore the larger capitals beat the smaller.

The competition to make labor more productive draws individual competing capitals ever more to a single capital. The strongest capitals can, for a time, counter the falling rate of profit with volume of profit. Eventually the proportion of variable capital will fall so low that profits cannot be realized and economic crisis unfolds.

The emergence of joint stock companies: 'prophets and swindlers'

The company is the central organizational form for mature capitalism. It encompasses the same exploitative relationship between labor and capital except that the surplus from unpaid labor power is claimed by the company and ultimately returns to equity capital and to borrowed capital. Additionally, the corporate form allows capital to be fungible and transferrable, both as shares and as securities. Corporate capitalism encompasses a market in labor interacting with a market in capital, where capital has almost unimpeded freedom of movement.

In the UK, it was crises that heralded the dominant use of the company form. This transition was also facilitated by the rise of credit. Marx ([1867] 1954: 626) analyzes the credit system in *Capital I*:

the credit system which in its first stages furtively creeps in as the humble assistant of accumulation, drawing in to the hands of individual or associated capitalist, by invisible threads, the money resources which lie scattered over the surface of society, in larger or smaller amounts; but it soon becomes a new and terrible weapon in the battle of competition and is finally transformed into an enormous social mechanism for the centralisation of capitals.

The credit system, which first functions as a way for business owners to invest in production and is repaid on an agreed interest rate once surplus value is realized, becomes a mechanism to centralize control as never before and to advance finance over industry. Credit enables the dominance of joint stock companies and increasing scales of production well above the level achievable for privately owned capitals. Investment in joint stock companies is drawn from capitalists who expand their interest by using both their own funds and credit. "It is the abolition of capital as private property within the framework of capitalist production itself" (Marx [1894] 1962: 427). In this way private capital is in large part replaced by social capital—social, in that credit derives from the pooled resources of many persons.

The destruction and replacement of private capital with social capital aligns it with the social nature of production. Capital derived from social funds combine with collective labor in the 'social production' of commodities. Marx sees the rise of social capital as a transitional phase before the production process, divorced from private ownership, becomes social property. For Marx, this is because labor in part owns its own appropriated surplus value. The pooled funds of workers put other and/or the same workers into the production process. The cooperative is an example of this transitional phase—workers are joint capital holders and workers hold a joint claim to the fruits of their labor.[3]

However, as Marx ([1894] 1962: 431) is quick to point out, this transitional moment, though realized in legal institutions like the cooperative, is distorted by credit and the joint stock company, which enable social capital and the gains accruing to social capital, to be appropriated by those capitalists who wield financial power. This is a smaller and more powerful group of capitalists who use finance and credit to purchase entitlements to surplus value in the form of shares, across many different companies.

A further degenerative effect of credit and the joint stock company is that the owners of capital become concerned not with the activities of the company in which they have shares, but with the values and transfers of other shares. In the joint stock company, social capital "exists in the form of stock, [and] its movement and transfer become purely a result of gambling on the stock exchange, where the little fish are swallowed by the sharks and the lambs by the stock exchange wolves" (Marx [1894] 1962: 430). Capital becomes speculative under the joint stock company in which a recklessness in pursuit of profit accelerates crises (Marx [1894] 1962: 432). This is because a "large part of the social capital is employed by people that do not own it and therefore tackle things quite differently than the owner, who anxiously weighs the limitations of his private capital in so far as he handles it himself" (Marx [1894] 1962: 431). The non-owning management, the "administrator of other people's capital" (Marx [1894] 1962: 427), is subject to the demands of the shareholder "money capitalist" who receive a form of interest "as mere compensation for owning capital" (Marx [1894] 1962: 427). The private entrepreneur capitalist managing his own business, will be concerned to protect that business (in order to protect returns). In contrast, the money capitalist is "entirely divorced from the function in the actual process of reproduction" and interested only in the returns on capital (Marx [1894] 1962: 427). They can remove their investment at any time and invest elsewhere. For Marx, capitalism under the joint stock company becomes "the most colossal form of gambling and swindling" (Marx [1894] 1962: 432).

Capital, liquidity, and the joint stock company

This 'gambling,' however, is dependent on capital becoming transferable and fungible without losing the entitlements of capital. It must become 'money capital.' In early capitalism, capital does not have that fluidity and the legal institutions which contain capital, such as the partnership, do not allow fluidity. The circuit of capital, $M - C \ldots P \ldots C' - M'$, involves a period when capital is bound to the production process, designated in this formula by the dots which "indicate that the circulation process is interrupted" (Marx [1894] 1962: 109). Money is the most mobile of all the elements of the circuit, but when invested in production it becomes capital and loses its fluidity. By transforming their money into capital, investors may claim entitlement to surplus value, but capital will not regain its fluidity until transformed into money again through the realization of surplus value in the market, the M' stage. Capital constantly strives for fluidity in order to reduce the risk of being bound to a particular production process. It tolerates being bound to production while profits are high but as the rewards at the M' stage diminish, it seeks more fluidity to seek out new value and reduce the risk of committed investment.

The legal facility to enable investment in shares as a form of money capital was developed in the nineteenth century. Legislative intervention and to a lesser degree judicial innovation enabled industrial capitalists to become money capitalists as the legal constraints to the movement of capital invested in companies were gradually removed. The UK's Bubble Act 1720, which prohibited the free transferability of shares without a corporate charter, thus rendering money invested in an unincorporated association bound to the original purchaser, was repealed in 1825. In 1844 the Joint Stock Companies Act allowed incorporation through registration. These two reforms legalized the free transferability of investments in companies. However, another constraint upon a share's transferability was the large size of shares, which made them difficult to sell. This was compounded by companies' tendency to issue shares with large uncalled capital, in effect de facto unlimited liability (Jeffrey 1946). The legal facility to break up shares into small denominations and to cancel uncalled capital was introduced in the Companies Act 1867.

Yet another innovation was the court's reformulation of the share as a claim to the surplus value alone, rather than an interest in the means of production. Until the early part of the nineteenth century the company share was treated in law as an equitable claim to the company's property and thus shareholders were co-owners in equity (Williston 1888). Their investment was bound to the production process. However, in the 1837 case *Bligh v Brent*[4] the share was held to be a claim to the surplus created by the productive assets and not a claim to the assets themselves. The company share, at least in larger companies, thereon ceased to be a portion of the equitable interest in the company as a whole. Instead the share became a legal and equitable interest in the surplus value alone. Legally severed from the company assets the share became a transferable property form (Ireland et al. 1987). Thus, the circuit of capital in the company was enabled through the transformation of shares into a transferable money form, with much of money's fluidity. Entitlements to surplus value can be sold at any point in the productive cycle, in markets that are legally, culturally, and geographically distinct from the markets in which the tangible products of the company are sold.

When profit rates were high and surplus value was best claimed by being bound to a particular business this liquidity was not sought. However, once profit rates fell, capital availed itself of this legal regime and enjoyed the fluidity offered by the joint stock company. In this way capitalists became uninterested and disassociated from the process of making labor more productive. They merely seek out profitable shares in order to access the surplus created through making labor more productive—a task undertaken by someone else. Thus, the joint stock company facilitates a whole range of mechanisms to extract value without direct involvement in making that value. In this way it

> reproduces a new variety of parasites in the shape of promoters, speculators and simply nominal directors; a whole system of swindling and cheating by means of corporation promotion, stock issuance, and stock speculation. It is private production without the control of private property.
>
> *Marx [1894] 1962: 429*

Marxism and the current crisis

The 2007 crisis and the resulting Great Recession are characterized by falls in the rate of profit, a massive extension of credit, and an explosion in new financial property forms tenuously linked to commodified claims to surplus value. The UK was at the center of the global financial crisis because it is predominantly a rentier economy, reliant on its role in international finance, credit, and a rising housing market. Like other governments, the UK governments' response to the crisis has aimed to protect capital at the expense of labor, resulting in an entrenched recession that has undermined the global economy. The company form has enabled this political policy through its capacity to sever interests within the organization (discussed above) so that polices can be directed to the protection and enhancement of capital alone.

The current crisis is the outcome of decades of strategies to redress the low profit rates, which became largely terminal from the 1970s, after years of post-war growth. From the 1980s onwards, governments in the UK and US responded to low returns on investment by rebalancing the power between labor and capital in favor of capital, enabling business to reduce the cost of wages, introduce flexible working practices, and suppress industrial action. Both governments reduced the legal rights labor had enjoyed in the post-war period through sustained attacks on the unions, including the passing of legislation that radically curtailed their powers. In the UK by the mid-1980s, this had enabled the government to break up labor-oriented manufacturing and mining industries that had become uncompetitive in the global economy. This lack of competitiveness was largely because the many nationalized industries in the UK had not sought to increase the productivity of labor, but rather to protect employment and employees (Lazonick [1991] 1993: 59). This would have been sustainable, had government policy supported labor as a social good, or, made labor-intensive industries globally competitive by investing in productivity. Thatcher's neoliberal government pursued neither of these policies, and effectively replaced those industries with the capital-oriented financial industry. This industry relied on the extraction of global values through its role as financier. In the remaining labor-oriented industries there was a partial recovery in the rate of profit because of the cheaper price of constant capital and given the depressed wages in the UK (Maito 2014: 5).

Governments in the UK and US bolstered capital by removing barriers to the creation and liquidity of fictitious commodities. In the US, prohibitions on the creation and trade of financial derivatives were removed (MacKenzie & Millo 2003). In the UK, financial interests were bolstered by years of lucrative purchases of the country's undervalued national industries, which were rapidly privatized (Talbot 2015). Mutual building societies were allowed to demutualize and become companies, enabling the distribution of their retained earnings to their new shareholders and freeing the societies from the tight controls on borrowing and lending applicable to mutuals (Talbot 2010). The newly liberated financial sector began to generate huge profits where it had previously made very modest returns (Duménil & Lévy 2005). Consequently investment shifted to finance rather than production, even for non-financial companies who began to engage in their own financial services and to invest in financial companies.

The move away from investing in production was no doubt exacerbated by a neoliberal ideology promoted in law and in corporate governance (and present in the UK Corporate Governance Codes since 1992) that promoted shareholder returns as the primary corporate goal. Managerial enthusiasm for high returns was undoubtedly spurred by the fact that the executives' remuneration was bound to share performance, a governance strategy to reduce agency costs (Jensen & Meckling 1976). However, the primary driver of this shift was the reduced return on investments in production. Investing in finance seemed like the cure to this terminal weakness. However, money does not create value, only labor creates value. The pre-crisis M − M' illusion, which seemed to magically bypass the C . . . P . . . C' process, was nothing more than a financial bubble destined to burst. The fictitious commodities it generated were increasingly difficult to value and were often over-valued. The profits made by global banks in the five years before the crash, estimated to be around US$855 billion, were slightly less than the amount paid by the public to bail them out, estimated at around US$1 trillion (Haldane & Madouros 2011). The public paid for these illusory profits while shareholders and directors have been allowed to hold on to their gains.

Most governments' response to the crisis has been to protect capital through mechanism such as quantitative easing (QE) and through lower corporate tax. This has amounted to a transfer from the general public to the wealthy. In the UK, QE benefited the richest 5 percent of UK households who gained around 40 percent of the resulting £600 billion increase in value on bonds and equities (Joyce et al. 2012). The QE supercharged equity purchases led to a rise in equity prices that had no relationship with the underlying performance of the productive assets. The result was that all the losses to the equity market in 2008 as the real value of investments became clearer, amounting to 28.4 percent for Financial Times Stock Exchange (FTSE) 100 companies, were replaced by a rise of 27.3 percent following the first injection of QE and continued to increase with each subsequent injection (FTSE 2015).

While the UK government removed tax support previously claimable by the many people working for inadequate wages, it reduced corporate tax to 18 percent. One study showed that in "the financial year 2012–13, the government spent £58.2bn on subsidies, grants and corporate tax benefits. It took just £41.3bn in corporation tax receipts" (Farnsworth 2015). The government *subsidizes* companies far in excess of the amount it garners from corporate tax. In contrast, the 'flexible labor market' has witnessed the rise of zero hour contracts (ONS 2015) and an average decline of 7.5 percent in real wages between 2009 and 2013 (ONS 2014).

Companies have taken advantage of historically low interest rates to engage in financial restructuring rather than develop their productive capacity. As the OECD (2015a: 227) notes "the implementation of such very supportive policy stances over a protracted period has not succeeded in reviving capital spending significantly." Instead, the low cost of debt relative to equity has encouraged companies to borrow to return funds to shareholders, through share repurchases (buybacks) and dividends. For instance, in 2014, US Standard and Poor's (S&P) 500 corporations bought back just over US$565 billion of their own shares, an amount equivalent to around three-quarters of their total capital expenditures (OECD 2015a).

Share repurchases are driven by the myopic drive for profit maximization demanded by shareholders, the parasitic behavior that Marx saw as inevitable in large companies. Today, shareholder value is created by squandering funds on financial restructuring at precisely the point when the economy needs to develop its productive capacity. However, productive companies are currently considered risky investments. Thus, investors are selling shares in high capital expenditure companies and buying shares in companies with low capital expenditure (OECD 2015a). In Angel Gurría's words, "stock markets in advanced economies are punishing firms that invest" (cited in OECD 2015b: 1). For most observers this is inexplicable. But for fluid profit-seeking capital it is entirely logical to eschew investment in production when profit rates are at a historic low, and to take advantage of the liberal and protected regime for financial securities.

The enhancement of share values is, of course, good news for investors. However, because profitability is not being achieved through production and through the use of labor, and where corporations are 'punished' for investing in their productive capacity, the workforce is excluded from this wealth. Furthermore, labor is on the frontline for any drop in capitalist returns. The downturn in Chinese production has reduced demand for raw materials globally, which has hit the extractive industries in particular. So, for example, when Anglo American's shares fell by 10 percent its response was to restructure, shedding over two-thirds of its workforce, from 135,000 to 50,000 (BBC 2015).

The responses of governments and corporate management to the Great Recession have been to protect capital at the expense of labor qua labor or labor qua citizens. The corporate form enables this because it legally separates production from title to profits (shares). Monetary and fiscal policies such as QE and cuts to corporate tax rates can directly enhance the value of shares, distinct from elements of production. The cost of the QE is borne by pension holders, the costs of low corporate tax is borne by the public, still subject to austerity measures. Share buybacks enhance the wealth of shareholders and play no role in developing the productive and innovative capacity of the company. Wages are low enough and working practices flexible enough to make increasing the productivity of labor otiose, a mere risky investment.

This has all massively increased levels of inequality between capital and labor. The OECD (2015c: 1) report on social inequality notes that:

> income inequality in OECD countries is at its highest level for the past half century. The average income of the richest 10% of the population is about nine times that of the poorest 10% across the OECD, up from seven times 25 years ago.

Inequality is even more pronounced as between the global North and the global South, although the wealthiest continue to prosper in all countries (Lakner & Milanovic 2016).

Problematically, inequality is not being tackled at the nation-state level through progressive taxation or increasing investments in education and other social goods. Instead, the typical response of many governments has been to reduce taxes for the rich, reduce investment in education and to cut benefits. Austerity measures to repay sovereign debts, often accrued during bank bailouts, are aimed at welfare and other measures that disproportionally affect the poorest. Because governments identify capital as the source of value, the wealthy qua investors and property owners, have enjoyed tax and other benefits. Governments are averse to governing, preferring to outsource their public duty to provide services to profit-driven companies who do not owe legal duties to the public. As a weak alternative to this duty, the OECD's unenforceable Principles of Corporate Governance recommends that where public functions have been "delegated to non-public bodies . . . the governance structure of any such delegated institutions should be transparent and encompass the public interest" (G20/OECD 2015: 15).

Conclusion: reform and the Marxian framework

The company's success as a legal institutional form lies in its superior mechanisms for organizing large-scale production and disciplining labor, and its ability to grow quickly through, for example, mergers, making it difficult for new capitals or smaller capitals to compete. This is particularly so in established industries although less so for innovative/disruptive technologies.

When large corporations with public stock emerge, they dominate access to credit that enables the centralization of ownership *and* control. Once capital in the company is able to act as money capital, the corporate form enables capital's destructive and parasitic tendencies. In so doing, the large corporation transforms production into speculation and heralds a new degenerative period of capitalism.

All capitalist extraction of value is built around the ability of capital to capture value from labor. Company law facilitates this by reifying this exploitative relationship as a transferable, fungible property form, the share—a perpetual title to the portion of labor's unpaid time. This process obfuscates the conflict between labor and capital. Moreover, capitals' ownership of shares designates a legal entitlement to have corporate activities and management decision-making oriented around delivering returns on their investment.

Political polices can provide greater compensation to labor in the form of welfare provisions and in the protection of organized labor groups, as they did to a greater extent in the post-war period. The law can require companies to protect corporate assets. However, in the current neoliberal period these parasitic strategies to counter falling growth and profit rates have been enabled and even encouraged. The result is that the snake is eating its own tail, as companies borrow to pay shareholders through share repurchases.

Reforms that curtail the legal powers of shareholders in the corporation are needed to protect the social production of society now dominated by the corporate form. Currently, company law empowers *shareholders* to dictate the productive capacity of society. Shareholders can, and do, sell off corporate assets and put labor out of work. Private equity purchases of companies are on the rise as the value of corporate assets exceeds the profit they can generate (Flood 2015). Shareholders can insist on mergers that are lucrative only for themselves and detrimental to employees and the community while the law (in the UK at least) imposes no fiduciary duties on them.

However, radical reform in company law has been dominated by progressive thought rather than a more dynamic and accurate Marxian framework. Beginning with Veblen and centering primarily around Adolf Berle, progressivism is marred by an inaccurate belief that shareholders do not and cannot exercise substantial control in the company. Veblen saw the role of shareholders as exploitative but passive in all but a concern for profit. They were 'absentee owners' purchasing shares in institutions purely for financial return (Veblen [1923] 1997: 330). The large public company allowed shareholders to absolve themselves from responsibility or "personal relation with the property which he owns and from which he derives an income" (Veblen [1923] 1997: 330). Problematically, although shareholders may bear little interest or knowledge of the production process from which they derive their income, it is their desire to 'make money,' which determines what that productive unit does (Veblen [1923] 1997: 211). Their interests do not necessarily coincide with the provision of useful and efficiently made things to society. This view is, of course, closer to Marx's own. However, Berle's (more popular) development on this theme was to view the increased share dispersal in large corporations as creating a new form of organization in which shareholders were entirely passive because they could no longer exercise control over management. Berle was largely concerned that as those who were left in control of the corporation were not property holders, they might have different motivations when governing the corporation. Possession and power, under the corporation, become divorced from ownership "as the corporation now emerges as the owner of the property" and as managers possess and control its activities (Berle 1959: 61). However, in *The Modern Corporation and Private Property* Berle & Means (1932) examined the socially progressive potential of a company free from shareholder demands and thus capable of exercising corporate decision-making in the interests of the wider community. They saw wider social changes, such as empowered labor unions as providing the necessary bulwark against overly powerful managers. Given the right incentives and controls, corporate managers as trained bureaucrats could guide the economy to a more socialized and egalitarian form.

Progressive thought, therefore, has centered on the issue of management accountability and the promotion of such strategies as improving fiduciary duties so that management makes more socially progressive decisions. Shareholders' possible malign influence is discounted as they are thought to be dispersed and powerless. Moreover some progressives have argued for more control rights for long-term shareholders who are reconceived as a benign force as against short-term shareholders like hedge funds. However, Marxians have been keen to emphasize that shareholder control is almost always malign. They have shown that increased share dispersal has actually enabled the centralization of capital around a small group of global investors (De Vroey 1975). They have shown that shareholder control, particularly when centralized and represented by finance, operates parasitically, demanding returns regardless of whether this destroys the productive company (Talbot 2013). Shareholders are neither powerless nor benign.

Marx's analysis provides a sound framework within which to understand the corporate economy and from which to formulate meaningful reform. He provides a theory that is essentially humanist in that it makes human endeavor the source of value. Marx and Marxian theorists have provided illustrations of the socially (and environmentally) regressive nature of shareholder-oriented goals and shareholder control rights. Thus, one of the first steps in making socially progressive reform is to make the early progressives' (inaccurate) assertion that shareholders are powerless into a legal reality.

Notes

1 The Joint Stock Companies Act 1844 enabled companies to be established through registration rather than the more expensive and complex methods of an Act of parliament or a charter granted by the state.
2 *Salomon v Salomon* [1897] AC 52.
3 A similar point has been made about pension funds today, which increase their value by investing in the stock market (Minns 1983). Pensioners ultimately benefit from the surplus extracted from unpaid labor-time, which of course includes the previous unpaid labor-time of the pensioners.
4 *Bligh v Brent* (1837) 2 Y & C 268.

References

BBC. 2015. Anglo American to cut workforce by 85,000 in restructuring. BBC, December 8. Available from http://www.bbc.co.uk/news/business-35038076 [Accessed December 8, 2015].
Berle, A.A. 1959. *Power Without Property: A New Development in American Political Economy*. New York: Harcourt, Brace and Company.
Berle, A.A. & Means G.C. 1932. *The Modern Corporation and Private Property*. London: Macmillan.
De Vroey, M. 1975. 'The corporation and the labor process: the separation of ownership from control in large corporations.' *Review of Radical Political Economics*, 7 (2): 1–10.
Duménil, G. & Lévy, D. 2005. 'Costs and benefits of neoliberalism: a class analysis,' *in*: G. Epstein (ed.), *Financialisation and the World Economy*. Cheltenham, UK: Edward Elgar, 17–46.
Farnsworth, K. 2015. The £93bn handshake: businesses pocket huge subsidies and tax breaks. *The Guardian*, July 7. Available from http://www.theguardian.com/politics/2015/jul/07/corporate-welfare-a-93bn-handshake [Accessed July 17, 2015]
Flood, C. 2015. Private equity attracts huge institutional interest. *Financial Times*, July 12. Available from http://www.ft.com/cms/s/0/cee7159e-209d-11e5-ab0f-6bb9974f25d0.html#axzz3flBLSv4e [Accessed December 12, 2015]
FTSE. 2015. Factsheet. Financial Times Stock Exchange, August. Available from http://www.ftse.com/Analytics/FactSheets/temp/505a76e8-1e06-4e0a-8e60-c5a2f85e5092.pdf [Accessed June 6, 2016]

G20/OECD. 2015. Principles of corporate governance. OECD Report to G20 Finance Ministers and Central Bank Governors. G20 Finance Ministers and Central Bank Governors Meeting 4–5 September 2015, Ankara, Turkey. Available from https://www.oecd.org/daf/ca/Corporate-Governance-Principles-ENG.pdf [Accessed July 4, 2016]

Haldane, A.G. & Madouros, V. 2011. What is the contribution of the financial sector? VoxEU, November 22. Available from http://www.voxeu.org/article/what-contribution-financial-sector [Accessed June 6, 2015]

Ireland, P., Grigg-Spall, I., & Kelly, D. 1987. 'The conceptual foundation of company law.' *Journal of Law and Society*, 14 (1): 1149–1162.

Jeffrey, J.B. 1946. 'The denomination and character of shares 1855–1885.' *Economic History Review*, 16 (1): 45–55.

Jensen, M. & Meckling, W. 1976. 'Theory of the firm: managerial behaviour, agency costs and ownership structure.' *Journal of Financial Economics*, 3 (4): 305–360.

Joyce, M., Miles, D., Scott, A., & Vayanos, D. 2012. 'Quantitative easing and unconventional monetary policy: an introduction.' *The Economic Journal*, 122 (564): 271–288.

Lakner, C. & Milanovic, B. 2016. 'Global income distribution: from the fall of the Berlin Wall to the great recession.' *The World Bank Economic Review*, 30 (2): 203–232.

Lazonick, W. [1991] 1993. *Business Organisation and the Myth of the Market Economy*. Cambridge: Cambridge University Press.

MacKenzie, D. & Millo, Y. 2003. 'Constructing a market, performing theory: the historical sociology of a financial derivatives exchange.' *American Journal of Sociology*, 109 (1), 107–145.

Maito, E.E. 2014. And yet it moves (down). *Weekly Worker*, August 14. Available from http://weeklyworker.co.uk/worker/1023/profit-debate-and-yet-it-moves-down [Accessed February 27, 2016]

Marx, K. [1867] 1954. *Capital: A Critical of Political Economy, Volume I*. Moscow: Foreign Languages Publishing House.

Marx K. [1894] 1962. *Capital: A Critique of Political Economy, Volume III*. Moscow: Foreign Languages Publishing House.

Minns, R. 1983. 'Pension funds: an alternative view.' *Capital & Class*, 7 (2): 103–115.

OECD. 2015a. Economic outlook, Volume 2015, Issue 1. OECD. Available from http://www.oecd.org/economy/outlook/Economic-Outlook-97-Lifting-investment-for-higher-sustainable-growth.pdf [Accessed December 12, 2015]

OECD. 2015b. Launch of the OECD business and finance outlook and opening high-level roundtable. OECD. Available from http://www.oecd.org/finance/launch-of-the-oecd-business-and-finance-outlook-and-opening-high-level-roundtable.htm [Accessed June 24, 2015]

OECD. 2015c. Inequality. OECD. Available from http://www.oecd.org/social/inequality.htm [Accessed June 30, 2015]

ONS. 2014. UK wages over the past four decades. Office of National Statistics, UK. Available from http://www.ons.gov.uk/ons/dcp171776_368928.pdf [Accessed July 20, 2015]

ONS. 2015. Analysis of employee contracts that do not guarantee a minimum number of hours. Office of National Statistics, UK. Available from http://www.ons.gov.uk/ons/dcp171776_396885.pdf [Accessed February 27, 2016]

Pashukanis, E.B. [1929] 1987. *Law and Marxism: A General Theory*. London: Pluto.

Polanyi, K. [1944] 2001. *The Great Transformation: The Political and Economic Origins of Our Time*. Boston: Beacon Press Books.

Shannon, H.A. 1932. 'The first five thousand limited liability companies and their duration.' *Economic History*, 2 (7): 296–424.

Talbot, L.E. 2010. 'Of insane forms: building societies from collectives to management controlled organisations to shareholder value organisations.' *Journal of Banking Regulation*, 11 (3): 223–240.

Talbot, L.E. 2013. 'Why shareholders shouldn't vote: a Marxist-progressive critique of shareholder empowerment.' *Modern Law Review*, 76 (5): 791–816.

Talbot, L.E. 2015. *Critical Company Law*, 2nd edn. London: Routledge.

Veblen, T. [1923] 1997. *Absentee Ownership Business Enterprise in Recent Times: The Case of America*. London: Transaction Publishers.

Williston, S. 1888. 'History of the law of business corporations before 1800: part II.' *Harvard Law Review*, 2 (4): 149–166.

17

Money and monetary regimes[1]

Pavlina R. Tcherneva

Introduction

Few institutions are as important to human welfare as that of money. Fewer still are as grossly misunderstood. Our knowledge and understanding of what money is, where it comes from, and what it does, is littered with pervasive myths.[2] Among these myths are: (i) that money is a creature of the market born out of the necessity to facilitate barter; (ii) that money is an object, usually of some intrinsic value (derived from precious metals) that is easily transportable and divisible; and (iii) that in and of itself, money has little economic significance (it is 'neutral'), thus serving only to simplify transactions but leaving employment, consumption, and investment decisions unaffected.

These myths pervading mainstream economic theory are known as the 'metallist view' of money (Goodhart 1998). They lead to several problematic assumptions and methodological practices within economics. First, since money is considered to be a market phenomenon, the state's control over the monetary system is treated as a significant market intervention that reduces market efficiency.[3] Second, if money is an object of intrinsic metallic value, it is assumed to be inherently scarce. Due to this scarcity, it is argued that government spending crowds out private consumption and investment. Additionally, the state's monopoly power over the currency issue is seen as a consequence of the state's appropriation of private monies that must be constrained at all costs, as the state (it is claimed) has the perverse incentive to overspend and debase the currency. Finally, because money is 'neutral,' conventional economic models are entirely void of money, finance, debt, or default.

Although the metallist view of the origins of money dominates mainstream economics, it finds no support in the academic literature from history, anthropology, numismatics, sociology, Assyriology, religion, or other disciplines. Debunking the conventional view is crucial, as it will upend all of the above propositions and illuminate the modern monetary system in ways the conventional view cannot.

This chapter presents a historically grounded analysis of the origins of money in the Western world, to illustrate that money predates markets. Not only is it *not* a 'creature of the market,' but a strong case can be made that money is instead a 'creature of the state,' however broadly defined. This proposition stands at the heart of the chartalist (or 'modern money') approach to money.

This chapter extends an earlier analysis of chartalism (Tcherneva 2006), and defines money as a *power* relation of a specific kind, namely a social credit-debt relation, that is codified by some authority or institution of power—be it an ancient religious authority, tribal chief, or an early administrative body, such as a Mesopotamian palace or a Greek polis, and later a monarchy, colonial power, or a modern nation state.

On money and power

A historical journey through the origins of money indicates that it is first and foremost a social relationship. More precisely, it is a power credit-debt relation, whereby the indebted party issues a liability that is held by the creditor as an asset. Behind this social relation, one can find various social power relations that codify human behavior in the specific historical context, and cultural and religious norms that govern the process of social provisioning.

There are several accounts of the historical origins of money. Economists commit a basic error when they conflate the origins of money with the origins of coinage (Innes 1913: 394; Knapp [1924] 1973: 1). The story of money's emergence from some hypothetical market exchange based on barter relationships finds no support in any other discipline outside of economics.

It is a well-established fact that money predates minting by nearly 3,000 years. Clay tablets (the earliest discovered forms of money) and various other objects that bear no 'intrinsic' value have circulated for thousands of years before the emergence of coinage or trade.[4] Indeed, clay tablets are themselves early checks or balance sheets, where the markings on the tablet specify how the debt can be extinguished (for example, a king's check would be inscribed 'Say to NN to give X to the bearer'), the collateral for the debt (someone's son or daughter), or the terms of debt slavery and bankruptcy.

Assyriologists trace the origins of money to the Mesopotamian temples and palaces, which developed an elaborate system of internal accounting of credits and debts (Hudson 2003). These large public institutions played a key role in establishing a general unit of account and store of value (initially for internal record keeping but also for administering prices). Money, in a sense, evolved as a *public good* introduced by public institutions in the process of standardizing prices and weights.

There is evidence that money also originated in ancient penal systems, which instituted compensation schedules of fines, similar to *wergild*, as a means of settling one's debt for inflicted wrongdoing on an injured party (Grierson 1997; Goodhart 1998; Wray 1998). These debts were settled according to a complex system of disbursements, which were eventually centralized into payments to the state for crimes. Subsequently, the central authority (be it a religious body, a tribal chief, or a political organization) added various fines, dues, fees, and taxes to the list of compulsory obligations of the population.

These two stories are not mutually exclusive. Since a system of debts for social transgressions existed in pre-Mesopotamian societies, it is highly likely that the measurement of social obligations (debts) was also used to measure equivalencies between commodities (Ingham 2004: 91). Henry's (2004) analysis of ancient Egypt also bridges the two accounts.

In Egypt, as in Mesopotamia, money emerged from the necessity of the ruling class to maintain accounts of agricultural crops and accumulated surpluses, but it also served as a means of accounting for payment of levies, foreign tributes, and tribal obligations to the kings and priests.[5] Henry (2004) argues that before societies were able to produce surplus, they had no use for money. Indeed, a substantial transformation of social relations from an egalitarian tribal society to one that is stratified and hierarchical was needed before money emerged. Once agricultural developments generated the economic surplus, taxation was used by authorities as a method of transferring part of that surplus (the real resources) from the population to the palaces. The central authority (the king) levied taxes on the population and determined how they could be settled, by establishing the unit of account used to denominate all debts to the state.

One of these units of account in the Old Kingdom was the *deben*, but no *debens* ever changed hands. It was purely a virtual and abstract measure for standardizing weights and prices, much like in the Mesopotamian palaces, though many different things represented one *deben*—wheat, copper, labor, etc. That is, once the unit of account was established, many 'things' measured in *debens* started circulating as the means of payment.

Graeber (2011) makes a compelling case that indeed, for most of human history, money has been 'virtual.' Today, the 'dollar' is also an abstract unit of measure and there are many things that answer to the name 'dollar'—notes, coins, and (mostly) electronic digits. Keynes also recognized that money is first and foremost a virtual state-administered unit of account, where the state has been able to determine its physical form for at least 4,000 years.

> The State, therefore, comes in first of all as the authority of law which enforces the payment of the thing which corresponds to the name or description in the contract. But it comes doubly when, in addition, it claims the right to determine and declare *what thing* corresponds to the name . . . . This right is claimed by all modern States and has been so claimed for some four thousand years at least. . . . To-day all civilized money is, beyond the possibility of dispute, chartalist.
>
> *Keynes 1930: 4–5*

In Ancient Greece, as in Ancient Egypt, the emergence of money was closely tied to the need of religious authorities to control the flow of the surplus. Money in other words becomes a public mechanism of redistribution of the economic surplus and justice. Semenova (2011:ii) explains:

> [In Ancient Greece] money emerged in the context of . . . socio-economic hierarchies and inequalities. Money was first embodied in the portions of sacrificial bull's flesh distributed by religious authorities during the rituals of communal sacrificial meals. Purporting to allocate to each his 'just' and 'equal' share, the redistributive rituals created a façade of social justice and equality via the use of money.

In sum, power, taxation, and religious tributes play a crucial role in all of these accounts of the origins of money. Taxation is the *motor* behind the transfer of real resources from subjects to authority, while money is the *vehicle*. The resource transfer was partly to provision the authority itself, and partly to allow the authority to redistribute the surplus to its subjects more 'equitably,' within the context of the prevailing cultural and religious social mores. In a sense, money is a *creature of the state, a public good*, and a *redistributive mechanism* employed by that state for good or ill.

On the myth of barter

In contrast to the historical account above, mainstream economists embrace the pervasive but historically unsubstantiated myth of barter.[6] Indeed, the definitive work from Cambridge anthropologist Caroline Humphrey (1985: 48) is steadfast in its conclusion: "No example of a barter economy, pure and simple, has ever been described, let alone the emergence from it of money; all available ethnography suggests that there never has been such a thing."

Barter arrangements of course did exist, but they were never a *coordinating mechanism* for social provisioning in any society. Graeber (2011: 37) suggests that barter itself is most likely a modern

Pavlina R. Tcherneva

and temporary phenomenon, observed among people familiar with the use of money, but for one reason or another, experiencing a breakdown in those monetary arrangements.

Debunking the myth of barter is key as it disproves the notion that money emerges from voluntary market transactions where agents engage in mutually beneficial exchange, where no single agent has any power over the other, and where the state introduces sizable market imperfection and inefficiencies. Because money is a social power relation, the socially embedded story of money tells us that it emerges as a *public good*, within the complexity of historically specific social debt obligations, whereby an authority serves as the arbiter of private and public debts, the agency which determines the unit of account (how all debts will be measured), and the enforcer of those debt settlements. That authority is the institution that imposes non-reciprocal obligations on the population and that assumes a redistributive role—in some cases in the interest of 'fairness' and 'justice,' while in other cases in the interest of colonization and slavery (more below). Placing power, authority, or some social agency that administers and enforces monetary debt arrangements at the center of the history of money also helps us understand modern monetary systems, and the powers and responsibilities of modern nation states to fulfill their modern redistributive functions.

This historical record is important because it: (i) delineates the nature of money as a social debt relationship; (ii) stresses the role of public institutions in the establishment of a standard unit of account by codifying accounting schemes, price lists, and private and public debts; (iii) shows that in all cases money was a pre-market phenomenon, representing initially an abstract unit of account and means of payment during a complex process of social provisioning, and only later a generalized medium of exchange; and (iv) underscores its inherent quality as a vehicle of redistribution. The next task is to use this historical understanding to illuminate modern monetary regimes and the policy space available for pursuing economic goals.

Modern money

The precise origins of money will never be known to us; what we do know is that it cannot be understood outside the powers of some authority or arbiter. In the modern context, however, money is not only a *public good*, but also a simple *public monopoly*. Modern nation states, like their ancient counterparts, also impose compulsory debts on the population and determine how they will be settled; now, however, they also have the exclusive power to issue the very thing (physical currency and electronic reserves) that settles those debt obligations (even if they abdicate this power, as is the case in some countries today). Private sector attempts to interfere with this power (for example through counterfeiting) are some of the most heavily prosecuted private offenses (more below).

Taxes

In the modern context, taxes assume an additional role. They still serve as an instrument of transferring real resources from the private to the public sector, but the way this transfer occurs is by creating demand for government-issued fiat currency. Modern governments settle their debts and pay for their expenditures by issuing their own liabilities—reserves, notes, coins, and government checks. The private sector, facing a series of compulsory obligations to the state, denominated in the state-administered and state-issued unit of account, must obtain the currency before it can settle its debts. Obviously, the issuer (the government) cannot collect taxes in currency it has not *already* issued. The way the private sector obtains currency from the issuer is by offering labor, goods, and services for sale to the government, paid in state currency.

In other words, in the modern context, taxes have two functions. First, they create demand for otherwise worthless paper currency (Mosler 1997–98; Wray 1998). Second, they serve as a means of provisioning the government in *real*, not in *financial*, terms. A monopoly currency issuer is never financially constrained by tax collections, as it always pays by issuing more of its own liabilities. It can spend as much currency/reserves as it wishes, so long as there are real goods and services for sale. And the state cannot possibly collect currency through taxes, before it has provided it through spending. The state does not need 'tax money' to spend; it needs real resources. A modern nation state in particular needs an army, public school teachers, police force, food inspectors, and any other resources necessary to fulfill their public purpose. In a way, the modern state, as in Ancient Greece, continues to serve a redistributive function in the economy, where it collects real resources (labor) from the private sector, and then redistributes them back to the private sector 'more equitably,' in the form of infrastructure, public education, government research and development, and via any other social welfare functions it is asked to fulfill by voters. The role of taxation in modern market economies remains the same as in ancient times: it is not a 'funding mechanism,' but a 'real resource transfer mechanism.'

On launching a new currency

Since taxes create demand for the currency, they have also been used as vehicle for launching new currencies. This can occur even in cases when the sovereign government is unable to fulfill its duties to the public by using its own national currency. For example, throughout the 1990s, Argentina operated under a monetary regime called a currency board, which required the government to maintain a fixed exchange rate with the US dollar, thereby abdicating monetary sovereignty and subjecting public spending decisions to the maintenance of the peg.

Such an arrangement severely constrains the ability of the government to spend national currency (pesos, in this case). New pesos in Argentina could be put in circulation only after the acquisition of foreign exchange (US dollars) held in Central Bank coffers. Argentina's government had to either earn or borrow dollars, before increasing its spending in pesos. As a net importer, Argentina bled US dollars throughout the 1990s, thereby reducing the amount of pesos in circulation, asphyxiating the economy and plunging it into what is now known as Argentina's 'lost decade.'

To deal with this economic crisis, Argentina's provinces used their constitutional power to issue notes, thereby circumventing the problem of a national currency shortage. The new notes (*patacones* or *lecops*, for example) began circulating overnight, even though the Argentinians themselves did not 'trust' the currency and there were no legal tender laws that required people to use it. Instead, the provinces allowed the public to pay its state taxes and public utility bills in the new notes, and in turn paid state employees with the new script. Taxes were a sufficient condition to create demand for a new fiat currency, and the provinces had to spend the currency *before* they could collect it in taxes. Taxes did not finance these provinces, instead they gave states more policy space to spend and conduct internal policy by launching these new currencies. The notes quickly circulated throughout the private economy and were used until the currency board was abandoned, monetary sovereignty in pesos was restored, and the Argentine government embarked on aggressive expansionary economic policy. This episode demonstrates that taxes do not finance the spending of the issuer of the currency; instead they serve as an effective vehicle for launching that new currency.

Taxes are also a powerful coercive mechanism. In Africa, for example, newly imposed head taxes compelled the colonized African tribes and communities to use the currency of the colonial powers, and became another method of colonialization and resource extraction (Rodney 1972;

Ake 1981). While the local population had previously no use for the colonial currency, with the imposition of taxes on the local population denominated in British pounds, French francs, or other colonial currency, tribes began to sell crops and labor in exchange for the colonial currency to settle the new tax obligation. It is, therefore, no surprise that the process of independence of any nation from colonial rule has been accompanied with the implementation of a new independent national currency, or with the assumption of full sovereign control over an existing national currency.

Monetary sovereignty as a prerequisite for political sovereignty

Let us consider the example of the former British colonies. As the British Empire began dissolving, newly independent nations began acquiring full monetary sovereignty. India, for instance, had been issuing its own notes—rupees—since 1862 (while still under British rule), but for most of that period up until independence, the monopoly note issue in India operated like a currency board (Weintraub & Schuler 2013). Only after independence did India assume full sovereign control over the rupee. Similarly, Australian colonies gradually began issuing some notes although they were all pegged to the British pound. The peg continued after the creation of the Federation in 1901 and up until the time the government assumed control over all currency matters and began issuing the Australian pound in 1910. Full independence required independent monetary sovereignty which Australia finally achieved in the period between the two world wars.

In a sense, the colonies remained tethered to the British Empire, through currency boards and hard peg currency arrangements keeping them dependent on monetary policy in the United Kingdom. In order to expand the domestic money supply, colonies had to export real goods and services to the former colonial power in exchange for the foreign currency (British pounds) against which they were pegged.

In a sense, the currency board was a method of continued colonial exploitation—a continued extraction of real resources and real goods and services, in exchange for foreign reserves. The board severely constrained the abilities of independent nations to conduct internal macroeconomic policy, so long as they promised convertibility of their national currencies into another. To complete the process of independence, colonies understood that monetary sovereignty was indispensable. Overtime, they abandoned these currency regimes (hard pegs and currency boards) and expanded the policy space to implement domestic policy.

Counterfeiting

The case of the American colonies' pursuit of independence from British rule is similar in many ways—having political sovereignty necessarily meant having monetary sovereignty as well. But this case is also instructive for another reason—it sheds new light on our understanding of money as a creature of the state by examining private sector financial fraud and counterfeiting.

Economists have no theory of counterfeiting. Because money is seen as a medium of exchange emerging from barter, the very limited writing on counterfeiting only examines the question of whether it may be 'efficient' (Kultti 1996). In general, counterfeiting is treated as a marginal and unimportant phenomenon that is not theorized.

The process of political independence of the American colonies went hand in hand with the process of monetary independence. As soon as the colonies declared independence and started the Revolutionary War, they began issuing their own currency to finance the war effort. The over-issuance of continentals is often used as an example of currency mismanagement by governments, leading to the swift depreciation of fiat currency from overspending. While it is true that financing the Revolutionary War required colonies to increase their spending at a rapid rate, a much under-appreciated fact is that the depreciation was much more the result of counterfeiting than overspending.[7]

Currency issue in the American colonies began 85 years before independence, as the colonies understood the need to emit the very thing that circulated within the colony for settlement of private and public debts (Rhodes 2012). These currency experiments worked reasonably well and gave the colonies significant economic independence, which prompted the British Empire to retaliate with the Currency Acts of 1751 and 1764, prohibiting the issue of new currency by the colonies.

As soon as the Revolutionary War was declared, colonies began to issue notes again, which they believed was their sovereign right. Several months before the war, however, British forces as well as crown loyalists in the Americas flooded the colonies with counterfeit notes. As Rhodes (2012: 35) put it, "[o]n the Eve of the Revolution, American counterfeiting had surpassed British imperialism as the No. 1 threat to Colonial currency."

After independence, there were various attempts to launch a unified national exclusive currency that failed when President Jackson vetoed the recharter of the Second Bank of the United States. Simultaneously, notes issued by individual states proliferated; so did private counterfeiting. There were as many as 10,000 different kinds of state-chartered notes, 6,000 of which were regularly falsified (Rhodes 2012: 35). When Lincoln's Legal Tender Act of 1862 designated the greenback as the national currency, counterfeiting remained widespread, even though it now carried significantly greater risks. The American colonies initially failed to crack down on Northern printers, but eventually the Treasury (established in 1789) began prosecuting counterfeiting of national currency with the full force of the law. It took a while to perfect the law enforcement process. In 1865, the Secret Service authorized by Lincoln was created precisely to defend this exclusive sovereign power to issue the national currency, and was charged with cracking down on counterfeiting. Benjamin Franklin recognized that, as much as issuing one's own currency is a prerequisite for sovereignty and independent internal policy, counterfeiting was an act of war against the sovereign (Rhodes 2012: 34). Sabotaging the exclusive prerogative of the government to issue the currency was done by devaluing it via massive over-issuance and by the inability to distinguish between the sovereign-issued and counterfeit notes.

Counterfeiting as an act of conflict has been used in other cases. Such are the cases of government-sponsored counterfeiting of US dollars under Stalin during the period between the two world wars (Krivitsky 2011), under Hitler during the Second World War (Operation Bernhard, forging British notes), and by the US during the Vietnam War (Asselin 2013: 189).

Revisiting stories of counterfeiting makes for tantalizing reading, but they are also theoretically important. As long as money has existed, so has counterfeiting. Numismatic work shows that counterfeiting of coins emerged as soon as the oldest coin was struck in Lydia (seventh century BCE) via clipping, shaving off, or melting, and all were punishable by death.

Counterfeiting was a problem in non-metallic money too. Indeed, capital punishment for forgery of bank notes was part of the legal code in England as late as the eighteenth century (Desan 2015). This is why, for example, the split tally stick had such an original design to avoid it. In medieval Europe, taxes were often levied in the form of wooden tallies, whereby the payments were recorded with notches on the stick that was then split in half (length-wise). This way the two halves both recorded the same notches, and the tax-paying serf kept one as proof of his tax payment. Clay tablets were also difficult to forge, as they represented detailed and complex schedules of tax assessments and payments, other debt obligations, and price equivalences. But it is likely that there have been attempts to tamper with their value as well, which necessitated the creation of the *bulla* (a seal where clay tokens were stored). The image (face value) of the clay tokens was often imprinted on the wet surface of the clay seal (the *bulla*) before it dried, to ensure that once the seal was broken to make payment, the value contained inside matched exactly the value claimed by the payee.

In other words, for most of known history, as long as money has existed as a creature of the state, private interests have wanted to manipulate its value; that is, a history of counterfeiting is a history of money as a creature of the state. It is a history of the ability of an authority to impose non-reciprocal obligations, set the unit of account for their payment, and enforce them. Conventional economic theory does not recognize money as a creature of the state. Consequently, it has under-theorized the importance of monetary sovereignty. Conventional economists see counterfeiting as an irregularity from generally smooth functioning markets (Kultti 1996). If, however, money is correctly considered as a creature of the state, then counterfeiting becomes a pervasive private sector market phenomenon that requires theorization. And as long as money has been a public good, the responsibility for both maintaining its purchasing power and for providing it in a manner consistent with domestic goals has rested with the government.

Hierarchy of money

The focus so far has been on state-issued liabilities and state-administered units of account. However, it is important to note that, since money is a debt or IOU, anyone can issue IOUs (Minsky 1986). The problem, as Minsky argued, is to get it accepted. Indeed, in modern capitalist economies, private agents finance their activities with position-making instruments—privately issued liabilities which have varied degrees of acceptability. Banks create bank money at the stroke of a pen via the process of lending. As the endogenous approach to money stresses, loans create deposits, which in the aggregate create purchasing power from private credit. In modern financial systems, Central Banks stand behind the liabilities of the banking sector to maintain a sound payments system and accept bank liabilities for payment of taxes, thereby making them as equally acceptable, as state-issued liabilities. The chartalist approach stresses that the multitude of private sector liabilities can be ranked in a hierarchical fashion, whereby the most acceptable and liquid forms of debt sit atop the money pyramid (Bell 2001) (see Figure 17.1).

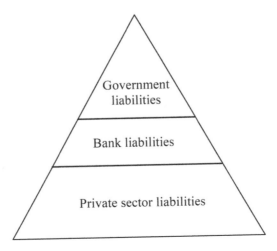

Figure 17.1 The hierarchy of money

The most important feature of this pyramid is that *every* economic unit, except the government, must deliver a third party's IOU (that sits somewhere higher in the pyramid) to settle its debt obligations. Firms and households settle their debts by delivering checks (bank liabilities) or notes and coins (Central Bank or Treasury liabilities). Banks settle debts among each other by delivering reserves (Central Bank's liabilities). The government is the *only* economic unit that settles its own debts by issuing more of its *own* liabilities. The state issues several types of liabilities: some are issued by its monetary agency (notes and reserves) and others are issued by its fiscal agency (coins, Treasury checks, and Treasury securities). The issue of each of these liabilities is the exclusive sovereign monopoly power of the state. The payment of one liability (Treasury check or Treasury security, for example) takes place when the state delivers another one of its liabilities (reserves).

While private contracts and debts clear in the state-issued unit of account (reserves), it is private finance that drives the capital development of modern market economies. It is also private finance that causes frequent financial and economic instability (Minsky 1986). Nevertheless, the final responsibility for the stability of the financial system rests with the state.

A capitalist system is a financial system, argued Minsky (1986). It is an evolving and innovating system, continuously looking for new profit opportunities by creating markets for new private sector liabilities. Banks create new position-making instruments, either for the purpose of financing the capital development of the economy or for financing 'finance.' The process of funding the acquisition of real or financial assets adds another dimension of instability to the capitalist system, and the process of financial innovation is often accompanied by creative accounting practices and fraud.

From this vantage point, as legal theories of finance illustrate, financial markets are essentially hybrid systems (neither private nor public), belonging neither purely to the state nor purely to the market. However, the law and its enforcement rest with the state, as private and public debt commitments are enshrined in law (legal contracts). Pistor (2013) argues that in the throes of a financial crisis, when the full enforcement of legal commitments will result in the self-destruction of the financial system, the full force of the law is suspended to ensure the survival of the financial system and prevailing financial relations. 'Where law is elastic,' she states, 'power becomes salient' (Pistor 2013: 29).

When Knapp proclaimed that 'money is a creature of law' ([1924] 1973: 1), he did not say that 'money is a creature of legal tender law' (as in Schumpeter 1954: 1090). In fact, Knapp explicitly rejected such an interpretation. Money is a creature of law because the state is the adjudicator and enforcer of non-reciprocal obligations and other private sector contracts.

Modern monetary regimes

'One nation, one currency' is the norm in modern economies (Goodhart 1998), where nation states assume full sovereign monopoly control over the currency issue. We nevertheless observe multiple cases of varying degrees of sovereignty, where states voluntarily impose on themselves different monetary restrictions or abdicate their monetary sovereignty altogether. Thus, we can classify monetary regimes according to different degrees of monetary sovereignty. At one end of the spectrum are fully sovereign monetary regimes. These are cases where the state issues non-convertible freely floating national currency and the two agencies of government—the Central Bank and the Treasury (or Ministry of Finance)—coordinate to clear government payments and guarantee all state liabilities that are denominated in the domestic currency. In these cases, the ability to execute internal domestic policy does not depend on the shortage of government finance, but on political considerations and the availability of *real domestic* resources that can be transferred

Pavlina R. Tcherneva

to the public sector for the purposes of achieving these objectives.[8] It must be noted that even fully sovereign monetary regimes have institutional peculiarities—laws and practices that may constrain government spending according to some self-imposed or legacy rules (for example, debt ceiling requirements in the US, or the inability of the Treasury to run an overdraft at its account at the Federal Reserve). But even in these cases, the rules may be suspended or circumvented, when the policy priorities dictate that the government must spend beyond these artificial constraints (think of the Federal Reserve creating a 'Treasury supplement'—essentially another account for the Treasury—at the stroke of a pen after the 2008 financial crisis, or of the routine practice of raising the debt limit in the US on an as-needed basis, political wrangling notwithstanding).

Other countries, however, face hard financial constraints in executing domestic policy. At the other end of the spectrum are countries that have completely abdicated monetary sovereignty, thus giving up the right to issue and manage their own national currency. This is the case of dollarized nations (Ecuador and small Caribbean nations, for example) and member states in the European Monetary Union. In both cases, relinquishing monetary sovereignty has transformed those countries from 'currency issuers' into 'currency users.'

To spend, the government of Ecuador must either earn or borrow dollars first. In this case, tax collections *do* raise revenue for the government. As an oil-exporting nation, Ecuador has not yet faced a dollar shortage, even though it has pursued aggressive development and pro-growth policies, while simultaneously strengthening the welfare safety net. But with a gradual liberalization of financial markets and an increased standard of living in Ecuador, one can envision a future when the country becomes a net importer, losing foreign exchange (dollars) faster than it earns it, and thereby experiencing a monetary contraction and an overall deflationary environment.

This of course is the case in the periphery countries of the Eurozone (EZ). They gave up their national currencies upon joining the monetary union. The situation is similar to that of Ecuador because, to conduct expansionary domestic policy, EZ governments must earn or borrow euros first. Net exports become the main channel for increasing a country's euro holdings (a strategy that describes the case of Germany, for example). But should a nation find itself in a net importing position, thereby losing euro reserves (as is the case in the periphery), the only way to fund government programs is by either borrowing euros, by raising domestic taxes for revenue, or by cutting those programs. The latter two mechanisms have a contractionary effect, which undermines a government's ability to pursue its policy agenda further. The former (raising revenue through borrowing) puts the periphery countries at the mercy of private markets' willingness to finance these already heavily indebted governments. It also puts the periphery countries in a vicious Ponzi finance cycle, where more heavily indebted nations face rising costs of borrowing, thereby increasing their overall indebtedness, while further undermining their ability to repay their debt.

The Eurozone has tried to 'solve' its economic problems by becoming a net exporter to the rest of the world. It is well understood that net exports cannot be a global solution to economic problems (as there must be net importers too), but within the Eurozone itself, it is highly likely that there will always be some countries that are in a net importing position.

The ECB is prohibited from financing Eurozone members by purchasing their government debt (the way the Bank of Japan or the Bank of England do, for example). Therefore, the Eurozone lacks a fundamental mechanism for executing independent macroeconomic policy. Thus, member countries have given up an unprecedented policy space to pursue domestic priorities, including the maintenance of some basic public sector functions or the implementation of pro-growth stimulus policies as needed. At the same time, the Eurozone as a whole lacks a central fiscal mechanism to conduct euro-wide economic policy, as is normally the case in other monetary unions with a full monetary sovereignty (US, Canada, or Australia).

Non-convertible sovereign free float (and dirty float) Pegged float (crawling band, crawling peg, horizontal band) Fixed exchange rates Currency board Dollarization Monetary union	Greatest policy space Smallest policy space

Figure 17.2 Modern monetary regimes and policy space

Countries that fall between the two extremes (full monetary sovereignty and no monetary sovereignty) will have different degrees of policy space available to them. They can be ranked as follows, from the most to the least amount of policy space: (i) *non-convertible freely floating sovereign currency regimes* as discussed above (US, Japan, UK, Canada, most countries in the world). In practice, these are often managed or dirty float systems, as Central Banks intervene in currency markets; (ii) *pegged floats*, where the domestic currency is pegged to a foreign currency at a specific value or within a band. These are either fixed or periodically adjusted, and vary from *crawling bands* to *crawling pegs* to *pegged within a horizontal band*; (iii) *fixed exchange rate regimes*, which promise direct convertibility into a foreign currency at a predetermined rate; (iv) *currency boards*: a much stricter form of fixed exchange rate system, where the monetary authority operates on auto-pilot to fulfill absolute and unlimited convertibility between its notes and the foreign currency; and, finally, (v) *dollarization* and (vi) *monetary unions*. (See Figure 17.2.)

As long as a nation commits to convertibility, it will depend (to varying degrees) on acquiring foreign currencies (foreign reserves) for expanding the domestic issue. The goal of maintaining a stable exchange rate with the foreign currency will often conflict with other policy objectives and thus impede efforts to deal with recessions or bank crises. For this reason, fixed exchange rate regimes are often abandoned in the middle of severe economic and financial crises, freeing additional policy space to conduct independent macroeconomic stabilization monetary or fiscal policy.

In fully sovereign monetary regimes, however, the economic possibilities facing a nation with a freely floating non-convertible national currency are constrained largely by political considerations and the availability of *real* resources to achieve those priorities, not by the availability of money.

The final issue to address, then, is how can this policy space be used by a monetarily sovereign government for achieving various policy goals? The answer to the question will also help debunk the final of the three myths introduced at the beginning of this chapter, namely that money is neutral and that, in and of itself, it does not affect employment and production decisions.

Money matters

A discussion of the full range of economic possibilities under sovereign monetary regimes is beyond the scope of this chapter. We will single out one problem that merits consideration, as it is pervasive, persistent, and pernicious—the problem of unemployment. Countries with different degrees of monetary sovereignty have different capacities to address this problem. But what is frequently overlooked is that unemployment is itself a result of current monetary arrangements.

Unemployment is a monetary phenomenon. From the viewpoint of firms, it means that, in the aggregate, expected costs and proceeds do not justify the employment of any more individual workers than firms are already employing. This is the effective demand problem identified by Keynes (1936). Note that effective demand can still be deficient (in the sense that profit expectations do not warrant any more hiring) even in a very strong economy. Firms are simply not in the business of providing jobs for all. They can be neither expected nor required to attain and maintain full employment over the long-run.

Providing full employment is the responsibility of government, because 'unemployment' is, to some extent, created by government. From the viewpoint of households, unemployment is evidence of someone wanting but not being able to obtain the currency. Recall that the tax which creates demand for the currency immediately creates unemployment. The population is required to fulfill a non-reciprocal obligation with the currency it does not have. The source of that currency is government. Thus the private sector provides real goods and services (labor) to government in exchange for that currency. The tax creates demand for government-issued money by creating unemployment in that currency (that is, labor which seeks remuneration). It is therefore incumbent on the monopoly issuer to provide its currency in a manner that is consistent with the objectives of full employment and price stability.

Recall that the government is also responsible for assuring that the currency is sound. Modern currencies are in part 'valuable' because the state keeps them in a constant state of scarcity, as evidenced by mass unemployment. But there is an alternative: the state can provide its currency in a manner that allows people to freely access it, while ensuring some internally stable floor for its value (Mosler 1997–98).

As the monopoly issuer of the currency, the state has the privilege of setting the prices for the goods and services it receives in exchange for the currency. But the state need not set all prices. It is sufficient to fix only one of them (the price of labor, for example) to anchor the value of its currency. Chartalists suggest that an ongoing public program that offers employment to anyone ready, willing, and able to work at a base wage can do the job (see Kaboub (2007) for the employer of last resort, job guarantee, and buffer stock employment proposals). Such a program will fluctuate counter-cyclically with the business cycle—expanding as private business hiring declines and shrinking as private sector employment picks up. The base wage will become the nominal anchor that establishes a conversion rate between the currency and labor.

While currency values are themselves determined in a complex manner, they essentially reflect what one can buy with the currency. The hourly wage of the buffer stock program pins down a basic conversion rate between labor and the currency. In other words, say, a $10/hour wage would anchor the currency in labor power and set the value of the dollar to be equal to six minutes of work. If the wage is doubled, then as a benchmark, one dollar will exchange for three minutes of work (or will erode in value by half). So when the emitter of the currency (the government) sets the exchange rate between the currency and the labor in the counter-cyclical buffer stock pool, it helps stabilize the value of its currency (for details see Mosler 1997–98; Wray 1998; Tcherneva 2012).

Freely floating non-convertible currencies today have no equivalent anchors. A full discussion of such a program is beyond the scope of this chapter. Our aim is merely to point out that in a world where the currency is a simple public monopoly: (i) unemployment is evidence that the currency is in short supply; (ii) taxes themselves create unemployment by creating private demand for the monopolist's currency; (iii) the monopolist has the power to set a conversion rate between its currency and labor hours; (iv) the monopolist can provide the currency on as-needed basis by maintaining the internal anchor; and (v) the buffer stock employment program can be used to create socially useful outputs, thereby allowing the monopoly currency issuer to fulfill its redistributive functions in a way that serves the public purposes.

Conclusion

This chapter began by articulating the view of money as an evolving social power relation within the process of social provisioning. The development of 'private monies' was not emphasized, not because it is unimportant (far from it), but because the role of the authority in codifying private contracts and transactions has been pervasive throughout history. From inception, money has been a 'creature of the state,' however broadly defined. The state, because of its unique power to impose compulsory obligations on its subjects and set the terms of their repayment, has always played some redistributive role in the process of social provisioning. This redistributive function is intrinsic to the state, irrespective of whether it is used for the good of the many or the good of the few.

In modern capitalist economies, the currency is a simple public monopoly and equilibrium market clearing models, based on the neutrality of money, are wholly inapplicable to the study of a monetary system. Nevertheless, pervasive mainstream economic myths about the origins and nature of money have alleged that the state's power over the monetary system is an unwarranted intrusion with significant disruptive effects. These myths have also given rise to monetary arrangements (such as currency boards or monetary unions) that radically constrain the policy options before modern nation states.

Not only cannot the birth of money be divorced from the power of the state but the entire monetary system resides within the set of rules and legal codes set forth by the state. Yet monetary regimes like the European Monetary Union have forced an incoherent division between nation states and their national currencies at great economic and human costs.

A proper understanding of the origins, role, and functions of money is essential for adequate assessment of contemporary economic problems and the policy space available to address them. It prompts us to think about the possible ways in which one could employ the monopoly powers of the state and design public policies to achieve a wide range of policy objectives, including full employment and price stability.

Notes

1 An earlier version of this chapter appeared in the *Journal of Self-Governance and Management Economics*, 2016.

2 The use of the term 'money' itself has been problematic, as it means different things to different people. Some economists use it to refer to liquidity, others treat it strictly as an object, yet others emphasize its abstract nature as unit of measure. This chapter aims to remedy this confusion.

3 See work on the inefficiency of seigniorage (Freeman 1993).

4 By 'trade' here we mean 'exchange' in the conventional sense—a market mechanism where prices serve an allocative role. Trade, in one form or another, has existed since very early times, and predates money itself. What is important about early trade is that, given available information, there was no attempt to establish 'equal' trade ratios (Henry 2004; Graeber 2011).

5 Henry (2004: 90) further adds that money cannot exist without power and authority. Societies based on hospitality and exchange simply had no use for it, while in a stratified society the ruling class is compelled to devise standard units of account, which measure not only the economic surplus collected in the form of taxes, but also the royal gifts and religious dues that were imposed on the population.

6 In the conventional view in economics, money emerges from barter as a means to efficiency solve the problem of the double coincidence of wants. Economists present these origins as a purely hypothetical, (even fictional) example of a barter system. Menger (1892) recognizes the lack of historical evidence supporting the metallist view and, therefore, posed a different question: "even if money did not originate from Barter, could it have?" He thus aimed to 'perfect' the conventional view of money by offering a mathematical solution to the hypothetical scenario of barter.

7 The Continental Congress had issued massive amount of notes to finance the War and some depreciation would have likely occurred anyway, but probably not enough to cause the total demise of the continental currency.

8 Note the emphasis on achieving *domestic* goals with *domestic real* resources. Countries like the US, which enjoy reserve-currency status, have the ability to acquire many foreign-produced real resources that countries without such a status do not. But the foregoing analysis does not depend on the reserve

currency status of a nation. 'Sovereignty' here means that the issuer of the currency cannot be forced into an involuntary default in its own currency. It also means that the sovereign *can*, irrespective of the nation's external position, employ whatever domestic resources are available for domestic goals. Resource-poor countries may not have sufficient *real* domestic resources, which may necessitate the purchase of foreign exchange, which will in turn have implications for the value of the domestic currency. But again, it will not necessitate an involuntary default in the domestic currency.

References

Ake, C. 1981. *A Political Economy of Africa*. Essex, UK: Longman Press.

Asselin, P. 2013. *Hanoi's Road to the Vietnam War: 1954–1965*. Berkeley, CA: University of California Press.

Bell, S. 2001. 'The role of the state and the hierarchy of money.' *Cambridge Journal of Economics*, 25 (2): 149–163.

Desan, C. 2015. *Making Money: Coin, Currency and the Coming of Capitalism*. Oxford, UK: Oxford University Press.

Freeman, S. 1993. The inefficiency of seigniorage from required reserves. Federal Reserve Bank of Dallas research paper 9334.

Goodhart, C.A.E. 1998. 'The two concepts of money: implications for the analysis of optimal currency areas.' *European Journal of Political Economy*, 14 (3): 407–432.

Graeber, D. 2011. *Debt: The First 5000 Years*. London: Melville House Publishing.

Grierson, P. 1997. *The Origins of Money*. London: Athlone Press.

Henry J.F. 2004. 'The social origins of money: the case of Egypt,' in: L.R. Wray (ed.), *Credit and State Theories of Money*. Cheltenham, UK: Edward Elgar, 79–98.

Hudson, M. 2003. 'The creditary/monetary debate in historical perspective,' in: S. Bell & E. Nell (eds.), *The State, the Market and the Euro*. Cheltenham, UK: Edward Elgar, 39–76.

Humphrey, C. 1985 'Barter and economic disintegration.' *Man*, New Series, 20 (1): 48–72.

Innes, A.M. 1913. 'What is money?' *Banking Law Journal*, 30 (May): 377–408.

Ingham, G. 2004. *The Nature of Money*. Cambridge, UK: Polity Press.

Kaboub, F. 2007. Employment guarantee programs: a survey of theories and policy experiences. Levy Economics Institute Working Paper No. 498. Annandale-on-Hudson, NY: The Levy Economics Institute.

Keynes, J.M. 1930. *A Treatise on Money*. London: Macmillan.

Keynes, J.M. 1936. *The General Theory of Employment, Interest and Money*. London: Macmillan.

Knapp, G.F. [1924] 1973. *The State Theory of Money*. Clifton, NY: Augustus M. Kelley.

Krivitsky, W.G. 2011. *In Stalin's Secret Service*. New York: Enigma Books.

Kultti, K. 1996. 'A monetary economy with counterfeiting.' *Journal of Economics*, 63 (2): 175–186.

Menger, C. 1892. 'On the origin of money.' *Economic Journal*, 2 (6): 239–255.

Minsky, H.P. 1986. *Stabilizing an Unstable Economy*. New Haven, CT: Yale University Press.

Mosler. W. 1997–98. 'Full employment and price stability.' *Journal of Post Keynesian Economics*, 20 (2): 167–182.

Pistor, K. 2013. 'A legal theory of finance.' *Journal of Comparative Economics*, 41 (2): 315–330.

Rhodes, K. 2012. 'The counterfeiting weapon.' *Federal Reserve Bank of Richmond, Econ Focus*, 16 (1): 34–37.

Rodney, W. 1972. *How Europe Underdeveloped Africa*. Washington, DC: Howard University Press.

Schumpeter, J.A. 1954. *History of Economic Analysis*. Oxford, UK: Oxford University Press.

Semenova, A. 2011. 'Would you barter with God? Why holy debts and not profane markets created money.' *American Journal of Economics and Sociology*, 70 (2): 376–400.

Tcherneva, P. 2006. 'Chartalism and the tax-driven approach to money,' in: P. Arestis & M. Sawyer (eds.), *Handbook of Alternative Monetary Economics*. Northampton, MA: Edward Elgar, 69–86.

Tcherneva, P. 2012. 'Employer of last resort,' in: King, J.E. (ed.), *The Elgar Companion to Post Keynesian Economics*, 2nd edn. Northampton, MA: Edward Elgar: 161–166.

Weintraub, C. & Schuler, K. 2013. 'India's Paper Currency Department (1862–1935) as a quasi currency board.' *Studies in Applied Economics*, December (9): 1–27. Available from http://krieger.jhu.edu/iae/economics/Indias_Paper_Currency_DepartmentWorkingPaper.pdf [Accessed August 16, 2015]

Wray, L.R. 1998. *Understanding Modern Money: The Key to Full Employment and Price Stability*. Cheltenham, UK: Edward Elgar.

18

Banks in developing countries

Radha Upadhyaya

Introduction

This chapter examines contending approaches to the role of banking in the financial systems of developing countries, with a particular focus on sub-Saharan Africa (SSA). The chapter begins by discussing the role that finance should play in the process of development, and continues with a discussion of the debates pertaining to the relationship of finance and development. The discussion shows that mainstream economics has focused on demonstrating a long-term correlation between finance and growth and the need for financial liberalization. Both mainstream and heterodox schools agree that financial liberalization failed to provide the perceived benefits of revenue mobilization, although they disagree on the reasons for this failure. Post-liberalization, mainstream studies have focused on understanding the level of competition within African banking sectors whereas heterodox economists have focused on the micro-finance sector with little attention to the commercial banking sector in SSA.

Studies on finance and development

The role of finance in development

The key role of financial institutions is intermediation—that is, transferring assets from savers to borrowers. Levine (1997) and Freixas & Rochet (1997) provide a review of mainstream studies on the causal link between finance and growth in terms of the functions of finance and the role of intermediaries in reducing information costs and transaction costs. Based on these theoretical and empirical links between finance and growth, it is commonly argued by mainstream economists that, due to adverse selection and moral hazard issues, information asymmetry and transactions costs can never be zero in any realistically defined financial market. Therefore, financial institutions are more efficient than individuals in transferring assets (Stiglitz & Weiss 1981).

Figure 18.1 summarizes the links between finance and growth from the mainstream perspective. It is widely agreed, especially in the mainstream tradition, that financial intermediaries reduce market frictions and provide certain functions that lead to growth. The main channels through which finance can facilitate growth are: first, by encouraging and mobilizing savings by providing a return on savings; second, by promoting the efficient allocation of resources because specialized

Figure 18.1 Theoretical links between finance and growth
Source: Levine (1997: 691).

Table 18.1 Simplified balance sheet of a developing country bank

Asset	Liability
Reserves	Deposits
Loans	Capital
Investments including government securities	

Table 18.2 Assets and liabilities at the bank and country level

	Asset	Liability
Bank-specific level	Loans to customers	Deposits from customers
Country level	Private credit / GDP	Liquid liabilities / GDP

financial institutions are more able to obtain information on borrowers, select projects, monitor ongoing projects, and ensure that contracts are enforced; third, by agglomerating capital that allows institutions to be more efficient in intermediation; and, fourth, by creating credit for firms and individuals that will generate employment and reduce poverty.

With specific reference to developing countries, the key role of finance is to encourage domestic resource mobilization. Tables 18.1 and 18.2 summarize a simplified balance sheet of a developing country bank and demonstrate how this translates into a national financial system.

In more developed financial markets, a bank's balance sheet will include a variety of instruments on both the liability and asset sides. However, in a developing country, a bank's balance sheet is relatively simple, with the main liability consisting of deposits and the main assets consisting of loans and investments in government securities.

As shown below, banking systems in SSA remain shallow and inefficient. Therefore, developing countries have relied heavily on external capital to fund development objectives (Serieux 2008).

Structural features of SSA banking systems

Understanding the structural characteristics of SSA banking systems is essential in order to appreciate the challenge faced by these banking systems to fulfill the needs for resource mobilization.

There are two main measures of size (or depth) of a financial system: the ratio of liquid liabilities to Gross Domestic Product (GDP) and the ratio of private credit to GDP. The former is a measure of the monetary resources mobilized by banks; the latter is a measure of the ability of banks to channel resources to borrowers and therefore of the growth potential of financial intermediation. At a bank-specific level, these measures refer to the liabilities (deposit mobilization) and assets (lending) sides of individual bank balance sheets. The interest rate spread—that is, the difference between the average lending rate and the average deposit rate—is the most common measure of bank (in)efficiency. The spread is often interpreted as a premium on the cost of external funds, introduced due to informational and enforcement frictions (Gertler & Rose 1994; Honohan & Beck 2007).

Table 18.3 presents financial depth indicators for SSA compared to other countries. While SSA financial systems have deepened since 2000, they remain shallow compared to those in other countries. Between 2000 and 2010, the ratio of private credit to GDP increased from 15 to 25 percent in SSA. In 2010, this ratio was 53 percent in upper-middle income countries and 130 percent in high-income countries. In the same year, the ratio of liquid liabilities to GDP averaged 37 percent in SSA, compared to 66 percent in upper-middle income countries and 120 percent in high-income countries. Furthermore, banking sectors in SSA are inefficient in terms of interest rate spreads. In 2010, the interest rates spread averaged 5 percent in SSA, compared to 3 percent in the East Asia and Pacific region and 2 percent in high-income countries. Moreover, banking sectors in SSA remain fragile with the ongoing occurrence of bank failures (Upadhyaya 2011).

In the following section we turn to the key debates and studies about finance and development, and financial liberalization. In particular, we consider a critical question: despite financial liberalization in SSA, why do most African countries still have a very poor record of domestic resource mobilization?

Studies on finance and growth

Both heterodox and mainstream economists claim that finance should lead to growth. But what is the evidence for this claim? Mainstream economists, for example, argue that "cross-country comparisons have shown the importance of a well-developed financial sector for long-term economic growth and poverty alleviation. Countries with better developed banking systems and capital markets enjoy higher growth rates" (Beck & Fuchs 2004: 1). They refer specifically to cross-country data that displays a positive relationship between financial development and growth.

The existence of an interrelation between financial deepening and growth was recognized by Goldsmith (1969), who constructed a financial interrelation ratio and showed that this ratio

Table 18.3 Comparison of financial depth indicators between SSA and other countries, 2000, 2005, and 2010

Countries	SSA			Upper-middle income countries			High-income countries		
Year	2000	2005	2010	2000	2005	2010	2000	2005	2010
Liquid liabilities/ GDP (%)	25	28	37	47	52	66	86	91	120
Private credit/ GDP (%)	15	17	25	38	40	53	82	98	130
Interest rate spread (%)	6	3	5	4	3	3	2	2	2

Source: Author's calculation from the World Bank Financial Indicators Database (Beck *et al.* 2000, 2009; Čihák *et al.* 2012).

Note: High-income countries with a GNP per capita in 1997 higher than $9,656; Upper-middle income countries with a GNP per capita between $3,126 and $9,655.

grew with a country's economic growth. However, Goldsmith was cautious in interpreting this interrelationship as causation.

Heterodox economists, like Goldsmith, argue that empirical studies on the relationship between finance and growth should be treated with caution (Harris 2012; Mavrotas 2005; Upadhyaya 2014). They question the idea that finance automatically leads to growth and often advocate for some form of state intervention in financial markets (Stein *et al.* 2002; Arestis *et al.* 2005). They note that conceptual mainstream studies on finance and growth are based largely on the work of McKinnon (1973) and Shaw (1973), who postulated a positive relationship between financial deepening and growth. The causal mechanism in the McKinnon-Shaw hypothesis stipulates that high (market-driven) interest rates will increase savings, which in turn increase growth. Therefore, it is insufficient to show that finance and growth are correlated; studies need to demonstrate that changes in interest rates lead to increased savings (Arestis & Demetriades 1997; Serieux 2008).

Heterodox economists highlight other cross-country studies similar to those cited above that failed to find support for the relationship between finance and growth, and therefore one cannot conclusively argue that finance always leads to growth (Ruziev 2006; Upadhyaya 2011; Harris 2012). For example, growth co-exists with negative real interest rates (Agarwala 1983; Khatkhate 1988). Similarly, single-country case studies also show ambiguous evidence. Four studies on Kenya, examining different periods between 1967 and 2005, find that savings are not responsive to real interest rate increases, and therefore conclude that financial development does not directly impact growth (Mwega *et al.* 1990; Oshikoya 1992; Kariuki 1995; Odhiambo 2008).

Two implications should be noted. First, the focus on growth equations and the need for economists to prove or disprove the relationship between finance and growth has masked the fundamental question: how and under what circumstances does finance actually lead to growth, and more specifically pro-poor growth which encourages development? Second, both mainstream and heterodox economists argue that financial intermediaries fulfill important functions that facilitate the growth. However, heterodox economists stress the complexity of the links between finance and development. Ruziev (2006: 90), for example, argues that

> in general, a more cautious suggestion is that economic development can occur without financial deepening, and financial development may not always lead to economic development. The former centrally planned economies of the socialist camp reached a considerable degree of economic development without any financial deepening. Whereas, although some offshore centers have developed sophisticated financial systems, economically they are still underdeveloped economies.

Therefore, there is no doubt that finance fulfills functions in the economy that lead to economic growth as discussed above. However, it is more important to understand the circumstances under which finance fulfills or does not fulfill these functions.

Studies on the impact of financial liberalization in SSA

Proponents of the 'finance and growth school' advocate an end to 'financial repression' and a need for financial liberalization (McKinnon 1973; Shaw 1973). From this mainstream perspective it is commonly argued that financial repression in SSA results in negative outcomes for the following reasons: first, low nominal interest rates often lead to negative real rates, discourage saving; second, large government deficits crowd out private sector expenditure; and third, small, and oligopolistic financial sectors (relative to the size of the economy) dominate by intermediation in short-term financial assets. These negative outcomes formed the rationale for financial liberalization, which was undertaken in most African countries in the 1980s and early 1990s as part of the structural adjustment policies advocated by the World Bank and the International Monetary Fund (IMF).

Financial liberalization advocated by mainstream economists as well as the World Bank and IMF involves the following: a movement towards market-determined interest rates; greater ease of entry into the banking sector, to encourage competition; a reduced fiscal dependence of the state on credit from the banking system (to allow for greater expansion of credit to the private sector); and a movement towards equilibrium exchange rates and, eventually, flexible exchange rate regimes with open capital accounts.

Such a policy approach has enjoyed few successes and suffered numerous unambiguous failures. On the 'positive' side, liberalization has furthered the integration of developing countries into global markets. Financial liberalization in this regard means that governments are able to raise (or borrow) funds from international capital markets. Middle-income consumers, in particular, have benefited from a wider array of financial services offered by local and international banks. Finally, some developing countries pursuing financial liberalization have experienced lower rates of inflation due to higher interest rates (Epstein & Grabel 2007). On the 'negative' side, there is general recognition in the literature that financial liberalization has not generated the expected increase in saving and investment, an improvement in financial sector intermediation, and a reduction in interest rate spreads (Brownbridge & Harvey 1998; Nissanke & Aryeetey 1998).

Experience from African countries suggests that credit available to the private sector did not increase after financial liberalization; in fact, banks shifted their portfolios towards government stocks (Nissanke & Aryeetey 1998; Serieux 2008). Instead of lending long-term funds, banks maintained highly liquid short-term portfolios and, consequently, non-performing loans increased (Nissanke & Aryeetey 1998). Furthermore, it has been recognized that financial liberalization was accompanied by increasing instability and a higher incidence of bank insolvencies (Soyibo & Adekanye 1992; Brownbridge 1998; Brownbridge & Harvey 1998). It should be noted that bank failures are extremely costly to the economy as a whole, particularly as they disrupt the payment system. It has been estimated that the fiscal cost of bank restructuring between 1984 and 1993 for 11 SSA countries was between 7 and 15 percent of their GDP (Popiel 1994). Heterodox economists point out that the key failure of liberalization is the perennially low level of savings and investment in SSA. The shift in policy stance from high levels of government intervention in the financial systems of SSA between the 1960s and 1980s to more liberalized financial systems since the 1990s has not increased savings and investment (Serieux 2008).

Overall, it can be argued that financial liberalization has not fulfilled the claims of proponents from mainstream economic and international organizations. However, there is still a significant debate as to why the reforms did not bear fruit. On the one hand, mainstream economists argue that liberalization failed due to the incompleteness of reforms, poor sequencing, an absence of government action, and poor initial conditions (see, for example, World Bank 1994). Heterodox economists, on the other hand, recognize the complex nature of financial liberalization and its effects. In countries such as Ghana and Malawi, reform was gradual; yet there have been few positive changes in financial indicators and outcomes similar to those in countries where reform was more rapid (Nissanke 2001). Thus, some heterodox economists emphasize that liberalization was a response to not only severe economic crises and acute macroeconomic instability but also the fragmentation and segmentation of financial markets (Brownbridge & Harvey 1998; Nissanke & Aryeetey 1998). Given the contending explanations of the causes and effects of financial liberalization, we now turn to studies on bank competition in Africa, which provide country-specific analyses of financial liberalization.

Studies on bank competition in Africa

Neoclassical economics assumes that increased competition will lead to lower costs and enhanced efficiency in the financial market. However, there is now a growing recognition, even within the mainstream literature, that assuming "competition is unambiguously good in banking is naïve" (Claessens & Laeven 2003: 4). It is argued that the information-intensive nature of banking implies that it is intrinsically less competitive than other sectors (Caprio & Levine 2002). Theoretically, an oligopolistic (or highly concentrated) banking sector can lead to more efficient market outcomes due to the economies of scale enjoyed by the larger banks, or to higher interest rate spreads and inefficiency due to collusive practices by the same banks (Buchs & Mathisen 2005). Therefore, contrary to the conventional neoclassical assumption, the link between competition and efficiency is not clear in the banking sector.

There is no doubt that SSA banking systems are highly concentrated, as shown in Table 18.4, where the bank concentration ratio is defined as the assets of the three largest banks as a proportion of the total assets of all commercial banks. While bank concentration ratios in SSA have fallen from 84 percent in 2000 to 72 percent in 2010, they are still high by international standards. In comparison, the 2010 bank concentration ratio for upper-middle income countries was 61 percent and for high-income countries it was 64 percent.

Despite the recognition that different countries may have different optimal levels of competition intensity (Vives 2001), empirical studies of African banking systems continue to follow a structure-conduct-performance (S-C-P) paradigm which assumes that a low level of competition is the main contributor to the poor performance of African banking. For example, using data from 13 African countries, Ncube (2007) argues that the oligopolistic nature of the banking sector is a key reason for high interest rate spreads. Furthermore, industrial organization studies show that not only competition is determined by concentration and market structure, but contestability is important (Baumol et al. 1982; Besanko & Thakor 1992).[1] Many empirical studies have measured competition defined in terms of contestability, generally following the seminal work by Panzar & Rosse (1987). The Panzar-Rosse model investigates the extent to which a change in factor input prices is reflected in (equilibrium) revenues earned by a specific bank. The model provides the H-statistic as a measure of the degree of competition, where a value between 0 and 1 (0 = monopoly and 1 = perfect competition) is regarded as monopolistic competition. Claessens & Laeven (2003) use this model to estimate the degree of competition in a cross-section of 50

Table 18.4 Bank concentration ratio in SSA and other countries, 2000, 2005, and 2010

Countries	Year	Bank concentration ratio (%)
SSA	2000	84.04
	2005	77.17
	2010	72.80
Upper-middle income countries	2000	64.43
	2005	64.10
	2010	61.06
High-income countries	2000	64.85
	2005	64.00
	2010	63.63

Source: Author's calculation based on the World Bank Financial Indicators Database (Beck *et al.* 2000, 2009; Čihák *et al.* 2012).

developed and developing countries for the period 1994 to 2001. Some studies by mainstream economists continue to use this methodology, including Buchs & Mathisen (2005) and Mugume (2006) for the Ugandan banking sector, and Musonda (2008) for the Zambian banking sector. These studies report an H-statistic between zero and one. This seems to be the 'default' result of applying the methodology and therefore the usefulness of this model to measure a degree of competition is questionable. In the banking sector, like any other sectors in the economy, perfect monopoly or perfect competition are not likely. Furthermore, the model is based on several restrictive assumptions including that banks are operating in (long-run) equilibrium. It can thus be argued that while these studies are sophisticated in their application of econometric and panel data analysis, they ignore the actual nature of competition in the banking sector, in particular the social and historical factors that shape the reputation of banks and their impact on banking sector competition. If we are concerned with whether an increase in competition is associated with banking performance or not, a deeper understanding of the banking sector in the socio-historical context is more useful.

Studies have been carried out by both the orthodox and heterodox schools to explain the reasons for the failures of liberalization. However, there is very little work by heterodox economists to explain, in particular, why banking systems in developing countries remain shallow and inefficient after financial liberalization. It should be noted that heterodox economists concur that finance does fulfill key functions in the economy, but the main question is to understand which circumstances allow finance to fulfill these functions. It may well be that the current theories and models used to explain banking systems are suitable for a deeper understanding of real issues and problems. We now turn to alternative heterodox concepts that offer a better explanation of the banking system in developing countries.

Heterodox approaches to understanding banks in developing countries

The lending relationship: knowledge creation

Contemporary mainstream banking theory focuses on the role of banks based on the functions they fulfill in reducing market frictions or transaction costs (Freixas & Rochet 1997). Information asymmetry is the key source of transaction cost that a bank overcomes when fulfilling its intermediation and information function (Bhattacharya & Thakor 1993). Stiglitz & Weiss (1981) place information asymmetry at the heart of the lending relationship and incorporate interest rates and default rates into their model, in which banks try to maximize their profit by obtaining a margin between deposit and loan rates. Borrowers try to maximize their profits through their choice of investment projects. Due to information asymmetry, banks are unable to distinguish 'good' borrowers from 'bad' borrowers. Furthermore, due to adverse selection and moral hazard, the normal market clearing system does not work. It simply encourages riskier borrowers to apply for loans. Therefore, banks practice a rule of thumb in order to keep interest rates lower than market conditions warrant. This has also led to the policy prescription advocated by the World Bank to develop credit registries and improve the legal environment (Honohan & Beck 2007).

It can be argued that while these mainstream models are useful in explaining the occurrence of credit rationing, there is still a need to understand the actual process of information production and how banks bridge information asymmetry in a country-specific context. Furthermore, viewing the lending relationship in terms of information asymmetry is too simplistic. An alternative approach to understanding the lending relationship is the concept of knowledge creation during the process of credit creation, as discussed by Dow (1998, 2002).

Dow, drawing on the works of, in particular, Keynes, Shackle, and Minsky, criticizes the extremely simplistic way in which information is understood in the Stiglitz–Weiss model. Dow argues that the major flaw with the Stiglitz–Weiss model is that its key result is not based on information asymmetry between a bank and a borrower, but on two much stronger assumptions—that is, borrowers have perfect information on the riskiness of investment projects, and borrowers conceal the actual risk of the project (Dow 1998, 2002).[2] These assumptions are necessary to minimize the importance of the borrower's risk and provide an explanation for credit rationing (Dow 1998). However, Dow's organizational theory indicates that borrowers also face uncertainty about project outcomes and, therefore, they can be either over- or under-optimistic (Dow 2002).

Furthermore, the Stiglitz–Weiss model assumes that *risk* can be reduced once the information asymmetry between a borrower and a lender is bridged. Dow (1998), following Shackle (1972) and Keynes' *Treatise on Probability* ([1921] 1973), argues that most knowledge is subject to uncertainty in terms of unquantifiable risk.[3] Therefore, according to Dow, the lending process should be seen as one in which both parties attempt to acquire or create knowledge in the uncertain world (Dow 1998, 2002). The application of this concept of knowledge creation to the context of credit market implies

> that it is in the nature of the banks' and borrowers' risk assessment processes that a strong element of judgement be employed. This is not the result of borrowers' intentionally concealing information in an opportunistic manner, but rather the nature of the process of knowledge acquisition in an uncertain world.
>
> *Dow 1998: 222*

As such, if lending and borrowing are not simply a matter of information, we should examine how factors located outside the market affect the lending-borrowing relationship. The following discussion draws on the concept of knowledge creation combined with the embeddedness of social factors in order to understand lending relationships in developing countries.

The lending relationship: social factors and trust

Outside of mainstream economics, social factors figure prominently in understanding lending relationships. The sociological theory of finance, for example, suggests that access to credit is not based entirely on the net present value of a project and transaction costs (Uzzi 1999); instead, banking transactions are *embedded* in social relations. Embeddedness, in turn, leads to the development of trust between borrowers and lenders and, therefore, affects access to and the price of credit (Uzzi 1999; Johnson 2003). The embeddedness argument is based on the work of Polanyi (1944) and Granovetter (1985) who stress "the role of concrete personal relations and structures of such [social] relations in generating trust and discouraging malfeasance" (Granovetter 1985: 490). Uzzi (1999: 482) defines social embeddedness as "the degree to which commercial transactions take place through social relations and networks of relations that use the exchange protocols associated with social, non-commercial attachments to govern business dealings."

In the specific context of lending relationships, therefore, social relations allow the exchange of knowledge and information and the development of trust between the lender and the borrower.[4] Such knowledge creation and trust encourage lenders to disburse loans to borrowers on a basis that cannot simply be captured by price factors and transaction costs.

In this respect, it is worthwhile to note Uzzi (1999)'s interesting sociological study of formal banking following the embeddedness approach. Using a combination of methods—interviews of bank managers and survey data from 2,400 middle-market firms in the United States—Uzzi tests the impact of arm's length ties versus embedded social relations between banks and borrowers. Arm's length ties are characterized by lean and irregular transactions, which take place without prolonged human or social contact between parties. Uzzi finds that firms having embedded social relations, rather than arm's length ties, with banks more likely to get funding at a lower interest rate. This argument is more nuanced than simply showing the importance of social relations in lending relations. That is, arm's length ties and embedded relationships are *complementary* rather than mutually exclusive; one type of relationship helps overcome the limitations of the other type of relationship. Therefore, while a firm with embedded relationships with a bank is more likely to get funding, it is also equally likely to make an effort to repay the loan if the firm is also able to meet most financial criteria (Uzzi 1999). The corollary is that banks with a mix of arm's length ties and embedded relationships are likely to have more capability of producing information and monitoring their borrowers.

The lending relationship: heterodox economic studies

There have been few heterodox studies examining banks in SSA. One study is Upadhyaya (2011), which analyzes qualitative data to understand the constraints banks in developing countries face when making lending decisions. This study concludes that some of the constraints include: the need to educate clients, particularly small and medium sized borrowers even on basic issues such as developing management accounts; the unreliability of financial information (therefore the need to compliment hard and soft information on borrowers); and, over-reliance by banks on name lending (that is, the process whereby the owners of the bank know the 'names' of borrowers as they are from the same community, and a loan is given purely on the perceived reputation of the borrower)—but this strategy is no longer working due to changing social relations.

Upadhyaya (2011) also shows that: changing social factors have a pervasive effect on the quality of asset portfolio of banks and this impact is complex and not unidirectional; to be able to effectively monitor clients, banks need to develop a mix of arm's length ties and embedded relationships; embedded relationships should not be discouraged by regulation; and, while credit registries can be useful they do not replace the need for banks to really understand their clients.

Studies on financialization

Financialization is a concept that heterodox economists and scholars from a variety of disciplines have adopted to describe the structural changes in the advanced economies since the early 2000s (Zwan 2014). Studies of financialization interrogate how an increasingly autonomous realm of global finance has altered the underlying logic of the capitalist economy such that finance capital has come to dominate industrial capital and, consequently, the increasing fragility of economies has become global (Newman 2009; Zwan 2014). Zwan (2014) provides a useful schema of financialization in industrialized countries divided into three main groups: the emergence of a new regime of accumulation, the ascendancy of the shareholder value orientation, and the financialization of everyday life.

The concept of financialization has also been applied to emerging economies such as Brazil and Turkey. For example, it is shown that the liberalization of capital flows and the increased participation of foreign investors buying short-term Brazilian assets made it very difficult for the government to effectively manage exchange rates in Brazil; as a result, the Brazilian real depreciated, which was not in line with the fundamentals of the economy (Kaltenbrunner 2010). In the case of Turkey, there has been a historic rise in consumer credit driven by both supply and demand factors (Karacimen 2014).

A few studies have examined the effect of financialization on the poor in developing countries. Newman (2009), for example, investigates the influence of financialization on the structure of coffee value chains since the decline of the International Coffee Agreement in 1989 and the liberalization of coffee markets in countries such as Uganda and Tanzania. This study also demonstrates how the use of financial instruments for private risk management helps stabilize incomes for the largest downstream actors at the cost of producers in developing countries. At the level of retail financial markets, Krige (2012) links the rise of illegal Ponzi and legal multi-level marketing schemes in South Africa to both the context of post-apartheid South Africa, with its discourse of 'economic empowerment' and 'entrepreneurship', and the wider neoliberal policy in the context of financialization.

The studies discussed above imply that financialization as a concept needs a more nuanced understanding when it comes to developing countries, particularly those countries where the level of credit in relation to GDP remains low. There is some evidence from the Kenyan context that while the banking sector has deepened and become increasingly dominated by local banks, lending to agriculture and manufacturing sectors, which are key for the development of the economy, has been declining (Upadhyaya & Johnson 2015). Therefore, while agriculture represents 25.9 percent of Kenyan GDP, lending to agriculture as a proportion of total lending dropped from 8.7 percent in 2000 to 4.9 percent in 2012. Furthermore, lending to manufacturing dropped from 21.4 percent in 2000 to 13.5 percent in 2012. The growth in credit is due largely to increased lending to households—from 3.3 percent in 2000 to 24.6 percent in 2012 (Upadhyaya & Johnson 2015). It should be noted, however, that in developing countries not all lending to households should be considered as consumption or unproductive lending, as people leverage their borrowing to invest in productive areas, including agriculture and small enterprises (Johnson 2003). Nonetheless, the empirical analysis presented above raises concerns that the changing structure of lending does not reflect the stated goals of the country, which aim for manufacturing to grow at 10 percent per annum (Upadhyaya & Johnson 2015).

Conclusions

This chapter reviewed studies on banking in developing countries, with a focus on SSA. Most studies on this particular issue are conducted by mainstream economists and fall in two main categories: first, cross-country and single-country studies that attempt to show an empirical link between finance and growth. These studies are methodologically weak, as they do not attempt to reveal the country-specific mechanisms that channel finance into growth; second, single-country case studies employ the 'structure-conduct-performance' paradigm, which assumes that the poor performance of African banking is attributable to high levels of concentration and low levels of competition. These studies, however, do not explain why economies of scale in banking do not always lead to efficiency, and why economies of scale can lead to better reputation and stability that has a complex effect on competition in the banking sector. While heterodox economists have actively participated in financial liberalization debates, there have been only a handful of heterodox studies that attempt to understand banking sectors in developing countries. In order to fill this lacuna, we examined three concepts that are useful in providing a heterodox understanding of banks in developing countries: knowledge creation as opposed to information asymmetry, and the embeddedness of credit relations in social relations. These two concepts are useful insofar as we are concerned with the reality of lending relations in developing countries. The third concept, financialization, was examined to show that there is considerable room for heterodox economists to extend this concept to developing countries, as it pertains to the relationship between the banking system and development.

Notes

1 Competitive outcomes are possible in concentrated systems, and collusive actions can be sustained even in the presence of many firms. Therefore, it is the threat of entry—contestability—that is more important.
2 Although Greenwald & Stiglitz (1993) recognize that production is a risky process, this is not translated in their formal model, where it is assumed that borrowers face quantifiable measurable risk (Dow 1998).
3 Shackle (1972) criticizes the probabilistic approach to decision-making theory, and emphasizes that the use of probability relies on past events and therefore, by their nature, methods that rely on probability cannot adequately capture the future.
4 It should be acknowledged that when we use the term 'trust', we use it in a very narrow context of the relationship between the bank and the borrower. In the specific context of finance, we do not look at the development of trust between banks, which is also essential for the smooth functioning of the payment system.

References

Agarwala, R. 1983. Price distortions and growth in developing countries. World Bank Policy Research Working Paper 575.
Arestis, P. & Demetriades, P. 1997. 'Financial development and economic growth: assessing the evidence.' *Economic Journal*, 107 (442): 783–799.
Arestis, P., Nissanke, M., & Stein, H. 2005. 'Finance and development: institutional and policy alternatives to financial liberalisation theory.' *Eastern Economic Journal*, 31 (2): 245–263.
Baumol, W., Panzar, J., & Willig, R. 1982. *Contestable Markets and the Theory of Industrial Structure*. San Diego, CA: Harcourt Brace Jovanovich.
Beck, T. & Fuchs, M. 2004. Structural issues in the Kenyan financial system: improving competition and access. World Bank Policy Research Working Paper 3363.
Beck, T., Demirgüç-Kunt, A., & Levine, R. 2000. 'A new database on financial development and structure.' *World Bank Economic Review*, 14 (3): 597–605.
Beck, T., Demirgüç-Kunt, A., & Levine, R. 2009. Financial Institutions and Markets across Countries and over Time: Data and Analysis. World Bank Policy Research Working Paper 4943.
Besanko, D. & Thakor, A. 1992. 'Banking deregulation: allocational consequences of relaxing entry barriers.' *Journal of Banking and Finance*, 16 (5): 909–932.
Bhattacharya, S. & Thakor, A.V. 1993. 'Contemporary banking theory.' *Journal of Financial Intermediation*, 3 (1): 2–50.
Brownbridge, M. 1998. 'Financial distress in local banks in Kenya, Nigeria, Uganda and Zambia: causes and implications for regulatory policy.' *Development Policy Review*, 16 (2): 173–188.
Brownbridge, M. & Harvey, C. 1998. *Banking in Africa*. Trenton, NJ: Africa World Press.
Buchs, T. & Mathisen, J. 2005. 'Competition and efficiency in banking: behavioral evidence from Ghana.' *IMF Working Paper*, 5 (17): 1–26.
Caprio, G. & Levine, R. 2002. Corporate governance in finance: concepts and international observations. Paper presented at the World Bank, IMF and Brookings Institution Conference on the Building the Pillars of Financial Sector Governance: The Roles of Public and Private Sectors.
Cihák, M., Demirgüç-Kunt, A., Feyen, E., & Levine, R. 2012. Benchmarking financial development around the world. World Bank Policy Research Working Paper 6175.
Claessens, S. & Laeven, L. 2003. What drives bank competition? Some international evidence. World Bank Policy Research Working Paper 3113.
Dow, S. 1998. 'Knowledge, information and credit creation,' in: R. Rotheim (ed.), *New Keynesian Economics/Post Keynesian Alternatives*. London: Routledge, 214–226.
Dow, S. 2002. *Economic Methodology: An Inquiry*. Oxford: Oxford University Press.
Epstein, G. & Grabel, I. 2007. Training module 3: financial policy. International Poverty Centre.
Freixas, X. & Rochet, J.-C. 1997. *Microeconomics of Banking*, 4th edn. Cambridge, MA: MIT Press.
Gertler, M. & Rose, A. 1994. 'Finance, public policy and growth,' in: G. Caprio, I. Atiyas, & P. Honohan (eds.), *Financial Reform: Theory and Experience*. Cambridge, UK: Cambridge University Press, 13–48.

Goldsmith, R. 1969. *Financial Structure and Development*. New Haven, CT: Yale University Press.

Granovetter, M. 1985. 'Economic action and social structure: the problem of embeddedness.' *The American Journal of Sociology*, 91 (3): 481–510.

Greenwald, B. & Stiglitz, J. 1993. 'Financial market imperfections and business cycles.' *Quarterly Journal of Economics*, 108 (1): 77–114.

Harris, L. 2012. 'From financial development to economic growth and vice versa: a review of international experience and policy lessons for Africa.' *Journal of African Economics*, 21 (AERC Supplement 1): i89–i106.

Honohan, P. & Beck, T. 2007. *Making Finance Work for Africa*. Washington, DC: The World Bank.

Johnson, S. 2003. "Moving mountains": an institutional analysis of financial markets using evidence from Kenya. PhD dissertation. University of Bath, UK.

Kaltenbrunner, A. 2010. 'International financialization and depreciation: the Brazilian Real in the international financial crisis.' *Competition and Change*, 14 (3–4): 296–323

Karacimen, E. 2014. 'Financialization in Turkey: the case of consumer debt.' *Journal of Balkan and Near Eastern Studies*, 16 (2): 161–180.

Kariuki, P. 1995. 'The impact of interest rate liberalisation on financial savings: the case of Kenya.' *African Review of Money, Finance and Banking*, 95 (1–2): 5–23.

Keynes, J.M. [1921] 1973. *A Treatise on Probability*. Reprinted in *The Collected Works of J.M. Keynes, Vol. VIII*. London: Macmillan.

Khatkhate, D. 1988. 'Assessing the impact of interest rates in less developed countries.' *World Development*, 16 (5): 577–588.

Krige, D. 2012. 'Field of dreams, field of schemes: ponzi finance and multi-level marketing in South Africa.' *Africa*, 82 (1): 69–92.

Levine, R. 1997. 'Financial development and economic growth: views and agenda.' *Journal of Economic Literature*, 35 (2): 688–726.

Mavrotas, G. (2005). 'Savings and financial sector development: assessing the evidence,' *in*: C. Green, C. Kirkpatrick, & V. Murinde (eds.), *Finance and Development: Surveys of Theory, Evidence and Policy*. Cheltenham, UK: Edward Elgar, 29–61.

McKinnon, R. 1973. *Money and Capital in Economic Development*. Washington, DC: Brookings Institute.

Mugume, A. 2006. Market structure and performance in Uganda's banking industry. Paper presented at the AERC Biannual Workshop 2006. Nairobi, Kenya.

Musonda, A. 2008. Deregulation, market power and competition: an empirical investigation of the Zambian banking industry. Paper presented at the CSAE Conference on Economic Development in Africa. Oxford, UK.

Mwega, F., Ngola, S., & Mwangi, N. 1990. Real interest rates and the mobilization of private savings in Africa. African Economic Research Consortium (AERC) Research Paper 2.

Ncube, M. 2007. 'Financial services and economic development in Africa.' *Journal of African Economies*, 16 (Suppl. 1): 13–57.

Newman, S.A. 2009. 'Financialization and changes in the social relations along commodity chains: the case of coffee.' *Review of Radical Political Economics*, 41 (4): 539–559.

Nissanke, M. 2001. 'Financing enterprise development in sub-Saharan Africa.' *Cambridge Journal of Economics*, 25 (3): 343–367.

Nissanke, M. & Aryeetey, E. 1998. *Financial Integration and Development: Liberalisation and Reform in sub-Saharan Africa*. London: Routledge.

Odhiambo, N. 2008. 'Financial depth, savings and economic growth in Kenya: a dynamic causal linkage.' *Economic Modelling*, 25 (4): 704–713.

Oshikoya, T. 1992. 'Interest rate liberalisation, savings, investment and growth: the case of Kenya.' *Savings and Development*, 16 (3): 305–320.

Panzar, J. & Rosse, J. 1987. 'Testing for 'monopoly' equilibrium.' *Journal of Industrial Economics*, 35 (4): 443–456.

Polanyi, K. 1944. *The Great Transformation: The Political and Economic Origins of Our Time*. Boston: Beacon Press.

Popiel, P. 1994. Financial systems in Sub-Saharan Africa. World Bank Discussion Papers Africa Technical Department Series 260.

Ruziev, K. 2006. Money and banks in transition economies: the case of Uzbekistan. PhD dissertation. University of Stirling, Scotland.

Serieux, J. 2008. Financial liberalisation and domestic resource mobilisation in Africa: an assessment. International Poverty Centre Working Paper 45.

Shackle, G. 1972. *Epistemics and Economics*. Cambridge, UK: Cambridge University Press.

Shaw, E. 1973. *Financial Deepening in Economic Development*. New York: Oxford University Press.

Soyibo, A. & Adekanye, F. 1992. The Nigerian banking system in the context of policies of financial regulation and deregulation. African Economic Research Consortium (AERC) Research Paper 17.

Stein, H., Ajakaiye, O., & Lewis, P. 2002. 'Financial deregulation and banking crises: an introduction to theoretical, institutional and policy issues,' *in*: H. Stein, O. Ajakaiye, & P. Lewis (eds.), *Deregulation and the Banking Crisis in Nigeria: A Comparative Study*. London: Palgrave, 1–20.

Stiglitz, J. & Weiss, A. 1981. 'Credit rationing in markets with imperfect information.' *American Economic Review*, 71 (3): 393–410.

Upadhyaya, R. 2011. Analysing the sources and impact of segmentation in the banking sector: a case study of Kenya. PhD dissertation. School of Oriental and African Studies, University of London, London, UK.

Upadhyaya, R. 2014. 'Financial sector development in Sub-Saharan Africa: a survey of empirical literature,' *in*: K. Ruziev & N. Perdikis (eds.), *Development and Financial Reform in Emerging Economies*. London: Pickering & Chatto, 167–182.

Upadhyaya, R. & Johnson, S. 2015. 'Evolution of Kenya's banking sector 2000–2012,' *in*: A. Heyer & M. King (eds.), *The Kenyan Financial Transformation*. Nairobi: FSD Kenya, 15–61.

Uzzi, B. 1999. 'Embeddedness in the making of financial capital: how social relations and networks benefit firms seeking financing.' *American Sociological Review*, 64 (4): 481–505.

Vives, X. 2001. 'Competition in the changing world of banking.' *Oxford Review of Economic Policy*, 17 (4): 535–547.

World Bank. 1994. *Adjustment in Africa: Reforms, Results and the Road Ahead*. Washington, DC: World Bank.

Zwan, N.v.d. 2014. 'Making sense of financialization.' *Socio-Economic Review*, 12 (1): 99–129.

19

Shadow banking

Benjamin Wilhelm

Introduction

An analysis of the shadow banking system provides at least two insights into the legal underpinnings of the financial system. On the one hand, shadow banking operates on a global or transnational scale, which makes it difficult to relate it to a single national legal framework. On the other hand, shadow banking displays the effects of an ineffective legal framework when 'adverse' economic conditions arise. The Financial Stability Board defines shadow banking as "the system of credit intermediation that involves entities and activities outside the regular banking system" (FSB 2011a: 3) and it has recently been "at the heart of the credit crisis" (Pozsar 2008: 17). Indeed, the systemic importance of shadow banking for global finance came to light during the financial crisis of 2007–2008. Paul McCulley (2014), who first coined the term 'shadow banking' in 2007, refers to the balance of private and public forces that were distorted before and during this financial crisis. Since then, regulators have endeavored to rebalance the banking system (IOSCO 2009; BCBS 2011; Bakk-Simon *et al.* 2012; IMF 2014; ESRB 2015; FSB 2015a).

Economically, shadow banking performs banking-like practices; legally, however, it holds a privileged accounting position, which comes with lower or no capital requirements compared to the traditional banking sector (Ordoñez 2013; Plantin 2014; Ferrante 2015). Hence, a pure economic analysis is limited in understanding the role of shadow banking. Instead, exploring the interplay of financial regulation and shadow banking activities will provide a more comprehensive picture of the institutional evolution of the financial practices which stabilize and destabilize the financial system.

After the so-called run on the shadow banking system in 2008, the integration of shadow banking practices into the regulatory frameworks has been discussed (Joint Forum 2008; IOSCO 2008; BCBS 2009; FSB 2011b). The Financial Stability Board (FSB) and others support the development of 'non-bank financing' as it "provides a valuable alternative to bank funding and helps support real economic activity" (FSB 2015b: 1). However, the question of what this actually means for the rebalancing of the financial system is still debatable; as highlighted by McCulley, the question is one of 'if, and how, shadow banking may function in its tamed version.'

This chapter illuminates the practices and regulatory aspects of the workings of the shadow banking system. The first section of the chapter points to the institutional qualities of shadow banking as a fundamental part of the broader financial system. The second section presents a view of the inner workings of shadow banking, which are better understood from a legal perspective than from an economic one. The chapter's third section lays out the present regulatory adaptations and how they affect the current state of shadow banking. The chapter argues that, in order to understand the shadow banking system, a more finely tuned institutional perspective must be supplemented with a perspective on the social and political contexts which condition (and are also conditioned by) the practices of shadow banking.

Institutionalizing shadow banking

The inclusion of shadow banking within regulatory regimes impacts on how intervention in economic systems occurs (Bundesbank 2014; Pozsar 2015). This, in turn, creates a new mode of governing international financial markets that further increases the homogeneity of financial practices and the interconnectivity of risks (Shin 2009). The financial crisis of 2007–2008 further underlines the importance of shadow banking for the functioning of the internationalized capitalist system. Its collapse, starting with the Lehman Brothers' failure in 2008, indicates the interconnectedness of financial institutions and the systemic vulnerability of the international financial architecture.

Mainstream economics has retained its unquestioned explanations of the present position of shadow banking—greed, moral hazard, asymmetric information, lack of transparency, and false regulation. However, Hodgson (2015) suggests that, in terms of the broader working of capitalism, it is the institutional environment of shadow banking that affects the practice of financial exchange. Furthermore, the influence of shadow banking goes beyond the financial sector. That is, shadow banking enforces not only a 'homeowner society' via the repackaging of mortgages into saleable assets but also further integration of financial institutions at the global level. Consequently, shadow banking introduces an additional systemic risk (embedded in new forms of credit and in collateral provision across state borders) that calls for new regulatory measures if such risk is to be contained.

Heterodox economists generally do not limit their analyses to only economic phenomena. Rather, heterodox economic analyses of finance are situated within the social and institutional context, including social norms and sanctions. The legitimacy of these institutions is represented through regulatory regimes as the basis for financial interaction. Since financial transactions are increasingly less contained within national boundaries, they must be governed by complex international regulatory mechanisms. Hence, to understand financial interaction within and beyond state-based legal frameworks, one has to understand international regulatory relations, which have recently been broadened and, consequently, created new forms of 'financial innovation.'[1]

Pre- and post-crisis regulatory measures show a tendency to enhance resilience against a crisis, rather than focusing on specific risk characteristics and hedging strategies. Their focus places a greater emphasis on bank equity than on external ratings, and more reliance on trading through third parties (that is, clearing counterparties) than on bilateral interbank markets (that is, over-the-counter transactions). The emphasis on resilience indicates that crisis is increasingly recognized as a common phenomenon. Such recognition is considerably different from the widely accepted view represented by the applied risk models that dominated before the recent global financial crisis. Thus, the rediscovery of the 'Minsky moment' (BIS 2008; Nesvetailova 2014; Ordoñez & Gorton 2014) reconfigured the way in which possible future crises can be conjectured in an economic and regulatory sense.

In addition, the 'Bagehot moment' (Mehrling 2012) marks the decisive position of the central banks during the collapse of the shadow banking system. The new state of financial affairs created through regulatory reform places pressure on the normal business behavior not only of banks (and the configuration of their financial assets in line with the new regulatory demands), but also of central banks (CGFS 2015). Especially for central banks in the face of a low interest rate environment, financial regulation seems to be a key instrument to adjust the lending behavior of banks and the economy at large.

The new dynamic components of regulatory control provide, among other mechanisms, new tools to govern financial affairs from a regulatory perspective. From this point of view, the new role of the European Central Bank as the main agency of European banking supervision appears to be a logical step towards the adoption of the 'new normal' in economic governance from a distance (Mehrling 2012, 2014). The new configuration and transmission of central bank policies have thereby expanded and become more complicated. These new policies might thus more closely resemble adjustable tools vis-à-vis the development of a future shadow banking system.[2]

In the past few years, some heterodox economic perspectives have developed an analysis of the financial system based on Schumpeterian (Ülgen 2014), Kaleckian/Minskian (Wray 2009; Ryoo 2013; Fisher & Bernardo 2014), or more general Post Keynesian (Guttmann 2012; Lavoie 2013) models. Ülgen (2014), for instance, places emphasis on the self-reflexivity of the financial system ('finance to finance' versus 'finance to production'), which disputes the unquestioned role of banking as a functional step to finance Schumpeterian innovation. A Minskian perspective of unstable capitalism, he argues, enables a better perspective on the destructive capacities of finance.

Wray (2009) draws on Veblen to explicate the transition from commercial to financial capitalism (or Minsky's money manager capitalism). He argues that in the present system private debt plays the leading role for economic growth, and securitization becomes central to the mode of accumulation. Post Keynesians present a systemic perspective on the present accumulation regime denoted as 'financialization' (Lavoie 2013). Since the 1980s, neoliberal economic policies, such as deregulation, privatization, the intensification of competition, and labor market flexibility, have restructured the economic system in favor of money managers.

One point of commonality between these heterodox perspectives is the rejection of the efficient markets theory formalized by Fama (1970, 1991). Moreover, heterodox analyses of the crisis demonstrate that even a broader understanding of economics might be insufficient to understand the setting of shadow banking in the contemporary mode of accumulation with an increasingly homogeneous global regulatory setting becoming evident. Complementing an economic perspective, the question that arises from a socio-political viewpoint revolves around the way certain financial orders flourish and others do not, independently of *a posteriori* rational explanations, and how political decisions regarding regulation trigger the evolution of the financial system.

Shadow banking is an impediment to better economic governance and regulatory systems. Both aspects suggest the need for interdisciplinary research by heterodox economists, financial lawyers, sociologists, historians, and political scientists. In this way, shadow banking can be understood as the result of a socio-political system, demonstrating how a value system transcends national boundaries and how its institutions provide for financial flows accordingly. In the present low interest rate environment, the 'search for yield' does not only challenge the current regulatory space but also resets socio-political 'normality.' It provides a new regulatory context for banks as well as for the insurance market or syndicated leveraged loan market (Lysandrou & Nesvetailova 2015; Joint Forum 2015). Financial investors have to adjust their balance sheets and product portfolios. Such an adjustment changes not only the availability of credit for the real sector of the economy but also the financial flows of large institutional investors.

The changes in international regulatory frameworks for banks are well represented by the transition from Basel II to Basel III. Basel II provisions only cover counterparty risk and accentuate the internal governance of financial institutions. Basel III focuses on 'credit value adjustment' and encompasses broader market fluctuations such as consumption, industrial production, and foreign exchange. As demonstrated by the recent financial crisis, value adjustments for whole asset categories (for valuations dominantly performed in the shadow banking sector) can cause even more systemic interruption as the actual defaults of specific assets increase. The crisis effects of mark-to-market valuation[3] may increase due to the growing need for interest-bearing assets and hence new forms of collateral to securitize remain the dominant form of market-based credit provision (BCBS & IOSCO 2015).

'Efficiency' in regulatory terms denotes the need to pursue maturity transformation off-balance sheet in order not to be subject to higher regulatory capital ratios. Banks can outsource an established cash flow and free their balance sheet for further investment (Gorton & Souleles 2005). The interlinking of special purpose vehicles solved this problem. They also allowed for an expansion of seemingly secure assets backed by seemingly reliable hedging strategies based on 'normal' probability distributions of future events (Merton 1974; BCBS 2005). The bankruptcy prone off-balance sheet construction of the shadow banking system failed when the banks rescued their sponsored special purpose vehicles (SPVs) more out of fear of losing further credibility within a tumbling financial market than because of contractual obligations. Exposure to special investment vehicles (a type of SPV) shrank from $297 billion in 2007 to $45 billion in 2008 (Joint Forum 2009).

The image of shadow banking as a 'money market funding of capital market lending' (Mehrling *et al.* 2015) suggests an abstract understanding of the cash flow across traditional and shadow banking institutions. Indeed, shadow banking is often presented as the other side of banking, although it is the largest (investment) banks that make broad usage of arbitrage opportunities via the cash flow structure of the shadow banking system (Joint Forum 2009, 2015).

Mehrling's (2012) inclusive vision of a functioning market-based credit system misses the reality of a global regulatory structure not backed by a sovereign entity like a self-contained nation state during the post-Second World War period of the last century. The next section sheds more light on how shadow banking can be explained and understood in a different way, focusing on the legal structures that enable and restrict certain cash flows or privilege particular financial products.

A legal view of shadow banking

After the global financial crisis, the G20 (2010) called for tighter regulation of the shadow banking system, as it was marked as a primary source for the global spread of financial turmoil. The Financial Stability Board (FSB 2011b) is the main forum for setting the regulatory agenda for a more stable international financial architecture. Together with the Basle Committee on Banking Supervision (BCBS 2011) and the International Organization of Securities Commissions (IOSCO 2009), the FSB is to provide the means to rebalance and thus to stabilize the architecture of the international financial system.

Even though the FSB took up the new notion of shadow banking as brought forward by the G20, issues such as securitization (Plantin 2011), special purpose vehicles (Gorton & Souleles 2005), off-balance sheet activities by banks (BCBS 1986) and the associated systemic risk (Hellwig 1995), and macro prudential regulation (Borio 2005) had long been discussed before the crisis. The new notion of shadow banking—non-bank intermediation chains for market-based credit provision—served as a node for a widespread regulatory agenda (FSB 2013). Research on re-intermediation practices (Rajan 2005), mark-to-market accounting (Plantin *et al.* 2005, 2007), and credit ratings through value-at-risk calculations (Fender & Kiff 2004) has highlighted in detail the systemic challenges posed by what is now called shadow banking.

Shadow banking is commonly defined as non-bank intermediation[4] (FSB 2011b). What distinguishes banks from these non-banking entities is that the latter have no direct access to central bank liquidity; nor are they secured through a deposit insurance scheme. Hence, the run on the shadow banking system, which came to a height around the time of the Lehman Brothers' failure in September 2008, had been fostered by the knowledge about the lack of institutional resources in times of crisis. It is thus commonly acknowledged that the trigger of the financial crisis was very similar to the ones associated with traditional banking crises in the light of which deposit insurance and the lender of last resort function (meaning contemporary central banks) had been put in place (Brunnermeier 2009; Moe 2012).

The shadow banking system relies on mainstream financial economics offering mathematical models to transfer the risk, for instance, of maturity or liquidity transformation (Bouvard *et al.* 2015). Maturity transformation practiced by banks means providing long-term loans and financing them through short-term debt. The shadow banking system performs a similar function although in reverse order and without the regulatory cushion. In order to reverse the maturity order, debt is transformed into a standardized category backed by risk calculations, credit insurance, collateral pools, and credit ratings. Thereby, long-term credit like mortgages can be transformed into well-tradable assets. Such a market-based credit system transfers (at least in theory) the attached risks directly to the holders of these assets (often banks themselves), without the traditional banking sector as an intermediary.

Legal entities, sometimes called SPVs or Other Financial Entities (OFEs), form a chain of different functions through which investors and creditors can be linked to the traditional banking system and therefore to the traditional back-up systems and regulatory obligations. Investments in the shadow banking system thus do not work in the 'boring finance' way—that is, when banks hold low interest-bearing deposits or government bonds through which they leverage investments in higher interest-bearing longer term credit portfolios. Rather, shadow banking can be understood as an off-balance sheet arrangement, which fosters and promotes new practices of securitization.

Thus, the 'shadowy' part of banking is created via directing financial flows through non-bank financial institutions, where the whole setting is mainly created by banks that charge for its usage but have no legal responsibility for its sustainability.[5] It is the legal structure that enables (or does not forbid) what can be created, sold, and then included in the respective capital structures. Here, Hodgson's (2015) legal institutionalism therefore points to 'a disaggregated view.' In this respect, Lysandrou & Nesvetailova's (2015) recent study provides a better understanding of the practice of shadow banking than the aggregation of monetary amounts that arguably represent the shadow banking system. As evidenced by Pozsar *et al.*'s (2010) mapping exercise, shadow banking is a way to legally enable certain financial products, which in turn interconnect the financial system in critical ways. These cannot be understood by merely looking at the size of monetary aggregates.

As such, the institutional structure allows the shadow banking system to create highly rated short-term products with interest rates above government bonds and significantly above the interbank rates, which are of interest especially to money market mutual funds (Bengtsson 2013; Chernenko & Sunderam 2014). The shadow banking system is able to absorb long-term or lower-rated products, which increase the demand for debt to be securitized; in fact, it establishes a fee-based originate-to-distribute arrangement through which earnings can be realized through transferring, for instance, default risks to investors (Brunnermeier 2009).[6] Consequently, the system enables banks to manage their balance sheet in a way that makes it more 'attractive' for their shareholders (FSF 2008). This arrangement can also abate the high-risk appetite of other institutional investors through its ability to differentiate risk exposures. The main activity to achieve this is a mixture of risk mitigation strategies, such as liquidity facilities, credit default swaps

(CDSs), or cash-flow waterfalls to produce what turns out as 'pseudo-risk-less' securities (Stein 2010), safe in good times but very risky in bad ones.

Securities—collateral backed financial instruments—function as a form of money within the shadow banking system, through which one is able to gain income in the form of interest payments correlated to the risk one is willing to take. Standard securities enable the pooling of multiple loans; this strategy has the benefit of not being exposed to total failure if a specific credit cannot be serviced. The second layer of securitization, the securitization of securities or so-called collateralized debt obligations (CDOs), provides risk stratification through trenching—that is, the creation of a so-called waterfall of cash flows from the upper tranches to the lower ones from which a calculated proportion of creditors can service their payment obligations. In the case of losses, this means that cash flows related to securities will first serve the upper tranches (super senior or senior tranches) before the intermediate (the mezzanine tranche) and finally the lowest positioned tranches (junior or equity tranches). In addition, and in order to further reduce risk exposures, financial innovation provides credit insurance for special investment vehicles and security tranches in the form of credit default swaps. In this way, insured upper tranches can receive the highest (triple A) credit ratings, whereas lower tranches can satisfy the hunger for higher returns (mezzanine tranches with B ratings, or unrated junior or equity tranches). Though usually only very secure assets are assigned the lowest default probability, based on such financial engineering, securities based on sub-prime mortgages can receive the highest triple A credit rating by the dominant rating agencies.[7]

This 'entanglement' points to the need for comprehensive regulation that does not rely predominantly on credit ratings. In the context of systemic disruptions, a change in credit ratings has similar effects to those of mark-to-market accounting, creating a high demand for liquidity in non-liquid times. What actually has been created is an enlargement of the capital basis for banks along with other opaque legal entities involved in creating financial products in order to hide their financial relations to banking institutions. The next section turns to the regulatory debate about shadow banking.

Regulatory reform and its consequences

As outlined above, shadow banking provides a new way to create debt in a seemingly very profitable and, at the same time, low-risk way, at least as long as most parts of the financial system remain intact. However, as indicated by the Asian Financial Crisis and the failure of Long-Term Capital Management, an emergence of 'super portfolios' disrupts the effectiveness of hedging strategies (see MacKenzie 2003), especially if a seemingly highly improbable event challenges the financial order systematically. CDOs, for instance, can be highly efficient if the financial system complies with the projected risk trajectory, assuming that systemic events might happen once in a 1,000 years (implying that a financial system would last that long and that a single event could be imagined in similar distance from present times). The watering down of eligibility criteria for individual creditors and financial products has been long ignored. The systemic success of shadow banking produces new risk configurations through massive supply and demand for private debt—a self-reinforcing, systemic effect that should have been prevented by the pre-global financial crisis regulatory framework.

Considering that activities pertaining to the shadow banking system "often generate benefits for the financial system and real economy, for example by providing alternative financing to the economy and by creating competition in financial markets that may lead to innovation, efficient credit allocation and cost reduction" (FSB 2012: 3), ex post regulatory proposals can also be read as a blueprint to enable such intermediation chains and risk mitigation strategies.

The Basel framework for banking regulation interconnected the international banking system more closely by providing common standards, especially for capital requirements and capital transactions. Consequently, securitization can be pursued within an internationalized market through a common understanding of risk, allowing for the decreased hindrance of financial exchange by national borders. The different jurisdictional provisions concerning banking enable a practice of cherry picking the most suitable legal framework for enhancing and modifying the respective business strategies of financial firms.

As the Joint Forum (2009: 18) highlights: "because the Basel II framework is more risk sensitive, it is likely to have a material effect on bank investors in terms of their interest in various types of securities." The heightened sensitivity of financial regulation compared to the Basel I framework for financial practices creates incentives for the increased compliance of asset portfolios with the risk hierarchies implemented via Basel II. What looked like a success of the regulatory process, however, turned out to be a trigger in demand for tailored investment products suitable for the respective risk portfolios of banks and provided by shadow banking, which thus became an incremental part of global financial intermediation (Plantin 2014).

One driver of this change was the inclusion of a portfolio invariant risk conception in regulatory standards. This established a singular understanding of risk, meaning that risk could be calculated and compared independently of its spatial, temporal, or institutional origin (Kessler & Wilhelm 2013). Thus, "diversification effects would depend on how well a new loan fits into an existing portfolio" (BCBS 2005: 4). The portfolio in question is made up of risk-weighted assets, which undergo a mark-to-market valuation. In this way, banks are asked to manage their balance sheets according to market variations in a shared governance system to keep up with the regulatory demands concerning their respective capital requirements.

Credit ratings for financial institutions and financial products provide a widespread standard along which the risk structure of a bank's balance sheet can be calculated. When market developments are retained in the projected range of risk frames, credit ratings provide the 'facts,' which "suffice to determine the capital charges of credit instruments" (BCBS 2005: 4). The underlying formulae to calculate the needed regulatory capital contain, however, several assumptions about the functioning of markets (for example, differentiated risk weights for sovereign bonds and car loans). After a crisis, however, these assumptions seem to apply only if ratings had not been built into financial instruments, thus aligning the balance sheets of banks to regulatory requirements and potentially providing for a shared crisis trigger when ratings change for financial product categories.

One assumption built into the capital requirements calculation is that capital charges for long-term obligations should be higher than for short-term exposure. Lower capital charges for short-term investments and similar investment strategies create investment incentives and, thereby, demand for such products by money market funds. An increasing demand for an 'efficient' maturity transformation stimulates the need for (seemingly less riskier) short-term debt leading in turn to an increase in the rollover of long-term investments through the issuance of short-term securitized debt. To do so, the shadow banking system makes use of collateralized liabilities which can be produced more 'efficiently' off the traditional and regulated banking sector's balance sheets (Plantin 2014).

Still needed to create such money-like securities is a high degree of standardization, that is, a high degree of information insensitivity paired with broadly accepted standards of transparency. Both aspects are achieved through the regulation of risk weights of securitization categories (especially asset classes like securities backed by prime mortgages), as well as external ratings provided by credit rating agencies. This combination creates an 'opaque' and, at the same time, a clear basis for investment decisions in favor of asset-backed securities and securities thereof (Gorton 2015).

There is a sense of there being enough information about abstract categories like a senior tranche of a mortgage portfolio, as well as a sense that the construction of structured investment products is immune to detailed disclosures of the performance of single mortgages. Thus, the rollover risk created through the transformation of single mortgages with long-term maturity into short-term securities can be eliminated, especially via the use of 'risk neutral' special investment vehicles. Only through such a legal structure can the exchange of collateralized products function in a money-like fashion.

Although trust in, and the liquidity of, shadow banking practices has vanished, regulators across the globe still try to refine the legal structure to make market-based banking more resilient (ECB & BoE 2014; ESRB 2015; FSB 2015a; BCBS & IOSCO 2015; IMF 2015). These efforts commonly agree about the need to provide more granular data about distinctive investment products, as well as the need to better understand how financial institutions are linked. Therefore, the importance of central clearing counterparties has risen due to further adjustment of the Basel scheme (BCBS 2011). The calculation of risk is now related to how banks interact ('interconnectedness'), to their lending along economic cycles ('pro-cyclicality'), to their indebtedness ('leverage ratio'), as well as to the size of banking institutions ('too-big-to-fail'). Each source of risk is now counterbalanced by increased capital buffers (higher risk weights) or lending and borrowing limits (a leverage ratio) to be fully implemented by 2019.

The regulatory net within the European Union (EU), for instance, has been transformed fundamentally since 2008 in response to the global financial crisis. The European Commission proposed new or reformed directives and regulations that change the modes of financial interaction. Institutions like the European Banking Authority, the European Insurance and Occupational Pension Authority, the European Securities and Markets Authority, and the European Systemic Risk Board provide further insights into market operations. Together, these developments impact on a more general conception of financial markets in the EU.

The systemic interconnectedness of the credit system via shadow banking and across jurisdictions has been enabled by common regulatory constructions and complementary cash flows across the Atlantic. Regulatory agencies, private associations, individual, national, and regional actors are all accountable for triggering the build-up of systemic risk and its consequences, although, as separate entities, they are perhaps unaware of creating an unprotected credit system inherently prone to runs. The systemic disruption of the financial system after the Lehman Brothers' failure created the need for further integration of the international financial order for credit and debt. This paradoxical situation—that is, regulating interconnectedness via a broader common regulatory framework—may not be resolved without understanding the socio-political underpinnings of the financial system. Further regulation may defer but not avoid systemic sensitivity.

Conclusion: heterodox economics and shadow banking

Shadow banking reflects the increasing homogeneity of the global financial rules that have been pushed into the direction of globally shared categories for financial regulation and practices. This shift is accompanied by not only an unprecedented compatibility of the varieties of international financial capitalism, but also a synchronicity of reactions and consequences in times of crisis. Thereby, financial regulation becomes part of the production of global categories for risk, resilience, or even safety. These aspects, however, are not restricted to the economic domain; nor can they be separated from the socio-political production of purposes or value systems for financial relations. Heterodox economics, in contrast with the mainstream view, provides several pathways to understand the present regime of accumulation. Heterodox economics allows not only an abstract analysis of certain value regimes like currencies, government bonds, or other debt securities, but also an evaluation of the conjunction of financial and societal relations. The orchestration of shadow and traditional banking will not work within a clear-cut regulatory (global) space, but will allow variegation of specificities beyond financial relations. The socio-political aspect of finance and the financial aspect of politics and society have far reaching implications for the reasoning of one value system against another. In this context, finance is one analytical entry point to understand variegation and its associated socio-political hierarchies.

In this regard, the balance of public and private forces points to an ongoing struggle that is not restricted to the field of finance. The preference for private over public debt, debt over taxes, or growth over sustainability structures the financial world; finance, however, enables specific relations over others when conducted in the social world. This points to a rather old concept in institutional economics, that is, how to value the future, expressed in the notion of 'futurity' by John R. Commons (1925: 376) at a time when economics was closer to sociology, history, and other social science disciplines.

The notion of futurity allows for the analysis of conceptions of the future rooted in the present and for the structuring of financial flows. In this way, a broader understanding of the socio-political production for imaginary thinking is needed, which considers the institutionalizations of future imaginations in the present. Possibly one of the most prominent accounts may be represented by pension schemes; one of the most popular can be seen in science fiction movies as guidance for technological innovation.

The problem of shadow banking shows the 'plumbing' of such imaginaries, as it directs monetary resources accordingly. The recent global financial crisis and its widespread consequences raised questions not only about economic theory but also about the political systems governing global relations. After its seemingly local origin, the market interruption challenged long-standing practices of central banks, transnational banking, and international financial regulation. The crisis intervened into economic and political procedures previously perceived as the norm for financial interactions. Systemic interruptions, hence, provide a context within which not only the failure of rules comes to light, but also the assumptions about the normal perception of a time to come.

Notes

1 Financial innovation cannot be reduced to individual financial products; rather, it is the way in which financial flows are reconfigured and thereby create new connections between financial products and new organizational nodes (that is, financial institutions organizing exchanges). For a more detailed explanation see Guttmann (2016: Ch. 5).
2 One should not overlook the increasing involvement of central banks in financial exchanges as a counterparty connected to a greater number of financial institutions; and also via their balance sheets and the assets covering a more extensive spectrum of involvement.
3 Mark-to-market accounting is an asset value measurement method based on current market prices that directly link market volatilities to balance sheet exposures, such as securities for trading purposes. This means that capital ratios have to adapt to current market conditions, and that there has to be a market for such financial products in order to generate a market price—both aspects are rather critical for the soundness of financial institutions in the contexts of market turmoil or crisis.
4 Often this practice is also understood as dis-intermediation or a market-based credit system, as the main intermediaries between creditors and debtors (banks) are not directly involved. For the purpose of creating products suitable for a market-based credit system, such as Mortgage Backed Securities, the original mortgage contract has to pass thorough several legal entities, which extend the intermediation chain.
5 Money Market Mutual Funds, for instance, had been main drivers for the repackaging of mortgage loans into differentiated securities as they provide an alternative to government bonds in terms of the probability of default assumptions though promising higher returns.
6 The move from an originate-to-hold to an originate-to-distribute business model also marks the changing incentive structure for risk evaluations. There might be a greater incentive to look at the underlying

collateral if banks want to hold a credit they originated to maturity than when they never held the asset but only orchestrate its legal creation. In the latter case, profit does not arise from interest but from fees, which encourage an expansion of the financial manufacturing industry, that is, shadow banking.

7 The role of credit rating agencies in misrepresenting the actual risk of structured financial products should not be understated, though there is a broad discussion on their role in generating the crisis dynamics through their conflicts of interest in the rating of financial products by the institutions that profit from higher rating results. This chapter however discusses more specifically the internal function of shadow banking.

References

Bakk-Simon, K., Borgioli, S., Giron, C., Hampell, H., Maddaloni, A., Racine, F., & Rosati, S. 2012. Shadow banking in the Euro area: an overview. European Central Bank Occasional Paper Series, No. 133. Available from https://www.ecb.europa.eu/pub/pdf/scpops/ecbocp133.pdf [Accessed March 15, 2016]

BCBS. 1986. The management of banks' off-balance-sheet exposures. Basel Committee on Banking Supervision, March.

BCBS. 2005. An explanatory note on the Basel II IRB risk weight functions. Basel Committee on Banking Supervision, July.

BCBS. 2009. Strengthening the resilience of the banking sector: consultative document. Basel Committee on Banking Supervision, December.

BCBS. 2011. Basel III: A global regulatory framework for more resilient banks and banking systems. Basel Committee on Banking Supervision, December.

BCBS & IOSCO. 2015. Criteria for identifying simple, transparent and comparable securitisations. Basel Committee on Banking Supervision & International Organization of Securities Commissions, July.

Bengtsson, E. 2013. 'Shadow banking and financial stability: European money market funds in the global financial crisis.' *Journal of International Money and Finance*, 32 (3): 579–594.

BIS. 2008. BIS 78th annual report. Bank for International Settlements, June.

Borio, C. 2005. 'Monetary and financial stability: so close and yet so far?' *National Institute Economic Review*, 192 (1): 84–101.

Bouvard, M., Chaigneau, P., & Motta, A.D. 2015. 'Transparency in the financial system: rollover risk and crises.' *Journal of Finance*, 70 (4): 1805–1837.

Brunnermeier, M.K. 2009. 'Deciphering the liquidity and credit crunch 2007–2008.' *Journal of Economic Perspectives*, 23 (1): 77–100.

Bundesbank. 2014. The shadow banking system in the Euro area: overview and monetary policy implications. Deutsche Bundesbank Monthly Report, March.

CGFS. 2015. Regulatory change and monetary policy. Committee on the Global Financial System Markets Committee, CGFS Papers No. 544.

Chernenko, S. & Sunderam, A. 2014. 'Frictions in shadow banking: evidence from the lending behavior of money market mutual funds.' *Review of Financial Studies*, 27 (6): 1717–1750.

Commons, J.R. 1925. 'Law and economics.' *Yale Law Journal*, 34 (4): 371–382.

ECB & BoE. 2014. The case for a better functioning securitisation market in the European Union. A Discussion Paper. European Central Bank and Bank of England, May.

ESRB. 2015. ESRB annual report 2014. European Systemic Risk Board, July.

Fama, E.F. 1970. 'Efficient capital markets: a review of theory and empirical work.' *Journal of Finance*, 25 (2): 383–417.

Fama, E.F. 1991. 'Efficient capital markets II.' *Journal of Finance*, 46 (5): 1575–1617.

Fender, I. & Kiff, J. 2014. CDO rating methodology: some thoughts on model risk and its implications. BIS Working Paper No. 163. Available from http://www.bis.org/publ/work163.htm [Accessed March 15, 2016]

Ferrante, F. 2015. A model of endogenous loan quality and the collapse of the shadow banking system. Finance and Economics Discussion Series 2015–021.

Fisher, E. & Bernardo, J.L. 2014. The political economy of shadow banking: debt, finance, and distributive politics under a Kalecki–Goodwin–Minsky SFC framework. Levy Economics Institute Working Paper No. 801. Available from https://www.ecb.europa.eu/pub/pdf/scpops/ecbocp133.pdf [Accessed March 15, 2016]

FSB. 2011a. Shadow Banking: scoping the issues. Financial Stability Board, April 12.

FSB. 2011b. Shadow banking: strengthening oversight and regulation: recommendations of the Financial Stability Board. Financial Stability Board, October 27.

FSB. 2012. Strengthening oversight and regulation of shadow banking: policy framework for strengthening oversight and regulation of shadow banking entities. Financial Stability Board, November 18.

FSB. 2013. Strengthening oversight and regulation of shadow banking: policy framework for strengthening oversight and regulation of shadow banking entities. Financial Stability Board, August 29.

FSB. 2015a. Transforming shadow banking into resilient market-based finance: an overview of progress. Financial Stability Board, November 12.

FSB. 2015b. Transforming shadow banking into resilient market-based finance: standards and processes for global securities financing data collection and aggregation. Financial Stability Board, November 18.

FSF. 2008. Report of the financial stability forum on enhancing market and institutional resilience. Financial Stability Forum, April 7.

G20. 2010. The G20 Seoul summit leaders' declaration. Group of 20, November 11–12.

Gorton, G.B. 2015. *The Maze of Banking: History, Theory, Crisis*. Oxford: Oxford University Press.

Gorton, G.B. & Souleles, N. 2005. Special purpose vehicles and securitization. NBER Working Paper 11190. Available from https://www.ecb.europa.eu/pub/pdf/scpops/ecbocp133.pdf [Accessed March 15, 2016]

Guttmann, R. 2012. 'The heterodox notion of structural crisis.' *Review of Keynesian Economics*, 3 (2): 194–212.

Guttmann, R. 2016. *Finance-Led Capitalism. Shadow Banking, Re-Regulation, and the Future of Global Markets*. Basingstoke, UK: Palgrave Macmillan.

Hellwig, M. 1995. 'Systemic aspects of risk management in banking and finance.' *Swiss Journal of Economics and Statistics*, 131 (4): 723–737.

Hodgson, G. 2015. *Conceptualizing Capitalism: Institutions, Evolution, Future*. Chicago: University of Chicago Press.

IMF. 2014. Risk taking, liquidity, and shadow banking: curbing excess while promoting growth. International Monetary Fund, Global Financial Stability Report, October.

IMF. 2015. Navigating monetary policy: challenges and managing risks. International Monetary Fund, Global Financial Stability Report, April.

IOSCO. 2008. Report on the subprime crisis: final report. International Organization of Securities Commissions, May.

IOSCO 2009. Unregulated financial markets and products. International Organization of Securities Commissions, May.

Joint Forum. 2008. Credit risk transfer developments from 2005 to 2007, July.

Joint Forum. 2009. Report on special purpose entities, September.

Joint Forum. 2015. Consultative document: developments in credit risk management across sectors: current practices and recommendations, February.

Kessler, O. & Wilhelm, B. 2013. 'Financialization and the three utopias of shadow banking.' *Competition & Change*, 17 (3): 248–264.

Lavoie, M. 2013. 'Financialization, neo-liberalism, and securitization.' *Journal of Post Keynesian Economics*, 35 (2): 215–233.

Lysandrou, P. & Nesvetailova, A. 2015. 'The role of shadow banking entities in the financial crisis: a disaggregated view.' *Review of International Political Economy*, 22 (2): 257–279.

MacKenzie, D. 2003. 'Long-Term Capital Management and the sociology of arbitrage.' *Economy and Society*, 32 (3): 349–380.

McCulley, P. 2014. Shadow banking: its past and its future challenges. September 13. Available from https://www.youtube.com/watch?v=5R17Rp-fjqc [Accessed March 15, 2016]

Mehrling, P. 2012. 'Three principles for market-based credit regulation.' *American Economic Review*, 102 (3): 107–112.

Mehrling, P. 2014. Why central banking should be re-imagined. BIS Papers No. 79.

Mehrling, P., Pozsar, Z., Sweeney, J., & Neilson, D.H. 2015. 'Bagehot was a shadow banker: shadow banking, central banking, and the future of global finance,' *in*: S. Claessens, D. Evanoff, L. Laeven, & G. Kaufman (eds.), *Shadow Banking Within and Across National Borders*. Hackensack, NJ: World Scientific, 81–97.

Merton, R.C. 1974. 'On the pricing of corporate debt: the risk structure of interest rates.' *Journal of Finance*, 29 (2): 449–470.

Moe, T.G. 2012. Shadow banking and the limits of central bank liquidity support: how to achieve a better balance between global and official liquidity. Levy Economics Institute Working Paper No. 712. Available from http://www.levyinstitute.org/pubs/wp_712.pdf [Accessed March 15, 2016]

Nesvetailova, A. 2014. 'A crisis of the overcrowded future: shadow banking and the political economy of financial innovation.' *New Political Economy*, 20 (3): 431–453.

Ordóñez, G. 2013. Sustainable shadow banking. Working Paper. Available from http://www.sas.upenn.edu/~ordonez/pdfs/Shadow.pdf [Accessed March 15, 2016]

Ordóñez, G. & Gorton, G.B. 2014. 'Collateral crises.' *American Economic Review*, 104 (2): 1–37.

Plantin, G. 2011. Good securitization, bad securitization. IMES Discussion Paper Series, 2011-E-4. Available from http://www.imes.boj.or.jp/research/papers/english/11-E-04.pdf [Accessed March 15, 2016]

Plantin, G. 2014. 'Shadow banking and bank capital regulation.' *Review of Financial Studies*, 28 (1): 146–175.

Plantin, G., Sapra, H., & Shin, H.S. 2005. 'Marking to market, liquidity, and financial stability.' *Monetary and Economic Studies*, 23 (S-1): 133–164.

Plantin, G., Sapra, H., & Shin, H.S. 2007. Marking to market: panacea or pandora's box? Working Paper. Available from https://www.princeton.edu/~hsshin/www/mtm.pdf [Accessed March 15, 2016]

Pozsar, Z. 2008. 'The rise and fall of the shadow banking system.' *Regional Financial Review*, 44 (July): 13–15.

Pozsar, Z. 2015. A macro view of shadow banking: levered betas and wholesale funding in the context of secular stagnation. Working Paper, January 31. Available from http://ssrn.com/abstract=2558945 [Accessed March 15, 2016]

Pozsar, Z., Adrian, T., Ashcraft, A., & Boesky, H. 2010. Shadow banking. Federal Reserve Bank of New York Staff Reports No. 458.

Rajan, R. 2005. Has financial development made the world riskier? NBER Working Paper 11728. Available from http://www.nber.org/papers/w11728V [Accessed March 15, 2016]

Ryoo, S. 2013. 'Bank profitability, leverage and financial instability: a Minsky–Harrod model.' *Cambridge Journal of Economics*, 37 (5): 1127–1160.

Shin, H.S. 2009. Financial intermediation and the post-crisis financial system. BIS Working Paper No. 304. Available from http://www.bis.org/publ/work304.pdf [Accessed March 15, 2016]

Stein, J. 2010. 'Securitization, shadow banking, and financial fragility.' *Daedalus*, 139 (4): 41–51.

Ülgen, F. 2014. 'Schumpeterian economic development and financial innovations: a conflicting evolution.' *Journal of Institutional Economics*, 10 (2): 257–277.

Wray, L.R. 2009. 'The rise and fall of money manager capitalism: a Minskian approach.' *Cambridge Journal of Economics*, 33 (4): 807–828.

20

The informal economy in theory and policy

Prospects for well-being

Elizabeth Hill

The activities and processes that constitute what we call 'the economy' are typically characterized in formal terms based on strict definitions. This is true across mainstream and heterodox traditions alike. Many of these definitions and frameworks of analysis, however, sideline a large number of activities that contribute directly to the process of capitalist provisioning and human well-being.

Feminist and environmental approaches to economics have highlighted some of these problems and challenged orthodox conceptions of the economy in their work on reproductive labor, care, nature, and the environment. In this literature, mainstream economic ideas of 'value,' 'work,' 'production,' and 'reproduction' are contested and exposed as blind to essential economic processes and relations of capitalist accumulation (Mies 1986; Waring 1988; Daly & Cobb 1989; Beneria 2003). In the field of development economics, orthodox theories of capitalist development and economic growth in post-colonial economies have been challenged by studies on the livelihood strategies practiced in the new urban centers of the developing economies in Asia, Africa, and Latin America. These studies have produced a rich body of theoretical and empirical scholarship that focuses on economic activities that do not conform to mainstream understandings of the regular or 'formal economy.'

Scholars coined the concept 'the informal sector' to help them analyze these alternative economic activities and their relationship to the mainstream capitalist economy (Hart 1973). Since the 1970s scholarship on the informal sector and processes of economic informality has burgeoned as economic development in the post-colonial world has not produced widespread formalization of the economy and informal economic activities have become entrenched. Informality is also a nascent feature of the contemporary Chinese economy and other ex-communist states, and a growing phenomenon in many post-industrial economies, sparking the interest of academics outside the development economics community (Leonard 1998; ILO 2013a).

Scholars from orthodox and some heterodox traditions have contributed to the theoretical literature on informality,[1] trying to explain the prevalence of informal economic activities and their contribution to employment, economic growth, and development. In recent years, scholarship on the reproduction and extension of informal employment and production relations has been linked to global processes of capital accumulation (Carr & Chen 2002; Chen 2006; Meagher

2013). However, expectations about the prospects of the informal economy differ: mainstream economists highlight the entrepreneurial potential of informal workers and their informal enterprises, while many heterodox scholars focus on the dynamics of exploitation and under-development, which, they argue, define the informal economy. This chapter will explore the theoretical tensions that shape the debate on the informal economy and its role in economic and human development. It begins with a short account of the evolution of the informal economy as an analytical idea and the debates around definition and measurement. The chapter then explores the social relations that structure the informal economy including the relationship between informality, gender, and poverty. The final section provides a short analysis of the global policy debate about how economic security and well-being of informal workers can be improved. This is the critical issue given the prevalence of the informal economy around the world and its direct association with socio-economic insecurity and poverty.

The informal economy in theory

The informal economy refers to economic activities, processes, and practices that are not orga-nized according to the regular rules, customs, and norms of capitalist economic institutions. Instead, informal economic activities occur beyond the purview of the state and regulatory regimes. Informality within the economy was originally identified by economists working on theories of economic development and growth in the post-colonial era of the 1950s. The first theories of economic development were premised on dualistic models of the economy in which economic activities were divided into the 'traditional' and 'modern' sectors (Lewis 1954; Harris & Todaro 1970). Price incentives in the form of higher wages were expected to attract labor away from traditional economic activities and into the modern industrial sec-tor. This shift in the allocation of labor out of marginal, unproductive, and survival-oriented activities and into formal processes of capitalist production would then provide the founda-tion for national economic growth (Lewis 1954). As labor relocated and capitalist economic development took hold in the newly independent nations in Africa, Asia, and Latin America, it was assumed the traditional, informal economy would slowly fade away and become an arti-fact of economic history. This has not occurred. Instead, economic informality has become a common and embedded feature of many developing countries, and is resurgent in some post-industrial economies.

Mainstream development economists were not only wrong about the transience of the informal economy, but also about the dynamism of informal economic activities, their contribu-tion to livelihood and connection to the formal economy. Keith Hart's (1973) study of Ghana was the first to challenge the underlying assumptions of orthodox dualistic approaches to economic development. Empirical data collected among urban migrants to Ghana's capital, Accra, showed that many of the economic activities economists previously deemed 'traditional' or informal and hence marginal and unproductive constituted a dynamic and productive sector of the modern Ghanaian economy. Hart's study established that inflation, low wages, and a surplus supply of labor in the urban labor market of Accra had led to the emergence of a high degree of infor-mality in the economic activities of workers he defined as the 'sub-proletariat.' These empirical findings led to Hart's coining of the 'informal sector' concept, based on an analytical distinction between workers employed in the 'formal sector' and those employed in the 'informal sector' of the economy.

According to Hart, the difference between the two sectors was the degree to which work was rationalized, controlled, and predictable. Workers recruited on a permanent and regular basis for fixed rewards were deemed to be part of the 'formal sector' and workers who were self-employed, unable to find work in the formal sector due to a lack of opportunities and training constituted the 'informal sector' (Hart 1973: 68). Hart found that workers in Accra were active participants in a range of informal economic activities that provided many of the city's essential services, were productive, and generated growth and employment. Models of economic development, he argued, needed to recognize both informal and formal economic structures, and support the productive, employment, and growth-generating capacity of informal workers and their activities.

The ILO World Employment Program in Kenya was also studying the informal sector at this time, but from the point of view of the enterprise. The Kenya study differentiates between the characteristics of informal and formal enterprises[2] and, similarly to Hart, concluded that the bulk of informal activities were productive, economically efficient, and profit making: "a sector of thriving economic activity and a source of Kenya's future wealth" (ILO 1972: 5). The ILO's focus on the employment and growth potential of informal enterprises challenged orthodox approaches to economic development and growth in post-colonial economies. While the dualists saw low productivity and residual survival-based strategies, Hart and the ILO saw productivity and innovation. They argued the state needed to change its approach to informal workers and their enterprises and instead of ignoring them, develop inclusive policies of economic support.

Hart and the ILO's ground-breaking and upbeat studies of the informal economy as a hub of economic dynamism were disputed by many scholars working from a heterodox perspective. Drawing on Latin American dependency theory (Frank 1967) and world systems theory (Wallerstein 1974), micro-studies from across the developing world emphasized the structural nature of the relationship between informal and formal sector activities as one of dependence and exploitation (Leys 1973; King 1974; Obregon 1974; LeBrun & Gerry 1975; Breman 1976; Gerry 1978; Moser 1978; Davies 1979; Santos 1979; Portes *et al.* 1989). In these studies scholars argue that informal and formal economic activities are deeply integrated according to relations of structural exploitation which constrain the potential for growth and accumulation among informal activities. They conclude that, in a competitive global market place, it is the informal economy that provides the cheap goods and services that underwrite capital accumulation in the formal economy. Recent scholarship on global value chains has bolstered the appeal of this approach.

Contrary to this hypothesis is the work of scholars working in a socio-legalist tradition—an approach exemplified in the work of Hernando de Soto (1989, 2000). De Soto argues the informal economy persists and is becoming widespread because of the excessive transaction costs imposed on economic activities by 'mercantilist-style' government regulations and bureaucratic controls that serve the interests of wealthy elites and inflict excessive compliance costs on regular people wanting to make a living. According to this school of thought, bureaucratic constraints and high barriers to entry are the driver of expanded informality—the only logical, survival-based mass alternative form of economic organization. Legalists argue that governments should simplify the bureaucratic and regulatory system so informal workers can gain legal recognition and access to the productive resources that will enhance productivity and allow them to accumulate capital. This optimistic free market approach to the informal economy has been adopted by mainstream economic development institutions such as the World Bank and a number of governments in Latin America and Eastern Europe, who see private initiative and enterprise as the fundamental building blocks of economic development.

These competing approaches to understanding what lies behind the prevalence and recent growth in economic informality reflect different economic and ideological traditions. None of them, however, captures the vast heterogeneity that defines the informal economy. Informal work as a survival strategy has a long history in developing economies where formal jobs are rare. This is also becoming a strategy used in times of economic crisis such as the Great Recession of 2008

(Horn 2009). However, informal employment is not always the choice of the worker. Increasingly, informality is the choice of employers and companies wanting to avoid the regulatory costs associated with formally organized economic production and employment. Much of the current growth in informal wage labor is the result of formal jobs being informalized through processes of contracting out and the expansion of other non-standard production and employment relationships. The extension of global production chains and new trade relationships often rely upon competition between workers and can affect the shape of the informal economy and workers' employment options (Standing 1999).

In the early twenty-first century, theoretical literature on the informal economy has taken a pragmatic turn with old ways of framing the debate giving way to more open, inclusive, and dynamic approaches that better capture the heterogeneity and dynamism of the informal economy across the development spectrum. These pragmatic responses are based on an acknowledgment that economic informality is not a historical anomaly but a 'normal' and regular feature of capitalist economies (Jutting & de Laiglesia 2009). It is now generally recognized that the informal economy provides employment for hundreds of millions of people around the world and that informal enterprises generate a significant amount of national Gross Domestic Product (GDP). It is also commonly accepted that the informal economy is integrated in complex ways into formal processes of production, distribution, and exchange, and that people who perform informal work are scattered across a myriad of occupations producing legal goods and services.

Within this more pragmatic approach informal employment has become the focus. This is captured in the ILO's reformulation of informality as a continuum of economic relationships and activities organized according to the extent to which work is rationalized and employment is regulated. At one end of the continuum are highly formalized economic activities. At the other are those activities that are most informal (ILO 2002). Informal employment is problematized as unregulated, insecure, and mostly very poorly paid, with workers highly exposed to the risk of poverty. This approach has influenced policy makers who interpret worker vulnerability and the 'gap' in workers' basic rights, legal protection, representation, and access to basic social security provisions as 'problems' in need of redress. In policy circles, this approach has culminated in the 'formalization debate,' which will be discussed in the final section of this chapter (ILC 2015).

Mapping and measuring the informal economy

Running parallel to the theoretical debate has been an international discussion about how to improve data collection on informal employment, the value of production in the informal economy, and its contribution to national economic growth (Charmes 2012). In 1993 the International Conference of Labour Statisticians (ICLS) passed a resolution on the informal sector to be included in national labor force and economic surveys. The definition focused on characteristics of the enterprise in which people worked, stipulating that:

> These [informal] units typically operate at a low level of organization, with little or no division between labour and capital as factors of production and on a small scale. Labour relations – where they exist – are based mostly on casual employment, kinship or personal and social relations rather than contractual arrangements with formal guarantees. . . . Production units of the informal sector have the characteristic features of household enterprises. . . .
>
> *ILO 1993: Point 5*

The definition provided a useful foundation but excluded a number of important economic activities including agricultural and related activities, households producing goods for their own use, domestic housework, care work, paid domestic work, and volunteer services. In 1997 the Delhi Group on Informal Sector Statistics was set up by the United Nations (UN) Statistical Commission to improve and develop the definition and data collection. This work culminated in a second resolution on the informal economy by the ICLS in 2003 and included an extended definition based on a conceptual framework that combines an enterprise-based concept of employment in the informal sector with a broader jobs-focused concept of informal employment. This expanded definition redefined the informal economy in terms of informal employment in which economic informality is determined by the level of protection and regulation of work, irrespective of the type of employment arrangement or whether the type of economic unit people operate or work for are informal enterprises, formal enterprises or households:

> Employees are considered to have informal jobs if their employment relationship is, in law or in practice, not subject to national labor legislation, income taxation, social protection or entitlement to certain employment benefits (advance notice of dismissal, severance pay, paid annual or sick leave, etc.).
>
> *ILO 2003: 51*

The expanded definition includes casual, short-term, and seasonal workers, own-account workers engaged in their own informal enterprise; employers in their own informal sector enterprises; contributing family workers; members of informal producers' cooperatives; employees holding informal jobs; and own-account workers producing goods for their household use. It also includes workers in formal sector enterprises who are not entitled to basic protection and social security.

Improved statistical guidelines and increased interest in the informal economy by governments and policy makers have led to a rise in the collection and reporting of both the size of the informal economy and its contribution to national growth. A recent study by Vanek *et al.* (2014) shows that informal employment is growing. In developing economies, informality is expanding into new and unexpected places—including the formal economy. In India, for instance, growth in informal employment has been most pronounced in the formal sector as contracting out of what were previously secure, regular, public, and private sector jobs has become common. This reflects a broader trend towards informalization in many OECD economies where neoliberal policy approaches to production and human resource management have seen an escalation in the contracting out of key business services. This is prevalent in both the private and public sectors. Employment in the service economy has been particularly vulnerable to the development of fixed-term and increasingly insecure forms of employment.

In developing countries, informal employment is a prevalent feature of the economy even when the agricultural sector is not counted. In most regions, informality defines more than half of non-agricultural employment: 82 percent in South Asia, 66 percent in sub-Saharan Africa, 65 percent in East and South East Asia, and 51 percent in Latin America. In the Middle East and North Africa, informal employment makes up 45 percent of non-agricultural employment, while Eastern Europe and Central Asia have a low level of informality at only 10 percent reflecting a history of central planning. In China, 33 percent of non-agricultural employment is informal (Vanek *et al.* 2014: 8).

Statistics on informal employment are commonly limited to the non-agricultural economy. However, it is important not to lose sight of agricultural employment when evaluating the reach of the informal economy. The vast majority of agricultural work is informally organized—either as self-employment or as casual/daily waged labor—with no basic social security or labor protection measures available to workers. Temporary labor migrants employed informally in another country are also not normally included in informal labor statistics. The informal nature of much of temporary labor migration is particularly pronounced in the case of female domestic workers who work in countries where the employment conditions of domestic workers are informal, and regulation and social security is absent (ILO 2013b: 41–45).

The mapping and measurement of informal employment in OECD economies is only just beginning. It is complicated by different models of the welfare state in which some countries provide universal health and social protection benefits to all citizens, and others deliver social protection as a workplace entitlement, but only for those engaged in standard employment relationships. This has made identifying a set of employment categories that reflect the ICLS's 2003 conceptual framework difficult. In the most recent data, the categories of non-standard employment, atypical jobs, temporary, and part-time work are considered proxies for informality because they tend to deliver low employment security and limited access to social protection entitlements. These forms of non-standard or informal work are becoming a regular feature in OECD economies (ILO 2013a).

The associated rise in labor insecurity or 'precarious labor' is an idea increasingly cited in the literature on changing employment in post-industrial economies. Guy Standing (2011) argues the conditions of 'precarity' are a structural feature of global capitalism in the early twenty-first century, and that the neoliberal turn in many OECD economies is producing a new social class of workers denied the social and economic benefits gained by organized labor during the twentieth century. In this, and other literature on the changing nature of work, the focus is on the political economy of growing informalization. Emergent forms of informal employment in rich countries may not directly mirror those in low- and middle-income countries, but they do share many features in common and are producing a new class of working poor (Shipler 2004; ILO 2013a).

In addition to the large number of jobs provided by the informal economy, informal economic activities also make an important contribution to national and global GDP. Calculating the value of informal work and production is complex and the available data is not as complete as that for employment, but recent estimates of the contribution of the informal economy to GDP are high. If agriculture is included in the calculation, then informal economic activities account for nearly two-thirds of GDP in sub-Saharan Africa, 54 percent in India, and nearly one-third of Latin America's GDP. When agricultural activities are excluded, then informal economic activities contribute half of GDP in sub-Saharan Africa, 46 percent in India, and one-quarter of Latin America GDP (Charmes 2012: 128). Estimates are not available for OECD economies but given the rapid expansion of informal employment in many of these countries, it is expected that the economic value produced by these workers is also growing.

Exploitation and vulnerability: the social and spatial relations of informal work

Why does the informal economy persist even as economic growth, improved education, and health have come to many developing countries? Why is it an emerging feature of developed economies? And why is informality a 'problem'?

The persistent reproduction and expansion of the informal economy in many countries can be understood as a function of its capacity to meet both the needs of the low-skilled masses for employment and the interests of global capital for cheap labor. That is to say, the informal economy has a dual function. The mismatch between growth in the working age population and the number of formal employment opportunities in many developing economies leaves the unskilled masses with no option except to create their own employment opportunities as wage laborers or in self-employment. Much informal employment is a survival strategy, a form of employment of last resort.

At the same time as the need for employment pushes people into informal forms of work, there is also a pull factor operating in these markets. Capital, both local and global, is attracted by a large pool of low-wage and unregulated labor that can be easily integrated into local and global production. Many of these workers operate essentially as industrial outworkers, often in their homes across Asia, Africa, and Latin America doing piece-rate work for global sporting, electronics, or garment companies. Periodically, reports of unrestrained exploitation, devastation, or death in informal workplaces become global news (Doherty 2012). Nevertheless, global value chains remain an important feature of global production and trade. The relationship between trade and employment is complex with empirical research showing that trade does produce new employment opportunities for the unskilled, but many of these, at least in the short-term, tend to be informal and marked by associated forms of socio-economic insecurity and vulnerability (Carr & Chen 2002; Bacchetta et al. 2009).[3]

Informal employment is closely linked to economic insecurity, poverty, and inequality. While not everyone who is informally employed is poor, there is a strong correlation between poverty and participation in informal employment. This is due to the exploitative nature of the social relations that structure informal employment, production, and exchange (Hill 2010). In contrast to 'normal' capital-labor relations, informal labor is incompletely separated from the means of production and subject to a range of non-capitalist methods of surplus production and accumulation. In the informal economy, exploitation is enhanced by the absence of formal employment contracts that normally offer some protection. Instead, labor control is maintained via a complex web of social and cultural relationships that are superimposed on unregulated labor market structures and operate beyond the purview of the state.

The insecurities and vulnerabilities associated with informal employment are therefore derived from both the worker's employment status, and the location of their work. Informal workers are located in all forms of industry including agriculture, retail, manufacturing, and a myriad of services. Within this complex array of economic activities, the economic insecurity and vulnerability that defines informal employment are closely linked to a worker's status as self-employed, as wage labor, or a dependent contractor (Carre 2013). The following four categories capture the various employment modalities that structure the informal economy and mediate a worker's relationship with formal institutional and regulatory systems.

The self-employed. This category includes employers, own-account workers, and unpaid contributing family workers. The self-employed are not formally employed by another person, and work ostensibly on their own behalf in either their own small enterprise or as an independent contractor in a longer production chain. Employment as an independent contractor or 'micro-entrepreneur' is often presented as an autonomous form of economic activity in which the worker maintains a level of control over the working day. However, as sole traders responsible for the entire production and distribution process, many self-employed workers enter into permanent relationships with contractors and retailers in an attempt to secure continuous flows of employment. Social relations of gender, class, ethnicity, and class shape these informal relationships, allowing contactors to set the terms of production and exchange in their own favor. Difficulties in procuring official licenses that allow the self-employed to trade freely in a secure and regular environment also hamper productivity and economic security. In the absence of appropriate documentation, workers remain vulnerable to harassment and exploitation by local authorities in the form of bribery or the confiscation of goods. These structural forms of economic insecurity and exploitation are intensified by a lack of access to social security provisions such as paid sick leave, unemployment benefits, life insurance, and paid parental leave.

Wage employment. This includes casual day laborers, and short-term piece-rate and contract workers. Wage laborers may be employed on a regular basis but without a contract of employment. Casual workers rely on labor contractors or individual employers for the provision of work and can be employed on a monthly wage, a fixed daily rate, or on a piece-rate where they are paid according to the number of times a specific task is completed. Informal wage employment is typically insecure, subject to seasonal variations, and transient. Without an official employment contract workers are not protected by national labor laws and have no workplace entitlement to social security. With no formal employment contract, workers are vulnerable to the non-payment and under-payment of wages.

Dependent contractors. This category includes industrial outworkers. Dependent contractors are formally dependent workers who enter into a direct relationship with either the factory from where the worker collects the raw materials ready for processing, or with a sub-contractor who delivers the raw materials to the worker's home. These workers are paid on a piece-rate basis, with the total wage determined by the employer/contractor after production has been completed. The contractor or factory representative assesses the quality of the product, and sets the wage. Products deemed to be of poor quality or spoiled are deducted from the total wage, even when the quality of the finished product is directly related to the low quality of the original raw materials supplied. Gender, class, ethnic, and caste hierarchies are deployed to maximize the subordination and exploitation of dependent contractors.

The spatial relations of informal production. Where informal workers perform their work has a substantial impact on the social relations of informal production and the reward for work. Many informal workers—self-employed, dependent contractors, and domestic and personal service workers—are located in private homes, either their own, or that of their employer. The private nature of the home-based setting contributes to the potential for exploitative work conditions, and constrains worker socio-economic security. Home-based workers are particularly vulnerable due to their social isolation and the lack of protective labor laws. The individualized work experience of home-based employment makes it very easy for contractors and employers to use personal threats and misinformation to exploit workers, as well as to keep wages at a minimum and the hours of work long. In most countries, industrial laws do not regulate work undertaken in the private space of one's own home or that of an employer, leaving workers with no protective regulatory framework.

Informal work performed in public spaces is also problematic. Vendors, waste collectors, construction, and transport workers perform their jobs on the streets where they compete for physical space and legitimacy with formal economy enterprises, private cars, and citizens. Informal workers trading in public are often harassed by authorities and abused by members of the public for using communal spaces to trade, even as they provide many of the essential services of the city. Lack of essential infrastructure, such as secure market places, shelter, drinking water, and public amenities adds to worker vulnerability curbing productivity and income earned.

Informality, poverty, and gender

The social and spatial relations of the different structures of informal employment mean that the socio-economic security and well-being of workers is largely determined by their employment status. This produces a stratified effect on the relationship between informal employment and the risk of poverty, with marked differences in outcome for employers, 'regular' wage earners, own-account operators, casual wage-workers, home-based and industrial workers, and those engaged in unpaid family work (see Figure 20.1).

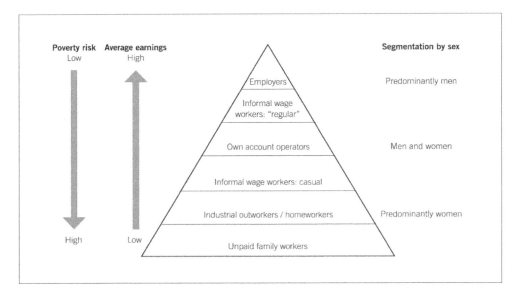

Figure 20.1 WIEGO model of informal employment: hierarchy of earnings and poverty risk by employment status and sex
Source: Chen (2012: 9).

Employers engaging in the informal economy tend to receive the highest average earnings and be least prone to the risk of poverty because they are least exposed to productivity and income-limiting dynamics in their daily work lives. Regular wage earners employed informally are not as protected and are exposed to a range of exploitative practices that constrain their earnings and put them at some risk of poverty. Own-account operators and or casual/daily wage-workers are much more vulnerable, as they face systemic forms of exploitation as discussed above. But variation in the relations of exploitation associated with different employment relationships causes the wages of regular wage earners to be higher than those of own-account workers who are more highly exposed to the risk of poverty.

The workers most vulnerable to exploitative and productivity-limiting practices are industrial outworkers and other 'self-employed' home-based workers. Vulnerability is reflected (and reproduced) in the low wages they receive and the associated risk of poverty. For all informal workers, limited access to protective labor laws and social security entitlements means that misadventure or natural disaster has a compounding negative impact on socio-economic security and well-being, leaving many informal workers vulnerable to chronic poverty. The link between informal employment and poverty has been observed in India: for example, informal workers are twice as likely (20.5 percent) as formal workers (11.3 percent) to be poor (NCEUS 2007: 24).

Gender is another stratifying feature of informal employment and its economic returns. In Latin America, sub-Saharan Africa, South Asia, and China, informal employment is a greater source of non-agricultural work for women compared to men (Vanek *et al.* 2014: 8).[4] Moreover, within the informal economy, women tend to be disproportionately concentrated in the less secure, lower-paid types of employment as informal wage-workers, casual, and home-based workers. Men dominate the relatively more secure higher-waged forms of informal employment.

This is not only the result of direct discrimination, but also a reflection of the prevailing sexual division of labor (UN Women 2015). Across both developing and developed economies, women are assumed to be the primary carers of dependent family members and primarily responsible for the labor of social reproduction. This limits their capacity to perform paid work and a lack of supportive social infrastructure such as childcare and aged care services mean that the majority of women have limited choices about the type of paid work they do. In most cases, women seek employment that enables them to combine caring and household reproduction with paid work. This inevitably limits women's productivity and hence economic security.

These structures of gender inequality are reflected in the very high rates of self-employed women in the informal economy, and their concentration in home-based forms of work—both of which severely limit productivity and wage-earning capacity. In all developing regions, self-employment constitutes a greater share of informal employment (non-agriculture) than wage employment, representing nearly one-third of total non-agricultural employment world-wide (ILO 2013a). Furthermore, women in all regions (except Eastern Europe and Central Asia) are more likely than men to be self-employed (ILO 2013a). Gendered hierarchies mean women are doubly exposed to the risk of poverty: they are more likely than men to be employed in the informal economy which typically delivers lower rates of pay than formal employment; and, women's employment status locates them disproportionately towards the bottom of the informal labor market pyramid performing work that is highly vulnerable to exploitation, low wages, and poverty. This makes the informal economy and employment a key domain for researchers and policy advocates interested in women's poverty, gender equity, and empowerment.

Discussion: the global policy agenda—opportunities and contradictions

Since the 1990s, scholarship on the informal economy has burgeoned. Most of the research has been focused on improving data collection and policy initiatives. National labor force survey tools have been developed to improve the enumeration of the size and value of the informal economy, and informality has become a regular feature of policy debates on economic development and women's workforce participation in developing countries in particular. An international consensus—at least in policy circles—on what defines 'informality' has also been settled, with a focus on the relationship between employment and social security.

Informal workers have established their own membership-based organizations and lobbied for new forms of social security and workplace rights. Street vendors around the world advocate for their interests through global organizations such as StreetNet International. Home-based workers organize through HomeNet South East Asia and HomeNet South Asia. Domestic workers have organized the first global union run by women—the International Domestic Workers' Federation (IDWF). These and other national, regional, and local level informal worker organizations have successfully joined with other policy advocacy forums to secure, among other things, two international labor conventions directly aimed at improving employment and livelihoods of some informal workers: the ILO Convention on Home Work No. 177 (1996) and the ILO Domestic Workers Convention No. 189 (2011). Both conventions provide guidelines for countries to recognize, protect, and regulate informal workers.

These statistical, conceptual, organizational, and regulatory initiatives are supported by an international consensus that economic growth must be inclusive and that such inclusivity relies fundamentally on the availability of decent employment. The most recent articulation of this view is the UN Sustainable Development Goal 8, which aims to 'promote inclusive and sustainable economic growth, employment and decent work for all' (SDG 8).[5] This follows up the ILO's 2013 declaration that formalizing the informal economy is one of the Organization's eight areas of critical importance.

The International Labour Conference's 'Recommendation 204' sets out a coherent agenda for global action promoting transition from the informal to the formal economy along three pathways: the transition of workers and economic units from the informal to the formal economy; the creation of enterprises and decent jobs in the formal economy; and, preventing the informalization of formal jobs (ILC 2015). The Recommendation provides guidelines on mainstreaming economic formalization through appropriate legal and policy frameworks, employment policies, rights and social protection, good governance, social dialogue, and worker organization.

The Recommendation highlights the need for a policy framework that promotes informal worker access to the formal conditions of employment, including social security, maternity protection, decent working conditions, minimum wage, and affordable quality childcare. For small informal enterprises, the focus is on policies that reduce the barriers to and costs of formal registration and compliance, and that improve access to credit and insurance products and business training and skill development programs. Guidelines for improving industrial relations are also included and emphasize freedom of association and collective bargaining. It is important to note that Recommendation 204 is not directed solely at developing economies. The policy measures directly challenge the shift towards contracting-out, casualization, and other forms of precarious informal models of employment that have become so pervasive in OECD economies.

In many respects, the UN's SDG 8 and the ILC's Recommendation 204 call for the maintenance and extension of the post-World War II industrial relations compact that underwrote widespread prosperity and well-being in the industrialized countries. Achieving this type of policy shift will be a complex and difficult task, both practically and politically. Policy advocates argue that formalization needs to be understood as "a gradual, ongoing process of incrementally incorporating informal workers and economic units into the formal economy through strengthening them and extending their rights, protection and benefits" (WIEGO 2014). What is not discussed is the controversial nature of the formalization/decent work agenda. Formalization of the informal economy would support inclusive growth, but it would also threaten current global dynamics of capitalist development and accumulation in which the informal economy is a fundamental but subordinate feature. It is not certain if global capital would stand by while the conditions of informality that currently underwrite global competition and capital accumulation are challenged.

The formalization agenda is also likely to be politically difficult. Policies to formalize the informal economy through increased regulation and social security provision challenge the prevailing neoliberal culture of governance in both rich and poor countries, including ideas of small government, free markets, and limited social spending. The contradiction between the demands of the international policy agenda and the logic of global structures of capital accumulation and governance suggests that transformation in the socio-economic security and well-being of informal workers will not be a simple matter of technical or administrative change. Instead, access to decent formal employment will require worker organization and struggle beyond what has already been achieved through global labor conventions, national bills for social security, and provincial level agreements for improved wages and conditions for informal workers. The informal workforce is vast and continues to grow. Perhaps contemporary concerns about the negative relationship between inequality and economic growth will provoke increased impetus for global change.

Notes

1 The language used to describe 'informality' in the economy varies across the literature and includes the informal sector, the informal economy, informal enterprises, economic informality, and informal employment. In the statistical literature the terminology used has very specific meanings. In much of the general literature these terms are often used interchangeably and refer to economic activities and processes that are not bound by formal regulations of the state.
2 Informal sector enterprises were characterized by ease of entry into the market; a reliance on indigenous resources; family ownership of the enterprise; small scale of operation; dominance of labor-intensive production processes by workers who acquired their skills outside of formal training institutions; and operation in unregulated and competitive markets. Formal sector enterprises were characterized by difficulty of entry into the market; their reliance on foreign resources; corporate ownership; large-scale operations in regulated markets protected by tariffs, quotas' and trade licenses; and the use of capital-intensive and imported technology by workers who were formally trained (ILO 1972).
3 A recent analysis of the literature on the relationship between trade openness and economic informality concludes that while in most cases "trade reforms increase the incidence of informal employment, . . . [the] impact on informal sector wages is ambiguous and depends on circumstances and country specificities" (Bacchetta *et al.* 2009: 67).
4 This varies across regions but is most marked in sub-Saharan Africa where 74 percent of women non-agricultural workers are informally employed compared to 61 percent of men; and in Latin America where 54 percent of women non-agricultural workers are informally employed in comparison to 48 percent of men.
5 http://www.un.org/sustainabledevelopment/sustainable-development-goals/

References

Bacchetta, M., Ernst, E., & Bustamante, J. P. 2009. Globalization and informal jobs in developing countries. Geneva: ILO-WTO co-publication. Available from https://www.wto.org/English/res_e/booksp_e/jobs_devel_countries_e.pdf [Accessed August 21, 2015]

Beneria, L. 2003. *Gender, Development, and Globalization: Economics As If All People Mattered.* New York: Routledge.

Breman, J. 1976. 'A dualistic labour system? A critique of the 'informal sector' concept.' *Economic & Political Weekly*, 11: 1870–1876, 1905–1908, 1939–1944.

Carr, M. & Chen, M.A. 2002. Globalization and the informal economy: how global trade and investment impact on the working poor. Working Paper on the Informal Economy 2002/1. Geneva: International Labour Office.

Carre, F. 2013. Defining and categorizing organizations of informal workers in developing and developed countries. WIEGO Organizing Brief No. 8, September. Cambridge, MA: WIEGO.

Charmes, J. 2012. 'The informal economy worldwide: trends and characteristics.' *Margin: The Journal of Applied Economic Research*, 6 (2):103–132.

Chen, M. 2006. 'Rethinking the informal economy: linkages with the formal sector and the formal regulatory environment,' *in*: B. Guha-Khasnobis, R. Kanbur, & E. Ostrom (eds.), *Linking the Formal and Informal Economy: Concepts and Policies.* Oxford: Oxford University Press, 77–92.

Chen, M. 2012. The informal economy: definitions, theories and policies. WIEGO Working Paper No. 1. Cambridge, MA: WIEGO. Available from http://wiego.org/sites/wiego.org/files/publications/files/Chen_WIEGO_WP1.pdf [Accessed February 18, 2016]

Daly, H.E. & Cobb, J.B. 1989. *For the Common Good: Redirecting the Economy Toward Community, the Environment, and a Sustainable Future.* Boston: Beacon Press.

Davies, R. 1979. 'Informal sector or subordinate mode of production? A model,' *in*: R. Bromley & C. Gerry (eds.), *Casual Work and Poverty in Third World Cities.* New York: John Wiley & Sons, 87–104.

De Soto, H. 1989. *The Other Path: The Invisible Revolution in the Third World.* London: I.B. Tauris.

De Soto, H. 2000. *The Mystery of Capital: Why Capitalism Triumphs in the West and Fails Everywhere Else.* New York: Basic Books.

Doherty, B. 2012. 'Poor children made to stitch sports balls in sweatshops.' *Sydney Morning Herald*, September 22.

Gerry, C. 1978. 'Petty production and capitalist production in Dakar: the crisis of the self employed.' *World Development*, 6 (9–10): 1147–1160.

Frank, A.G. 1967. *Capitalism and Underdevelopment in Latin America.* New York: Monthly Review Press.

Frank, A.G. 1975. *On Capitalist Underdevelopment.* Bombay: Oxford University Press.

Harris, J.R. & Todaro, M. 1970 'Migration, unemployment and development: a two sector analysis.' *American Economic Review,* 60 (1): 126–142.

Hart, K. 1973. 'Informal income opportunities and urban employment in Ghana.' *The Journal of Modern African Studies,* 11 (1): 61–89.

Hill, E. 2010. *Worker Identity, Agency and Economic Development: Women's Empowerment in the Indian Informal Economy.* London: Routledge.

Horn, Z. 2009. No cushion to fall back on: the global economic crisis and informal workers. WIEGO Inclusive Cities Study. Available from http://wiego.org/sites/wiego.org/files/publications/files/Horn_ GEC_Study_2009.pdf [Accessed August 20, 2015]

International Labour Conference (ILC). 2015. Recommendation 204 concerning the transition from the informal economy, adopted by the Conference at its one hundred and fourth session, Geneva, 12 June. Available from http://www.ilo.org/wcmsp5/groups/public/—ed_norm/—relconf/documents/meeting document/wcms_377774.pdf [Accessed August 21, 2015]

International Labour Organisation (ILO). 1972. *Employment, Incomes and Equality: A Strategy for Increasing Productive Employment in Kenya.* Geneva: International Labour Office.

International Labour Organisation. 1993. *Report of the Conference.* The XVth International Conference of Labour Statisticians. January 19–28, Geneva: International Labour Office.

International Labour Organisation. 2002. *Decent Work and the Informal Economy: Report VI.* International Labour Conference, 90th Session. Geneva: International Labour Office.

International Labour Organisation. 2003. *Report 1: General Report.* Seventeenth Conference of Labour Statisticians. November 24–December 3. Geneva: International Labour Office.

International Labour Organisation. 2013a. *Women and Men in the Informal Economy: A Statistical Picture,* 2nd edn. Geneva: International Labour Office

International Labour Organisation. 2013b. *Domestic Workers Across the World: Global and Regional Statistics and the Extent of Legal Protection.* Geneva: International Labour Office.

Jutting, J.P. & de Laiglesia, J.R. (eds.) 2009. *Is Informal Normal? Towards More and Better Jobs in Developing Countries.* Paris: OECD.

King, K. 1974. 'Kenya's informal machine makers: a study of small scale industry in Kenya's emergent artisan society.' *World Development,* 2 (4–5): 9–28.

LeBrun, O & Gerry, C. 1975. 'Petty producers and capitalism.' *Review of African Political Economy,* 2 (3): 20–32.

Leonard, M. 1998. *Invisible Work, Invisible Workers: The Informal Economy in Europe and the US.* New York: St. Martin's Press.

Lewis, A.W 1954. 'Economic development with unlimited Supplies of labor.' *The Manchester School,* 22 (2): 139–191.

Leys, C. 1973. 'Interpreting African development: reflections on the ILO report on employment, incomes, and inequality in Kenya.' *African Affairs,* 72 (289): 419–429.

Meagher, K. 2013. Unlocking the informal economy: a literature review on linkages between formal and informal economies in developing countries. WIEGO Working Paper 27, Cambridge, MA: WIEGO.

Mies, M. 1986. *Patriarchy and Accumulation on a World Scale: Women in the International Division of Labour.* London. Zed Books.

Moser, C. 1978. 'Informal sector or petty commodity production: dualism or dependence in urban development?' *World Development,* 6 (9/10): 1041–1064.

National Commission for Enterprises in the Unorganized Sector (NCEUS). 2007. *Report on Conditions of Work and Promotion of Livelihoods in the Unorganized Sector.* New Delhi: Government of India.

Obregon, A. 1974. 'The marginal pole of the economy and the marginalised labour force.' *Economy & Society,* 3 (4): 393–428.

Portes, A., Castells, M., & Benton, L. (eds.) 1989. *The Informal Economy.* Baltimore, MD: The Johns Hopkins University Press.

Santos, M. 1979. *The Shared Space: Two Circuits of the Urban Economy in Underdeveloped Countries.* London: Methuen.

Shipler, D.K. 2004. *The Working Poor: Invisible in America.* New York: Vintage.

Standing, G. 1999. *Global Labour Flexibility: Seeking Distributive Justice.* New York: St. Martin's Press.

Standing, G. 2011. *The Precariat: The New Dangerous Class.* London: Bloomsbury Academic.

UN Women. 2015. *Progress of the World's Women 2015–2016: Transforming Economies, Realising Rights.* Available from http://progress.unwomen.org/en/2015/pdf/UNW_progressreport.pdf [Accessed August 20, 2015]

Vanek, J., Chen, M.A., Carre, F., Heintz, J., & Hussmanns, R. 2014. Statistics on the informal economy: definitions, regional estimates & challenges. WIEGO Working Paper (Statistics) No. 2, April. Cambridge, MA: WIEGO.

Wallerstein, I. 1974. *The Modern World System I: Capitalist Agriculture and the Origins of the European World-Economy in the Sixteenth Century.* New York: Academic Press.

Waring, M. 1988. *Counting for Nothing: What Men Value and What Women are Worth.* North Sydney: Allen & Unwin.

WIEGO. 2014. WIEGO Network Platform: transitioning from the informal to the formal economy in the interests of workers in the informal economy. Available from http://wiego.org/sites/wiego.org/files/resources/files/WIEGO-Platform-ILO-2014.pdf [Accessed on August 15, 2015]

21

Inequality and poverty

Marcella Corsi and Giulio Guarini

It will be seen how in place of the *wealth* and *poverty* of political economy come the *rich human being* and rich human need. The *rich* human being is simultaneously the human being *in need of* totality of human life—activities—the man in whom his own realization exists as an inner necessity, as *need*.

Karl Marx, *The Economic and Philosophic Manuscripts of 1844*

Introduction

A unanimously agreed idea of what heterodox economics is and where its borders are does not exist. So far, after decades of debate, opinions remain divided on the subject (Lee 2012; Elsner 2013). Thus, in dealing with inequality and poverty, we define here heterodox economics on the basis of the relationship with classical economics, on the one hand, and the attention to 'diversity,' on the other. Generally, the contemporary mainstream economic literature assumes that economic behavior can be explained through the same process applying to all individuals, at most exhibiting quantitative differences in the extent of certain individual properties (the approach of *heterogeneity*). Some heterodox approaches, as well as other social science disciplines, assume instead that individuals can be grouped into aggregates for the sake of analysis, and each group is subject to its own laws of behavior, fundamentally influenced by the socio-economic environment: the approach of *diversity* (D'Ippoliti 2011). By drawing on the classical economists, an approach based on the concept of diversity, we base our discussion on the consideration that individuals are characterized by different income levels, and are subject, some more than others, to the risks of social exclusion and poverty.

Social exclusion affects the most vulnerable individuals more severely, creating treacherous social traps; the effects of which can only be mitigated through social institutions. This implies a potential capacity for social innovation on the part of public institutions, in initiating inclusive actions adapted to address the persistent problems of social reality.

This chapter consists of two main sections. In the first section, we consider income inequality, with particular reference to the stochastic approach to the distribution of personal income. Then, in the second section, we discuss social exclusion, focusing on some theoretical and empirical dimensions of poverty, namely in the labor market, financial market, and the education system.

In this broad framework, we mostly refer to the contributions made by classical economists and by Amartya Sen, the founder of the capability and human development approach. We integrate these contributions with specific complementary perspectives, such as that of feminist economics. The main thread linking this discussion is an objective to achieve social justice within the capitalistic economic system. According to the classical viewpoint, economics is a social science, intrinsically interconnected with social, cultural, and political contexts (Martins 2011, 2012). Inequality and social exclusion represent two of the main economic aspects that can negatively influence economic and civil development. On the one hand, for a given level of poverty, a significant worsening of income distribution can generate social insecurity and political instability. On the other hand, for a given level of income distribution, an increase in poverty makes the economic system unable to ensure basic social conditions in terms of health and education. For this reason, the classical economists, although from different theoretical and political positions, evaluate inequality and poverty as two separate and distinct topics, but belonging to the same framework of economic development.

Income inequality

The nature, causes, and consequences of economic inequality have been widely investigated by economists; the first notable analysis of these topics was by Adam Smith. In *The Wealth of Nations*, Smith states that personal income distribution is affected by the institutional aspects of society but is independent of the economy; in this sense, as a result of economic growth, individual incomes move upwards rather proportionally (Smith [1776] 1976: 80, 159). In contrast, in the *Principles of Political Economy*, John Stuart Mill (1848: 699) addresses a concern that economic progress could change the income shares accrued to the middle classes, without improving the economic condition of the poorest sections of the population. However, it is with David Ricardo, and later with Karl Marx, that the distribution of income becomes a central theme of classical political economy, focusing on the social antagonisms within the process of distribution of the surplus in society and among its classes.

Income distribution remains important in Jean-Baptiste Say's work who explicitly considers personal income distribution as an indispensable element of the analysis of the demand for a good. According to Say, if a product price decreases in relation to individual incomes, more and more consumers will demand it, while less and less will demand it as it becomes more expensive (Say 1836: 272–273).

The same approach characterizes the work of Vilfredo Pareto, who for the first time describes the shape of the income curve as the basis of his analysis of aggregate demand (Pareto [1897] 1964). Even if different from the original Paretian one, the hypothesis that the frequency distribution of earners could be considered a stable relationship, and of general validity, subsequently stimulated a large number of analyses aimed at providing an adequate description of the phenomenon and/or at identifying its determining variables.

The degree of inequality in the distribution of personal incomes can be considered the result of a conflict between two sets of forces:

The forces of diversification: (i) institutional and social norms that tend to favor wealthy people and their heirs, guaranteeing a monopoly of certain occupations and certain properties; and, (ii) the impossibility of acquiring those qualifications that give access to certain income levels (age, race, gender, etc.).

The forces of assimilation: (i) progressive taxes, (ii) inheritance taxes, and (iii) social services, which together provide those on the lowest income with better opportunities to increase their standard of living and limit the tendency of the rich and their heirs to become richer (Champernowne 1973: 190).

There are some forces of change that modulate the distribution of income to make it converge towards equilibrium; however, "for the presence of pulses to change (which act for a short period of time) and for the gradual modification of the same forces of change, such an equilibrium distribution is never reached" (Champernowne 1973: 9).

The Pareto approach, and more generally the stochastic approach to income distribution also discussed by Gibrat (1930) and Champernowne (1973), among others, has made a significant contribution to the understanding of income differentials with its analysis of the empirical laws of income distribution. All models have, as a common starting point, the observation of the existence of inequality seen as an asymmetry of income distribution, in which a large portion of total income goes to a small portion of the population. This empirical observation can be explained by assuming that every individual gets income by virtue of his or her own characteristics. The distribution of income depends on the distribution of the qualifications necessary to obtain such income: income differences between individuals in a community reflect their different qualifications. The characteristics normally taken into account are individual skills, personal wealth, and occupation, which are by assumption considered freely tradable between income earners. However, these characteristics must be complemented by other qualifications that are not sold but significantly affect the opportunities of an individual to receive a certain income level: age, sex, social status, race, and disability (defined as grounds for disadvantage or prejudice).

Moreover, it should be borne in mind that individual qualifications are not independent of the social structure of the community in question, as well as the contingent economic conditions. In particular, economic factors influence the distribution of income, which in turn influences access to qualifications and their relative value. Inertial phenomena (habits, conventions, and institutional factors) are at the basis of the strong dependence of the distribution of current income from that of the past. In these terms, income distribution is both malleable (could be different) and persistent. Economic structures as well as collective values recognized by society create such a lack of flexibility in income distribution (Sen 1992).

Within the heterodox literature on inequality, an original and important contribution focused on gender inequality is offered by feminist economics. According to Robeyns (2003), the feminist viewpoint introduces three relevant elements to the analysis of inequality. The first general point is that every economic issue is *gender-conditioned*. While mainstream economics considers inequality, and in particular the gender gap, to be an 'accident' in respect of the theoretical hypothesis of equilibrium and socio-economic harmony, the feminist view affirms that the economy is not gender neutral, and gender inequality can represent both the cause and the effect of most economic processes. Thus, an inequality analysis that does not take into account gender is not neutral, but *de facto* follows a masculine perspective and this creates false gender neutrality (Okin 1989).

Second, feminist studies explore the issue of inequality within the household. While mainstream works assume that the household represents a homogeneous and compact unit of analysis, feminists argue that a good level of household income can hide relevant economic discrimination among its members, especially women, which generates serious economic exclusion. Thus the mainstream assumption of an equal income distribution among household members is theoretically incorrect and politically pernicious.

Finally, feminist analyses take into account economic relations outside of formal market exchange. In fact, different forms of discrimination and inequality can be found in informal economic contexts. The investigation of activities, such as care work and household labor, enlarges the field of research, offering a new spectrum in which to consider gender inequalities.

Thus, the feminist view enriches the inequality debate not only by considering gender inequality, that is one of the pillars of social injustice, but also by introducing the aforementioned elements of analysis that are also useful to evaluate other kinds of inequality, such as inter-generational inequality or ethnic inequality within informal markets.

In the era of globalization, the international dimension of inequality is becoming more and more fundamental. According to Milanovic (2013), the increasing movement of people, financial capital, and technologies make the generation of individual income dependent on global dynamics. Furthermore, the perception and the satisfaction deriving from individual economic status are strongly influenced by the globalization of information and faster flows of persons and commodities. In the world of today where economic borders are becoming more and more opaque, inequality among individuals should be analyzed with an international approach that combines inter-state inequality with intra-state inequality. To this end, Milanovic (2013) indicates three kinds of inequality: the first considers inequality across nations, the second integrates the first one by measuring population sizes, while the third, called 'global inequality,' is individual-centered, and is calculated on the basis of individual income without accounting for nationality.

Social exclusion and human development

The human development approach is the main reference point for policy development at national and international levels. Human development, according to Amartya Sen, is the process of determining individual and collective well-being. It is a process in which each person turns the resources at his or her disposal to acquiring the constituent elements of well-being and quality of life. These elements, otherwise known as 'states of being and doing,' are called 'functionings.' The effective freedom to acquire *functionings* is a capability; the transformation of resources in capabilities depends on conversion factors that are both subjective and linked to the social, economic, and institutional context, as well as on choice factors that intervene in the passage of the set of capabilities to that of functionings. Figure 21.1 illustrates the aforementioned process of human development.

Each person participates in this process both as an individual and as a member of a community. Capabilities have an intrinsic value because the very fact of having the freedom to pursue all opportunities offered by the economic and social system is an element that improves the quality of life. They also have an instrumental value because they are the precondition for improving one's quality of life. Each individual may acquire resources independently of his or her well-being, and this ability is called *freedom of agency*, that is the ability of the individuals "to promote their own well-being, but also to bring about changes in their community" (Sen 1999: 19). It may involve either resources related to the individual (*weak agency*) or resources that concern the welfare of others (*strong agency*) (Sen 1999).

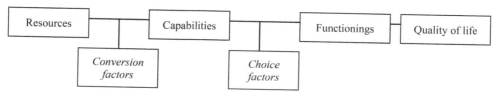

Figure 21.1   The process of human development

The role of institutions is to provide the instrumental freedoms that fall in the conversion factors. According to Sen (1999), these are: political freedoms, such as direct and indirect participation in political life; economic infrastructure that allows for production, consumption, and the exchange of goods and services; social opportunities, understood as goods and services that help to improve the quality of life; guarantees of transparency concerning the rules of the game in the market but also in institutions; and, social security against the risks linked to poverty.

According to Robeyns (2003), this approach can be integrated into a feminist study of gender inequalities both by considering the human development process as a specific gender conversion factor, and/or by re-interpreting the human development process as gendered capabilities and functionings.

The definition of social exclusion

The concept of social exclusion is complex and difficult to define. The discourse on social exclusion offers operational definitions that highlight important aspects that facilitate its analysis. Sen does not formulate a precise definition of social exclusion, but outlines several of its characteristics. According to Sen (1999), poverty is capability deprivation, meaning the inability to live a minimally decent life, while social exclusion can be understood as the permanence of this condition. For example, we can define social exclusion as a permanent deprivation of those capabilities needed in order to be fully integrated in society.

For the definition of these capabilities, we can refer to some of their constituents. First of all, these capabilities involve the element of *social justice*, which implies,

> [h]aving the social bases of self-respect and non-humiliation; being able to be treated as a dignified being whose worth is equal to that of others. This entails provisions of nondiscrimination on the basis of race, sex, sexual orientation, ethnicity, caste, religion, national origin.
>
> *Nussbaum 2003: 42*

A second element is that of active participation that can be defined as the ability "to relate to others and to take part in the life of the community" (Sen 2000: 13). Finally, social exclusion can be defined as the deprivation of *social capabilities*, that is,

> to be integrated in networks; to commit oneself to a project within a group, aimed at serving a common good, a social interest; to take part in decision making in a political society; to have specific attachments to others (friendship, love); to try to value others' objectives, considering them as ends.
>
> *Sen 2000: 13*

Social exclusion affects both individual and collective agency, and in particular self-help, defined as "the ability of the people to help themselves and to influence the world" (Sen 2000: 13). Social exclusion can reduce agency and self-help through the reduction of "the critical consciousness of the poor to express their social discontent, think critically about their problems and actively resolve these problems" (Sen 1999: 18). This greatly reduces the quality of life of individuals because self-help interacts positively with instrumental freedoms. In fact, it allows individuals to be able to perform voice actions to promote their own needs; it is an economic facility because it can generate income by creating new social opportunities and reducing the imbalance of powers; it can improve transparency in the community bringing out trust and reciprocity; and, it can strengthen social protection.

Social capital, defined "as the set of social relations and networks enabling the poor to form and sustain self-help groups" (Ibrahim 2006: 409), can positively influence collective action in several ways: it spreads trust and reciprocity, helps in making collective decisions (regarding the objectives and the distribution of benefits), allows the dissemination of information and coordination of activities, and protects community members from possible economic shocks. Furthermore, it encourages participation in local decision-making processes and helps to ensure new individual and collective rights. Social capital may be the only real resource for vulnerable people, "because poor people (by definition) have little economic capital and face formidable obstacles in acquiring human capital (that is education), social capital is disproportionately important to their welfare"(Putnam 2000: 18).

The process of social exclusion

The generators of the process of social exclusion are the so-called 'drivers of exclusion,' that is, the inputs that convert personal and context vulnerability into actual social exclusion. There are three different drivers of social exclusion: active exclusion, passive exclusion, and self-exclusion.

Active exclusion occurs due to discriminatory actions by powerful public or private groups concerning policy decisions that victims are not able to prevent or counteract. These power groups are socially and culturally identifiable. *Passive exclusion* occurs due to changes in the structure and organization of society and institutions. Specifically, there may be social, cultural, and economic changes that lead to such exclusion. Finally, *self-exclusion* occurs when individuals or groups self-marginalize due to their natural attitudes, behaviors, and values. They are thus responsible for their own exclusion.

Social exclusion involves complex processes in which drivers may be central or residual with respect to structural changes, or may depend on the ineffectiveness of policies (*structural dislocation*). Furthermore, social exclusion may be regarded as an integral part of capitalist development: in this case, the policy will aim to transform the structural causes (*structural dualism*), rather than reabsorbing them. Finally, social exclusion can be seen as a result of the ineffectiveness of community policies due to the separation between economic and social policies, as well as due to the gap existing between community institutions and the needs of citizens, and the content of economic policies such as excessive flexibility of the labor market (*institutional exclusion*).

Globalization is a phenomenon that affects directly and indirectly both the drivers of social exclusion and vulnerability factors. It is therefore appropriate to analyze the relationship between social exclusion and globalization. Globalization may be defined as:

a process (or set of processes) which embodies a transformation in the spatial organisation of social relations and transactions – assessed in terms of their extensity, intensity, velocity and impact – generating transcontinental or interregional flows and networks of activity, interaction and the exercise of power.

Beall 2002: 43

From this definition, three typical effects of the globalization process emerge. First, there is a widening of social, economic, and political relationships beyond national borders. In addition, there is an intensification of the interconnection between financial, trade, and migration flows, due to the development of communication systems and transportation. Finally, the local impact of global events becomes more remarkable as the boundary between the global and the local level becomes more fluid.

Following McGrew (2000), we can identify some interpretations of the link between globalization and social exclusion. From the *neoliberal* view, what prevails is an optimistic view that general welfare is achieved, with the end of the so-called Third World, through the establishment of a single global market and a steady thinning of public interventions in the organization of the economic system. International institutions, such as the International Monetary Fund, the World Bank, and the World Trade Organization, are the only institutions that can facilitate the formation of a single global system, while nation states are entities with less and less powers and organizational capacities to regulate global phenomena. In this context, social exclusion is an unpleasant but inevitable side effect to the global economic process. In rich countries, the excluded belong to those who are directly affected by trade liberalization, with the ensuing reduction in privileges and social security.

From a *radical* view, globalization reinforces transnational capital resulting in global inequalities and marginalization of poor countries; the world is divided into smaller blocks, in which the OECD countries are the main leaders. In this context, attention to the new concept of social exclusion is a way to reduce economic inequality produced by the global mechanisms.

Finally, from the *transformationalist* view, globalization is seen as a period of major structural changes across the world, which witnesses the formation of new global systems, new hierarchies, and new mechanisms of inclusion and exclusion. From this perspective, it becomes essential to study the distribution of power between regions and groups in terms of methods, tools, distribution of income, and organization. Social exclusion is analyzed by studying social relations present in the formal and informal institutions and their changes with developments in international relations, their social impacts, and their reactions. Castells (1998) argues that "globalization proceeds selectively, including and excluding segments of economies and societies in and out of the networks of information, wealth and power that characterize the new dominant system" (Castells 1998: 161–162).

Another element that affects the process of social exclusion and the degree of vulnerability of individuals is *social stratification*. Social stratifications vary in different aspects: in the number of layers, in the difference between the first and the last layer, in the dimension of each layer, in the layer composition (in terms of gender, social, economic, cultural, ethnic characteristics), and in the degree of movement between the layers of the individuals. In this context, *social mobility* is defined as the passage of a proportion of individuals from a layer to another, in ascending or descending direction. It is intergenerational if the comparison is between parents and children; intragenerational, if the comparison is between two different periods with respect to the same individual. Social exclusion can thus be a form of downward social mobility or social immobility.

Poverty and social exclusion

Poverty can be classified into two main categories: absolute and relative. Absolute poverty means that people lack a minimum amount of income that satisfies basic needs for survival. Relative poverty refers to a condition of people not receiving enough income to maintain an average standard of living measured for a particular society and time. A measure of relative poverty can be converted into a measure of inequality and of social exclusion.

The transition from the concept of poverty to that of social exclusion involves the passage from a one-dimensional to a multi-dimensional vision, from a pre-eminence of social elements over economic ones to an interest in the quality of social relations. Social exclusion is not an alternative concept of poverty, but it is a way to clarify its understanding. According to Jackson (1999), social exclusion and poverty are interrelated, albeit distinct, concepts: poverty often results from social exclusion. According to Atkinson (1998), social exclusion is due to poverty and/or inequality. Some people may be excluded without being poor while others, although poor, may not be excluded (especially in depressed areas, where they can live under a minimum threshold, but still participate in social life).

There is a strong interaction between social exclusion and poverty. And there may be a cumulative vicious circle whereby poverty and social exclusion feed each other. The transition from poverty as *deprivation of means* to poverty as *deprivation of capabilities* involves shifting attention from the lack of means to their inadequacy in respect to capabilities and to the conversion of means into substantial freedoms.

Exclusion from the labor market

The prevalence of unemployment, especially long-term unemployment, is perhaps the single most important contributor to the persistence of social exclusion on a large scale. According to Sen (1996), we can consider three aspects of the link between unemployment and social exclusion: *income aspects*, *recognition aspects*, and *production aspects*.

As to *income aspects*, unemployment is directly linked to economic deprivation. Sen (1997) argues that it is inappropriate to affirm that non-participation in the labor market is not a major problem because there is a welfare system that can guarantee social benefits and a minimum income. In fact, this approach is not sustainable in the long-run, since being out of the labor market has a fiscal cost for society. Moreover, the exclusion from the labor market can be a real deprivation of capabilities, making the individual unable to participate in economic life.

As to *recognition aspects*, unemployment can cause severe psychological damages: some empirical studies emphasize the positive correlation between suicide rates and conditions of permanent unemployment (see Boor 1980; Platt 1984). Moreover, there may be related health effects, with a subsequent negative impact on social relations: there is a loss of social relations, starting within the family.

Finally, concerning *production aspects*, there is a negative effect on education. On the one hand, there is a loss of learning, since we learn *by doing*, and we therefore unlearn *by not doing*. On the other hand, there is a decline in cognitive ability caused by mistrust and resignation. When it becomes difficult to be employed, competition between workers emerges, directly affecting those most vulnerable. Long-term unemployment may cause the individual to develop negative feelings against the society that does not include them, leading, in some cases, to the risk of illegal activity. Figure 21.2 illustrates the relationship between the aforementioned concepts.

Figure 21.2 The relationship between unemployment and social exclusion

Financial exclusion

Financial exclusion can be defined as "a process whereby people encounter difficulties accessing and/or using financial services and products in the mainstream market that are appropriate to their needs and enable them to lead a normal social life in the society in which they belong" (European Commission 2008: 9).

It is in fact difficult to estimate those who are excluded from the financial system and in particular those who have no access to credit because exclusion can have different temporal (temporary and permanent) dynamics, and because the supply of financial services is typically very complex. There are different types of financial services, the exclusion from which can be indicative for our analysis (see Figure 21.3). For example, exclusion from banking transactions, such as receiving regular payments (salaries, pensions, public subsidies), the ability to cash checks, to pay utilities electronically, to pay goods without cash, and to send remittances (in the case of migrants). Such financial exclusion, being inherent in the basic economic activities of a developed society, causes economic and social marginalization. Moreover, it implies the exclusion from all other financial services and it reduces security in the management of money.

Another form of financial exclusion is an inability to access a bank account due to a low income and a lack of proper identification documents in the case of immigrants. The 'unbanked' are those individuals who do not have an account in a bank. In the case of businesses, the same problem is manifested in a lack of access to credit. This results in the exclusion from credit, such as loans, from the possession of a credit card, and from overdraft banking. This exclusion often leads 'unbanked' individuals (and businesses) to rely on risky informal and illegal channels as a source of funds.

Finally, there is the exclusion from insurance services. It is important to consider this exclusion with regard to poverty because private insurance services are increasingly replacing social welfare benefits. Therefore, such exclusion creates the risk of failing to meet a minimum standard of living.

The causes of financial exclusion can be both exogenous and endogenous. For individuals, exogenous causes are employment instability, poor health, low levels of education, and gender or migrant status. For example, families are in a vulnerable position when they are not owners of their home, when they live in a marginal geographical area with dependent people such as children and elderly people, and when they are single-parent (especially single-mother) families. Finally, exogenous causes of financial exclusion for companies can be: their small size, the economic vulnerability of the owner, the local character of the goods or services sold, an inadequate infrastructural context.

Below we analyze the main causes of financial exclusion that are endogenous to the financial market. The first is *credit rationing* due to the phenomenon of 'enforcement': the higher the

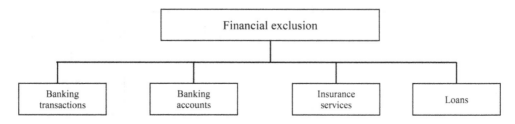

Figure 21.3 The dimension of financial exclusion

cost of compliance with the contract terms for reasons related to the national legal system or to local regulations, the greater the tendency of the creditor to avoid low-income individuals, who require very small financing and mostly reside in areas where the cost is higher (for formal and informal rules). Another factor of credit rationing is the costs of transaction, that is, the costs associated with contract preparation, access to information, trading, and the monitoring of compliance with the contract. Obviously, with the same transaction costs, individuals requesting a small amount of credit do not generate a profitable lending. Another endogenous element of financial exclusion is the inadequate geographical distribution of creditors: the lower the spread, the more difficult is the adaptation of credit offers to customer requests, especially for the most marginalized clients. Another element is the cost of the loan, the price, and other conditions of lending (such as evaluation time, documentation, amount and duration of the loan, repayment frequency, possibility of re-negotiation), which can make a loan too onerous and then make access to credit impossible for vulnerable people or businesses.

Financial crime and the associated social problems have a negative impact on the banking sector too, which can in turn induce further credit rationing. The negative effects of crime on banks are twofold: an increase in the cost of trading and an increasing difficulty for banks to assess the financial conditions of their customers due to asymmetric information. As a result, credit rationing in many crime-affected areas becomes a characteristic phenomenon of the banking system. A high level of crime involves higher interest rates, but does not seem to affect the supply of revolving credit. In general, the negative impact of crime on credit suppliers decreases as the size of the debtor increases.

The importance (in terms of quality and quantity) of collaterals in credit contracts is higher in areas of high criminal intensity because both conditions of businesses are more opaque, and banks want to protect their own investments from the high risk of insolvency. Crime generates greater information asymmetry between banks and their customers; in the case of banks, it increases the chance of adverse selection in the time of evaluating the financing plans for customers, while in the case of customers there is an increase of moral hazard in fulfilling contracts. As to loans to large companies, these problems tend to present lesser information problems since they are relatively more transparent and efficient.

Exclusion from the education system

Education is an effective tool of social inclusion. With regard to the acquisition of education, according to the *credentialist* approach, a higher education degree reflects an individual's skill. In the labor market, under conditions of incomplete information, the demand for labor relies on qualifications as an indication of the ability of workers. The worker, in turn, tries to obtain a higher level of education so as to secure a greater probability of receiving a higher salary. In this case, the differences in education levels reflect differences in the innate capacities of individuals.

According to the mainstream economic approach, it is possible to take action to reduce inequalities in education by lowering costs and, therefore, obstacles to accessing education. On the other hand, for the *credentialist* approach, it is inefficient to intervene in educational inequalities if the educational system rewards the best ones. While mainstream policies focus on access to education to give everyone the chance to earn more in the future, according to the *credentialist* approach, institutions must focus on making the education system efficient so that it rewards merit.

Empirical analyses have estimated the different factors that influence the acquisition of education; among the main ones are family background, the effectiveness of the education system, as well as the labor market in relation to the opportunity to train during their working career. A very topical element of social exclusion is the intergenerational effect of education. Income inequality leads to inequality in education levels. Beyond that, there is the persistence of inter-generational deprivation of education: deprivation of a parent increases the likelihood of deprivation of the children. In essence, the deprivation of education carries a lower expected income, a lower probability of children's education, and a lower probability of employment. Deprivation of education or skills causes harm to individuals by predisposing them to social exclusion, but also hampers economic growth, as it limits the expansion of education, which is one of the main means to economic development.

The minimum level of education under which exclusion occurs is in fact dependent on both internal factors, such as the degree of development and the degree of inequality of the territory concerned, and on exogenous factors, such as socio-economic change at the global level. Certainly, the two types of factors interact, but it is good to consider them separately from the point of view of policy actions because the acquisition of an adequate level of education is a fundamental prerequisite for social inclusion.

Conclusion

In discussing inequality and poverty, this chapter has first focused on income inequality, following a classical approach complemented by a stochastic approach to the distribution of personal income. It has then devoted attention to the link between human development, social exclusion, and poverty, focusing on some theoretical and empirical dimensions of exclusion such as exclusion from labor market, financial market, and education.

In analyzing the process of human development, we have referred to Sen's capability approach, examining a process of expanding resources that can be transformed into real opportunities available to individuals and communities. The transformation of resources in real freedoms to achieve desired objectives depends on factors of individual and social conversion, as well as on factors of choice leading each individual to actually implement available opportunities.

Social exclusion, as a condition, is characterized by being multi-dimensional, involving social and economic factors that affect both individuals and entire social groups. In summary, social exclusion and poverty appear to be an inability of individuals to participate in economic and civil life and gain access to social services. It is the result of the interaction between emerging factors of potential exclusion, the so-called drivers of exclusion, which may have a structural, institutional, and behavioral nature, and pre-existing vulnerability factors. This process tends to be cumulative, meaning it can create traps; drivers of a type of exclusion can become vulnerability factors for other types of exclusion (for instance, unemployment is certainly a driver of exclusion, but can also become a risk factor for financial exclusion). Traps can also occur because of the negative externalities that the social exclusion of an individual or a community can generate in relation to other subjects. If an individual resides in an area of high social disadvantage, s/he may have difficulty in accessing credit, while not having any personal risk factor. In this context, social exclusion seems to strike repeatedly and in a multi-dimensional way the most vulnerable subjects and regions.

Acknowledgments

Many thanks are due to the *Handbook* editors for their useful comments. The usual disclaimer applies.

References

Atkinson, A.B. 1998. 'Social exclusion, poverty and unemployment,' in: A.B. Atkinson & J. Hills (eds.), *Exclusion, Employment and Opportunity*. London: Centre for Analysis of Social Exclusion, London School of Economics, 1–20.

Beall, J. 2002. 'Globalization and social exclusion in cities: framing the debate with lessons from Africa and Asia.' *Environment and Urbanization*, 14 (1): 41–51.

Boor, M. 1980. 'Relationship between unemployment rates and suicide rates in eight countries, 1962–1979.' *Psychological Reports* (Missoula, MT), 47 (3):1095–1101.

Castells, M. 1998. *End of the Millennium*. Oxford: Wiley-Blackwell.

Champernowne, D.G. 1973. *The Distribution of Income Between Persons*. Cambridge: Cambridge University Press.

D'Ippoliti, C. 2011. *Economics and Diversity*. New York: Routledge.

Elsner, W. 2013. 'State and future of the 'Citadel' and of the heterodoxies in economics: challenges and dangers, convergences and cooperation.' *European Journal of Economics and Economic Policies: Intervention*, 10 (3): 286–298.

European Commission. 2008. *Financial Services Provision and Prevention of Financial Exclusion*. Brussels: European Commission.

Gibrat, R. 1930. *Les Inégalités Economiques*. Paris: Librairie du Recueil Sirey.

Ibrahim, S.S. 2006. 'From individual to collective capabilities: the capability approach as a conceptual framework for self-help.' *Journal of Human Development and Capabilities*, 7 (3): 397–416.

Jackson, C. 1999. 'Social exclusion and gender: does one size fit all?' *The European Journal of Development Research*, 11 (1): 125–146.

Lee, F.S. 2012. 'Heterodox economics and its critics.' *Review of Political Economy*, 24 (2): 337–351.

Martins, N.O. 2011. 'The revival of classical political economy and the Cambridge tradition: from scarcity theory to surplus theory.' *Review of Political Economy*, 23 (1): 111–131.

Martins, N.O. 2012. 'Sen, Sraffa and the revival of classical political economy.' *Journal of Economic Methodology*, 19 (2): 143–157.

McGrew, A. 2000. 'Sustainable globalization? The global politics of development and exclusion in the New World Order,' in: T. Allen & A. Thomas (eds.), *Poverty and Development into the 21st Century*. Oxford: Oxford University Press, 345–364.

Milanovic, B. 2013. 'Global income inequality in numbers: in history and now.' *Global Policy*, 4 (2): 198–208.

Mill, J.S. 1848. *Principles of Political Economy*. London: Longmans, Green and Co.

Nussbaum, M.C. 2003. 'Capabilities as fundamental entitlements: Sen and social justice.' *Feminist Economics*, 9 (2–3): 33–59.

Okin, S. 1989. *Justice, Gender and the Family*. New York: Basic Books.

Pareto, V. [1897] 1964. '*Cours d'économie politique*,' in: G. Busino (ed.), *Oeuvres Complètes*. Genève–Paris: Droz.

Platt, S. 1984. 'Unemployment and suicidal behavior: A review of the literature.' *Social Science and Medicine*, 19 (2): 93–115.

Putnam, R. 2000. *Bowling Alone: The Collapse and Revival of American Community*. New York: Simon and Schuster.

Robeyns, I. 2003. 'Sen's capability approach and gender inequality: selecting relevant capabilities.' *Feminist Economics*, 9 (2–3): 61–92.

Say, J.-B. 1836. *Cours Complet d'Économie Politique Pratique*. Bruxelles: Dumont.

Sen, A.K. 1992. *Inequality Re-examined*. Oxford: Clarendon Press.

Sen, A.K. 1996. 'Employment, institutions and technology: some policy issues.' *International Labour Review*, 135 (3–4): 445–471.

Sen, A.K. 1997. 'Inequality, unemployment and contemporary Europe.' *International Labour Review*, 136 (2): 155–171.

Sen, A.K. 1999. *Development as Freedom*. Oxford: Oxford University Press.

Sen, A.K. 2000. Social exclusion: concept, application and scrutiny. Social development papers 1. Available from http://www.adb.org/sites/default/files/publication/29778/social-exclusion.pdf [Accessed July 26, 2016]

Smith, A. [1776] 1976. *An Inquiry into the Nature and Causes of the Wealth of Nations*, in: R.H. Campbell, A.S. Skinner, & W.B. Todd (eds.), *The Works and Correspondence of Adam Smith*, Vol. II, Oxford: Oxford University Press.

Part IV

The dynamics of capitalist socio-economic structure

22

The accumulation of capital
An analytical and historical overview

Ramaa Vasudevan

Introduction

The investigation of the process of accumulation of capital forms a rich and distinctive terrain of heterodox economic analysis. The models of economic growth in classical, Marxian, and Post Keynesian approaches differ from the orthodox neoclassical tradition of savings-driven, supply-side models derived from the Solow-Swan growth model (Taylor 2004; Foley & Michl 2010). Apart from the distinctive analysis of economic growth that is centered on the re-investment of profits in production, these traditions share a common conception of the accumulation of capital as an irreversible historical process, taking place in the context of capitalist institutions. The abstract models of steady-state growth represented by Marx's expanded reproduction scheme or the Cambridge growth equation are only the starting point for the analysis of the process of accumulation. In order to comprehend the complex dynamics of capitalist accumulation, "economic analysis requires to be supplemented by comparative historical anthropology" (Robinson 1956: 59).

Within the neoclassical framework, the growth of technology and the labor force are proximate determinants of the long-run growth path, around which the economy fluctuates when subject to external shocks. The new endogenous growth models in the Solow tradition incorporate endogenous technical change. The fundamental role of institutions in fostering or hampering growth is also recognized as a factor explaining the differential growth performance across countries. However, the investigation of the concrete, non-linear "path of development of an accumulating economy through historical time" (Minsky 1986: 285) that can be found within the different heterodox traditions has no real parallel in neoclassical analysis.

Heterodoxy goes beyond 'theories of growth' in its analysis of capitalist dynamics. Accumulation is intertwined in the process of institutional and technological change propelled by the forces of capitalist competition. The development and evolution of the financial system shapes the path of capitalist accumulation. Its trajectory is turbulent and punctuated by crisis.

In this chapter, we present a broad overview of the heterodox approaches to the capital accumulation process, from both an analytical and historical perspective.

The analytical framework of heterodox traditions

Before embarking on a more historically grounded elaboration of heterodox approaches to the accumulation of capital, we will identify the analytical characteristics of heterodox approaches that distinguish themselves from the neoclassical approach. The focus here is more specifically on Marxian and Post Keynesian/structuralist approaches.[1] We do not elaborate the theories of growth, focusing instead on the different dimensions of the analysis of the accumulation process.[2]

Beyond the steady-state growth model

In neoclassical savings-driven growth theory, the rate of growth of the labor force is treated as an exogenous factor determining growth. The assumption of the substitutability of capital and labor ensures that labor markets clear and there is full employment of labor.

The investment-driven growth models of Post Keynesian and structuralist theories, in contrast, break with Say's law and the assumption of the full employment of labor,[3] and extend the Keynesian principle of effective demand to the long-run (Taylor 2004). Marx also rejects Say's law, and locates the sources of demand within the circuit of capital (Foley 1985). Growth in the classical and Marxian models is driven by the re-investment of profits. In the absence of a specification of the investment function governing the rate of re-investment of profits, growth will tend to be 'profit-led.' However, effective demand plays a role in the short-run in classical and Marxian models of growth, when capacity utilization differs from the normal capacity utilization level (Shaikh 1991; Duménil & Lévy 1999).

Gibson (2010) makes the argument that the exogenous factor in the Post Keynesian growth model is demand. Aggregate demand is, in turn, based on animal spirits.[4] The counterpart to animal spirits as an exogenous factor in Marxian growth models would be the evolution of class relations. Class relations govern the rate of surplus extraction in production, its distribution, and the incentives for technological innovation. The exogenous impact of animal spirits or class struggle allows both the Post Keynesian and Marxian analyses of growth to be open to 'history.'

This openness paves the way for a conception of the complex qualitative dynamic of accumulation that transcends the underlying abstract model of growth that informs the Marxian and Post Keynesian visions. It also situates the accumulation process firmly in the context of dynamic transformation of capitalist social relations.

The context of capitalist social relations

The point of departure of heterodox analysis is the fundamental division of the capitalist economy into capitalist entrepreneurs and workers. For Marx, this social-class relation was the key to understanding the capitalist economy; he was thus concerned with discovering the 'laws of accumulation' that emerged in the context of capitalist social relations. Capitalism is understood as a totality of relations and processes organized around the accumulation of capital through production, circulation, and the recommitment of surplus to production. However, accumulation involves not just the production and capitalization of surplus value but also the transformation of the production process and the reproduction and extension of capitalist social relations.

The capitalist entrepreneur making decisions under conditions of fundamental uncertainty is, similarly, at the heart of Post Keynesian analysis of accumulation. The economy consists of groups with conflicting interests that are held together by rules of the game that are "largely concerned with the manner in which work and property are combined in production and with the rights that they give to shares in the proceeds" (Robinson 1956: 4). For capitalist accumulation to proceed smoothly, the cycle of production has to be completed and the proceeds from this cycle to be ploughed back into financing a new cycle.

Accumulation, in Marx's framework, also entails the processes of concentration (as individual capitals grow larger) and centralization (as capitals merge with and acquire other capitals). This has led to the postulation of a monopoly phase of capitalism with a consequent tendency towards stagnation (Baran & Sweezy 1966). Contrary to this view, it has been argued that concentration and centralization do not abolish competition, but rather reflect and intensify it (Shaikh 1978). The growth of monopolies and oligopolies also impinges on the accumulation process within the Post Keynesian framework. Firms fix prices in terms of a mark-up that reflects monopoly power. Growing monopoly power can lead to secular stagnation, as a decline in effective demand triggers a cutback in capacity utilization, investment, and accumulation.

Both Marxian and Post Keynesian analyses, thus, give primacy to the decisions of capitalist entrepreneurs in search of profits as the source of accumulation and view the process of accumulation as an integrated system of real and financial stocks and flows that are continually reproduced and extended. They are also concerned with how the changing structure, organization, and scale of individual firms and capitals conditions the accumulation process.

Centrality of profits and distribution

Profits and profitability are central to the accumulation process in the Marxian and Post Keynesian traditions. The analysis of the rate of profit in the Marxian tradition is rooted in the sphere of production and is determined by technology (organic composition of capital) and distribution (rate of exploitation). The profit rate (r) can be expressed as

$$r = \frac{P}{K} = \frac{P}{Y} \cdot \frac{Y}{K} = \pi \cdot k$$

where P is aggregate profits, K is the aggregate stock of capital, Y is aggregate income, π is the profit share, and k the ratio of aggregate output to capital stock.

In Kaleckian models, the profit rate is determined by a mark-up that reflects monopoly power in the market.[5] Investment demand and capacity utilization determine profits. The profit rate can thus be decomposed as

$$r = \frac{P}{Y} \cdot \frac{Y}{Y^*} \cdot \frac{Y^*}{K} = \pi \cdot u \cdot k$$

where Y^* is capacity output, u is the capacity utilization ratio, and k is the capacity output to capital stock ratio.

In the classical and Marxian traditions, profitability regulates growth and accumulation. The growth model of the expanded reproduction scheme boils down to the Cambridge growth equation:

$$g = s_\pi r$$

where g is the rate of growth of capital stock, r is the rate of profit, and s_π is the propensity to save out of profits or the rate of re-investment of profits (under the assumption that workers do not save).

Ramaa Vasudevan

In Post Keynesian and structuralist traditions that derive from Kaldor, Kalecki, and Robinson, profitability affects growth and accumulation through the investment function:[6]

$$g = g_k (\alpha, u, r)$$

or in an alternative formulation

$$g = g_k (\alpha, u, \pi)$$

where α represents animal spirits. The investment function gives rise to dynamic patterns that are either profit-led and exhilarationist, or wage-led and stagnationist (Marglin & Bhaduri 1990; Taylor 2004).

The primacy of the processes determining distribution is common to both Marxian and Post Keynesian approaches. The former emphasizes class relations, and how distributive outcomes are determined in the sphere of production. Demand varies with changing distribution between wages and profits in Post Keynesian models. The inclusion of Goodwin-style distributive curves, linking the distribution to capacity utilization, into these models incorporates the manner in which the changing bargaining power of workers determines distribution.

Technological change

Technological change plays an integral role in the accumulation of capital. The Marxian notion of competition is that of the turbulent reciprocal interaction of capitals. That "battle of competition is fought by the cheapening of commodities," and thus necessitates cost-cutting innovations (Marx [1867] 1976: 626). In a similar vein, Robinson (1956: 6) argues that "the capitalist rules of the game foster large-scale production and the use of elaborate techniques" and that the "capitalist entrepreneur . . . is impelled to do so by the competitive struggle to undersell others."

Drawing on Myrdal's principle of cumulative and circular causation and Verdoorn's law, Kaldor (1961) put forward an analysis of growth and accumulation, which stressed increasing returns to scale and path dependence. Verdoorn's law, relating the growth rate of output and of productivity, can be explained as an outcome of returns to scale from the division of labor with the expansion of the market, and of gains from 'learning by doing.'

Marx noted the tendency towards a rising organic composition of capital in the course of capitalist accumulation. Within capitalist social relations, technological change takes a particular form of substituting capital for labor and deploying more machinery to enhance labor productivity. Post Keynesian models in the Kaldorian tradition also incorporate such factor-biased induced technological progress. They introduce a technical progress function that relates productivity growth to capital intensity or investment per worker. The growth of real wages induces capitalists to adopt labor-saving technical innovations (Foley & Michl 1999; Taylor 2004)

The idea of endogenous technical change has now been incorporated in the neoclassical endogenous growth models as well. However, in the Post Keynesian framework, technological change is endogenous in the sense of being demand-determined and explicable in terms of the growth and distribution outcomes that are engendered by the process of accumulation (Setterfield 2010). In Marxian models, technological change is endogenous; it is determined by the specific context of class relations in which competition compels innovation. In both of these heterodox approaches, technology develops and responds in a social and historical context.

Institutional change

The accumulation process is shaped by historically specific institutions that govern the organization of production and the distribution of income. Institutions are not simply a factor determining growth, but also a mechanism by which the more complex process of accumulation is mediated and regulated.

Régulation theory and the Social Structures of Accumulation (SSA) approach that draw on both Marxian and Keynesian theoretical traditions explicitly demarcate periods based on the institutional evolution of capitalism. These approaches explain long-term patterns in accumulation in terms of a network of social institutions and social norms. The SSA approach delineates the institutional framework that fosters and stabilizes accumulation and enhances the power and profits of the capitalist class (Gordon *et al.* 1982; Kotz & McDonough 2010). *Régulation* theory is framed in terms of the impact on the modes of *régulation* and regimes of accumulation on the contradictory tendencies that are inherent in the Marxian laws of accumulation (Aglietta 1979).

Marxian analysis is rooted in the investigation of social-class relations. Capital accumulation derives from the exploitation of wage labor and the appropriation, by the capitalist, of the surplus produced by the worker in the production process.[7] Marx's historically grounded account of the process of 'primitive accumulation,' the evolution of large-scale industry, and the reshaping of the organization of work and working conditions provides an institutionally textured concrete analysis of the accumulation process.

Post Keynesian analysis of accumulation is framed around the specification of the macroeconomic regime—"a process of income generation embedded within a historically specific institutional framework" (Setterfield & Cornwall 2002: 67). The institutions, though enduring, are not 'immutable,' so that a particular steady-state growth path is conditional on the reproduction over time of a specific institutional structure (Setterfield 2011). The principal, institutionally driven characteristics that define a pattern of accumulation comprise the macroeconomic structure, the system of production, rules of coordination, and the international order (Glyn *et al.* 1990).[8]

While Post Keynesian analysis of accumulation tends to address institutions through their impact on macroeconomic structures, Marxian analysis of capital accumulation derives from the institutional structures that shape capital-labor relations in the process of production. Fundamental to these approaches is the recognition of the dynamic nature of institutional structures, which is conditioned by, and in turn conditions, the accumulation process. This consideration is what sets these approaches apart from the neoclassical approach, where the role of 'good institutions' (in particular property rights and rule of law) is simply added on as another determinant of growth.

Finance

Heterodox analyses share a vision of the capitalist economy as an intrinsically financial system. The theory of capitalist production and the theory of money and finance are integrated. The mechanisms of finance, including the development of a market for debt and modes of corporate finance, evolve along with capitalist accumulation.

Neoclassical growth empirics investigate the relationship between both the depth and quality of financial markets and growth. The conventional understanding of a positive relationship between finance and growth within neoclassical approaches has been recently revisited and revised. The functioning of the shadow banking system has also come under scrutiny after the collapse of Lehman Brothers in 2008. However, for an in-depth understanding of the manner in which finance impinges on accumulation dynamics, one has to turn to heterodox analyses, which view the evolution of the credit system and financial relations as being crucial to the expansion and development of capitalism.

Finance paved the way for the emergence of large-scale industry, in particular where large outlays for fixed capital are needed. It is the monetary complement to the large bursts of innovations that enable an extension of the circular flow of income in the Schumpeterian framework. Finance also plays a critical role in the centralization of capital in Marx's conception of accumulation.

Marx ([1895] 1981) outlined the division of the capitalist class into financial capitalists and industrial capitalists. With the concentration and organization of money capital in the form of large financial institutions, the power and dominance of finance over the accumulation process is entrenched more deeply. The 'general managers of money capital' are not simply intermediaries mobilizing and channeling surpluses but confront industrial and commercial capital as powerful interests. Credit offers "command over capital and property of others" (Marx [1895] 1981:570).

Post Keynesian analyses, analogously, distinguish the entrepreneur from the speculative rentier. Minsky (1996), writing in the context of 'money-manager capitalism,' which saw a large share of liabilities of corporations being held by financial institutions and large institutional investors, elaborates how this development leads to the domination of speculation over enterprise.

In these approaches, the balance and interconnection of the real and financial flows is integral to the dynamics of capitalist accumulation; these changing balances have an impact on production and distribution. The notion of fictitious capital was elaborated by Marx in the context of financial assets representing titles to future flows of income; these are valued by the capitalization of these future flows at the prevailing rate of interest. The notion of fictitious capital foreshadows Minsky's ([1986] 2008) formulation of the endogenous generation of financial instability. Minsky theorizes the emergence of financial instability in terms of the divergent movements of the prices for current output and those of financial and capital assets and the impetus to speculative and Ponzi positions during periods of stability and prosperity.

Both Marx and Minsky share a conception of the dual character of finance. The growth of finance fosters accumulation, but also exacerbates fragility. On the one hand, finance furthers the material development of technology and the creation of the world market; on the other hand, however, it accelerates the violent outbreak of contradiction and crises of accumulation by fueling excessive speculation (Marx [1895] 1981:572). It "acts as the sometimes dampening sometimes amplifying governor for investment" (Minsky [1975] 2008:127). In both of these heterodox traditions, the process of accumulation is embedded in and inseparable from the evolution of the financial system.

Crisis and instability

Accumulation is not a smooth and harmonious process. The trajectory of capitalist accumulation is subject to both cyclical turbulence and more profound structural crises. In contrast to the neoclassical framework, departures from the steady state are not necessarily triggered by exogenous shocks and there are no automatic stabilization mechanisms to restore the economy to a steady-state path.

Cyclical patterns can emerge endogenously in heterodox models from the instability of investment through the multiplier-accelerator mechanism (in the Post Keynesian models), or through labor market dynamics in Goodwin cycles (which have been incorporated in both Marxian and structuralist models). The imbalances between the real and the financial sector, the cyclical expansion, and rupture of the network of debt also cause cyclical patterns in both Marxian and Post Keynesian frameworks. But even apart from these cyclical fluctuations, the trajectory of accumulation is punctuated by periodic systemic breakdowns.

In Post Keynesian analysis, fundamental uncertainty associated with expectations of future profits imparts volatility and unpredictability to investment, and can lead to breakdowns. On the one hand, excessive investor pessimism that manifests itself in a liquidity trap can trigger a collapse of investment demand. On the other hand, attempts to depress real wages below a threshold that reflects socially acceptable norms can trigger a wage-price spiral. The floor to lowering real wages poses 'an inflationary barrier' to the growth of profits and investment (Robinson 1956, 1962). The Keynesian dilemma arises because the level of activity has to lie above a threshold level that ensures financial viability on the one hand, and below the level of the inflationary barrier on the other (Patnaik 2008). The rupture of the accumulation process is not amenable to automatic resolution. Intervention by the state and new institutional arrangements to stimulate demand and redistribute income is necessary before accumulation can be resumed.

There is no single theory of crisis in Marxian scholarship. If we sidestep the debates, Marxian accounts of the causal mechanisms of crisis fall into two broad categories: a crisis of aggregate demand and a crisis of profitability (Basu & Vasudevan 2013). The first category highlights the tendency towards the widening gap between the growing productivity of workers and their falling share of the gains from productivity growth. The crisis—a realization crisis—is characterized by difficulty of maintaining aggregate demand in the context of large and growing surplus and expresses a core contradiction of the pattern of accumulation—the 'tendency for the rate of exploitation' to rise (Foley 2012). The second category focuses on 'the tendency of the falling rate of profit' caused by the specific pattern of technical change that promotes mechanization and rising capital investment as the means of increasing labor productivity. These two tendencies express the contradictory nature of capitalist accumulation, and demonstrate that crises are moments of forcible resolution of these inherent contradictory tendencies.

Parallels can be drawn between the two contradictory tendencies in Marxian analysis and the dilemmas of Post Keynesian analysis. On the one hand, the accumulation process is subject to disruption when there is a shortfall in aggregate demand consequent to the collapse of investor confidence or to excessive surpluses as the share of workers is squeezed. On the other hand, falling profitability, as the economy hits the inflationary barrier or is confronted with falling capital productivity (rising organic composition), also leads to a rupture in the accumulation process. The contradictions and dilemmas of accumulation thus relate both to the inadequacy of aggregate demand and to declining profitability.

An integrated analysis of accumulation

The foregoing overview of the Marxian and Post Keynesian theoretical-analytical framework highlights the common core of these approaches to the accumulation process that distinguish them from the mainstream analysis, while clarifying some of the critical differences between them. This bare-bones overview of the theoretical approaches to capital accumulation can be given some flesh through a concrete analysis of the historical trajectory of accumulation. Such an exposition will allow for a better appreciation of the distinctive analysis of accumulation that these heterodox traditions share. Instead of simply focusing on the quantitative aspect of the growth in scale of the economy, the heterodox analysis seeks to comprehend the interlinked, qualitative dimensions of the process of accumulation. While institutions, technology, and even the development of finance are seen as causal factors determining growth in neoclassical growth theory, there is no counterpart to the holistic, historically informed analysis of accumulation that is characteristic of the broader heterodox tradition.

Ramaa Vasudevan

Accumulation in the post-war US

Instead of attempting to present a sweeping, encompassing account of the historical process of the accumulation of capital, we focus more narrowly on the post-war experience of the United States (US) in order to illustrate the manner in which Marxian and Post Keynesian traditions comprehend the concrete process of accumulation. While this account of the historical trajectory of the accumulation of capital is US-centric, it serves as a lens through which the rich distinctiveness of the heterodox approach can be illuminated.

A stylized view of the US economy

In the spirit of Kaldor (1961: 178), who built his abstract model of growth on the basis of "the characteristic features of the economic process recorded by experience," we present a 'stylized view' of the three broad trends and tendencies in the post-war history of the US economy that are of relevance to understanding the dynamics of capitalist accumulation in the recent historical period. These are the trends in income inequality, the share of finance, and the profitability; they are the pivot around which we survey the heterodox analyses of two distinct phases in the path of accumulation of the post-Second World War US. This demarcation of two distinct phases is also relevant to other advanced capitalist economies (see Glyn et al. 1990).

Figure 22.1 presents the share of the top one percent in the US income distribution. Inequality, represented by the share of the top percentile, rose in the early decades of the twentieth century until the onset of the Great Depression. The post-Second World War decades were characterized by declining inequality until the 1970s. Since then, the share of the top percentile has risen sharply, indicating a resurgence of the trend of rising inequality.

Finance as a share of income, and financial assets as a ratio to income, in the US (presented in Figure 22.2) both rose until around 1932. The period of the Great Depression and the Second

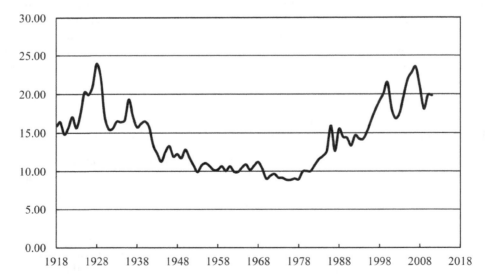

Figure 22.1 Share of the top 1 percent in household incomes, USA

Note: The Y axis displays the share of the top percentile of households in income distribution as a percentage of the total income of all households in the US.

Source: Emmanuel Saez and Thomas Piketty dataset (available from http://eml.berkeley.edu/~saez/).

World War saw a decline in the share of finance. The post-war period was marked by a steady rise in finance, which had significantly surpassed its inter-war peak in the nineties. Financial assets rose to be more than three times Gross Domestic Product (GDP) after 2000.

Figure 22.3 presents the trends in the decomposition of the profit rate in the tradition of Foley & Michl (1999). The trends in profitability are decomposed into the trends in the profit

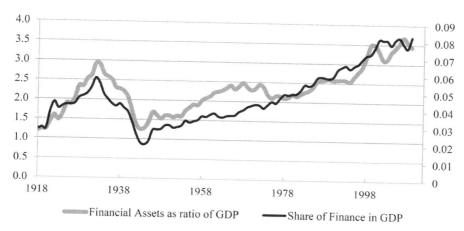

Figure 22.2 The rise of finance

Note: The share of the financial sector in GDP (ratio) is displayed on the right axis and financial assets as a ratio of GDP on the left axis.

Source: Thomas Phillipon dataset (available from http://pages.stern.nyu.edu/~tphilipp/research.htm).

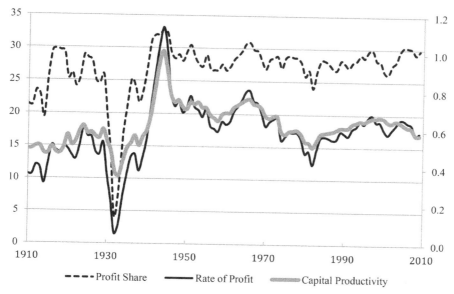

Figure 22.3 Decomposition of the profit rate

Note: The profit share (P/Y) and the rate of profit (P/K) are displayed on the left axis; capital productivity (Y/K) on the right axis.

Source: Duménil & Lévy dataset (available from http://www.jourdan.ens.fr/levy/biblioa.htm).

share and capital productivity. Capital productivity rose in the early decades of the twentieth century until around the mid-1940s. Since the mid-1960s, after a period of fluctuations with no discernible trend, capital productivity declined until the mid-1980s. The 1990s witnessed a slow rise in capital productivity. This trend reversed in 2000 (Basu & Vasudevan 2013). The profit rate rose between 1910 and 1945 (apart from the sharp break during the Great Depression). Since then, profitability has displayed a declining trend. This trend was broken in the 1980s (Basu & Vasudevan 2013).

These stylized facts suggest a break in the post-Second World War trajectory of capitalist accumulation around the 1970s. This post-war period can be divided into two distinct periods. The period before the 1970s is characterized by declining inequality, a share of finance that is slowly rising but relatively small, and declining profitability after the peak in the mid-1960s, along with falling capital productivity. After the 1970s, the US economy witnessed a sharp rise in inequality and a surge in the share of finance to unprecedented levels, along with a break in the trend of declining profitability. The two periods have been characterized as the Golden Age and the neoliberal age, respectively. This periodization reflects a fundamental transformation of the institutional and technological parameters that shape the accumulation process. This transformation is itself viewed as a response to the crisis that unfolded in the 1970s.

From the Golden Age to the neoliberal age

Before setting out the distinctive manner in which the Post Keynesian and Marxian traditions analyze the recent path of accumulation in the US, we briefly outline some of the defining institutional and macroeconomic features of the two periods.

The decades immediately following the Second World War were characterized by buoyant expansion and prosperity in the US. The edifice of the welfare state and a social safety net had been established in the wake of the Great Depression, under the New Deal. The role of the Federal Reserve as a lender of last resort evolved with the implementation of deposit insurance and the implicit guarantee of mortgages. At the same time, the regulatory structure instituted under the Glass–Steagall Act of 1933 legislated for the separation of commercial and investment banking activity and sought to rein in speculation. Under the prevailing Fordist work-contract, unionized workers agreed to cede control over the workplace and entered into productivity bargains in exchange for the assurance of better work conditions and wages. As a consequence, income inequality declined as real wages kept pace with labor productivity. A progressive tax regime with high marginal tax rates at the top income brackets also helped curb incomes at the top.

Internationally, the Bretton Woods System—hinged around the peg of the US dollar to gold and capital controls—facilitated relatively stable patterns of international capital flows. This period, also referred to as the Golden Age, came to a close in the 1970s, when the US (and other advanced capitalist countries) experienced soaring inflation and stagnation accompanied by a decline in capital productivity and profitability.

The 1980s launched the neoliberal period. The regulatory apparatus and the social safety net set up under the New Deal were rolled back as the imperative to combat inflation became the focus of macroeconomic policies. Monetary policy came to play a more central role in managing the economy and public spending faced increased scrutiny and cutbacks. Financial and labor markets were deregulated and the legislative framework that sought to rein in speculative investment activity was dismantled. The financial institutions entered a period of rapid innovation and growth. Tax breaks for the top income groups were initiated under the Reagan administration. Unions came under attack and collective bargaining systems were eroded. The Fordist work organizational system was replaced by lean production systems based on zero-inventory, just-in-time systems, a flexible unorganized workforce, and the outsourcing and offshoring of production. Real wages remained stagnant even as labor productivity rose sharply. Private borrowing and household debt grew as the banking sector expanded its reach. Both inequality and the share of finance began to rise sharply. Profitability and investment grew in the 1990s, but the 2000s saw a sharp decline in capital productivity and the rate of growth of investment also fell. A new international payments regime based on a floating dollar with liberalized international capital markets emerged after the collapse of the Bretton Woods System. Liberalized capital and trade flows facilitated the global relocation of production.

Post Keynesian analysis of post-war accumulation

The transformation of the macroeconomic regime/structure plays a significant role in the historical development of US capitalism within the Post Keynesian framework. During the Golden Age, counter-cyclical fiscal policy under the prevailing Keynesian consensus helped maintain aggregate demand. This commitment to reducing unemployment through demand management policies buttressed accumulation.

A key feature of this period was the close link between the growth rate of labor productivity and real wages—"the golden rule," which was "embedded in the particular institutions of the wage-determination process" (Glyn *et al.* 1990: 58). Strong national unions and minimum wage regulations helped establish broader wage norms. The social bargain over the distribution of the gains in labor productivity underpinned the golden rule. The lower cost of job loss, in the context of the social safety net and demand management policies enshrined in Keynesian consensus, also buttressed the bargaining position of workers and undermined the ability of capital to discipline workers (Marglin 1990).[9]

The rise in real wages in the late 1960s and 1970s, along with flagging labor productivity, broke the balance between wage and productivity growth. Inflationary pressures built up and profits were squeezed (Bowles *et al.* 1983; Glyn *et al.* 1990; Setterfield & Cornwall 2002).

Stagflation persisted through the 1970s, as the way was paved for the resurgence of monetarism and the eclipse of the Keynesian policy consensus. The priority was to contain inflation with a sharp hike in interest rates in 1979; monetary tightening thus paved the way for a new macroeconomic regime based on a neoliberal policy agenda favoring deregulation and rollback of the state's role in stabilizing demand and maintaining the social wage. The pattern of co-respective competition and the avoidance of predatory pricing and pre-emptive investment that had contributed to stability was replaced by one of coercive competition, cutthroat pricing, and over-investment. The increased vulnerability of workers helped keep real wages stagnant. Labor productivity grew much faster than real wages, and the social bargain that was the centerpiece of the Golden Age was dismantled. Expansionary policies to restore the economy from recessions now depended on a form of asset-Keynesianism with a permissive monetary regime fueling the growth of the financial sector. Demand was maintained in the face of stagnant wages by an unsustainable dynamic of debt accumulation. The collapse of this dynamic with the bursting of the housing bubble precipitated the problem of insufficient aggregate demand.

The relatively "stable pattern of cyclical growth with rising inflation" in the Golden Age thus gave way to a "combination of real and financial trends that supported fairly steady growth with moderate inflation on one hand and rising income inequality and financial instability on the other" (Taylor 2013: 208).

Ramaa Vasudevan

Marxian analysis of post-war accumulation

The point of departure in Marxian approaches is the balance of class forces and how class tensions are mediated through institutional arrangements. The capital-labor accord and the rise of the welfare state are, in this framework, a systemic response to the crisis of the 1930s. At issue, in this crisis, was the problem of maintaining aggregate demand in a context of growing surpluses.

These specific institutions of the Golden Age were crucial in resolving the crisis after the Second World War. The capital-labor accord committed workers, through their unions, to maintain high levels of productivity while sharing some of the gains though rising wages and benefits. The social acceptance of the role of the state in regulating demand and managing class conflict helped stabilize accumulation. By the 1960s, in the face of worker resistance to further increases in productivity, the limits of Taylorization as a strategy to maintain favorable trends in productivity became evident and profitability began to decline (Bowles *et al.* 1987). Falling profitability in this period has been ascribed in the literature to falling capital productivity (Shaikh 1987), the pressure of rising wages (Body & Crotty 1975), "excessive competition" (Brenner 2006), and the stagnationist tendencies of monopoly capitalism (Sweezy & Magdoff 1981).

Capital launched a full-scale offensive pushing back against its declining shares of income and wealth in the post-Second World War period. The imperative from the point of view of capital was to force concessions from the unions and put a lid on rising wages. A sharp increase in unemployment was necessary to undermine worker security and the power of unions in order to intensify exploitation and ensure the restoration of profitability. With the Volcker shock of 1979, the fight against inflation was deployed as a tool for restructuring class relations. This coup of finance ushered in a period of consolidating the power of financial and corporate capital in the US alongside a concerted attack on labor (Duménil & Lévy 2004). The growing gap between labor productivity and real wages was symptomatic of the ratcheting up of the rate of exploitation and surplus extraction. The trend of declining profitability was broken. The growing concentration and centralization of corporate capital alongside a global reorganization of production further consolidated the power of capital. Growing inequality and the rising power of finance posed fresh constraints to the accumulation process. The resolution of the crisis of the 1970s had thus set in motion trends that led to the current crisis.

Summing up

The above account of Post Keynesian and Marxian analysis of accumulation in the US of the post-Second World War period does not do justice to the vast and rich literature and the debates within it. It does, however, showcase the distinctive heterodox conception of how accumulation is shaped by institutional and technological developments, the contradictions and dilemmas that emerge, and how crises bring about a profound structural transformation in their wake.

What is remarkable, however, is the broad convergence in both accounts, not only with respect to the differentiation and characterization of the core features of the two periods but also with regard to their analysis of the distinct constraints to accumulation. The social compromise and its dismantling is central to both accounts of the Golden Age. Furthermore, both strands identify the trends of rising household indebtedness, growing US trade deficits, and the dependence on the rest of the world to finance this deficit as threats to the sustainability of the macroeconomic trajectory (Godley 1999; Duménil & Lévy 2010) in the neoliberal period. The structural constraints of the neoliberal mode of accumulation arises from the weakened capacity to generate aggregate demand as the pace of investment slows down and consumption spending becomes the primary driver of demand; they are also impacted by the growth in inequality as exploitation is intensified and capital successfully pursues its quest for higher incomes. The disproportionate growth and unraveling of the financial system is also of significance in both approaches (Wray 2009; Lapavitsas 2013)

Accumulation in the neoliberal period has been characterized by the twin forces of globalization and financialization. These processes are tied to the growing power and changing role of the top managerial executive of large multinational corporations with the rise to dominance of the ideology of the maximization of shareholder value. Recent literature in the heterodox tradition addresses the significance of financialization and the new role of the managerial class in transforming the dynamic of accumulation. This literature demonstrates how heterodox approaches can respond to the concrete forms in which the capitalist economic system evolves.

Some open questions

The motor of capitalist economies is the accumulation of capital. Despite important differences, Post Keynesian and Marxian traditions share enough common ground in their approach to point towards a coherent alternative to neoclassical approaches to growth. Instead of deriving their abstract analytical framework from the assumptions of the optimizing behavior of atomistic agents, the conception of capitalist accumulation is based on the investigation of observed patterns and regularities in the trajectory of capitalist accumulation. Accumulation is understood as a totality of reciprocal interactions and relations between different dimensions and parts of the economic system.

What are some of the directions, which a heterodox research agenda could usefully pursue?

Recurrent and newly emerging empirical regularities and patterns in the global economy, both historically and in terms of a wider geographical spread, need further investigation and analysis. Such analysis would be the empirical foundation for broadening and deepening the understanding of the trajectory of capitalist accumulation.

The task of building more plausible and realistic microfoundations for the analysis of accumulation is another area which heterodox research needs to explore. Plausible microfoundations would need to comprehend the complexity of the reciprocal interactions that drives capitalist dynamics.

Finally, the methodological framework of heterodox traditions is particularly well-equipped to address some of the emerging challenges that confront the future of capitalist accumulation. The urgent dilemmas posed by climate change and the ecological crisis for the accumulation of capital is one such pressing question. Another potentially important question is that of the implications for capitalist dynamics of the institutional and technological changes that are unfolding in the wake of the growth of the information-based technology driven 'a new economy.'

These questions are by no means exhaustive but are suggestive of the distinctive ways in which heterodox economics can contribute to deepening the understanding the capital accumulation process in the contemporary global capitalist economy.

Notes

1 The term heterodox economics is a bit of a catch-all term encompassing approaches ranging from Marxians, Sraffians, and Post Keynesians to Austrians. This chapter does not address the debate on what constitutes heterodox economics. Instead of attempting the heroic task of dealing with the full range of heterodox approaches in the space of a single chapter, the chapter is limited to the Marxian and Post Keynesian strands.
2 Foley & Taylor (2006: 77) identify the core features that unify heterodox perspectives as "a focus on the functional distribution of income; the avoidance of model closures that are imply full employment of a

given labor force; differential modeling of the consumption and savings decisions workers and capitalists; the adoption of an investment demand function independent savings decisions; and a separate treatment of the firm as an economic agent independent of its owner households."

3 Full employment (à la Kaldor) or labor-constrained models (à la Goodwin) are special cases, but growth is in the general case constrained by capital not labor (Foley & Michl 2010). The supply of labor is explicitly endogenous in structuralist growth models where inflows to and outflows from the workforce, in response to the pace of accumulation, regulate employment. In classical-Marxian models, induced labor-saving technological change, with rising wages or tight labor markets, would replenish the reserve army of labor (Foley & Michl 2010).

4 Uncertainty has a bearing on animal spirits and class conflict would be an important source of uncertainty (Setterfield 2011).

5 Palley (2013), however, distinguishes between firms' market monopoly power and workers' bargaining power as two independent determinants of profit share.

6 Robinson (1962) elaborates the double-sided nature of the relation between profits and rate of accumulation with the rate of accumulation also affecting the rate of profit.

7 We use 'surplus' throughout the chapter to refer to national income less wages paid to productive labor.

8 The macroeconomic structure encapsulates "macroeconomic relations which ensure the perpetuation [of] the growth path including that between wages and productivity, profits and capital employed, and investment and consumption." The system of production refers to "general principles governing the techniques of production and the organization of work." The rules of coordination ensure the compatibility between individual behavior and the macroeconomic pattern (Glyn *et al.* 1990: 40–41).

9 Such a regime also characterized other advanced capitalist economies (see Glyn *et al.* 1990).

References

Aglietta, M. 1979. *A Theory of Capitalist Regulation*. London: Verso.

Baran, P. & Sweezy, P. 1966. *Monopoly Capital: An Essay on the American Economic and Social order*. New York: Monthly Review Press.

Basu, D. & Vasudevan, R. 2013. 'Technology, distribution and the rate of profit in the US economy: understanding the current crisis.' *Cambridge Journal of Economics*, 37 (1): 57–89.

Body, R. & Crotty, J. 1975. 'Class conflict and macro policy: the political business cycle.' *Review of Radical Political Economy*, 7 (1): 1–19.

Bowles, S., Gordon, D., & Weisskopf, T.E. 1983. *Beyond the Waste Land*. New York: Anchor Press-Doubleday.

Brenner, R. 2006. *Economics of Global Turbulence*. London: Verso.

Duménil, G. & Lévy, D. 1999. 'Being Keynesian in the short term and classical in the long term.' *The Manchester School*, 67 (6): 684–716.

Duménil, G. & Lévy, D. 2004. *Capital Resurgent*. Cambridge, MA: Harvard University Press.

Duménil, G. & Lévy, D. 2010. *The Crisis of Neoliberalism*. Cambridge, MA: Harvard University Press.

Foley, D.K. 1985. 'Say's Law in Marx and Keynes.' *Cahiers d'economie politique*, 10/11: 183–194.

Foley, D.K. 2012. 'The political economy of post crisis capitalism.' *South Atlantic Quarterly*, 111 (2): 251–263.

Foley, D.K. & Michl, T. 1999. *Growth and Distribution*. Cambridge, MA: Harvard University Press.

Foley, D.K. & Michl, T. 2010. 'A classical growth model,' *in*: M. Setterfield (ed.), *Handbook of Alternative Theories of Economic Growth*. Cheltenham, UK: Edward Elgar, 49–63.

Foley, D.K. & Taylor, L. 2006. 'A heterodox growth and distribution model,' *in*: N. Salvadori (ed.), *Economic Growth and Distribution: On the Causes of the Wealth of Nations*. Cheltenham, UK: Edward Elgar, 75–99.

Gibson, B. 2010. 'A structuralist growth model,' *in*: M. Setterfield (ed.), *Handbook of Alternative Theories of Economic Growth*. Cheltenham, UK: Edward Elgar, 17–48.

Glyn, A., Hughes, A., Liepeitz, A., & Singh, A. 1990. 'The rise and fall of the Golden Age,' *in*: S. Marglin & J. Schor (eds.), *The Golden Age of Capitalism: Reinterpreting the Post War Experience*. Oxford: Clarendon Press, 39–125.

Godley, W. 1999. Seven unsustainable processes: medium-term prospects and policies for the United States and the world. Levy Economics Institute Special Report. Available from http://www.levyinstitute.org/pubs/sevenproc.pdf [Accessed July 10, 2015]

Gordon, D., Edwards, R., & Reich, M. 1982. *Segmented Work, Divided Workers*. Cambridge, UK: Cambridge University Press.

Kaldor, N. 1961. 'Capital accumulation and economic growth,' *in*: F.A. Lutz & D.C. Hague (eds.), *Theory of Capital*. London: Macmillan, 177–222.

Kotz, D. & McDonough, T. 2010. 'Global neoliberalism and the contemporary social structure of accumulation,' *in*: T. McDonough, M. Reich, & D. Kotz (eds.), *Contemporary Capitalism and its Crisis: Social Structure of Accumulation Theory for the 21st Century*. New York: Cambridge University Press, 93–120.

Lapavitsas, C. 2013. *Profiting without Producing: How Finance Exploits Us All*. London: Verso.

Marglin, S. 1990. 'The lessons of the Golden Age,' *in*: S. Marglin & J. Schor (eds.), *The Golden Age of Capitalism: Reinterpreting the Post War Experience*. Oxford: Clarendon Press, 1–38.

Marglin, S. & Bhaduri, A. 1990. 'Unemployment and the real wage: the economic basis for contesting ideologies.' *Cambridge Journal of Economics*, 14 (4): 375–393.

Marx, K. [1867] 1976. *Capital, Volume I*. London: Penguin.

Marx, K. [1895] 1981. *Capital, Volume III*. London: Penguin

Minsky, H. [1975] 2008. *John Maynard Keynes*. New York: McGraw-Hill.

Minsky, H. [1986] 2008. *Stabilizing an Unstable Economy*. New York: McGraw-Hill.

Minsky, H. 1996. Uncertainty and the institutional structure of financial capitalism. Levy Economics Institute Working Paper 155. Available from http://www.levyinstitute.org/pubs/wp155.pdf [Accessed July 15, 2015]

Palley T.I. 2013. 'A Kaldor–Hicks–Goodwin–Tobin–Kalecki model of growth and distribution.' *Metroeconomica*, 64 (2): 319–345.

Patnaik, P. 2008. *The Value of Money*. New Delhi: Tulika Books.

Robinson, J. 1956. *The Accumulation of Capital*. London: Macmillan.

Robinson, J. 1962. *Essays in the Theory of Economic Growth*. Berlin: Springer.

Setterfield, M. 2010. 'An introduction to alternative theories of economic growth,' *in*: M. Setterfield (ed.), *Handbook of Alternative Theories of Economic Growth*. Cheltenham, UK: Edward Elgar, 1–17.

Setterfield, M. 2011. 'Anticipations of the crisis: on the similarities between Post-Keynesian economics and Regulation theory.' *Revue de la Régulation*, 10 (2). Available from http://regulation.revues.org/9366?gathStatIcon=true [Accessed July 19, 2016]

Setterfield, M. & Cornwall, J. 2002. 'A neo-Kaldorian perspective on the rise and decline of the golden age,' *in*: M. Setterfield (ed.), *The Economics of Demand led Growth: Challenging the Supply Side Vision of the Long Run*. Cheltenham, UK: Edward Elgar, 67–86.

Shaikh, A. 1978. 'Political economy and Dobb's theory of crisis.' *Cambridge Journal of Economics*, 2 (2): 233–251.

Shaikh, A. 1987. 'Falling rate of profit and the economic crisis in the US,' *in*: R.I. Cherry (ed.), *The Imperiled Economy, Book I*. New York: Monthly Review Press, 115–126.

Shaikh A. 1991. 'A dynamic approach to the theory of effective demand,' *in*: D.B. Papadimitriou (ed.), *Profits, Deficits, and Instability*. New York: Macmillan, 271–294.

Sweezy, P. & Magdoff, H. 1981. *The Deepening Crisis of US Capitalism*. New York: Monthly Review Press.

Taylor, L. 2004. *Reconstructing Macroeconomics*. Cambridge, MA: Harvard University Press.

Taylor, L. 2013. *Maynard's Revenge: The Collapse of Free Market Economics*. Cambridge, MA: Harvard University Press.

Wray, L.R. 2009. 'The rise and fall of money manager capitalism: a Minskian approach.' *Cambridge Journal of Economics*, 33 (4): 807–828.

23

A heterodox reconstruction
of trade theory

Yan Liang

Introduction

Mainstream economists almost unanimously support unrestricted trade (Fuller & Geide-Stevenson 2003). Some believe that free trade is the only proposition in social science that "is both true and non-trivial" (Samuelson 1948: 683), while others even argue that it has become "something of an article of faith" (MacDonald & Markusen 1985: 277) in modern economics.[1] However, as Joan Robinson aptly points out, "there is no branch of economics in which there is a wider gap between orthodox doctrine and actual problems than in the theory of international trade" (Robinson 1973: 14).

Heterodox economists, such as Post Keynesians, institutionalists, feminists, and dependency theorists, have long challenged mainstream trade theory and the policy implications thereof. They unveil unrealistic assumptions underlying traditional trade theory, critique the alleged efficiency-enhancing patterns of trade, and question the faith in the mutual benefits of trade. Heterodox trade theory, however, goes much beyond the constructive critiques of mainstream theories. Although there is no single 'heterodox trade theory,' different heterodox traditions share the same dissatisfaction with mainstream trade theory. These traditions are complementary and can be integrated into an effective and coherent approach to study the nature and impacts of international trade.

This chapter will examine the pitfalls of mainstream trade theory from the heterodox economics perspectives of the Post Keynesian and institutionalist traditions, and present alternative analytical frameworks to study the nature and impacts of trade. The structure is as follows. The second section presents a brief heterodox critique of mainstream trade theory on both the theoretical and empirical grounds, which provides the starting point to introduce alternative heterodox theories. The third section presents a tentative Post Keynesian-institutional framework to analyze the nature and patterns of trade, as well as the macroeconomic and developmental implications of trade. This section also provides some policy suggestions that radically differ from the free trade regime. The last section contains some concluding remarks.

A heterodox critique of mainstream trade theory

Comparative advantage theory is the cornerstone of mainstream trade theory. The theory consists of both a normative dimension that asserts that free trade is advantageous for all participating nations, and a positive dimension that describes how each nation automatically specializes according to its comparative advantages.[2] In Ricardo's original model ([1817] 2004), it is not explained how countries gain their comparative advantages, which are manifested in relatively lower production costs and hence lower export prices. This point was taken up later by neoclassical economists. The Heckscher–Ohlin–Samuelson (HOS) model builds upon Ricardian comparative advantage and further provides explanations for what accounts for comparative advantages (Heckscher 1919; Ohlin 1933; Samuelson 1948). It also extends the analysis of the impacts of trade, such as factor price changes and income distribution within and across countries. Simply put, the HOS model holds that each nation has a comparative advantage "in the production of commodities into which enter considerable amounts of factors abundant and cheap" (Ohlin 1933: 20). That is, the abundance in naturally endowed resources and production factors allows a country to lower production costs and hence enjoy the comparative (cost) advantage.

Despite mainstream's ubiquitous support of comparative advantage theory, the theory stands on very shaky theoretical and empirical grounds. First, it is an *ahistorical* and *asocial* theoretical construct. In developing the theory of comparative advantage, Ricardo used the example of the division of labor between Portugal and England in wine and cloth production to illustrate the voluntary, efficient, and mutually beneficial specialization and trade. Yet, the reality is that during the last years of the seventeenth century, Portugal imposed a protectionist policy, which prohibited its people from wearing foreign cloth in order to improve its own domestic cloth production. Meanwhile, British people preferred the lighter French wines to the heavier Portuguese wines, but wars with France and France's protectionist policy prompted Britain to find other sources of wines. Due to Portugal's dependence on Britain's military help to maintain its colonies, Portugal eventually signed the Methuen Treaty in 1703, which stipulated that Portugal lift restrictions on English cloth and woolen manufacturers; in return, Britain guaranteed a lower tax on Portuguese wine than on French wine (Felipe & Vernengo 2002–3). As Magdoff (1978: 156) points out, "[t]he comparative advantage that mattered was rooted not in soil or labor productivity, but in the superiority of British sea power and in Portugal's inability to hold on to its overseas empire without the protection of the British navy."

Stated alternatively, what Ricardo presumed as a voluntary and natural division of labor was in fact an outcome of a power struggle and a relationship of dominance and compromise. And the result was far from being mutually beneficial. Portuguese cloth manufacture was destroyed in its infancy and its wine production affected negatively the investment in corn and other food-stuffs. In contrast, Britain expanded its garment and textile industry and as a result enjoyed rapid industrial development and favorable trade balances. Similar stories can be told for many trading partners,[3] and in particular, between Western Europe and Asia, where the division of labor was not equal, voluntary, or mutually beneficial (see, for example, Pomeranz 2000). As Felipe & Vernengo (2002–3: 58) put it, "comparative advantage was 'historically created' as a result of colonialism, wars, nationalist rivalries, and military power."

Second, the theory of comparative advantage is built upon unrealistic and shaky assumptions. These faulty assumptions include full employment, the perfect mobility of labor and other resources between industries within a country, the immobility of capital and labor across borders, and, last but not the least, trade always remains balanced between two countries. Extending Say's law to an open economy, mainstream economists hold that trading based on comparative advantage would only re-allocate resources toward the most efficient uses, without generating unemployment as the resources shifted away from one industry will be redeployed in another. However, as heterodox economists incisively point out, the division of labor and specialization could lead to rising unemployment and thus undermine the benefits of trade.

In addition, without full employment and fixed income, trade imbalances could trigger income adjustments, not price adjustments.

Dismissal of the full employment assumption and Say's law marks a radical departure of Post Keynesian theory from the classical–neoclassical model. The assumption of perfect labor mobility between industries is equally bogus. Labor embodies specific skills and experiences within one industry, and as labor is required to switch from one to another industry, they may not be readily employable. This shows that the division of labor and industrial restructuring resulting from trade incurs some adjustment costs, which could be high and should not be easily ignored.

Capital immobility is yet another necessary but indefensible assumption. Ricardo was aware of the fact that as Portugal produces both wine and cloth cheaper than Britain, under capital mobility "the wine and the cloth should both be made in Portugal, and therefore . . . the capital and labor of England employed in making cloth, should be removed to Portugal for that purpose" (Ricardo [1817] 2004: 79). To avoid capital and labor mobility and resurrect comparative advantage theory, Ricardo resorted to the insecurity of foreign investments and "a natural disinclination which every man has to quit the country of his birth and connections, and entrust himself with all his habits fixed, to a strange government and new laws" (Ricardo [1817] 2004: 79). This argument, although a kernel of truth, is too arbitrary and cannot be generalized given today's global economy.[4] Daly & Cobb's ([1989] 1994: 217) argument is worth quoting at length:

> A classic example is a lawyer who is a better typist than her secretary. Even though the lawyer has an absolute advantage over the secretary both in knowledge of the law and in typing, she nevertheless finds it advantageous to specialize in law (her comparative advantage) and employ the secretary to do the typing. Since there is no possibility for labor power or any other productive capacity to flow out of the secretary and into the lawyer in response to absolute advantage, the assumption of factor immobility is guaranteed, and the principle of comparative advantage works. But the argument cannot be generalized to nations without the explicit requirement that their productive capacities (factors) not flow across national borders.

Finally, the assumption that trade is always balanced is theoretically flawed and empirically unfounded. The classical–neoclassical theory assumes balanced trade and this argument rests on two premises: first, international trade is purely a barter exchange and Say's law applies—the revenues of exports are by default to be used for imports; and second, should countries try to pursue net surpluses, the price-specie principle would render their efforts unattainable. That is, if a country's trade surplus rises, its 'gold' (foreign exchange) reserves increase, which increases the money supply and hence prices and hence undercuts its export competitiveness and induces imports. Provided that the price elasticities of demand for exports and imports work properly (the so-called Marshall-Lerner conditions), the country's trade balance will be restored through such a relative price/real exchange rate adjustment.

The exchange rate is solely determined by trade flows. The currency of the nation that experiences a trade deficit—and thus an outflow of money—will be depreciated and the currency of the nation that has a trade surplus will be appreciated. Thus, the commodities produced in the deficit nation will become cheaper internationally while those from the surplus nation will become more expensive. "When exports become equal to imports in money value, the exchange rate will stop moving and equilibrium will exist" (Eicher *et al.* 2009: 65). As a prominent macroeconomics textbook puts it, "[i]n the long run, we can reasonably assume that trade will be roughly balanced. . . . If trade is balanced in the long run, the long-run exchange rate must be such as to ensure trade balance" (Blanchard 1997: 276).[5] However, both premises that guarantee balanced trade are shaky.

Following Keynes' (1930) insights, Post Keynesians have emphatically noted the difference between a barter and a monetary economy. Export revenues may be used entirely for imports in the former economy, but that is not the case in the latter where monetary accumulation becomes the overriding objective of economic activities. On the other hand, exchange rate adjustments may not automatically eliminate trade imbalances as the exchange rate is not determined exclusively by trade in goods and services.

All these flaws in comparative advantage theory render it an unconvincing explanation as to why countries trade, how they trade, and what impacts trade brings forth. The mainstream reactions to these challenges are mainly twofold. One is to resort to 'long-run' reasoning, presuming that under idealistic conditions in the long-run (which would range between ten and 75 years!), international trade would work the way the theory prescribes. Another approach is to acknowledge the 'imperfections' of real world conditions and develop 'new trade theory,' which shows that free trade does not necessarily benefit all, given imperfect competition, economies of scale, and the uneven distribution of skills, knowledge, and institutions across countries (Shaikh 2003). And yet, despite all the problems free trade entails, new trade theory still holds that free trade policy works the best.

A Post Keynesian-institutionalist theory of trade

In this section, an alternative trade framework is presented. The first subsection considers the Post Keynesian framework that emphasizes uncertainty, monetary production, and the impacts of trade on effective demand and cumulative growth; the second subsection focuses on the institutionalist insights into trade, technological progress, and economic development.

Trade, effective demand, and cumulative export-led growth

Burbidge (1979: 139) wrote over three decades ago that "no formal post-Keynesian treatment of international trade has yet appeared that would correspond to the orthodox, neoclassical theory." Although a formal Post Keynesian trade theory is yet to be established, substantial developments in Post Keynesian trade theories have been made in the past three decades. Post Keynesians, by extending and elaborating the work of John Maynard Keynes, Joan Robinson, Michał Kalecki, Nicholas Kaldor, and others, provide many insights into the nature and patterns of international trade, as well as its macroeconomic and developmental implications.

As mentioned above, neoclassical trade theory is largely a micro-based theory that ignores the monetary nature and macroeconomic effects of trade. Neoclassical economic theory presumes sufficient aggregate demand and full employment (Dillard 1988), and their trade theory is based on this faulty foundation. In stark contrast, Post Keynesian trade theories emphasize the impacts of trade on effective demand. They also highlight the monetary profit-driven incentives to trade, which could lead firms and countries to run persistent trade imbalances. Trade deficits could lead to a drain on effective demand and hence slow down economic growth. Capital outflows and the resultant reduction in labor productivity and real wages could again lead to a reduction in wage-led consumption (Prasch 1996); domestic investment may also fall as a result. In short, from a Post Keynesian perspective, international trade must be cast into a monetary production framework where uncertainty, money, effective demand, and income adjustments matter.

Yan Liang

Unlike neoclassical theory where comparative advantage dictates the division of labor and trade pattern, Post Keynesian theory insists that absolute advantage or competitive advantage rules. As Burbidge (1979: 142) puts it, "the pattern of trade emerges, for a fixed set of exchange rates, depends on the ratio of average hourly earnings to average labor productivity (direct costs per unit of output) across the countries, measured, say, in U.S. dollars (cost) per unit of output." Stated alternatively, the relative prices of international goods (and hence a nation's terms of trade) are regulated in the same way as relative national prices. In both cases, high-cost producers lose out to low-cost ones and suffer trade deficits, which will correspond with capital inflows (for example, borrowing). Contrary to the theory of comparative advantage, there are no automatic price/exchange rate adjustments that will ensure that all countries are equal.[6] Rather, trade imbalances are the norm both because of the nature of a monetary economy and due to the ineffectiveness of exchange rate adjustment.

In a monetary production economy where monetary profits motivate firms to produce and trade, there is no guarantee that export revenues will automatically translate into import purchases. As Milberg (2002: 242) states, "the trade surplus country accrues liquid assets; there is no reason to assume these [liquid assets] will be converted into non-liquid assets, much less into foreign-produced non-liquid assets. Saving is thus the mechanism which creates the possibility of . . . persistently unbalanced trade." In addition, in a monetary production economy where effective demand could fall short of supply, trade imbalances may trigger income adjustments, which could in turn lead to cumulative, instead of self-reversing, outcomes (more below).

With capital mobility, exchange rates are largely determined by capital flows because the scale of capital flows significantly dwarf that of trade flows in the contemporary world economy. Should a country run trade deficits and a loose monetary base, its money supply will fall (*ceteris paribus*) and hence the interest rate will rise. As a result, it will attract capital inflows, which sustains its trade deficits—that is, it can rely on foreign borrowing to finance net imports. In this case, the exchange rate will not depreciate but appreciate, perpetuating, instead of improving, trade deficits. Indeed, the daily turnover in the foreign exchange markets reached US$5.3 trillion in 2013 (BIS 2015) whereas the total yearly exports were US$23.4 trillion (WTO 2014). This suggests that capital is much more fluid and mobile compared to flows of goods and services across borders. In short, the value of a currency is influenced by financial and currency markets on the basis of supply and demand (Harvey *et al.* 2010); the changes in currency value do not respond solely to trade imbalances and cannot guarantee to restore balanced trade.

Empirical evidence also points to persistent trade imbalances. The textbook version of the 'long-run' lasts ten years or more, during which a trade balance would be restored. But over most of the post-war period, the US has run a trade deficit while Japan has had a trade surplus (Arndt & Richardson 1987). More recently, UNCTAD (2004) reports that

> [a]n important feature of the LDC [less developed countries] economies is that they almost all have persistent and high trade deficit. In the period 1999–2001, the trade deficit was over 10 percent of GDP in 25 out of 44 LDCs for which data are available, and over 20 per cent of GDP in 8 of them.
>
> *Quoted in Skarstein 2007: 351*

Ultimately, without exchange rate adjustments, it is the differentials in real wages and technologies across nations that determine their international competitiveness (Shaikh 1980, 2003; Milberg 1994). In this case, competitive or absolute advantage governs patterns of trade. Unless countries can reduce real wage costs of production or improve production technology, they will lose out in trade. The presumed price/exchange rate adjustments will not work to redress trade imbalances, as exchange rates are not entirely determined by trade flows.

As Deprez (1995: 438–440) explains, in a monetary production economy the terms of trade are determined partly by the "subjective elements," including liquidity premiums, marginal user costs, and marginal efficiency of capital that are different and changing across economies; all these changes "dictate these subjective values" and hence shape the evolutions of terms of trade, which may or may not serve to rebalance trade. Without full employment and a fixed level of income, income adjustments could be the mechanism that redresses trade imbalances.[7] That is, "with unemployment allowed to exist in the model, the effect of the initial trade imbalance of the higher cost country is not to bring about price changes, but changes in income (employment) and/or real interest rates" (Turnell 2001: 7). The effect of income adjustments can be further illustrated in the balance-of-payments-constrained-growth-model below. This model is a significant contribution of the Post Keynesians in that it goes far beyond comparative advantage theory, which focuses merely on the micro level efficiency-enhancing effect of trade; instead, the Post Keynesians connect the effects of trade with aggregate demand and economic growth at the macro level.

The seminal paper by Thirlwall (1979) presents the balance-of-payments-constrained-growth-model, which connects trade balances with aggregate demand and growth rates. In this model, the growth of exports and imports is determined by the growth of world income and domestic income, respectively, as well the rate of change of relative prices. Substituting these into the balance-of-payments equation, expressed in growth rates, yields the growth of domestic income as a function of the growth of world income, the rate of changes of relative prices, and the growth of net international capital flows. Given that relative prices play a negligible role,[8] we can derive that the growth rate of domestic income consistent with the balance-of-payments equilibrium is determined by world income growth multiplied by the ratio of income elasticities of export and import. In mathematical form,

$$\dot{y} = \frac{\varepsilon \, \dot{y}^*}{\pi}$$

where $\dot{y}$ and $\dot{y}^*$ are domestic and world income growth rates, respectively, and ε and π are the income elasticities of export and import, respectively. This model is essentially an extension of Harrod's (1933) model, which holds that exports play an independent role in determining output and employment, that is, the export-led model of growth. In essence, 'Thirlwall's Law' reflects the importance of demand constraints and income adjustment applied to an open economy, where a balance-of-payments deficit cannot be self-equilibrating through internal or external price adjustments but it does through income adjustments. A balance-of-payment deficit would slow down domestic income growth to the level compatible with world income growth; whereas a balance-of-payment surplus would allow domestic income growth to exceed world growth.

The flip side of the balance-of-payment constraint is the idea of cumulative export-led growth. Harrod (1933) first introduced the notion of the foreign trade multiplier.[9] It is based on the idea that it is the income adjustment that brings the equality of exports and imports (for example, if a trade deficit occurs, the home income would have to reduce imports to restore trade balance), and therefore, the foreign trade multiplier is equal to the reciprocal of the marginal propensity to import. Based on this theory, Kaldor (1976) developed the cumulative export-led model that consists of four equations: first, output growth is a function of export growth; second, export growth is a function of changes in relative prices and world income growth; third, relative price changes are a function of wage and productivity growth; and lastly, productivity growth is a function of output growth (Verdoorn's Law). Under this structure, the faster the growth of exports, the faster is the growth of output, and *vice versa*. Therefore, working through the demand side and dynamic productivity changes, trade could lead to cumulative growth. The Verdoorn-Kaldor 'laws' of productivity growth provide rich grounds to explore the impacts of trade on dynamic long-term technical change and productivity growth.[10]

Empirical tests of these models have yielded reasonably good results. In the original study by Thirlwall (1979) of 18 developed countries during 1951–1973 and 1953–1976, the rank correlations between the actual growth rate and the growth rate predicted by the dynamic Harrod trade multiplier model were 0.891 and 0.764. Other studies typically reached a rank correlation of over 0.7 (McCombie & Thirlwall 2004: 9). Also studies that test the average deviation of the actual growth rate from the predicted rate turn out to be less than one percentage point (see, for example, Andersen 1993; Atesoglu 1993), which again shows the strong explanatory power of the model.

Trade, technological change, and economic development

Neoclassical trade theory, represented by the HOS model, is premised on fixed endowments and static efficiency gains through resource re-allocation. However, this theory cannot explain rapid and varying technological changes in different countries at different time periods; nor can it provide useful policy suggestions for countries to improve their technological development. Neoclassicals insist that given endowed resources, free trade alone has "the potential for development and convergence between rich and poor countries" (Kiely 2007: 15). Institutionalists, however, have long understood that "a country's resource endowment is formed out of its specific historical experience with economic development" (Prasch 1996: 49). Technology, demand conditions, and innovative efforts all matter for the creation and development of productive 'resources'; because resources are not; they 'become.' After all, "resources are not things or stuff or materials; they are a set of capabilities" (De Gregori 1987: 1243).

These capabilities are not fixed or given to a country; they are fostered and developed through historical processes. Moreover, "[i]ncremental and path-dependent change are important components of the totality of technical change . . . these changes are endogenous to the economic system" (Prasch 1996: 50–51). With such an understanding, heterodox economists have a much better explanation for how countries trade and the effects of trade on development. For example, the rapid rise in manufacturing production and trade in the United States during 1860–1929 was not a result of the discovery of pre-set fixed endowments and free trade; rather, "American industry developed behind relatively high tariffs combined with the once non-trivial economic barrier provide by two vast oceans" (Prasch 1996: 52). Similarly, state-led industrial policy and tariff and non-tariff protection lie behind the success of numerous other countries, from Great Britain and Germany to Japan and South Korea. It is not surprising to find that a growing market share of a nation is "strongly positively correlated" with faster productivity growth and an increase in technological capability (Fagerberg 1996: 40–41).

Comparative advantage theory holds that trade is mutually beneficial regardless of what countries specialize in. Specializing in manufacturing goods or agricultural goods should not make a difference so long as countries adhere to their fixed endowments and trade based on their comparative advantages. Inferior productivity or technology will not prevent countries from enjoying the benefits of free trade, because

> [i]nternational competition does not put countries out of business. There are strong equilibrating forces that normally ensure that any country remains able to sell a range of goods in

world markets, and to balance its trade on average over the long run, even if its productivity, technology, and product quality are inferior to those of other nations . . . both in theory and in practice, countries with lagging productivity are still able to balance their international trade, because what drives trade is comparative rather than absolute advantage.

Krugman 1991: 811, 814

This proposition, however, is vehemently dismissed by heterodox economists. As Cypher & Dietz (1998: 307, original emphasis) emphatically state, "[i]t may not be specialization per se that is so important for a country's future as *is the choice of what to specialize in.*" Their dynamic comparative advantage model, following the Prebisch-Singer hypothesis (PSH), reveals that the North (producers of manufactured goods) gains doubly from trade at the expense of the South (producers of primary goods) due to the evolution of the terms of trade.

More specifically, both Prebisch (1950) and Singer (1949) argued that gains from specialization in primary production may be offset by the balance-of-payments consequences due to the unfavorable terms of trade and the income elasticity of demand for primary goods. They further argued that: first, free trade tends to lead developing countries to specialize in primary goods and developed countries to specialize in manufactured goods; and, second, as a result of specializing in primary goods, developing countries suffer secular declining terms of trade and volatility in commodity prices.

The reason that primary goods tend to have unfavorable terms of trade is twofold. One is the different market structures of manufactured products and primary goods (Toye & Toye 2003). The former is typically featured by mark-up pricing and the unionization of labor, which buttress the unit prices of manufactured goods. The other factor is differing technical progress, which not only favors the manufacturing sector regarding productivity growth but also in terms of future demand (primary goods have lower income and price elasticity of demand compared to manufactured goods). Thus producers in developed countries (or 'the center') are able to maintain high prices and workers enjoying rising wages due to increasing productivity, while in developing countries (or 'the periphery') firms face declining prices as they compete with other primary producers and workers encounter stagnant or declining wages as unemployment rises. Therefore, the terms of trade of developing countries deteriorate over the long-run, which undermines their development process (Singer 1984).

The PSH has been empirically tested widely and the results mostly support the theory. A prominent UN study finds that the terms of trade between agricultural goods and manufactured goods decline over time to the detriment of the former (de Larrinoa Arcal *et al.* 2000). Ocampo & Parra (2003) trace the evolution of the terms of trade between commodities and manufactures in the twentieth century and find that the relative price series for 24 commodities and of eight indices had a significant deterioration in the barter terms of trade. Their investigation shows that far reaching changes in the world economy during the 1920s and 1980s led to a stepwise deterioration of nearly 1 percent real price reduction every year for raw materials.

In a more recent study, Harvey *et al.* (2010) investigate 25 commodity prices spanning the seventeenth to the twenty-first centuries. In their study, 11 price series present a significant downward trend overall or some fraction of the sample period and in the very long-run, and a secular deteriorating trend is found for a significant proportion of primary commodities. In another study that examines the secular trend and short-run volatility of primary commodity prices, Arezki *et al.* (2013) examine 25 series of primary commodity prices, some of which date back to 1650. This study finds that a majority of the price series display downward trends, despite the rising demand of primary commodities by emerging markets and the falling costs of transportation. This also echoes earlier findings that real commodity prices exhibit increasing variability since the early 1970s after the breakdown of the Bretton Woods exchange regime (Reinhart & Wickham 1994; Cuddington & Liang 1999).

Two important implications can be drawn from the PSH. First, free trade does not yield equal benefits to trading countries that are in different developmental stages and technological levels; nor does it unconditionally promote economic development. Second, the PSH shows that there is large room for state interventions. For example, some price stabilization schemes are needed for primary commodity exports and cushions need to be built in for foreign exchange reserves as windfalls from favorable commodity prices could be temporary and easily relapsed.[11] More importantly, developing countries should institute industrial policies to diversify their economies and become less dependent on primary commodity exports. All these are contrary to free trade policies that are derived from comparative advantage theory.

Although today's advanced countries deliberately used tariffs, subsidies, and other protective policies as they developed and became competitive, they forcefully prescribe free trade policies for developing countries. As Chang (2002: 1) writes,

> [c]riticizing the British preaching of free trade to his country, Ulysses Grant, the Civil War hero and the US President between 1868–1876, retorted that 'within 200 years, when America has gotten out of protection all that I can offer, it too will adopt free trade.'

And yet, the 'unholy trinity' (the IMF, World Bank, and WTO), and the advanced capitalist countries behind it, cajole and force developing countries to lower tariffs and eliminate subsidies, adhere to WTO rules in intellectual property rights, customs procedures, sanitary standards, the treatment of foreign investors, and adopt various liberalization and privatization 'reforms' (Rodrik 2001).

Indeed, contrary to what free trade advocates preach, countries that avoided wholesale liberal policies but follow highly selective trade policies have enjoyed successful development experiences. These countries include Japan, South Korea, Taiwan, and other Asian Tigers. In contrast, countries that did pursue free trade—Chile (1974–1979), Mexico (1985–1988), and Argentina (1991)—have suffered great setbacks in industrial development and incurred prohibitive social costs (Agosin & Tussie 1993). As Burbidge (1979: 150) states "it would seem that, to gain ground, the less developed countries must somehow jump over the technological gap that separates them from the more developed countries and set up their own manufacturing sectors." In short, the institutionalists focus on the technological determination of trade patterns and the dynamic impacts of trade on development lead them to propose industrial and protectionist trade policies to promote developmental-friendly trade as opposed to free trade.

Conclusions

Ricardian comparative advantage theory and the HOS model hold that the relative prices of production, derived from countries' natural endowments of productive resources, govern international trade. Following the endowments and natural division of labor, countries specialize in what they produce relatively more efficiently (or less inefficiently) and trade, which allows them to enhance resource allocation and static efficiency. Trade will remain balanced (at least in the 'long-run') thanks to relative price/exchange rate adjustments. In this case, countries participating in trade always gain. Based on the theory, free trade is unconditionally advocated as a way to promote development and convergence. However, heterodox economists, particularly, Post Keynesians and institutionalists, forcefully challenge this mainstream trade theory and its policy implications.

Based on a monetary production framework where uncertainty, monetary incentives, effective demand, and unemployment play an important role, Post Keynesians argue that almost all the assumptions of comparative advantage theory are false. Trade is not a net barter that always remains balanced and mutually beneficial. In contrast, because of monetary incentives, countries that happen to enjoy absolute advantages (due to lower labor costs or superior technology) and run a trade surplus may have no incentives to eliminate the surpluses; and there is no automatic terms of trade/exchange rate adjustment that could restore the balance. Trade imbalances could trigger adverse income adjustments in the deficit countries, which could bring forth a cumulative, vicious cycle of falling income and employment, falling productivity, worsening trade competitiveness, and so on.

Institutionalists, on the other hand, emphasize that patterns of specialization are not determined by naturally endowed resources and not equally beneficial to the center and peripheral countries. Because resources can be 'created' through the development of technology, countries should not be confined to their natural endowments and static comparative advantages, given the unfavorable terms of trade changes resulted from primary goods production and export.

Post Keynesian and institutionalist trade theory provides a powerful alternative to the mainstream theory in accounting for the patterns and impacts of trade; in addition, they propose dramatically different policies based on the theory. At the country level, the balance of payments could constrain growth; and, therefore, automatic market forces cannot be relied on to achieve trade balances. Kaldor (1981: 593) wrote three decades ago that "under more realistic assumptions unrestricted trade is likely to lead to a loss of welfare to particular regions or countries." To say that unregulated international trade is automatically beneficial because of some 'principle of comparative advantage' is to offer a verbal formula in place of the causal processes, laws, and institutions that actually shape actions and events (Culbertson 1984: 10).

Although beggar-thy-neighbor policies may help individual countries promote demand and growth, it will not work at the aggregate level. So other demand-enhancing policies must be in place and given its macroeconomic impacts, trade should not be unconstrained; instead, policies that will improve trade competitiveness and generate positive trade balances should be instituted. From an institutionalist perspective, countries should strive to diversify their industries and upgrade technologies. At the international level, developing countries should not be forced to be open to free trade. As Gunnar Myrdal (1956: 292) proposes, a "double-standard morality" should be promoted where under-developed countries "not only have good reasons but are virtually forced to control their imports and subsidize their exports—indeed, to practice systematic protection—if they are not to give up their drive for economic development."

Notes

1 There exists a "virtual unanimity among economists, whatever their ideological position on other issues, that international free trade is in the best interests of trading countries and of the world" (Friedman & Friedman 2004: 1; see also Bhagwati 2002: 3–4; Winters et al. 2004: 72, 78, 106).

2 As Milberg (2004: 56–57) summarizes the view that international trade leads to "the happy result that all countries will be able successfully to participate in international trade in the sense that they will benefit from such trade and be able to generate export revenues equal to the value of imports."

3 Economic historian Carlo Cipolla's discussions about Italy's and Spain's shift of specialization away from industry as a result of international trade provide revealing insights into how trade and specialization can in fact hinder a country's development. By contrast, England became an economic power, not because of laissez-faire but by direct government actions like the prohibition of Spanish wool or the wearing of foreign cloth, and the support of shipping and the merchant marine. Likewise, the United States economy grew to a dominant position in the decades following the Civil War because of a wall of tariffs protecting them from European competition (Culbertson 1989: 70–74).

4 Neoclassical economists first adopted Ricardo's argument (for example, Haberler 1930: 350) and later developed the factor price equalization theorem that renders capital and labor movements superfluous, as capital and labor would earn the same returns at home or abroad (Samuelson 1948). This theorem states that international trade leads to the same result as if capital and labor were mobile. Hence, there is no necessity for their international mobility. However, there is no evidence that factor prices equalize worldwide (Subasat 2003: 152) and models that allow for labor and capital movement show that comparative advantages do not determine trade patterns (see, for example, Brewer 1985; Jones 2000).

5 Other neoclassical theories define the 'long-run,' when balanced trade and purchasing power parity would hold, to be on the order of 75 years or longer (Rogoff 1996), a time span that is theoretically arbitrary and practically meaningless.

6 "The basic issue is that in an economy operating at less than full employment, trade deficits will not bring the appropriate relative price adjustments necessary to induce resource re-allocation necessary to bring balanced trade" (Milberg 1994: 228).

7 Indeed, in today's global economy, full employment is rather an exception than a norm. "Even in the fifteen most economically liberalized nations, unemployment rates have ranged between 1.0% and 16.6% in the last two decades" (Schumacher 2013: 94).

8 This is so either because in the long-run the purchasing power parity holds or due to the small and negligible price elasticities of demand (McCombie & Thirlwall 2004).

9 Thirlwall's Law can be considered as dynamic version of Harrod's foreign trade multiplier. In a more complex model (McCombie 1985) shows that Thirlwall's Law could be generally regarded as Hick's 'super-multiplier' in the sense that a growth in export would not only increase the growth of income through the Harrod foreign trade multiplier, but it also increases domestic components of demand, thereby increasing the growth rate even more.

10 Robert Blecker (1994) has shown the existence of a causal relationship between capital mobility, trade flows, the stagnation of wages and the slowing of economic growth in the United States.

11 As Kaldor (1976) points out, events that force up the prices of primary products relative to manufactured goods will only last temporarily. Ultimately, the prices of manufactured goods, which are purchased by primary producers, will increase and shift income distribution toward developed countries.

References

Agosin, M.R. & Tussie, D. 1993. 'Trade and growth: new dilemmas in trade policy–an overview,' in: M.R Agosin & D. Tussie (eds.), *Trade and Growth: New Dilemmas in Trade Policy*. New York: St. Martin's Press, 1–32.

Andersen, P.S. 1993. 'The 45° rule revisited.' *Applied Economics*, 25 (10): 1279–1284.

Arezki, R., Hadri, K., Loungani, P., & Rao, Y. 2013. Testing the Prebisch–Singer hypothesis since 1650: evidence from panel techniques that allow for multiple breaks. IMF Working Paper. Washington, DC: International Monetary Fund.

Arndt, S.W. & Richardson, J.D. 1987. Real-financial linkages among open economies. NBER Working Paper 2230.

Atesoglu, H.S. 1993. 'Balance of payments constrained growth: Evidence from the United States.' *Journal of Post Keynesian Economics*, 15 (4): 507–514.

Bhagwati, J.N. 2002. *Free Trade Today*. Princeton, NJ: Princeton University Press.

Bank of International Settlements (BIS). 2015. Statistics: triennial central bank survey of foreign exchange and derivative market activity in 2013. Available from http://www.bis.org/publ/rpfx13.htm [Accessed September 16, 2015]

Blanchard, O. 1997. *Macroeconomics*, 2nd edn. New York: Prentice Hall.

Blecker, R. 1994. 'The new economic stagnation and the contradiction of economic policy making,' in: M. Bernstein & D. Adler (eds.), *Understanding America's Economic Decline*. New York: Cambridge University Press, 276–310.

Brewer, A. 1985. 'Trade with fixed real wages and mobile capital.' *Journal of International Economics*, 18 (1–2): 177–186.

Burbidge, J.B. 1979. 'The international dimension,' in: A.S. Eichner (ed.), *A Guide to Post-Keynesian Economics*. White Plains, NY: M.E. Sharpe, 139–150.

Chang, H.-J. 2002. *Kicking Away the Ladder*. London: Anthem Press.

Cuddington, J. & Liang, H. 1999. Commodity price volatility across exchange rate regimes. Unpublished paper. Washington, DC: Department of Economics, Georgetown University.

Culbertson, J.M. 1984. *International Trade and the Future of the West*. Madison, WI: 21st Century.

Culbertson, J.M. 1989. *The Trade Threat and U.S. Trade Policy*. Madison, WI: 21st Century.

Cypher, J.M. & Dietz, J.L. 1998. 'Static and dynamic comparative advantage: a multi-period analysis with declining terms of trade.' *Journal of Economic Issues*, 32 (2): 305–314.

Daly, H.E. & Cobb Jr., J.B. [1989] 1994. *For the Common Good: Redirecting the Economy Toward Community, the Environment, and a Sustainable Future*. Boston: Beacon Press.

Deprez, J. 1995. 'Technology and the terms of trade: considering expectational, structural, and institutional factors.' *Journal of Economic Issues*, 29 (2): 534–543.

Dillard 1988. 'The barter illusion in classical and neoclassical economics.' *Eastern Economic Journal*, 16 (4): 299–318.

Eicher, T.S., Mutti, J.H., & Turnovsky, M.H. 2009. *International Economics*, 7th edn. London: Routledge.

Fagerberg, J. 1996. 'Technology and competitiveness.' *Oxford Review of Economic Policy*, 12 (3): 39–51.

Felipe, J. & Vernengo, M. 2002–3. 'Demystifying the principles of comparative advantage implications for developing countries.' *International Journal of Political Economy*, 32 (4): 49–75.

Friedman, M. & Friedman, R. 2004. 'The case for free trade,' in: *Globalization and World Capitalism: A Debate*. The Cato Institute, May 25. Available from https://docs.google.com/document/d/1B3KJ0GoJiPijUkc b8p9oJB8PlAIGMy4xrXYIoAhVqCA/edit?hl=en_US [Accessed January 18, 2016]

Fuller, D. & Geide-Stevenson, D. 2003. 'Consensus among economists: revisited.' *The Journal of Economic Education*, 34 (4): 369–387.

De Gregori, T.R. 1987. 'Resources are not; they become: an institutional theory.' *Journal of Economic Issues*, 21 (3): 1241–1263.

Haberler, G. 1930. 'Die Theorie der komparativen Kosten und ihre Auswertung für die Begründung des Freihandels.' *Weltwirtschaftliches Archiv*, 32: 349–370; translated and reprinted in Anthony Y.C. Koo (ed.), 1985. *Selected Essays of Gottfried Haberler*. Cambridge, MA: MIT Press, 3–19.

Harrod, R.F. 1933. *International Economics*. Cambridge: Cambridge University Press.

Harvey, D.I., Kellard, N.M., Madsen, J.B., & Wohar, M.E. 2010. 'The Prebisch–Singer hypothesis: four centuries of evidence.' *Review of Economics and Statistics*, 92 (2): 367–377.

Heckscher, E. 1919. 'The effect of foreign trade on the distribution of income.' *Ekonomisk Tidskrift*, 21: 497–512; English translation, American Economic Association (ed.) 1949. *Readings in the Theory of International Trade*. Philadelphia: Blakiston, 272–300.

Jones, R.W. 2000. *Globalization and the Theory of Input Trade: The Ohlin Lectures 8*. Cambridge, MA: MIT Press.

Kaldor, N. 1976. 'Inflation and recession in the world economy.' *Economic Journal*, 86 (344): 703–714.

Kaldor, N. 1981. 'The role of increasing returns, technical progress and cumulative causation in the theory of international trade and economic growth.' *Économie Appliquée*, 34 (4): 593–617.

Keynes, J.M. 1930. *A Treatise on Money*. London: Macmillan.

Kiely, R. 2007. *The New Political Economy of Development: Globalisation, Imperialism and Hegemony*. Basingstoke, UK: Palgrave Macmillan.

Krugman, P. 1991. 'Myths and realities of US competitiveness.' *Science*, 254 (5033): 811–815.

de Larrinoa Arcal, Y.F. & Maetz, M. 2000. 'Trends in world agriculture and trade,' in: *Multilateral Trade Negotiations On Agriculture: A Resource Manual*. Rome: Food and Agriculture Organization of the United Nations. Available from http://www.fao.org/docrep/003/x7352e/x7352e01.htm [Accessed February 4, 2016]

MacDonald, G.M. & Markusen, J.R. 1985. 'A rehabilitation of absolute advantage.' *Journal of Political Economy*, 93 (2): 277–297.

Magdoff, H. 1978. *Imperialism: From the Colonial Age to the Present*. New York: Monthly Review Press.

McCombie, J.S.L. 1985. 'Economic growth, the Harrod foreign trade multiplier and the Hicks super-multiplier.' *Applied Economics*, 17 (1): 52–72.

McCombie, J. & Thirlwall, T. 2004. *Essays on Balance of Payments Constrained Growth: Theory and Evidence*. London and New York: Routledge.

Milberg, W. 1994. 'Is absolute advantage passe? Towards a Post Keynesian/Marxian theory of international trade,' in: M. Glick (ed.), *Competition, Technology and Money: Classical and Post Keynesian Perspectives*. Cheltenham, UK: Edward Elgar, 220–236.

Milberg, W. 2002. 'Say's Law in the open economy: Keynes's rejection of the theory of comparative advantage,' in: S.C. Dow & J. Hillard (eds.), *Keynes, Uncertainty and the Global Economy: Beyond Keynes*. Cheltenham, UK: Edward Elgar, 239–253.

Milberg, W. 2004. 'The changing structure of trade linked to global production system: what are the policy implications?' *International Labour Review*, 143 (1–2): 45–90.

Myrdal, G. 1956. *An International Economy: Problems and Prospects*. New York: Harper & Brothers Publishers.

Ocampo, J.A. & Parra, M.A. 2003. 'The terms of trade for commodities in the twentieth century.' *CEPAL Review*, 79 (April): 7–35.

Ohlin, B. 1933. *Interregional and International Trade*. Cambridge, MA: Harvard University Press.

Pomeranz, K. 2000. *The Great Divergence: China, Europe, and the Making of the Modern World Economy*. Princeton, NJ: Princeton University Press.

Prasch, R. 1996. 'Reassessing the theory of comparative advantage.' *Review of Political Economy*, 8 (1): 37–54.

Prebisch, R. 1950. *The Economic Development of Latin America and Its Principal Problems*. New York: United Nations.

Reinhart, C. & Wickham, P. 1994. Commodity prices: cyclical weakness or secular decline? MPRA paper No. 8173. Available from http://mpra.ub.uni-muenchen.de/8173/ [Accessed February 4, 2016]

Ricardo, D. [1817] 2004. *The Principles of Political Economy and Taxation*. Mineola, NY: Dover Publications.

Robinson, J. 1973. 'The need for a reconsideration of the theory of international trade,' in: *Collected Economic Papers, Vol. 4*. Oxford: Basil Blackwell, 14–24.

Rodrik, D. 2001. The global governance of trade: as if trade really mattered. Background Paper to the UNDP Project on Trade and Sustainable Human Development, October. New York: United Nations Development Programme.

Rogoff, K. 1996. 'The purchasing power parity puzzle.' *Journal of Economic Literature*, 34 (2): 647–668.

Samuelson, P. 1948. 'International trade and the equalization of factor prices.' *Economic Journal*, 58 (230): 163–184.

Schumacher, R. 2013. 'Deconstructing the theory of comparative advantage.' *World Economic Review*, 2: 83–105.

Shaikh, A. 1980. 'The law of international exchange,' in: E. Nell (ed.), *Growth, Profits and Property*. Cambridge, UK: Cambridge University Press, 204–234.

Shaikh, A. 2003. *Globalization and the Myth of Free Trade*. London and New York: Routledge.

Singer, H.W. 1949. 'Economic progress in underdeveloped countries.' *Social Research: An International Quarterly of Political and Social Science*, 16 (1): 1–11.

Singer, H.W. 1984. 'The terms of trade controversy and the evolution of soft financing: early years in the UN,' in: G.M. Meier & D. Seers (eds.), *Pioneers in Development*. Washington, DC: The World Bank, 275–303.

Skarstein, R. 2007. 'Free trade: a dead end for underdeveloped economies.' *Review of Political Economy*, 19 (3): 347–367.

Subasat, T. 2003. 'What does the Heckscher–Ohlin model contribute to international trade theory? A critical assessment.' *Review of Radical Political Economics*, 35 (2): 148–165.

Thirlwall, A.P. 1979. 'The balance of payments constraint as an explanation of international growth rate differences.' *Banca Nazionale del Lavoro Quarterly Review*, 128 (791): 45–53.

Toye, J.F.J. & Toye. R. 2003. 'The origins and interpretation of the Prebisch–Singer thesis.' *History of Political Economy*, 35 (3): 437–467.

Turnell, S. 2001. The right to employment: extending the core labour standards and trade debate. Macquarie Economics Research Papers 1/2001. Sydney: Macquarie University.

UNCTAD. 2004. *The Least Developed Countries Report 2004: Linking International Trade with Poverty Reduction*. New York & Geneva: UNCTAD.

Winters, L.A., McCulloch, N., & McKay, A. 2004. 'Trade liberalization and poverty: the evidence so far.' *Journal of Economic Literature*, 42 (1): 72–115.

World Trade Organization (WTO). 2014. Statistical database. Available from http://stat.wto.org/StatisticalProgram/WSDBStatProgramHome.aspx?Language=E [Accessed March 21, 2015]

24

Analyzing the organization of global production
Thoughts from the periphery

Víctor Ramiro Fernández and Gabriel Brondino

Introduction

By the end of the 1970s, the 'Golden Age' of capitalism that started in the post–Second World War years came to an end. The institutional arrangements that sustained a strong process of capital accumulation had now become a straitjacket for its continued expansion. There began a process of considerable institutional and productive transformations, which scholars are still trying to explain. One of the most important dimensions of this transformation is related to changes in the global organization of production. A restructuring of supply chains in multiple locations involving multiple firms operating in a highly coordinated way through market exchanges has been evidenced. This stands in sharp contrast to the vertically integrated conglomerates distinctive of the Fordist mode of accumulation.

The question of how these changes emerged and what are their theoretical and practical implications remains a contested field of discussion among scholars. The central variable in most explanations is technological change. For new institutional economics, changes in technology create new rents for potential innovators that demand institutional rearrangements. In this sense, the technological shifts of the 1970s and 1980s opened up attractive rent opportunities that could only be seized by breaking down the vertically integrated corporations (Langlois 2003). A similar position, though in a neo-Schumpeterian vein, is held by Perez (1985).

Although we do not deny the importance of these elements, we believe that they fall short in providing a comprehensive explanation of the complexity of the changes. In this sense, it is legitimate to ask to what extent one can explain these transformations by abstracting them from other transformations that have occurred within the capitalist system in the advent of the 1970s world crisis, in terms of class struggle, the policy priorities of states, and geopolitics. It is also relevant to investigate the particular impact that these changes have had on the periphery of the capitalist system and the way in which this periphery is involved in the 'spatial solution' of capitalism in general and in global productive transformations in particular.

We will attempt to provide a theoretical framework to analyze these changes in the context of recent historical transformations of the capitalist system, as well as to evaluate the particular way in which the periphery has been incorporated into these transformations.

Understanding capitalist transformations
in a *longue durée* perspective

> Capitalism is the first and only historical system that has become global in scale and scope. Mapping this transformation over time is a particularly challenging task.
>
> *Arrighi 2004: 527*

Classical political economists considered the conflict and power relations between the owners of means of production (capitalists) and the direct producers (laborers) to be a central feature of capitalism. The main conflict concerned the distribution of the social surplus. For given normal conditions of production, "one class cannot have more without the other class having less" (Garegnani 1984:301). According to Marx, it was the merit of Ricardo to point out the economic contradiction between this "intrinsic relation" (Marx 1963: 525).

The production of commodities is structured in terms of chains, which are constituted by the exchange relations established between capitalists. Each chain can be seen as a network of inputs (including labor) required for the production of final goods (Hopkins & Wallerstein 1977). The conflictive relation between the labor force and capitalist agencies underlies each node of the chain. That is why, in addition to competing in final product markets, capitalist agencies also attempt to displace the distributional conflict to other nodes of the chain. In this way they aim to get the largest share of the surplus generated in the chain (or other chains).

There is no defined territorial scope for the constitution of commodity chains. As World Systems theorists have shown, because territories are delimited by the inter-state system, inter-capitalist competition is not disconnected from inter-state competition for power and leadership. In this sense, the formation of global commodity chains is not an unintended outcome derived solely from the autonomous decisions of capitalists. Commodity chains also have "occurred under the leadership of particular communities and blocs of governmental and business agencies which were uniquely well placed to turn to their own advantage the unintended consequences of the actions of other agencies" (Arrighi 1994: 10).

A state that accumulates enough power can lead the system in a desired direction and, in doing so, be "perceived as pursuing a general interest" (Arrighi 1994: 30). Under the leadership of the hegemonic power, states are ranked into three broad groups (Fiori 2009): first, states developed under the tutelage of the hegemon, mainly by geopolitical motives; second, states that adopt autonomous development strategies to catch-up with the leader (these projects are not always permitted by the hegemonic power and may be blocked); and third, a group of heterogeneous states, which constitute the periphery of the system. In this 'center-periphery structure,' some states can change their position but the structure as a whole is stable over time (Arrighi & Drangel 1986; Babones 2005).

This political structure of center-periphery relations influences the exchange and production relations of commodity chains. Peripheral states usually provide primary and secondary specialized inputs to central states. According to Latin American structuralist authors, exchange between the center and the periphery is unequal since central states commonly provide political protection within their domestic borders both to labor and capital, while peripheral states are more limited in their ability to do so. This differential in protection means a different distributive arrangement in the center than in the periphery, which in the end implies an unequal terms of trade (Prebisch 1962).

To sum up, the emergence of a hegemonic state implies a particular inter-state structure, configuring and articulating a center-periphery hierarchy. This structure is supported by a particular configuration of global commodity chains. In each node of the chain, capitalist agencies attempt to displace the distributive conflict to other nodes or other chains. This displacement is reinforced and mediated by the center-periphery relations. Capitalist agencies located in central states are usually more successful in translating the conflict to nodes located in peripheral states.[1]

This way, inter-capitalist and inter-state competition ultimately resolves itself in a particular configuration of global capital accumulation. The configuration will depend on the form of these two types of competition (Arrighi & Drangel 1986).[2] But this configuration is not definitive and competitive pressures are always latent.

As capital accumulates, it may have difficulties in finding outlets for its production and realizing the expected normal profitability. This may lead to a breakdown in the accumulation process and leave large shares of labor and productive capacity underutilized in some areas of production. When the crisis becomes deep enough, a global restructuring of capital accumulation occurs. As Marxian critical geography authors claim, the crisis is usually resolved by restructuring the production process. This restructuring is accomplished by incorporating new spaces for capital accumulation, that is, a 'spatial fix' (Harvey 1981, 2001). Since the fundamental contradictions of the crisis are not solved, this solution is also a temporal fix, that is, it only delays further in time the always latent distributive conflict.

There arises resistance to new spatial-temporal fixes. Some fractions of capital, as well as local institutions and part of the labor force, cannot relocate. This is important in the sense that it is not necessary for a capitalist to actually move but to have a potential place of relocation. The mere possibility of a spatial fix is enough for the mobile fractions of capital to have leverage to negotiate concessions for obtaining higher profits (Bluestone & Harrison 1982). Resistance also comes from inter-state competition, since relocation of productive activities may empower the recipient territory/state and cause geopolitical shifts in the balance of power (Harvey 1981; Arrighi 2004).

If for capitalist agencies only the possibility of a new spatial fix is sufficient, what are the main determinants that make this menace credible? What enables global restructuring of productive chains? Certainly, the institutional and technological advances are fundamental determinants (Perez 1985), but they cannot be understood without considering the general picture of inter-state competition and distributive conflict.

Recent transformations of global production

The rise of the Golden Age

By the end of the Second World War, the United States (US) had consolidated its global political power and assumed the leadership of the inter-state system. This hegemony was continuously threatened by a particular group of states centered around the Soviet Union (USSR). Under these circumstances, the US pursued an active foreign policy in those states that had geographical proximity to the territories controlled by the USSR. Specifically, the strategy had two pillars: economic and political reconstruction of Europe, and an impulse for development in East Asia.

As military tension between state blocs began to rise, internal political pressure from the working class in Western central states was increasing, especially in Western Europe. Labor organizations gained strength in wage negotiations and, in the face of the 'menace' of communism, concentrated capital adopted a defensive strategy. National states acted as mediators of this transitory agreement between the two factions. Negotiations were highly centralized, since they were developed by big economic groups and trade unions (Brenner 2004). The agreements allowed—in central states—for an extended process of formation of the Keynesian welfare states, which, regardless of their domestic specificities (Esping-Andersen 1990) converged in encouraging a unique growth process through social spending and full employment policies (Marglin & Schor 1990).

The presence of big economic groups and concentrated capital was the result of rapid industrial development at the end of the nineteenth and beginning of the twentieth centuries. The development of transportation and communication systems (railroads and telephone network, among others) within domestic borders enlarged the size of national markets. Since commodity chains were configured mainly inside the national borders, a market expansion allowed for a larger division of labor and higher productivity (Kaldor 1970). The majority of industrial production processes were characterized by a proliferation of production techniques based on the constitution of an assembly line that allowed a technical division of labor within the firm or corporation (Scott 1988). In the context of wage negotiations tied to productivity growth, capitalist agencies had to exploit the maximum scale of operations in order to maintain the rate of profits. The basic form of industrial organization that capital adopted was vertical integration of the supply chain (Langlois 2003). The rigidity of this type of organization required an environment of stable demand, which was guaranteed by the implementation of the full employment policies mentioned above.

This type of productive organization conditioned the industrialization strategies of peripheral states. Since the main supply chains operated at the domestic level, the most relevant option for development was the creation of industrial supply chains and the proper articulation of its nodes. But for this strategy to be viable it was necessary that markets be large enough to benefit from scale economies and from vertical integration. As technology came mostly from the central states, it was also necessary to provide attractive conditions for transnational companies. Even if these two conditions were fulfilled, in order for the industrialization process to be eventually successful in international markets—that is, to alter the traditional export pattern—a source of external demand (mainly from the central states) was also necessary.

However, not all peripheral states were equally able to carry out this strategy, so they adapted in different ways and performed differently. It is beyond the scope of this chapter to offer a comprehensive analysis of the causes of this differential economic performance, specifically between East Asian (EA) and Latin American (LA) regions. Instead, by highlighting the different elements that intervened in this outcome, we aim to show, first, that the periphery is never constituted by a homogeneous group of states, and second, how inter-state and inter-capitalist competition has affected the periphery in different ways, and hence influenced the organization of global production and the international division of labor.

Economic performance was affected by three main aspects: (i) the geopolitical strategy of the central states—the US, in particular; (ii) the capacity of the state to steer industrialization; and (iii) the nature and extent of land reform.

In the LA region, development projects were mostly geopolitically conditioned. Industrialization was permitted, as long as it was not a threat to the political leadership and economic interests of the US. Also, the region was discouraged from engaging in integration processes that could form a potential regional bloc which limited the power of both hegemons. At the same time, there were internal restrictions due fundamentally to the state's ineffectiveness in solving the distributive struggle and to command the accumulation process (Fiori 1992). The state's role was confined to that of an authoritative intervention related to the cyclical deactivation of popular sectors (O'Donnell 1973).

These conditions had a clear impact on the configuration of the productive structure of most LA states, which were markedly heterogeneous (Pinto 1970). The nodes of production of higher productivity were dominated by the presence of large foreign corporations. These nodes were poorly articulated with the nodes of lower productivity, which absorbed the surplus labor. As a result, the labor force was segmented into two broad sectors, formal and informal (Chena 2010). This had a clear impact on the capacity of the working class to organize, which was less than that of the central states. Nevertheless, when social conflict began to arise, the final way out of the conflict was 'truncating' the industrialization process through authoritative governments (Fajnzylber 1985).

In contrast, industrialization projects in the EA region were authorized and even encouraged by the hegemonic state (Glassman 2011). Within this geopolitical context, the process was directed through nation states of strong authoritative nature, high technical quality, and with a very coherent and centralized strategy (Evans 1995; Woo-Cumings 1999). These elements permitted, on the one hand, both domestic and foreign big capital to be disciplined (Amsden 1992); on the other hand, they allowed for the unionization of the working class to be hindered. Finally, in contrast to the LA region, agrarian reforms in the EA region fragmented the capitalist class and limited its conditioning capacity (Kay 2002).

The process of industrialization under economies of scale with vertical integration managed to advance in the sensitive nodes and, at the same time, to be extended spatially in the EA area through a process of regional integration known as *flying geese* (Akamatsu 1962).

It is in this stage—and considering these specificities—that attention should be given in order to analyze the subsequent differential in economic development between both regions. During this period, international trade between peripheral and central countries maintained a structure similar to that in force during the period of British hegemony. In general, trade at that time consisted of final goods; central countries exchanged industrial goods, while peripheral countries participated in international trade by exporting primary goods. The possibility of developing integrated industries allowed EA states to join trade networks exporting manufactures of increasing complexity. This differential led to a different integration in global commodity chains.

Crisis and restructuring

By the late 1960s and early 1970s, the first signals of exhaustion of the post-Second World War expansion cycle become visible. The reconstruction of Western European states in general, and the German economy in particular (together with Japan), increased both inter-state and inter-capitalist competitive pressures. The emergence of China in global politics and the global economy also contributed to the questioning of American hegemony.[3]

Distributive tensions in central countries reached critical levels. By the end of the 1960s, demands for higher wages increased rapidly (Cavalieri *et al.* 2004). This, together with the abrupt increment in the international oil price, increased inflationary pressures. In such a context, during the 1980s, the majority of central states applied disinflationary policies based on higher interest rates combined with demand adjustment policies (Serrano 2003). The resulting rise in unemployment was a key element to discipline the working class and to contain wage demands.

In this scenario, a fraction of the capitalist class sought to relocate part of the nodes of production outside national spaces (Ross & Trachte 1990), and through changes in the capitalist strategy, a new spatial-temporal fix began to emerge. One of the most visible aspects of this new 'fix' was the restructuring of global commodity chains. This restructuring was made possible by technological advances that occurred in the transportation and communication systems, and in the sphere of production, on the one hand, and the process of financialization, on the other hand.

The development and refinement of tools and machines governed by electronic control mechanisms allowed greater flexibility in production processes (Alcorta 1994). This flexibility created the possibility to break down the production process into elementary units that unskilled labor could easily perform. This allowed the replacement of skilled high-wage labor of the center with low-wage labor of peripheral regions (Fröbel *et al.* 1977). As for connective technology, the development of jet aircraft and the introduction of containerization reduced substantially the costs for transporting heavy and bulky freight. In communication systems, technological developments in satellites and optical fibers vastly increased the speed and capacity of communications networks (Dicken 2011: 81–97).

Finally, the production restructuring should not be considered as detached from the growing process of financialization, meaning the "increasing role of financial motives, financial markets, financial actors and financial institutions in the operation of the domestic and international economies" (Epstein 2005: 3). In this framework, profit making in the pattern of accumulation "occurs increasingly through financial channels rather than through trade and commodity production" (Krippner 2005: 181).

Financialization played a vital role in relocating investments through space and time as well as in developing new forms of organization of capital and its production system. The deregulation wave of capital markets across the world gave greater flexibility of movement to those fractions of capital that became globalized. But as it facilitated the transfer of capital from one location to other, finance capital also began to take a stake in the organization of global commodity chains (Milberg 2009). Moreover, the industrial and financial forms of capital has reached such a level of development that transnational companies can be considered to be the "organizational modality of finance capital" (Serfati 2008: 35).

With these techniques and in the context of high capital mobility, a new form of economies of scale became relevant, and so the industrial organization of most productive sectors began to change. Business enterprises began to externalize a great part of the activities that constituted their supply chain, and most of these activities began to take place in new geographical territories. In this new setting, production is organized through numerous firms dispersedly located, but operating simultaneously in real time. In each node of production, specialization also means generalization. For example, a firm that participates in the stage of assembling products does not assemble for one particular firm, but assembles a variety of products for different firms (Langlois 2003). Hence, supply chains are now disintegrated on a multi-firm, multi-location basis, where in each location there exists a clustering of firms that specialize in a given set of activities.

By connecting the literature on international business and economic geography, it is possible to observe how an increasing process of outsourcing led by transnational corporations co-exists with a multiplicity of heterogeneous and unequal local clusters (Mudambi 2008). In other words, spatial dispersion and agglomerative logics are part of the new economic geography of capitalism. Overall, mediated by the financialization process, technological transformations provided the foundation for the spatial reorganization of production in order to temporarily fix the distributive crisis of the central states. Within this spatial-temporal fix, space is at the same time shrinking and expanding. That is, while more spaces are being incorporated into global production, within this larger space, firms cluster according to the type of activity they perform (Harvey 2003).

These transformations also have had repercussion in the activities of national states and the manner in which they regulate the constitution of these networks. Under the new spatial-temporal arrangement, states no longer seek to insulate local actors from international market pressures, but are compelled to provide competitive support so its 'national' capital can develop global competence (*Competition state*) (Cerny 1997). Far from representing an absent state, it represents one immersed in 'strategic activism,' related to the strengthening of its capitalist economic agents in the global competitive process through the securing of commercial, technological, and financial support (Weiss 2005) and subordination of social policies to the structural demands of competitiveness (Jessop 1993). The changes in national strategies and the process of restructuration of global capital affected the peripheral states and, due to the geopolitical articulation configured during the Golden Age, the manner in which they became involved in the new global economy was different.

Traditional commercial articulation between the center and the periphery lost relevance in the total trade flow, in terms of final goods exchange. At the same time, productive disarticulation within national spaces and the novel forms of operation of capitalist agencies altered the role of foreign direct investment. Under current circumstances, even if the market is large enough to allow for production to take place in the periphery, transnational companies do not replicate the same production processes used in the center, but participate in the nodes that are functional to their global strategy of maximizing profits.

Considering the cases of the EA and LA regions, the different forms of involvement meant a subsequent difference in performance between the two regions. Due to its successful industrialization process in previous years, the EA region became involved in the most dynamic nodes (industries with high technological complexity) of supply chains. The LA region, on the other hand, dismantled a great portion of its industrial structure and specialized in some productive nodes using advanced technological capabilities mostly oriented towards the exploitation of natural resources.

The argument developed so far reveals the inextricable connection between changes in the global organization of production and inter-state and inter-capitalist competition that have converged historically in different spatial-temporal fixes, and configured center-periphery relations. As we stated in the introduction, conventional explanations of the organization of global production does not incorporate these elements and how they figure in the analysis. We will critically discuss the Global Value Chain (GVC) approach given that it is the one that gained most popularity among academic scholars and has become relevant for the formulation and assessment of public policies.

Recent changes in global production in light of the contributions of the Global Value Chain approach

Fundamentals of the GVC approach

The origin of the GVC approach traces back to the term Commodity Chain (CC) discussed earlier, which was coined by Hopkins and Wallerstein (1977). Gary Gereffi first introduced the concept of Global Commodity Chain but later changed it to Global Value Chain to avoid the disproportionate attention given to the notion of commodities in relation to primary products (Bair 2005). While the notion of CC was advanced in a broader theoretical framework aimed at explaining the macro-historical dynamics of capitalism, GVC was introduced as an attempt to construct a novel tool for understanding the current specificities of the globalization process. Notwithstanding their heterodox roots, the transition to GVC had several mutations of important interpretative implications.

The GVC approach aims at analyzing the networks of enterprises that do business at a global level in activities that transcend national and regional boundaries. The focus is on the organizational logic of different global industries and the role of firms that comprise those industries. In order to analyze such networks, the concepts of governance and upgrading have been developed for understanding the top-down and bottom-up dynamics that constitute the global chain, and which organize its functioning.

The top-down approach is developed through the concept of *governance*, which is used to unravel the way in which large firms obtain governance over the GVC and additionally fix its dynamics based on the control over certain strategic functions (Gereffi *et al.* 2005). The GVC literature broadly distinguishes between 'producer-driven' and 'buyer-driven' value chain governance.[4] 'Producer-driven' chains are usually found in sectors with high technological and capital requirements, where capital and proprietary know-how constitute the main entry barriers (for example, automobiles, aircrafts, and computers). In these chains, producers tend to keep control of capital-intensive operations and sub-contract more labor-intensive functions, often in the form of vertically integrated networks. 'Buyer-driven' chains are found generally in more labor-intensive sectors, where the cost of information, product design, advertising, and advanced supply management systems set entry barriers (for example, clothing, footwear, and many agro-food commodities). In these chains, production functions are usually outsourced and key actors concentrate on branding, design and marketing functions.

The bottom-up approach is developed through the concept of *upgrading*, the purpose of which is to examine the processes and ways in which firms that do not govern the chain (and are therefore subordinated) climb steps in the international ladder of value-added activities, moving from low-value to high-value activities to increase the benefits of participating in GVCs (Bair & Gereffi 2003). To this end, three essential forms of upgrading are distinguished: (i) the upgrading of a product (improving its quality or design); (ii) the upgrading of a process (in scale and speed, and efficiency and productivity); and, (iii) functional upgrading (acquisition of new functions to increase the added value of activities in the chain) (Gereffi 1999).

Based upon these concepts, the main contribution of GVC to the study of the current globalization process has been to understand the way in which space and economic activities interact and evolve along different stages of production of each global economic network, and the way in which value is produced and distributed among those networks, not only focused on manufacturing nodes, but also including marketing and distribution (Giuliani *et al.* 2005).

The receptiveness of mainstream economics to this approach was slow. In recent years, the use of the GVC approach has spread among economists studying trade and development; mainly among those working in multilateral economic institutions (Ravenhill 2014). This can be seen through the overwhelming presence of its conceptual apparatus in the policy recommendations of international institutions, as well as in the development proposals of national and regional governments.[5]

Critical discussion

Despite its contributions, there are several omissions and critical simplifications in the GVC approach that have significant implications. Many of these omitted issues are related to the elements we have considered in our analysis.

First, by proposing an analysis of the changes in the process of production restricted to a limited period—specifically, that of globalization—in which all that is considered are the novel ways of production organization and coordination of distribution, the forms of governance, and the types of upgrade, the approach loses the historical perspective of capitalism highlighted in the second section of this chapter. The GVC approach is also focused on sectors and specific activities. This method of *slicing* the chain (Bernstein & Campling 2006) has the corresponding disadvantage of losing sight of the analysis of capitalism as a whole, and of the interaction of the commodity chain with other entities and agencies.

Second, the lack of a holistic and historical perspective of capitalism is accompanied by disregard for the contradictory, hierarchical, and unstable logic of capitalist development. This neglects the cyclical form and recurrent crisis under which global production processes are developed and their relation to the spatial fixes (as discussed in the second section of this chapter). Disregard for these logics is rooted in the conception (more or less explicit) of power underlying this approach (Fernández 2014). The notion of power as domination, that is the capacity to impose one's will over others, is displaced and replaced by another—grounded in theories of network relationships—in which power is related to *co-production* and *collective endeavors* (Hess 2008).[6] This association, in the absence of a historical and holistic perspective, restricts the capacity to consider the way in which conflictive relations are reinstalled and reprocessed at the level of spaces and actors.

With respect to actors, the GVC approach focuses mainly on firms and the relationships between them (Bair 2008). This neglects not only the role of labor (Newsome *et al.* 2015), but also disregards the conflictual relationship between workers and capitalists, which is central to the analysis of crisis and emergent spatial fixes.

With respect to space, the sectoral perspective and the adopted method of slicing chains together with the poor treatment of power, has restricted the GVC approach's relevance and the way in which global commodity chains contribute to shape centers and peripheries. The approach has been in general reluctant to take into account the complex set of global geopolitical elements, as well as the specificities of national trajectories (Fernández 2014). In sum, in the GVC approach prevails a global–local conception (Werner *et al.* 2014) that is imposed without a clear recognition of national spaces and peripheral specificities. In this conception, the leading firms build forms of global governance while local instances appear as strategic spaces for developing clusters of Small and Medium Enterprises (SME) internally organized to enhance upgrading in the GVC (Humphrey & Schmitz 2000).

As we have seen, all these elements are important to understand how central states and their leading firms control the strategic functions of the commodity chain and establish a hierarchical link with peripheral states, where most activities of low complexity and remuneration are performed. However, within this approach, and as a part of the globalization process, the state has been diluted to be like any other public organization acting to complement firms (Sturgeon 2013), and whose performance should be evaluated in terms of the effectiveness of the reversion in the unequal position of local actors in the commodity chain.[7] This omission and reduction does not recognize the historically unique specific role of the state in particular and the inter-state system in general in the regulation of accumulation cycles, and, within these, in the development and transformation of global and national processes of production.

The 'invisibility' of the state also affects the linking of the role of geopolitics and national trajectories previously mentioned. Under the inter-state system constituted in the new scenario of globalization, it is essential to take into account the strategic role played by the US in the periphery, as we discussed earlier, since the post-Second World War years (Glassman 2011), together with the different historical national trajectories of peripheral states (Kohli 2012). It is from the confluence of both elements, and from the centering of the analysis on the state, that plausible explanations arise for the different developments of the EA and LA regions. The respective regional responses to the constitution of leading firms with governance capacity in global commodity chains (as in the case of Japan, South Korea, and Taiwan) leads to region-specific and upgrading strategies to reach the core nodes of the chains (as in the case of China).

To sum up, the GVC approach excludes the role central and peripheral states have played in the new spatial fix intervening in the constitution of governance and development of upgrading in the global supply chains. As we have seen, *competition states* act as supporters of leading firms located in the center in developing resources and infrastructure to enhance their international competitiveness (Block 2008). This amplifies the differences in the capacity of firms from central states for constituting and positioning in the global commodity chain.

Finally, there is a remarkable absence of finance and financialization issues in the GVC approach and its conceptual apparatus (Williams 2000). When finance and financialization are introduced, two additional aspects become critical for the analysis of the links between producers from peripheral states and transnational capital. First, relations between leading firms from the center and the peripheral regions are more shaped by speculative motives than by productive purposes (Newman 2009). Second, global firms of the chain have privileged access to financial instruments, in contrast to economic actors from the periphery. In order to improve their functions and positions in the commodity chains through new financial investments, these economic actors depend on the assistance offered by either leading firms or national and international coordinated programs from international institutions through development and financial assistance. In consequence, the financialization process (as well as the financial system) tends to increase asymmetric control of power within the chain, and establishes entry barriers mostly for small actors.

Concluding remarks

In this chapter, we have provided an analysis of the main aspects involved in the changes in the organization of global production in the context of the recent transformations of the capitalist economic system. We have highlighted the necessity to observe these transformations as a part of the cyclical process of crisis and the subsequent restructuring through new spatial fixes of the capitalist system that do not alter its fundamental contradictions and center-periphery configuration but rather reinforce them.

Based on this conceptual framework, we have presented a critical assessment of the GVC approach, the mainstream analysis of recent transformations in global production. We have examined their analytical tools and demonstrated how the omissions and simplifications of the approach limit its capacity to understand how these transformations condition the way in which different actors and spaces manage to face the process of global productive restructuring and position themselves in the commodity chain.

The most problematic arguments that stand out are related to the adoption of a perspective limited to the globalization period and centered on the analysis of sectors and interfirm relations in which power is associated with co-production and collective endeavors. In our view, such arguments omit the historical and holistic perspective under which the contradictory nature of capitalism can be fully grasped. Such omissions encourage disregard for the role of labor and its conflictual relation with capital, as well as denial of the center-periphery spatial configuration. These omissions are reinforced through a weak treatment of the state (both in its center and periphery characterizations), the nullification of geopolitics and national trajectories, and the exclusion of the process of financialization in the formation and functioning of global chains.

Considering the growing institutionalization of the GVC approach, the effects of the simplifying assumptions and omissions are not restricted to limited interpretations within the academic field. Quite the contrary. The institutional strategies derived from the framework tend to derail a dynamic global insertion of the periphery supported by integral accumulation strategies that overcome the heterogeneous and unequal socio-productive structures.

In this way, an articulation of the omitted elements in the dominant perspective is important: to attain a more adequate explanation of the context and factors that influence the process of global restructuring of production in capitalism and to account for the distinct way this process takes place within the periphery; and to also elaborate the multi-scalar strategies that allow peripheral spaces to participate in the process of global restructuring in a way that is capable of reversing—or at least reducing—its subordination and elevating the position of labor.

Notes

1 Peripheral states are not homogeneous. Recall that in the process of global configuration of commodity chains, geopolitical interests of the hegemon may benefit some regions and block initiative of others. The institutional trajectory of each peripheral state also plays an important role in this process.
2 Arrighi (1994: Ch. 1), for instance, identifies in the history of capitalism four partly overlapping 'systemic cycles of accumulation' of increasing scale and decreasing duration.
3 Whether the US has lost the inter-state leadership to China is still a matter of discussion among scholars (Fiori *et al.* 2008). The trouble arises from the fact that the Chinese economy is sometimes seen as complementary to the US hegemony and sometimes as an opponent and potential substitute for its leadership (Medeiros 2006).
4 A recent study suggests a broader classification of types of governance (Ponte & Sturgeon 2013).
5 See Fernández (2014) and Werner *et al.* (2014), and the official documents of World Bank, UNCTAD, OECD, ILO, and IDB cited there.
6 The poor treatment given to power in the GVC approach co-exists in similar perspectives like that of Global Production Networks (GPN) (Henderson *et al.* 2002, Coe *et al.* 2008). GPN presents itself as a complementary perspective to GVC but critical regarding some elements of the latter approach. However, the approach fails to offer a systematic and articulated problematization of these issues, so part of the critics advanced to GVC in this section also apply to GPN.
7 Recent warnings made about the absence of the state in GVC have been mainly concerned with highlighting its new adaptive role in the novel conditions of global production (Lee *et al.* 2014), disregarding—and even considering anachronistic—the strategic role played by the developmental state in moving up from a peripheral position in the world system. See the special issue on GVC and GNP of the *Review of International Political Economy* (volume 21, issue 1, 2014).

References

Akamatsu, K. 1962. 'A historical pattern of economic growth in developing countries.' *The Developing Economies*, 1 (Supplement s1): 3–25.
Alcorta, L. 1994. 'The impact of new technologies on scale in manufacturing industries: issues and evidence.' *World Development*, 22 (5): 755–769.
Amsden, A. 1992. *Asia's Next Giant: South Korea and Late Industrialization*. New York & Oxford: Oxford University Press.
Arrighi, G. 1994. *The Long Twentieth Century: Money, Power, and the Origins of Our Times*. London: Verso.
Arrighi, G. 2004. 'Spatial and other 'fixes' of historical capitalism.' *Journal of World-Systems Research*, 10 (2): 527–539.
Arrighi, G. & Drangel, J. 1986. 'The stratification of the world-economy: an exploration of the semiperipheral zone.' *Review (Fernand Braudel Center)*, 10 (1): 9–74.
Babones, S. 2005. 'The country-level income structure of the world-economy.' *Journal of World-Systems Research*, 11 (1): 29–55.
Bair, J. 2005. 'Global capitalism and commodity chains: looking back, going forward.' *Competition & Change*, 9 (2): 153–180.
Bair, J. 2008. 'Analysing global economic organization: embedded networks and global chains compared.' *Economy and Society*, 37 (3): 339–364.
Bair, J. & Gereffi, G. 2003. 'Upgrading, uneven development, and jobs in the North American apparel industry.' *Global Networks*, 3 (2): 143–169.
Bernstein, H. & Campling, L. 2006. 'Commodity studies and commodity fetishism I: trading down.' *Journal of Agrarian Change*, 6 (2): 239–264.
Block, F. 2008. 'Swimming against the current: the rise of a hidden developmental state in the United States.' *Politics & Society*, 36 (2): 169–206.
Bluestone, B. & Harrison, B. 1982. *The Deindustrialization of America: Plant Closings, Community Abandonment, and the Dismantling of Basic Industry*. New York: Basic Books.
Brenner, N. 2004. *New State Spaces: Urban Governance and the Rescaling of Statehood*. Oxford & New York: Oxford University Press.
Cavalieri, T., Garegnani, P., & Lucii, M. 2004. 'Anatomia di una sconfitta.' *La rivista del manifesto*, 48: 44–50.
Cerny, P.G. 1997. 'Paradoxes of the competition state: the dynamics of political globalization.' *Government and Opposition*, 32 (2): 251–274.

Chena, P.I. 2010. 'La heterogeneidad estructural vista desde tres teorías alternativas: el caso de Argentina.' *Comercio Exterior*, 60 (2): 99–115.

Coe, N.M., Dicken, P., & Hess, M. 2008. 'Global production networks: realizing the potential.' *Journal of Economic Geography*, 8 (3): 271–295.

Dicken, P. 2011. *Global Shift: Mapping the Changing Contours of the World Economy*, 6th edn. New York: The Guildford Press.

Epstein, G. 2005. 'Introduction,' in: *Financialization and the World Economy*. Cheltenham, UK: Edward Elgar Publishing, 3–17.

Esping-Andersen, G. 1990. *The Three Worlds of Welfare Capitalism*. Princeton, NJ: Princeton University Press.

Evans, P.B. 1995. *Embedded Autonomy: States and Industrial Transformation*. Princeton, NJ: Princeton University Press.

Fajnzylber, F. 1985. *La industrialización trunca de América Latina*. Buenos Aires: Grupo Editor Latinoamericano.

Fernández, V.R. 2014. 'Global value chains in global political networks: tool for development or neoliberal device?' *Review of Radical Political Economics*, 47 (2): 209–230.

Fiori, J., Medeiros, C., & Serrano, F. 2008. *O mito do colapso do poder americano*. Rio de Janeiro: Editora Record.

Fiori, J.L. 1992. 'Economía política del Estado desarrollista en Brasil.' *Revista de la CEPAL*, 47: 187–201.

Fiori, J.L. 2009. 'O poder global e a nova geopolítica das nações.' *Crítica y Emancipación*, 1 (2): 157–183.

Fröbel, F., Heinrichs, J., & Kreye, O. 1977. 'The tendency towards a new international division of labor: the utilization of a world-wide labor force for manufacturing oriented to the world market.' *Review (Fernand Braudel Center)*, 1 (1): 73–88.

Garegnani, P. 1984. 'Value and distribution in the classical economists and Marx.' *Oxford Economic Papers*, 36 (2): 291–325.

Gereffi, G. 1999. 'International trade and industrial upgrading in the apparel commodity chain.' *Journal of International Economics*, 48 (1): 37–70.

Gereffi, G., Humphrey, J., & Sturgeon, T. 2005. 'The governance of global value chains.' *Review of International Political Economy*, 12 (1): 78–104.

Giuliani, E., Pietrobelli, C., & Rabellotti, R. 2005. 'Upgrading in global value chains: lessons from Latin American clusters.' *World Development*, 33 (4): 549–573.

Glassman, J. 2011. 'The geo-political economy of global production networks.' *Geography Compass*, 5 (4): 154–164.

Harvey, D. 1981. 'The spatial fix – Hegel, Von Thünen, and Marx.' *Antipode*, 13 (3): 1–12.

Harvey, D. 2001. 'Globalization and the spatial fix.' *Geographische revue*, 3 (2): 23–30.

Harvey, D. 2003. *The New Imperialism*. Oxford & New York: Oxford University Press.

Henderson, J., Dicken, P., Hess, M., Coe, N., & Yeung, H.W.C. 2002. 'Global production networks and the analysis of economic development.' *Review of International Political Economy*, 9 (3): 436–464.

Hess, M. 2008. 'Governance, value chains and networks: an afterword.' *Economy and Society*, 37 (3): 452–459.

Hopkins, T.K. & Wallerstein, I. 1977. 'Patterns of development of the modern world-system.' *Review (Fernand Braudel Center)*, 1 (2): 111–145.

Humphrey, J. & Schmitz, H. 2000. Governance and upgrading linking industrial cluster and global value chain research. IDS Working Paper 120. Brighton, UK: Institute of Development Studies.

Jessop, B. 1993. 'Towards a Schumpeterian workfare state? Preliminary remarks on post-Fordist political economy.' *Studies in Political Economy*, 40: 7–39.

Kaldor, N. 1970. 'The case for regional policies.' *Scottish Journal of Political Economy*, 17 (3): 337–348.

Kay, C. 2002. 'Why East Asia overtook Latin America: Agrarian reform, industrialisation and development.' *Third World Quarterly*, 23 (6): 1073–1102.

Kohli, A. 2012. 'Coping with globalization: Asian versus Latin American strategies of development, 1980–2010.' *Revista de Economia Política*, 32 (4): 531–556.

Krippner, G.R. 2005. 'The financialization of the American economy.' *Socio-Economic Review*, 3 (2): 173–208.

Langlois, R.N. 2003. 'The vanishing hand: the changing dynamics of industrial capitalism.' *Industrial and Corporate Change*, 12 (2): 351–385.

Lee, Y.-S., Heo, I., & Kim, H. 2014. 'The role of the state as an inter-scalar mediator in globalizing liquid crystal display industry development in South Korea.' *Review of International Political Economy*, 21 (1): 102–129.

Marglin, S. & Schor, J. (eds.) 1990. *The Golden Age of Capitalism: Reinterpreting the Postwar Experience*. Oxford: Clarendon Press.

Marx, K. 1963. *Theories of Surplus Value*. Part II. Moscow: Progress Publishers.

Medeiros, C. 2006. 'A China como um duplo pólo na economia mundial e a recentralização da economia asiática.' *Revista de Economia Política*, 26 (3): 381–400.

Milberg, W. 2009. 'Shifting sources and uses of profits: sustaining US financialization with global value chains.' *Economy and Society*, 37 (3): 420–4514.

Mudambi, R. 2008. 'Location, control and innovation in knowledge-intensive industries.' *Journal of Economic Geography*, 8 (5): 699–725.

Newman, S.A. 2009. 'Financialization and changes in the social relations along commodity chains: the case of coffee.' *Review of Radical Political Economics*, 41 (4): 539–559.

Newsome, K., Taylor, P., Bair, J., & Rainnie, A. 2015. *Putting Labour in Its Place: Labour Process Analysis and Global Value Chains.* New York: Palgrave Macmillan.

O'Donnell, G. 1973. *Modernization and Bureaucratic-Authoritarianism Studies in South American Politics.* Berkeley, CA: Institute of International Studies-University of California.

Perez, C. 1985. 'Microelectronics, long waves and world structural change: new perspectives for developing countries.' *World Development*, 13 (3): 441–463.

Pinto, A. 1970. 'Naturaleza e implicaciones de la 'heterogeneidad estructural' de la América Latina.' *El Trimestre Económico*, 37 (145(1)): 83–100.

Ponte, S. & Sturgeon, T. 2013. 'Explaining governance in global value chains: a modular theory-building effort.' *Review of International Political Economy*, 21 (1): 195–223.

Prebisch, R. 1962. 'The economic development of Latin America and its principal problems.' *Economic Bulletin for Latin America*, 7 (1): 1–22.

Ravenhill, J. 2014. 'Global value chains and development.' *Review of International Political Economy*, 21 (1): 264–274.

Ross, R. & Trachte, K. 1990. *Global Capitalism: The New Leviathan.* Albany, NY: State University of New York Press.

Scott, A.J. 1988. 'Flexible production systems and regional development: the rise of new industrial spaces in North America and western Europe.' *International Journal of Urban and Regional Research*, 12 (2): 171–186.

Serfati, C. 2008. 'Financial dimensions of transnational corporations, global value chain and technological innovation.' *Journal of Innovation Economics & Management*, 2 (2): 35–61.

Serrano, F. 2003. 'From 'static' gold to the floating dollar.' *Contributions to Political Economy*, 22 (1): 87–102.

Sturgeon, T.J. 2013. *Global Value Chains and Economic Globalization: Towards a New Measurement Framework.* Eurostat.

Weiss, L. 2005. 'Global governance, national strategies: how industrialized states make room to move under the WTO.' *Review of International Political Economy*, 12 (5): 723–749.

Werner, M., Bair, J., and Fernández, V.R. 2014. 'Linking up to development? Global value chains and the making of a post-Washington consensus.' *Development and Change*, 45 (6): 1219–1247.

Williams, K. 2000. 'From shareholder value to present-day capitalism.' *Economy and Society*, 29 (1): 1–12.

Woo-Cumings, M. 1999. *The Developmental State.* Ithaca, NY: Cornell University Press.

25

Labor processes and outcomes
An institutional-heterodox framework

Siobhan Austen

Introduction

The institutional-heterodox[1] tradition of analyzing labor market processes and outcomes is long and rich, pre-dating by a long margin current mainstream labor economics. A single chapter cannot attempt to do justice to the extensive contributions of heterodox economists over many centuries on core labor issues such as wage outcomes, bargaining and unions, and the reproduction of labor. Interested readers can access numerous volumes of work on institutional and other heterodox perspectives on labor processes and outcomes, including several that have been published in recent decades (see, for example, Kaufman 1993, 2004; Champlin & Knoedler 2004; Blyton *et al.* 2008). The ambitions of this chapter are, thus, relatively constrained; limited to providing a review of some relatively recent developments in institutional economics that are potentially relevant to the future direction of this important field of study.

A key focus of the chapter is on the Institutional Analysis and Design (IAD) framework, devised by Elinor Ostrom and her colleagues to assist in the development of theories of behavior in a diverse range of situations (Ostrom 2005: 6; May & Summerfield 2012: 29). While the majority of previous discussions of Ostrom's work have focused on her analysis of common pool environmental resources, this chapter examines the potential of the IAD framework for the development of institutional-heterodox theories and empirical analyses of labor situations.

Some readers of this chapter may have a negative view of Ostrom's institutional analysis. For example, Hayden (2011) asserts that Ostrom makes a number of critical mistakes in her use of deontic logic, in her definition of an individual, the way she distinguishes frameworks, theories, and models, her assumptions about the rationality of individuals, and her definitions of 'rules.' Other readers may share the perspective of Hyman (2004) that, contrary to Ostrom's position, it is neither possible nor desirable to attempt an integrative theory of labor processes and outcomes.

In response, however, it must be noted that Ostrom did not claim that the IAD framework was either complete or inviolable. In 2005 she introduced her book on the framework as "a progress report on a long-term project" and expressed her wish that this project "be continued . . . by many others into the future" (Ostrom 2005: 1). Thus, while Ostrom expressed a belief that it *was* possible to identify a framework to guide studies of individual and collective behavior in a diverse range of situations, and through the IAD framework she made suggestions on its possible form, she also emphasized that the component parts (or building blocks) of such a theoretical framework for the social sciences was open for discussion and debate. By critically exploring the IAD framework it is possible to enter this debate and, possibly, shape a theoretical framework to reflect the themes and concerns of institutional-heterodox economics.

The pursuit of institutional-heterodox theoretical frameworks for studies of labor issues is an important undertaking, despite the risks and challenges involved. Such frameworks can provide heterodox economists who want to investigate labor issues a clear alternative to mainstream economic concepts.[2] On the one hand, relying on mainstream concepts risks the production of analyses that buttress existing patterns of power and are detrimental to the well-being of, especially, vulnerable workers. On the other hand, proceeding without an explicit theory risks relying on ad hoc causal explanations and aimless or unstructured empiricism. Theoretical frameworks can help guide and contextualize the making of hypotheses and assumptions about phenomena of concern, such as the wage and other outcomes achieved by workers. They can also guide the specification of variables in empirical work on labor markets, help determine the appropriate level of precision for variables in statistical and other analyses, and assist with the interpretation of data. The IAD framework, while not perfect, does offer a well-developed meta-theoretical language that can translate key ideas in institutional economics. As such, it may add value to ongoing institutional-heterodox scholarship on labor processes and outcomes, and for these reasons it is an important resource for institutional-heterodox labor scholars to consider.

The chapter's discussion is organized into four sections. The first section summarizes the key features of the IAD framework, drawing heavily on the detailed description provided by Ostrom in her 2005 book *Understanding Institutional Diversity*. The second part of the chapter relates the meta-theoretical language of the IAD framework to key concepts in institutional analyses of labor processes and outcomes. The third part makes several observations about the possible ways in which the IAD framework could be used to guide institutional-heterodox economists in studies of labor processes and outcomes. The final section adds some comments on the challenges and risks involved in taking such an approach.

Background to the IAD framework

The IAD framework takes a very particular approach to the analysis of social phenomena. It is based on the premise that the component parts of social hierarchies can be 'unpacked' to discern the universal factors that influence both human behavior and the outcomes of social interaction. In the IAD framework the key components (or 'holons') of social hierarchies are 'action arenas,' 'action situations,' and 'actors.' The framework unpacks these holons into a number of constituent elements that are perceived to be consequential for all human behavior and outcomes.

Importantly, the IAD approach emphasizes that each component in the social hierarchy is at the same time both a whole (or holon) comprised of many parts, *and* a part of a whole. As such, it describes each holon as being shaped by the features of broader institutional, material, and biological environments. Thus emphasis is continually given to the institutional context of observed human action in particular, and to the influence of this context on the nature and distribution of economic and social outcomes.

The notion that social hierarchies are comprised of components that are, at the same time, both autonomous units (a whole composed of smaller parts) *and* dependent parts of a larger whole was adapted by Ostrom and her colleagues from the philosophical psychology of Arthur Koestler. In his 1967 treatise, *The Ghost in the Machine*, Koestler (1967) coined the term 'holon' to refer to the whole–part entities that comprise all hierarchical systems, and devised a 'holonic' approach to reflect those systems where each entity (holon) exists, or takes on significance, only in a context of relationships with both the elements (sub-holons) it is made up of and the structure it belongs to.

Koestler developed holon theory to address issues in psychology that were similar to problems that Ostrom and other institutionalists perceive in economics. Koestler aimed to provide a framework that could unify and integrate reductionist and mechanistic worldviews in psychology with alternative holistic and humanistic worldviews; that could reflect the importance and relevance of evolutionary processes; and that was suited to analyses at the micro level of individuality and the macro-level of collectivity (Edwards 2013). Ostrom was attempting to develop a framework that could address the crafting and sustenance of institutions, and take account of their influence on human behavior, without sacrificing useful insights provided by rational choice theory (see, for example, Ostrom 2005: 103). She was deeply concerned with the evolution of the institutional environment (see, for example, Ostrom 2005: 121; May & Summerfield 2012: 28). And she was motivated to develop a framework with the capacity to guide analysis at multiple levels (see, for example, Ostrom 2005: 6).

The key holons in the IAD framework are summarized in Figure 25.1. Of particular importance is the *action situation*. This is a 'social space' within which sets of actors interact, for example, over the production and/or exchange of a particular good or service. Each action situation can, in turn, be 'unpacked' into a number of lower-level holons that are consequential for the types of *interactions* (or processes) within, and the *outcomes* that flow from, different situations. For example, in workplace situations the interactions between workers and employers can be analyzed, in part, with reference to the participants' valuation of alternative actions and outcomes, the way they process information, and how they make decisions.

The IAD framework also identifies how action situations are themselves part of a larger whole—the *action arena*. Each action arena is made up of a number of related action situations. For example, we can think of an industry or occupation as comprising a large number of workplace and other action situations, within which workers, employers, managers, clients, regulators, and others interact over the production and exchange of particular goods or services. In turn, action arenas (and their constituent situations) exist within a broad contextual environment that comprises the *attributes of the biophysical world* (which, for market situations, encompasses the physical characteristics of the good or service being produced); the *attributes of the more general*

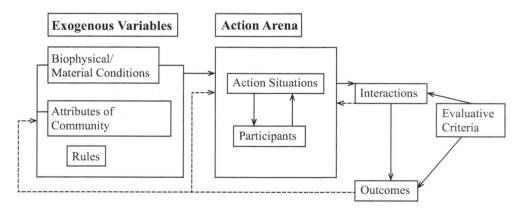

Figure 25.1   The IAD framework
Source: Ostrom (2005: 15).

community (including the values generally accepted, prevailing levels of trust, and social norms); and the current set of *rules in use*, that is "the shared understandings by participants about the enforced prescriptions concerning what actions (or outcomes) are required, prohibited, or permitted" (Ostrom 2005: 18).

As such, the IAD framework reflects the original institutionalist idea that human behavior is constituted by culture and it is context specific. According to its language, the way in which participants perceive their biophysical and social environment, and the set of their possible actions, will be shaped by the features of the 'attributes of community' holon. A shared culture will also increase the likelihood that participants in action situations will have shared (or at least similar) mental models, and this will promote the coordination of their actions. The transmission of cultural values across generations (through processes such as socialization) will be a potential source of stability in the processes and outcomes of given situations over extended periods of time.

The 'rules in use' holon is a further important 'institutional' aspect of the IAD framework. Rules shape the interactions in and outcomes of situations in a variety of ways. For example, they determine: the eligibility of individuals to participate in different situations; the actions that may and may not be taken in particular situations; the processes that must be followed; the information that must or must not be provided; and the rewards for different actions. Reflecting the somewhat functional explanation of rules that Ostrom favored,[3] the IAD framework also incorporates feedback loops, to account for the way in which, for example, participants may respond to particular outcomes by engaging in efforts to either change or reinforce the structure of their action arenas, including the design of its rules (as indicated by the line at the bottom of Figure 25.1).

A further important aspect of the IAD framework that is not immediately apparent in the above diagram is its *hierarchical* design. The framework describes *operational* level situations, where an existing set of rules structures the interactions of the participants of action situations. For example, the interactions of workers and managers in workplace situations are regulated by a set of current rules on working times, qualifications, staffing ratios, etc. However, the IAD framework also identifies a number of higher-level situations, including *collective choice* situations where, for example, negotiations take place about the rules to be applied in operational level situations in a particular action arena. At a higher level still, the framework describes *constitutional* situations, where decisions are made about who can participate in the collective and operational-level situations, and how.

The IAD framework and current institutional analyses of labor situations

By the end of her life, Ostrom had specified major elements of the IAD framework. While it was not complete, it had already proved useful in guiding theoretical and empirical work on Common Pool Resource (CPR) situations. The awarding of the Nobel Memorial Prize in Economic Sciences[4] to Ostrom in 2009, "for her analysis of economic governance, especially the commons" (Nobelprize.org 2009), is a testament to the generally high regard for her work.

The relevance and usefulness of the IAD framework to institutional-heterodox studies of situations other than those involving CPRs is a less settled issue, as the comments of Hayden (2011) suggest. The question of whether the framework might be used, for example, to facilitate institutional-heterodox studies of labor processes and outcomes thus far has not been considered at all. To help redress this gap, the following paragraphs examine whether the language of the IAD framework can capture key features of recent institutional scholarship on labor economics, and contrast this to neoclassical labor economics (NLE). The focus of the discussion of institutional labor economics is on the work of Bruce Kaufman, a leading figure in the field with a keen interest in developing its theoretical foundations.[5] Kaufman's objectives and approach appear to be similar to Ostrom's. He generally emphasizes the importance of achieving a "realistic model of the human agent," echoing the focus on participants and their actions that features in the IAD framework (Kaufman 2010: 85). However, at the same time, Kaufman also stresses the relevance of "hierarchical firms" and the "institutional infrastructure of laws, cultures, social/ ethical norms, and historical traditions" in the determination of labor processes and their outcomes (Kaufman 2010: 85). His particular approach to institutional economics, which appears to contrast Hayden's, increases the potential for synergies with the IAD approach.

Kaufman builds explicitly on a long and complex history of institutional labor economics, including the systems theory approach of John Dunlop (1958). Systems theory has a number of similarities to the IAD approach. It focuses on understanding actors: workers and their organizations, managers and their organizations, and government agencies concerned with the workplace. It emphasizes the importance of institutions and context, describing interactions between actors as occurring within, and determined by, an 'environmental context' comprised of technology (the production process, the size of the plant, the required job skills, etc.), market or budgetary constraints (the degree of competition in the product and labor market, the amount of profit, etc.), and the power relations and status of the actors (including the laws affecting union organization and bargaining power, and the amount of rule-making authority vested in management).[6] Dunlop's detailed theoretical work focused on how labor outcomes varied with the level of product market competition and the 'web of rules' governing relations between unions, corporations, and the state (see, for example, Kerr et al. 1960).

Reflecting the fact that his work took place in the United States (US) in the 1950s, at a time characterized by the growth of large companies and relatively high levels of unionism, Dunlop focused on institutionalized procedures regulating the interests of trade unions, corporations, and the state. In contrast, the focus of Kaufman's theoretical work is more squarely centered on the interface between markets, on the one hand, and the interactions that take place between workers and employers (or managers) in workplace situations, on the other hand. His approach contrasts the sole focus of NLE on markets, but it also contrasts other institutional-heterodox labor scholarship that focuses on the underlying tensions and conflicts associated with capitalist relations of production and accumulation.

The set of *outcomes* from labor situations that Kaufman considers are broadly defined, ultimately comprising of efficiency as well as "social justice, democratic procedures, and individual self-development" (Kaufman 2012: 441). In line with institutional principles, Kaufman prioritizes the 'quality of work life,' or human rights and interests. This is an important contrast to NLE, which, as Joseph Stiglitz (2000: 31) observes, appears to have been designed "to undermine the rights and position of labor." Also in contrast with NLE, Kaufman identifies the economic surplus produced by most labor situations, which translates into a strong concern for the distribution of the outcomes of labor situations. However, Kaufman's work does not give the same priority to economic surplus as is provided in radical/Marxian analyses of labor outcomes or in the Fabian tradition of the Webbs (for an overview, see Kaufman & Gall 2015: 411).

As noted above, Kaufman's studies of labor processes focus on the *employment relationship*. This relationship encompasses the cooperative and conflicting interactions between employers and workers within a workplace situation and is typically both personal and ongoing, in contrast to the "one-time market-mediated anonymous exchange[s]" described in NLE (Kaufman 2010: 16). NLE assumes that interactions in labor situations take place among autonomous buyers and sellers of labor services. It describes the interactions as simply being concerned with the negotiation/re-negotiation of a complete contract that specifies all the terms for the exchange of a particular labor service. It assumes that perfect competition will deliver a price vector to coordinate the interactions of buyers and sellers of labor and will ultimately produce optimal outcomes.

In highlighting the importance of employment relationships, Kaufman emphasizes the boundaries between the coordination of labor in markets (through contracts, prices, and competition) and the coordination of labor services within workplace situations (through the employment relationship). He notes that—in most workplace situations—contracts, prices, and competition play a relatively minor role in the coordination of labor. Labor contracts are typically *incomplete*, in that they commonly only specify aspects such as the annual salary or hourly wage rate to be paid, and the broad set of tasks and responsibilities to be undertaken. Labor contracts typically leave out the details of all the tasks workers may be asked to perform and do not specify a range of important issues, such as whether wage premiums will be paid for the performance of additional roles. Reflecting themes in institutional economics more generally, Kaufman highlights that *administrative rules*, rather than market prices govern wage rates and procedures for the allocation of labor within most workplace situations. Wage rates "rather than being solely market-determined as assumed in the core version of NLE, are always and everywhere managed/administered prices, albeit shaped and constrained by market forces" (Kaufman 2010: 87).

The importance of employment relationships is given a particular theoretical explanation by Kaufman; one that highlights the role of significant transaction costs that limit the mobility of labor and other resources. This appears to reflect the influence on his thinking of concepts from new institutional economics. Kaufman (2010) uses insights provided by Coase (1937) in his theory of the firm to highlight how market-based exchange can involve substantial transactions costs, especially when specific and/or complex skills and other resources are required for the production of a good or service. Firms are treated as institutional arrangements that act to reduce these costs. Importantly, this logic also implies that within the boundaries of a firm, non-market mechanisms, such as an employment relationship, will be used to allocate labor. The boundaries between markets and firms imply that processes and outcomes within organizations are separated, at least to some degree, from the influences of labor market competition, and that administrative rules, rather than market prices will be most important in the determination of wage rates.

The importance attached to the employment relationship has broad implications for the form of labor economics favored by Kaufman. He shifts our attention towards achieving alternative types of *employment systems* that can govern interactions within workplace situations (and their consequences), and away from a sole focus on market factors. Studies of "the configuration of structures, policies, programs, and practices that firms adopt to obtain and dismiss, develop, motivate, coordinate, and govern the labor input" are suggested by Kaufman's approach (Kaufman 2010: 98). To coin a phrase used by Ostrom (2005: 8), he sets as an important challenge for labor scholars to "dig under the surface" of different labor situations to obtain a good understanding of what employment system is being used and why.

Kaufman (2012) also suggests a particular approach to the theoretical analysis of employment relationships and systems. He suggests a model where the authority to select an employment system in the workplace situation rests with the employer, and the selection of a particular system is assumed to be based on each system's relative payoff to the employer. Workers and their unions are ascribed a more reactionary/defensive set of actions in this model, related to their (limited) authority to reject and/or negotiate the features of the employment system.

Kaufman's model features *fundamental power asymmetries*. The ownership of the means of production, supported by the legal right given to owners of capital to manage their businesses, shifts the balance of power in workplace situations towards employers (Kaufman 2012: 443). "Mobility costs, a reserve of unemployed job seekers in most years, and in many cases quickly exhausted financial resources" are viewed as further constraints on the bargaining power of workers (Kaufman 2010: 92).

This perspective is shared, and indeed is given greater emphasis, in radical/Marxian analyses of labor processes and outcomes. Both approaches highlight the tendency for employment systems to promote employers' interests, with potentially deeply negative consequences for workers' outcomes. These are in stark contrast to the NLE assumption of competitive firms with no market power and its prediction of outcomes that are both efficient and fair.

Kaufman's model also assumes that while employers have the authority to select an employment system for their workplace situation, they cannot compel workers to supply their effort. As such, employers' payoffs from alternative employment systems depend in part on their ability to achieve the cooperation of workers. This reflects a further precept of institutional labor economics, and one shared by Marx ([1867] 1907), that the ability of firms to profit from the hiring of labor depends on their ability to convert labor-time into productive effort and work (see Kaufman & Gall 2015: 411). The lack of complete control by managers over labor can lead to efforts to influence work intensity or impose discipline. However, more positive approaches to the governance of employment relationships are also possible. For example, norms of reciprocity, fairness, and trust may be utilized in the design of employment systems. Kaufman (2010: 95) notes, for example, that an internal labor market system can help to engender the "distinctly human aspects of labor, such as commitment, morale, and trust," while a commodity/machine model of labor favors "the emergence of an adversarial low-trust 'prisoner's dilemma' form of employment relationship and consequent poor firm performance."

Underlying this type of theorizing are several additional, important assumptions. First, participants in workplace situations are assumed to value a range of outcomes for themselves and others and adopt contextually relevant norms of behavior.[7] Fairness is also assumed to be an important determinant of work effort, and workers have a (conditional) willingness to cooperate with their employer and co-workers (see Kaufman 2010: 96, 2012: 448–450). These are an important contrast to simplistic NLE models, which assume purely self-regarding preferences.

Due to the influence of employment systems, and the presence of economic surplus, the outcomes from labor situations are *indeterminate* in Kaufman's model, in contrast to the NLE prediction of a single wage/employment outcome from a given set of supply and demand factors. Kaufman (2012: 444) follows an approach favored by Ostrom by representing employment relationships as *games* "with numerous alternative outcomes."[8] His model of employment systems also predicts nominal wage rigidity and allows for the possibility of persistent unemployment (Kaufman 2012: 448–450), establishing a further crucial contrast with the NLE propositions of wage variability and full employment.

Other important features of Kaufman's institutional labor economics include a focus on the contextual environment of labor situations. In parallel to the 'biophysical/material conditions' holon in the IAD framework, Kaufman (2012) refers to the *market context*, which encompasses the level of product market and labor market competition. Reflecting a major theme in the original labor economics of John Commons (1934), unemployment is modeled as a powerful coercive influence on workers' levels of cooperation (effort). Thus, workers who have few options for obtaining work or income will be vulnerable to the monopsony power held by employers, and, thus, to poor wage and other outcomes (Kaufman 2012: 453). In contrast, imperfect competition in product markets and full employment will be more conducive to employment systems that deliver higher wages and better working conditions.

In parallel to the 'rules in use' holon in the IAD framework, Kaufman emphasizes the critical importance of the *web of rules* in the determination of labor processes and outcomes, especially through its influence on the distribution of bargaining power between the participants in labor situations (for an overview see Kaufman & Gall 2015: 413). Examples of important rules in labor arenas include: protective labor laws, such as those mandating minimum wage payments and working conditions; social insurance/safety net programs that influence workers' ability to leave their current labor situation; rules governing the ability of workers to form trade unions; and, rules affecting the ability of trade unions and their members to engage in industrial action. It can be noted that Kaufman, in tandem with other institutional-heterodox labor scholars, ascribes a positive role to trade unions in offsetting for example monopsony power and by helping to achieve the coordination and enforcement of workplace governance systems. In contrast, NLE treats unions as a market imperfection and inimical to economic efficiency.

In sum, the institutional labor economics promoted by Kaufman, following in the tradition established by Dunlop, has a range of features that are consistent with the theoretical approach that underlies the IAD framework. To illustrate these similarities, the following diagram relates the concepts used by Kaufman to the features of the IAD framework (as was summarized in Figure 25.1). The components on the left-hand side of Figure 25.2 show how Kaufman places each labor arena in the context of its 'material' conditions. Also shown is the emphasis that Kaufman gives to the reality and importance of institutions, including norms and conventions, as well as the 'web of rules.' Both components are viewed as playing a role in determining the distribution of bargaining power in labor arenas, in shaping and regulating the actions of individuals in labor situations, and, ultimately, in influencing the distribution of the economic surplus and the quality of working life. Figure 25.2 also highlights Kaufman's particular concern with workplace situations where an employment relationship structures the interactions between workers and managers, and an employment system, determined at a higher level of the organizational or industry hierarchy, governs these relationships.

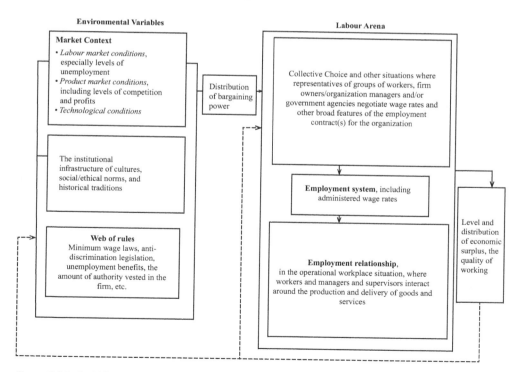

Figure 25.2 An IAD version of Kaufman's framework

The similarities between the IAD framework and Kaufman's theoretical work suggest that the framework may play a useful role in institutional-heterodox labor studies However, some may question whether the IAD framework *adds value* to institutional-heterodox scholarship in labor economics. For example, some might argue that there is no need to translate Kaufman's models into the IAD framework because there is already sufficient detail in his theoretical analysis to guide a rich program of institutional labor research on employment systems. Others might assert that the IAD framework has little relevance to types of institutional-heterodox scholarship other than Kaufman's. The following section discusses these issues.

The IAD framework and the future of institutional-heterodox analyses of labor processes and outcomes

While it is undoubtedly true that institutional-heterodox studies of labor processes and outcomes can and will proceed without the adoption of the IAD framework, there are various ways in which the framework can make an important contribution. First, the hierarchical design of the framework offers a useful way of identifying the range of different types of labor situations relevant to the determination of wages and other outcomes, and their interrelationships. This can add value to institutional-heterodox projects by assisting the task of identifying (and contextualizing) the broad range of issues that are relevant to labor processes and outcomes.

As noted above, a large part of Kaufman's work focuses on operational situations, where the relationship between workers and an employer is governed by the firm's employment system. His work provides important insights to the determination of wage rates and working conditions. However, the IAD framework helps to highlight the range of higher-level situations in occupational and industry labor arenas that are also critical to wage and other outcomes. These include, first, the 'collective choice' situations, where, for example, negotiations take place about the rules to be applied in the various operational level situations in a particular labor arena. The framework also highlights the importance of constitutional situations where, for example, industrial laws are formulated that determine who can participate in the negotiation of wage rates and conditions, and the range of allowable wages and conditions they can consider. These situations exist at the national and international level.

A further attribute of the IAD framework is the coherent approach it sets out for the investigation of a range of labor situations. The framework generally suggests an approach that focuses on 'unpacking' the characteristics of participants and other aspects of different labor situations that are relevant to the negotiation of wage rates and working conditions. However, it is supportive of various lines of inquiry including investigations of the market, institutional, and other determinants of the bargaining power of participants in labor situations, and the relationships and links between different situations, at various levels, in particular labor arenas.

Labor arenas are undoubtedly enormously complex, and the range of elements affecting outcomes such as wages and working conditions is very large. Effective institutional-heterodox studies of labor processes and outcomes will typically only be able to focus on one element or holon of a labor arena at a time. The IAD framework is useful, however, in identifying the context of particular studies and it can play a valuable role in facilitating interdisciplinary studies of labor processes and outcomes.

A range of factors will influence the focus of particular studies, including the scholar's discipline-specific knowledge and priorities. Many heterodox labor scholars will focus on the contextual environment holons that shape the processes and outcomes from labor situations. Those with an interest in behavioral economics are likely to focus on the characteristics of participants in workplace and other situations, especially the characteristics relating to information processing and decision-making. Those with an interest in economic sociology are likely to be more concerned with the features of the community attributes holon, and the consequences of particular norms and conventions for formal and informal labor processes and outcomes.

Illustrating the potential uses of the IAD framework

In a recent feminist economic study, we prioritized gendered social norms (in the community attributes holon) and rules, and analyze how these norms shaped the interactions in and outcomes from the Australian aged care work arena[9] (see Austen *et al.* 2016). The study was especially concerned with the role played by social norms in explaining the lower wages and poor working conditions of the predominantly female aged care workforce. It documented strong connections between normative attitudes about the (lack of) skills involved in work performed by women in the home and the patterns of interactions of workers and managers in aged care work situations. The study linked these patterns to the absence of a wage premium for adverse working conditions in aged care.

An IAD approach was not essential for this study of the impact of gendered social norms on wage outcomes. A number of other studies have explored the influence on market wage rates of commonly held perceptions of the skills and/or difficulty associated with work performed by women and men (see Fraser 2000; England *et al.* 2002; Palmer & Eveline 2012). However, the IAD framework added value to our study by highlighting the potential importance of feedback links from individual workplace situations to key collective choice situations. That is, the framework provided a way to express how negotiations at a higher level of the social hierarchy determine the 'rules' relating to the administered wages and conditions that must be adhered to in Australian workplace aged care situations (see Austen *et al.* 2016). The IAD framework also helped us to theorize about the relationship between the taboos surrounding the issue of dirty work,[10] which made aged care workers reluctant to talk about these aspects of their work, and the conduct of wage negotiations in the relevant collective choice situations. We found that the reluctance of parties to wage negotiations (in collective choice situations) to talk about the issue of dirty work was an important factor contributing to misrecognition of aged care workers' skills and a failure to adequately reflect the contributions of aged care workers in the setting of wage rates in the sector.

The study also used concepts relating to constitutional choice situations to emphasize the importance of labor laws and government funding for the wage outcomes and working conditions of aged care workers. The influence of collective choice situations was demonstrated when new legislation, which enabled trade unions to apply for equal remuneration orders, resulted in substantial increases in the wage rates paid to social and community sector workers (see Austen *et al.* 2013).

Nancy Folbre (2009) identified a further, novel application of IAD analysis in her discussion of the awarding of the Nobel Memorial Prize to Ostrom. Folbre observed that the IAD framework can be used to understand the importance of group dynamics in the economic profession. Academic disciplines, similar to local communities in CPR situations, develop boundary and other rules to protect the common property of a collective reputation—the disciplinary 'brand.' Some of these initiatives play a positive role. However, institutional failure also results because the participants in the relevant collective action situations develop rules and other institutions aimed at protecting themselves from competition and to reinforce their own priorities. In economics, for example, particular definitions of quality and, indeed, of economics have been imposed. Folbre argues that successful governance of the 'economics commons' requires openness, flexibility, and democracy, and for this reason she was strongly supportive of the awarding of the 2009 Nobel Memorial Prize to Elinor Ostrom.

Discussion and conclusion

This chapter has presented a positive assessment of the potential usefulness of the IAD framework for institutional-heterodox studies of labor processes and outcomes. The chapter has emphasized the ability to 'translate' some recent scholarship in institutional labor economics into the language of the IAD framework, and the potential for the framework to highlight the features that distinguish institutional from neoclassical labor economics. The chapter has also identified the potential to use the IAD framework as a 'road map' for ongoing institutional-heterodox investigations of labor processes and outcomes. Because the IAD framework comprises a well-developed, structured taxonomy of concepts, it provides a 'map' that conforms to current notions of a 'scientific' approach. Because the framework is meta-theoretical it can help identify opportunities for integrating knowledge and techniques from other disciplines into institutional-heterodox analyses of labor processes and outcomes.

Beyond the IAD framework, Ostrom's work on CPR situations also has the potential to inform the methodology of institutional-heterodox labor scholarship. In her work, Ostrom used a variety of methods to integrate detailed descriptive data on the rules and other institutions affecting particular CPR situations with theoretical models that sought to identify the determinants of interactions and outcomes in a range of situations. As Boettke *et al.* (2013: 414) explain, Ostrom combined "thin descriptions" of interactions between boundedly rational individuals with the "dirty" empirical methods of anthropologists and historians, including comparative case studies and fieldwork.

Ostrom seemed particularly concerned to make economics useful at the local level. She was critical of any tendency to apply a single idealized 'plan' to all situations ("the particular niches in that terrain"):

> If the social sciences are to be relevant for analyses of policy problems, the challenge will be to integrate efforts to map the broad terrain and efforts to develop tractable models for particular niches in that terrain.
>
> *Ostrom 1990: 214–215*

Ostrom argued that this 'localized' approach would also make economics more, rather than less 'scientific,' as it would more closely match the approach taken in the physical sciences. She noted how in engineering, for example, the approach taken to designing motors reflects an appreciation that the function of motors depends both on particular settings that the motor will need to operate in, as well as the underlying laws relating to the operation of all motors. Similarly, in meteorology, weather patterns are understood to reflect both general patterns of air movement and temperatures, as well as particular locational factors, such as topography. 'Good science,' according to Ostrom, involves taking account of, and tailoring analysis to, particular characteristics of situations, which vary over both time and space.

This type of methodological approach is an important advance on current practice in much of labor economics. NLE is currently dominated by attempts to apply 'thin' models, including simplistic supply and demand representations of a labor 'market,' to the analyses of all labor processes and outcomes. The lack of realism of these descriptions makes them largely irrelevant to the design of most labor policy and practice.

Kaufman and other institutional labor economists have responded to the failure of NLE by devising more realistic models of labor processes, informed by the detailed descriptions of labor market institutions provided by early institutional economists. Some of the important features of Kaufman's models have been described in this chapter. However, going forward, 'thin' modeling needs to be complemented with empirical research using methods that are capable of delivering detailed descriptions of local labor situations and the institutions that govern them. Without these details, it is unlikely that research will support the design of positive policy interventions relevant to the circumstances and experiences of specific groups of workers.

The IAD framework can help to identify the types of situations, arenas, rules, and other contextual factors that are relevant to particular, local labor processes and outcomes. In doing so, it can help guide the identification of appropriate methodologies for particular studies. However, of course, scholars are always left with the key decisions and challenges. One of these is to decide the weight to place on the individual versus the social determinants of labor processes and outcomes. In Ostrom's work, the tendency was to shift the focus of analysis towards the interactions between individuals, based on her presumption that purposeful individuals can and do shape their environments, including surrounding institutions (see Muller-Jentsch 2004, for an overview of this approach in industrial relations). While this produces some useful insights on, for example, the importance of individual's other-regarding preferences, it diminishes the importance placed on the inherent power relationships that underpin institutions and situations. Institutional-heterodox studies of labor processes and outcomes must ensure that any tendency to focus on 'micro' considerations, or the constituent part-wholes of labor situations, is balanced with detailed and full analyses of the way employment relationships and industrial relations systems are embedded in capitalist relations of production and accumulation (for a broader perspective, see Hyman 1975: 11; Heilbroner & Milberg 1995: 68–96).

It is important to stress, in closing, that the IAD, as a meta-theoretical framework, does not dictate an emphasis on individuals, their agency and their interactions. The framework is capable of expressing the theories and models of labor processes and outcomes from each of the institutional-heterodox (and other) traditions and, thus, reflect different perspectives on the nature, origins, and impacts of the institutions affecting labor situations. To the extent that the framework can facilitate an exchange of ideas between the different institutional-heterodox traditions in labor economics and assist with the identification of programs of research, it will make an important and valuable difference to studies of labor processes and outcomes.

Acknowledgments

This manuscript has benefited from the thoughtful attention and useful comments and suggestions of Bruce Kaufman, the editors of the *Handbook*, and my colleagues at Curtin University. Any errors are mine.

Notes

1 This chapter adopts a broad definition of heterodox labor economics as approaches that reject the fundamentalist ideas of mainstream economics, such as of automatic equilibrating processes and asocial optimizing individuals.
2 Steve Keen made a similar observation in his discussion of microeconomics teaching, when he noted that: "A great strength of traditional economics is the absence of a well-developed alternative. The pressure to teach *something* often results in orthodox economics ruling the roost" (2009: 120, italics in original).
3 Ostrom (2005: 18) asserted that rules are "often self-consciously crafted by individuals to change the structure of repetitive situations that they themselves face in an attempt to improve the outcomes that they achieve."
4 Formally known as the Sveriges Riksbank Prize in Economic Sciences in Memory of Alfred Nobel.
5 Kaufman (2010: 82) describes his project in general terms as "an effort to construct a multidisciplinary and quasi-heterodox type of social labor economics."

6 Muller-Jentsch (2004) describes a range of alternative theories of industrial relations, including various Marxian standpoints that are critical of Dunlop, such as the political economy of Hyman (1975) and Kelly (1998).

7 Kaufman also assumes that participants in labor situations are boundedly rational. However, in contrast to Ostrom, the implications of this characteristic of the participant holon are not the focus of Kaufman's detailed theoretical work.

8 A related concept is *areas of indeterminancy*, which refers to the variety of wage and other outcomes that can emerge from the interactions between different groups of employers and workers in labor situations.

9 This study focused on paid care work, in contrast to feminist economic studies of unpaid work.

10 Age care work includes aspects, such as toileting care recipients, that are commonly seen as dirty work. The work can involve dangerous direct contact with bodily products and with the products of infection, and aged care workers also commonly encounter aggressive patients.

References

Austen, S., Jefferson, T., & Preston, A. 2013. 'Contrasting economic analyses of gender, work and pay: Lessons from an equal remuneration case.' *Journal of Industrial Relations*, 55 (1): 60–79.

Austen, S., Jefferson, T., Lewin, G., Ong, R., & Sharp, R. 2016 'Recognition: Applications in care work.' *Cambridge Journal of Economics*, 40 (4): 1037–1054.

Blyton, P., Bacon, N., Fiorito, J., & Heery, E. (eds.) 2008. *The Sage Handbook of Industrial Relations*. London: Sage.

Boettke, P., Lemke, J., & Palagashvili, L. 2013. 'Riding in cars with boys: Elinor Ostrom's adventures with the police.' *Journal of Institutional Economics*, 9 (4): 407–425.

Champlin, D. & Knoedler, J. (eds.) 2004. *The Institutionalist Tradition in Labor Economics*. Armonk, NY: M.E. Sharpe.

Coase, R. 1937. 'The nature of the firm.' *Economica*, 4 (16): 386–405.

Commons, J.R. 1934. *Institutional Economics: Its Place in Political Economy*. New York: Macmillan.

Dunlop, J. 1958. *Industrial Relations Systems*. New York: Holt.

Edwards, M. 2013. A brief history of holons. *Integral Worlds*. Available from http://www.integralworld.net/edwards13.html [Accessed February 10, 2015]

England, P., Budig, M., & Folbre, N. 2002. 'Wages of virtue: The relative pay of care work.' *Social Problems*, 49 (4): 455–473.

Folbre, N. 2009. 'The economics club.' *The New York Times*, October 19. Available from http://economix.blogs.nytimes.com/2009/10/19/the-economics-club/ [Accessed March 13, 2015]

Fraser, N. 2000. 'Rethinking recognition.' *New Left Review*, 3 (May/June): 107–120.

Hayden, F.G. 2011. 'Usefulness to Original Institutional Economics (OIE) of normative criteria theory in the frameworks of Elinor Ostrom's Institutional Analysis and Development (IAD) and Paul A. Sabatier's Advocacy Coalition Framework (ACF).' *Journal of Economic Issues*, 45 (2): 465–474.

Heilbroner, R. & Milberg, W. 1995. *The Crisis of Vision in Modern Economic Thought*. Cambridge: Cambridge University Press.

Hyman, R. 1975. *Industrial Relations: A Marxist Introduction*. London: Macmillan.

Hyman, R. 2004. 'Is industrial relations theory always ethnocentric?' *in:* B. Kaufman (ed.), *Theoretical Perspective on Work and the Employment Relationship*. Madison, WI: IRRA, 265–292.

Kaufman, B. 1993. *The Origins and Evolution of the Field of Industrial Relations in the United States*. Ithaca, NY: ILR Press.

Kaufman, B. (ed.) 2004. *Theoretical Perspectives on Work and the Employment Relationship*. Madison, WI: IRRA.

Kaufman, B. 2010. 'The theoretical foundation of industrial relations and its implications.' *Industrial and Labor Relations Review*, 64 (1): 74–108.

Kaufman, B. 2012. 'An institutional economic analysis of labor unions.' *Industrial Relations*, 51 (S1): 438–471.

Kaufman, B. & Gall, G. 2015. 'Advancing industrial relations theory: an analytical synthesis of British-American and pluralist-radical ideas.' *Industrial Relations Quarterly Review*, 70 (3): 407–431.

Keen, S. 2009. 'A pluralist approach to microeconomics,' *in:* J. Reardon (ed.), *The Handbook of Pluralist Economics Education*. Abingdon: Routledge, 120–149.

Kelly, J. 1998. *Rethinking Industrial Relations: Mobilization, Collectivism, and Long Waves*. London: Routledge.

Kerr, C., Dunlop, J., Harbison, F., & Myers, C. 1960. *Industrialism and Industrial Man*. Cambridge, MA: Harvard University Press.

Koestler, A. 1967. *The Ghost in the Machine*. London: Arkana.

Marx, K. [1867] 1906. *Capital: A Critique of Political Economy, Vol. 1*. New York: Random House.

May, A. & Summerfield, G. 2012. 'Creating a space where gender matters: Elinor Ostrom (1933–2012) talks with Ann Mari May and Gale Summerfield.' *Feminist Economics*, 18 (4): 25–37.

Muller-Jentsch, W. 2004. 'Theoretical approaches to industrial relations,' *in*: B. Kaufman (ed.), *Theoretical Perspectives on Work and the Employment Relationship*. Ithaca, NY: Cornell University Press.

Nobelprize.org. 2009. The Sveriges Riksbank Prize in Economic Sciences in Memory of Alfred Nobel 2009. Available from http://www.nobelprize.org/nobel_prizes/economics/laureates/2009 [Accessed March 13, 2015]

Ostrom, E. 1990. *Governing the Commons: The Evolution of Institutions for Collective Action*. New York: Cambridge University Press.

Ostrom, E. 2005. *Understanding Institutional Diversity*. Princeton, NJ: Princeton University Press.

Palmer, E. & Eveline, J. 2012. 'Sustaining low pay in aged care work.' *Gender, Work and Organization*, 19 (3): 254–275.

Stiglitz, J. 2000. 'Democratic development as the fruits of labor.' *Perspectives on Work*, 4: 31–38.

26
Heterodox theories of the business cycle

Matías Vernengo

Introduction

The discussion of economic fluctuations dates back to the nineteenth century, to the classical political economists. However, these scholars were essentially concerned with the process of capital accumulation, and did not develop a proper theory of cycles. Arguably, economic fluctuations in most pre-capitalist societies were irregular and highly related to shocks to agricultural production. Most discussions related to what eventually would become part of business cycle theory were related to the acceptance or rejection of Say's law and the possibility of a general crisis. The marginalist revolution that brought the neoclassical model to the center of the economics discipline, in contrast, suggested that the system did have a tendency to the full utilization of resources, including labor. In this view, crises and eventually cycles were either deviations from the optimal output level or changes to the optimal level itself, caused by shocks in both cases—monetary in the former and real in the latter.

Keynesian economics resurrected the classical political economy notion that the system was prone to crises, and that it could settle at a stable and sub-optimal position in the long-run. Keynes did not advance a theory of the economic cycle in the *General Theory* (GT), and his discussion in that book suggests that shocks were central for him, particularly shocks that he referred to as the 'marginal efficiency of capital' (MEC) (Keynes 1936: 313). However, Keynesian scholars developed a family of models that incorporated Keynes' principle of effective demand, in which business cycles occurred in the absence of shocks. Further, the trend, and fluctuations of economic growth were intertwined, and it was impossible to disassociate the process of economic growth and cycles.

The economic system, in this sense, was prone to fluctuations, and economic policy had to be geared towards reducing the negative effects of the downward phase of the cycle and to stimulate the boom. Shocks, both real and monetary, can still play a role in heterodox models of the cycle, but they essentially exacerbate the tendencies of an already unstable economy. These heterodox views of the economic cycle, based on endogenous mechanisms that generate fluctuations, were essentially abandoned by the mainstream of the economics discipline after the rise of monetarism in the 1960s and new classical economics and real business cycles in the 1970s. Nevertheless, heterodox scholars remain of the view that an endogenous theory of cycles is necessary to understand the inherent instability of capitalism.

The rest of this chapter is structured in three sections. The following section analyzes the contributions of the classical political economists, with an emphasis on the works in the Marxian tradition, which have been the most influential development within this framework. Particular attention is paid to the role of the predator-prey model in generating economic fluctuations. The following section looks at heterodox Keynesian models, starting with Keynes, and then with his followers. They emphasize the relevance of the interaction of the multiplier and accelerator mechanisms, and the role of structural instability, as the main sources of business fluctuations. A brief conclusion forms the final section.

Marxian theories of the business cycle

Classical political economy discussions of crisis can be seen as the impetus for theories of economic fluctuations. David Ricardo and Robert Malthus famously debated the possibility of a general glut, with the former denying its possibility. The Ricardian view was that in the long-run a generalized over-production crisis could not occur, since supply created its own demand. For Ricardo this basically meant that generally production resulted from the desire to consume. In other words, supply by definition was the result of demand. Hence, for Ricardo, while crises could occur in the short-run since some products would not meet demand, in the long-run producers would learn from their mistakes and supply only goods which were socially useful, and that would provide them with the purchasing power to fulfill their own consumption desires. Ricardo suggested that nobody would continue to produce something for which there is no demand over the long-run. Note that while in Ricardo's view capitalists re-invested all their savings, and capital was fully utilized, the same was not true for labor. The level of output was fixed in this classical model.

Marx was critical of Say's law, and for that reason is probably the first relevant author to discuss the possibilities of recurring crises as an inherent feature of capitalist societies. The Ricardian view is grounded in what Marx referred to as the 'simplest form of the circulation of commodities,' or simple exchange, where commodities were produced for exchange for commodities, with money being just an intermediary, C-M-C′ (commodity-money-new commodity). In this case, Say's law was operative, since it was true that production occurred as a result of a desire to consume. Yet, Marx suggested that, in capitalist societies, accumulation, and not consumption, is the basis of material production. In other words, capitalists produce to accumulate profits in monetary terms, or M-C-M′, and realization crises, the problem in the last leg of the transition from commodity to money (C-M′), might be a feature of the economy. While Say's law would be valid in a simple reproduction system, it would be invalid in a capitalist economy.

By the middle of the nineteenth century, there was a more widespread understanding that economic crises are periodical in industrialized economies.[1] Several scholars criticized Say's law, most notably Malthus, Sismondi, and Rodbertus. These criticisms developed into what is sometimes referred to as under-consumptionist theories of crises. The most famous of the under-consumptionist theories was that of John Hobson, an anti-imperialist British economist who argued that as the process of accumulation accelerated and profits became concentrated in fewer hands, the opportunities for profitable investment were reduced, and the lack of demand would make it impossible to increase production on a larger scale. Both the role of under-consumption, particularly with Rosa Luxemburg and later Paul Sweezy, and of monopoly capital, with Rudolf Hilferding and afterwards with Paul Baran and Sweezy, would contribute to Marxian theories of crises. Marxian scholars have been, for the most part, the ones extending the old and forgotten tradition of classical political economy.

Marxian theories of the business cycle have a common thread—that is, the role of the rate of profit is the main variable to understand fluctuations. Profit squeeze theories, which became popular in the 1960s, suggest that in booms the reserve army of the unemployed shrinks, the bargaining power of workers will increase, and higher wages will tend to squeeze the profits of the capitalists, who will refrain from investing as a result. The crisis that ensues will also contain the seeds of the recovery, since as higher unemployment reduces the bargaining power of the labor force, wages will tend to fall behind, and the profit rate will recover, leading to a renewed process of accumulation.[2]

The main difference between alternative Marxian explanations of business cycle fluctuations is the mechanism by which the rate of profit changes over time. In addition, it is important to understand that these theories differ from long-term arguments about the effects of a profit squeeze on accumulation, and on the possibility of a generalized crisis of capitalism.[3]

Richard Goodwin's contribution is one of the most idiosyncratic and probably one of the most important developments of Marxian ideas on the business cycle. Goodwin ([1967] 1982), adapting an idea from biological sciences, the so-called predator-prey model, notes that the fluctuations of the profit rate that are central to the explanation of cycles are also intrinsically connected to the process of economic accumulation and growth. The Goodwin model provides an example of cyclical growth—that is, the notion that the process of economic growth is highly unstable, and that fluctuations of economic activity are intrinsically connected to the process of capital accumulation and growth.

In Goodwin's model investment is a function of profits, and in a booming economy with profits increasing, capital accumulates, and output and employment increase as well. However, as employment increases the economy moves towards full employment, and the share of wages in total income rises, reducing profits, and eventually has a negative impact on investment and employment. As profits fall, investment is reduced, and output and employment also decline. Yet, as unemployment increases, wage pressures diminish, and the whole cycle starts anew. The wage share acts as a predator, preying on profits,[4] so to speak, which is the fuel of the economy.

Central to Goodwin's argument is that savings out of profit determine investment. In a classical political economy fashion, all wages are consumed, while profits are saved and used for investment. Additionally, employment grows with output which, in turn, follows investment. Employment grows with capital accumulation, adjusted by the increase in labor productivity and the growth of the labor force. In other words, employment is directly related to profits, and inversely related to the wage share. In fact, Goodwin's view of the labor market is perfectly compatible with mainstream marginalist views, in which firms demand more labor as it becomes less expensive. The wage share grows with real wages, and in the steady-state economy the wage share is constant, and the real wage grows with productivity, as in marginalist models. In Goodwin's view, real wages increase in the proximity of full employment, which would be seen as the upper limit of the cycle.

In addition, in a downturn the wage share falls, not because the bargaining power of workers is reduced and real wages fall, but because real wages do not grow at the same pace than labor productivity, and that is what allows for the restoration of profitability; a very 'un-Marxian' result as noted by Goodwin ([1967] 1982: 169). The Goodwin model represents a hybrid of Marxian and neoclassical views, or what might be termed a Marxian-marginalist theory of the business cycle. The idea of the predator-prey, however, might be preserved in models in which the idea of distribution determined by marginal productivities and the tendency to full employment are abandoned, and in which the role of the bargaining power of the labor class assumes a more determinant role.[5]

One last family of Marxian theories warrants noting as part of the classical political economy tradition on the economic cycle, namely, Nikolai Kondratieff's long cycles. This would be roughly 50-year cycles, longer than the decennial business cycles on which most theories concentrate. Like other theories, the basis for the cycle is that the process of replacing capital goods is not smooth. But Kondratieff suggested that major innovations tended to cluster and to lead to long cycles. Most economists find the empirical evidence for Kondratieff cycles to be weak, and sometimes the weaker notion of Kondratieff waves is used instead.[6] The long wave theories of Kondratieff influenced the development of the Social Structure of Accumulation (SSA) approach, which emphasizes a broader set of variables to understand the process of economic development. In this sense, fluctuations are not only explained by changes in the rate of profit movements, but more importantly by the set of institutions that fosters capitalist accumulation.[7]

It is important to emphasize that classical political economy views on the cycle in general tend to assume that investment behavior, driven by the rate of profit, is the essential driving force of the economic cycle. In this view, investment is *profit-led*; in other words, firms increase or decrease capacity utilization on the basis of the rate of profit, or the returns to investment.[8] However, many modern Marxian models assume that this is the actual rate of profit, while for classical political economy investment was related to the normal rate of profit. In that view, as noted by Garegnani (1992), firms would invest if the actual profit is above the normal rate of profit, which is equivalent to say that they need additional capacity to adjust to demand requirements. In other words, firms must adjust their capacity to demand, and there is a normal level of capacity utilization. In this view, expected demand might have a role in the determination of investment and, hence, the cycle. This view was later developed in Keynesian models in which an expansion in the wage share might be stimulating to the economy. In the alternative view, which was followed by certain Marxian scholars like Kalecki, the system would be *wage-led*, even though the effects of income distribution on output, employment, and growth may be ambiguous.

Keynesian theories of the business cycle

Keynesian theories of the business cycle start from the notion that changes in income equilibrate savings to investment *ex post*, and the level of economic activity is determined by effective demand. Further, the system does not have a tendency towards full employment. In that sense, the economy can fluctuate in the long-run, with wage and price flexibility, around a normal position that is below full utilization of labor and capital. Unemployment is the norm. Keynes was not directly concerned in the GT with business cycles *per se*, even though he discussed the issue towards the end of the book. His main concern was with what he referred to as 'unemployment equilibrium.'

Keynes ([1936] 1964) argues that autonomous investment decisions are central for the determination of the level of output, and these are taken in an environment of true non-probabilistic uncertainty about the future. Investment is governed by long-term expectations, which could be interpreted as being affected by the prospects of future demand. The fluctuation of investment, associated with what Keynes referred to as *animal spirits*, leads to the fluctuation of the level of output and employment, basically following the multiplier process. Keynes suggested that it was the cyclical changes in investment, which he associated with the marginal efficiency of capital that determined business cycle fluctuations.[9] Keynes ([1936] 1964: 317) thought, also in conventional fashion, that to revive investment was not easy, in particular because of the "uncontrollable and disobedient psychology of the business world" and also since the return of confidence was "insusceptible to control in an economy of individualist capitalism." But he did not rely completely on 'confidence fairies,' to use a more modern expression.

The socialization of investment, by which Keynes ([1936] 1964: 375–376) meant basically public investment, was necessary to get the economy out of the crisis, but would, in his view, "be quite compatible with some measure of individualism, yet it would mean the euthanasia of the rentier." The rentier class, to which Keynes belonged, lived from financial returns, and the idea of the euthanasia of rentiers basically meant maintaining relatively low rates of interest. Although Keynes' reasons were essentially conventional, associated with stimulating investment which according to marginalist theory occurs at low rates of remuneration, the euthanasia of the rentier meant that debtors, in general, but in particular the state, would be less burdened and that would allow for the economy to be maintained closer to a permanent boom. After all, Keynes ([1936] 1964: 322) argued in Chapter 22 of the GT that the: "right remedy for the trade cycle is not to be found in abolishing booms and thus keeping us permanently in a semi-slump; but in abolishing slumps and thus keeping us permanently in a quasi-boom." It is important to note, however, that cycles, in Keynes' conception, depend on shocks, which are associated with the state of long-term expectations and the state of confidence, meaning that business cycles are essentially exogenous.

There is no explanation of the shocks, and of the reasons why advanced capitalist economies seem to go through persistent fluctuations. In that sense, mainstream economists suggest that demand shocks to either the goods market equilibrium or the monetary market can be seen as reasonably within the scope of what Keynes suggested caused the cycle. However, that would be a model in which there is no tendency to full employment as a result of income distribution and debt-deflation effects, and more in line with heterodox Keynesian views.[10] It would fall to Keynes' followers in Cambridge and Oxford to develop an endogenous theory of the cycle, that is, one that did not depend on external shocks.

The multiplier-accelerator interaction

Kalecki ([1933] 1971), who advanced the principle of effective demand independently of Keynes, and Harrod (1936), a disciple of Keynes, developed an early theory of the cycle based on the interaction of Keynes' multiplier process with the concept of the accelerator. The American institutionalist economist John Maurice Clark developed the idea of the accelerator.[11] The accelerator resulted from the institutionalists' preoccupation with empirical evidence on business cycles, pioneered by Wesley Mitchell, the founder of the National Bureau of Economic Research (NBER). The notion is relatively simple: firms will invest, that is, buy equipment and installations and increase the stock of capital, to the extent that future demand is expected to increase. In other words, firms will try to maintain a desired or normal capacity utilization level, which will mean a desired ratio of output to capital. Capacity or supply will adjust to demand, and investment will be dependent on expectations of future income, or derived demand.

The interaction of the multiplier and the accelerator provides a simple explanation for economic cycles that are endogenous, and that under certain conditions can be persistent and for that reason might not require external shocks to explain economic fluctuations, even if shocks do occur and are frequent. Kalecki ([1933] 1971) emphasized the role of time lags between the placing of investment, the demand for new equipment, and the delivery of the new equipment, indicating the dual role of investment as part of demand, but as creating productive capacity in the future. Further, Kalecki suggested that investment orders are a positive function of autonomous demand and a negative function of the existing capital stock. In other words, if demand is growing firms will add capacity and invest, but if capacity is already built and the existing stock of capital is large, they will not. Investment requires the maintenance of a particular ratio of the flow of income to the stock of capital. Note that capital goods depreciate, and, as a result, a certain amount is demanded just for replacement.

Assuming that expectations about future demand are high, then investment will increase and through the multiplier effect it will have a reinforcing effect on income. The increase in income, in turn, will lead, according to the accelerator, to an increase in investment, leading to an economic boom. However, as investment increases, eventually new investment orders will exceed the replacement requirements, and the capital stock will also rise. This will have a negative effect on the rate of increase in investment, and new investment orders will slow down first, and then decrease. The decreasing orders will have a negative impact on demand, and through the multiplier, lead to a reduction in the level of income, creating the conditions for a recession. Falling income will imply lower investment, following the accelerator, and even further collapse of income. In a depression, investment orders will collapse and at some point they will fall below the replacement requirements associated with depreciation, leading to a reduction in the stock of capital. Finally, the falling stock of capital will make the need for investment inevitable, and this will lead to more demand and a recovery.

The essential mechanism of the business cycle in the Kaleckian model is connected to the lags between the demand effect and the capacity effect of investment. Kalecki (1954) assumed that shocks will provide the initial spark for the business cycle, and the multiplier-accelerator mechanism will keep it going.[12] He noted also that only under very specific circumstances will the cycle recur, and that additional shocks will be necessary to avoid a dampened cycle. Further, fluctuations will occur around levels of output which imply an average rate of unemployment considerably below the peak reached in the boom, and the existence of what he referred to as the reserve army of unemployed, following Marx, will be a characteristic of the cycle. In other words, fluctuations will occur around a normal position that involves significant unemployment, as Keynes argued.[13]

Kaldor (1940) developed a model, later formalized by Hicks (1950) and Goodwin (1951), which allowed for the economic cycle to recur even in the absence of external shocks. The central difference in the Kaldorian model was the introduction of non-linear investment and savings functions. The idea was not to deny the existence of stochastic shocks or time lags, but to demonstrate that the economic system will also fluctuate in their absence, and that in a broad sense the capitalist system was inherently unstable. In other words, Kaldor introduced a non-linear accelerator and multiplier. At low levels of income, investment will not change much with an increase in income, since the large amount of spare capacity will preclude additional investment. Also, at high levels of income, investment will be insensitive to changes in income, since the capital goods sector that produces investment goods will be close to full capacity. The investment schedule is shown in Figure 26.1.

Further, the savings function too will be non-linear, with a high propensity to save—the inverse of the multiplier—at low and high levels of income, and a lower propensity to save at intermediate levels of income. The idea is that at low levels of income, the propensity to save is low, since consumption cannot fall below a certain minimum that is socially acceptable, and at higher levels of income the savings rate increases, and at very high levels of income the savings rate increases explosively, since the rich can save almost all their additional income. The non-linear multiplier follows from different patterns of consumption associated with income distribution. The savings function will resemble the S-curve depicted in Figure 26.1.

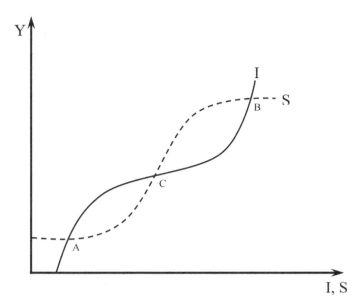

Figure 26.1 Non-linear multiplier-accelerator

In this case, there may be multiple equilibria between investment and savings, and some will be unstable. Whenever investment (I) is bigger than savings (S), the multiplier process will imply higher income, and *vice versa* when investment is smaller than savings. In Figure 26.1, A and B will be stable equilibria, while C will be unstable, since whenever the income level is above A and B investment is smaller than savings, and income will decrease, while the opposite is true above C.

Further, Kaldor (1940) assumed that an initial shock would move one of the schedules. That is, both the investment schedule (I) and the savings curve (S) will shift generating the initial instability. Assume that the economy starts at the high output equilibrium at point B. Then the exhaustion of investment opportunities will lead to a shift of the investment curve upwards, meaning less investment (I) for the same level of income (Y). At the high level of income, consumption patterns will also change and the S schedule will move downward, implying less savings (S) at the same level of income (Y). The high income equilibrium level becomes unstable in a downward direction (B+C), as depicted in the graph on the right of Figure 26.2; for a given level of income above the equilibrium between I and S, I will be smaller than S as income will be decreasing. As the level of income decreases, however, and income collapses, the fall in investment leads to a situation in which the purchase of new equipment is insufficient to cover capital replacement needs. A shift of the whole investment schedule down and to the right, until it is tangent to the savings curve, as shown in the left-hand graph in Figure 26.2, will take place. In this situation, at the original level of income S will be smaller than I, and income will be increasing in the direction of the new equilibrium. The low level of income equilibrium will become upwardly unstable (A+C equilibrium), and the original situation will be re-established, with a continuous cycle.[14]

In the Kaldorian non-linear cycle model, once the economic system is perturbed, fluctuations will inherently recur as a result of the interaction between the multiplier and the accelerator.

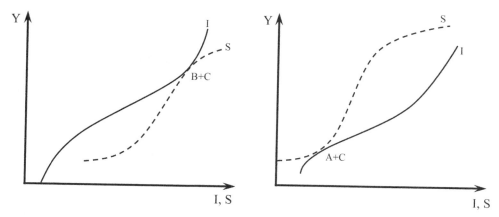

Figure 26.2 Cyclical instability

The system will be in *perpetuum mobile*. Goodwin's (1951) limit-cycle model showed that the non-linear interaction between the multiplier and accelerator leads to regular fluctuations without the need for exogenous shocks, time lags, or particular parameter values.[15] These models were essentially abandoned by the mainstream in the 1970s, not because they have theoretical or methodological flaws, or because of the empirical evidence favoring the multiplier and accelerator effects. The models were discarded with the rediscovery of the notion of the natural rate of unemployment, and the notion that the economic system is self-adjusting to full employment.[16]

Even though the multiplier and accelerator effects seem to be empirically relevant and point to the role of demand in economic fluctuations, it is important to understand that the Keynesian notion of the instability of capitalism is not completely illuminated by the models discussed so far. It is also important to note that the heterodox Keynesian business cycle models imply that the forces explaining fluctuations are also directly and intrinsically connected to structural changes and economic growth. Trend and cycle are to some extent inseparable.

Financial fragility and structural instability

The interaction of the multiplier and accelerator means that the trend, which depends on the accelerator, that is, on the adjustment of capacity (supply) to demand, is intrinsically connected to fluctuations. In this sense, one cannot separate cycles and growth, and Keynes' notion that, to avoid the worst types of recession, policy should aim at maintaining a quasi-boom all the time makes sense. Note that demand forces, not supply conditions, determine the maximum level of output, below which the economy fluctuates.[17]

In addition, the Keynesian approach to the cycle based on the interaction of the multiplier and the accelerator suggests that the economic system is dynamically unstable—that is, not only does it regularly fluctuate around a sub-optimal level of activity, but also the system is within certain conditions that are structurally stable. This is the reason that Keynes ([1936] 1964: 249) suggests: "it is an outstanding characteristic of the economic system in which we live, that, whilst it is subject to severe fluctuations in respect to output and employment, it is not violently unstable." Keynes emphasized the role of monetary and financial factors in the characterization of instability.

Vercelli (1984) argues that Keynes' theory must be re-interpreted in light of the difference between the concepts of dynamic and structural instability. Dynamic instability is simply the divergence from equilibrium, while stability will be convergence. Harrodian knife-edge instability is the most evident example. Structural instability, on the other hand, is associated with the qualitative change in behavior of the system after being disturbed. The Minskian financial instability hypothesis (FIH) exemplifies the idea of structural instability. Vercelli (2000) argues that the degree of financial fragility can be measured as the minimum threshold of the shock required for inducing a firm into insolvency and leading it to bankruptcy.[18] The behavior of the system is such that a small shock is able to change the qualitative behavior of firms, from stable to unstable, following Minsky's (1986) notion that 'stability is destabilizing.' The behavior of the system is characterized by fluctuations that are cyclical although not regular, and this results from the endogenous properties of the system rather than exogenous shocks.[19]

Alternatively, the differences between the inter-war Gold Standard and the so-called Bretton Woods period (often referred to as the Golden Age of capitalism for its high rates of economic growth around the globe) are a good example of the difference between dynamically and structurally unstable economic systems. In both cases, the economy fluctuates around a demand-determined average level of output and employment. However, the inter-war Gold Standard system, with no clear hegemonic leader, forced countries to maintain relatively high rates of interest, and created a burden on indebted agents, including governments and thus reducing their ability to expand demand. On the other hand, during the Bretton Woods period, the existence of capital controls, which allowed for lower interest rates without fear of capital flight, and central banks committed to full employment policies, the economies of advanced countries fluctuated around positions that were closer to the full utilization of the labor force.

In both cases, the economy is dynamically unstable, within certain margins, but dynamically stable from a general perspective. Yet, in the inter-war Gold Standard system the change in the hegemonic center from the United Kingdom to the United States (US) led to a change in the qualitative behavior of the economy and to significant structural instability, leading to the Great Depression.[20] In that sense policy regimes, in particular the functioning of the international monetary system are central to the Keynesian view for the determination of whether the economy will fluctuate around a position that is closer, or not, to full employment. In this sense, heterodox Keynesian theories of the cycle, like Marxian views reflected in the SSA approach, suggest that business cycles are not always the same in different historical circumstances.

Conclusion

Heterodox views of the business cycle build on the old classical political economy notion that the economic system is inherently unstable. Contrary to the mainstream view that the cycle is a result of shocks, either monetary or real, which affect the economy, heterodox scholars suggest that the system has mechanisms by which fluctuations are inherent and will occur even in the absence of shocks. Shocks obviously do occur, and demand or monetary shocks tend to be more common than real shocks. But it is difficult to explain the relative regularity of cycles if shocks are their only source.

Also, since the economy fluctuates around a normal capacity utilization that is only by chance the maximum level of capacity utilization, in fact a rare phenomenon, the shocks are non-mean reverting, that is, the economy does not necessarily return to the same trend. This accounts for the fact that Gross Domestic Product follows a random path that is not explained by real shocks affecting the optimal output level, as implied by real business cycle scholars.

Marxian models of the cycle emphasize the role of profits in the explanation of economic fluctuations. An important mechanism that allows for recurrent fluctuations is based on the predator-prey mechanism. The behavior of investment, which is dependent on the profit rate, and the effects of a growing economy on the bargaining power of workers and the wage share, are combined to create the conditions for cyclical movements. In the heterodox Keynesian view, output fluctuates because investment is affected by expected demand, leading through the accelerator to an adjustment of capacity to demand, but investment affects actual income through the multiplier. Higher than expected demand leads to higher income, and higher income leads to more demand, and *vice versa* when expected demand falls.

Both Marxian and heterodox Keynesian scholars tend to emphasize the broader institutional framework that makes capitalism unstable. While Marxian authors emphasize the relevance of what has become known as social structures of accumulation, Post Keynesian authors tend to emphasize the monetary and financial elements that produce instability. In many ways, these views remain compatible, even if some specific models are not and they emphasize different elements of the capitalist system.

Finally, the heterodox view of economic cycles suggests that cycles and growth are intertwined. That is, the process of growth and the wealth of nations occur concomitantly with booms and recessions. Cycles can be smoothed out by appropriate economic policy but they cannot be completely eliminated.

Acknowledgments

The author thanks the comments of the editors on a preliminary version of the paper.

Notes

1 For the most part, the pioneers of business cycle analysis were marginalists or proto-marginalists. Clément Juglar, among the proto-marginalist authors, is normally considered the pioneer of business cycle theory. Juglar emphasized the role of monetary factors in explaining crises and, in particular, the speculation and the up- and down-swings of business confidence. There is little theoretical discussion in his analysis of why prices increase during booms, and what causes over-production and sudden collapse.

2 There is a myriad of models in this vein with applications to the US and several other advanced capitalist economies. Sherman (1979) summarizes these views. An important contribution by Weisskopf (1979) argues that cyclical declines in the profit rate are central to explaining economic crises. For a more recent analysis along these lines see Bakir & Campbell (2006). Bakir & Campbell (2013) expand the analysis to encompass the effects of the rate of profit in the financial sector, which in their view becomes more relevant in the more recent fluctuations of the US economy.

3 Besides the cyclical profit squeeze, and the secular decline in the profit rate, associated with the rising organic composition of capital, the third type of crisis that can lead to a Marxian model of crises, and to a theory of business cycle, will be under-consumption. For Marxian models that try to adapt the Keynesian idea of effective demand, see Shaikh (1989).

4 Alternatively, one can think of wages being predatory to employment, which is how the Goodwin model is often portrayed. For a contemporary discussion applied to the US economy, see Barbosa-Filho & Taylor (2006) and see Taylor (2011) for an extended version including financial aspects.

5 Palley (2009) develops a Keynesian model in which the predator-prey dynamics plays a role.

6 Shaikh (1992) suggests that Marx's theory of the secular decline of the profit rate is at the basis of long wave fluctuations. There is an extensive literature on the validity, or not, of Marx's tendency of the falling rate of profit and the so-called Okishio Theorem, which is beyond the scope of this chapter.

7 Gordon *et al.* (1994: 18) argue, regarding the post-war social structure of accumulation, that: "The prosperity of the 1960s undermined the postwar capital-labor accord by giving labor and other non-capitalist groups greater economic and political power, thereby destabilizing one of the principal institutional arrangements that had made the long boom possible." So the relative strength of the labor force, and the institutions associated with the international monetary regime of Bretton Woods, that included capital

controls and allowed for low interest rates were all central elements of the relatively benign cycles of this era. The classic discussion of SSA is Bowles *et al.* (1983), and the contributions in Kotz *et al.* (1994). For a recent discussion of the collapse of the neoliberal SSA and its consequences for the last crisis in the US see Kotz (2013).

8 In a sense, if causality comes from profits, which correspond to savings, to investment, then essentially the logic of Say's law prevails.

9 On the necessity of breaking with the marginalist theory of distribution in order to show that the system does not have a tendency to full employment see Camara-Neto & Vernengo (2012).

10 Traditional marginalist arguments based on Keynes and Pigou effects, the so-called real balance effects, show that the economic system can have a tendency to full employment with flexible prices. In Chapter 19 of the GT, Keynes shows that a reduction in wages and prices might lead to worsening income distribution, lower spending, and lower output and employment, as well as bankruptcy of debtors and the collapse of investment. In both cases, the system will not tend to full employment, and wage flexibility can make things worse.

11 For a discussion of Clark's views on the multiplier-accelerator interaction see Fiorito & Vernengo (2009). The interaction of the multiplier and the accelerator as the main mechanism for explaining the cycle was at some point accepted by proponents of the neoclassical synthesis, like John Hicks and Paul Samuelson. For a recent application of the multiplier-accelerator model to the US economy see Baghestani & Mott (2014).

12 The shocks will be propagated by the multiplier-accelerator mechanism. The methodology of separating the impulse that leads to the cycle from the propagation mechanism was devised by Ragnar Frisch and Eugene Slutzky and is dominant in mainstream economics, even though the propagation mechanism rarely includes the multiplier-accelerator mechanism. In mainstream models, shocks to demand or to supply lead to a readjustment to equilibrium; in the case of the latter, that is, real shocks, the actual equilibrium of the economy moves. In that sense, models that emphasize demand shocks suggest that cycles are deviations from the optimal level, while real business cycles (RBC) imply that the cycle is a change of the optimal level itself. For monetary and real mainstream cycle models see Erceg (2008) and McGrattan (2008), respectively.

13 Kalecki ([1943] 1971) would additionally suggest in his famous 'Political Aspects of Full Employment' that political economy factors are all central in determining whether an economy will fluctuate around full employment. In his view, capitalists have a vested interest in maintaining a certain amount of unemployed workers in order to reduce their bargaining power. This has led to a prolific literature within the mainstream on political business cycles. In heterodox circles, the Kaleckian idea has been seen as more relevant to understand the social basis of sound finance, and austerity policies, than as the basis for understanding output fluctuation.

14 For a detailed presentation of the model and the further theoretical developments of the Kaldorian non-linear cycle see Targetti (1992). The Kaldorian model can be seen as a simple prototype of more complex non-linear models.

15 For a modern presentation of heterodox Keynesian models of the business cycle, extended to deal with debt issues, and emphasizing both multiplier-accelerator and predator-prey mechanisms see Palley (2009).

16 The mainstream, on the contrary, suggests that supply conditions determine the capacity limit, often associated in modern macroeconomics to Milton Friedman's natural rate of unemployment. Friedman (1968: 2) cites the Pigou effect, but none of the replies to its limitations like, for example Kalecki (1944), the basis for his argument to be the tendency to a natural rate of unemployment. Probably the most important development in this respect was the development of RBC theories, and the notion that cycles are equilibrium reactions to stochastic shocks to the economy, and the evidence presented by Nelson & Plosser (1982) that output follows a random path. This has created a notion that cycles are better understood as stochastic shocks, and deviations of the optimal level, that is, a changing natural rate. Note, however, that this is predicated on the notion that the relevant shocks are supply-side shocks, but it is very hard to believe that the Great Depression, or the more recent Great Recession were caused by supply-side shocks. It would be more reasonable to assume that demand shocks affect an economy that fluctuates around sub-optimal levels, and that the very idea of the natural rate should be abandoned (Galbraith 1997). In that sense, while shocks play a role, it is clear, given their continued empirical relevance, that multiplier and accelerator effects do matter.

17 In this case, the interaction of the multiplier and the accelerator is used to obtain the normal level of output, in a supermultiplier model. These models bring together elements of the old classical

political economy tradition with the ideas of heterodox Keynesians. For these, see Serrano (1995) and Bortis (1997).

18 In his pure flow model, this financial fragility measure is simply associated with a fall in profits or an increase in interest rates. For firms there is a threshold of financial fragility beyond which they do not wish to go. More importantly, following Hyman Minsky, Vercelli (2000: 146) suggests that firms that are in a safe zone regarding financial fragility will, as a result of competition, invest and incur more fragile financial structures, moving from hedge, to speculative, and from that to Ponzi situations. This view is central within Post Keynesian theories of the cycle.

19 Vercelli suggests that the model has similarities with Keynesian accelerator-multiplier models, in particular with the Goodwin non-linear cycle. It is worth noticing that Minsky's PhD dissertation did rely on the interaction between the multiplier and accelerator mechanisms (Minsky 2004). Regarding the endogenous nature of fluctuations, Minsky (1986: 324) argues that: "A sophisticated, complex, and dynamic financial system . . . endogenously generates serious destabilizing forces so that serious depressions are natural consequences of noninterventionist capitalism." Most discussions of Minsky's model are related to financial crises rather than as part of a theory of the business cycle. For a short exposition of Minsky's crisis theory see Wray (2011).

20 Kindleberger's ([1973] 1986) hegemonic stability theory suggests that the absence of a clear hegemon— being able to act as an international lender of last resort and as a source of demand in distress conditions— causes instability. This can be seen as an example of structural instability, and a broader explanation for the Great Depression.

References

Baghestani, H. & Mott, T. 2014. 'Asymmetries in the relation between investment and output.' *Journal of Post Keynesian Economics*, 37 (2): 357–365.

Bakir, E. & Campbell, A. 2006. 'The effect of neoliberalism on the fall in the rate of profit in business cycles.' *Review of Radical Political Economics*, 38 (3): 365–373.

Bakir, E. & Campbell, A. 2013. 'The financial rate of profit: what is it, and how has it behaved in the United States?' *Review of Radical Political Economics*, 45 (3): 295–304.

Barbosa-Filho, N.H. & Taylor, L. 2006. 'Distributive and demand cycles in the U.S. economy – a structuralist Goodwin model.' *Metroeconomica*, 57 (3): 389–411.

Bortis, H. 1997. *Institutions, Behaviour and Economic Theory: A Contribution to Classical-Keynesian Political Economy*. Cambridge: Cambridge University Press.

Bowles, S., Gordon, D., & Weisskopf, T. 1983. *Beyond the Wasteland: A Democratic Alternative to Economic Decline*. Garden City, NY: Anchor Press/Doubleday.

Camara-Neto, A.F. & Vernengo, M. 2012. 'Keynes after Sraffa and Kaldor: effective demand, accumulation and productivity growth,' *in*: T. Cate (ed.), *Keynes's General Theory: Seventy-Five Years Later*. Cheltenham, UK: Edward Elgar, 222–237.

Erceg, C. 2008. 'Monetary business cycle models (sticky prices and wages),' *in*: S. Durlauf & L. Blume (eds.), *The New Palgrave Dictionary of Economics*, 2nd online edn. New York: Palgrave Macmillan.

Fiorito, L. & Vernengo, M. 2009. 'The other J.M.: John Maurice Clark and the Keynesian Revolution.' *Journal of Economic Issues*, 43 (4): 899–916.

Friedman, M. 1968. 'The role of monetary policy.' *American Economic Review*, 58 (1): 1–17.

Galbraith, J.K. 1997. 'Time to ditch the NAIRU.' *Journal of Economic Perspectives*, 11 (1): 93–108.

Garegnani, P. 1992. 'Some notes for an analysis of accumulation,' *in*: J. Halevi, D. Laibman, & E. Nell (eds.), *Beyond the Steady State: A Revival of Growth Theory*. New York: St. Martin's Press.

Goodwin, R. 1951. 'The nonlinear accelerator and the persistence of business cycles.' *Econometrica*, 19 (1): 1–17.

Goodwin, R. [1967] 1982. 'A growth cycle,' *in*: R. Goodwin, *Essays in Economic Dynamics*. London: Macmillan.

Gordon, D., Edwards, R., & Reich, M. 1994. 'Long swings and stages of capitalism,' *in*: D. Kotz, T. McDonough, & M. Reich (eds.), *Social Structures of Accumulation: The Political Economy of Growth and Crisis*. Cambridge: Cambridge University Press.

Harrod, R. 1936. *The Trade Cycle: An Essay*. Oxford: Clarendon Press.

Hicks, J.R. 1950. *A Contribution to the Theory of the Trade Cycle*. Oxford: Oxford University Press.

Kaldor, N. 1940. 'A model of the trade cycle.' *Economic Journal*, 50 (197): 78–92.

Kalecki, M. [1933] 1971. 'Outline of a theory of the business cycle,' *in*: *Selected Essays on the Dynamics of the Capitalist Economy, 1933–1970*. Cambridge: Cambridge University Press, 1–14.

Kalecki, M. [1943] 1971. 'The political aspects of full employment,' *in*: *Selected Essays on the Dynamics of Capitalist Economies, 1933–1970*. Cambridge: Cambridge University Press, 138–145.

Kalecki, M. 1944. 'Professor Pigou on "The Classical Stationary State": a comment.' *Economic Journal*, 54 (213): 131–132.

Kalecki, M. 1954. *Theory of Economic Dynamics*. London: George Allen and Unwin.

Keynes, J.M. [1936] 1964. *The General Theory of Employment, Interest and Money*. New York: Harcourt Brace Jovanovich.

Kindleberger, C. P. [1973] 1986. *The World in Depression, 1929–1939*. Berkeley, CA: University of California Press.

Kotz, D. 2013. 'Social structures of accumulation, the rate of profit, and economic crises,' *in*: J. Wicks-Lim & R. Pollin (eds.), *Capitalism on Trial: Explorations in the Tradition of Thomas E. Weisskopf*. Cheltenham, UK: Edward Elgar.

Kotz, D., McDonough, T., & Reich, M. 1994. *Social Structures of Accumulation: The Political Economy of Growth and Crisis*. Cambridge: Cambridge University Press.

McGrattan, E. 2008. 'Real business cycles,' *in*: S. Durlauf & L. Blume (eds.), *The New Palgrave Dictionary of Economics*, 2nd online edn. New York: Palgrave Macmillan.

Minsky, H. 1986. *Stabilizing an Unstable Economy*. New Haven, CT: Yale University Press.

Minsky, H. 2004. *Induced Investment and Business Cycles*. Cheltenham, UK: Edward Elgar.

Nelson, C.R & Plosser, C.I. 1982. 'Trends and random walks in macroeconomic time series: some evidence and implications.' *Journal of Monetary Economics*, 10 (2): 139–162.

Palley, T. 2009. The simple analytics of debt-driven business cycles. Political Economy Research Institute, University of Massachusetts at Amherst Working Paper No. 200.

Serrano, F. 1995. 'Long period effective demand and the Sraffian supermultiplier.' *Contributions to Political Economy*, 14 (1): 67–90.

Shaikh, A. 1989. 'Accumulation, finance, and effective demand in Marx, Keynes, and Kalecki,' *in*: W. Semmler (ed.), *Financial Dynamics and Business Cycles: New Perspectives*. Armonk, NY: M.E. Sharpe, 65–86.

Shaikh, A. 1992. 'The falling rate of profit as the cause of long waves: theory and empirical evidence,' *in*: A. Kleinknecht, E. Mandel, & I. Wallerstein (eds.), *New Findings in Long Wave Research*. New York: St. Martin's Press, 174–195.

Sherman, H. 1979. 'A Marxist theory of the business cycle.' *Review of Radical Political Economics*, 11 (1): 1–23.

Targetti, F. 1992. *Nicholas Kaldor: The Economics and Politics of Capitalism as a Dynamic System*. Oxford: Clarendon Press.

Taylor, L. 2011. 'Growth, cycles, asset prices and finance.' *Metroeconomica*, 63 (1): 40–63.

Vercelli, A. 1984. 'Fluctuations and growth: Keynes, Schumpeter, Marx and the structural instability of capitalism,' *in*: R. Goodwin, M. Krüger, & A. Vercelli (eds.), *Nonlinear Models of Fluctuating Growth*. Berlin: Springer-Verlag, 209–231.

Vercelli, A. 2000. 'Structural financial instability and cyclical fluctuations.' *Structural Change and Economic Dynamics*, 11 (1): 139–156.

Weisskopf, T. 1979. 'Marxian crisis theory and the rate of profit in the postwar U.S. economy.' *Cambridge Journal of Economics*, 3 (4): 341–378.

Wray, L.R. 2011. 'Minsky crisis,' *in*: S. Durlauf & L. Blume (eds.), *The New Palgrave Dictionary of Economics*, 2nd online edn. Palgrave Macmillan.

27

Heterodox theories of economic growth

Özgür Orhangazi

Introduction

The sources and dynamics of economic growth have occupied a central place in economics since its beginning. The main concern of the classical political economists was explaining the growth and distribution of income. While the rise of the marginalist school pushed this question aside for some time, the 1940s saw growth economics brought back to center stage. Starting with Harrod's (1939) growth model, there emerged a voluminous literature that analyzes the determinants of economic growth and its pace.

The search for the determinants of economic growth was accompanied by questions of: whether capitalist economies tend towards stable growth at full employment; and whether fluctuations in growth are due to endogenous or exogenous reasons. The dominant neoclassical thinking in economics suggests that under conditions of perfect competition and minimal state intervention, capitalist economies generate a stable growth path at full employment. Any fluctuation around or deviation from this path is attributed to factors outside the economic system. Heterodox theories of economic growth, on the other hand, question the validity, attainability, and stability of long-term economic growth at full employment, while theorizing on the fluctuations in growth as inherent to the capitalist economic system.

In this chapter, I present an overview of the foundational ideas and main issues in heterodox growth theories, paying specific attention to Post Keynesian and Marxian contributions.[1] While it is not possible to do justice to the whole heterodox literature on economic growth within one chapter, this chapter is intended as an accessible entry point to the many different ways of heterodox growth theorizing. To that end, I set aside the details of the formal theoretical models as well as issues of economic development and the link between growth and development. I start in the next section with Post Keynesian models in general, then move on to models that focus on growth in developing countries, and finally discuss various Marxian approaches to economic growth. In the following section I outline some common features of various heterodox growth theories and discuss the relevance of heterodox growth theories with respect to the recent 'secular stagnation' debate. Finally, a brief overview of recent work that is critical of growth itself is presented.

From Harrod-Domar to Kaleckian models

Modern growth theory finds its origins in the works of Roy Harrod and Evsey Domar. Harrod (1939), influenced by the ideas of Keynes, studies whether the short-run conclusions of the Keynesian theory in terms of growth and employment are valid also for the long-run. Domar (1946) takes into consideration the capacity effects of investment and looks for an equilibrium growth rate that will give constant capacity utilization.[2]

Incorporating Keynesian characteristics both in terms of methodology and the theoretical construction of the model, Harrod's (1939) analysis demonstrates the multiplier mechanism as well as the acceleration principle as the dynamic of economic growth. Harrod suggests the existence of a 'warranted' growth path—in the sense that the sales and capacity expectations of the firms and the outcomes are on average consistent with each other. However, he notices two problems with this path. First, there is no mechanism to ensure that this 'warranted' rate of growth will be equal to the actual or the 'natural' rate (that is, the growth rate of the labor force). Second, there is no mechanism for expectations and outcomes to be equal to each other and hence, the warranted path is likely to be unstable.

These conclusions essentially depend on Harrod's theorization of firms' investment behavior. The decisions of firms are directly determined by the level of aggregate demand, particularly through the capacity utilization rate. Harrod argues that once the actual growth rate deviates from the warranted growth rate, there are no mechanisms to bring them back to equilibrium; rather, the accelerator principle will lead to further deviations. For example, when the capacity utilization rate exceeds the desired level, firms undertake investment. However, this investment, through multiplier effects, leads to a worsening of the initial disequilibrium. As investment is determined independently from the savings, it is possible to have an investment-saving inequality *ex ante*. *Ex post*, investment creates an equal amount of savings. Hence, income, employment and savings are determined by the *ex ante* investment decisions and their workings through the multiplier process. In other words, market signals can generate disequilibrium—that is, the market system fails to ensure permanent equilibrium in goods and labor markets. As a result, the short-run Keynesian conclusions will be valid in the long-run as well and this serious problem, according to Harrod, can only be solved through government interventions.[3]

Harrod's approach and conclusions are in sharp contrast to the neoclassical presupposition that the market system generates an equilibrium with efficient outcomes under conditions of perfect competition. His arguments, especially the instability conclusion, triggered studies that led to what is known as the 'neoclassical solution.' Solow (1956) and Swan (1956) modified Harrod's model with a set of strong assumptions so that the model would give a stable growth rate at full employment through relative price variation and factor substitution. Hence, the instability of the warranted growth rate disappeared in the neoclassical growth models.[4] Various neoclassical growth models developed later were dedicated to showing long-run equilibrium within the same general framework, albeit under different conditions and assumptions. A second generation of neoclassical growth models emerged, known as 'new growth models' or 'endogenous growth models,' which treat technological progress as an endogenous variable (Romer 1986; Lucas 1988). Post Keynesian growth theory, on the other hand, developed through a number of key contributions made by economists such as Nicholas Kaldor, Luigi Pasinetti, Joan Robinson, and Michał Kalecki, who provided the main ideas and the building blocks of modern Post Keynesian growth models.

Kaldor (1957) argues that steady growth is a 'stylized fact' of capitalist economies and therefore needs to be explained. He introduces a growth model in which a steady growth equilibrium at full employment can exist and be stable depending on the values of the parameters. However, similar to Harrod, Kaldor also argues that there are no mechanisms that will give the right parameters to ensure stable long-run growth. Kaldor's model was later criticized for its full employment assumption and the lack of an explanation as to how full employment is reached and for its insufficient explanation of the determinants of autonomous investment, which Kaldor considered to be a main driver of economic growth (Skott 1989a). However, the most well-known criticism of Kaldor came from Pasinetti (1962), who argues that whereas in Kaldor's model there are different savings propensities from wages and profits, the dynamic implications of this model are ignored because if workers save they will gradually own capital stock and as a result they will receive two types of income. Kaldor (1966a) responded to Pasinetti's criticism and a long debate ensued around the implications of this issue.[5] Later, Kaldor (1966b) put forward a number of theses on growth, arguing that manufacturing is the engine of growth as it has increasing returns to scale and draws resources from other sectors inducing productivity growth in those sectors as well.

Robinson (1962) argues that with a constant rate of capacity utilization, the rate of growth will be equal to the accumulation rate. She introduces the idea that the accumulation rate is determined by the expected profit rate. This means accumulation determines the realized profit rate, which sets the expectations for the following period. In this framework, firms invest and savings adjust to the rate of investment. Robinson rejects the steady-state equilibrium models of growth and argues that models need to be historically and institutionally specific and the investment functions should take into account these historical and institutional factors as well as Keynes' 'animal spirits.'[6]

Kalecki's ideas provided the basis for a family of modern heterodox growth models. Kalecki combined elements from both Keynesian and Marxian approaches, which made him influential among both Post Keynesians and Neo-Marxians. It is also well known that Kalecki introduced the idea of the importance of aggregate demand in the determination of output and employment before Keynes (Kalecki 1971). In fact, famous dictum ascribed to him that workers spend what they get and capitalists get what they spend follows along the lines of Post Keynesian theory of distribution. He also used ideas consistent with Marxian class struggle arguments. For example, he argued that powerful trade union movements could reduce profitability.[7] For Kalecki the modern capitalist system is characterized by imperfect competition and firms are price makers. They set a mark-up over costs depending on the degree of oligopoly. The normal operation of capitalism generates both excess capacity and unemployment. A key argument is that the level of demand affects the capacity utilization rate and long-run growth is driven by investment. This makes the analysis of the determinants of investment important. In the short-run, an increase in oligopolization leads to increasing mark-ups and a redistribution of income in favor of profits, which then has a negative impact on investment through its negative effect on aggregate demand. In the long-run, investment is determined by technological progress and innovations, which also tend to slow down due to increasing oligopolization.

In this regard, Kalecki's arguments have similarities with Steindl (1952), who argues that the industry is transitioning from a competitive structure towards monopolization, which he calls a process of 'absolute concentration' or mature or oligopolistic capitalism. Steindl also argues that oligopolies lead to demand shortfall problems as they cause an increase in profits that are not used since oligopolist firms are likely to have excess capacity and they will not invest in the absence of competition and demand. As a result, a self-enforcing stagnation tendency emerges in capitalism.

A family of 'Kaleckian' growth models are based on these ideas of Kalecki. Rowthorn (1981) explicates the basis for most of the Kaleckian approaches to economic growth.[8] In Rowthorn (1981) economic growth is led by wages. In an economy operating below full capacity, an increase in nominal wages leads to an increase in the share of wages within total income. This generates an increase in aggregate demand that leads to higher output levels. As a result, a higher utilization of capital is observed and profits on the existing capital stock increase. In the process, it is also possible that increased capacity utilization leads to economies of scale and this will counteract the increased cost of higher wages. Capitalists respond to these changes by investing. Hence, capacity utilization and profits are the two main variables determining investment in Rowthorn's formulation.

The idea that the rate of profits determines accumulation was formalized by Robinson (1962), while the idea that capacity utilization affects investment was first introduced by Steindl (1952). Steindl argues that excess capacity exists because, first, firms prefer to build capacity ahead of demand and, second, in oligopolistic markets they use excess capacity as a barrier to entry. The indivisibility of capital goods further adds to excess capacity. In Steindl, an increase in capacity utilization, therefore, leads to investment. In this type of Kaleckian formulation, the industrial structure becomes quite important as the degree of oligopoly determines the mark-up rate, which directly affects the relative shares of wages and profits within total income. While investment determines savings in a Keynesian fashion, the main difference from the short-run Keynesian formulation is the argument that the accumulation of capital (investment-capital ratio) determines income distribution (profit rate).

Following Marglin & Bhaduri (1990) and Bhaduri & Marglin (1990), a distinction between wage-led and profit-led growth models became one of the major features of the Kaleckian approach to economic growth. These scholars introduced the idea that a profit-led economic growth would also be possible with a different investment model. Bhaduri & Marglin (1990) argue that investment and savings are functions of the profit share and capacity utilization, which is an indicator of expected demand. Their use of the profit share instead of the profit rate stems from the argument that when investment is specified as a function of capacity utilization and the profit rate, this specification makes only wage-led growth possible and rules out the possibility of profit-led growth. In their model, the system is called 'exhilarationist' (profit-led), if investment responds strongly to profitability. In this case, a higher profit share leads to higher capacity utilization. And the system is called 'stagnationist' (wage-led), if a higher profit share leads to lower capacity utilization. In a wage-led regime, an increase in the wage share leads to increased economic activity and growth due to workers' higher marginal propensity to consume. In a profit-led regime it has the opposite effect and demand is led by profits. Hence, the issue is basically about the relationship between income distribution and aggregate demand. A profit-led regime is possible whereas a wage-led growth may fail to create the necessary growth in capacity and lead to a crisis of under-accumulation. Bhaduri & Marglin (1990) and Marglin & Bhaduri (1990) also present an intermediate case—'conflictual stagnationist.' In this case, aggregate demand can be weakly wage-led, while at the same time growth is profit-led.

While these models are usually set up for the case of a closed economy, reformulations for the open economy case are possible. In an open economy, an increase in wages can decrease export competitiveness by raising labor costs and also decrease profits, leading to lower investment. If the negative impact of the trade balance on growth is greater than the positive impact of increased domestic demand due to higher wages, the net effect on accumulation will be negative. The economy can be wage-led only if the increase in demand is large enough to outweigh the negative effect of net exports. In other words, wage-led growth is only possible if the economy is relatively closed to foreign trade—that is, exports and imports have low price elasticities, imports are a small percentage of Gross Domestic Product (GDP) and they have low income elasticity (Blecker 1989, 1999).

It is also suggested that even though some economies can be considered to be profit-led, the world economy as a whole would still be wage-led if the international competitive results cancel each other out at the global level (Onaran & Galanis 2012; Lavoie & Stockhammer 2012).

If this is the case, then a global redistribution of income towards wages will have expansionary consequences even in profit-led economies. A large empirical literature examines various economies and tries to determine whether they are wage-led or profit-led although no consensus is reached.[9] Blecker (2015) suggests that the lack of consensus may be because insufficient attention has been given to the time dimension in these empirical studies. According to his arguments, demand is more likely to be profit-led (or weakly wage-led) in the short-run and wage-led in the long-run (or strongly wage-led). The reasoning behind this argument is that the positive effects of higher profits and higher net exports on accumulation are stronger in the short-run, whereas the positive effects of higher wages on aggregate demand are stronger in the long-run.

Following Keynes' (1933) theory of monetary production, the Post Keynesian tradition began incorporating monetary variables and the role of financial markets into growth models by the 1980s. More recently, a group of scholars developed models to account for the effects of financialization on growth, following the empirical findings of Krippner (2005), Stockhammer (2008), and Orhangazi (2008a, b), who show that a process of financialization is at work in advanced economies in the post-1980 era.

The impact of financialization on economic growth occurs through three channels. First, increasing shareholder power and changing financial market requirements can have a negative impact on investment. This literature argues that financialization is associated with increasing power of shareholders vis-à-vis firm management and workers, and with the increased involvement of non-financial firms in financial investments. As a result, firm management has changed its focus from long-run growth objectives to short-term profitability. Second, increased indebtedness can create an expansionary impetus in the short-run (in particular through increased household consumption financed by debt) and a contractionary effect as well as potential instability in the long-run. Third, financialization contributes to increased income inequality with negative effects on aggregate demand (for example, Boyer 2000; Hein & van Treeck 2010; Hein 2012).[10] As a result, some argue that two possible growth regimes arise: a debt-led consumption boom regime, and an export-led mercantilist regime (Hein 2014).

An interesting case is made by Stockhammer & Michell (2014) who argue that an economy characterized by a Marxian-type reserve army of labor and a Minskian-type debt channel could exhibit the characteristics of a profit-led demand economy even though it actually is wage-led. As a result, a rising capacity utilization, a shrinking reserve army of labor, and rising debt can all exist at the same time. If the negative effects of increasing debt on aggregate demand and growth dominate, then the economy would appear to be profit-led, when this coincides with increasing wages and decreasing growth rates.[11]

Growth in the South

Another heterodox perspective on economic growth that specifically focuses on developing economies is the 'structural approach,' which emphasizes the importance of different structures across sectors and countries. It was originally formulated as a critique of mainstream growth theory, especially in regards to its trade and stabilization policy implications for developing countries. While it is not possible to present a single, synthetic model of the structural approach to economic growth, works in this tradition can broadly be grouped into three: the original ECLAC (United Nations Commission for Latin America and the Caribbean) approach of the 1950s and 1960s, based on Prebisch (1950); Latin American neo-structuralism of the 1970s; and Taylor-type structuralist macroeconomic models of the 1980s and 1990s.

The ECLAC approach argues that the world economy should be considered as a whole, within which a center and a periphery can be identified. The center and the periphery have structural differences that, taken together, create an international division of labor and a single world economic system. In this system, growth in the periphery depends on the conditions in the center. The periphery specializes in low-value-added products (mostly agricultural products) and this specialization leads to a trade-dependent growth path. However, given different income elasticities of imports in the core and the periphery, the world system creates a deterioration in the terms of trade against the periphery and causes structural balance-of-payments problems as well as structural unemployment in the periphery. More importantly, this setup fails to produce industrialization, which is a necessary condition for long-run economic growth. Hence, the proponents of this approach argue that a set of industrial policies, including state investment in key industries, infant industry protections, controls on exchange rates, and promotion of foreign direct investment, are needed for economic growth.

The second group of structuralist analyses—the neo-structuralist theories—focuses more on short-run issues such as debt crises, trade deficits, and stabilization policies starting in the 1970s. The third group is usually identified with Taylor's work (see, for example, Taylor 1983, 1985, 1991). Taylor presents a critique of the dominant economic policies, especially of the one-size-fits-all policies imposed upon developing economies to solve problems such as trade imbalances and high inflation. He has developed a series of formal macroeconomic models based on Kaleckian ideas and brought growth and distribution into consideration. Taylor emphasizes that the models have to be more flexible and take into consideration different structures in these economies, a position that is in sharp contrast to the mainstream approach. For example, he introduces mark-up pricing in certain sectors; the idea of endogenous money to show that tight monetary policy may restrict production but not decrease inflation; and the role of financial markets and institutions in economic growth for developing economies.

A related analysis that includes structural features as well as ideas from Harrod, Kalecki, and Prebisch, is the balance-of-payments-constrained-growth-model, which suggests that international trade places limits on economic growth (Thirlwall 1979).[12] According to this model, a country's growth rate cannot exceed the rate that is consistent with the current account's balance equilibrium, unless it can finance its deficits indefinitely. There are limits to the trade deficit to GDP ratio and the foreign debt to GDP ratio. When these limits are exceeded, international financial markets are likely to put downward pressure on the currency, making a financial crisis likely. In contrast to mainstream theories of trade and growth, the balance-of-payments-constrained-growth-approach stresses the potentially negative effects on economic growth of trade openness. This does not imply that it refutes the contribution of exports to economic growth; on the contrary, it recognizes the importance of exports to the growth process, as an increase in economic growth is likely to lead to higher import requirements and hence higher foreign exchange needs. Thirlwall's model, like Harrods's and Kaldor's, highlights that there is no mechanism to guarantee a growth rate consistent with current account balance equilibrium and full employment.

Marxian approaches to growth

Works in the Marxian tradition are concerned mainly with disruptions to economic growth. Some important Marxian growth theories deserve careful examination. Goodwin (1967), to begin with, brings Marx's concept of the reserve army of labor into growth modeling. In his model, the size of the reserve army of labor (or the rate of unemployment) determines workers' bargaining power. Low unemployment increases the bargaining power of workers, which then leads to an increase in the share of wages in total income. An increase in wages, however, hurts profitability and has a negative effect on investment and hence the rate of accumulation and employment. Therefore, a cyclical growth path emerges out of the interaction between the rate of unemployment, the wage share of total income, and investment. A large body of literature followed Goodwin (1967), extending and generalizing his contribution.[13] These models do not attempt, however, to integrate all Marxian ideas and focus primarily on the labor market, with distribution outcomes which investment accommodates without any demand problems.[14]

Other formal growth analyses within the Marxian tradition, in general, start with an economy with two classes (capitalists and workers), an unlimited labor supply and an income distribution determined by class struggle.[15] In this economy, workers do not save and capitalists use their savings for investment, which expands output and employment. Hence, in the classical-Marxian model, growth depends on savings, which leads to capital accumulation. In the absence of any demand problems, then, a more unequal income distribution leads to higher income for capitalists, higher investment and higher economic growth. While in Post Keynesian models changes in wages affect the growth rate through their effects on demand and then capacity utilization; in the classical-Marxian models real wages affect the profit rate, which determines the rate of accumulation and growth.

In the classical-Marxian approach, in contrast to the Post Keynesian tradition, economic growth is determined on the supply side through technological change due to competition and class struggle. Some argue for a potential convergence between the two approaches by suggesting that while in the short-run aggregate demand will determine the level of capacity utilization, in the long-run the Marxian tendencies will dominate (Duménil & Lévy 1999, 2014; Dutt 2011). A Marxian approach to growth emphasizing the demand side is Baran & Sweezy's (1966) monopoly capitalism approach, which is influenced by the arguments of Kalecki and Steindl. They suggest that increased market concentration gives firms pricing power, resulting in increased mark-up rates and higher profit shares in the economy. Hence, an increased degree of oligopoly results in a tendency for economic stagnation and continued economic growth requires external factors such as public spending, export markets, epochal innovations, and so on.

Another Marxian approach to long-term economic growth is Social Structure of Accumulation (SSA) theory. In its original formulation it was a theory of how crises are resolved (Gordon 1978) and quickly developed into a theory that explains both long periods of economic growth and how they end (Gordon 1980; Gordon et al. 1982; Kotz et al. 1994; McDonough et al. 2010).[16] SSA theory is built on the Marxian idea that the economy and social and political institutions constitute a whole system, and that capitalism creates periods of growth, crisis, and slowdown. Therefore, instead of only focusing on economic models and variables, the whole institutional structure needs to be examined.

As such, SSA theory has some parallels to both Kondratieff's (1925, 1935) and Schumpeter's (1939) concerns about explaining periods of long-term growth followed by slowdowns—known as long waves. Kondratieff (1925, 1935) identifies three long waves and argues that the main determinant of these long waves is the replacement need of long-lived capital goods. Schumpeter (1939), on the other hand, views major innovations as the driving force behind the long waves (for example, cotton textiles and iron 1790–1815; railways, steam, and steel 1845–1873; electricity and industrial chemistry 1895–1913).

SSA theory's approach to economic growth can be summarized as follows. Stable economic growth occurs when a set of economic and political institutions are in place that favor capital accumulation. These institutions are referred to as a social structure of accumulation and they promote accumulation and growth by regulating key relationships in the economy to create stability and predictability, while ensuring sufficient profitability and aggregate demand over time. In the absence of these conditions, the economy may suffer from instability and/or stagnation. For example, the social structure of accumulation in the post-Second World War United States (US) economy included institutions such as an increased involvement of the state in the economy through investment and regulations, limited competition among firms, a 'tacit' deal between capital and labor, and US leadership in the world economy, among other things.

The key driver of accumulation according to SSA theory is also profitability, but profitability by itself is insufficient, as capitalists will only invest if they have confidence in the outcome of that investment. This confidence is provided by a set of institutions that are favorable to capital accumulation as well as to stability. As such, power is also an important determinant in the sense that profitability is ensured by the power of the capitalists over other classes and groups in the society (Gordon *et al.* 1987). For example, a crucial feature of the institutional structure in the post-Second World War US economy was the enhanced power of the capitalists. A key idea in this approach is that while a social structure of accumulation can promote stable growth for a long time, it eventually runs into a crisis, as institutions became obstacles rather than promoters of economic growth. Then there follows a 'structural' or a 'long-run' economic crisis that is only resolved through a reconstruction of the institutions and a transformation to a new social structure of accumulation.

Some common themes and current relevance

As should be clear by now, heterodox scholarship on economic growth includes many different perspectives which are not possible to combine into one synthetic heterodox model of economic growth. Furthermore, cross-influences between heterodox schools of thought sometimes make it difficult to classify one into a particular school of thought. However, it is still possible to identify some common themes even though the particular significance attributed to a theme may vary from one approach to the other. Five common themes can be identified.

The role of aggregate demand: Keynes assigned a significant role to aggregate demand in the short-run. Various heterodox growth models examine whether aggregate demand is also a significant determinant of long-run growth. Post Keynesian growth literature takes this issue as central and suggests that aggregate demand affects long-term growth through different channels.

Distribution: Issues of distribution also play a central role in many heterodox growth models. Distribution is not only considered as one of the potential determinants of economic growth and technical change, but also as an economic outcome that is important in and of itself.

Instability: Potential instability of the growth process and its sources are taken seriously by heterodox approaches. Even when formal models with steady-state equilibrium analysis are used, heterodox economists are concerned with the attainability and sustainability of equilibrium. Contrary to mainstream growth theories, the possibility that economic growth is a cyclical process rather than a steady one and is inherently unbalanced is usually entertained in the heterodox growth literature.

Competition and technical change: The role of competition and technical change is treated differently from mainstream analysis, in that technical change is considered as being not just endogenous but also endogenous to the outcomes such as growth and distribution. The degree of competition, for example, has an impact on technical change as well as on growth and distribution.

The role of institutions: The role of institutional structures feature prominently in heterodox growth theories as they rule out hypothetical perfect competition without state intervention and attempt to produce more realistic models and understandings of economic growth.

The debate on the determinants of long-run growth seems to have made a comeback recently as the recovery from the 2008 financial crisis and the ensuing Great Recession has been quite weak in the US as well as in other developed economies. An emerging literature discusses the possibility of a secular stagnation, which inevitably includes a discussion on the determinants of economic growth.

The literature can broadly be divided into two opposing groups: supply-side and demand-side approaches. For example, Gordon (2012, 2014) argues that a main driver of growth is technological change; however, recently technological change has failed to promote high rates of economic growth. Summers (2014), on the other hand, draws attention to demand-side factors such as reduced investment demand that is partly due to the need for less capital investment in new technologies; declining population growth and increasing inequality. Ball et al. (2014) similarly challenges the view that aggregate demand does not matter for long-run growth as, they argue, even a short period of depression can have significant effects on the long-run path of potential GDP.

Within this debate, however, references to the history of economic thought on growth are scarce. Hein (2015), noting this fact, presents an argument based on Steindl (1952) and argues that what modern capitalist economies are facing is an aggregate demand constraint and Steindl's approach is very relevant to the debate on secular stagnation. Hein also stresses that the changing institutional structure, especially the rise of financialization, has a significant role in changing the growth path. Furthermore, Kotz & Basu (2016), following the SSA approach, make the argument that the lack of rapid economic growth results from the inability of the current social structure of accumulation to promote normal conditions of accumulation and growth.

Growth critiques

A discussion of the heterodox literature on economic growth would be incomplete without highlighting two recent lines of the critique of economic growth itself: the critique of growth as a measure of social welfare and the critique of growth economics for its neglect of environmental costs.

The first critique is based on the argument that the growth of GDP itself is not a reliable indicator of social welfare (van den Bergh 2009; van den Bergh & Kallis 2012). The GDP measure suffers from a number of problems. First of all, it only measures the costs of market activities but not their benefits, while completely ignoring non-market or informal activities. Second, it does not present a good approximation of social welfare. Not only is there no evidence that GDP accurately represents social welfare, but also it is quite possible that subjective well-being and the growth of GDP can move in opposite directions. Third, the use of natural resources and the costs to the environment are not accounted for in the growth framework (van den Bergh & Kallis 2012).

In fact, ecological economists have been concerned with this last point for some time.[17] Recent contributions by some heterodox economists pay attention to the environmental costs of economic growth and suggested investment in a 'green economy.' Pollin (2015), for example, argues that protecting the environment and generating job opportunities are not necessarily conflicting goals. Large-scale investment in energy efficiency and renewable energy resources can generate growth while contributing to the protection of the environment. In fact, he suggests that this can also counter the current stagnation tendency. Another line of thought is developed under the title of 'degrowth,' which is a concept used to suggest an intentional policy of downscaling the economy so as to ensure it remains consistent with biophysical boundaries (Kallis et al. 2012).

Notes

1 Some of the ideas discussed in this chapter feature in Vasudevan (this volume) in the context of capital accumulation and Vernengo (this volume) in the context of business cycles.
2 Hein (2014: 47) notes that the standard textbook version of the Harrod-Domar growth model ignores their main questions and is presented as "a neoclassical model with a built-in-rigidity" without any attention to the role of aggregate demand for growth.

3 For the use of Harrodian ideas by contemporary heterodox economists, see Skott (1989a, b, 2010) and Fazzari et al. (2013).
4 This created the famous capital controversy between the neoclassical and Post Keynesian economists (Harcourt 1972). The main issue in the capital controversy was that in neoclassical theory the real interest rate is determined by the marginal productivity of capital at the aggregate level. However, in order to determine the marginal productivity of capital, the real interest rate needs to be given. Skott (1989a) argues that while aggregation is at the center of the controversy, this is essentially a manifestation of a deep disagreement on the static notion of equilibrium.
5 For the Pasinetti theorem, see Asimakopulos (1988), Skott (1989a), or King (2002: 70–71).
6 For an overview of Robinson's approach and a comparison with Kaldor and Pasinetti, see Kregel (1975).
7 On the issue of unemployment, Kalecki (1971: 138–145) argues that attaining full employment is possible in modern capitalism as we now have a good understanding of capitalist economies thanks to Keynes. He argues that full employment, through its impact on demand, could also contribute to capitalists' profitability. However, capitalists will still not want full employment policies; not because it will hurt their profitability but because it would threaten their control over the workplace in particular and political institutions in general (see also Pollin 2012). Kalecki (1971) reasoned that this opposition to full employment can create political business cycles. Later, Steindl (1979) argues that this opposition is likely to contribute to the stagnation tendency.
8 For other earlier formalizations see Steindl (1979), Taylor (1983, 1985), and Dutt (1984, 1987).
9 See, for example, Hein & Vogel (2008), Hein & Tarassow (2010), Blecker (2011), Stockhammer (2011), Lavoie & Stockhammer (2012).
10 See Hein (2014: Chapter 10) for a review of Post Keynesian models of financialization.
11 There is also a growing literature on stock-flow consistent dynamic modeling, based on the idea that growth models need to properly account relevant stocks and flows between them (see Godley & Lavoie 2007; Keen 2013).
12 For a review of the model and its empirical applications, see Thirlwall (2011).
13 See Desai (1973), Shah & Desai (1981), and Goodwin et al. (1984).
14 Skott (1989a) presents a model taking into consideration both the role of labor's bargaining power and effective demand and argues that a cyclical growth path similar to Goodwin's (1967) is possible, although the underlying mechanisms can be different.
15 Harris (1978), Marglin (1984), Dutt (1990), and Foley & Michl (1999) cover classical Marxian approaches to growth.
16 See McDonough (2010) for a review of the recent SSA literature.
17 See Kallis et al. (2012) for an overview of the ecological economics literature on growth.

References

Asimakopulos, A. 1988. 'Post-Keynesian theories of distribution,' in: A. Asimakopulos (ed.), Theories of Income Distribution. Boston: Kluwer, 133–158.
Ball, L., DeLong B., & Summers, L. 2014. Fiscal policy and full employment. Washington, DC: Center on Budget and Policy Priorities.
Baran, P. & Sweezy. P. 1966. Monopoly Capital. Harmondsworth, UK: Penguin.
Bhaduri, A. & Marglin, S. 1990. 'Unemployment and the real wage: the economic basis for contesting political ideologies.' Cambridge Journal of Economics, 14 (4): 375–393.
Blecker, R.A. 1989. 'International competition, income distribution and economic growth.' Cambridge Journal of Economics, 13 (3): 395–412.
Blecker, R.A. 1999. 'Kaleckian macro models for open Economies,' in: J. Deprez & J.T. Harvey (eds.), Foundations of International Economics: Post-Keynesian Perspectives. London: Routledge, 116–150.
Blecker, R.A. 2011. 'Open economy models of distribution and growth,' in: E. Hein & E. Stockhammer (eds.), A Modern Guide to Keynesian Macroeconomics and Economic Policies. Cheltenham, UK: Edward Elgar, 215–239.
Blecker, R.A. 2015. Wage-led versus profit-led demand regimes: the long and the short of it. Paper presented at the Eastern Economics Association conference, New York.
Boyer, R. 2000. 'Is a finance-led growth regime a viable alternative to Fordism? A preliminary analysis.' Economy and Society, 29 (1): 111–145.
Desai, M. 1973. 'Growth cycles and inflation in a model of the class struggle.' Journal of Economic Theory, 6 (6): 527–545.

Domar, E.D. 1946. 'Capital expansion, rate of growth and employment.' *Econometrica*, 14 (2): 137–147.

Duménil, G. & Lévy, D. 1999. 'Being Keynesian in the short term and classical in the long term: the traverse to classical long-term equilibrium.' *The Manchester School*, 67 (6): 684–716.

Duménil, G. & Lévy, D. 2014. 'A reply to Amitava Dutt: the role of aggregate demand in the long run.' *Cambridge Journal of Economics*, 38 (5): 1285–1292.

Dutt, A.K. 1984. 'Stagnation, income distribution and monopoly power.' *Cambridge Journal of Economics*, 8 (1): 25–40.

Dutt, A.K. 1987. 'Alternative closures again: a comment on "growth, distribution and inflation".' *Cambridge Journal of Economics*, 11 (1): 75–82.

Dutt, A.K. 1990. *Growth, Distribution and Uneven Development*. Cambridge, UK: Cambridge University Press.

Dutt, A.K. 2011. 'The role of aggregate demand in classical-Marxian models of economic growth.' *Cambridge Journal of Economics*, 35 (2): 357–382.

Fazzari, S.M., Ferri, P.E., Greenberg, E.G., & Variato, A.M. 2013. 'Aggregate demand, instability and growth.' *Review of Keynesian Economics*, 1 (1): 1–21.

Foley, D.K. & Michl, T.R. 1999. *Growth and Distribution*. Cambridge, MA: Harvard University Press.

Godley, W. & Lavoie, M. 2007. *Monetary Economics: An Integrated Approach to Credit, Money, Income, Production and Wealth*. Basingstoke, UK: Palgrave Macmillan.

Goodwin, R.M. 1967. 'A growth cycle,' in: C.H. Feinstein (ed.), *Socialism, Capitalism and Growth*. Cambridge: Cambridge University Press, 54–58.

Goodwin, R.M., Krüger, M., & Vercelli. A. 1984. *Non-linear Models of Fluctuating Growth*. Berlin: Springer.

Gordon, D.M. 1978. 'Up and down the long roller coaster,' in: Union for Radical Political Economics (ed.), *US Capitalism in Crisis*, New York: Union for Radical Political Economics, 22–35.

Gordon, D.M. 1980. 'Stages of accumulation and long economic cycles,' in: T.K. Hopkins & I. Wallerstein (eds.), *Processes of the World System*. Beverly Hills, CA: Sage, 9–45.

Gordon, D.M., Edwards, R. C., & Reich, M. 1982. *Segmented Work, Divided Workers: the Historical Transformations of Labor in the United States*. New York: Cambridge University Press.

Gordon, D.M., Weisskopf, T.E., & Bowles, S. 1987. 'Power accumulation and crisis: the rise and demise of the postwar social structure of accumulation,' in: R. Cherry & T. Michl (eds.), *The Imperiled Economy, Book I: Macroeconomics from a Left Perspective*. New York: Union for Radical Political Economics, 43–55.

Gordon, R.J. 2012. Is the US economic growth over? Faltering innovation confronts the six headwinds. National Bureau of Economic Research Working Paper 18315. Available from http://www.nber.org/papers/w18315 [Accessed February 8, 2016]

Gordon, R.J. 2014. The demise of US economic growth: Restatement, rebuttal and reflections. National Bureau of Economic Research Working Paper 19895. Available from http://www.nber.org/papers/w19895 [Accessed February 8, 2016]

Harcourt, G.C. 1972. *Some Cambridge Controversies in the Theory of Capital*. Cambridge, UK: Cambridge University Press.

Harris, D.J. 1978. *Capital Accumulation and Income Distribution*. London: Routledge & Kegan Paul.

Harrod, R. 1939. 'An essay in dynamic theory.' *Economic Journal*, 49 (193): 14–33.

Hein, E. 2012. *The Macroeconomics of Finance-dominated Capitalism and its Crisis*. Cheltenham, UK: Edward Elgar.

Hein, E. 2014. *Distribution and Growth after Keynes: A Post-Keynesian Guide*. Cheltenham, UK: Edward Elgar.

Hein, E. 2015. Secular stagnation or stagnation policy? Steindl after Summers. Levy Economics Institute Working Paper No. 846. Available from http://www.levyinstitute.org/pubs/wp_846.pdf [Accessed February 8, 2016]

Hein, E. & Tarassow, A. 2010. 'Distribution, aggregate demand and productivity growth: theory and empirical results for six OECD countries based on a post-Kaleckian model.' *Cambridge Journal of Economics*, 34 (4): 727–754.

Hein, E. & van Treeck, T. 2010. '"Financialisation" in post-Keynesian models of distribution and growth–a systematic review,' in: M. Setterfield (ed.), *Handbook of Alternative Theories of Economic Growth*. Cheltenham, UK: Edward Elgar, 277–292.

Hein, E. & Vogel, L. 2008. 'Distribution and growth reconsidered–empirical results for six OECD countries.' *Cambridge Journal of Economics*, 32 (3): 479–511.

Kaldor, N. 1957. 'A model of economic growth.' *Economic Journal*, 67 (268): 591–624.

Kaldor, N. 1966a. 'Marginal productivity and the macroeconomic theories of distribution.' *Review of Economic Studies*, 33 (4): 309–319.

Kaldor, N. 1966b. *Causes of the Slow Rate of Economic Growth of the United Kingdom.* Cambridge, UK: Cambridge University Press.

Kalecki, M. 1971. *Selected Essays on the Dynamics of the Capitalist Economy, 1933–70.* Cambridge, UK: Cambridge University Press.

Kallis, G., Kerschner, C., & Martinez-Alier, J. 2012. 'In defense of degrowth.' *Ecological Economics*, 70 (5): 873–880.

Keen, S. 2013. 'A monetary Minsky model of the Great Moderation and the Great Recession.' *Journal of Economic Behavior and Organization*, 86: 221–235.

Keynes, J.M. [1933] 1987. 'A monetary theory of production,' in: D. Moggridge (ed.), *The Collected Writings of J.M. Keynes, Vol. XIII.* London: Macmillan, 408–411.

King, J.E. 2002. *A History of Post Keynesian Economics since 1936.* Cheltenham, UK: Edward Elgar.

Kondratieff, N.D. [1925] 1975. 'The major economic cycles,' in translation; *Review*, II (4): 519–562.

Kondratieff, N.D. 1935. 'The long waves in economic life.' *Review of Economic Statistics*, 17 (6): 105–115.

Kotz, D.M., McDonough, T., & Reich, M. 1994. *Social Structures of Accumulation: The Political Economy of Growth and Crisis.* New York: Cambridge University Press.

Kotz, D.M. & Basu, D. 2016. Stagnation and institutional structures. Paper presented at the Allied Social Sciences Associations Annual Meetings, San Francisco, January 4.

Kregel, J.A. 1975. *The Reconstruction of Political Economy: An Introduction to Post-Keynesian Economics.* London: Macmillan.

Krippner, G.R. 2005. 'The financialization of the American economy.' *Socio-Economic Review*, 3 (2): 173–208.

Lavoie, M. & Stockhammer, E. 2012. Wage-led growth: concept, theories, and policies. Conditions of Work and Employment Series No. 41, International Labour Organisation.

Lucas, R.E. 1988. 'On the mechanics of economic development.' *Journal of Monetary Economics*, 22 (1): 3–42.

Marglin, S.A. 1984. *Growth, Distribution and Prices.* Cambridge, MA: Harvard University Press.

Marglin, S.A. & Bhaduri, A. 1990. 'Profit squeeze and Keynesian theory,' in: S. Marglin & J. Schor (eds.), *The Golden Age of Capitalism: Reinterpreting the Postwar Experience.* Oxford: Oxford University Press, 153–186.

McDonough, T. 2010. 'The state of the art of social structure of accumulation theory,' in: T. McDonough, M. Reich, & D. Kotz (eds.), *Contemporary Capitalism and its Crises: Social Structure of Accumulation Theory for the 21st Century.* Cambridge, UK: Cambridge University Press, 23–44.

McDonough, T., Reich, M., & Kotz, D. (eds.) 2010. *Contemporary Capitalism and its Crises: Social Structure of Accumulation Theory for the 21st Century.* Cambridge: Cambridge University Press.

Onaran, Ö. & Galanis, G. 2012. Is aggregate demand wage-or profit-led? National and global effects. Conditions of Work and Employment Series, No. 31, International Labour Organisation.

Orhangazi, Ö. 2008a. 'Financialisation and capital accumulation in the non-financial corporate sector: a theoretical and empirical investigation on the US economy: 1973–2003.' *Cambridge Journal of Economics*, 32 (6): 863–886.

Orhangazi, Ö. 2008b. *Financialization and the US Economy.* Cheltenham, UK: Edward Elgar.

Pasinetti, L. 1962. 'Rate of profit and income distribution in relation to the rate of economic growth.' *The Review of Economic Studies*, 29 (4): 267–279.

Pollin, R. 2012. *Back to Full Employment.* Cambridge, MA: MIT Press.

Pollin, R. 2015. *Greening the Global Economy.* Cambridge, MA: MIT Press.

Prebisch, R. 1950. *The Economic Development of Latin America and its Principal Problems.* Lake Success, NY: United Nations Department of Economic Affairs.

Robinson, J. 1962. *Economic Philosophy.* London: Macmillan.

Romer, P.M. 1986. 'Increasing returns and long-run growth.' *Journal of Political Economy*, 94 (5): 1002–1037.

Rowthorn, B. 1981. 'Demand, real wages and economic growth.' *Thames Papers in Political Economy*, Autumn: 1–39.

Schumpeter, J.A. 1939. *Business Cycles: A Theoretical, Historical and Statistical Analysis of the Capitalist Process, Vols. I and II.* New York: McGraw-Hill.

Shah, A. & Desai, M. 1981. 'Growth cycles with induced technical change.' *Economic Journal*, 91 (364): 1006–1010.

Skott, P. 1989a. *Conflict and Effective Demand in Economic Growth.* Cambridge, UK: Cambridge University Press.

Skott, P. 1989b. 'Effective demand, class struggle and cyclical growth.' *International Economic Review*, 30 (1): 231–247.

Skott, P. 2010. 'Growth, instability and cycles: Harrodian and Kaleckian models of accumulation and income distribution,' in: M. Setterfield (ed.), *Handbook of Alternative Theories of Economic Growth*. Cheltenham, UK: Edward Elgar, 108–131.

Solow, R.M. 1956. 'A contribution to the theory of economic growth.' *Quarterly Journal of Economics*, 70 (1): 65–94.

Steindl, J. 1952. *Maturity and Stagnation in American Capitalism*. Oxford: Blackwell; 2nd edn. New York: Monthly Review Press.

Steindl, J. 1979. 'Stagnation theory and stagnation policy.' *Cambridge Journal of Economics*, 3 (1): 1–14.

Stockhammer, E. 2008. 'Some stylized facts on the finance-dominated accumulation regime.' *Competition and Change*, 12 (2): 189–207.

Stockhammer, E. 2011. 'Wage-led growth: an introduction.' *International Journal of Labor Research*, 3 (2): 167–188.

Stockhammer, E. & Michell, J. 2014. Pseudo-Goodwin cycles in a Minsky model. Post Keynesian Economics Study Group Working Paper 1405. Available from http://www.postkeynesian.net/downloads/working-papers/PKWP1405.pdf [Accessed February 8, 2016]

Summers, L.H. 2014. 'US economic prospects: secular stagnation, hysteresis and the zero lower bound.' *Business Economics*, 49 (2): 65–73.

Swan, T.W. 1956. 'Economic growth and capital accumulation.' *The Economic Record*, 32 (2): 334–361.

Taylor, L. 1983. *Structuralist Macroeconomics*. New York: Basic Books.

Taylor, L. 1985. 'A stagnationist model of economic growth.' *Cambridge Journal of Economics*, 9 (4): 383–403.

Taylor, L. 1991. *Income Distribution, Inflation, and Growth*. Cambridge, MA: MIT Press.

Thirlwall, A. 2011. 'Balance of payments constrained growth models: history and overview.' *PSL Quarterly Review*, 64 (259): 207–251.

Thirlwall, A. 1979. 'The balance of payments constraint as an explanation of international growth rate differences.' *Banca Nazionale del Lavoro Quarterly Review*, 128 (791): 45–53.

van den Bergh, J.C.J.M. 2009. 'The GDP paradox.' *Journal of Economic Psychology*, 30 (2): 117–135.

van den Bergh, J.C.J.M. & Kallis, B.G. 2012. 'Growth, a-Growth or degrowth to stay within planetary boundaries?' *Journal of Economic Issues*, 46 (4): 909–919.

28

Financialization and the crises of capitalism

Petra Dünhaupt

Introduction

Marx highlighted the contradictions of capitalism, and argued that capitalism is but a stage on the way to a final societal form (Wallerstein 1974). Despite its contradictions and potential limits, capitalism continues to survive, by periodically redesigning and renewing its structure. Followers of Marx categorized these developments within capitalist history into different stages or periods, elaborating on the weaknesses of the system. Thus, the tendency of crisis plays a central role in Marxian tradition, exposing the limitations of the system and forcing new periods of capitalist development (Clarke 1994). The theory of capitalism can be approached by three different levels of analysis, one of which is a stage theory that analyzes the structural manifestations of the law of value in the stages of mercantilism, liberalism, and imperialism (Albritton 1986).[1] The analysis of different stages of development is also of central importance in the Post Keynesian tradition. Institutions have a profound impact on economies and hence economies need to be regarded from a historical perspective (Kriesler 2013).

Since the 1980s, the financial sector and its role have increased significantly. This development is often referred to as *financialization*. Authors working in the heterodox traditions have raised the question whether the changing role of finance manifests a new era in the history of capitalism.

The first section of the chapter provides some general discussion on the term financialization and presents some stylized facts, which highlight the rise of finance. The second section begins with a brief review of the Marxian argument that capitalism is prone to crisis. Also reviewed are two schools of thought in the Marxian tradition—the Social Structure of Accumulation (SSA) approach and the Monthly Review school—which consider financialization as the latest stage of capitalism. Both highlight the contradictions imposed by financialization that disrupt the growth process as well as the fragilities imposed by its growth regime.[2] The third section examines Post Keynesian theory, which emphasizes potential destabilizing factors that are germane to the phenomenon of financialization and the finance-led growth regime. The last section provides a comparative summary.

The development of financialization

As stressed by Epstein (2005), financialization is one of three terms often used to characterize the past three decades of capitalism—the other two being neoliberalism and globalization.

He defines financialization as "the increasing role of financial motives, financial markets, financial actors and financial institutions in the operation of the domestic and international economies" (Epstein 2005: 3). According to Dore (2008: 1097),

> 'Financialization' is a bit like 'globalization'—a convenient word for a bundle of more or less discrete structural changes in the economies of the industrialized world. As with globalization, the changes are interlinked and tend to have similar consequences in the distribution of power, income, and wealth, and in the pattern of economic growth.

Financialization has many dimensions and relates to numerous different economic entities (Stockhammer 2013; Epstein 2015). One key dimension is the spectacular rise of the financial sector. Greenwood & Scharfstein (2013) report a massive growth of the financial sector over the past 30 years in the United States (US), measured either by the financial sector's share of Gross Domestic Product (GDP), the volume of financial assets, employment, and average wages in the financial sector. But the growth of finance is not specific to the US; similar developments can also be found in other OECD countries although not as extreme as in the US (Philippon & Reshel 2013). The rise of the financial sector also manifests itself through profit shares. In the US, the share of total profits attributable to financial corporations has risen constantly: its share amounted to 13 percent on average in the 1960s, in the 2000s it increased to an average of 28 percent, and reached a peak in 2002, of 37 percent.[3] Recent research shows a similar trend for many OECD countries,[4] though with a few exceptions—for example, Germany (Detzer et al. 2013).

The rise of the financial sector is also mirrored by the rise in financial activity compared to real productive activity (Stockhammer 2013). Figure 28.1 shows the stock market capitalization as a share of GDP for Germany, France, the UK, and the US for the period from 1975 to 2011.

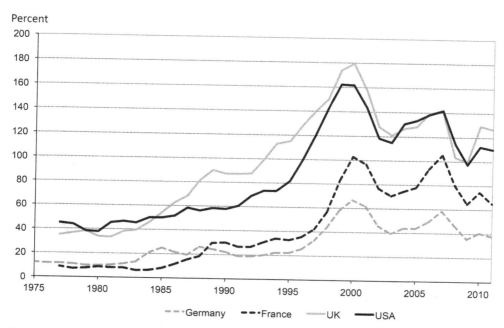

Figure 28.1 Stock market capitalization as a share of GDP: Germany, France, UK, and US, 1975–2011

Source: Beck *et al.* (2000; updated in 2013) author's calculation.

Stock market capitalization has grown rapidly in all countries since the mid-1980s, and even more so since the mid-1990s. In the UK and US, since the early or mid-1990s, stock market capitalization has outpaced GDP significantly.[5]

Figure 28.2 presents the stock value traded as a share of GDP for the same countries and time period. The change in this indicator is even more pronounced: since the mid-1990s, it has risen in all countries. In the UK and especially in the US, the trading activity has picked up tremendously, exceeding GDP over three (the UK in 2008) or four times (the US in 2009).

A further dimension of financialization relates to the rise in financial activity and financial orientation pursued by non-financial corporations. The rise in the shareholder value movement as a concept of corporate governance changed managerial focus from the long-term growth objective of the firm to the short-term objective of favoring shareholders' interests (Stockhammer 2004; Lin & Tomaskovic-Devey 2013; Epstein 2015). The increase in non-financial corporations' engagement in financial activities is also reflected in the following data.

Figure 28.3 shows net dividends and net interest payments as a share of net operating surplus for US non-financial corporations from 1960 to 2010. Until the mid-1980s, dividend payments as a share of net operating surplus fluctuated around 20 percent; yet, by the mid-2000s it was over 40 percent. In contrast, net interest payments as a share of the net operating surplus has followed a downward trend since the early1990s—this is partly attributed to the high interest rate policy in the US. However, in 2000, the proportion of net interest payments recovered temporarily, reflecting high debt levels related to the 'new economy boom' (ECB 2012).

Moreover, non-financial corporations heavily relied on stock repurchases to increase stock prices. According to Lazonick (2010, 2011), between 2000 and 2009 S&P 500 companies spent 58

Percent

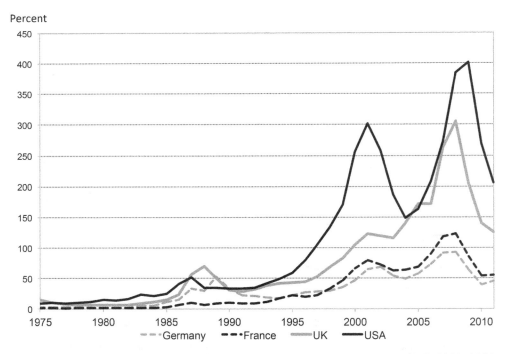

Figure 28.2 Stock value traded as a share of GDP: Germany, France, UK, and US, 1975–2011
Source: Beck *et al.* (2000; updated in 2013) author's calculation.

percent of their net income to repurchase their own stocks and disbursed 41 percent as dividends. According to the European Central Bank (ECB 2007), the increase in dividend payments and stock buybacks are also a common practice undertaken by firms in the Euro area. Moreover, it is reported that those non-financial companies investing in their own equity curtailed real investment in productive capacity. Taken together, non-financial corporations have replaced the old strategy of 'retain and invest' with 'downsize and distribute' (Lazonick & O'Sullivan 2000).

Finally, another aspect of financialization that appears in many OECD countries is the rise in debt in different sectors (Epstein 2015). Particularly household debt relative to disposable income has risen sharply, as illustrated in Table 28.1 for Germany, Greece, Japan, the UK, and the US for the years 1995, 2000, 2005, and 2010. All countries considered here have a tendency of rising debt ratios from the mid-1990s to the Great Recession. High household debt ratios are potential sources of instability, since in a recession it might be difficult to service debt (Stockhammer 2013).

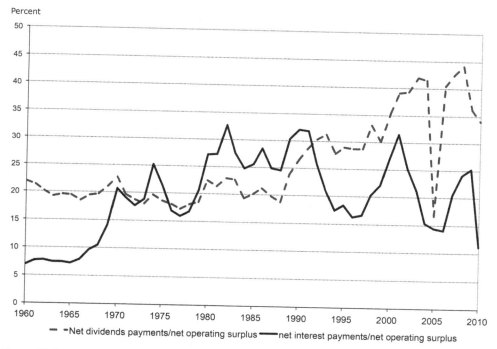

Figure 28.3 Net dividends and net interest payments as a share of net operating surplus of non-financial corporations: US, 1960–2010
Source: Bureau of Economic Analysis (BEA), NIPA tables; author's calculation.

Table 28.1 Household debts as a percentage of net disposable income

	Germany	Greece	Japan	UK	US
1995	97.21	–	137.36	–	94.47
2000	116.52	–	140.74	118.94	103.50
2005	108.10	63.0	137.88	167.16	134.58
2010	98.25	101.1	131.90	158.73	127.23

Source: OECD Financial Indicators 2015; Greece in OECD (2014).

Petra Dünhaupt

Financialization as a new stage of capitalism

The possibility of crises in the Marxian framework

Though Marx himself never developed a full-fledged crisis theory, he seems to "associate crises with the tendency for the rate of profit to fall, with tendencies to overproduction, underconsumption, disproportionality and overaccumulation with respect to labour" (Clarke 1994: 7). Central to Marxian macrotheory are the capitalist mode of production and the 'circuits of capital.' The mode of production is made by the forces and social relations of production, whereas the circuits of capital describe the stages of the capital accumulation process (Crotty 1986; Foley & Duménil 2008).

In the beginning of a production process (circuit one), the capitalist invests a certain amount of capital consisting of constant capital (M), the means of production, and variable capital, labor. During the production process (circuit two), the invested capital is transformed, creating surplus value—the value of the created commodity (C) exceeds the original value by a surplus. Finally, the commodities are sold and turned into money (M' and M' > M) (circuit three) (Marx 1887). From this follows Marx's famous short schema: M-C-M'.

Marxian crisis theories address the variables in the circuits of capital framework as well as the institutional foundations of the circuits (Kenway 1983; Crotty 1986; Evans 2004). There are three major mechanisms that supposedly lead to a crisis. The first mechanism relates to the tendency of the falling rate of profit. Following Marx's reasoning, during the capital accumulation process the organic composition of capital, which is defined as the ratio of constant capital to variable capital, increases. This, however, leads to a decline in the rate of profit, which is defined as the ratio of surplus value to total capital. Therefore, in the long-run, a rise in the organic composition of capital results in a fall in the rate of profit. The second mechanism potentially leading to a crisis relates to the distribution of income and under-consumption. Generally, workers spend all of their income on consumption. Hence, a redistribution of income at the expense of labor leads to a decline in demand for the produced commodities and, given the mismatch in supply and demand, ultimately to a failure to realize surplus value. The third mechanism potentially contributing to crisis relates to power relations. Here, a decline in the 'industrial reserve army' strengthens workers' bargaining power vis-à-vis capitalists, probably leading to higher wages. A rise in the share of labor income potentially contributes to a decline in the rate of profit—that is, a 'profit squeeze'—and hence to a fall in the rate of accumulation (Weisskopf 1992).

In the following, two schools of thought in the Marxian tradition, which consider financialization as the latest stage of capitalism, are examined in detail.

Social Structure of Accumulation theory

SSA theory conceptualizes capitalism in consecutive cycles, each lasting about 50–60 years. These cycles, or stages, are divided into phases of growth and stagnation. A crisis follows from stagnation; it constitutes the beginning of a new SSA (McDonough et al. 2010). SSA theory seeks to identify the institutional arrangements that support economic expansion. Here, institutions refer to a set of transnational and international organizations or customs—for example, the World Bank or the bargaining power of trade unions (Lippit 2010). SSA theorists describe their conceptualization as a mixture of Marxian and Keynesian economics. In line with Marxian economics, crisis tendencies emerge as a result of class struggle—that is, conflicts between capitalists and workers or within the capitalist class—and become an obstacle to further accumulation.

Similarly to Keynesian economics, SSA theory acknowledges that volatile investment decisions are shaped by expectation.

Recent work defines "SSA as a coherent, long-lasting institutional structure that promotes profit-making and serves as a framework for capital accumulation" (Kotz & McDonough 2010: 98). Based on this definition, Kotz & McDonough (2010) argue that since the early 1980s a new SSA—global neoliberalism—is in place. The neoliberal institutional structure is characterized by a free market ideology, which involves the demise of state regulatory structures and a shift of power from labor to capital. At a global level, the neoliberal SSA is characterized by a tremendous rise in cross-border movements of goods and capital, and the geographical extension of global production chains. At a domestic level, the neoliberal SSA changes the capital-labor relation; above all, the weakening of trade union bargaining power, while labor relations also change considerably. A further defining feature is a reconfiguration of the role of the state. The belief in the self-adjustment of markets has led to the dismantling of the welfare state, reducing tax rates, deregulation, and privatization of state-owned enterprises.

Kotz (2011) elaborates on historical circumstances that enabled the emergence of neoliberalism. The previous SSA is often referred to as 'regulated capitalism'[6] in which the state played an active role in regulating economic activity, both at the domestic and global level. Moreover, while welfare states were developing, there was a compromise between capital and labor (Kotz 2011). This SSA fell into a crisis in the 1970s. Consequently, it was replaced by the neoliberal SSA. According to Kotz (2011), the crisis of the 'regulated capitalism' SSA together with the rise in global economic integration, the belief in the free market doctrine, and the declining threat from the socialist countries are all key causes for the global neoliberal SSA to emerge. Further, he argues that the neoliberal institutional environment served as a favorable setting for financialization to develop.

Though neoliberalism and the deregulation of the financial sector paved the way for financialization, it is argued that "financialization is an ever-present tendency in corporate capitalism" (Kotz 2011: 15). In this view, financialization refers to the rise of the financial sector and its changing role. In the past, the financial sector's core business involved activities supporting the non-financial sector—for example, the provision of loan-based finance. During the neoliberal SSA, the financial industry detached itself from its core business and increasingly engaged in financial market-based activities. As a result, financial corporations increased their share in corporate profits.

SSA theory suggests that each stage of capitalism has a main contradiction with respect to economic growth, which eventually leads to a crisis (Kotz 2008, 2011). The contradictions of the neoliberal SSA are in one way or another related to financialization.

The institutional structure of the neoliberal SSA provides on the one hand a favorable environment for the creation of surplus value, while on the other hand it creates a problem for its realization, given the redistribution of income from labor to capital and the rise in income inequality. Two features that relate to financialization resolved the realization problem: first, the financial sector's increasing engagement in speculative and risky financial market activities, and second, the rising occurrence of asset price bubbles. The redistribution of income towards profits and the increase in top income shares resulted in a vast amount of investable funds, which exceeded available productive investment opportunities and hence contributed to the emergence of asset bubbles. In light of these asset bubbles, households' consumption was increasingly financed through debt and was based on the wealth effect (Kotz 2009).

Turning back to traditional Marxian crisis theories, at first glance the realization problem of surplus value during the neoliberal SSA appears as a crisis of under-consumption. However, the lack of demand was compensated by debt-financed consumption. Thus, the structural crisis of the neoliberal SSA can be considered as a crisis of over-investment (Kotz 2012). Over-investment refers to an excess demand for fixed capital in relation to the level of aggregate demand and can be prompted by asset bubbles. In light of rising debt-financed consumption by households, firms' investment in capital stock rises to match the increase in consumption demand. Further, firms' excess expectation regarding future profitability might also lead to a rise in investment spending. However, when the bubble bursts, firms' capacity to repay debts diminish and consumption spending declines, but excess fixed capital remains (Kotz 2013).

During the neoliberal SSA, economic growth was generated, on the one hand, by the rise in debt-financed consumption to compensate for wage stagnation caused by neoliberalism and, on the other hand, by financial speculation and asset bubbles. That said, economic expansion in the neoliberal era depends on debt and asset bubbles (Kotz 2008) and the world economic crisis seems to mark the end of the neoliberal SSA (Kotz 2011).

The Monthly Review school

The Monthly Review school relates financialization to economic stagnation. Inspired by Kalecki's work on monopolization and investment, Steindl (1952) seeks to explain economic stagnation by linking the emergence of oligopolistic industries to a reduction in investment expenditure and, hence, to a decline in overall economic activity. Baran & Sweezy (1966) further elaborate on the stagnation thesis. In their view, the emergence of large corporate enterprises in oligopolistic and monopolistic industries leads not only to widening profit margins but also to a rise in the overall profit share and economic surplus.[7] However, corporations face a dilemma. On the one hand, they seek to maximize profits and accumulate capital. On the other hand, they face problems in maintaining their profit margins and hence avoiding over-production and price reductions. Such a tendency results in a reduction in capacity utilization (Foster 2007). Ultimately, the economy falls into stagnation. Though monopolistic corporate enterprises generate huge surpluses, investment in capital stock remains low.

According to Foster & McChesney (2009), since the early 1970s, a crisis of over-accumulation and stagnation has appeared repeatedly, while at the same time the 'financial superstructure' has been growing. From the 1970s onwards, corporations started to channel surpluses into financial products instead of investing in fixed capital goods (Magdoff & Sweezy 1987). The money that was channeled into financial markets contributed to asset price inflation. Due to low investment in capital stock, growth was mainly generated through the debt-financed consumption of the household sector via the 'wealth effect.' Debt levels of other sectors of the economy increased as well, which led to a rise in instability of the economy as a whole (Foster 2008).

Foster (2006, 2007, 2008, 2010a, b) argues that by the late 1970s, capitalism entered a new phase, which he calls 'monopoly-finance capital.' The defining features of this phase are, among others, the accelerating increase in financial bubbles and financial speculation. Though profits of financial corporations have risen as a share of total corporate profits, Foster argues that the divide between financial and non-financial corporations has become less clear, given the increasing reliance of non-financial corporations on financial activities. Moreover, he observes the rise in income inequality as another defining feature, which generates a rise in households' indebtedness induced by stagnating or falling real wages. According to Foster (2007), a more unequal distribution of income is a prerequisite for the functioning of monopoly-finance capital, given the "demand for new cash infusions to keep speculative bubbles expanding." Foster (2007) thus regards neoliberalism as "the ideological counterpart of monopoly-finance capital" reflecting "to some extent the new imperatives of capital brought on by financial globalization."

In summary, the main argument brought forward by the Monthly Review school is that it is stagnation that generates financialization. The genuine problem from this perspective is "the system of class exploitation rooted in production" (Foster 2008). Recalling Marx's schema, it appears that M leads to M′, leaving out the production of commodities (Foster & McChesney 2009).

Destabilizing factors in the Post Keynesian school

Post Keynesian economics rests on the principle of effective demand, which determines the level of output and employment. Fundamental uncertainty and expectations are defining features of the capitalist monetary production economy, which is shaped by social norms and institutions. Class and power relations determine income and wealth distribution (Arestis 1996; Stockhammer 2015b). With these core theoretical and methodological commitments, it follows that there are three main forces that can potentially destabilize the economy (Goda 2013): an increase in uncertainty, the endogeneity of money and financial fragility, and changes in income distribution.

In a world of fundamental uncertainty, entrepreneurs' investment decisions are subject to expectations about future profitability. In an uncertain monetary production economy, individuals might restrain from consumption and investment and hold their money in liquid assets (Ferrari-Filho & Camargo Conceicao 2005).

Hyman Minsky (1986) developed the financial instability hypothesis that links the role of pro-cyclical credit to the business cycle, and that increasing instability renders an economy prone to crisis. When an economy is booming, investors become more optimistic about their future investments and, therefore, they are keen to borrow and credit expands. The lenders also have positive expectations about the future and become more willing to lend, even for high-risk investment projects. Minsky emphasizes the behavior of borrowers who increase their debts during the boom to buy assets. The underlying motive is to exploit short-term capital gains that result from the difference in increasing asset prices and the interest rates paid on the borrowed funds. However, the investors' sentiments change when the economy slows down, because the interest paid on the borrowed funds might possibly exceed the increase in asset prices. Borrowers start to sell off their assets. During an economic downturn, the demand for credit decreases as the investors' expectations of the future become more pessimistic. This causes both borrowers and lenders to proceed with greater caution (Kindleberger & Aliber 2005). Consequently, financial fragility might arise and an economy moves from 'hedge finance' through 'speculative finance' and finally ends with 'Ponzi finance' (Minsky 1986).

Further disruptions might emerge from changes in the distribution of income. In Post Keynesian models of distribution and growth, the redistribution between wages and profits feeds back on consumption demand, given different propensities to save from rentiers', managers', and workers' income, thereby, affecting overall aggregate demand and growth (Hein 2010; Hein & van Treeck 2010a, b; Onaran et al. 2011). However, redistribution also impacts on firms' investment through different channels, either directly or indirectly via profits or capacity utilization. Based on these contradictory effects of redistribution between capital and labor, Bhaduri & Marglin (1990) argue that aggregate demand and long-run growth may either be 'wage-led' or 'profit-led.' In recent years, multiple studies based on this framework show that in the medium- to long-term, demand in most OECD countries seems to be wage-led (see, for example, Naastepad & Storm 2007; Hein & Vogel 2008). Therefore, a decline in labor's income share partially causes a reduction in aggregate demand and growth.

The macroeconomics of financialization

Like Marxian theories delineated above, a view that capitalist development is divided into historical stages is inherent to the Post Keynesian approach. The most recent phase of capitalism is often referred to as 'finance-dominated' or 'money manager' capitalism. In this framework, financialization is defined as a combination of three phenomena: a rise in shareholder value orientation of the firm, redistribution of income and wealth in favor of shareholders and managers at the expense of ordinary workers and employees, and more opportunities for debt-financed consumption (van Treeck 2012).

On theoretical grounds, it is argued that financialization might impact investment, consumption, and distribution. With regard to firms' investment in capital stock, it is argued that an increase in shareholder value orientation might have two effects on the management. First, given shareholders' increasing demand for higher dividends, internal funds necessary for investment purposes decline. Moreover, investment is increasingly financed through debt, leading to rising obligations in interest payments.[8] Second, the alignment of shareholders' and managers' interests through variable remuneration in the form of stock options changes managerial preferences from high growth rates to high short-term profitability. Thereby, financialization depresses management's animal spirits (Hein 2010). In regard to consumption, financialization has opened up the possibilities for consumption based on the wealth effect and financed by debt. Finally, it is argued that financialization impacts on the distribution of income. Regarding functional income distribution, it is argued that at least in the medium-term, shareholders' rising demand for dividend payouts come at the expense of the share of wages in national income. This notion is based on Kalecki's mark-up pricing theory, which assumes that in the medium-term the markup is dividend-elastic. Hence firms are able to increase dividend payments, which constitute an increase in overhead costs and in the mark-up (Hein 2014).

With regard to investment, empirical evidence lends support to the hypothesis that financialization has indeed contributed to a slowdown in accumulation through the 'preference channel' and 'internal means of finance channel.' Firms that pursue short-term profits substitute financial investment for real investment in capital stock (Stockhammer 2004; Orhangazi 2008). Moreover, real investment is also dampened by a rise in interest and dividend payments (Orhangazi 2008; van Treeck 2008). However, the negative impact of financialization on real investment seems to concern larger firms rather than small firms (Davis 2013).

Empirical studies also show that the 'wealth effect' of either stock market or housing price changes substantially alters consumer spending (Slacalek 2009; Sousa 2009). However, regional differences exist. The wealth effect from changing house prices appears to be more relevant in Anglo-Saxon countries compared to countries like France, Germany, Spain, and Japan (Girouard et al. 2006).

There seems to be a consensus in the literature that rising household indebtedness is related to income inequality (Kumhof & Ranciere 2010; Rajan 2010). In times of stagnating or declining incomes, households increasingly go into debt to maintain their standard of living (Goldstein 2012) and to finance conspicuous consumption in order to 'keep up with the Joneses' (Frank 2007). At the same time, households took advantage of new financial opportunities to finance consumption. It is argued that the rise in borrowing reflects a broader transformation in household behavior towards more risk taking. Empirical evidence suggests that household indebtedness and the use of financial products has risen among all income recipients (Fligstein & Goldstein 2015).

Empirical studies suggest that financialization also has an impact upon income distribution. First, in most OECD countries, financialization favors property owners, which is measured by a rise in rentiers' income shares (Power *et al.* 2003; Epstein & Jayadev 2005; Dünhaupt 2012). Moreover, it appears that financialization has also contributed to the decline in labor's share of income (Lin & Tomaskovic-Devey 2013; Köhler *et al.* 2015; Stockhammer 2015a; Dünhaupt 2017) and to the rise in personal income inequality (Kus 2012; Dünhaupt 2014).

Post Keynesians have incorporated elements of financialization into macroeconomic models of distribution and growth. The crux of their analysis is the development of functional income distribution and the responsiveness of consumption out of labor and rentier income, and the investment activity of corporations.[9] According to Post Keynesian theory, different growth regimes can emerge under financialization with more or less favorable outcomes (Boyer 2000; Hein 2012). In a 'finance-led growth' regime, the spread of the shareholder value doctrine has a positive effect on growth—although redistribution from labor to rentier income takes place, consumption remains strong due to a high propensity to consume out of rentiers' income and due to debt-financed consumption related to a strong wealth effect. Moreover, investment is stimulated via the accelerator mechanism. The second growth regime is called 'profits without investment' that resembles the first regime with the only difference being that there is no stimulation of investment. The third growth regime is called the 'contractive' regime. As the name suggests, the rise in firms' payout ratio has a negative effect on capacity utilization, profit, and capital accumulation. Moreover, consumption remains low in this regime (Hein 2014).

Empirical studies suggest that before the 2007 crisis many OECD countries pursued a 'profits without investment' regime, which is characterized by rising levels of profits in spite of weak real investment (van Treeck *et al.* 2007; van Treeck & Sturn 2012; Hein & Mundt 2012; Hein 2014).

From a macroeconomic perspective, a 'profits without investment' regime is only possible if demand is generated by another component—that is, consumption, government deficits, or export surpluses. This becomes apparent from Kalecki's (1965: 49) famous profit equation:

Gross profits net of taxes = Gross investment + Export surplus + Budget deficit − Workers' saving + Capitalists' consumption

Since the early 1980s in the US GDP growth has been mainly driven by private consumption, whereas investment in capital stock has increased rather moderately, except during the New Economy boom in the late 1990s. Hence, until the Great Recession, US growth relied mainly on debt-led consumption, expansionary fiscal policy, and capital imports. According to Palley (2009), Minsky's financial instability hypothesis can be considered an explanation as to why the US economy did not end up in stagnation much earlier: the tremendous rise in borrowing was enabled by financial innovation and deregulation, which increased financial fragility.

However, the debt-led consumption boom growth model was practiced by not only the US but also other countries, such as the UK, Spain, Ireland, and Greece. Falling labor income shares and low investment in capital stock are associated with another growth model, 'export-led mercantilist,' which emerged in other countries. Countries that relied on this growth model experienced only weak domestic demand and were strongly dependent on international trade, running current account surpluses. Here, Japan and Germany are prominent examples (Hein 2012).[10]

Both growth models contributed to the rise in global imbalances until the beginning of the Great Recession in 2008–09. Enabled by the liberalization of international capital markets and the removal of capital controls, countries that pursue the 'debt-led consumption boom' strategy depend, on the one hand, on global markets' credit supply resulting in current account deficits. On the other hand, those countries also depend on domestic demand through borrowing by households against rising house and asset prices. 'Export-led mercantilist' countries, however, run current account surpluses and depend strongly on global demand.

Many Post Keynesians argue that in light of falling labor shares and rising income inequality, financialization fostered the emergence of these highly fragile growth regimes through its effects on investment and consumption (see, for example, Hein 2012; Hein & Mundt 2012; van Treeck & Sturn 2012; Stockhammer 2013). The world economic and financial crisis that started in the US in 2007 has undermined the sustainability of both systems. Apparently, the debt-led consumption boom came to a halt, as household indebtedness became unsustainable. On the flipside, export-mercantilist countries were affected as well, given the decline in global demand and the devaluation of their capital exports (Hein 2014).

Comparative summary

The topic of financialization encompasses many themes and can be addressed from a number of angles. The purpose of this chapter has been to review and introduce the literature focusing on financialization as the latest stage of capitalism. All heterodox approaches considered here agree that since the late 1970s or early 1980s capitalism has entered a new stage—'global neoliberalism,' 'monopoly finance capitalism,' or 'finance-led capitalism.' It is apparent that each heterodox approach has a special focus of attention.

The basic narrative in all approaches draws on the same elements. First, in the era of neoliberalism and financialization, wages stagnate and income is redistributed from labor to capital. However, the rise in income inequality does not lead to a decline in consumption demand and a crisis of under-consumption. Second, consumption demand is debt-financed along with asset price inflation. At the same time, the financial sector is liberalized and deregulated and financial speculation increases.

While the basic narrative is quite similar, major differences stem from both the relationship between neoliberalism and financialization and the question of whether financialization can be considered as a cause or effect.

Proponents of the SSA theory argue that neoliberalism is the main characteristic of the recent phase of capitalism. According to this view, neoliberalism fosters the emergence of inequality, the shift in financial practices, and asset bubbles. While a crisis of under-consumption could be avoided by the rise of debt-financed consumption, a crisis of over-accumulation of fixed capital emerges. The latter can be considered as a crisis of capitalism in general. Furthermore, it is argued that "financialization is an ever-present tendency in corporate capitalism and, once neoliberalism released the constraints against it, it developed rapidly in the favorable neoliberal institutional context" (Kotz 2011: 15). Even though neoliberalism is identified as the root problem which allowed financialization to appear and which furthered a structural crisis of capitalism, it is argued that a reversal towards a more social-democratic form of capitalism is insufficient, since it is capitalism as an economic system *per se* that is inherently unstable.

The position of the Monthly Review school is reminiscent of the position taken by SSA theory in the sense that the contradictions of capitalism are considered the main problem. In the era of monopoly-finance capitalism, the high degree of monopolization and industrial maturity result in deep-seated stagnation tendencies. Consumption and investment are not sufficient to absorb the high surpluses that are generated. These surpluses are channeled into debt-leveraged speculation. It is argued that capitalist economies are trapped in a circle of stagnation and financialization. In contrast to proponents of the SSA School, the Monthly Review school argues that it is financialization that leads to neoliberalism. Financialization is a response to a stagnation-prone economy, while neoliberalism is the ideological counterpart of monopoly-finance capitalism. More importantly, there is no cure to the system, since "the fault is in the system" (Foster & McChesney 2010).

For Post Keynesians, financialization and neoliberalism are two complementary concepts. According to Palley (2013: 1),

> financialization corresponds to financial neoliberalism which is characterized by domination of the macro economy and economic policy by financial sector interests. According to this definition, financialization is a particular form of neoliberalism. That means neoliberalism is the driving force behind financialization and the latter cannot be understood without an understanding of the former.

In this view, the rise of finance emanates from the deregulation and liberalization of the financial (and economic) system. That is to say, financialization is the cause rather than the effect. Financialization affects the macroeconomy via four channels—income distribution, investment in capital stock, household debt, and net exports and current account balances. In light of falling labor income shares and depressed investment in capital stock, Post Keynesians argue that 'profits without investment' regimes emerged, which are either driven by debt-led consumption or rising export surpluses. Both regimes, however, are prone to crisis. As a remedy, it is argued that economic structures dominated by financialization should be addressed on four dimensions: re-regulation and downsizing of the financial sector, redistribution of income from top to bottom and from capital to labor, re-orientation of macroeconomic policies towards stabilizing domestic demand at non-inflationary full employment levels, and re-creation of international monetary and economic policy coordination.[11]

Notes

1 As highlighted by Albritton (1986), there are many more categorizations of capitalist history; for example, the classification into competitive and monopoly capitalism or laissez-faire, monopoly, and state monopoly capitalism.

2 For an excellent review of the French *Régulation*, Social Structure of Accumulation, and Post Keynesian approaches, see Hein et al. (2015). See also Lapavitsas (2011, 2013) for a review of economic and sociological literature on financialization and his own analysis of financialization, which draws on classical Marxism.

3 BEA NIPA Table 6.16. Available at http://www.bea.gov/national/nipaweb/DownSS2.asp. See also Crotty (2007).

4 See FESSUD Studies in Financial Systems. http://fessud.eu/studies-in-financial-systems/

5 Part of this rise can be attributed to the increase in financial innovation and the introduction of new financial instruments (see Grabel 1997).

6 The regulated capitalist SSA, which is also called 'post-war SSA,' lasted from the end of World War II until the late 1970s. Many authors (Gordon et al. 1987; Wolfson & Kotz 2010) argue that the crisis of the post-war SSA was one of profit squeeze, brought about by a relative rise in labor's power and rising real wages.

7 Economic surplus is defined as the difference between "what a society produces and the costs of producing it" (Baran & Sweezy 1966: 9).

8 This theoretical claim is called into question by recent research. See, for example, Jo (2015) and Kliman & Williams (2015).

9 Certainly, financialization might also impact on aggregate demand and growth via its direct effects on consumption and investment behavior. Further influences are related to macroeconomic policies, government demand management, and the overall macroeconomic policy regime (see Hein & Mundt 2012).

10 A very good overview and a range of specific country studies on this topic are provided by Hein et al. (2016).

11 Compare Hein (2016) and the literature quoted in the document.

References

Albritton, R. 1986. 'Stages of capitalist development.' *Studies in Political Economy*, 19 (Spring): 113–139.

Arestis, P. 1996. 'Post-Keynesian economics: towards coherence.' *Cambridge Journal of Economics*, 20 (1): 111–135.

Baran, P. & Sweezy, P. 1966. *Monopoly Capital*. New York: Monthly Review Press.

Beck, T., Demirgüç-Kunt, A., & Levine, R. 2000. 'A new database on financial development and structure.' *World Bank Economic Review*, 14 (3): 597–605.

Bhaduri, A. & Marglin, S. 1990. 'Unemployment and the real wage: the economic basis for contesting political ideologies.' *Cambridge Journal of Economics*, 14 (4): 375–393.

Boyer, R. 2000. 'Is a finance-led growth regime a viable alternative to Fordism? A preliminary analysis.' *Economy and Society*, 29 (1): 111–145.

Clarke, S. 1994. *Marx's Theory of Crisis*. Basingstoke, UK: Macmillan Press.

Crotty, J. 1986. 'Marx, Keynes and Minsky on the instability of the capitalist growth process and the nature of government economic policy,' in: D. Bramhall & S. Helburn (eds.), *Marx, Keynes and Schumpeter: A Centenary Celebration of Dissent*. Armonk, NY: M.E Sharpe, 297–326.

Crotty, J. 2007. If financial market competition is so intense, why are financial firm profits so high? Reflections on the current 'golden age' of finance. PERI Working Paper No. 134.

Davis, L. 2013. Financialization and the nonfinancial corporation: an investigation of firm-level investment behavior in the U.S., 1971–2011. University of Massachusetts Amherst Working Paper 2013–08.

Detzer, D., Dodig, N., Evans, T., Hein, E., & Herr, H. 2013. The German financial system. FESSUD Studies in Financial Systems No. 3.

Dünhaupt, P. 2012. 'Financialization and the rentier income share–evidence from the USA and Germany.' *International Review of Applied Economics*, 26 (4): 465–487.

Dünhaupt, P. 2014. An empirical assessment of the contribution of financialization and corporate governance to the rise in income inequality. IPE Working Paper 41/2014.

Dünhaupt, P. 2017. 'Determinants of labor's income share in the era of financialisation.' *Cambridge Journal of Economics*, 41 (1): 283–306.

Dore, R. 2008. 'Financialization of the global economy.' *Industrial and Corporate Change*, 17 (6): 1097–1112.

ECB. 2007. 'Share buybacks in the Euro area.' *European Central Bank Monthly Bulletin*, May: 103–111.

ECB. 2012. 'Corporate indebtedness in the euro area.' *European Central Bank Monthly Bulletin*, February: 87–103.

Epstein, G. (ed.) 2005. *Financialization and the World Economy*. Cheltenham, UK: Edward Elgar.

Epstein, G. 2015. Financialization: there's something happening here. PERI Working Paper No. 394.

Epstein, G. & Jayadev, A. 2005. 'The rise of rentier incomes in OECD countries: Financialization, central bank policy and labor solidarity,' in: G. Epstein (ed.), *Financialization and the World Economy*. Cheltenham, UK: Edward Elgar, 46–74.

Evans, T. 2004. 'Marxian and post-Keynesian theories of finance and the business cycle.' *Capital & Class*, 28 (2): 47–100.

Ferrari-Filho, F. & Camargo Conseicao, O.A. 2005. 'The concept of uncertainty in Post Keynesian theory and in institutional economics.' *Journal of Economic Issues*, 39 (3): 579–594.

Fligstein, N. & Goldstein, A. 2015. 'The emergence of a finance culture in American households, 1989–2007.' *Socio-Economic Review*, 13 (3): 575–601.

Foley, D. & Duménil, G. 2008. 'Marxian transformation problem,' in: S.N. Durlauf & L.E. Blume (eds.), *The New Palgrave Dictionary of Economics*, 2nd online edn. Palgrave Macmillan.

Foster, J.B. 2006. 'Monopoly-finance capital.' *Monthly Review*, 58 (7). Available from http://monthlyreview.org/2006/12/01/monopoly-finance-capital [Accessed April 26, 2016]

Foster, J.B. 2007. 'The financialization of capitalism.' *Monthly Review*, 58 (11). Available from http://monthlyreview.org/2007/04/01/the-financialization-of-capitalism/ [Accessed April 26, 2016]

Foster, J.B. 2008. 'The financialization of capital and the crisis.' *Monthly Review*, 59 (11). Available from http://monthlyreview.org/2008/04/01/the-financialization-of-capital-and-the-crisis [Accessed April 26, 2016]

Foster, J.B. 2010a. 'The age of monopoly-finance capital.' *Monthly Review*, 61 (9). Available from http://monthlyreview.org/2010/02/01/the-age-of-monopoly-finance-capital [Accessed April 26, 2016]

Foster, J.B. 2010b. 'The financialization of accumulation.' *Monthly Review*, 62 (5). Available from http://monthlyreview.org/2010/10/01/the-financialization-of-accumulation [Accessed April 26, 2016]

Foster, J.B. & McChesney, R.W. 2009. 'Monopoly-finance capital and the paradox of accumulation.' *Monthly Review*, 61 (5). Available from http://monthlyreview.org/2009/10/01/monopoly-finance-capital-and-the-paradox-of-accumulation [Accessed April 26, 2016]

Foster, J.B. & McChesney, R.W. 2010. 'Listen Keynesians, it's the system! Response to Palley.' *Monthly Review*, 61 (11). Available from https://monthlyreview.org/2010/04/01/listen-keynesians-its-the-system-response-to-palley/ [Accessed April 26, 2016]

Frank, R. 2007. *Falling Behind: How Rising Inequality Harms the Middle Class*. Berkeley, CA: University of California Press.

Girouard, N., Kennedy, M., van den Noord, P., & André, C. 2006. Recent house price developments: the role of fundamentals. OECD Economics Department Working Paper, No. 475.

Goda, T. 2013. The role of income inequality in crisis theories and in the subprime crisis. Post Keynesian Economics Study Group Working Paper 1305.

Goldstein, A. 2012. Income, consumption, and household indebtedness in the U.S., 1989–2007. Department of Sociology, University of California. Unpublished Manuscript.

Gordon, D., Weisskopf, T., & Bowles, S. 1987. 'Power, accumulation and crisis: the rise and demise of the postwar social structure of accumulation,' *in*: R. Cherry, C. D'Onofrio, C. Kurdas, T. Michl, F. Moseley, & M.I. Naples (eds.), *The Imperiled Economy: Book I: Macroeconomics from a Left Perspective*. New York: Union for Radical Political Economics, 43–58.

Grabel, I. 1997. 'Savings, investment, and functional efficiency: a comparative examination of national financial complexes,' *in*: R. Pollin (ed.), *The Macroeconomics of Saving, Finance and Investment*. Ann Arbor, MI: The University of Michigan Press, 251–297.

Greenwood, R. & Scharfstein, D. 2013. 'The growth of finance.' *Journal of Economic Perspectives*, 27 (2): 3–28.

Hein, E. 2010. 'Shareholder value orientation, distribution and growth: short- and medium-run effects in a Kaleckian model.' *Metroeconomica*, 61 (2): 302–332.

Hein, E. 2012. *The Macroeconomics of Finance-Dominated Capitalism – And Its Crisis*. Cheltenham, UK: Edward Elgar.

Hein, E. 2014. *Distribution and Growth after Keynes: A Post-Keynesian Guide*. Cheltenham, UK: Edward Elgar.

Hein, E. 2016. Causes and consequences of the financial crisis and the implications for a more resilient financial and economic system. IPE Working Paper 61/2016.

Hein, E. & Mundt, M. 2012. Financialisation and the requirements and potentials for wage-led recovery: a review focusing on the G20. Conditions of Work and Employment Series No. 37, International Labour Organisation.

Hein, E. & van Treeck, T. 2010a. "Financialisation' in post-Keynesian models of distribution and growth: a systematic review,' *in*: M. Setterfield (ed.), *Handbook of Alternative Theories of Economic Growth*. Cheltenham, UK: Edward Elgar, 277–292.

Hein, E. & van Treeck, T. 2010b. "Financialisation' and rising shareholder power in Kaleckian/post-Kaleckian models of distribution and growth.' *Review of Political Economy*, 22 (2): 205–233.

Hein, E. & Vogel, L. 2008. 'Distribution and growth reconsidered: empirical results for six OECD countries.' *Cambridge Journal of Economics*, 32 (3): 479–511.

Hein, E., Detzer, D., & Dodig, N. (eds.) 2016. *Financialization and the Financial and Economic Crisis: Country Studies*. Cheltenham, UK: Edward Elgar.

Hein, E., Dodig, N., & Budyldina, N. 2015. 'The transition towards finance-dominated capitalism: French Regulation School, Social Structures of Accumulation and post-Keynesian approaches compared,' *in*: E. Hein, D. Detzer, & N. Dodig (eds.), *The Demise of Finance-dominated Capitalism: Explaining the Financial and Economic Crises*. Cheltenham, UK: Edward Elgar, 7–53.

Jo, T.-H. 2015. 'Financing investment under fundamental uncertainty and instability: a heterodox microeconomic view.' *Bulletin of Political Economy*, 9 (1): 33–54.

Kalecki, M. 1965. *Theory of Economic Dynamics*, 2nd edn. London: George Allen and Unwin.

Kenway, P. 1983. 'Marx, Keynes and the possibility of crisis,' *in*: J. Eatwell & M. Milgate (eds.), *Keynes's Economics and the Theory of Value and Distribution*. New York: Oxford University Press, 149–166.

Kindleberger, C & Aliber, R. 2005. *Maniacs, Panics, and Crashes. A History of Financial Crises*, 5th edn. Hoboken, NJ: John Wiley & Sons.

Kliman, A. & Williams, S.D. 2015. 'Why 'financialization' hasn't depressed US productive investment.' *Cambridge Journal of Economics*, 39 (1): 67–92.

Köhler, K., Guschanski, A., & Stockhammer, E. 2015. How does financialization affect functional income distribution? A theoretical clarification and empirical assessment. Kingston University Economics Discussion Paper 2015-5.

Kotz, D. 2008. 'Contradictions of economic growth in the neoliberal era: accumulation and crisis in the contemporary U.S. economy.' *Review of Radical Political Economics*, 40 (2): 174–188.

Kotz, D. 2009. 'The financial and economic crisis of 2008: a systemic crisis of neoliberal capitalism.' *Review of Radical Political Economics*, 41 (3): 305–317.

Kotz, D. 2011. 'Financialization and neoliberalism,' *in*: G. Teeple & S. McBride (eds.), *Relations of Global Power: Neoliberal Order and Disorder*. Toronto: University of Toronto Press.

Kotz, D. 2012. Social structures of accumulation, the rate of profit, and economic crises. PERI Working Paper No. 329. University of Massachusetts Amherst.

Kotz, D. 2013. 'The current economic crisis in the U.S.: a crisis of over-investment.' *Review of Radical Political Economics*, 45 (3) 284–294.

Kotz, D. & McDonough, T. 2010. 'Global neoliberalism and the contemporary social structure of accumulation,' *in*: T. McDonough, M. Reich, & D. Kotz (eds.), *Contemporary Capitalism and its Crises: Social Structure of Accumulation Theory for the 21st Century*. New York: Cambridge University Press, 93–120.

Kriesler, P. 2013. 'Post-Keynesian perspectives on economic development and growth,' *in*: G.C. Harcourt & P. Kriesler (eds.), *The Oxford Handbook of Post-Keynesian Economics, Volume 1: Theory and Origins*. New York: Oxford University Press, 539–555.

Kumhof, M. & Ranciere, R. 2010. Inequality, leverage and crises. IMF Working Paper 10/268.

Kus, B. 2012. 'Financialisation and income inequality in OECD nations: 1995–2007.' *The Economic and Social Review*, 43 (4): 477–495.

Lapavitsas, C. 2011. 'Theorizing financialization.' *Work, Employment and Society*, 25 (4): 611–626.

Lapavitsas, C. 2013. 'The financialization of capitalism: 'profits without producing'.' *City: Analysis of Urban Trends, Culture, Theory, Policy, Action*, 17 (6): 792–805.

Lazonick, W. 2010. 'The explosion of executive pay and the erosion of American prosperity.' *Entreprises et Histoire*, 57: 141–164.

Lazonick, W. 2011. The innovative enterprise and the developmental state: toward an economics of 'organizational success.' Paper presented at the conference of the Institute for New Economic Thinking, Bretton Woods, NH, April 10.

Lazonick, W. & O'Sullivan, M. 2000. 'Maximizing shareholder value: a new ideology for corporate governance.' *Economy and Society*, 29 (1): 13–35.

Lin, K.-H. & Tomaskovic-Devey, D. 2013. 'Financialization and US income inequality 1970–2008.' *American Journal of Sociology*, 118 (5): 1284–1329.

Lippit, V. 2010. 'Social structure of accumulation theory,' *in*: T. McDonough, M. Reich, & D. Kotz, (eds.), *Contemporary Capitalism and its Crises: Social Structure of Accumulation Theory for the 21st Century*. New York: Cambridge University Press, 45–71.

Magdoff, H. & Sweezy, P.M. 1987. *Stagnation and the Financial Explosion*. New York: Monthly Review Press.

Marx, K. 1887. *Capital: A Critique of Political Economy, Volume 1*. Moscow: Progress Publisher.

McDonough, T., Reich, M., & Kotz, D. 2010. 'Introduction: social structure of accumulation theory for the 21st Century,' *in*: T. McDonough, M. Reich, & D. Kotz (eds.), *Contemporary Capitalism and its Crises: Social Structure of Accumulation Theory for the 21st Century*. New York: Cambridge University Press, 1–8.

Minsky, H. 1986. *Stabilizing an Unstable Economy*. New Haven, CT: Yale University Press.

Naastepad, C.W.M. & Storm, S. 2007. 'OECD demand regimes (1960–2000).' *Journal of Post Keynesian Economics*, 29 (2): 211–246.

OECD. 2015. Financial indicators. Available from https://stats.oecd.org/Index.aspx?DataSetCode=FIN_IND_FBS [Accessed April 26, 2016]

OECD. 2014. 'Household debt,' *in*: *Nationals Accounts at a Glance 2014*. Paris: OECD Publishing, 80–81.

Onaran, Ö., Stockhammer, E., & Grafl, L. 2011. 'Financialization, distribution, and aggregate demand in the US.' *Cambridge Journal of Economics*, 35 (4): 637–662.

Orhangazi, Ö. 2008. 'Financialisation and capital accumulation in the non-financial corporate sector: a theoretical and empirical investigation on the US economy: 1973–2003.' *Cambridge Journal of Economics*, 32 (6): 863–886.

Palley, T. 2009. The limits of Minsky's financial instability hypothesis as an explanation of the crisis. IMK Working Paper 11/2009.

Palley, T. 2013. *Financialization: The Economics of Finance Capital Domination*. New York: Palgrave Macmillan.

Philippon, T. & Reshel, A. 2013. 'An international look at the growth of modern finance.' *Journal of Economic Perspectives*, 27 (2): 73-96.

Power, D., Epstein, G., & Abrena, M. 2003. Trends in rentier incomes in OECD countries. 1960–2000. PERI Working Paper No. 58a.

Rajan, R. 2010. *Fault Lines: How Hidden Fractures Still Threaten The World Economy*. Princeton, NJ: Princeton University Press.

Slacalek, J. 2009. What drives personal consumption? The role of housing and financial wealth. ECB Working Paper, No. 1117.

Steindl, J. [1952] 1976. *Maturity and Stagnation.* New York: Monthly Review Press.

Sousa, R. 2009. Wealth effects on consumption: evidence from the Euro area. ECB Working Paper, No. 1050.

Stockhammer, E. 2004. 'Financialisation and the slowdown of accumulation.' *Cambridge Journal of Economics,* 28 (5): 719–741.

Stockhammer, E. 2013. 'Financialization and the global economy,' *in*: M. Wolfson & G. Epstein (eds.), *The Handbook of the Political Economy of Financial Crises.* New York: Oxford University Press, 512–525.

Stockhammer, E. 2015a. 'Determinants of the wage share: a panel analysis of advanced and developing countries.' *British Journal of Industrial Relations.* doi: 10.1111/bjir.12165.

Stockhammer, E. 2015b. Neoliberal growth models, monetary union and the Euro crisis: a Post-Keynesian perspective. Post Keynesian Economics Study Group Working Paper 1510.

van Treeck, T. 2008. 'Reconsidering the investment-profit nexus in finance-led economies: an ARDL-based approach.' *Metroeconomica,* 59 (3): 371–404.

van Treeck, T. 2012. 'Financialization,' *in*: J. King (ed.), *The Elgar Companion to Post Keynesian Economics,* 2nd edn. Northampton, MA: Edward Elgar.

van Treeck, T. & Sturn, S. 2012. Income inequality as a cause of the great recession? A survey of current debates. Conditions of Work and Employment Series No. 39, International Labour Organisation.

van Treeck, T., Hein, E., & Dünhaupt. P. 2007. Finanzsystem und wirtschaftliche Entwicklung, neuere Tendenzen in den USA und in Deutschland. IMK Studies 5/2007.

Wallerstein, I. 1974. 'The rise and future demise of the world capitalist system: concepts for comparative analysis.' *Comparative Studies in Society and History,* 16 (4): 387–415.

Weisskopf, T. 1992. 'Marxian crisis theory and the contradictions of late twentieth-century capitalism.' *Rethinking Marxism,* 4 (4): 368–391.

Wolfson, M & Kotz, D. 2010. 'A reconceptualization of social structure of accumulation theory,' *in*: T. McDonough, M. Reich, & D. Kotz (eds.), *Contemporary Capitalism and its Crises—Social Structure of Accumulation Theory for the 21st Century.* New York: Cambridge University Press, 72–90.

29

Theories of international development
The Post Keynesian and Marxian alternatives

John Marangos

Introduction

In 1989, John Williamson (1990) presented the term 'Washington Consensus' (WC) to describe the consensus between the Washington-based United States Executive Branch, the International Monetary Fund (IMF) and the World Bank (WB). These three entities are the main financiers of developing economies. Originally, the WC term was associated with the policies and conditionalities imposed by 'Washington' upon Latin America. Subsequently, the perceived 'success' in Latin America gained international appeal, making the WC the dominant set of policies and conditionalities for international development. Nevertheless, the WC evolved as a prescription for international development under the burden of condemnation, assessment, and ever-changing economic conditions. By 2003, the WC policy-set for international development was modified. Accordingly, Kuczynski & Williamson (2003) substituted the original term with a new name, 'After the Washington Consensus' (AWC), designating a supposedly 'new' set of policy reforms for developing economies which did not significantly deviate from the original WC.

Williamson (1990) identifies ten WC policy instruments regarding fiscal discipline, public expenditure priorities, tax reform, financial liberalization, exchange rates, trade liberalization, foreign direct investment, privatization, deregulation, property rights, and institution building. The AWC is an attempt to remedy the defects of the original WC while maintaining its fundamental tenets. Even though the original goal of the AWC was to accelerate economic growth, the goal was expanded to include improving income distribution. It appears that there is significant but incomplete overlap between the WC and AWC; some reforms are the same, while others were added in the AWC, such as institution building, income distribution, and the social sector.

The dominance of the WC and the AWC for international development is based on mainstream economics and has been imposed by Washington upon debt-stranded developing countries. Consequently, there is a need for an alternative to the static mainstream model of international development. The purpose of this chapter is to develop dynamic alternative schemes and recommendations for international development based on heterodox economics, in particular pulling from the Post Keynesian and Marxian traditions.

The Post Keynesian approach to international development

Post Keynesians reject the WC and AWC reforms due to the conditions surrounding their implementation, the content of the policies, and the rapid pace at which they are implemented. Post Keynesians argue that debt-ridden developing countries are effectively blackmailed into applying austere macroeconomic discipline and free markets policies which are at the root of economic crises.

From a Post Keynesian standpoint, the AWC and WC are unrealistic and impractical blueprints which ignore "specific historical and institutional conditions prevailing in developing countries" and completely abandon the "Keynesian notion of aggregate demand and income distribution set within a nonergodic world" (Gnos & Rochon 2004: 190). The free market goal of the WC and the AWC is not the actual economy we encounter. According to Davidson (2004), the WC and AWC are only applicable if the three classical axioms are satisfied: neutrality of money, gross substitution between goods, and an ergodic economic environment. For this reason, Keynes expressed serious skepticism that in the long-run the economic system was self-adjusting and argued that full employment was "a rare and short-lived experience" (Peterson 1987: 1591). In the following, I outline the policies proposed by Post Keynesians, based on Keynes' ideas, about how to bring developing countries out of their current disadvantaged state. The dynamic Post Keynesian perspective for international development aims to establish a civilized social provisioning process based on a social–democratic capitalist system, along with a variety of property forms and a market with state intervention within a democratic political system (Davidson & Davidson 1996; Marangos 2000).[1]

The WC and the AWC require developing countries to sustain primary surpluses, even in periods of recession, since fiscal deficits are held to ignite inflation. This policy stance warrants elaboration. Keynes is known for heavy criticism regarding the effectiveness of fiscal discipline, especially in times of recession. Deficits are the result of recession (Camara-Neto & Vernengo 2004: 335). So, avoiding deficits and recessions requires stabilizing the cycle by stabilizing investment through public investment. Private investments are not necessarily superior to public investments (Chang & Grabel 2004a: 195).

Davidson (2004), referring to Keynes, suggests that developing countries embrace a national investment program directed to achieving full employment and shun inflation targeting that damages the economy by diminishing output and employment. There is no clear relationship between fiscal deficits and inflation (Ocampo 2002: 398; Gnos & Rochon 2004: 190; Saad-Filho 2007: 522). Fiscal policy should instead target economic stabilization, investment programs, and incentives for the private sector to support the government's social provisioning goals (Saad-Filho 2007: 524). Unfortunately the WC and AWC have driven a substantial decline in public investment, adversely affecting private investment (Camara-Neto & Vernengo 2004: 341; Saad-Filho 2007: 521). The elimination of industrial policies and sectoral incentives has also had a negative effect on manufacturing investment, a sector that had been traditionally heavily protected and subsidized in developing countries.

It is not surprising that a significant proportion of public expenditure reduction falls upon those groups with the least political and economic power: the poor, the unemployed, and the sick (Chang & Grabel 2004a: 191; Saad-Filho 2007). Hence, one of the main concerns regarding the WC policies is that income distribution is not even mentioned. Meanwhile in the AWC, the unequal distribution of income is framed as the result of volatility. The IMF's and World Bank's obsession with fiscal austerity, inspired by the WC and the AWC, restricts economic growth and public expenditures and so harms social provisioning. "Cross-country and historical experience show that strategic, well-designed and well-managed programmes of public expenditure are critical to the promotion of economic growth, investment and the alleviation of social ills" (Chang & Grabel 2004a: 197).

Post Keynesians express heavy skepticism on the emphasis placed by the WC and the AWC on buttressing the social safety net rather than on expanding the modern welfare state; effectively, subordinating social provisioning to market-based reforms (Ocampo 2004: 310). Public expenditures in education, health, and infrastructure "are clear pre- and co-requisites for private investment" expected to *crowd in* private investment (Chang & Grabel 2004a: 183). Consequently, the position of Post Keynesians is establishing a modern welfare state and directing expenditure on social programs, including retraining the structurally unemployed.

For the Post Keynesians, the development of a tax system should be based, not only on revenue considerations, but also on the social and cultural background of the society. Preventing tax evasion is at least as important as expenditure reduction in the face of budget deficits (Chang & Grabel 2004b: 288). Meanwhile, the aforementioned fiscal policies require a modern tax system and an expanded tax base (Saad-Filho 2007: 522–523). Davidson & Davidson (1996: 91–92) hold that there is a definite link between tax compliance and civic values. In a dynamic civilized social provisioning society of the Post Keynesian mold, there is a conscious payment of taxes by members of the society and non-compliance is not considered an alternative. Non-compliance is the result of the diminishing role of civic values in a society. The development of a civilized society in the Post Keynesian framework encourages tax-paying norms consistent with civic values, where individuals would have had to pay their taxes as part of their moral duty. "In a civilized society where civic values and self-interest flourish, the citizens must be willing not only to die for their country but also to pay for it" (Davidson & Davidson 1996: 217). The Post Keynesians propose establishing a modern tax system, expanding the tax base, increasing tax revenues, redistributing income, and strong enforcement of the existing tax laws; the reduction or elimination of the deductions, exemptions, and loopholes favoring the well-off; increase in the tax rates; taxing wealth and large or second properties in rural and urban areas; and taxing interest income, capital gains, financial transactions, and international capital flows.

Financial liberalization, defined as freeing financial markets from any intervention and allowing the market to determine the allocation of credit, is a source of financial instability and crises. Arestis (2004: 256) suggests that the "appalling performance of financial liberalization policies should not be surprising [as] it can be readily explained by its problematic theoretical nature and its poor performance at the empirical level." The financial liberalization proposition is based on an ideological commitment to free markets that is grounded neither in empirical evidence nor economic theory. Financial fragility, in contrast to WC and AWC perception, is not the result of accidents, policy errors, government failure, or exogenous shocks. Rather, financial fragility is built into the market capitalist system as Minsky long ago pointed out (Nissanke & Stein 2003: 296). From a Post Keynesian standpoint, interest rate liberalization has a negative effect on investment, financial liberalization is less likely to enhance long-term growth prospects, and a free banking system is unable to respond effectively to financial crises (Arestis 2004: 258).

Post Keynesians accentuate the need for greater regulation of financial markets together with a relatively closed capital account that will allow for lower interest payments, lower debt servicing spending, and more space for public investment. Interest rate policies should target a stable and permanently low level of interest rates and state-directed credit to specific parts of the economy (Arestis 2004: 262, 265). "If there is any single idea that Keynes propounded in *The General Theory* and adhered to throughout his life it was the necessity for interest rates to be low if capitalism is to function effectively" (Peterson 1987: 1617).

Davidson (2004: 217) holds that "the Washington Consensus has created perverse incentives that set nations against nations in a process that perpetuates a world of slow growth (if not stagnation)." By chasing the 'competitive exchange rate' instructed by the WC and the AWC with the intention of making domestic industries more competitive in the absence of capital controls, risks stability and capital flight. Unemployment becomes a problem for not only the competing economies, but also the trading partners of the 'successful' export-led country. Even if the search for a 'competitive exchange rate' were to succeed, the end result would still tend to increase the global inequality of income and likely reduce domestic living standards and social provisioning. Chang & Grabel (2004a: 179) support an adjustable pegged exchange rate regime matched with capital controls. Kregel (2008: 551) recommends an exchange rate anchor as part of domestic price stabilization policy. In other words, "whatever the exchange rate regime, it must be managed carefully" (Saad-Filho 2007: 529).

The theory of comparative advantage rests on outdated assumptions about technology, industrial structure, macroeconomic conditions, and the mobility of labor and capital (Chang & Grabel 2004a: 60). Any efforts by many nations to obtain competitive gains by implementing policies that will reduce the domestic monetary costs of labor or the exchange rate can only foster further global stagnation and recession. Each nation that attempts to regain a competitive edge induces similar depressionary policies in other economies. In addition to this, trade liberalization around the world is partially biased, as products produced in developing countries are subject to the highest levels of protectionism in developed economies. Seeing that trade liberalization can disproportionately affect the poor, the pro-poor strategies require the regulation of the balance of payments (Saad-Filho 2007: 528).

Davidson (2004: 218) and Ocampo (2002: 397) propose an international trade reform program built on Keynes' Bretton Woods proposals. These were designed to obtain an international agreement without surrendering monetary policy, domestic banking systems, or fiscal policies, and also to allow a sufficient degree of freedom to governments to pursue their goals. Davidson's (2004) reform plan for international trade, updating Keynes' proposals, takes into account those dynamic systemic features that were at the basis of Bretton Woods' success: fixed but adjustable exchange rates; capital flow restrictions; and reduction of trade imbalances, initiated by surplus nations. The creation of the International Clearing Union would require only an international agreement among its national members, preserving the core of the Keynes Plan.[2]

Keynes (1980: 276) was firm that movements of capital should be controlled as "we cannot hope to control rates of interest at home if movements of capital moneys out of the country are unrestricted." For Post Keynesians, capital controls are the necessary complement to Keynes' fiscal policy proposals and are also necessary for the socialization of investment and social provisioning. It appears that a sustainable growth path is a precondition for private capital inflows (Chang & Grabel 2004a: 16; Camara-Neto & Vernengo 2004: 337).

The race for foreign direct investment (FDI) serves as a formidable constraint to the promotion of expansionary, redistributive and labor rights policies (Chang & Grabel 2004a: 23). However, not all investment by multinational corporations (MNCs) can be prone to flight. Investment decisions by MNCs are grounded on factors such as a large domestic market, an educated workforce, rising incomes, economic growth, and sound infrastructure. So, FDI can be regulated and achieve developmental objectives as part of a national development strategy and/or industry policy. In the meantime, there is no single appropriate strategy for all types of FDI and for all developing countries. Policies regarding FDI must be tailored to the particular dynamic conditions of each industry, sector, and economy. It is growth that stimulates FDI and not the other way around (Chang & Grabel 2004a: 143). In sum, the Post Keynesians conjoin FDI with national development strategy or industry policy instead of dismantling the FDI regulatory framework as required by the WC and AWC.

In a number of developing countries, many state-owned enterprises (SOEs) became a source of budget deficit and wastefulness, but this is not a widespread feature of SOEs. Without a doubt, developed countries kept some SOEs that are quite successful. For the reason that it is easier to control state-owned enterprises, compared to private firms, the experiences of France, Austria, Finland, Norway, Italy, and Asia demonstrate a dynamic state-owned sector that played a key role in industrial development (Chang & Grabel 2004a: 87). Meanwhile, the experiences of developing countries subject to the WC and AWC privatization mandate reveal badly designed privatization programs, rent-seeking in the regulation of privatized enterprises, and the transfer of resources to insiders (Chang & Grabel 2004b: 288; Ocampo 2004: 312). There is a heavy expression of skepticism in establishing an unambiguous causal empirical link between the size of the SOE sector and economic growth. There is no evidence that a large SOE sector unavoidably causes countries to perform poorly. Consequently, economic and social development does not require a substantial change in property ownership. This is because ownership *per se* is less important than competition, the incentive structure, and the nature of regulatory policies (Marangos 2002). Thus, the policy recommendation from the Post Keynesians is to maintain SOEs as an engine of socio-economic development and a source of social provisioning.

The liberalization of the labor market is defended by neoclassical-Keynesians because unemployment is attributable to short-term wage and price rigidities or, in an open economy, to non-competitive exchange rates (Davidson 2004). However, labor market liberalization contributes to increasing income inequality, while the centralized wage bargaining system counter-attacks such trends. In addition, labor market "flexibility should never be seen as a substitute for adequate macroeconomic policies" (Ocampo 2004: 311). In an unstable macroeconomic environment, further flexibility increases uncertainty and firms respond by reducing 'formal' labor employment and/or eroding working conditions. Flexibility has negative externalities, such as damage to job security (Ocampo 2002: 403–404). Therefore, government intervention should encourage productivity growth, better working conditions, increasing the minimum wage and reducing wage dispersion, supporting trade unions, and offering tax and other incentives to firms to invest in targeted sectors that introduce new technologies and high wages (Saad-Filho 2007: 525).

The importance of property rights for an entrepreneurial market economy cannot be questioned (Davidson 2004: 209). Therefore, it is important from a Post Keynesian perspective to reform the land tenure systems in developing countries (Saad-Filho 2007: 526). However, Post Keynesians hold that property rights are only one element of the institutional framework for an entrepreneurial market provisioning process. The neglect of institutions in the WC was injurious to economic development (Ocampo 2004: 309).

Economic and social institutions, indispensable for a market economy of the Post Keynesian mold, must be subject to a democratic political process. This is because differences in the effectiveness of economic institutions are ingrained in ideological standpoints that can only be resolved via a democratic political process. This stance by the Post Keynesians signifies the actuality. There is no such thing as a unique institutional design of a market economy in terms of economic dynamism and stability, income distribution, social cohesion, and social provisioning. "The institutional heterogeneity is apparent" among countries today (Chang & Grabel 2004b: 278). Moreover, institutional development is essentially endogenous to each society and depends on a learning process and numerous historical determinants (Ocampo 2004: 312). It is not the role of 'Washington' to impose a dominant institutional structure. Instead, the Post Keynesians argue that institutions are endogenous to each society so as to guarantee social cohesion and social provisioning, and to manage conflict in the establishment of a civilized society.

The Marxian approach to international development

The growth dynamics of capitalism and its dependence on the financial system is fundamental to the Marxian approach to international development. Marxians view capitalism as a dynamic historical process characterized by constant change. Development of capitalism is uneven; divergence is the rule and convergence the exception. These are central conclusions of the Marxian analysis of accumulation. These are to be viewed in contradistinction to the equilibrium approach of the neoclassical economics and the WC and the AWC. Stated simply, neoclassical economists insist on abstracting economics from all social relations and institutional arrangements. The real history of capitalism is lost and the idiosyncrasies of institutions, history, and culture are disregarded. Subsequently, capitalist relations can only allegedly advance naturally from human nature (Bracarense 2013: 335).

In this dynamic process, capitalist development or non-development is the outcome of the interaction between domestic and international forces. What Marxians bring to the table in the creation and dynamics of capitalist development and crisis is class analysis, exploitation, modes of production, surplus value, and power. 'Class' denotes people grouped together by a common relation, including ownership relation, to productive activity (Lippit 1988: 20). While most mainstream development theorists continue to argue that developing countries should emulate developed capitalist countries and see development policy as a way of speeding up the process (Bracarense 2013: 334), the Marxian dynamic process of international development paves the way for socialism as an alternative economic system of social provisioning. Socialism has a well-defined set of ends and values of freedom, democracy, social justice, community, efficiency, self-management, solidarity, prevention of exploitation of the weak, reduction of alienation, greater equality of opportunity, income, wealth, status and power, and the satisfaction of basic needs. In the socialist dynamic process, the working class prevails in the decision-making process at any level of the society.

Marxians argue that under-development has its roots to colonialism and imperialism, while at the same time colonialism and imperialism are part of the same dynamic process of capitalist development (Bracarense 2013: 336). The incorporation of the colonies into the world capitalist system established power structures that allow the former to develop by expropriating surplus for the benefit of the latter. "This process inevitably leads to the 'development of underdevelopment' in the periphery" (Ayres & Clark 1998: 89). Eventually, economic development takes place when the dominant domestic and foreign classes controlling the surplus value realize that it is in their interest to use the surplus in a way that will promote national development. Only then, the ruling classes invest in, for example, infrastructure, education, and health care provisioning (Lippit 1988: 23). That is to say, development reflects the specific class interests that set development in motion. During this dynamic process, countries must get rid of their cultural and social idiosyncrasies that separate them from capitalist world. They must replicate world capitalism, eliminate social peculiarities by applying the WC and the AWC. In contrast, Marxians abandon the dichotomized view such as 'developed' and 'developing' and 'center' and 'periphery.' Instead, they adopt a decentralized view of social change (Bracarense 2013: 339) with the ultimate goal of achieving socialism and genuine social provisioning.

The IMF and the WB have played a central role as a broker between creditors and debtors and as a global enforcer of the capitalist rules of the game mainly by imposing the WC and the AWC. In contrast to the Marxian goals of socialism, the IMF is placing the cost of capitalist under-development on citizens rather than those responsible for the crisis. Clearly, the international debt crisis not only made developing countries more dependent on the fetishized world of money and finance, but also led to increased levels of exploitation of the working class and greater misery for the mass of the population (Ayres & Clark 1998: 110). Marxians demand the repudiation of the debt (Cleaver 1989: 39), given that it is not a legitimate burden acquired by the majority of the people. They argue that there is no moral or ethical reason for continuing to repay the illegitimate debt. From a working-class standpoint, capitalists borrowed to increase exploitation and misery for the mass of the population. In the following, I outline the policies proposed by Marxians on how to bring developing countries out of their current disadvantaged state.

Budget deficits increased in developing countries because of the concentration of economic and political power run by dominant groups pursuing their own class and individual interests. Marxians suggest that fiscal deficits be avoided due to their implications for income distribution, planned allocation of resources, economic power, and social provisioning. Deficit financing can undermine state autonomy and result in the diminution of sovereignty, especially when financed with foreign savings, since the use of foreign savings increases the probability of government policy being constrained by foreign creditors and/or agencies. The hegemony produced by foreign debt establishes a high degree of default risk if government policies do not serve the interests of external financers (Harris 1991: 115–116). The global recession undermined the debtor countries' ability to benefit from any reductions in foreign exchange and the rise in interest rates dramatically raised the cost of debt, further increasing depression. The enormous increases in debt servicing thus had significant negative consequences for development. Marxians therefore reject the use of deficit financing and argue that it is a mechanism through which developing countries are used to stabilize international capitalist finance.

No society appears to be too poor as a surplus value exists that can be used either to sustain capital formation or to fight wars or build monuments (Lippit 1988: 18). The use of the surplus value is conditioned on the prevailing class power and modes of production. The dominant capitalist class appropriates and uses surplus value in a way that is mandated by their class interests. Some uses of the surplus sustain development and social provisioning, for example investment. Other methods perpetuate non-development, for example luxury consumption, warfare, or monument construction (Lippit 1988: 18). If the working classes are in power in socialism, the pattern of development will reflect the interest of the majority of the population. The provision of basic needs such as education, housing, health care, the absence of exploitation, and racial and gender inequalities, the reduction of unemployment and achievement of economic growth denote socialist social provisioning. Marxians also insist that the state should establish and facilitate the establishment of democratic institutions, which allow for the full participation of the masses. This would require adoption of an educational policy that raises the political and class consciousness of the masses. Intensification of the class struggle for the realization of non-capitalist development must be the ultimate purpose of such an educational policy.

Overall, developing countries collect comparatively few taxes (Weller 2007: 369). Marxians are in favor of raising more revenue through greater progressivity; high capitalist incomes would provide tax revenue and reduce income inequality through transfer payments and social provisioning, increasing aggregate consumption. More efficient tax collection could improve revenues through using modern information technology, reorganizing local tax collection authorities, implementing effective self-assessment, and establishing credible deterrents for tax evasion. The result should be more revenue, greater fairness, improved transparency, and a larger formal sector. A consumption tax, such as Value-Added Tax (VAT), is regressive and, as such, is rejected by Marxians. In addition, Ricardian equivalence does not hold (Harris 1991:112). It is aggregate expenditure that drives tax revenues and not the other way around.

Marxians are quite conscious of the class nature of credit and of debt and the manner in which financial capital is used against workers. Credit, debt, and capital cannot be appropriated by the working class, but must be destroyed in communism. Then again, when money and credit cannot be destroyed, it must be used to advance working-class interests under socialist social provisioning. In comparison to financial liberalization which essentially invites foreign banking and savings to the economy, Marxians focus on increasing domestic banking and national savings.

In line with this thought, industry must be financed and controlled by domestic sources. If industry is externally financed, national control may be lost (Ayres & Clark 1998: 108).

The rapid rise in interest rates in the early 1980s raised the cost of debt repayments and ushered in the global recession in growth, which reduced foreign earnings necessary to repay the debt. Inflation of external credit led to the debt crisis and the invitation of the IMF to reschedule the debt. Mandel (1962) evaluates 'indebtedness' within the framework of a theory of capitalist crisis and credit creation, and suggests that the international indebtedness of developing countries diminishes the impact of the capitalist crisis by reducing the scale of the global downturn and by stimulating growth. "Debt is therefore viewed as a necessary consequence of the intrinsic laws of global capital accumulation" (Yaghmaian 1989: 102). Consequently, developing countries are no longer passive recipients of debt, but consciously accumulate debt as an integral component of their industrialization and economic development and also as a process of integration in the fetishized world of money and finance. Developing countries' indebtedness is thus an intrinsic tendency of capitalist development during the stage of the internationalization of productive capital. Decisively, "debt is a structural tendency that is primarily governed by the dynamics of global accumulation, as opposed to abrupt fluctuations in the world commodity and financial markets" (Yaghmaian 1989: 103–104) for which financial liberalization is an essential prerequisite.

A system of internationally negotiated controls on capital flight was necessary, whereby countries would have been required to return capital that was moved abroad in violation of a nation's laws. Such returned funds would have been confiscated if the owner was convicted of illegal capital flight, providing a powerful deterrent. "We need to penetrate the fetishism of money and question the changes in class relations that underlay the rearrangements of world capital flows" (Cleaver 1989: 22).

Through the socialist customs union, a fixed exchange system will eliminate the instability and negative outcomes caused by the flexible exchange rate system. Depreciation of the local currency hurts social provisioning and working-class consumption of imported goods, which in many countries includes basic subsistence goods (Cleaver 1989: 31). The concept of comparative advantage had its origins not so much in economics as in politics. It was created within the context of colonialism, war, nationalist rivalries, and military power. Prices and wages are the products of specific historical processes. Experience revealed that free trade did not benefit everyone equally. Trade liberalization did not facilitate the closing of the technology gap, which is central to industrial development. Developing countries face growing global protectionism with respect to advanced technology and most transfers are intrafirm. In the same way, knowledge is increasingly tied up in patents, which are controlled by multinational corporations. Developing countries have traditionally relied on cheap labor to attract foreign investment, but this policy does not necessarily bring access to technology. Furthermore, the tightening of controls over technological knowledge creates barriers to entry into high technology industries and thereby inhibits the transformation of developing countries (Ayres & Clark 1998: 112). MNCs have higher import propensities, industrial exports have a higher resource content and lower manufacturing valued added than locally owned firms (OECD 1988: 71). Efforts by developing countries to impose domestic content levels have generally failed due to the power of MNCs (Ayres & Clark 1998: 109).

The expansion of mutually beneficial international trade requires government planning. A customs union of several socialist countries is feasible, comprising a common market with close cooperation, a common external tariff, and perhaps a common currency. The socialist customs union will provide the means to avoid the destructive elements of free international trade with the capitalist countries and, at the same time, will become a vehicle for the development of socialism. A supranational planning body will ensure that prevailing regulations and interventions in member socialist countries encourage social provisioning, equality, and ecological responsibility. The socialist customs union is underpinned by the notion that "the precondition for the free development of each would be the free development of all" (Blackburn 1991: 233). The social-ist customs union will be based on an international socialist market, guided by a supranational planning body based on the principles of consultation, debate, democracy, and self-government among member states.

Marxians emphasize the importance of independent industrialization. However, that does not exclude participation of foreign capital in the socialist economy. The mandate of socialism is to provide for social provisioning and to equalize incomes in the national economy, meaning domestic incomes could increase through the participation of foreign capital. The socialist con-trol of investment would, however, require some regulation of foreign investment. Meanwhile, socialist countries will be able to use their custom union members' resources without damaging the socialist cause and falling into the trap of providing concessions to international capital by eliminating restrictions. This is because FDI in developing countries is attracted to poor labor conditions and low wages, contributing to the growth of exports while resulting in distorted development (Ayres & Clark 1998: 113).

In his later Marxian-oriented work, Hymer (1972) investigates how FDI by MNCs gives rise to 'the law of uneven development,' whereby the interests of developing countries are subordi-nated to those of the elite in developed nations who effectively control MNCs and FDI. This hierarchical organization of the world "pulls and tears at the social and political fabric and erodes the cohesiveness of national states" (Hymer 1972: 133). Thus, while Hymer acknowledges the private welfare-enhancing role of MNCs and FDI, he concludes that the impact of FDI on social welfare is harmful as "it creates hierarchy rather than equality, and it spreads its benefits unequally" (Hymer 1972: 133).

The IMF and the WB demand and pressure for privatization to break workers' leverage with the state. Privatization in developing countries has simply resulted in enriching the capitalists, without any benefit to the workers or to production. For the Marxians, the distribution of ownership is a major concern because it determines the distribution of power and influences equity, efficiency, and social provisioning. Because markets do not approximate perfect competi-tion and are instead dominated by domestic and international monopolies, the distribution of property increases inequalities. Developing economies typically lack domestic capitalists with the necessary financial capital to purchase enterprises, making foreign ownership the only means of privatization. It was not by coincidence that foreign capital came to the 'rescue' of developing economies. This is an act of purposeful action by developed economies, ensuring that foreign ownership was the only permissible method of privatization. A debt crisis process implicitly has the goal of initiating the destruction of any institutional barrier, thus inhibiting the penetration, influence, and power of foreign capital. The IMF is responsible for creating the depression in developing economies. In such an environment, the only interested buyers come from abroad at a price "for next to nothing" (Gowan 1995: 45). Equally important has been the pressure exerted on governments in developing economies to sell state assets and public utilities to MNCs (the only possible buyers) in order to reduce fiscal deficits, lower inflation, and discipline the labor market by inducing high unemployment. Competition, not the lack of it, is the source of instability, crises, and uneven development and not a cause of equilibrium or development. In the labor market, the rigidity of wages is not the cause of unemployment. Wage or price flex-ibility is neither a necessary nor a sufficient condition for full employment equilibrium. The 1970s 'anti-inflationary policy' was a synonym for 'anti-wage policy' (Cleaver 1989: 28). Overall, state-owned enterprises should remain state-owned from a Marxist point of view to be used as vehicles of socialist social provisioning.

Socialism is typically defined as the public ownership of land and capital. But socialist development does not call for an exclusive commitment to state ownership. It is the dominance of working-class interests rather than state ownership that defines the socialist social formation (Lippit 1988: 23). Forms of ownership are determined by, among other things, the varying degree of concentration of the productive forces. Diverse forms of technology gave rise to diverse forms of socialization, as technology is not neutral (Barratt-Brown 1995: 361). Thus, to impose a common form of ownership is inconsistent with social reality. It could hardly have been correct to describe the progress of socialism as a mechanical increase in the share of state-owned assets at the expense of other forms of ownership. The simplistic view that state property is clearly superior to all other forms of ownership cannot be sustained. Markets and planning in conjunction with a number of different kinds of ownership institutions, both private and collective, are suitable in socialism.

Marxians argue that state ownership *per se* does not guarantee efficiency. If the structure of state ownership conflicts with the changing economic realities, state ownership could be a negative rather than a positive element in economic development. State property is no longer seen as sufficient, or even necessary, for socialism. Within the socialist economic system, and based on state property, a variety of property forms can exist. Thus, all forms of property—individual, cooperative, and state—are important and are consistent with socialism. Capital will be socialized and rented to firms. Private property is considered complementary to state and group ownership. Individuals should be permitted to operate their own enterprise, being the most effective structure for the development of labor-intensive activities and the service sector, subject to certain regulations administered by local government.

Marx emphasized the importance of supporting institutions for accumulation and the fact that institutional choice did not take place in a vacuum. Moreover, given human behavior, the institutions have to be altered so that the social provisioning was consistent with the social interests of efficiency, equity, self-management, and solidarity. From a Marxian perspective, orthodox economists continue to overlook the significant role of class relations in the institutions of socio-economic development. Ruccio (2011) states that existing institutions within developing countries often serve to create and to reproduce relations of capitalist exploitation, as well as appropriation of surplus value created by the direct producers. The surplus generated is utilized to strengthen the exploitative institutions in safeguarding the institutional conditions of surplus value extraction. From a Marxian point of view, Ruccio (2011) proposes institutions that impede the appropriation of surplus value through capitalist forms of exploitation and that promote alternative forms for redistribution of surplus in a non-exploitative way for socio-economic development and social provisioning. Ruccio (2011: 575–576) also suggests the implementation of "rules and norms that make it possible for the direct producers themselves to appropriate and distribute the surplus they create."

Conclusion: linkages and contradistinctions

This chapter presents the Post Keynesian and Marxian perspectives on international development. To give structure to the debate, the analysis was concentrated on identifying the reactions of these heterodox schools to the specific policies of the WC and the AWC. In particular, fiscal discipline, public expenditure priorities, tax reform, financial liberalization, exchange rates, trade liberalization, foreign direct investment, privatization, deregulation, property rights, and institutions building were examined in detail. Unquestionably, these policies are not the only preconditions for economic prosperity.

The dynamic Post Keynesian and Marxian approaches developed in this chapter may appear at first sight contradistinctive. The dynamic process of Post Keynesian perspective for international development is to establish a civilized capitalist social provisioning process, whereas the dynamic process of the Marxian perspective for international development is to establish socialism as an alternative economic system of social provisioning. Nevertheless, Marx (1904: 12) clearly stated that

> no social order ever disappears before all the productive forces for which there is room in it have been developed; and new higher relations of production never appear before the material conditions of their existence have matured in the womb of the old society itself.

When each social order of social provisioning has exhausted the dynamic nature all the productive forces, the new social order of social provisioning appears. Socialism, in other words, would not be possible until capitalism had exhausted its potential for further development either in the neoclassical or Post Keynesian mode. Consequently, the dynamics of international development in developing economies pass through the dominant neoclassical paradigm in the form of the WC and AWC to a civilized capitalist social provisioning process and then to socialism as an alternative economic system of social provisioning, based on Marxian historical materialism.

For Post Keynesians the dynamic nature of social provisioning ends in the form of a civilized capitalist economic system, whereas for Marxians the dynamic nature of social provisioning unfolds in the form of a socialist economic system of social provisioning. The linkages between the Post Keynesian and Marxian approaches to international development are unsurprising. Linkages exist with respect to public expenditure (priorities on social programs), tax reform (aggregate expenditure drives tax revenues), exchange rates (fixed exchange rate), trade liberalization (clearing/customs union), privatization (maintain state-owned enterprises), deregulation (government intervention in the labor market), property rights (all forms of property are consistent), and institutions building (endogenous created). Contradistinctions are present with respect to fiscal discipline (deficits should target full employment versus fiscal deficits should be shunned) and financial liberalization (low level of interest rates versus financing only through domestic sources). The linkages between heterodox approaches, in this case Post Keynesian and Marxian, have the potential to advance heterodox theories of international development in theory and practice. This is a thought-provoking and crucial objective for all heterodox economists.

Acknowledgments

I am grateful to Shaina Sorrel and Sean Alley for their valuable comments.

Notes

1 The Post Keynesianism approach discussed in this chapter refers mainly to American or fundamentalist Post Keynesianism. It is acknowledged that this is a narrow view of Post Keynesianism, excluding those who hold a radical vision of society (including Kaleckians, Sraffians, and radical political economists).
2 For an application of the plan for international trade in Eastern Europe in the form of an Eastern European Clearing Union, see Marangos (2001).

References

Arestis, P. 2004. 'Washington consensus and financial liberalization.' *Journal of Post Keynesian Economics*, 27 (2): 251–271.
Ayres, R. & Clark, D. 1998. 'Capitalism, industrialisation and development in Latin America: the dependency paradigm revisited.' *Capital & Class*, 22 (1): 89–118.
Barratt-Brown, M. 1995. *Models in Political Economy*, 2nd edn. Melbourne: Penguin Books.

Blackburn, R. 1991. 'Fin de Siecle: Socialism after the Crash,' *in*: R. Blackburn (ed.), *After the Fall: The Failure of Communism and the Future of Socialism*. London: Verso, 173–249.

Bracarense, N. 2013. 'Contract zones: development theory and the 'cultural turn.' *Review of Radical Political Economics*, 45 (3): 333–340.

Camara-Neto, A.F. & Vernengo, M. 2004. 'Fiscal policy and the Washington Consensus: a Post Keynesian perspective.' *Journal of Post Keynesian Economics*, 27 (2): 333–343.

Chang, H.-J. & Grabel, I. 2004a. *Reclaiming Development. An Alternative Economic Policy Manual*. London: Zed Books.

Chang, H.-J. & Grabel, I. 2004b. 'Reclaiming development from the Washington Consensus.' *Journal of Post Keynesian Economics*, 27 (2): 273–291.

Cleaver, H. 1989. 'Close the IMF, abolish debt and end development: a class analysis of the international debt crisis.' *Capital & Class*, 13 (3): 17–50.

Davidson, G. & Davidson, P. 1996. *Economics for a Civilised Society*, 2nd edn. London: Macmillan.

Davidson, P. 2004. 'A Post Keynesian view of the Washington Consensus and how to improve it.' *Journal of Post Keynesian Economics*, 27 (2): 208–230.

Gnos, C. & Rochon, L.P. 2004. 'What is next for the Washington Consensus? The fifteenth anniversary 1989–2004.' *Journal of Post Keynesian Economics*, 27 (2): 187–193.

Gowan, P. 1995. 'Neo-liberal theory and practice for Eastern Europe.' *New Left Review*, 213 (September/October): 3–60.

Harris, L. 1991. 'The role of budget deficits in development strategies.' *Review of Radical Political Economics*, 23 (1&2): 111–117.

Hymer, S.H. 1972. *The Multinational Corporation and the Law of Uneven Development*. New Haven, CT: Yale University Press.

Keynes, J.M. 1980. *The Collected Writings of John Maynard Keynes, Vol. XXV: Activities 1940–1944. Shaping the Post-War World: The Clearing Union*. London: Macmillan.

Kregel, J.A. 2008. 'The discrete charm of the Washington Consensus.' *Journal of Post Keynesian Economics*, 30 (4): 541–560.

Kuczynski, P.P. & J. Williamson. 2003. *After the Washington Consensus*. Washington, DC: Institute for International Studies.

Lippit, V.D. 1988. 'Class structure, modes of production and economic development.' *Review of Radical Political Economics*, 20 (2&3): 18–24.

Mandel, E. 1962. *Marxist Economic Theory, Volume 1*. New York: Monthly Review Press.

Marangos, J. 2000. 'A Post Keynesian view of transition to market capitalism: developing a civilized society.' *Journal of Post Keynesian Economics*, 23 (4): 689–704.

Marangos, J. 2001. 'International trade policies for transition economies: the Post Keynesian alternative.' *Journal of Post Keynesian Economics*, 23 (4): 689–704.

Marangos, J. 2002. 'A Post Keynesian critique of privatization policies in transition economies.' *Journal of International Development*, 14 (5): 573–589.

Marx, K. 1904. *A Contribution to the Critique of Political Economy*. Chicago: Charles H. Kerr & Company.

Nissanke, M. & Stein, H. 2003. 'Financial globalization and economic development: toward an institutional foundation.' *Eastern Economic Journal*, 29 (2): 287–308.

Ocampo, J.A. 2002. 'Rethinking the development agenda.' *Cambridge Journal of Economics*, 26 (3): 393–407.

Ocampo, J.A. 2004. 'Beyond the Washington Consensus: what do we mean?' *Journal of Post Keynesian Economics*, 27 (2): 293–314.

OECD. 1988. *The Newly Industrialized Countries: Challenge and Opportunity for OECD Countries*. Paris: OECD.

Peterson, W.C. 1987. 'Macroeconomic theory and policy in an institutional perspective.' *Journal of Economic Issues*, 21 (4): 1587–1621.

Ruccio, D.F. 2011. 'Development, institutions and class.' *Journal of Institutional Economics*, 7 (4): 571–576.

Saad-Filho, A. 2007. 'Life beyond the Washington Consensus: an introduction to pro-poor macroeconomics policies.' *Review of Political Economy*, 19 (4): 513–537.

Weller, C.E. 2007. 'The benefits of progressive taxation in economic development.' *Review of Radical Political Economics*, 39 (3): 368–376.

Williamson, J. 1990. 'What Washington means by policy reform,' *in*: J. Williamson (ed.), *Latin American Adjustment: How Much Has Happened?* Washington, DC: Institute for International Economics, 7–20.

Yaghmaian, B. 1989. 'Economic development and the determinants of third world debt.' *Review of Radical Political Economics*, 21 (3): 99–104.

30

Energy, environment, and the economy

Anders Ekeland and Bent Arne Sæther

Environment and economics in the age of Anthropocene

Until the early 1960s, the economics discipline had largely ignored nature. This is true for mainstream neoclassical economics as well as for Post Keynesian, Marxist, institutionalist, and other heterodox schools of economic thought. Centuries ago, the physiocrats and classical political economists were concerned with the limitations of resources, in particular the pressure from a growing population on limited areas of arable land. In the nineteenth and twentieth centuries such concerns were more or less absent until texts such as Rachel Carson's *Silent Spring* (1962) gave the first signal that humans were severely damaging the environment. Ten years later came *The Limits to Growth* (Meadows *et al.* 1972), initiating a discussion of how the limits to growth can be measured and how 'hard' these environmental limits are.

Our history is a history of human modification of nature. The provisioning process depends on nature and affects nature. In particular, the process depends on the methods available for converting solar radiation into useful energy. Advances in such technologies have triggered the transformation of societies and our relation to nature. Contemporary societies are strongly shaped by the revolution that is usually referred to as 'industrial,' but which was fundamentally an energy revolution. It was a transition from a reliance on photosynthesis to the use of immense quantities of solar energy that are stored as fossil fuels. Wrigley (2010: 39), writing about England, estimates that even by 1800 one-third of the country's land would have to be covered by forests to produce a similar amount of energy as was being produced from coal at the time.

Since the transition to a fossil-based economy, human activities have gradually degraded our surroundings on a vast scale, including the climate. With access to seemingly unlimited amounts of cheap energy, "the massive power to produce has been accompanied by an equally great rise in the power to destroy" (Wrigley 2010: 2). The global average temperature is rising following ten millennia of stability: biodiversity is being depleted at an alarming rate due mainly to the massive conversion of land made possible by fossil-based technology and machinery. We have entered what has been termed the *Anthropocene* (Crutzen 2002), a new geological age where human activity is decisively shaping the geo-physical landscape (ice caps, sea level), and the conditions for Darwinian selection processes among the species by the rapid increase in the global temperature.

When nature finally returned to economics, only a minority of economists took on the 'new' challenge. Two fields stand out since they had nature specifically in focus. Within the mainstream, environmental economics commenced in the 1960s. The Association of Environmental and Resource Economists (AERE) was founded in 1979. Outside of the mainstream, ecological economics emerged a few years later and the International Society for Ecological Economics (ISEE) was established in 1988. In addition, ecological currents have emerged in all the major schools of heterodox economic thought.

Setting ecological and green economics aside, ecological issues are the special interest of a minority in all heterodox schools of thought. Due to limitations of space we have chosen to focus on ecological, Marxian, and Post Keynesian economics, which we discuss in the next three sections. In the final section, we briefly outline a number of issues and challenges for heterodox economists related to ecological problems and sustainable development.

Ecological economics

When the ISEE was established in 1988, it offered some radically different perspectives from those dominating economics (Spash 1999), but also became an umbrella for very different currents. Concern was expressed by some natural scientists who felt a need to collaborate with economists to better translate their scientific results into policies. There were neoclassical economists who were deeply concerned about the weak engagement with environmental and resource problems within the discipline. In addition, there were economists who rejected the neoclassical paradigm and wished to build a heterodox, interdisciplinary alternative (Spash 1999; Røpke 2004).

A shared vision and a deep division

In the introduction to their anthology of ecological economics, Martinez-Alier & Røpke (2008: xxx) argue that all the contributors to the two volumes

> share the pre-analytical vision that the human economy is an open system inside the framework of a closed system in the thermodynamic sense. Instead of describing the relationship between the economy and nature in terms of interfaces between two basically different systems (with nature providing resources, sink capacity and direct utility for the economy), it is emphasized that the human economy is embedded in nature, and that the economic process can also be conceptualized as natural, biophysical processes.

The fact that the economy is an 'open' sub-system means that there is an exchange of matter and energy with the rest of the biosphere. The biosphere, on the other hand, is a closed system when it comes to matter. In practice, no matter enters or leaves the biosphere from outer space. With energy, it is different. Solar radiation flows into the biosphere and heat is released into outer space. It is the delicate balance of this exchange that is disturbed by emissions originating in human activity. All human production uses energy to convert matter, and can be described as a natural, biophysical, or metabolic process. The form of the metabolism, in particular our ability to capture solar energy and convert it to useful forms, goes a long way in defining the provisioning process.

This fundamental view calls for trans-disciplinarity, which has been a vision of ecological economics from the outset (Costanza et al. 2015: 87). Ecological economics wanted to avoid methodological narrowness and isolation from other disciplines. Methodological pluralism has been a principle of ecological economics from the very beginning (Norgaard 1989), and this has included mainstream economics. In their well-known textbook in ecological economics,

Daly & Farley (2011: xxv) state that they "draw out the useful elements of neoclassical economic theory and integrate them into ecological economics." The explicit tolerance of neoclassical economics by key persons in the ISEE has led to the situation where the ISEE journal, *Ecological Economics*, has been dominated by mainstream articles (Anderson & M'Gonigle 2012; Plumecocq 2014).

Spash (2012: 46) argues that the neoclassical model is opposed to the pre-analytical vision within ecological economics. He explicitly rejects what he calls "unstructured and uncritical pluralism" and calls for a pluralism based on "commonalities . . . between ecological economics and heterodox schools of thought" (Spash 2012: 45). These very different views of what constitutes real pluralism indicate the very different methodological approaches inside the ISEE.

Scale and limits to growth

The methodological division notwithstanding, there are some key and shared elements of ecological economics that distinguish the field from the mainstream approach, and which could pose a challenge also to some heterodox economists. First, and most importantly, it is a view that the scale of the economy matters in a finite world. Second, ecosystem processes are complex, and uncertainty is consequently a pervasive feature. Third, a skepticism about the scope for 'technological fixes' and for substitutability between nature and human-made capital, leads to adherence to a strong sustainability principle. Finally, the focus on limitations to growth makes both inter- and intragenerational equity a core issue.

The idea that production cannot grow indefinitely was widely shared by classical economists (Dale 2013). Thomas Malthus, Adam Smith, and John Stuart Mill foresaw a future state characterized by stable population and production. Whereas Malthus and Smith held a dismal view on the future state, Mill specifically argued that a stable state would not mean the end of mental, moral, and social progress. Such ideas were marginalized during most of the twentieth century, particularly in the post-Second World War growth period, but re-emerged as environmental problems became increasingly manifest.

Some early contributions have been very important in shaping ecological economics. Georgescu-Roegen (1971) claims that the laws of thermodynamics will ultimately create limits to long-term growth. Kenneth Boulding (1966) launches the term 'spaceship Earth' as an image for our existence within boundaries, and argues forcefully that man must go from a 'cowboy economy' designed to maximize Gross Domestic Product (GDP) to a 'spaceman economy' where throughput must be minimized. In 1972, Georgescu-Roegen's disciple, Herman Daly, developed the concept of the 'steady-state economy':

> A steady-state economy is one that develops qualitatively (by improvement in science, technology and ethics) without growing quantitatively in physical dimensions; it lives on a diet – a constant metabolic flow of resources from depletion to pollution (the entropic throughput) maintained at a level that is both sufficient for a good life and within the assimilative and regenerative capacities of the containing ecosystem.
>
> *Daly 2015: 53*

Whereas the mainstream sees an almost unlimited scope for reduction in resource use and environmental damage per produced unit, ecological economists express much less confidence in a 'technical fix' (Costanza *et al.* 2015: 118). Daly (2015) sees limited prospects for 'absolute decoupling' of resource use from GDP. The 'dematerialization' of the economy is limited by the input-output structure of production. Even 'weightless' goods such as information and literature need substantial physical input. The lexicographic structure of human needs and wants implies that "a million recipes on the Internet" have no meaning to us "unless we first have sufficient food on the plate" (Daly 2015: 4).

Still absent from conventional economics, including environmental economics, the limits to growth debate is developing within and close to the ecological economics community including an exploration of *degrowth*, a concept first elaborated by André Gorz (1994). This concept became a "slogan against economic growth . . . and developed into a social movement" (Demaria *et al.* 2013: 192). This debate is also informed by insight concerning the dubious links between real income and welfare. Several studies indicate that beyond certain income levels, well below those found in today's advanced capitalist economies, the self-reported well-being of the population increases slowly, if at all (Easterlin 1995; Jackson *et al.* 2004).

Distribution and values

In contrast to mainstream economists, heterodox economists, including ecological economists, view economics as value-laden. There are several reasons for this position. In a 'full world,' that is a world where human activities begin to transgress the carrying capacity of ecosystems, and with limited scope for decoupling, economic growth cannot resolve conflicts over income, wealth, and resources. Therefore, distribution, both between generations and within each generation, becomes one of three major concerns for ecological economics: the other two concerns are scale and efficiency (Common & Stagl 2005; Daly & Farley 2011). Daly & Farley (2011: 13) argue that "Ecological economics also considers efficient allocation important, but it is secondary to the issues of scale and distribution."

Further, when existing human preferences come into conflict with planetary boundaries and sustainability, the former must be subordinate to the latter. As ecological economics sees preferences as socially constructed, the inevitable conflicts of interests should be solved by broad public discussions about what must and can be sustainable social consumption norms (Jackson *et al.* 2004).

Complexity, resilience, and precaution

In a world of limited substitution possibilities and deep uncertainty about natural processes and thresholds, sustainability depends on the protection and management of nature qua ecosystems and resources. They cannot be measured and aggregated in any straightforward way. A key concept in this respect is *resilience*, defined as the capacity of a system to absorb shocks and to remain functional. As elaborated by Holling (1973), this concept implies that ecosystems can have multiple 'stability domains' and move from one state to another, while people have limited knowledge regarding mechanisms and thresholds in the ecosystems. This concept thus takes the focus away from the search for a single, stable equilibrium. If achieving sustainability is a central concern, maintaining ecosystems' resilience must become a key criterion.

The limits to growth, and the inability of conventional national accounts to capture the ecological consequences of economic activity, have led environmental and ecological economists to look for indicators to replace or complement GDP. The first attempts to track and measure the material part of economic metabolism were made when, in 1969, Robert Ayres and Allen Kneese constructed material balances for the United States economy, and thus created the basis for modern material flow analysis (Fischer-Kowalski 1998).

Several indicators have been constructed to better capture ecological sustainability. A prominent example is 'the ecological footprint' (Wackernagel & Rees 1996), which attempts to measure humanity's direct and indirect demand for the reproductive capacity of the Earth. In the political sphere, for example, the World Wildlife Fund (WWF) announced a certain date as the 'World Overshoot Day' (WWF 2014), the date when the ecological footprint equals the Earth's total reproductive capacity.[1] Daly & Farley (2011: 33) note that: "Scholars may have statistical arguments over the best measures of carrying capacity demanded and supplied, but the basic qualitative conclusion of unsustainable trends is hard to deny."

While the mainstream tends to prescribe policies based on optimality considerations utilizing, for example, a cost-benefit analysis, ecological economists generally support the *precautionary principle* (UNCED 1993). This principle states that where there are threats of serious or irreversible damage, lack of scientific certainty should not be used as a reason to postpone protective action. It "shifts the burden of proof" away from the environment to those promoting potentially harmful economic activities. The major ecological problems of our time are exactly marked by uncertainty and ignorance, not manageable risk (Spash 2012: 43).

Marxian economics and the environment

Since the rise of the New Left in the 1960s, there has been an ongoing debate about Marx and ecology. Howard Parson, Elmar Altvater, Paul Burkett, and John Bellamy Foster have been prominent authors arguing that there is a fundamentally correct ecological understanding in Marx and Engels (Foster & Burkett 2016). Other Marxists, such as Murray Bookchin, André Gorz, Ted Benton, James O'Connor, Joel Kovel, Daniel Tanuro, and Kate Soper, while agreeing that there clearly are insights to build on, find Marx and Engels falling short on one or more important points (Benton 1996). Then there are those who find the views of Marx and Engels fundamentally problematic, such as Martinez-Alier, Robin Eckersly, and Alain Lipietz (Lipietz 2000; see also the responses in the following issue of *Capitalism Nature Socialism*).

The metabolic rift

The first two groups agree that Marx and Engels have some insight on important ecological problems of their time. They point to Marx's concept of the *metabolic rift* caused by capitalism. This concept was inspired by the writings of the leading German agricultural scientist, Justus von Liebig, who pointed out that British 'high farming' was not sustainable because it was dependent on long-distance imports of fertilizers such as guano from Peru. Useful, local nutrients ended up as urban pollution in the form of human and animal waste instead of being recycled (Foster 2000, 2002).

The difference between Marx and subsequent Marxian scholars was signaled in Marx's critique of the first program of the German Social Democratic party, the so-called 'Gotha Programme,' where Marx pointed out that "labor is not the source of all wealth. Nature is just as much the source of use values" (Marx [1875] 1970: Chapter 1), a point made in various places in *Das Kapital*. It is often argued that Marx and Engels had a naïve, productivist, 'man-masters-Nature' attitude. The following quote from Engels is often used as evidence to the contrary. It is from Engel's posthumously published book manuscript, 'The Dialectics of Nature.'

> Let us not, however, flatter ourselves overmuch on account of our human victories over nature. For each such victory nature takes its revenge on us. Each victory, it is true, in the first place brings about the results we expected, but in the second and third places it has quite different, unforeseen effects which only too often cancel the first.

Engels then gives several examples of such effects in previous times, and concludes:

Thus at every step we are reminded that we by no means rule over nature like a conqueror over a foreign people, like someone standing outside nature – but that we, with flesh, blood and brain, belong to nature, and exist in its midst, and that all our mastery of it consists in the fact that we have the advantage over all other creatures of being able to learn its laws and apply them correctly.

Engels [1925] 2015: 195

Did Marx and Engels have an eco-centric worldview, or was it overly anthropocentric? Joel Kovel (2012: 211) states that while Marx is clearly not Promethean, "there remains in his work a foreshortening of the intrinsic value of nature." Robyn Eckersly (cited in Benton 1996: 276) states that if orthodox eco-Marxists "would be prepared to defend ecosystem preservationism, it would be on purely human-centered, instrumental grounds." While the discussion about anthropo- versus eco-centrism is fairly abstract, it does manifest itself through different attitudes to the question of population control and lifestyle (Benton 1996: 292).

The energy debates

A recurrent topic has been the question of exchange-value and energy, often related to the work of Sergei Podolinsky, a Ukrainian socialist contemporary of Marx and Engels. Podolinsky is described as an important forerunner of ecological economics, credited with "the concept of energy return to energy input in different types of land use" (Martinez-Alier 1987: 5). Martinez-Alier argues that Marx and Engels (and later also Marxians) had a negative reaction to Podolinsky's efforts to develop an energy-based value theory. By the same token, a leading eco-Marxian, James O'Connor (1988), argues that Marx turned a 'deaf ear' to Podolinsky.

The 'Podolinsky affair' actually raises two separate issues: the theoretical possibility of an energy-based theory of value, a question most Marxian authors answer in the negative, and Marx and Engels' reaction to Podolinsky. Foster & Burkett (2016) present a detailed discussion of the 'Podolinsky affair' from the perspectives of both value theory and the history of economic thought. While disagreeing with Podolinsky, they conclude that Marx and Engels took him seriously.

Also relevant are the views of Marx and Engels on exhaustible resources. Tanuro (2010: 93) sees positive ecological aspects in Marx, but concludes that "this vision is rendered largely inoperative by a serious error in the treatment of energy." The reason for this negative conclusion is Marx's failure to distinguish between renewable and non-renewable energy resources, the *forms* of energy, and by doing so indirectly disarmed the labor movement from seeing this important distinction. Foster & Burkett (2016), on the other hand, point to textual evidence. For example, Engels writes to Marx:

What Podolinsky has entirely forgotten is that man as a worker is not merely a fixer of *present* solar heat but a still greater squanderer of *past* solar heat. The stores of energy, coal, ores, forests, etc., we succeed in squandering you [Marx] know better than I. From this point of view even fishing and hunting appear not as the fixation of new sun heat but as the using up and incipient waste of solar energy already accumulated.

Marx & Engels 1992: 411, italics in original

Although there is textual evidence that Marx and Engels were aware of this difference; they did not make it into a central question.

The question of energy involves a discussion of whether Engels rejected the second law of thermodynamics as argued by, for example, Daniel Bensaïd and Martinez-Alier. Foster &

Burkett (2016) argue that Engels did not oppose the second law of thermodynamics; he was just opposed to the conclusion about a 'heat death' of the universe as were many leading physicists at that time, and making a distinction about a closed system and the basically unknown dynamics of the total universe.

Ecology and political change

Subsequent Marxian scholars have not produced a major work on *political* ecology in the sense of socialist environmental policies. So the debate within the New Left commences with the works of Marx and Engels (see Foster (2000) and Foster & Burkett (2016) for references). Karl Polanyi (1944) has also clearly influenced the debate with his notion of labor and nature (land) as 'fictitious' commodities and the 'double movement' against the destruction of labor and land by free markets. O'Connor (1988) characterizes his view as 'Polanyian-Marxist.'

An important issue in the contemporary debate is the role of ecology in relation to the need for a change from capitalism to socialism and the forces driving such a change. Central to this debate has been the concept of a 'second contradiction' of capitalism launched by O'Connor (1988). O'Connor argues that in addition to the traditional contradiction between labor and capital, there is a second contradiction between capital and its natural conditions of production. He further argues that:

> Marx never put two and two together to argue that 'natural barriers' may be capitalistically produced barriers, that is a 'second' capitalized nature. In other words, there may exist a contradiction of capitalism which leads to an 'ecological' theory of crisis and social transformation.
>
> *O'Connor 1988: 14*

O'Connor stresses the increasing costs related to repairing environmental damage in a broad sense as increasing the possibility of a capitalist crisis. O'Connor does not pose squarely the question of all the natural phenomena that do not have a price. Critics claim the concept of the 'second contradiction' concept is limited. For example, many global environmental problems do not show up as 'reinternalized' monetary costs for firms; and even if they do, like global warming, it is too late, since the tipping points have been passed (Foster 2002).

Considering actual policies and real movements, what matters is not so much what Marx said *per se*, but what Marxians do. An author from the Marxian-inspired *Régulation* school, Alain Lipietz (2000: 69) distinguishes between Marx's writings, and ideas and the movements inspired by Marx that were "vanishing from the earth." A key point in Lipietz's argument is that contradictions in modern society, "while strongly overdetermined by capitalist relations," are not "reducible to them"; instead contradictions are 'horizontal,' that is, between the individual and the community rather than between rulers and ruled (2000: 79).

Postscript: the early Soviet years

Often, the ecological disasters of the Soviet Union are used as an indicator that Marxism is basically 'productivist.' In the early years of the Revolution, however, the Bolsheviks had a quite different policy. Before the Revolution in 1917 the conservationist movement in Russia proposed creating natural preserves, *zapovedniki*—areas which should be kept free from any human intervention besides scientific observation. Lenin signed the decree on the first *zapovednik* in 1919, and in the next decade a total of 61 *zapovedniki* were created. Gare (1996: 121) states that "ecological concepts were accepted into mainstream science in the Soviet Union in a way that contrasts radically with the marginal place similar ideas have occupied in the West up to the present," and that, regarding state policy, "it could be fairly argued that the Soviet Union led the world in ecology." Stalin replaced this 'path' by a 'productivist' one. The Soviet ecologists became "the most trenchant critics of the implementation of the Five Year Plan" and "opposed the damming of rivers without due care for the ecological effects" (Gare 1993: 124).

Post Keynesian economics and the environment

Observing the severe 1970s recession, Joan Robinson (1977) points out that economists must address natural resource constraints and pollution problems. While most economists looked for signs of growth, she posed an important question: "The greatest of all economic questions, but one that in fact is never asked: What is growth for?" (Robinson 1977: 1337). Robinson resurrected Keynes' vision of a future when 'the economic problem' will have been solved, and people will focus on "our real problems – the problems of life and of human relations, of creation and behavior and religion" (Keynes [1931] 2009: 2). However, Keynes never developed this perspective into a more comprehensive analysis of sustainability, and ecological constraints have not been the focus of Post Keynesian analyses. Ecological economists have criticized Post Keynesians for promoting economic growth and ignoring the ecological constraints, having a 'growth mania' (Daly 2007: 26; Spash & Schandl 2009). Spash & Schandl (2009: 55) see an excuse for Keynes himself, but less so for the Post Keynesians who, in spite of their claim of realism, have "persisted in this partial and limited view of reality for half a century." An obvious explanation for the lack of focus on ecological limits is that the Post Keynesian approach emerged out of the concern with unemployment (Mearman 2007).

Nevertheless, some positive changes are occurring. A major attempt has been made to bring ecological and Post Keynesian economics together over environmental issues (Holt et al. 2009). The contributions in this book verify differences in focus, but also indicate that the two schools share a number of insights and basic ideas. Two recently published handbooks—The Elgar Companion to Post Keynesian Economics (King 2012) and The Oxford Handbook of Post-Keynesian Economics (Harcourt & Kriesler 2013) include chapters on the environment and sustainability.

Mearman (2010) further points to several developments in Post Keynesian economics that are promising for a better understanding of environmental issues. At the ontological and methodological levels, there is the development of 'Babylonism' and critical realism, both open to a pluralist approach to economics, although Mearman (2010: 25) also admits that these developments "have not been universally accepted by Post-Keynesians."

Production, consumption, and sustainability

The outcome of the Cambridge capital controversy was that the concept of aggregate capital is inherently flawed, a result which can be applied also to 'natural capital' (Winnett 2012: 175; Perry 2013: 5). The Post Keynesian production function has fixed technical coefficients in the short-term, and is open to technological change in the long-term. Kronenberg (2010) claims that Post Keynesian production theory is compatible with ecological economics by rejecting gross substitution. As a consequence, Post Keynesians in general have favored a 'strong' version of sustainability, that is a definition where nature cannot smoothly be substituted for by man-made capital (Perry 2013: 5; Holt 2016: 363). The Post Keynesian view is thus in line with that of ecological economics as opposed to the conventional, 'weak' version of neoclassical economics.

Anders Ekeland, Bent Arne Sæther

Consumption is understood and analyzed differently to neoclassical consumption theory because needs are seen as satiable and separable, and some needs are subordinate to others. Thus, "the notions of gross substitution and trade-offs, which are so important for neoclassical economics, are brought down to a minor phenomenon which only operates within narrow boundaries" (Lavoie 2010: 142). Agents do not optimize in the neoclassical sense, but make decisions based on procedural rationality. Moreover, consumer tastes are also seen as outcomes of societal processes. Criticizing mainstream methods of contingent valuation, Winnett (2012: 173) poses the question "where does a person's notion of an appropriate price come from if not from social practice?"

In Post Keynesian theory, market prices will thus reflect neither resource scarcity nor inherent consumer preferences. Such an approach will "presumably not" encompass the neoclassical concept of externalities (Winnett 2012: 173). In similar vein, Perry (2013: 5) argues that in a Pasinetti-type model, pollution would "constitute a joint product," a concept also emphasized by some ecological economists (Baumgärtner et al. 2001).

Policies and power

Post Keynesians do not accept the mainstream doctrine that prices can be corrected to produce optimal outcomes. Limited substitution possibilities, fundamental uncertainty as well as equity considerations, are reasons why more trust should be placed in regulatory instruments than price incentives in environmental policy (Earl & Wakeley 2010). Still, environmental taxes can have a role to play. Perry (2013: 8) points out that in a Kaleckian model, such taxes may have a stronger influence in the long-run than in the short-run. Additional elements in such a policy will be public investment to ensure structural change, and government efforts to secure finance for green investment made necessary by the uncertain private profitability of such investments. The 'Green New Deal' concept, launched in the wake of the financial crisis of 2007, can be seen as a merger of environmental and Keynesian (though not specifically Post Keynesian) policies (Courvisanos 2012: 521; Winnett 2012: 172).

When sketching Post Keynesian ecological macroeconomics, Fontana & Sawyer (2016: 186) present a model that explicitly acknowledges economic growth as a 'double-edged sword' that can not only help to reduce unemployment, but also cause severe environmental problems. Without a smooth neoclassical self-adjustment, natural constraints can lower capacity utilization and employment. Fontana & Sawyer (2016: 193) go on to argue that "governmental policies and changing social norms are likely to be more successful than market forces in bringing the growth of output towards a sustainable path." It should be noted that although Post Keynesian assumptions deviate from those of neoclassical growth models, their discussion and the policy conclusions are quite close to what can be found in works by mainstream economists.

Heterodox economics for sustainability

We need economic theories that guide actions on urgent ecological problems. As humanity faces potentially devastating global warming, a rapid extinction of biodiversity, and other serious environmental problems, theories and policies for full employment and more equal distributions can no longer be formulated without taking into consideration the ecological consequences. The ecological impacts of economic activities cannot be treated as add-ons to more important policy issues. The question is *whether heterodox economics is up to the challenge* on all the levels needed, from fundamental methodological levels to political levels.

422

The static and marginalist nature of the dominant neoclassical economics renders it unable to cope with uncertain and fundamentally dynamic processes in society and nature, and with the magnitude of the transitions needed from an economy based on fossil energy to one built on renewable energy. This concern is increasingly recognized by many economists, policymakers, and the general public. This means that heterodox theory will be—indeed must become—more relevant in the future. But one question arises: Are heterodox economic schools focused on the urgent problems related to energy, climate, and environment? The answer is negative. Our reading of Post Keynesian and Marxian literature reveals that most economists of these schools have ignored ecological aspects. Nevertheless, some positive changes are taking place, and the engagement of economists of other schools, such as the original institutionalists, has been more vigorous.[2] Heterodox economists must relate to the challenges from ecological economists. This leads us to *the issues of growth*—that is, the ecological limits to growth, the drivers of growth, and the question of what can and should grow and what cannot. Humanity is not on a sustainable growth path and must make a transition to a sustainable one—a path that is based on renewable energy and with considerably less material throughput per capita than the average of advanced capitalist economies. For one thing, this daunting task calls for a new macroeconomics[3] where the key question is an 'optimal control' problem, that is how to get from where we are to where we need to be in the near future. Second, theories supporting systemic changes must include an understanding of political power. They must put forward proposals that can mobilize the actual, existing political forces, such as Left-Green political parties, trade unions, and the environmental movement. Integration must run both ways. Ecological issues cannot be analyzed in isolation. How can alliances be built over a green transition, full employment, and decent work in the age of automation? Heterodox economics must measure its success by its contribution bringing humanity closer to sustainability.

The question concerning policy formation is, of course, multi-faceted. Institutional economists in particular have raised the issue of how economic behavior is shaped by the social context. As consumers, we follow a different logic than that of the citizen. This is highly relevant for the role of a deliberate democracy, and the role of the market as a part of this, or as an alternative. A key issue is *the role of prices* in environmental policies. The idea of 'the correct price' in mainstream environmental economics is based on flawed assumptions. This does not imply that carbon taxes and other price-based instruments cannot play a prominent role. Martinez-Alier (1995) argues for 'ecologically corrected prices,' that is, prices that are not 'optimal' in any sense. The price of fossil fuels will be the most fundamental price, and the distributional effects will be a major factor in this price-setting process. Heterodox economists of different schools should commence a dialogue as to their understanding of how the economy works, and how policies and strategies should be shaped.

Some forward-looking economists within the mainstream and some frontrunners in the economic establishment are already sketching a transition of the economy based on the present structures of property and power. This raises the issue of whether existing capitalism can also be sustainable in a social and ecological sense—that is, to what extent the ecological limits challenge the very functioning of our economy. All in all, the various schools of heterodox economics place too much emphasis on 'old' issues, failing to see both the need for and the potential in an ecologically based economics. Pointing out the limitations of neoclassical economics, including criticizing its ideological role, will be very important until its hegemony is broken. Focusing on ecological issues is key to achieving that. Green economist Molly Scott Cato (2012: 1033) calls for "putting the planet and politics back into economics." The first step must be to bring the planet and ecological politics into heterodox economics.

Notes

1 In 2016 the Overshoot Day is estimated to be August 8. The date arrives approximately one week earlier each year.
2 See, for example, Vatn (2005, 2015) for comprehensive contributions from an institutional economist with a long-time participation in the ecological economics community. See also Spash & Villena (1998) for an evaluation of the relation between original institutionalism and ecological economics.
3 For an overview of the origins and the state of the art of ecological macroeconomics, see Rezai & Stagl (2016).

References

Anderson, B. & M'Gonigle, M. 2012. 'Does ecological economics have a future?' *Ecological Economics*, 84 (2): 37–48.

Baumgärtner, S., Dyckhoff, H., Faber, M., Proops, J., & Schiller, J. 2001. 'The concept of joint production and ecological economics.' *Ecological Economics*, 36 (3): 365–372.

Benton, T. (ed.) 1996. *The Greening of Marxism*. New York: Guildford Press.

Boulding, K. 1966. 'The economics of the coming spaceship earth,' *in*: H. Jarrett (ed.), *Environmental Quality in a Growing Economy*. Baltimore, MD: Johns Hopkins University Press, 3–14.

Carson, R. 1962. *Silent Spring*. Boston: Houghton Mifflin.

Cato, M.S. 2012. 'Green economics: putting the planet and politics back into economics.' *Cambridge Journal of Economics*, 36 (5): 1033–1049.

Common, M. & Stagl, S. 2005. *Ecological Economics: An Introduction*. Cambridge: Cambridge University Press.

Costanza, R., Cumberland, J.H., Daly, H., Goodland, R., Norgaard, R.B., Kubiszewski, I., & Franko, C. 2015. *An Introduction to Ecological Economics*, 2nd edn. Boca Raton, FL: CRC Press.

Courvisanos, J. 2012. 'Sustainable development,' *in*: J.E. King (ed.), *The Elgar Companion to Post-Keynesian Economics*, 2nd edn. Cheltenham, UK: Edward Elgar, 515–523.

Crutzen, P. 2002. 'Geology of mankind: the Anthropocene.' *Nature*, 415 (6867): 23.

Dale, G. 2013. 'Critiques of growth in classical political economy: Mill's stationary state and a Marxian response.' *New Political Economy*, 18 (3): 431–457.

Daly, H.E. 2007. *Ecological Economics and Sustainable Development: Selected Essays of Herman Daly*. Cheltenham, UK: Edward Elgar.

Daly, H.E. 2015. *Essays Against Growthism*. Bristol, UK: World Economic Association.

Daly, H.E. & Farley, J. 2011: *Ecological Economics: Principles and Applications*, 2nd edn. Washington, DC: Island Press.

Demaria, F., Schneider, F., Sekulova, F., & Martinez-Alier, J. 2013. 'What is degrowth? From an activist slogan to a social movement.' *Environmental Values*, 22 (2): 191–215.

Earl, P.E. & Wakeley, T. 2010. 'Price-based versus standard-based approaches to reducing car addiction and other environmentally destructive activities,' *in*: R. P.F. Holt, C.L. Spash, & S. Pressman (eds.), *Post-Keynesian and Ecological Economics: Confronting Environmental Issues*. Cheltenham, UK: Edward Elgar, 158–177.

Easterlin, R.A. 1995. 'Will rising income of all increase the happiness of all?' *Journal of Economic Behavior and Organization*, 27 (1): 35–47.

Engels, F. [1925] 2015. *The Dialectics of Nature: Explanation about Dialectical Materialism*. Tamil Nadu, India: Leopard Books.

Fischer-Kowalski, M. 1998. 'The intellectual history of materials flow analysis, Part I, 1860–1970.' *Journal of Industrial Ecology*, 2 (1): 61–78.

Fontana, G. & Sawyer, M. 2016. 'Towards a post-Keynesian ecological macroeconomics.' *Ecological Economics*, 121 (January): 186–195.

Foster, J.B. 2000. *Marx Ecology: Materialism and Nature*. New York: Monthly Review Press

Foster, J.B. 2002. 'The nature of the contradiction.' *Monthly Review*, 54 (4). Available from http://monthlyreview.org/2002/09/01/capitalism-and-ecology [Accessed September 22, 2016]

Foster, J.B. & Burkett, P. 2016. *Marx and the Earth: An Anti-Critique*. Leiden, Netherlands: Brill

Gare, A. 1996. 'Soviet environmentalism, the path not taken,' *in*: T. Benton (ed.), *The Greening of Marxism*. New York: Guildford Press, 111–128.

Georgescu-Roegen, N. 1971. *The Entropy Law and the Economic Process*. Cambridge, MA: Harvard University Press.

Gorz, A. 1994, *Capitalism, Socialism, Ecology.* London: Verso.

Harcourt, G.C. & Kriesler, P. 2013. *The Oxford Handbook of Post-Keynesian Economics,* two volumes. Oxford: Oxford University Press.

Holling, C.S. 1973. 'Resilience and stability of ecological systems.' *Annual Review of Ecological Systems,* 4 (November): 1–24.

Holt, R. 2016. 'Sustainable development,' *in:* L.-P. Rochon & S. Rossi (eds.), *An Introduction to Macroeconomics: A Heterodox Approach to Economic Analysis.* Cheltenham, UK: Edward Elgar, 359–380.

Holt, R., Pressman, S., & Spash C. (eds.) 2009. *Post-Keynesian and Ecological Economics: Confronting Ecological Issues.* Cheltenham, UK: Edward Elgar.

Jackson, T., Jager, W., & Stagl, S. 2004. 'Beyond insatiability – needs theory, consumption and sustainability,' *in:* L.A. Reisch & Inge Røpke (eds.), *The Ecological Economics of Consumption.* Cheltenham, UK: Edward Elgar, 79–110.

Keynes, J.M. [1931] 2009. *Essays in Persuasion.* New York: Classic House Books.

King, J.E. 2012. *The Elgar Companion to Post Keynesian Economics,* 2nd edn. Cheltenham, UK: Edward Elgar.

Kovel, J. 2002. *The Enemy of Nature: The End of Capitalism or the End of the World?* London: Zed Books.

Kronenberg, T. 2010. 'Finding common ground between ecological economics and post-Keynesian economics.' *Ecological Economics,* 69 (7): 1488–1494.

Lavoie, M. 2010. 'Post-Keynesian consumer choice theory and ecological economics,' *in:* R. P.F. Holt, C.L. Spash, & S. Pressman (eds.), *Post-Keynesian and Ecological Economics: Confronting Environmental Issues.* Cheltenham, UK: Edward Elgar, 141–157.

Lipietz, A. 2000. 'Political ecology and the future of Marxism.' *Capitalism Nature Socialism,* 11 (1): 69–85.

Martinez-Alier, J. 1987. *Ecological Economics.* Oxford: Basil Blackwell.

Martinez-Alier, J. 1995. 'Distributional issues in ecological economics.' *Review of Social Economy,* 53 (4): 511–528.

Martinez-Alier, J. & Røpke, I. (eds.) 2008: *Recent Developments in Ecological Economics.* Cheltenham, UK: Edgar Elgar.

Marx, K. [1875] 1970. *Critique of the Gotha Programme.* Moscow: Progress Publishers.

Marx, K. & Engels, F. 1992. *Collected Works, Vol. 46.* New York: International Publishers.

Meadows, D.H., Meadows, D.L., Randers, J., & Behrens, W. 1972. *The Limits to Growth.* New York: Universe Books.

Mearman A. 2007. 'Post-Keynesian economics and the environment: waking up and smelling the coffee burning?' *International Journal of Green Economics,* 1 (3/4): 374–380.

Mearman, A. 2010. 'Recent developments in Post-Keynesian methodology and their relevance for understanding environmental issues,' *in:* R.P.F. Holt, C.L. Spash, & S. Pressman (eds.), *Post-Keynesian and Ecological Economics: Confronting Environmental Issues.* Cheltenham, UK: Edward Elgar, 27–46.

Norgaard, R.B. 1989. 'The case for methodological pluralism.' *Ecological Economics,* 1 (1): 37–57.

O'Connor, J. 1988. 'Capitalism, nature, socialism: a theoretical introduction.' *Capitalism Nature Socialism,* 1 (1): 11–38.

Perry, N. 2013. 'Environmental economics and policy,' *in:* G.C. Harcourt & P. Kriesler (eds.), *The Oxford Handbook of Post-Keynesian Economics, Volume 2: Critiques and Methodology.* Oxford: Oxford University Press, 391–411.

Plumecocq, G. 2014. 'The second generation of ecological economics: how far has the apple fallen from the tree?' *Ecological Economics,* 107 (November): 457–468.

Polyani, K. 1944. *The Great Transformation.* Boston: Beacon Press.

Rezai, A. & Stagl, S. 2016. 'Ecological macroeconomics: introduction and review.' *Ecological Economics,* 121 (January): 181–185.

Robinson, J. 1977. 'What are the questions?' *Journal of Economic Literature,* 15 (4): 1318–1339.

Røpke, I. 2004. 'The early history of modern ecological economics.' *Ecological Economics,* 50 (3/4): 293–314.

Spash, C.L. 1999. 'The development of environmental thinking in economics.' *Environmental Values,* 8 (4): 413–435.

Spash, C.L. 2012. 'New foundations for ecological economics.' *Ecological Economics,* 77 (May): 36–47.

Spash, C.L. & Schandl, H. 2009. 'Challenges for Post-Keynesian growth theory: utopia meets environmental and social reality,' *in:* R. P.F. Holt, C.L. Spash, & S. Pressman (eds.), *Post-Keynesian and Ecological Economics: Confronting Environmental Issues.* Cheltenham, UK: Edward Elgar, 47–76.

Spash, C.L. & Villena, M.G. 1998. Exploring the approach of institutional economics to the environment. Environment Series Number 11. Department of Land Economy, University of Cambridge, UK.

Tanuro, D. 2010. 'Marxism, energy, and ecology: the moment of truth.' *Capitalism Nature Socialism*, 21 (4): 89–101.

UNCED. 1993. *The Earth Summit: The United Nations Conference on Environment and Development*. London: Graham and Trotman.

Vatn, A. 2005. *Institutions and the Environment*. Cheltenham, UK: Edward Elgar.

Vatn, A. 2015. *Environmental Governance: Institutions, Policies and Actions*. Cheltenham, UK: Edward Elgar.

Wackernagel, M. & Rees, W.E. 1996. *Our Ecological Footprint: Reducing Human Impact on the Earth*. British Columbia, Canada: New Society Publishers.

Winnett, A. 2012. 'Environmental economics,' *in*: J.E. King (ed.), *The Elgar Companion to Post Keynesian Economics*, 2nd edn. Cheltenham, UK: Edward Elgar, 170–175.

Wrigley, E.A. 2010. *Energy and the English Industrial Revolution*. Cambridge: Cambridge University Press.

WWF. 2014. 'Living planet report 2014.' Washington, DC: World Wildlife Fund. Available from http://www.worldwildlife.org/pages/living-planet-report-2014 [Accessed August 8, 2016]

Part V

Transforming the capitalist social provisioning process

31

An exit strategy from capitalism's ecological crisis

Lynne Chester

Introduction

Nature is continuously impacted by the process of capitalist accumulation. Nature is converted, redefined, and transformed into sites of production for profit through a process of re-ordering which requires material and energy inputs, and produces waste. The high dependency of capitalism on the extraction and burning of fossil fuels as sources of energy is one critical cause of escalating and irreparable ecological degradation.

The ecological crisis is one dimension of the contemporary crisis of capitalism. Other dimensions include the energy and economic crises. The common cause for all three crises lies in the capitalist model of economic growth and the accumulation process. Nevertheless, policy responses are directed at addressing particular aspects of a crisis (for example, carbon emissions). Discourse and proposed policy solutions reflect little understanding of the interrelationships—or the points of intersection—between these three crises. This has meant each crisis is treated as quite separate.

The ecological crisis discourse focuses almost exclusively on climate change and not the multi-dimensional nature of the crisis. Policy responses, strongly informed by mainstream economics, are narrowly directed at the manifestations of problems—not causes—and underscored by a conceptualization of nature as providing stocks and services and being capable of management. Alternative policy prescriptions advocated by heterodox scholars fall within a dichotomy reflecting different social ontological views: those advocating the reform of capitalism using the same mechanisms which have embedded the ecological crisis (for example, ecological economics, steady-state economics); and, those proposing another system of economic organization (for example, ecological Marxism, socialist ecology) which is highly unlikely before irreversible ecological changes catastrophic for human well-being. This chapter proposes another policy approach to an exit strategy from capitalism's ecological crisis which accounts for the multiple interdependent spheres constituting capitalism and the need to address the root cause, not symptoms, of the crisis.

The chapter is structured in four parts. The first section outlines the contours of the policy narrative for solutions to the ecological crisis and posits an alternative approach to overcome the inherent weaknesses in the dichotomy of heterodox policy prescriptions. The second section of the chapter outlines the social ontological view—the relation of capitalist accumulation and nature—in which the chapter's subsequent discussion of a proposed policy approach is grounded. A third section presents a preliminary contribution to the proposed complex policy task. The interdependencies of the ecological, economic, and energy spheres is discussed using the current three crises as a lens though which to understand that relationship. A final section concludes that an effective exit strategy from the ecological crisis must: address its multiple dimensions and interdependencies with capitalism's other spheres; be directed at the accumulation process not the symptoms of ecological degradation; and, thus requires a restructuring of the existing mode of *régulation* to create a new regime of accumulation.

The contours of the policy narrative

Within many social and natural science discourses, the ecological crisis is treated solely in terms of climate change caused by escalating greenhouse gas emissions as a result of capitalism's high dependency on fossil fuels for energy. Climate change is one of the nine interdependent planetary boundaries identified by the Stockholm Resilience Centre Project as critical to "maintaining an earth-system environment in which humanity can exist safely" (Foster *et al.* 2010: 14). Drawing from scientific knowledge to quantify these boundaries, this Project concluded: three boundaries have been breached—climate change, rate of biodiversity loss, changes to the nitrogen cycle; and the boundaries for land system change, global freshwater use, ocean acidification, ozone depletion, and the nitrogen and phosphorous cycles (that impact soil fertility and thus food production) are on the brink (Rockström *et al.* 2009).[1]

> The mapping out of planetary boundaries in this way gives us a better sense of the real threat to the earth system [sic]. Although in recent years the environmental threat has come to be seen by many as simply a question of climate change, protecting the planet requires that we attend to all these planetary boundaries, and others not yet determined. The essential problem is the unavoidable fact that an expanding economic system is placing additional burdens on a fixed earth system to the point of planetary overload.
>
> *Foster* et al. *2010: 17–18*

Despite the multi-dimensional nature of the ecological crisis commonly being subsumed into the hallmark of climate change, there is widespread acknowledgment that "humans constitute the dominant driver of change to the Earth System" (Rockström *et al.* 2009: 2), which is the biophysical and socio-economic processes and cycles determining, through their interactions, the planet's environmental state. However, dominant policy prescriptions—based on mainstream economic theory—are framed to minimize negative externalities to the air, water, soil, living organisms, and the built environment instead of setting ecological boundaries for human development. The planet's ecosystems (the environment) are deemed to provide "stocks of resources, flows of ecosystem services, or low-cost natural infrastructure" (Lohmann 2016: 484) and to be capable of management.

The regulation of mineral extraction, water supply and waste disposal, marketable property rights over forests, fisheries and water sources, land use planning, wetlands mitigation banking, emissions permits, fishing catch quotas, legal liability for oil spills, and charges for effluent or emissions are exemplars of the different techniques initiated by capitalism to manage the environment. These techniques focus on the manifest problem—not the cause—with each treated as a commodity. Markets are regarded as the optimal solution. For example, pollution is defined as "something to be aggregated, regulated and traded . . . using any means available, not something that occurred at particular sites and had to be fought using specified technologies" (Lohmann 2016: 484). In addition, entities have been deemed as " 'renewable resources' which were supposed to be indefinitely exploitable as long as a calculable, more or less linear schedule for their replenishment was respected" (*ibid.*).

Mainstream policy prescriptions are framed around price, the elasticities of supply and demand, demand forecasting, and the deregulation of markets. One prominent example is the strategy proposed by the renowned climate scientist James Hansen (2012) to reduce CO_2 emissions before global warming spirals out of human control. Hansen advocates making CO_2 emissions prohibitively expensive through the imposition of a uniform fee on fossil fuel companies for each tonne of carbon produced at source. All revenue collected would be redistributed to the population on a per capita basis to compensate for the significant price impacts of the fee on all commodities produced and transported using fossil fuels.

Coincidently to the development of policies to manage the environment, the concept of sustainable development was "transformed, stripped of its critical content, and reconfigured" (Carruthers 2001: 93) to become virtually synonymous with sustained economic growth. This concept was excised of the connotation of "grassroots engagement, equality and social justice, local empowerment and low-impact development" (Dale *et al.* 2016: 3) and there has been a conflation of sustainability (the ecological problem) with development (the economic problem) (Paton 2008: 94). Continual economic growth has been promoted and accepted as axiomatic to sustainable development. Thus the environment has been reconceptualized by mainstream economics, policymakers, and supranational organizations as an economic not an ecological problem and a recast concept of sustainability adopted as a commonly accepted policy goal. Hence, the ecological challenge is perceived through an economic prism with the emphasis on "reducing the environmental impact of each unit of economic activity" (Gibbs & Healey 1997: 195) through market measures and legitimizing particular levels of environmental damage.

Ecological economics directly responded to the mainstream's depiction of the environment "as simply the sum of a discrete collection of resources and an incidental backdrop to economic activity" (Rosewarne 2002: 185). Methodologically pluralist, ecological economics is distinguishable from mainstream economics through *inter alia* its: condemnation of reliance on technology to solve the problems of scarcity and waste; respect for the complexity and holism of natural systems; scientific approach; use of key ecological concepts such as capacities for assimilation, regeneration, and carrying; vision of the earth as being thermodynamically closed; valuing of nature in biophysical terms; and, an emphasis on issues of distribution and justice.[2] Ecological sustainability is the primary objective and the approach of ecological economics can be broadly described as to:

> First, establish the ecological limits of sustainable scale and establish policies that assure the throughput of the economy stays within these limits. Second, establish a fair and just distribution of resources using systems of property rights and transfers . . . Third, once the scale and distribution problems are solved, market-based mechanisms can be used to allocate resources efficiently.
>
> *Costanza* et al. *1997: 83*

So, notwithstanding differences with mainstream economics, ecological economics advocates the use of mainstream policy measures—property rights and market-based mechanisms—to achieve ecological sustainability. In other words, the ecological destruction of capitalism will be overcome by the reform of capitalism using the same policy measures that have accelerated that destruction. This approach is exemplified by Hahnel (2011) who offers an ecological economics perspective of the environmental crisis and advocates tackling climate change with the mainstream policy measures of regulation, taxes, and tradable permits using property rights, zoning, transfer development rights, and community management. "The centre of gravity of the ecological economic policy options thus tends to be set in reaction to the parameters of the existing policy framework and to what is practicable within this framework" (Rosewarne 2002: 188) despite often being represented as green economics.

In the early 2000s and particularly in the aftermath of the global financial crisis of 2008, "as sustainable development—the discourse and project—lost its way, it gradually, inexorably, found itself folded into a new framework: green economy and 'green growth'" (Dale et al. 2016: 4). Nature is now explicitly conceptualized as a form of capital to be produced, converted, and accumulated. Green growth is promoted as the panacea for both the ecological and economic crises: the creation of new markets, a stronger commodification of nature and new profit opportunities will stimulate a new cycle of growth. The obstacles created by ecological degradation—for example, the exhaustion of local resources, excessive waste, illness, too much CO_2—are viewed as the source of opportunities for new forms of capital accumulation (Kenis & Lievens 2016). The green capitalism project has, however, not halted—or dented—the ecological crisis because capitalism's DNA of unlimited growth and profits cannot be aligned with the contradictory goal of arresting and redressing the ecological crisis (Smith, R. 2011).

Support has also been expressed for Herman Daly's (1973) notion of a steady-state economy: *"an economy with constant stocks of people and artifacts, maintained at some desired, sufficient levels by low rates of maintenance 'throughput',* that is, by the lowest feasible flows of matter and energy" (Daly 1991: 17, original emphasis). Achievement of Daly's steady-state is premised on the mainstream policy instruments of private property rights and markets although he does advocate some centralized planning to set quotas and controls on the use of particular resources. "Once the level of resource throughout is reduced to a sustainable level, the pattern of consumption will automatically adapt, thanks to the market. Let the market determine efficient allocation" (Daly 1996: 16). In other words, by reducing growth and consumption, capitalism can be reconstructed to be a steady-state economy using the same mechanisms that support its current form of economic organization.

Degrowth is another strategy proposed to reduce the economic growth of capitalist economies (Latouche 2004). This strategy has been criticized for being vague about how the output level can be reduced and perpetually maintained in a steady state, and inequitable application of the concept to both wealthy and poor countries (Foster 2011).

Similar criticisms can be leveled at Jonathon Porritt's notion of sustainable capitalism. Porritt (2007: 137) is of the view that "there is no inherent, fixed or non-negotiable aspect of capitalism" that makes sustainability unattainable. He contends that humanity faces two conflicting imperatives—a biological imperative to limit consumption growth and a political imperative to raise living standards—and proclaims the solution to be a better quality of growth with wise consumption, primarily achieved by repackaging the idea of natural limits to gain the understanding and acceptance of the majority. The mechanisms to undertake this repackaging and create Porritt's sustainable capitalism are the "usual levers—government intervention, consumer preference, international diplomacy, education and so on" (*ibid*: 138) and "properly regulated markets" (*ibid*: 90).

For the proponents of a steady-state economy, degrowth or Porritt's sustainable capitalism, "growth is seen as entirely *subjective*, optional, not built into capitalist economies. So it can be dispensed with, exorcised, [manipulated] and capitalism can carry on in something like 'statis'" (Smith, R. 2010: 30, original emphasis).

Ecofeminism, social ecology, deep ecology, and ecological Marxism present more radical alternatives to those proposing the reform or reconstruction of capitalism to deal with the ecological crisis. Technological fixes and the notion of green markets are rejected. Radical ecological alternatives are also political projects with considerable emphasis placed on transforming the power relations that structure human interactions with the natural environment (for example, patriarchal relations). Given the scale and pace of change needed to address the ecological crisis and its inexorable relationship with capitalism's incessant drive to accumulate, "what is required is an ecological revolution that would need to be also a social revolution" (Foster *et al.* 2010: 426). A social revolution is needed to create a just and sustainable society. An ecological revolution, it is posited, requires short-term strategies such as leaving fossil fuels in the ground, reducing carbon emissions as quickly as possible to near zero, direct intervention of the state through expenditure and regulation, and 'contraction and convergence' in greenhouse gas emissions between the North and the South. "The long-term strategy for ecological revolution throughout the globe involves the building of a society of substantive equality—the struggle for socialism" (*ibid*: 441). Sustainable human development, the restoration of harmony between humans and nature and thus elimination of the ecological rift, so the argument goes, will only be achieved through: (i) social ownership and social use of nature, (ii) social production organized by workers and regulation of the metabolic relation between humans and nature, and (iii) satisfaction of present and future communal needs. As to how a 'universal revolt' against capitalism will occur to eliminate the ecological rift is, however, not well defined or concretized. Discussion of what will actually be required in the necessary transition that capitalism must undergo is vague.

This discussion of the policy prescriptions to resolve the ecological crisis reveals different conceptualizations of the problem and the economic-environment relation. Some view nature as separate from the accumulation process; others consider nature as a form of capital; and, others perceive nature as being shaped, re-ordered, and transformed by accumulation. For mainstream economics, the environment can be neatly eviscerated from its role within the economic system and commodities and markets can be designed to minimize detrimental effects to the environment. This worldview of mainstream economics, presupposed by its formalistic methods, reflects a quite distinct ontological view of social reality—capitalism is a closed economic system with no exogenous influences. The externalities of production like pollution are not regarded as pervasive or intrinsic but as capable of being internalized—to maintain a closed system—through treatment as economic costs. Ecological economics, steady-state economics, and degrowth, on the other hand, share a different social ontological view of reality—the growth of capitalism has caused ecological destruction and herein lies the cure; the objective of capitalist growth can be recalibrated to ameliorate the ecological crisis. The more radical approaches such as ecological Marxism and socialist ecology see the capitalist mode of production as structured around conflictual social relations and the capitalist economy is organized around the accumulation of capital. Hence, the key to solving the ecological crisis lies in changing these relations and the accumulation process to create an alternative economic system.

The more salient point about heterodox policy prescriptions to solve the ecological crisis is this: these policies pose a dualism of *either* reforming capitalism (using the same measures which have not halted but embedded the ecological crisis) *or* changing capitalism to another system of economic organization (without clearly articulating how this will occur). The options provided by this dualism are unsatisfactory. The contention that capitalism can be reformed to resolve the ecological crisis (or any other crisis)—using markets, prices, and commodification—is not supported by history or reality. Energy efficient light bulbs, appliances, and buildings, carbon trading and carbon taxes, waste recycling, organically produced food, and other 'techniques' introduced to 'manage' environmental problems have failed to halt the ecological crisis. The scientific evidence (for example, the Stockholm Resilience Centre Project) indicates that action is needed now to prevent significant—and irreversible—global human-induced environmental change, and action to address cause *not* effect. Yet to achieve, for example, global agreement to limit warming to 1.5 degrees above pre-industrial levels, technological solutions are being considered which will not address the root cause *per se* and will result in ecosystem damage eclipsing the benefits of lower warming (Hamilton 2016). However, at the other end of the policy spectrum, the prospects to achieve an alternate socio-economic system—before irreversible changes catastrophic for human well-being—seem highly improbable.

I suggest that there is another option to this policy dichotomy impasse although this will require a significant shift in thinking. The model of social and economic organization represented by capitalism constitutes multiple *interdependent* spheres such as the economic, cultural, social, political, ecological, technological, energy, and spatial. These spheres are interdependent because a change in one will impact other spheres. A common example of this relationship is evidenced by capitalism's increasing use of fossil fuels as a source of energy (energy sphere) which, in turn, contributes significantly to greenhouse gas emissions causing environmental damage (ecological sphere). Other examples of these interdependencies between spheres are: government subsidies, other funding forms and taxation (political and economic spheres) to encourage the use of fossil fuels (economic, energy, and spatial spheres), to provide relief to low-income households from rising electricity prices (energy and social spheres), to encourage the use of renewable energy sources (technological, energy, and spatial spheres), or to facilitate the operation of carbon trading markets or a reduction in carbon emissions (economic and ecological spheres). Consequently, if a strategy focuses solely on the ecological sphere—through the manifestations of environmental degradation—it will be ineffective because both the root cause and these interdependencies between spheres, and thus their influence, are ignored.

To provide a preliminary contribution to this obviously complex policy task, this chapter now considers the relationship between the economic, energy, and ecological spheres—three dimensions of the current crisis of capitalism—and their interdependent relationship with the accumulation process. However, before doing so, it is necessary to set out the nature of the core problem—the relation of capitalist accumulation and nature. It is this social ontological view in which the subsequent discussion of the three spheres—through the lenses of their respective crises—is grounded.

The core problem: capitalist accumulation and nature

Accumulation, the process by which capitalism is reproduced and expanded over time, must ensure the maintenance and reproduction of two fundamental social relations (the commodity relation and the wage relation) otherwise crises will occur. Certain conditions—regularities—sustain core elements of these social relations to ensure the hegemony of capitalism although their historical form will evolve. As the chapter in this volume by Labrousse & Michel demonstrates, these regularities are denoted by the accumulation regime, a period of relatively stable capitalist development, and reflected in the social and economic patterns that define a particular combination of production and consumption as well as sustaining the accumulation process between crises (Boyer & Saillard 2002).

The conjunction of five institutional forms—the mode of *régulation*—governs and secures the accumulation regime although the inherent tensions and contradictions of capitalism's social relations will never totally disappear and thus crises can occur. These institutional forms are the monetary and financial regimes, the form of competition, the wage-labor nexus, the form of the state, and a national economy's international integration. These institutions of the mode embed macroeconomic coherence. Capitalism has developed in *stages*, given its propensity for crisis, and each stage exhibits its own distinctive conjunction of institutions (and relation with nature).

The cycles of capital accumulation require reproduction and intensification to realize profits from initial investments. Commodification is critical to ongoing capital accumulation, of creating new objects of production and extending existing objects, objects around which profits can be realized and capital accumulated. Hence, the importance of the mode of *régulation*—to ensure opportunities for new sites of accumulation—and particularly the critical role played by the state in securing the other institutional forms and their overall complementarity.

Capitalism's relation with nature can be considered in a number of ways, the first being the abstraction of nature as an object of production (Smith, N. 2006, 2010). Accordingly, the dictates of accumulation require continuous expansion of the capitalist mode of production and hence the never-ending quest for sources of material resources. "Nature becomes a *universal means of production* in the sense that it not only provides the subjects, objects, and instruments of production, but is also in its totality an appendage to the production process" (Smith, N. 2010: 71, original emphasis). Nature is appropriated and subordinated to capitalism's logic. That is, nature is produced literally through "alteration of the form of received nature . . . [and] the universal production of nature was written into the DNA of capitalist ambition from the start; neoliberal globalization is only its latest incarnation" (Smith, N. 2006: 22).

A more concrete notion of nature is as an indefinite resource and condition of production required by capitalism (O'Connor 1998). Natural resources such as fossil fuels, water, forests, fish, and other species form one of the three conditions necessary for capitalist production, the other two being the built environment and the reproduction of human labor power. This use of nature, propelled by the drive to accumulate, however, causes ecological destruction ranging from smaller scale dis-amenities (such as pollution of local waterways, excessive noise, and traffic congestion) to destruction on a much larger and more widespread scale (such as global warming, soil erosion, deforestation, desertification, and species extinction). To maintain or repair the natural conditions of production imposes costs, which threaten profitability and thus ongoing accumulation. O'Connor (1998) deems these costs to form part of the second contradiction of capitalism, the possibility of an economic crisis from the supply side, that is, from an undermining of the conditions of production.[3]

These conceptions of nature lead to the view that the imperative to accumulate means nature, performing a tap-and-sink role, is subjected to continuous reorganization. Capitalist production continuously re-orders nature and re-ordered nature presents bounds or parameters to economic activity: "the economic process is not an isolated, self-sustaining process. This process cannot go on without a continuous exchange which alters the environment in a cumulative way and without being, in turn, influenced by these alterations" (Georgescu-Roegen 1975: 348). Capitalism converts nature into sites of production for profit through a process of re-ordering, which requires material and energy inputs, and produces waste. Processes of production also both redefine and transform nature: industrial areas are designated; a region becomes a mining area with the establishment of mining operations; spaces for recreational use arise from the destruction of others and the relocation of human recreational needs; forests are replaced by agricultural activities; and river systems are reconfigured by canals, dams, and weirs (Altvater 1989).

It is this conversion, redefinition, and transformation of nature by the process of accumulation that has caused ecological degradation which has escalated with the evolution of capitalism. Moreover, each stage of capitalism has displayed a distinct economic-environment relation, the scope and form of which is given *definition* by the mode of *régulation* specific to that stage of capitalism. The institutional forms of the mode, particularly in the post-Fordist era, have increasingly included ecological *régulation*—a range of actions and policies primarily initiated by the state to deal with the symptoms of ecological degradation (that is, environmental managerialism).

These actions and policies are clear indicators of the scope and form of the economic-environment relation because they are directed at removal or alleviation of impediments to accumulation exemplified by various types of environmental degradation. They are evidence of the *type and form* of interaction between the capitalist economic system and the environment: for example, the trading schemes to purportedly reduce greenhouse gas emissions due to capitalism's thirst for energy from fossil fuels; the environmental impact assessments commonly conducted for new infrastructure projects and used to negotiate compromises for projects to proceed; the fishing quotas imposed to allegedly ensure species survival but also maintain economic activity; the legislation imposing penalties for large-scale oil spills (but not preventing or prohibiting); and, local land use planning and development regulations which legitimate certain levels of environmental damage from the erection of buildings and vehicle access to national parks and ocean beaches. These examples characterize, delineate, describe, and thus define aspects of the contemporary capitalist economic-environment relation.

It should also be noted that the conversion, redefinition, and transformation of nature by accumulation does not occur with the same logic as that for accumulation because of the entropic nature of capitalist production. The process of capital accumulation is one of circularity and reversibility. The surplus is appropriated and re-invested in an expanded production process to create a growing surplus. On the other hand, the transformation of nature and consumption of energy is irreversible because production processes cause ecological destruction as well as an increase in entropy.

The contribution of energy, through the combustion of fuels, to accumulation processes is reflected through the intensification and expansion of production processes to generate commodities for profit realization. The direct relationship of higher energy inputs to the increased output of production, and economic growth, is well recognized as is the importance of fossil fuels since the industrial revolution (see, for example, Warr & Ayres 2010; Stern & Kander 2012).[4] A fossil fuel regime provided the basis for the Fordist growth regime and, by 1973, more than 86 percent of the world's energy consumption was provided by fossil fuels (Koch 2012: 82).

Energy from fossil fuels "fulfils almost perfectly the requirements of the capitalist process of accumulation. It fits into capitalism's societal relation to nature" (Altvater 2006: 41). Fossil fuels are transportable around the world so the supply of energy does not necessarily limit the choice of production locations. Nor do fossil fuels impose constraints on the timing of their combustion being able to be stored and thus "used 24 hours a day 365 days a year with constant intensity, allowing the organisation of production processes independently of social time schedules, biological and other natural rhythms" (*ibid.*). Technological changes have also provided greater flexibility for production processes to use fossil fuels and further eliminated spatial, temporal, and energy restrictions impacting on the processes of accumulation and economic growth. The use of fossil fuel energy is inextricable from the development and evolution of capitalism.

The foregoing social ontological view means a methodological approach that focuses on the institutional forms—of the mode of *régulation*—that shape the social relations of capitalism instead of objects such as the environment or planetary boundaries. It also underscores the next section's discussion of the relationship between the economic, energy, and ecological spheres— three dimensions of the current crisis of capitalism—and their interdependent relationship with the accumulation process.

The interdependencies of the ecological, economic, and energy spheres

The economic sphere

The capital crisis that began in 2007 shifted, from within the financial system and centered on the banks, to become a fiscal crisis of nation states. From the "greatest secular bull market in U.S. stock market history . . . the always-innovative financial sector . . . found new sources of profit in the home-ownership boom that was taking place" (Lippit 2014: 144). A housing bubble ensued and then a rise in United States (US) foreclosures quickly spread to Europe. Financial losses quickly spread to other financial institutions in North America, Europe, the United Kingdom (UK), and the rest of the world.

The consequent financial turmoil led to unprecedented interventions in financial markets by central banks and government fiscal stimulus packages to maintain the stability of the financial system and avert an economic crisis. Significant support was provided by governments to the financial sector, often commonly generalized as bank bailouts and quantitative easing.[5] Forms of financial sector support included: capital injections to recapitalize banks; asset purchases and direct lending to financial institutions; central bank support through credit lines; purchase of asset-backed securities and asset swaps, guarantees for financial sector liabilities; and, upfront government financing. Overall, the headline support for the financial sector and upfront government financing was the equivalent of more than 100 percent of GDP for the UK and nearly 90 percent for the US (IMF 2009: 7).

Central banks also lowered interest rates to stimulate spending as governments around the world progressively adopted fiscal stimulus of which around two-thirds were expenditure measures (*ibid*: 16). The magnitude and speed of fiscal stimulus packages and financial bailouts led some to suggest that nation states had returned to their former 'Keynesian ways.' To view these measures as a reversion to Keynesian economic management overlooks the absence of commensurate institutional change characteristic of that era. It also overlooks the subsequent austerity measures that were rapidly implemented by governments to reduce budget deficits and soaring public debt, and avert a sovereign debt crisis (Konzelmann 2014: 25).

Austerity measures, to reduce budget deficits, have placed a higher reliance on expenditure cuts targeted at the social wage, public sector labor, and environmental programs than on increasing or introducing taxation measures. The expenditure cuts are directed at making savings primarily at the expense of labor and those on the lowest incomes.

The speed and sharpness of the policy reversal—from stimulus to austerity—destabilized recovery, and led to high and longlasting unemployment as well as strong public opposition. Paradoxically, the contractionary impact of austerity measures depressed economic growth and increased public debt. Moreover, the 1980s liberalization of financial markets and the subsequent application of regulatory laissez-faire to finance led to innovations (such as derivatives, securitizations, and sub-prime mortgages) "so powerful that they destabilised the whole economic system" (Boyer 2013: 29). Without a recovery of accumulation, finance has created a situation, which threatens the conditions of its existence "like a snake biting its own tail" (*ibid*: 34) because governments will not be able to fund further bailouts.

The energy sphere

"Between 1950 and 2000 the global human population more than doubled from 2.5 to 6 billion, but in these same decades consumption of major natural resources soared more than 6 fold on average" (Smith *et al.* 2016: 136). The scale and intensity of energy use has been driven by significant changes to the energy regime, technology, and economic organization. Oil became the world's main transport fuel from 1930 and has caused widespread ecological degradation through spills, leaks, blowouts, and fires from the industry's exploration and construction projects, pipelines, and refineries. The chainsaw, rail transport, and the car led to deforestation, air, land, and water impacts, spatial implications, and added impetus to the oil industry's growth to meet fuel needs. The spread of industrialization and the production norms of Fordism, throughout the 1940s to the 1970s, further escalated energy use and pollution. China and India also emerged in the late twentieth century as key energy consumers.

The fossil fuels of oil, coal, and gas currently meet 82 percent of the world's demand for energy (IEA 2015a). Oil remains the largest single energy source at around 33 percent of total world consumption. Coal provides a further 30 percent and gas contributes around 24 percent (British Petroleum 2015). Fossil fuel consumption has been actively supported by direct government subsidies, estimated to be equivalent to 6.5 percent of global GDP (IMF 2015) and government energy policies (see, for example, European Commission 2010, 2014).

Oil, coal, and gas produce nearly 70 percent of the world's electricity (IEA 2014). Electricity accounts for more than 22 percent of the world's final energy consumption and for 42 percent of the world's carbon emissions (IEA 2015b). Electricity sectors around the world have been radically restructured. Competition has increased, there is less government ownership of electricity assets, a stronger regulatory role has been assumed by government, and electricity derivatives have been created to manage price volatility.

Restructured electricity sectors are exhibiting outcomes contrary to the proclaimed benefits. There is increasing market concentration and generation companies have been found to exercise market power causing considerable wholesale price volatility (Chester 2012). New generation and network capacity is required to meet future demand, to replace old coal-fired generation plants, to provide capacity following the progressive closure of Germany's nuclear electricity plants, and to meet, for example, European renewable energy and efficiency targets and new environmental standards. Policy uncertainty, in the wake of the economic crisis, has led to little new investment in long-term supply capacity and the inadequacy of short-term capacity is becoming evident (OFGEM 2012). A further critical outcome has been the rapid escalation in household electricity prices far in excess of general price and wage movements. These increases are causing low-income households to pay higher proportions of income and expenditure to meet energy bills. Consequently, energy impoverishment—hardship, deprivation, and social exclusion from rising energy prices—has become systemic and widespread among low-income households (Chester 2013).

The ecological sphere

Capitalism's ecological legacy is marked by global warming, biodiversity loss, soil erosion, desertification, deforestation, and pollution of air and water. As noted earlier, transformation of the twentieth century's energy regime, new technologies, the spread of industrialization and Fordism, government subsidies and policies, and the emergence of China and India as key energy consumers, have driven the scale and intensity of the world's energy use and the overwhelming dominance of fossil fuels. This energy use has provoked substantial ecological change, the extent of which has been exacerbated by globalization and further changes arising from capitalist accumulation. Greater integration of the international trading system has transformed ecologies to meet world demand (for example, rainforests converted to beef cattle ranches and coffee plantations), the creation of petrochemicals—derived from oil—has produced toxic pollutants producing durable waste like plastics, and genetic modification has impacted *inter alia* pest control, fertilizers, recycling, pollination, and food production.

Environmental concerns became more prevalent from the 1960s and, as discussed earlier, capitalism responded with the creation of 'techniques' (ecological commodities) to manage the environment. Supranational organizations (for example, United Nations Commission on Environment and Development) were created to promote economic growth as mandatory for environmental improvement. Concurrently, a growing body of scientific evidence detailed the scale, intensity, and implications of the ecological degradation caused by capitalism, particularly in terms of the impact of carbon emissions on global warming and climate change. Fossil fuel use is the primary contributor to emissions growth, and deforestation to a lesser extent. International negotiations led to the 1997 Kyoto Protocol, an international agreement by 37 industrialized countries and the European Union to reduce greenhouse gas emissions, and subsequently a global target of limiting the long-term rise in the average temperature to less than 2 degrees Celsius. The UK Government commissioned the 2006 Stern Review on the economics of climate change. These actions, and more, reinforced a global agenda of economic and environmental integration.

By end 2015, more than 140 countries had initiated energy efficiency programs and around 170 countries had set renewable energy targets, mandating a proportion of energy demand be provided from renewable sources (REN21 2016). Government policies, regulatory instruments, tax concessions, subsidies and direct expenditure have been implemented to stimulate the commercial development of renewable energy sources. Nevertheless, global investment in renewable energy was estimated at US$270 billion in 2014 compared to fossil fuel subsidies of US$5 trillion (UNEP 2015). Carbon pricing—predominantly trading schemes—has been introduced in 40 countries and 20 cities, regions, and states although this accounts for only 12 percent of global emissions (World Bank 2015). The World Bank (2012) estimated carbon trading to have reached US$176 billion in 2011, the growth of which has been accompanied by a rapid growth in another form of derivatives—carbon derivatives.

Despite actions by government and the creation of new markets, the world is not on track to limit global warming to 1.5 degrees Celsius nor reverse the damage of other widespread ecological degradation. Austerity policies also have weakened the commitments of nation states to reduce fossil fuel use through expenditure cuts to renewable energy, energy efficiency, and other environmental programs. In addition, large transnational companies are continuing to invest in locating and extracting new fossil fuel reserves while record-breaking temperatures and extreme weather events, rising sea levels, mudslides, earthquakes, wildfires, and droughts are becoming more frequent and intense, causing considerable damage and loss of life.

The dialectical relationship of the three spheres and the implications for an exit strategy

Financial market liberalization induced financial innovation leading to the creation of derivatives. From the liberalization of energy markets, ostensibly to place far greater reliance on market-determined prices and investment, increase competition, and reduce government involvement and consumer prices, another form of derivative—for electricity wholesale prices—emerged. Similarly carbon derivatives emerged after the creation of carbon trading markets as the favored policy measure to limit the growth in emissions.

Carbon and electricity derivatives are not simply complements to emission permit and wholesale electricity trading. Trading in derivatives is a hedge against the risk of purchasing emission permits or wholesale electricity price volatility. Yet this facility facilitates a much more extensive engagement with financial markets as hedge funds and a wide range of investors enter the carbon and wholesale electricity markets in search of arbitrage opportunities. Moreover, speculative behavior dominates derivatives trading, and speculation is the dominant characteristic of the financial sector. As witnessed over the course of the global financial crisis, products designed to reduce volatility appear to have contributed to new forms of volatility.

Restructured energy markets and new carbon markets—interrelated with financial markets—provided new sites of accumulation. Carbon trading has not reduced emissions growth and ecological degradation continues despite the marketization of nature and the introduction of 'environmental programs' such as renewable energy targets and policies. Market concentration, the exercise of market power, and volatile wholesale energy prices characterize restructured energy markets which are also marked by insufficient investment in new capacity threatening energy supply, and rapidly rising household energy prices, the cumulative effect of which is now widespread and embedded energy impoverishment.

Financial liberalization and innovation led to the global financial crisis and the subsequent economic crisis and austerity measures which are strongly skewed towards social wage expenditure cuts, directly impacting labor, and environmental programs. The impact of fiscal austerity measures on labor is compounded by household energy impoverishment for which there have been piecemeal ineffective policy responses, also impacted by fiscal consolidation.

Figure 31.1 provides a high-level synthesis of the interactions between the three spheres and the role played by finance and markets.

The responses by nation states to the current economic crisis are aggravating dimensions of the energy and ecological crises and not transforming a finance-led accumulation regime, which, all in turn, pose threats to recovery from the economic crisis. This conjunction of the

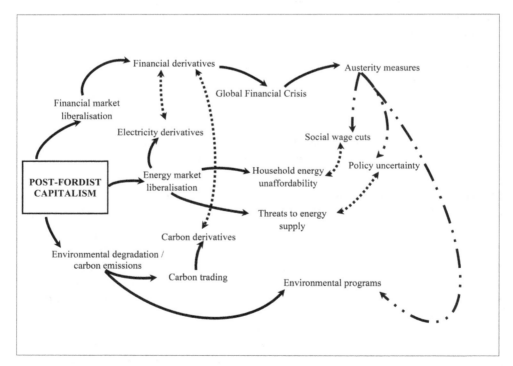

Figure 31.1 The conjunction of capitalism's economic, energy, and ecological spheres

three crises is driven by the dialectical relationship between the economic, energy, and ecological spheres, each performing a significant role in shaping and reshaping the form of each other. An ecological exit strategy will be ineffective unless it addresses this critical relationship, the heart of which is the accumulation process and the powerful role of finance. Capitalism's insatiable quest for accumulation intersects with all spheres constituting capitalism and it is this relationship that holds the key to resolving the ecological and all other crises.

Thus, an effective exit strategy from the ecological crisis must be structured to address *concurrently* the multiple dimensions of the ecological crisis—not just that of global warming and climate change—*and*, in so doing, must also be framed to take into account the interdependencies of the ecological sphere with the economic, energy, and other spheres. Both aspects are critical. It cannot be one or the other given the interdependencies between the spheres of capitalism. Moreover, the focus of policies and actions initiated by the state must be directed at the accumulation process *not* the symptoms of ecological degradation. Consequently, all institutional forms of the mode of *régulation* must be the constituent elements of an exit strategy.

Capitalism's resilience—despite its contradictory tendencies to erode its own natural and social conditions of production—is due to the mode of *régulation*. The mode's role is to secure accumulation. An effective exit strategy from the ecological crisis lies with a restructuring of the institutional forms of capitalism's mode of *régulation*, which includes a fundamental recalibration of the relationship between finance and productive capital. Thus the mode's institutional forms must be restructured to support and sustain a *new* capitalist formation: not reform the structures of the existing form *or* replace them with another form of economic and social organization but establish a new form (stage) of capitalism—a new regime of capitalist accumulation in which the imperative of ecological preservation is compatible with capitalism's mode of production.

Notes

1 For the remaining two boundaries—atmospheric aerosol loading and chemical pollution—it was concluded that there are as yet insufficient physical measures.
2 Ecological economics is discussed in Chapter 30 by Ekeland & Sæther in this volume.
3 The first contradiction is the tendency for a demand-side crisis given capital's drive to increase profits from greater production with less labor but the corollary occurs of reduced consumption by labor leading to lower profits.
4 Capital accumulation contributes to, but is not synonymous with, economic growth.
5 'Bank bailouts' is a euphemism for bank recapitalization. Quantitative easing, often labeled an 'unconventional' monetary policy tool, refers to increasing the size of a central bank's reserves by purchasing large quantities of long-term securities which puts upward pressure on their prices and downward pressure on their yield and attempts to stimulate investment in long-term securities. Banks then have access to additional liquidity that can be used to extend new credit.

References

Altvater, E. 1989. 'Ecological and economic modalities of time and space.' *Capitalism Nature Socialism*, 1 (3): 59–70.
Altvater, E. 2006. 'The social and natural environment of fossil capitalism,' *in*: L. Panitch & C. Leys (eds.), *Socialist Register 2007: Coming to Terms with Nature*. New Delhi: Leftwood Books, 37–59.
Boyer, R. 2013. 'The present crisis: a trump for a renewed political economy.' *Review of Political Economy*, 25 (1): 1–38.
Boyer, R. & Saillard, Y. 2002. 'A summary of régulation theory,' *in*: R. Boyer & Y. Saillard (eds.), *Régulation Theory: The State of the Art*. London: Routledge, 36–44.
British Petroleum. 2015. *BP Statistical Review of World Energy*. Available from https://www.bp.com/content/dam/bp/pdf/energy-economics/statistical-review-2015/bp-statistical-review-of-world-energy-2015-full-report.pdf [Accessed July 26, 2015]

Carruthers, D. 2001. 'From opposition to orthodoxy: the remaking of sustainable development.' *Journal of Third World Studies*, 18 (2): 93–112.

Chester, L. 2012. 'Unravelling the roles played by derivatives and market power in electricity price formation.' *Heterodox Economics: Social Provisioning in Crisis-prone Capitalism, Refereed Papers: 11th Annual Conference, Australian Society of Heterodox Economists*, University of New South Wales, December 3–4.

Chester, L. 2013. The impacts and consequences for low-income households of rising energy prices. Unpublished report funded by the Consumer Advocacy Panel, Australian Energy Market Commission. Available from http://www.householdenergyuse.com [Accessed October 10, 2013]

Costanza, R., Perrings, C., & Cleveland, C.J. 1997. *The Development of Ecological Economics*. Cheltenham, UK: Edward Elgar.

Dale, G., Mathai, M.V., & Puppim de Oliveira, J.A. (eds.) 2016. *Green Growth: Ideology, Political Economy and the Alternatives*. London: Zed Books.

Daly, H. 1973. *Towards a Steady-State Economy*. San Francisco: W.H. Freeman & Co.

Daly, H. 1991. *Steady-state Economics*. London: Earthscan.

Daly, H. 1996. *Beyond Growth*. Boston: Beacon.

European Commission. 2010. *Energy 2020: A Strategy for Competitive, Sustainable and Secure Energy*. Brussels, COM(2010) 639 final. Available from http://eur-lex.europa.eu/LexUriServ/LexUriServ.do?uri=COM:2010:0639:FIN:EN:PDF [Accessed April 14, 2011]

European Commission. 2014. *A Policy Framework for Climate and Energy in the Period from 2020 and 2030*. Brussels, COM(2014) 15 final. Available from http://eur-lex.europa.eu/legal-content/EN/TXT/PDF/?uri=CELEX:52014DC0015&from=EN [Accessed October 19, 2014]

Foster, J.B. 2011. 'Capitalism and degrowth: an impossibility theorem.' *Monthly Review*, 62 (8). Available from http://monthlyreview.org/2011/01/01/capitalism-and-degrowth-an-impossibility-theorem/ [Accessed February 2, 2011]

Foster, J.B., Clark, B., & York, R. 2010. *The Ecological Rift: Capitalism's War on the Earth*. New York: Monthly Review Press.

Georgescu-Roegen, N. 1975. 'Energy and economic myths.' *Southern Economic Journal*, 41 (3): 347–381.

Gibbs, D. & Healey, M. 1997. 'Industrial geography and the environment.' *Applied Geography*, 17 (3): 193–201.

Hahnel, R. 2011. *Green Economics: Confronting the Ecological Crisis*. Armonk, NY: M.E. Sharpe.

Hamilton, C. 2016. 'Limiting the planet to 1.5 degrees C of warming is crucial, but it won't be easy.' *Scientific American*, 26 September. Available from http://blogs.scientificamerican.com/guest-blog/limiting-the-planet-to-1-5-degrees-c-of-warming-is-crucial-but-it-won-t-be-easy/ [Accessed September 28, 2016]

Hansen, J. 2012. 'Storms of my grandchildren's opa.' Available from http://www.mediafire.com/view/5sl1uqrw9f1xf9j/20121213_StormsOfOpa.pdf [Accessed April 12, 2013]

International Energy Agency (IEA). 2014. *Key World Energy Statistics*. Available from http://www.iea.org/publications/freepublications/publication/keyworld2014.pdf [Accessed December 8, 2014]

International Energy Agency (IEA). 2015a. *World Energy Outlook 2014*. Paris: OECD & IEA.

International Energy Agency (IEA). 2015b. *CO_2 Emissions from Fuel Combustion: 2015 Edition*. Available from http://www.oecd-ilibrary.org.ezproxy1.library.usyd.edu.au/energy/co2-emissions-from-fuel-combustion-2015_co2_fuel-2015-en [Accessed December 8, 2015]

International Monetary Fund (IMF). 2009. Fiscal implications of the global economic and financial crisis. IMF Staff Position Note SPN/09/13. Available from http://https://www.imf.org/external/pubs/ft/spn/2009/spn0913.pdf [Accessed September 20, 2012]

International Monetary Fund (IMF). 2015. Counting the cost of energy subsidies. Available from http://www.imf.org/external/pubs/ft/survey/so/2015/new070215a.htm [Accessed August 10, 2015]

Kenis, A. & Lievens, M. 2016. 'Greening the economy or economizing the green project? When environmental concerns are turned into a means to save the market.' *Review of Radical Political Economics*, 48 (2): 217–234.

Koch, M. 2012. *Capitalism and Climate Change: Theoretical Discussion, Historical Development and Policy Responses*. Basingstoke, UK: Palgrave Macmillan.

Konzelmann, S. 2014. 'The political economics of austerity.' *Cambridge Journal of Economics*, 38 (4): 701–741.

Latouche, S. 2004. 'Degrowth economics.' *Le Monde Diplomatique*, 17 November. Available from http://mondediplo.com/2004/11/14latouche [Accessed February 2, 2011]

Lippit, V.D. 2014. 'The neoliberal era and the financial crisis in the light of SSA theory.' *Review of Radical Political Economics*, 46 (2): 141–161.

Lohmann, L. 2016. 'Neoliberalism's climate,' in: S. Springer, K. Birch, & J. MacLeavy (eds.), *The Handbook of Neoliberalism*. New York: Routledge, 480–492.

O'Connor, J. 1998. *Natural Causes: Essays in Ecological Marxism.* New York: The Guildford Press.

Office of Gas and Electricity Markets (OFGEM). 2012. Electricity Capacity Assessment, 126/12, 5 October 2012. Available from http://http://www.ofgem.gov.uk/Markets/WhlMkts/monitoring-energy-security/ elec-capacity-assessment/Documents1/Electricity%20Capacity%20Assessment%202012.pdf [Accessed August 15, 2014]

Paton, J. 2008. 'What's *left* of sustainable development?' *Journal of Australian Political Economy*, 62: 94–119.

Porritt, J. 2007. *Capitalism as if the World Matters.* London: Earthscan.

REN21. 2016. *Renewables 2016 Global Status Report.* Available from http://www.ren21.net/status-of-renewables/global-status-report/ [Accessed July 20, 2016]

Rockström, J., Steffen, W., Noone, K., Persson, Å., Chapin, F.S. III, Lambin, E., Lenton, T.M., Scheffer, M., Folke, C., Schellnhuber, H., Nykvist, B., De Wit, C.A., Hughes, T., van der Leeuw, S., Rodhe, H., Sörlin, S., Snyder, P.K., Costanza, R., Svedin, U., Falkenmark, M., Karlberg, L., Corell, R.W., Fabry, V.J., Hansen, J., Walker, B., Liverman, D., Richardson, K., Crutzen, P., & Foley, J. 2009. 'Planetary boundaries: exploring the safe operating space for humanity.' *Ecology and Society*, 14 (2). Available from http://www.ecology andsociety.org/issues/article.php/3180 [Accessed November 22, 2012]

Rosewarne, S. 2002. 'Towards an ecological political ecology.' *Journal of Australian Political Economy*, 50 (December): 179–199.

Smith, N. 2006. 'Nature as accumulation strategy,' *in*: L. Panitch & C. Leys (eds.), *Socialist Register 2007: Coming to Terms with Nature.* New Delhi: Leftwood Books, 16–36.

Smith, N. 2010. *Uneven Development: Nature, Capital and the Production of Space.* 3rd edn. Verso: London.

Smith, R. 2010. 'Beyond growth or beyond capitalism?' *Real-World Economics Review*, 53: 28–42. Available from http://www.paecon.net/PAEReview/issue53/Smith53.pdf [Accessed May 18, 2014]

Smith, R. 2011. 'Green capitalism: the god that failed.' *Real-World Economics Review*, 56: 112–144. Available from http://www.paecon.net/PAEReview/issue56/Smith56.pdf [Accessed May 18, 2014]

Smith, R., Neil, W., & Zimmerman, K. 2016. 'Capitalism, corporations and ecological crisis: a dialogue concerning *Green Capitalism*.' *Real-World Economics Review*, 76: 136–145. Available from http://www. paecon.net/PAEReview/issue76/Smith-et-al76.pdf [Accessed September 29, 2016]

Stern, D.I. & Kander, A. 2012. 'The role of energy in the industrial revolution and modern economic growth.' *The Energy Journal*, 33 (3): 125–152.

United Nations Environment Programme (UNEP). 2015. *Global Trends in Renewable Energy Investment 2015.* Report prepared by Frankfurt School-UNEP Centre/BNEF. Available from http://www.unep.org/ publications/ [Accessed August 10, 2015]

Warr, B.S. & Ayres, R.U. 2010. 'Evidence of causality between the quantity and quality of energy consumption and economic growth.' *Energy*, 35 (4): 1688–1693.

World Bank. 2012. *State and Trends on the Carbon Market 2012.* Available from http://documents.world bank.org/curated/en/749521468179970954/State-and-trends-of-the-carbon-market-2012 [Accessed December 13, 2012]

World Bank. 2015. *State and Trends of Carbon Pricing 2015.* Available from http://documents.worldbank.org/ curated/en/636161467995665933/State-and-trends-of-carbon-pricing-2015 [Accessed August 10, 2015]

32

Restructuring financial systems with human advancement in mind

Wesley C. Marshall

Introduction

The global financial crisis that erupted in 2007 struck at the heart of the global economy. It not only occurred within the world's most powerful economic institutions in the geographical center of economic power, but the enormous sums of money involved also forced many to rethink the nature of money, reaching the heart of economics as an academic discipline. The meteoric rise of the shadow banking system (SBS) and its collapse and bailout lead to the irrefutable observation that money is not scarce. The subsequent global policy of propping up financial asset prices while restricting productive investment, employment, and production is neither economically nor politically sustainable. However, the alternative of abundant funding for full employment and production is also problematic, as simply producing more smoke and steel can no longer be a way forward.

This chapter draws on the traditions of institutionalism and Post Keynesianism in order to demonstrate how we have arrived at our current juncture, and uses the guidance of Keynes to point towards a set of basic principles and structures that can attend to the needs of a truly transformative alternative to today's financialized global morass. Only after the non-scarcity of money is openly recognized and understood by society can the perhaps even more difficult task of working towards the realization of full human potential in the face of existential threat be undertaken. As will be argued, the many historical lessons offered by global finance point to the fact that designing global, regional, national, and local financial structures for such a task can be done. In order to provide for greater production and employment under the guidance of human advancement, the most difficult part will be attaining the minimal public understanding of finance necessary to establish the political will to restructure the financial system.

To show how a democratically determined financial system at the service of humanity has worked in the past, and why economic interests have created a public misunderstanding of finance and its operations in order to exclude the possibility of this happening again, this chapter is organized in the following way: first, we examine how mainstream economics disingenuously deals with institutions that can create money out of nothing. Then, we explore the nature of these institutions and how they are controlled. We then turn our focus to banking in order to synthesize our main points regarding the integral functioning of public and private finances and their appreciation within society as a whole, in order to close with several considerations regarding abundant money and its potential uses and abuses in current society.

Money and its institutions

Following the Veblenian tradition of critically associating institutions with economic power, this chapter looks at the three key money-creating institutions and pillars of the financial system in the United States (US)—the central bank, the treasury, and private banks—under the key fundamental assumption that a handful of global banks constitute the dominant political faction of capital in current western capitalism.

In past decades, as the academic debate regarding the monetarist counter-revolution gave way to the debate over financial globalization and then to financialization, a small group of global banks was gaining ever greater economic and political power. The growing dominance of these banks is at the center of financialization, succinctly defined by Epstein (2005: 3) as "the increasing role of financial motives, financial markets, financial actors and financial institutions in the operations of domestic and international economies." Such financial motives have conquered the market discipline of capitalism, as most clearly manifested by the too big to fail phenomenon, as well as the legal discipline of governments, as shown by the too big to prosecute doctrine.

The monopolistic power of global banks is easily seen in the domestic concentration of banking sectors that have later gone on to conquer other ones in the process of financial opening that has happened around the world. As we argue here, stemming from their core desire to be the monopolistic provider of credit, a handful of global banks that now dominate many economic and political systems have actively promoted a thought system that consistently rails against the state, lies about its abilities, and promotes laws to restrict its money-creating capabilities. National spaces of production have been transformed into international arenas of concentrated financial control. We certainly agree with Keynes' sentiment that "when the capital development of a country becomes the by-product of the activities of a casino, the job is likely to be ill done" (Keynes 1936: 159), except that these banks are not only monopolistic but 'criminal.'

As a result of decades of national policies of financial deregulation, de-supervision, and *de facto* de-criminalization—the three D's identified by Black (2005)—an increasingly criminogenic system has been created in which fraudulent practices have driven out legitimate ones. This fundamental driver of the financial crisis, originally and forcefully argued by Black and appreciated by James Galbraith (2014) in his most recent book, greatly explains how and why the largest and most important financial markets, such as foreign exchange, and prices, such as the London Interbank Offered Rate (LIBOR), have all come to be dominated by a handful of banks who systematically and criminally manipulate them (US DoJ 2015).

Yet to appreciate the evolution of money-creating institutions, the evolution of an institution that does not create money—academic economics—is also of great help. As Charles Ferguson showed in his documentary *Inside Job*, elite members of the academy have been bought off by the banking industry, a point taken up from academia by DeMartino (2011) and further developed by Ferguson (2013) himself.

Much as we can historically divide with some precision the golden and leaden ages of capitalism with the ending of the Bretton Woods monetary system in 1971, we can also set as a historical marker Hayek's winning of the Sveriges Riksbank Prize in Economic Sciences in Memory of Alfred Nobel in 1974 as the beginning of what Paul Krugman (2009) termed 'the dark age of macroeconomics.' In Hayek's prize acceptance speech, he claimed that as societies we should never attempt to master the forces of our social world. An openly avowed obscurantist winning a scientific award is worrisome, and indeed Hayek began the tradition of neoliberal economists being awarded the Nobel prize, despite repeatedly showing themselves to be poor 'scientists,' consistently getting wrong the issues that are most important for society and those that are supposedly their professional strengths (Black 2014).

Hayek (1944: 211) argues for the only acceptable possible existence of spontaneous market order, and that any sort of formal planning could only have disastrous consequences:

> Those who argue that we have to an astounding degree learned to master the forces of nature but are sadly behind in making successful use of the possibilities of social collaboration are quite right so far as this statement goes. But they are mistaken when they carry the comparison further and argue that we must learn to master the forces of society in the same manner in which we have learnt to master the forces of nature. This is not only the path to totalitarianism, but the path to the destruction of our civilisation and a certain way to block future progress.

Instead of arguing for greater knowledge as a force against overzealous, crooked or poor planners, Hayek (1944: 208) argues for less knowledge:

> there are fields where this craving for intelligibility cannot be fully satisfied and where at the same time a refusal to submit to anything we cannot understand must lead to the destruction of our civilisation. . . . A complex civilisation like ours is necessarily based on the individual adjusting himself to changes whose cause and nature he cannot understand.

We would counter with Joan Robinson's (1960: 17) saying that "the purpose of studying economics is not to acquire a set of ready-made answers to economic questions, but to learn how to avoid being deceived by economists." Indeed, from the early 1970s onwards, a dominant faction of mainstream economics has succeeded in essentially fooling all the people all the time. The political movement that was born in 1947 at the inaugural conference of the Mont Pelerin Society (MPS) and that originally called itself neoliberalism, was initially led by Hayek (Mirowski & Plehwe 2009; Burgin 2012; Mirowski 2013). The reins were then gradually passed to Milton Friedman—a co-founder himself—as his self-denominated 'monetarist counter-revolution' (Friedman 1970: 1) was making important inroads in public policy spheres.

The dumbing down of economics, which accompanied the increasing operational control of neoliberal economics over public policy, has been a two-pronged movement consisting of a publicity campaign designed to change public opinion, and of a purge of academic dissenters. Indeed, one of neoliberalism's great victories has been to convince societies at large that inflation rather than unemployment is humanity's greatest problem, and this can be seen as an important clue as to why banks seek to suppress knowledge. Unemployment is a fundamentally human problem, as the lack of employment opportunities devalues human existence, while inflation is fundamentally a banking problem—or at least a perceived banking problem. The propaganda efforts of neoliberalism, and of Friedman in particular, can best be seen in his PBS documentary *Free to Choose* (1980).

Efforts were made to change expert opinion as well. As Mirowski & Plehwe (2009: 7) notes, "among the key tasks perceived by MPS leaders was a neoliberal reeducation of capitalists." The evidence that the neoliberal economists who have led the monetarist counter-revolution are systematically paid for by banks and other financial institutions (Mirowski & Plehwe 2009; Mirowski 2013; Ferguson 2013) strongly suggests that the ever greater social dominance of neoliberalism has been a bank-led exercise in economic control. Indeed, Hoover (2003: 184) reports of a diplomatic cable at the end of the Second World War stating that "Wall Street looks on Hayek as the richest goldmine yet discovered and are peddling his views everywhere."

Mirowski (2013) has made an important contribution in highlighting Hayek's crucial role in creating Chicago school economics, and provided evidence to connect the interests of Wall Street and the school of thinking that has produced the greatest amount of academic backing for legislation that favors Wall Street.

The neoliberal pincer

The academic dominance of neoliberalism is well described by James Galbraith (2014: 70):

> Even those who objected with this vision had to engage with it. The layered complexity of the vision, the subtlety of the claims, meant that it took mental effort to come to grips with what was being said. To articulate a dissent without becoming a heretic was a difficult task. The profession would reward those who kept just a few points of departure from the pure model, and punish the rest. In this way, the debate stays within the tribe, and the purists, though sometimes embattled, preserve their importance.

In mainstream economics, any serious analysis about the nature of money, how it is used in reality, or how money-creating institutions can restrict the creation and circulation of money are strictly off-limits. The division of academic economic teaching between freshwater and saltwater economists (Galbraith 2014), who can get things wrong in different and predictable ways because they omit, eschew, or frankly lie about the most important facts in their analyses, leaves us with the pincer of neoliberal economics.

> By enabling the claim that macroeconomics is fully characterized by a divide between new Keynesian and new classical macroeconomics, new Keynesianism closes the pincer that excludes old Keynesianism. As long as that pincer holds, economics will remain under Friedman's shadow. Breaking the pincer requires surfacing the role of Friedman's thinking in new Keynesian economics and making clear the distinction between old Keynesian and new Keynesian economics.
>
> *Palley 2015: 632*

Galbraith (2014) and Palley (2015) come to similar conclusions. Much like Palley's neoliberal pincer, Galbraith speaks of the common methodology of both the freshwater and saltwater economists that knits them into a single community of 'serious economists,' excluding all others:

> a few economists challenged the assumption of rational behavior, questioned the belief that financial markets can be trusted and pointed to the long history of financial crises that had devastating economic consequences. But they were swimming against the tide, unable to make much headway against a pervasive and, in retrospect, foolish complacency.
>
> *Galbraith 2014: 80*

Such complacency may have been foolish, but the above researchers have shown that it was not unintentional. Indeed, the only scholars to get the crisis 'right' to varying degrees fall outside of the narrow limits of Palley's pincer: They represent the heretics that mainstream economics have made into "the unpersons of the profession" (Galbraith 2014: 80). To better appreciate the process through which critical economists were either purged from academia or pushed to its sidelines, there is no better guide than Fred Lee's *A History of Heterodox Economics* (2009), which goes through in great detail how the parameters used to evaluate academic success are continuously stacked against anyone who falls outside of the narrow freshwater-saltwater divide.

Today's deliberately confusing ontology regarding money and its institutions

Adding together the components of economists who are paid by banks or other financial companies, and that execute public policy that rewards failed banks at the expense of employment, we can understand financialization as the takeover of society by banks and other private money-creating institutions. We can therefore understand how academic economics has become an appendage of these interests and how the concurrent 'dark age of macroeconomics' is simply the creation and propagation of an obscurantist pseudo-science at the service of banks. Again, the application of an institutionalist perspective means that this should come as no surprise.

On the right side of the neoliberal pincer, from Friedman's views on money, to Stigler's regulatory capture, to Buchanan's public choice theory, and to Myerson's pleas for higher CEO pay in order to keep them from committing financial crimes (Black 2014), the Chicago school's Nobel prize winning economists consistently had their prophesies come true. Statements of how reality works that were absurd at face value when originally presented have become accurate descriptions of reality as the Chicago school's promotion of the deregulation, de-supervision, and the *de facto* de-criminalization of banking activities has fundamentally changed how financial systems work. On the other side of the pincer, we have a group that operates under a moniker—New Keynesians—that has little to do with its namesake, and that has had open adherents in the most important positions of power, such as Ben Bernanke and Mario Draghi.

In order to comprehend the victory of the monetarist counter-revolution in academic economics, the partial victory of Keynes' revolution must also be understood, for both it and its succeeding monetarist counter-revolution were top-down affairs. John Kenneth Galbraith notably referred to Keynes' as the Mandarin Revolution (Galbraith 1977: 224). Similarly, the subsequent monetarist counter-revolution, which led to the leaden period of capitalism and continual crisis, can most clearly be seen as an elite dominated *coup d'état* that occurred above the heads of democratic societies.

The Keynesian revolution, aimed at controlling state finances in order to eliminate unemployment, offered a brief historical respite from this scourge of humankind, establishing the financial conditions for full employment in many countries around the globe. While the steering wheel of state finances was used to attend to human demands, the grip of informed electorates over it was always tenuous. The political gains of the New Deal and those of post-war Britain that supported Keynes' revolution would certainly point to the conclusion that, at least in some times and places, the citizenry could identify full employment as a priority and as an achievable political goal. But even while at the operational level money and state finances were used towards the goal of full employment, the use of functional finance was only tenuously incorporated into the social sciences at the academic level. So while much of the electorate could certainly understand the importance of eliminating unemployment, the ways of getting there—the lessons of functional finance—never reached a critical permeation in academia or politics, and were washed away with disappointingly few taking note.

In the *General Theory*, Keynes (1936: 33) cryptically alludes to the "powers behind authority" and their support for the 'Ricardian economics' that held such sway over British society at the time of the *General Theory*'s writing. But Keynes' views on money were likewise cryptic. Trying to tease out Keynes' real understanding or opinion on the nature and role of money in society is an almost impossible task, for as Smithin (2013) points out, Keynes' conceptions of money both evolved and maintained contradictions throughout his writing. Many have suggested that Keynes was employing some sort of strategic ambivalence, for reasons explored below.

Reading more of Keynes is a good cure for such doubts. The New Keynesians, however, tread in the opposite direction. The only element of Keynesian thinking that really enters into their policy recommendations is the IS-LM curve—what the self-identified New Keynesian Paul Krugman (1998) called "the workhorse of practical policy analysis in macroeconomics." It is problematic for a group of economists to proclaim themselves Keynesians when they rely so heavily on only one of his supposed ideas. It becomes even more problematic when one considers that the IS-LM curve was never even suggested by Keynes himself. It becomes even more problematic when the man who did invent the IS-LM curve—John Hicks—formally recanted his invention (Davidson 2008).

Krugman (1998) states that the IS-LM curve is "not fit to be seen in polite intellectual company," yet he bases his policy recommendations on it. Considering the glaring lack of theory on banking (Smithin 2013: 252), and the fact that declared experts on the Great Depression cannot even contemplate bank failure as they "are not historians" (Bernanke 2000), reality becomes even more worrisome. When the same renowned academic heads the world's most influential central bank, then we are really in a dark age, in which the New Keynesians, the only public figures that associate themselves with the political left, cannot countenance banks damaging the economy, or the role of functional finance in healing it.

Money-creating institutions

In order to briefly trace the thread of how the most important money-creating institutions are consistently misrepresented by academia and how such institutions are used to favor the interest of banks over the interests of the public at large, we focus on the ontology of these institutions and their operations.

We begin our analysis with government spending. In his opinion piece mentioned earlier, Krugman (2009) puts forward several arguments against John Cochrane, who argues that "first, if money is not going to be printed, it has to come from somewhere. If the government borrows a dollar from you, that is a dollar that you do not spend. . . . This is just accounting, and does not need a complex argument about 'crowding out'." Krugman's response to Cochrane is that "what's so mind-boggling about this is that it commits one of the most basic fallacies in economics—interpreting an accounting identity as a behavioral relationship." Krugman correctly identifies Cochrane's error—government accounts are nothing more than accounting identities—but then Krugman goes on to commit the same error: "Yes, savings have to equal investment, but that's not something that mystically takes place, it's because any discrepancy between desired savings and desired investment causes something to happen that brings the two in line." An accounting identity means that no mystical actions are needed. It is simply a rule. If the government spends more on roads in a year than it takes in through taxation, that is a fiscal deficit.

Krugman once again does what he accuses Cochrane of. As opposed to "what mystically takes place," what "causes something to happen" leads the reader into a macro model, where desired savings and investment meet at an equilibrium point. This is a behavioral relationship, not an accounting relationship, as Krugman strongly implies.

Krugman could have simply accused Cochrane of flat out lying: "every dollar of increased government spending must correspond to one less dollar of private spending" is exactly what the accounting relationship does not say. We posit that Krugman must confuse the issue so much because the definition that public deficits are always a subsidy to businesses and households is such a bold political statement in itself. Krugman ends the opinion piece lamenting the "dark age of macroeconomics," while only muddying the issue himself. Seccareccia (1995) attended to this issue convincingly decades ago. As Baragar & Seccareccia (2008: 82) argue, this accounting identity by no means implies that private and public spending have to "even themselves out." Both can grow, or shrink, at any rate, but they always maintain the same relationship.

The neoliberal pincer therefore holds on public finance. Cochrane on the right and Krugman on the left both get it wrong in different ways, and the public is left without an explanation of the theoretical possibility of functional finance. Krugman bases his consistent support for the 'fiscal restriction' approach on the maxim that "yes, savings have to equal investment."

True to Palley's pincer or Galbraith's exclusionary saltwater-freshwater spectrum, public opinion is trapped between two misrepresentations of the truth, as also happens with public discourse regarding monetary or credit policies. The New Keynesian corollary to Bernanke's willing omission of the role of banks in the history of America's financial crises can be found in Krugman's inability to countenance the potential of money creation by banks. Krugman both ignores and omits the basic rules of monetary accommodation of the Federal Reserve (Fullwiler 2012), as well as the existence of an interbank market from which the SBS was spawned. By treating all money as exogenous—only available if the state prints it, and never created by banks—Krugman eschews even Friedman's understanding of 'inside and outside money,' referring to the money created by banks from the money created by the state (Friedman & Schwartz 1987).

Within the exclusionary saltwater-freshwater pincer, neither banks nor governments can create credit or money out of nothing more than social agreements, a proposition that has become ever less tenable in the face of the creation of more than US$ 800 trillion worth of derivatives and structured financial products in less than 20 years, and the US banking bailout of somewhere around US$ 30 trillion (Felkerson 2011). Such a massively obvious exception to standard economic theory has led to much questioning of economics as a profession.

The economist as social engineer: the brake and the accelerator

If we can build on the metaphor of the government holding the steering wheel of the car, which represents the state (Forstater 1999), we would like to add that there are two sets of brakes and accelerators (we will assume it is an automatic car). One set corresponds to monetary policy, and the other to fiscal policy. In both cases, the brakes are designed to take money out of circulation, and the accelerators to put money into circulation. On the fiscal side, the accelerator is the fiscal deficit, and the brakes are taxes. If the driver wishes the engine to engage—for the economy to expand—s/he can push more money into the economy through a variety of delivery methods, including public works, transfer payments, subsidies, public companies, public employment programs, etc. When a government spends nothing, the engine does not move out of state stimulus. This does not mean that it cannot move on its own. But if the driver wants to slow the economy down through fiscal spending, s/he can surely do so by stepping on the brake and applying taxes. The fiscal balance measures whether the state is giving or taking more or less money to the economy as a whole. If we had, for example, a 100 percent fiscal surplus, this would mean that the government would only be taking and not giving anything.

Under Lerner's (1943) functional finance, the fiscal accelerator should be applied through bond issuance. In this case, money is created *ex nihilo*, but not to a great degree. If a country runs a permanent deficit of 5 percent, the government has simply opted to forward investment, employment, consumption, and profit, later to be taken back in the form of taxes and returned to bondholders. But to assure economic expansion, more must be given than taken. This task is facilitated by the fiscal multiplier: as money is forwarded, it is multiplied as well. During the golden age, experience showed that countries can forward spending, or run fiscal deficits, in a perfectly sustainable fashion.

The monetary brake and accelerator have an extra step between them and the engine of the economy in general: banks, the gatekeepers of credit. This makes the monetary brake—the application of interest rates above the break-even level of profit expectations and interest rates—particularly effective. If a government is willing to raise interest rates to 25 percent and credibly guarantee its payment, then banks and other capitalists will invest more in government debt and less in productive investment and employment. Additionally, at least some amount of consumption should be directed towards savings. Whereas a government can run surpluses and hold on to more money than it pushes out into the system, banks can also hold on to more money than they lend out. This most commonly occurs when the central bank applies the brake. If the government does nothing, and simply allows private non-monopolistic banks to set the interest rates, no brake is applied by the state. However, under monopoly conditions, the banking system itself can apply the brake.

The accelerator of monetary policy is mostly ineffective, and when used, tends to simply 'flood' the engine. As years of zero interest rate policies and multiple rounds of 'quantitative easing' have shown, the accelerator is ill-suited for the task of getting the economy moving. The monetary accelerator only reaches the main engine of the economy through the antechamber that is the banking system. It is this element that the fiscal accelerator does not pass through on the way to the motor, that can become 'flooded,' when banks cannot or do not want to lend out the money that the state is pushing out. This phenomenon, academically known as 'pushing on a string,' can last indefinitely. Understanding the basic structural limitations of monetary policy helps to understand why this is.

With the monetarist counter-revolution well underway, John Kenneth Galbraith (1975: 305) notably stated that "only the enemies of capitalism will hope that, in the future, this small, perverse and unpredictable lever will be a major instrument in economic management." These words would prove ever more true a decade later, under the economic stewardship of Reagan and Thatcher.

Four decades after Galbraith's observation, years of continually applying the monetary accelerator have not only failed to get the economic motor going sufficiently, but have not changed mainstream economists' preference for using monetary rather than fiscal policy. This situation reflects the passing of the control of the car to those who represent bank interests, while simultaneously demonstrating how the monetary accelerator is only attached to money center banks. The overall economy is not awash with cash; it is only the banking sector ante-motor that is flooded. Yet neither side of the pincer relinquishes their obscurantism regarding how our current banking system creates and distributes money.

Banking

Fortunately, the debate around banking and macro financial issues does not occur in a vacuum, and there are concrete historical results that clearly point to the varied performance between different types of capitalism: golden age Keynesian versus leaden age Friedmanian. For us to understand why for 30 years the western world could grow at around 6.5 percent annually during the golden age of the post-Second World War as opposed to around 2 percent during the leaden age, with similar rates of inflation, we must understand how the international financial system operated, as well as appreciate the widespread application of functional finance under distinct national systems of production. Likewise, in order to understand why there were no systemic financial crises during the golden age period, we must rise above obscurantism and understand how banking systems operated and have changed. Let us start from the latter point.

The Organization for Economic Cooperation and Development (OECD) states in its *Bank Competition and Financial Stability* that

> In very broad terms, there are two quite different types of financial products:
>
> 1   Those primary instruments associated with consumption, savings and fixed capital formation that create wealth (usually associated with loans for trade credit and working capital, and securities – equity and debt); and
> 2   Those associated with wealth transfer between economic agents in the attempt: to hedge risks; to arbitrage prices, to gamble; and to reduce tax, regulatory and agency cost (management fees, custody, brokerage, etc.)
>
> *OECD 2011: 36*

The OECD distinguishes two forms of banking, with the first being more prevalent in the golden age, and the second in the leaden age. For expositional clarity, we can likewise take the example of housing in the two periods, in order to emphasize just how different macro outcomes can be under the two systems. In the US, housing was left to private banking, done at the local level through Savings and Loans (S&L) institutions. During the 1930s, the US Congress conferred upon S&Ls the role as principal agents of national housing policy. At the level of the federal government, during the golden age, regulations and subsidies guaranteed that fraud and bank failures were at a minimum (NCFIRRE 1993). Under these circumstances, popularized fairly accurately in Frank Capra's *It's a Wonderful Life*, banking is a relatively decentralized, unprofitable, and boring affair. Productive banking as above classified by the OECD can be seen through the 3×3×3 standard: pay depositors 3 percent, charge 3 percent more for loans, and be on the golf course by 3.

Issuing a home mortgage is an easy task for this type of banker. When examining a loan application, the banker can feel sure that the client will be good for her payment, provided that she is gainfully employed and has good recommendations. The credit agent can also feel sure that the client would be able to pay off her loan, as thanks to an active fiscal policy mass unemployment was unheard of. The credit agent therefore makes one bet on the creditworthiness of the individual and another on macroeconomic conditions. Again, under such conditions, such bets are easy and their payoffs are low. But this is the essence of banking serving its customers and the economy in general. With a handshake the credit circuit is born, and money is created from nothing, but only to a small degree in this case, as bets are small and risks are low.

Under Lerner's (1943) vision of functional finance, the accelerator of fiscal spending must be continually applied if both capital accumulation and production and employment are to expand. Continual deficits of, say, 5 percent, provide subsidies to families and businesses. Much of this subsidy is directed at maintaining a welfare state, where retirement, education, health care, and transportation are subsidized. With more disposable income to spend, aggregate demand and business profits rise. People can live with basic guarantees of living and can simultaneously act as vehicles between fiscal spending and business profits. During the golden age, functional finance and decentralized productive banking went hand in hand, and megabanks and monetary policy had little place.

Such traditional financial intermediation between savers and lenders was the result of a financial system designed for banks to be at the service of the economy, and not the other way around. The regulations enacted in the 1930s attended to the necessary conditions of such a system: banking was decentralized in its market structure; bets were relatively safe and spread thinly over the economy; opportunities for conflicts of interest between banks and their clients were minimized; and a system of regulation and supervision was established and maintained. The contrasts with the conditions that created the 2007–2009 crisis could not be more clear. While in the above scenario banks could be rightly called financial intermediaries, global banks can now be rightly called fraud intermediaries. Whereas risks were previously small and atomized, today they are centralized and world-stopping.

The subprime crisis arose in large part from the criminogenic environment created through decades of financial de-regulation, de-supervision, and *de facto* de-criminalization of the banking system. Once the Glass–Steagall Act was revoked in the US, commercial banks could again write bonds backed by future mortgage payments—the process of securitization. This fundamental transformation meant that it was often more profitable to sell off packaged loans than to hold them through to maturity. As volume was key to profits, and as financial fraud was no longer punished, banks had every incentive to massively defraud clients. On the front end, mortgages were fraudulently peddled to retail customers, while on the back end, structured financial products were fraudulently sold to institutional investors.

While apologists for bank interests state the mortgage fraud 'epidemic' (in the words of the FBI in 2004) was caused by the Community Reinvestment Act (FCIC 2011), they have few answers as to how or why these fraudulent loans claimed their first victims on the back end in Germany in 2007. The transition from a legitimate system that aligned bank interests with those of its clients to a criminal system in which banks could defraud with impunity, did not hurt only the retail customer.

As revealed by the Financial Crisis Inquiry Commission (FCIC), the ratio of managers' profits to debts created through collateralized debt obligations (CDO) was between approximately 1 to 50 and 1 to 100, depending on the complexity of the deal (FCIC 2011: 131). As such, the end result of defrauding clients on both ends of the CDO were profits for individual actors, and astronomical levels of debt that have been used to guarantee political impunity for banks, most clearly seen with the too big to fail–too big to prosecute doctrines. Incentive structures have been completely inversed since the golden age. Whereas banks were at the service of the economy in general before, now their profits often come from bankrupting clients on both the retail and wholesale level, and their political survival depends on how much damage they could potentially inflict upon the economy, in a current application of Kalecki's (1943) proposition that the captains of industry would sacrifice profits for political control.

The above quote from the OECD (2011) arrives as the core dynamics of traditional banking, of great benefit to the average person but not to the criminal banker, and offers great contrast to the shadowy banking system that entered into crisis in 2007. The OECD's insight is also helpful to our argument here, as it underlines how different structures can produce different results regardless of time. Appeals to return to a system that worked well before are often casually brushed aside as nostalgia, confusing how a system worked with a certain point in history.

This is why understanding the ontology of finance and understanding why some systems work better than others is such an important—and perhaps unsurprisingly unattended—area of study. Indeed, as helpful as the OECD quote is, it does not include the almost pure monetary creation of some parts of the SBS, nor does it explicitly mention fraud.

As we have tried to emphasize, if finance is to attend to the creation of investment, employment and wealth, it must attend to several core concepts. Banking must be decentralized, supervised, and regulated. The elements of the SBS that acted as the fraud intermediaries that drove the 2007–2009 crisis could not have operated if anti-monopoly and anti-fraud laws were applied. On a national level, a humble yet functional banking system has no need for a strong central bank, and fiscal policy—and not merely private bank loans—should be the mechanism used to assure that the economy is constantly and consistently forwarded money. In order to guarantee the international conditions for such policies, stable exchange rates and relatively closed financial systems are needed for national spaces of production to be relatively protected from what would otherwise be rough and disruptive seas of global finance. In the golden age, such financial stability led to lower interest rates and the possibility of long-term and stable productive investment.

Money and morals: concluding remarks

If economics as a social science should come to grips with the social convention of money being at the service of democratic and enlightened societies, then we must ask whether societies at large can responsibly manage the possibility of abundant money. To put it in less moral terms, given the planet's rapidly deteriorating ability to comfortably accommodate human life, considerations over whether functional finance would simply be adding fuel to the unsustainable material ambition of today's world must be addressed. Yet to address these we must return to a focus on morals. Keynes' (1931: 332) famous passages from 'Economic possibilities for our grandchildren,' that "for at least another hundred years we must pretend to ourselves and to everyone that fair is foul and foul is fair; for foul is useful and fair is not," hints at why he did not lay out functional finances as formally and clearly as Lerner did.

At the beginning of the 1970s, Schumacher (1973) offered the criticism that Keynes erred in calling for an advance towards the light through darkness. While Keynes' academic ambiguity regarding money certainly left room open for economists at the service of banks to greatly contribute to the conditions that created today's global financial morass. The ongoing global financial crisis on the other hand offers an unprecedented opportunity for Keynes' moral and political considerations regarding monetary abundance to be revisited, particularly in light of the increasingly clear motivations behind the obscurantism and false science that define the neoliberal pincer.

Indeed, as we are now almost a hundred years removed from the writing of Keynes' above quote, perhaps we should now ask whether we need to still pretend about money. But if there were to be a general recognition of the non-scarcity of money, then how should we use it?

Keynes provides guidance on the political and moral front. Although strictly speaking of the right to national self-sufficiency—and certainly most applicable to that—the below quote resonates with the basic premise of establishing functional finance in order to allow society to make informed decisions regarding spending. Once freed from the money motive, society can work towards what is truly worthwhile as it sees fit. Similarly, once countries can break their economic dependence from foreign financial actors and markets and become self-sufficient, nations as a whole can

> be our own masters, and to be as free as we can make ourselves from the interferences of the outside world. Thus, regarded from this point of view, the policy of an increased national self-sufficiency is to be considered not as an ideal in itself but as directed to the creation of an environment in which other ideals can be safely and conveniently pursued . . . that we all need to be as free as possible of interference from economic changes elsewhere, in order to make our own favorite experiments towards the ideal social republic of the future.
>
> *Keynes 1933: 760*

Demands for both full employment and dignified work are not mutually exclusive; capital productivity and full employment may be, however, particularly when there are no barriers in place to assure that capital and the forces of production share the same spaces and fates. If we are to guarantee a productive system and a financial system at the service of "our own favorite experiments," hopefully led by the effervescent creativity of the young from below, we must decentralize both our financial and productive systems. Despite many opinions that there can be 'no going back' in finance, we propose that the basic financial architecture of the US and the globe under Keynes' international monetary system was correct in spirit and function: a global system that minimizes international financial flows and maximizes home-grown credit and work, supported at the local level by a variety of credit institutions from which to start ventures, and at a national level by a system of functional finance in which the average worker can always have a month's advance instead of always being a dollar short.

As Galbraith (2008) mentioned towards the beginning of the crisis, simply increasing government payouts through already existing programs is an easy way of creating aggregate demand and improving social welfare. Government deficits can more easily and effectively go towards subsidizing everyday citizens than bailing out banks. Simply increasing social security payments, cutting tuition to state schools while adding more faculty and staff, or expanding the role and depth of Medicare, represent frictionless government subsidies paid at the household level. A basic appreciation of how our financial systems operate should eliminate controversy regarding this statement.

Perhaps achieving a general appreciation for a stable financial system is a more ambitious task than the creation of one. To insist, a stable financial system has much more to do with form and function than space and time. If the US and other countries are to once again have their private and public money-creating institutions act in concert with human advancement in mind, we will need: on the one hand, academic economists willing to rise above the neoliberal pincer and embrace the reality of money's non-scarcity—a calling that Post Keynesian economists have consistently embraced; and on the other hand, we will need public opinion at large to understand that attention to employment and consumption based on human needs and dignity—rather than the invidious accumulation of material goods—should be the end goal of that stable system and abundant money.

We certainly sympathize with Keynes' skepticism. Much like during his times, today's society may not be prepared for this. However, at this critical juncture, we conclude that this is our only possible way forward. Today's elite, guided by materialism and obscurantism, has clearly failed humanity. We hope that society can now truly heed Schumacher's (1973) position—which was never that far from Keynes'—that the only way out of the darkness of ignorance and into the light of knowledge and consciousness is through the path of truth, morals, and social science at the service of humanity.

References

Baragar, F. & Seccareccia, M. 2008. 'Financial restructuring: implications of recent Canadian macroeconomic developments.' *Studies in Political Economy*, 82 (Autumn): 61–83.

Bernanke, B. 2000. *Essays on the Great Depression*. Princeton, NJ: Princeton University Press.

Black, W. 2005. *The Best Way to Rob a Bank Is to Own One: How Corporate Executives and Politicians Looted the S&L Industry*. Austin, TX: University of Texas Press.

Black, W. 2014. Roger Myerson's paean to plutocracy. New Economic Perspectives. June 5. Available from http://neweconomicperspectives.org/2014/06/gary-beckers-nobel-prize-getting-wrong-family.html [Accessed December 31, 2015]

Burgin, A. 2012. *The Great Persuasion: Reinventing Free Markets since the Depression*. Cambridge, MA: Harvard University Press.

Davidson, P. 2008. 'Post WW II politics and Keynes's aborted revolutionary economic theory.' *Economia e Sociedade*, 17 (special issue): 549–568.

DeMartino, G. 2011. 'El economista como ingeniero social: la necesidad de ética profesional.' *Ola Financiera*, 11 (January–April): 65–90. Available from http://www.olafinanciera.unam.mx/new_web/11/pdfs/DeMartino_OlaFin-11.pdf [Accessed July 28, 2016]

Epstein, G. 2005. 'Introduction: Financialization and the world economy,' *in*: G. Epstein (ed.), *Financialization and the World Economy*. Northampton, MA: Edward Elgar, 3–16.

Felkerson, J. 2011. $29,000,000,000,000: A detailed look at the Fed's bailout by funding facility and recipient. Levy Economics Institute Working Paper No. 698. Available from http://www.levyinstitute.org/pubs/wp_698.pdf [Accessed July 31, 2016]

Ferguson, C. 2013. *Predator Nation: Corporate Criminals, Political Corruption, and the Hijacking of America*. New York: Crown Business.

Financial Crisis Inquiry Commission (FCIC). 2011. The financial crisis inquiry report: Final report of the National Commission of the Causes of the Financial and Economic Crisis in the United States. Washington, DC; United State Government Publishing Office. Available from https://www.gpo.gov/fdsys/pkg/GPO-FCIC/pdf/GPO-FCIC.pdf [Accessed June 1, 2016]

Forstater, M. 1999. Functional finance and full employment: Lessons from Lerner for today? Levy Economics Institute Working Paper 272. Available from http://www.levyinstitute.org/pubs/wp272.pdf [Accessed July 28, 2016]

Friedman, M. 1970. The counter-revolution in monetary theory. IEA Occasional paper 33. London: Institute of Economic Affairs. Available from http://0055d26.netsolhost.com/friedman/pdfs/other_academia/IEA.1970.pdf [Accessed July 28, 2016]

Friedman, M. 1980. *Free to choose*. A TV series by Public Broadcasting System.

Friedman, M. & Schwartz, A. 1987. 'Has government any role in money?' *in*: A.J. Schwartz (ed.), *Money in a Historical Perspective*. Chicago: University of Chicago Press, 289–314.

Fullwiler, S. 2012. Krugman's flashing neon sign. Naked Capitalism. April 2. Available from http://www.nakedcapitalism.com/2012/04/scott-fullwiler-krugmans-flashing-neon-sign.html [Accessed December 31, 2015]

Galbraith, James K. 2008. 'Colapso del monetarismo e irrelevancia del nuevo consenso monetario.' *Ola Financiera*, 1 (September/December): 1–17. Available from http://www.olafinanciera.unam.mx/new_web/01/pdfs/Galbraith-OlaFin-1.pdf [Accessed July 31, 2016]

Galbraith, James K. 2014. *The End of Normal: Why the Growth Economy Isn't Coming Back—and What to Do When It Doesn't*. New York: Simon and Schuster.

Galbraith, John K. 1975. *Money: From Whence It Came, Where It Went*. Boston: Houghton Mifflin.

Galbraith, John K. 1977. *The Age of Uncertainty*. Boston: Houghton Mifflin.

Hayek, F. 1944. *The Road to Serfdom*. Chicago: University of Chicago Press.

Hoover, K. 2003. *Economics as Ideology: Keynes, Laski, Hayek, and the Creation of Contemporary Politics*. New York: Rowman and Littlefield.

Kalecki, M. 1943. 'Political aspects of full employment.' *Political Quarterly*, 14 (4): 322–330.

Keynes, J.M. 1931. 'Economic possibilities for our grandchildren,' *in*: J.M. Keynes (ed.), *Essays in Persuasion*. London: Macmillan, 358–373.

Keynes, J.M. 1933. 'Economic self sufficiency.' *The Yale Review*, 22 (4): 755–769.

Keynes, J.M. 1936. *The General Theory of Employment, Interest, and Money*. London: Macmillan.

Krugman, P. 1998. Japan's trap. Available from http://web.mit.edu/krugman/www/japtrap.html [Accessed December 31, 2015]

Krugman, P. 2009. A dark age of macroeconomics (wonkish). *New York Times*. January 27.

Lee, F.S. 2009. *A History of Heterodox Economics: Challenging the Mainstream in the Twentieth Century*. London: Routledge.

Lerner, A. 1943. 'Functional finance and the federal debt.' *Social Research*, 10 (1): 38–51.

Mirowski, P. 2013. *Never Let a Good Crisis Go to Waste: How Neoliberalism Survived the Financial Crisis*. London: Verso Books.

Mirowski, P. & Plehwe, D. 2009. *The Road from Mont Pelerin: The Making of the Neoliberal Thought Collective*. Cambridge, MA: Harvard University Press.

National Commission on Financial Institution Reform, Recovery and Enforcement (NCFIRRE). 1993. Origins and causes of the S&L debacle: a blueprint for reform. A Report to the President and Congress of the United States. Washington, DC: US Government Printing Office.

Organization for Economic Cooperation and Development (OECD). 2011. *Bank Competition and Financial Stability*. Paris: OECD Publishing.

Palley, T. 2015. 'Milton Friedman's economics and political economy: an old Keynesian critique,' *in*: R. Cord (ed.), *Milton Friedman: Contributions to Economics and Public Policy*. Oxford: Oxford University Press, 631–656.

Robinson, J. 1960. *Collected Economic Papers, Vol. II*. Oxford: Basil Blackwell.

Schumacher, E.F. 1973. *Small is Beautiful: Economics as if People Mattered.* New York: Harper.

Seccareccia, M. 1995. 'Keynesianism and public investment: A left–Keynesian perspective on the role of government expenditures and debt.' *Studies in Political Economy*, 46 (Spring): 43–78.

Smithin, J. 2013. 'Keynes's theories of money and banking in the *Treatise* and *The General Theory.' Review of Keynesian Economics*, 1 (2): 242–256.

US DoJ (United States Department of Justice). 2015. Five major banks agree to parent-level guilty pleas. Office of Public Affairs. May 20. Available from https://www.justice.gov/opa/pr/five-major-banks-agree-parent-level-guilty-pleas [Accessed July 31, 2016]

33

Rethinking the role of the state

Anna Klimina

Introduction

Heterodox economists recognize that the state is central in establishing and modifying all market orders. Mainstream economists do not deny that markets cannot operate without the state's provision of "the legal-institutional process through and within which markets function" (Medema 2003: 434). However, they typically do not allow a role for the state beyond the minimal functions of producing and enforcing the institutional framework that best protects a free market economy, viewed as an evolutionary end-point. In contrast, many heterodox economists believe that the state should direct economic evolution by designing and nurturing institutions that secure greater equality, social justice, and full employment, outcomes that might not emerge as a result of "unfettered operation of laissez-faire capitalism" (Petr 1987: 1453; see also Commons [1934] 1961; Galbraith 1973; Stanfield 1992; Mayhew 2001; Whalen 2008). Consequently, they argue for a profound reconceptualization of the mainstream vision of a minimal state with little remedial involvement in the economy.

Although heterodox economists offer several possible alternatives to the mainstream support of an unfettered market, this chapter discusses a new vision for the state within the framework of the evolutionary-institutionalist school of heterodox economics, which offers more room to imagine the positive roles that the state could play in democratic reformation of capitalist economies. In the first place, "from their American beginnings," institutionalist scholars have been "proponents of an active state" (Mayhew 2001: 244) that "works for the betterment of [capitalist] society" (Commons [1934] 1961: 6). Furthermore, "as products of modern industrial culture, with its commitment to individual rights and democratic principles, institutionalists accept . . . tenets of liberalism" and celebrate Western values of individual freedom, human participation, pluralism, and respect for human rights (Waller 2006: 22). Their intention is to extend the remedial functions of government to enhance these values (Waller 2006: 22). Original institutional economics, then, draws on its democratic heritage and liberal values to reconceptualize the involvement of the state in market economies.

The broad overview of this reconceptualized state is presented in three stages. The first section demystifies prevailing assumptions about the state, which are centered on the expectation of an inevitable development of rent-seeking and corruption in government; and the desirability of a liberal market, with its minimal state, as the eventual end-point of economic evolution. The second section discusses key tenets of original institutional economics and its ensuing policies that will contribute most beneficially to the proposed new view of the state. The third section outlines the institutionalist concept of state control in state capitalist societies, in which a powerful state, as a large owner of society's productive property, has a huge potential to improve market economies and move them, in the words of Clarence Ayres (1973: xi–xii), "beyond [existing] capitalism."

Typical fallacies concerning the state

The first and most typical mainstream myth about the state is that self-interest automatically guides the behavior of all state agents. Therefore, state activism, beyond securing the free market institutions, would necessarily promote rent-seeking and corruption (Todaro & Smith 2014: 137). Consequently, mainstream scholars argue that a minimally active government is the best government (Becker 1958: 109). Notably, in the first part of the twentieth century, many (albeit not all) neoclassical scholars acknowledged that state intervention is necessary to correct market failures, such as those caused by externalities and unrestricted market power, situations that distort a competitive market's efficiency and create social losses (Pigou 1932: 174–183; Simons 1934: 4–5, 19–29). However, since the end of the 1950s, in response to developments in neoclassical theory of government intervention (Backhouse 2005: 358–360), most mainstream scholars began to see state involvement in correction of market failures as an inevitable promotion of corrupt behavior (Krueger 1974). In tandem with post-Second World War Chicago school scholars, public choice economics, which originated in the 1960s, is best known for its emphasis on government failures, belief in the efficiency of unregulated markets, and relentless advocacy for the abandonment of antitrust regulation (Director & Levi 1956; Buchanan & Tullock 1962; DiLorenzo & High 1988). Accordingly, "between 1970 and 2000 . . . an ideology favorable to [state] management of the economy gave way to one in which state action was seen as raising more problems than it solved" (Backhouse 2005: 355), and the conception of limited government has become dominant in mainstream anti-corruption discourse (Streeten 1993: 1292; Chang 1994: 297).

Thus rethinking the role of the state necessarily means dismissing this erroneous link between state activism and rent-seeking. It is unconvincing and inaccurate, based on an extreme distrust of government officials who are assumed to be universally motivated by egotistical ends and not at all by public purpose. We interpret this link, as suggested by Ha-Joon Chang, as "providing vision" for the future and "engineering"—through the "construction of new institutional vehicles for the realization of its vision"—socio-economic changes to national advantage (Chang 1994: 299, 300). As James Stanfield (1991: 775) observes, the "absence [in modern discourse] of a positive theory of the state is especially critical for institutionalists with their penchant for social democratic reform."

Another closely related myth about the state rests on a teleological vision of humankind's evolution, which considers societal progress as moving inevitably toward a single social construction (Lichtenstein 1996: 258). In mainstream economics, it means convergence on "an ideal limiting case" of a "liberal market order" (Evensky 2005: 12), regarded as a "civilization standard" (Cowen 2004: 71). From this perspective, mainstream scholars commonly view any increase in state control over the economy as an inefficient and therefore temporary phenomenon that will eventually give way to efficient free market capitalism, due to the forces of global competition and increased transparency (North 1990: 80–91; Boettke et al. 2008: 333–336). In this respect, the mainstream conception of "evolutionary convergence" is fundamentally anti-evolutionary and is similar to "the determinism of neoclassical equilibrium economics, with the equilibrium being a rut rather than a point" (Atkinson 1998: 886).

An equally anti-evolutionary conception of the state is rooted in an ideology of cultural determinism, which over-emphasizes the role of culture and history in defining the nature of the state. Cultural determinism is often used to justify non-democratic prospects for some societies around the globe. To illustrate, once obscure nationalist ideas of a 'Russian special way,' grounded in the belief that the country's inherited non-democratic institutions and cultural attitudes are immutable, have been revived in modern Russia and officially endorsed by the political elite as the preferred ideology. Russia is thus historically and culturally predestined—so goes the argument—to follow the traditional authoritarian path of development, which will always be incompatible with Western values, especially Western respect for democracy, pluralism, individual freedom, and the rule of law (Surkov 2008; Rozov 2012).

Rethinking the role of the state should thus begin with the rejection of such simplistic views of evolutionary processes, and the recognition of the course of societal progress as a divergent rather than convergent process. As a result, it cannot be determined in advance, but remains subject to any deviation brought about by citizens, who can direct and redirect the evolution of the state, typically by changing the legal framework in which a nation state operates.

The importance of human agency in changing the state and consequently, the path of socio-economic evolution, is a central premise of original institutional economics, whose "volitional, pragmatic and essentially democratic perspective on human societies" (Petr 1987: 1448) is foundational to the vision of the state developed in this chapter. The next section examines in detail the institutionalist perspectives on the state that we consider the most useful for outlining, in the section that follows, the institutionalist concept of state control in state capitalist societies.

Perspectives on the state in original institutional economics

All evolutionary-institutionalist scholars argue that a competitive market distributes goods in a socially unacceptable way and consequently support an active state. However, 'volitional' or 'constructivist' institutionalism offers a wider scope for this chapter's vision of the state's positive role in evolutionary restructuring of market economies "along more equitable and progressive lines" (Knoedler & Schneider 2010: 259). This strand of original institutional economics is based on John Commons' (1931: 655) belief that economic evolution is primarily guided by purposeful human action rather than non-deliberative processes. Such state intervention in economic affairs, Commons believed, is necessary for "making Capitalism good" (Commons [1934] 1964: 143). Below are the key tenets of original institutional economics and the envisioned policies for an activist state, which are the most appropriate and useful for this chapter's proposed new view of the state.

Economic evolution as a volitional process and belief in remedial possibilities, not-rent-seeking, for the state

Unlike mainstream economists, John Commons ([1934] 1961: 6) argues that the deliberative selection of institutions by the authorities is not merely a way to commence and secure the institutions of free market, but also a means to "harmonize" the market, which he understood as "naturally" prone to conflicts "in the world of scarcity and private property." The evolving market order, according to Commons, is largely premeditated by "the minds of men," who, "by individual or collective action, control evolution according to their own ideas of fitness" (Commons [1934] 1961: 120), thus constructing "order out of conflict" (Commons [1934] 1961: 109). Consequently, he emphasizes the important role of human volition, especially that of "authoritative agency" (Commons [1934] 1961: 120), in adjusting social institutions through dispute resolution, a premeditated legal action that supports the interests of "certain businesses or classes . . . rather than others," thus redesigning markets and guiding economic development (Commons [1924] 1968:137–138). Commons ([1934] 1961: 636) defines the outcome of volitional dispute resolution as "artificial" selection, an enforced "survival of good customs and punishment of bad customs," and emphasizes that "artificial selection" signifies "Purpose, Futurity, Planning, injected into and greatly controlling the struggle for life." Commons ([1934] 1961: 162) believes in the ameliorative nature of these "artificial selection" processes, and explains that "the visible hand of . . . courts" takes "over the customs of the time and place, in so far as deemed good" and enforces "these good customs on refractory individuals."

As Yngve Ramstad (1994: 111) notes, through Commons' metaphor of artificial selection, "it becomes evident that the market system is solely a human artifact, a set of arrangements purposefully selected to advance the well-being of the group (going concern) as a whole." Along with emphasizing deliberative court decisions in the course of reforming markets, Commons also underlines the important role of political power of the state in guiding evolution by establishing "the laws of the land" that "proportion the factors over which [the state] has control," "encourage certain businesses . . . rather than others," "open up certain areas, localities or resources, instead of others" (Commons 1909: 79), and balance "inducements to individuals and associations of individuals to act in one direction rather than other directions"(Commons [1924] 1968: 387).

Institutionalist economists have adopted Commons' perspective on the role of the state "as a creative entity" that provides "a sense of overall direction to the overall economic evolution" (Chang 1994: 307) and similarly acknowledge that it is through the "legislative, administrative and judicial decisions" of the state that the rights and freedoms in society get "their specific meaning" derived "from the clash of competing interests" (Samuels 1989: 426–428). Contemporary institutionalists go beyond Commons in their focus on the determining role of power relations in guiding the evolution of market economy; they view markets as essentially a product of perpetual interaction between economic and political forces that endlessly affect, reconstitute, and readjust the existing market design (Samuels & Schmid 1981; Mazzucato 2013). They acknowledge that the state's strategic position within the economy as "the only agent which may represent the interest of the whole society" (Chang 1994: 299) gives the state more opportunities to intentionally restructure market economies for the good of all of society, provided that the state uses its power to design, select, and nurture institutions that compensate for free market deficiencies and promote just development (Pressman 2006: 134).

While institutionalists typically believe in remedial possibilities for the state, they are not idealists who see the state as an autonomous independent entity. Rather, they acknowledge that the state is "captured by powerful corporations" and, therefore, acts as both "the executive committee of the great corporation and its planning system" (Galbraith 1973: 11) and as an "agency of the ruling class" (Solo 1978: 829). However, they do not view the state "as a passive agency of private economic interests" and "as hives of rent-seekers" (Mayhew 2001: 244). They are convinced that for many agents of the state the motives of seeking the public purpose and of instituting fairness are of vital importance (Stanfield 1991: 765). That is why they base their hope for liberation from the hegemony of corporate power and for full comprehensive human development on the countervailing power of the state. As Galbraith (1973: 10) declares, while acknowledging the reality that the state "is captured," necessary "remedial action"—that is, "the restriction of excessive resource use, organization to offset inadequate resource use, controls, actions to correct systemic inequality, protection of the environment, protection of the consumer"—"lies with the state."

In contemporary institutionalist analysis, Commons' metaphor of 'artificial selection' could thus be interpreted as an indication of both the state's ability and obligation to design, impose, and nurture institutions that will correct economic injustices and produce socially desirable outcomes. However, the institutionalist support for the use of the state's discretionary power to shape socio-economic development and thus guide economic evolution does not automatically indicate a belief in the teleological nature of social evolution or in the ability of the state to predict accurately the direction of movement in societal progress. It merely recognizes that active state control is necessary in order to secure socially just economic outcomes.

Non-teleological understanding of state endogeneity and recognition of importance of human agency

There is a well-established consensus among many institutionalists that the state should be seen "as endogenous to the economic system" (Cypher 2014: 252), and as evolving from each society's "unique cultural, social and political history" (Waller 2006: 31). From this perspective, a country's historical backwardness and lack of market institutions, particularly the absence of economic relations based on property and rule of law (for contract enforcement), is often considered the primary cultural-historic cause of corrupt and non-democratic states around the globe (Owen 1997; Klimina 2010).

On the other hand, while recognizing the role of history in influencing the form and character of the state, institutionalists also argue that the future of the state is not fully determined by its history (Atkinson 1998: 886). The nature of the state is also shaped by individuals who, singly and collectively, amend state institutions through rearranging power distribution. The institutionalist theory of human nature asserts that, "the individual with whom we are dealing is the Institutionalized Mind" (Commons [1924] 1968: 73), who is socially and culturally embedded and thus "cannot be comprehended outside the social whole" (Atkinson & Reed 1990: 1105). However, within the non-teleological conception of the state's evolution outlined in the previous section, individuals are also learning agents. They are "always-changing 'institutionalized personalities', sentient and thinking personalities" (Mayhew 2001: 240), who can adapt their activities and expectations to "incorporate changes into the existing order" (Hodgson 2000: 327). As Dugger & Sherman (1994: 107) accurately observe, "the individual is not a cultural marionette because individuals can and do transform their culture through collective action and even through individual action," while "culture itself is continually changing through myriad actions, inactions, and choices of individuals." Anne Mayhew (2001: 243) explains that the "social goals of individuals and of groups of individuals are shaped by visions of what is possible and by new understanding."

Consequently, many institutionalists argue that political change, the starting point for the desired economic change, does not originate exclusively from the state, but through a combination of pressure from citizenry and reforms from above. François Moreau (2004: 851) indicates that the state does not have "*a priori* privileged knowledge on the actions to be undertaken to increase social welfare." Glen Atkinson (1998: 886) explains that under conditions of pervasive uncertainty, when "there is no extant future path" but "only imagined likely and possible paths," "if the imagined likely future path is deemed undesirable then we [as active individuals] propose actions to create a possible alternative path." Finally, Knoedler & Schneider (2010: 266) insist that it is only through active individuals who "demand change," thus "reducing the power of elites to resist change," that adjustment of power balance in society takes place, such that "evolutionary change comes about."

The former Soviet Union's perestroika ('restructuring') movement of 1985–1991, led by then-leader Mikhail Gorbachev, is a case in point. Perestroika represents an attempt by a constructivist state to bring about a politically pluralistic society and a social-democratic market through adjustments to the balance of power in a formerly totalitarian society so that democratic change could evolve. Although perestroika was initially premeditated, imposed, and nurtured by the state, it was the political power of the public, the "power from below," that was intended to play a creative role in shaping the emerging democratic market order, whose overall design thus remained indeterminate. Of course, the Soviet Union did not have enough time to implement, let alone observe the long-term outcomes of constructivist perestroika policies. That renders premature any suggestion that those policies were unviable and idealistic.

Evolutionary-institutionalist vision of the policies of the constructivist state

Institutionalists differ on what constitutes an acceptable scope of state activism, despite their shared beliefs in both the necessity of state intervention to correct market deficiencies and the power of human agency to redirect the evolutionary development of national economies. Some institutionalist economists argue that changing the laws which grant more equitable protection to different interest groups, without direct "government intervention in a situation in which it has hitherto been absent," would be sufficient to reduce the degree of state capture, improve competitiveness, and engineer social change for the better (Samuels 1989: 427–428). In contrast, the majority of contemporary institutionalist scholars believe that only "through scientifically guided" broad government intervention "in the public interest," particularly through "social control of business," via "regulation and the development of new working rules," social "institutions can be reformed" for greater social benefit (Rutherford 1994a: 150–151).

In particular, this refers to the government regulation of private monopolies and oligopolies (Galbraith 1967; Eichner 1976). Furthermore, institutionalists and Post Keynesians argue that, in conditions of fundamental uncertainty, the state should act as an uncertainty-reducing institution (Pressman 2006: 133) and "as an entrepreneur whose task is to provide a vision for the society" and deliver the stable institutions "required to achieve the vision" (Chang 1994: 297). Accordingly, government policies should, first, decrease uncertainty by ensuring price stability, providing certain social safety nets, provisioning and diffusing information, guaranteeing public markets, and regulating industrial, environmental and technology policies; second, provide a level of public investment sufficient for achieving full employment; and third, equalize income distribution through progressive taxation and wide-ranging government spending programs (Pressman 2006; Holt 2013). Fiscal policy should be based on "functional finance" (Abba Lerner's term) rather than balanced budget considerations. According to Nevile (2012: 224), functional finance implies:

> that government expenditures and revenues should be determined so that total expenditure in an economy is at the rate which will produce full employment without inflation. This is to be done without any concern about whether the resulting budget is in surplus or deficit.

While in agreement with all the above policy proposals, some radical institutionalists push the argument for comprehensive government intervention even further. They call for an active progressive state to create or amend existing market institutions. Since such a state is in a better position to substantially improve equity distribution, it can use "economic surplus as a fund for social change" (Stanfield 1992: 130) to promote economic security, socially just amelioration, an end to alienation, and greater equality of wealth and resources through increase in opportunity and participation (Dugger 1987; Whalen 2008; Wrenn 2011). These scholars are also concerned with the distribution of the ownership of productive assets in society, arguing that property rights represent a fundamental form, and key source, of economic power (Neale 1991: 469). As Dowd

(1974: 129) notes in reference to the US economy "the power of the ruling class in the country has come principally from its ownership and control of the nation's productive wealth," while workers, as Bowles *et al.* (1983: 27) point out, have "little or no control over production process" and they are "clearly separated from management by layers of hierarchical authority and by significant differentials in income and social status." Radical institutionalists thus call for the state to encourage more equitable sharing of productive property, through various forms of collective ownership and worker participation in economic decision-making, as well as the initiation of new property in social investment, measures that should be aimed at advancing a "shared-prosperity" capitalism (Whalen 2008: 55).

Given these positions, it is logical to take the next step and envisage a progressivist agenda for the new form of economically powerful states that are emerging in some market economies. State capitalism can be an efficient means through which national economies are intentionally restructured along more democratic lines, provided that the state incorporates key institutionalist proposals for just development and uses its power to design and nurture institutions that compensate for market deficiencies and promote effective economic and political democracy. The next section discusses this issue in detail.

Institutionalist vision for state capitalism

State capitalism is typically denoted as a condition under which a national state controls a substantial part of society's capital, acts as a significant domestic investor and employer, and directs a considerable portion of international trade and investment (Pollard 2011: 4–5; Wooldridge 2012: 3–6). Defined this way, state capitalism is distinguishable from a merely interventionist state because here the state acts as the largest controller of the economy's means of production and, thus, as the largest appropriator and distributor of economic surplus. Furthermore, this definition presumes that the state exercises considerable power over socio-economic decisions in state capitalist societies.

Heterodox economists have not ignored state capitalism; however, negative reactions have emanated from scholars ranging from original institutionalist economists to Western Marxians. Western Marxians in particular view state capitalism as similar to the bureaucratic statist economy established in the Soviet Union, despite acknowledging that Soviet 'state capitalism' was not actually a capitalist economy (Laibman 1978: 25). They argue that Soviet state officials "appropriated economic surpluses" (Wolff & Resnick 2012: 326) generated by worker-producers, thus retaining the core capitalist division between surplus producers and surplus appropriators (Oppenheimer 2009: 436). Western Marxians often highlight the undemocratic character "of surplus centralization" in Soviet-style economies (Gabriel *et al.* 2008: 545), the exploitative use of the means of production by state's officials for the benefit of state elites (Cliff 1974: 159), perpetual worker alienation from control over surplus distribution (Bettelheim & Chavance 1981: 42), and the "hierarchical organization of a workplace" (Oppenheimer 2009: 436). In contrast, institutionalists associate state capitalism with mature capitalism, but their understanding of the term is similar to what Western Marxian scholars identify as "state monopoly capitalism," a condition under which a conglomeration of powerful private corporations dominates the state to assure maximal conditions for profit generation (O'Connor 1973). Similar to Marxian scholars, evolutionary-institutionalist economists such as Elliot (1984) emphasize and comprehensively examine worker alienation under state monopoly capitalism.

The present rise of state capitalism in the "big emergent markets of China, Russia, India and Brazil" is correctly linked in development literature to a national government's intention to "resist neoliberalism" (Wooldridge 2012: 3–4) and "gate globalization" (Ip 2013:16) in order to "control capital accumulation," "protect national economies," increase the "state's power over national resources," and advance the "state's political ambitions" (Bremmer 2009: 48). This calls for a re-imaging of state capitalism in heterodox economic literature to acknowledge its inherent promise.

Development scholars commonly admit that the primary purpose of state capitalism is to ensure that "market forces" protect the "ruling elite's political control" (Bremmer 2009: 50), rather than the maximization of wealth production. However, state capitalist governments still administer a core capitalist state, securing and promoting business interests of large state-run companies, which are typically sectoral monopolies or oligopolies. Governments "recognize that profitable state-owned enterprises make the state stronger" and thus stimulate, through financial support of large-scale enterprises in strategic sectors, the creation of "global champions" that enjoy "a special competitive advantage not possible for the private firms" (Musacchio & Lazzarini 2014: 8–9). Researchers also agree that under state capitalism, state-owned and state-controlled enterprises are often "more capital and knowledge-intensive, more productive and more profitable" than they were under state socialism (Vanteeva & Hickson 2012: 173–175).

State capitalism, this chapter argues, can accomplish more than just a successful nationalization of large-scale productive property to advance national strength. When pressured from below by citizens dissatisfied with excessive social inequality, non-democratic polity, non-transparent bureaucracy, and continuing worker alienation from power over surplus distribution (problems thoroughly documented in modern scholarly research on contemporary state capitalism), the state can, unlike private capitalist states, use its considerable power over socio-economic decisions to nurture the democratic fundamentals of the economy and promote a social-democratic welfare state. This is precisely the institutionalist vision for democratic state control in market-based societies that was outlined in the previous section.

The democratic promises inherent in state capitalism in emerging economies can be translated into the most mature capitalist economies as well. These economies are also characterized by a dominance of centralized and bureaucratically controlled large-scale corporations, but these corporations were not developed by design as in many developing and post-socialist economies. They emerged through concentration and centralization of capital, processes based on internal dynamics of competition and accumulation. Due to the nature of technology and market uncertainties, large companies and oligopolistic markets will remain a key part of any kind of market economy, whether private capitalist or state capitalist or any other variation. Furthermore, the existence of large-scale corporations is unavoidable, since large-scale corporations in mature economies, like corporations in emerging markets, are also driven by the demands of globalization, first of all, the globalization of corporate power. As a result, competition policies that merely attempt to control the size of modern corporations through forced division into smaller companies are counterproductive and "offer little to a progressive society eager to make good use of modern technology" and trends in globalization (Martin 1974: 772).

The most pressing issue when rethinking the role of the state in progressive transformation of modern capitalist economies, both mature and emerging, is how the state can conduct comprehensive democratic restructuring of an economy's large-scale industrial enterprises without their fragmentation. State capitalist economies are certainly in a better position than a modern private capitalist state to make progressive changes, because the state owns most of the corporations. Nevertheless, a modern private capitalist state can pursue beneficial regulation in the public interest, either as controlling shareholder, or, depending upon corporation specificity, as minor shareholder in large corporations' equity, using its influence and power to promote workplace democracy. Envisioning such a potentially benevolent state is aided through an analysis of one of the largest state capitalist countries, Russia, and the policy proposals, which are aimed at the democratic restructuring of highly concentrated state ownership of industrial assets.

Learning from reform of large-scale state ownership in state capitalist societies

The reform of large-scale state capitalist property proposed in this chapter entails, above all, a restructuring of large-scale state enterprises without also mandating large-scale private property rights. The necessity of such reform is clear from the persistent unsavory characteristics that still mark large-scale state capitalist property, including "lack of participatory democracy" (Xie *et al.* 2013: 445), "bureaucratic inefficiency" in management, and perpetual worker separation from power and resources (Schweickart 1992: 30–31). Arguably, the concept of multileveled state ownership, originally introduced during the Soviet Economic Reform of 1965 but developed thoroughly in the years of perestroika, can become a working template for democratic restructuring of large-scale state capitalist property. Undoubtedly inspired by progressive economists' ideas of democratic economic planning and by the worker ownership/participation movement, this concept conceives of three interdependent levels of ownership: the state level, the enterprise (firm) level, and the worker (employee) level (Mereste 1987; Torkanovski 1989). Without being entirely transformed into the property of production collectives or turned over into private hands, this tripartite version of large-scale ownership offers possibilities for worker co-ownership and co-decision, envisioned as including shared ownership in the firm's assets and participation in determining enterprise plans, allocation of resources, election of managers, and surplus-sharing, all of which would promote workplace democracy and end alienation. Since the oligopolistic industry remains the dominant form of state capitalist industrial structure, the democratization of state-owned large-scale enterprises will actually lead to "installing democratic and participatory processes" inside state enterprises by providing workers with significant control and decision-making rights. This would reinforce "serviceable aspects of their [state enterprise] performance," a re-application of William Dugger's (1987: 94–95) advice on reforms in the United States, and promote more equitable power distribution under state capitalism.

Furthermore, Russia's current efforts at modernization, aimed at ensuring sustainable and broad-based economic growth, will depend not only on major investment in high-tech industry, but also, crucially, on enhancing participatory democracy and ending worker alienation. As a progressive scholar Schweickart (1992: 31) argues, regarding similar perestroika modernization problems, "workplace democracy is the most appropriate, on both moral and economic grounds," to remedy "worker alienation and consequent low labour productivity," since only "working people [who are] . . . aroused and motivated have the capability to unlock their creative potential and turn things around."

Moreover, such a "tripartite power structure inside state ownership" that understands "ownership relations as essentially multileveled combines the advantages of participatory economics with the need for nationwide planning and coordination" (Emchenko 1987: 142–144). The state, functioning on behalf of the national economy as a whole, accomplishes that planning and coordination through economic means, especially through a "proper system of taxes" aimed at redistributing surplus to promote equality and at treating fairly "the external effects of property use" in a form of differential rents (Nekipelov 2009: 148–149). If the Russian state functions as a primary co-owner and an essential partner in the model of multileveled property ownership, the lack of informational transparency and necessary countrywide coordination that occurred under the much-criticized Yugoslavian system of worker-management, which privileged workers' ownership and sectoral interests above national economic goals, will be avoided, since the state will be in charge of enforcing the democratically determined social priorities. Major investment projects will be conducted and employment security will be protected according to these priorities, all within the state-controlled economy. Moreover, given the oligopolistic positions of state-owned and state-controlled enterprises, the state as the supreme co-owner can more easily intervene in order to ensure that large-scale producers are not acting against the interests of society. As Chang (2007: 23) rightly asserts, to increase competition among large-scale state companies the state could, for example, establish another state-owned enterprise, "given that it is feasible and socially productive."

Such power over productive assets would definitely give the state opportunity to strengthen social control in the public interest. While broad consensus regarding a market type of socialism does not yet exist in society, nor does the will to establish it (Sherman 2012: 496), there is an increasing readiness to gravitate to a strong social-democratic welfare state, a model which has been extensively discussed in progressive economic literature for decades. The time has come to use states' control over large productive property in order to give a social-democratic welfare state in state capitalist economies a second chance, thus transforming the entire social edifice in these countries. Furthermore, to secure more equitable sharing of economic surplus, 'new property' (Reich 1964) by way of social investment ('government-created wealth') should be generated and secured through state-supported access to jobs, state-guaranteed income programs, and a state-funded, wide-ranging system of social benefits. Acting as a key facilitator of "collective action to improve the adjustment of instituted power and status to the fuller unfolding means and purposes of generic humanity" (Stanfield 1991: 778) in order to build a truly democratic economy, state capitalism can become the agent of both economic and political democratization, and social control.

Taken as a whole, such a proposal implies that a progressive societal transformation through state capitalism is possible. The proposed concept of multileveled restructuring of large-scale state property along fairly inclusive and collective lines in state capitalist societies deserves to be put into place in economies whose state is ready to go "beyond capitalism" (Ayres 1973: xi–xii). Graciously recalling original and essential principles, Ayres (1973: xi–xii) reminds us:

> The values we seek are those of human life and well-being. The process by which we seek them is an experimental process, as it has always been. By pursuing this process we will go beyond capitalism, as our forebears went beyond the systems into which they were born. This is the message of institutionalism.

Conclusion

This chapter identifies key mainstream misperceptions about the state, including expectations of an inevitable development of rent-seeking and corruption in government, and a teleological assumption that humankind's evolution will inevitably converge on a liberal market order. These misperceptions prevent mainstream economics from developing a positive vision for state activism beyond securing necessary free market institutions. Original institutional economics provides a wider, more hopeful perspective, including a view of economic evolution as a volitional process, a belief in remedial possibilities for the state rather than inevitable rent-seeking behavior, and a conviction that "through scientifically guided government intervention, social institutions can be reformed and the economy planned for the greater social benefit" (Rutherford 1994b: 553). These basic tenets are foundational to the proposal in this chapter that under state capitalism (viewed as a new form of modern capitalism), the state as chief owner of society's productive property and principal controller of social surplus has both the capacity and opportunity to use its power over socio-economic decisions to nurture the democratic fundamentals of the economy and promote a ssocial-democratic welfare state.

References

Atkinson, G. 1998. 'Review of *Evolutionary Economics and Path Dependence* edited by L. Magnusson and J. Ottosson.' *Journal of Economic Issues*, 32 (3): 885–887.

Atkinson, G. & Reed, M. 1990. 'Institutional adjustment, instrumental efficiency, and reasonable value.' *Journal of Economic Issues*, 24 (4): 1095–1107.

Ayres, C. 1973. *Science: The False Messiah*. New York: Augustus M. Kelley.

Backhouse, R. 2005. 'The rise of free market economics: economists and the role of the state since 1970,' in: S. Medema & P. Boettke (eds.), *The Role of the Government in the History of Economic Thought*. London: Duke University Press, 355–392.

Becker, G.S. 1958. 'Competition and democracy.' *Journal of Law and Economics*, 1 (3): 105–109.

Bettelheim, C. & Chavance, B. 1981. 'Stalinism as the ideology of state capitalism.' *Review of Radical Political Economics*, 13 (1): 40–54.

Boettke, P., Coyne, C., & Leeson, P. 2008. 'Institutional stickiness and the new development economics.' *American Journal of Economics and Sociology*, 67 (2): 331–358.

Bowles, S., Gordon, D., & Weisskopf, T. 1983. *Beyond the Wasteland: A Democratic Alternative to Economic Decline*. Garden City, NY: Anchor Press.

Bremmer, I. 2009. 'State capitalism comes of age: the end of the free market?' *Foreign Affairs*, 88 (3): 40–55.

Buchanan, J. & Tullock, G. 1962. *The Calculus of Consent: Logical Foundations of Constitutional Democracy*. Chicago: The University of Chicago Press.

Chang, H.-J. 1994. 'State, institutions and structural change.' *Structural Change and Economic Dynamics*, 5 (2): 293–313.

Chang, H.-J. 2007. State-owned enterprise reform. UNDESA National Development Strategies Policy Notes. Available from http://esa.un.org/techcoop/documents/PN_SOEReformnote.pdf [Accessed October 17, 2013]

Cliff, T. 1974. *State Capitalism in Russia*. London: Pluto Press.

Commons, J.R. 1909. 'American shoemakers, 1648–1895: a sketch of industrial evolution.' *Quarterly Journal of Economics*, 24 (1): 39–84.

Commons, J.R. 1931. 'Institutional economics.' *American Economic Review*, 21 (4): 648–657.

Commons, J.R. [1934] 1961. *Institutional Economics*. Madison, WI: University of Wisconsin Press.

Commons, J.R. [1934] 1964. *Myself*. Madison, WI: University of Wisconsin Press.

Commons, J.R. [1924] 1968. *Legal Foundations of Capitalism*. Madison, WI: University of Wisconsin Press.

Cowen, T. 2004. *Creative Destruction: How Globalization Is Changing the World's Cultures*. Princeton, NJ: Princeton University Press.

Cypher, J.M. 2014. *The Process of Economic Development*, 4th edn. New York: Routledge.

DiLorenzo, T. & High, J. 1988. 'Antitrust and competition, historically considered.' *Economic Inquiry*, 26 (July): 423–435.

Director, A. & Levi, E. 1956. 'Law and the future: trade regulation.' *Northwestern University Law Review*, 51 (2): 281–296.

Dowd, D. 1974. *The Twisted Dream*. Cambridge, MA: Winthrop Publishers.

Dugger, W. 1987. 'Democratic economic planning and worker ownership.' *Journal of Economic Issues*, 21 (1): 87–99.

Dugger, W. & Sherman, H. 1994. 'Comparison of Marxism and institutionalism.' *Journal of Economic Issues*, 28 (1): 101–127.

Eichner, A.S. 1976. *The Megacorp and Oligopoly*. Armonk, NY: M.E. Sharpe.

Elliot, J. 1984. 'Karl Marx's theory of socio-institutional transformation in late-stage capitalism.' *Journal of Economic Issues*, 18 (2): 383–391.

Emchenko, V. 1987. *Methodology of the Analysis of the State Ownership* (in Russian). Kiev: Naukova Dumka.

Evensky, J. 2005. *Adam Smith's Moral Philosophy: A Historical and Contemporary Perspective on Markets, Law, Ethics, and Culture*. New York: Cambridge University Press.

Gabriel S., Resnick, S., & Wolff, R. 2008. 'State capitalism versus communism: what happened in the USSR and the PRC?' *Critical Sociology*, 34 (4): 539–556.

Galbraith, J.K. 1967. *The New Industrial State*. Boston: Houghton Mifflin.

Galbraith, J.K. 1973. 'Power and the useful economist.' *American Economic Review*, 63 (1): 1–11.

Hodgson, G. 2000. 'What is the essence of institutional economics?' *Journal of Economic Issues*, 34 (2): 317–329.

Holt, R. P.F. 2013. 'The Post-Keynesian critique of the mainstream theory of the state and the Post-Keynesian approaches to economic policy,' *in*: G.C. Harcourt & P. Kriesler (eds.), *The Oxford Handbook of Post-Keynesian Economics, Vol. 2*. New York: Oxford University Press, 290–309.

Ip, G. 2013. 'The gated globe.' Special Report. *The Economist*, October 12–18: 1–20

Klimina, A. 2010. 'On the risks of introducing a liberal plan in a traditionally autocratic society: the case of Russia.' *Journal of Economic Issues*, 44 (2): 513–522.

Knoedler, J. & Schneider, G. 2010. 'On institutionalist vision of a good economy.' *Forum for Social Economics*, 39 (3): 259–267.

Krueger, A. 1974. 'The political economy of rent-seeking society.' *American Economic Review*, 64 (3): 291–303.

Laibman, D. 1978. 'The "state capitalist" and "bureaucratic-exploitative" interpretations of the soviet social formation: a critique.' *Review of Radical Political Economics*, 10 (4): 24–34.

Lichtenstein, P. 1996. 'A new institutionalist story about the transformation of former socialist economies: a recounting and an assessment.' *Journal of Economic Issues*, 30 (1): 243–265.

Martin, D.D. 1974. 'Beyond capitalism: a role for markets?' *Journal of Economic Issues*, 8 (4): 771–784.

Mayhew, A. 2001. 'Human agency, cumulative causation, and the state: remarks upon receiving the Veblen-Commons Award.' *Journal of Economic Issues*, 35 (2): 239–250.

Mazzucato, M. 2013. *The Entrepreneurial State: Debunking Public vs. Private Sector Myths*. London: Anthem Press.

Medema, S. 2003. 'The economic role of government in the history of economic thought,' *in*: W. Samuels, J. Biddle, & J. Davis (eds.), *A Companion to The History of Economic Thought*. Malden, MA: Blackwell Publishing, 428–444.

Mereste, U. 1987. 'The theory of property and improvement of the economic mechanism.' *International Journal of Sociology*, 17 (4): 23–44.

Moreau, F. 2004. 'The role of the state in evolutionary economics.' *Cambridge Journal of Economics*, 28 (6): 847–874.

Musacchio, A. & Lazzarini, S.G. 2014. *Reinventing State Capitalism*. Cambridge, MA: Harvard University Press.

Neale, W.C. 1991. 'Society, state, and market: a Polanyian view of current change and turmoil in Eastern Europe.' *Journal of Economic Issues*, 25 (2): 467–473.

Nekipelov, A. 2009. 'Is it easy to catch a black cat in a dark room, even if it is there?' *in*: V. Kuvaldin (ed.), *Breakthrough to Freedom: Perestroika, a Critical Analysis*. Moscow: R. Valent Publishers, 144–151.

Nevile, J.W. 2012. 'Fiscal policy,' *in*: J.E. King (ed.), *The Elgar Companion to Post Keynesian Economics*, 2nd edn. Northampton, MA: Edward Elgar, 224–228.

North, D. 1990. *Institutions, Institutional Change and Economic Performance*. New York: Cambridge University Press.

O'Connor, J. 1973. *The Fiscal Crisis of the State*. New York: St. Martin's Press.

Oppenheimer, M. 2009. 'Some comments on "state capitalism".' *Critical Sociology*, 35 (3): 435–437.

Owen, T. 1997. 'Autocracy and the rule of law in Russian economic history,' *in*: J. Sachs & K. Pistor (eds.), *The Rule of Law and Economic Reform in Russia*. Boulder, CO: Westview Press, 23–40.

Petr, J. 1987. 'The nature and necessity of the mixed economy.' *Journal of Economic Issues*, 21 (4): 1445–1468.

Pigou, A. 1932. *The Economics of Welfare*, 3rd edn. London: Macmillan.

Pollard, V. 2011. 'State capitalist analysis – before the Russian revolution, in reaction to Stalin's consolidation of power, and after the cold war,' *in*: V. Pollard (ed.), *State Capitalism, Contentious Politics and Large-Scale Social Change*. Boston: Brill, 1–20.

Pressman, S. 2006. 'A Post-Keynesian theory of the state,' *in*: S. Pressman (ed.), *Alternative Theories of the State*. New York: Palgrave Macmillan, 113–138.

Ramstad, Y. 1994. 'On the nature of economic evolution: John R. Commons and the metaphor of artificial selection,' *in*: L. Magnusson (ed.), *Evolutionary and Neo-Schumpeterian Approaches to Economics*. Boston: Kluwer Academic Publishers, 65–122.

Reich, C. 1964. 'The new property.' *The Yale Law Journal*, 73 (5): 733–787.

Rozov, N. 2012. 'Geopolitics, geo-economics, and geoculture: the interrelation of dynamic spheres in the history of Russia.' *Russian Social Science Review*, 43 (6): 4–26.

Rutherford, M. 1994a. *Institutions in Economics: The Old and the New Institutionalism.* Cambridge: Cambridge University Press.

Rutherford, M. 1994b. 'Austrian economics and American (old) institutionalism,' in: P. Boettke (ed.), *The Elgar Companion to Austrian Economics.* Brookfield, VT: Edward Elgar, 529–534.

Samuels, W. 1989. 'Some fundamentals of the economic role of government.' *Journal of Economic Issues*, 23 (2): 427–433.

Samuels, W. & Schmid, A. 1981. *Law and Economics: An Institutional Perspective.* Boston: Martinus Nijhoff.

Schweickart, D. 1992. 'Socialism, democracy, market, planning: putting the pieces together.' *Review of Radical Political Economics*, 24 (1): 29–45.

Sherman, H. 2012. 'Socialism,' in: J.E. King (ed.), *The Elgar Companion to Post Keynesian Economics*, 2nd edn. Northampton, MA: Edward Elgar, 495–499.

Simons, H. 1934. *A Positive Program for Laissez-Faire: Some Proposals for a Liberal Economic Policy.* Chicago: Chicago University Press.

Solo, R. 1978. 'The Neo-Marxist theory of the state.' *Journal of Economic Issues*, 12 (4): 829–842.

Stanfield, J.R. 1991. 'The dichotomized state.' *Journal of Economic Issues*, 25 (3): 765–780.

Stanfield, J.R. 1992. 'The fund for social change,' in: J. Davis (ed.), *The Economic Surplus in Advanced Economies.* Brookfield, VT: Edward Elgar, 130–148.

Streeten, P. 1993. 'Markets and states: against minimalism.' *World Development*, 21 (8): 1281–1298.

Surkov, V. 2008. 'Russian political culture: the view from utopia.' *Russian Social Science Review*, 49 (6): 81–97.

Todaro, S. & Smith, S. 2014. *Economic Development*, 12th edn. New York: Pearson.

Torkanovski, E. 1989. 'The participation of working people in the management of production as a factor in heightening labor activism,' in: A. Jones & W. Moskoff (eds.), *Perestroika and the Economy: New Thinking in Soviet Economics.* Armonk, NY: M.E. Sharpe, 78–88.

Vanteeva, N. & Hickson, C. 2012. 'Whither corporate Russia?' *Comparative Economic Studies*, 54 (1): 173–201.

Waller, W.T. 2006. 'The pragmatic state: institutionalist perspectives on the state,' in: S. Pressman (ed.), *Alternative Theories of the State.* New York: Palgrave Macmillan, 13–33.

Whalen, C. 2008. 'Toward "wisely managed" capitalism: Post-Keynesian institutionalism and the creative state.' *Forum for Social Economics*, 37 (1): 43–60.

Wolff, R. & Resnick, S. 2012. *Contending Economic Theories: Neoclassical, Keynesian, and Marxist.* Cambridge: MIT Press.

Wooldridge, A. 2012. 'State capitalism: a visible hand.' *The Economist*, January 21–27: 1–20.

Wrenn, M. 2011. 'The economic surplus as a fund for social change and postneoliberal governance.' *Forum for Social Economics*, 40 (1): 99–117.

Xie, F., Li, A., & Li, Z. 2013. 'Can the socialist market economy in China adhere to socialism.' *Review of Radical Political Economics*, 45 (4): 440–448.

34

The twenty-first century capitalist revolution

How the governance of large firms shapes prosperity and inequality

Jordan Brennan

> In a system of corporate concentration the result of competition is some sort of planning; and planning does not reduce power but increases it. . . . The corporation is now, essentially, a non-statist political institution.
>
> *Adolf Berle 1955: 38, 44*

Introduction

Contemporary corporate governance literature tends to focus on, *inter alia*, intrafirm authority, board member composition, the incentive structure decision-makers face, and norms around compensation and accountability (Lütz *et al.* 2011). Some studies compare models of corporate governance across cultures to determine how differing structures affect business behavior and performance (Roe 1993), while others broaden the scope to include the interplay between corporate governance and political power (Gourevitch & Shinn 2005). For the most part, though, the discipline has evolved to focus on 'governance' in the most straightforward sense of the term applied to activities *within* the firm.

In some ways the term 'corporate governance' is an uneasy assemblage. The word 'corporate' conjures up modern notions of the economy, while 'governance' has connotations that are bound up with the polity. Contemporary presuppositions suggest that, in liberal capitalist settings at least, the economy is the domain of freedom insofar as order is generated through voluntary association. The polity, by contrast, is the domain of obedience insofar as order is generated through coercive laws.[1] The term 'governance' means "to rule over by right of authority" (Harper 2016). Derived from the thirteenth-century Old French *governer*, which meant 'to steer,' 'rule,' 'command,' and 'direct,' the verb 'to govern' is unambiguously bound up with notions of authority, obedience, and power. It is partly because mainstream economists tend to ignore or dismiss institutional power, even in corporate governance literature, that it has been left to heterodox economists to integrate power into the analysis of modern capitalism.

The innovative studies of the original institutional economists and Post Keynesians differ from contemporary corporate governance scholarship in two crucial respects: first, they explore corporate authority as it manifests itself both inside and outside the firm; second, their analysis recognizes that the modern corporation fundamentally altered the power dynamic in American political, economic, and social life. From the standpoint of the original institutional economics, 'corporate governance' is inextricably bound up with corporate power.

This chapter reviews some of the most profound heterodox thinking on corporate governance, including insights from original institutional economics, neo-Marxism, and Post Keynesianism. Rather than being bound by contemporary suppositions, 'corporate governance' will be viewed in an expansive manner and will include aspects as diverse as industrial production, market structure, price formation, business investment, and the distribution of income. The first section reviews some of the assumptions and concepts deployed by twentieth century heterodox economists—notably the original institutional economics of Thorstein Veblen and J.K. Galbraith, the neo-Marxism of Michał Kalecki, and the Post Keynesianism of Adolf Berle and Gardiner Means—to understand the power underpinnings of the modern corporation. The second and third sections utilize the ideas of the aforementioned thinkers to empirically explore the interplay between large firms and labor unions, on the one hand, and Gross Domestic Product (GDP) growth and income inequality, on the other. The fourth section closes by reflecting on how twenty-first century capitalism might be progressively transformed. The core argument is that the modern corporation may be validly understood as a power institution and that the amassment of this form of power has simultaneously depressed GDP growth and exacerbated income inequality. Meaningful attempts to transform neoliberal capitalism must find ways to constrain or redirect corporate power.

Corporate governance as the exercise of commodified power

Berle (1955: 1) posits that "no adequate study of twentieth-century capitalism exists" for the singular reason that mainstream economic thinking has failed to come to a satisfactory account of the modern corporation. Instead of economic activity being coordinated through the push and pull of market forces, and instead of business decisions unfolding under conditions of fundamental uncertainty, Berle claims that large firms plan supply and demand, shield themselves from market discipline through internal financing, make decisions under fairly predictable conditions, and administer prices. The modern corporation, Berle (1955: 44) concludes, should be treated as a "non-statist political institution." Berle's position is in large measure consistent with the original institutional economics founded by Veblen ([1904] 2005, [1923] 2004) and popularized by Galbraith (1952), which offered the most stinging critique of capitalism since Karl Marx.

As Veblen (1908a, 1908b) observes, neoclassical doctrine has failed to keep pace with changes in the institutional and behavioral realities of American capitalism, a failure most clearly manifest in the theory of capital. For neoclassical economists, capital is produced means of production or artifacts (output) used in the production process as inputs (as later reiterated by Samuelson & Nordhaus 2010: 352). Veblen argues that this definition of capital is untenable for two reasons. First, the assertion that capital is a material-productive entity breaks down in the face of 'capital mobility.' Veblen's acute vision notes that when capital 'moves' from one location in the industrial geography to another, this does not necessarily entail the movement of physical objects. The continuity of capital is not predicated on a transfer of stuff, but is derived from the maintenance of ownership—something that is not a physical fact. The continuity of capital is of an immaterial character, for it centers on legal rights and control ([1908] 2003: 196–197). The second argument centers on the recognition that 'capital goods,' understood as physically abiding productive entities, cannot be aggregated because they lack a homogeneous quality. Capital as a monetary magnitude may be homogeneous, but physical equipment is heterogeneous. This fact makes the aggregation of capital in neoclassical production functions impossible, thus undermining the marginal productivity theory of distribution.

One of Veblen's core contentions is that private ownership of industrial objects and land effectively enables proprietors to control the community's technological inheritance through the limitation of access. In Veblen's ([1923] 2004: 65–66) words:

> any person who has a legal right to withhold any part of the necessary industrial apparatus or materials from current use will be in a position to impose terms and exact obedience, on pain of rendering the community's joint stock of technology inoperative to that extent. Owner-ship of industrial equipment and natural resources confers such a right legally to enforce unemployment, and so to make the community's workmanship useless to that extent. This is the Natural Right of Investment.

Every definition of capital, be it neoclassical, Marxian, or institutionalist, recognizes the cen-trality of private ownership. The word 'private' is derived from the Latin *privare*, which means "to deprive," and *privatus*, which means "withdrawn from public life" (Harper 2016). 'Owner-ship,' to own, is derived from late Middle English *ownen*, which signifies "power," "authority," "dominion," or "to be master of." The popular understanding conceives of private ownership as a useful institution because it *enables* those who own, but Nitzan & Bichler (2009: 228) argue that its overriding purpose is to *disable* those who do not own. Institutionalized exclusion, they assert, is always a matter of organized power.

Without private ownership, capital could not exist. And without the modern state, private ownership could cease to exist. And the modern state, Weber ([1919] 1946: 82–83) argues, is a power institution whose authority rests on its monopoly on the legitimate use of violence. So Veblen is analytically and etymologically correct, in that the reality of capital makes no sense apart from private ownership and private ownership has no force or effect apart from the state and its monopoly on the legitimate use of violence. Power is 'in' the state and the state is 'in' capital. In sharp contrast to the neoclassical school of thought, Veblen ([1908] 2003: 200) contends:

> the substantial core of all capital is immaterial wealth . . . if such a view were accepted . . . the 'natural' distribution of incomes between capital and labor would 'go up in the air'. . . . The returns actually accruing to [the capitalist] . . . would be a measure of the differential advan-tage held by him by virtue of his having become legally seized of the material contrivances by which the technological achievements of the community are put into effect.

In this passage Veblen complicates, if not severs, the link between production and distribution. Using Veblen's ([1904] 2005, [1923] 2004) conceptual scheme, the modern corporation may be validly understood as a business institution, not an industrial unit. 'Business' is distinguishable from 'industry' in the same way that the legal, organizational, and institutional structure of the economy is distinct from its material, productive, and technological sphere. Business centers on pecuniary distribution and is institutionally embodied in the modern corporation. Industry cen-ters on production and is most clearly manifest in the 'machine process.' From this perspective, the modern corporation *governs* industrial production for the purposes of pecuniary distribu-tion. And contrary to the view that the distribution of income is a consequence of the innate productivity of the various 'factors of production,' using Veblen's ideas we may validly see the distribution of income as partially manifesting the (institutional) power of the firms' owners.

While Veblen supplies some of the language necessary to integrate power into economic analysis, the causal channels that link institutional structure, market power, and price formation remain unclear in his account. On the subject of price formation, Means (1935) supplies evidence indicating the existence of bifurcated price behavior in the United States. In concentrated markets with a few large firms, 'administered prices' prevail during the period of his study. An administered price is set for a period of time across a number of transactions. This rigidity suggests a degree of pricing discretion on the part of the seller. In less concentrated markets, classical competition and price formation are on display. Classical prices are flexible and change frequently, implying that the seller has little or no pricing discretion.[2] Means (1972) re-tests his hypothesis four decades later and finds that it has not been refuted.[3]

While Means establishes points of contact between market structure and non-classical price formation, it remains unclear how to rigorously conceive and empirically measure market power. It also remains unclear what the macro-distributive implications of oligopolistic market structures are. The Neo-Marxian economist, Michał Kalecki (1938, 1943), crystallizes the relationship between market power and distribution through his conception of the 'degree of monopoly.'[4] Kalecki argues that large firms in semi-monopolistic market structures set prices by marking up their average prime costs (materials and labor), with a higher mark-up signaling a greater degree of monopoly. Kalecki (1943: 51) imagines the strength of trade unions acting as a check on the market power of large firms insofar as a greater degree of monopoly "strengthens the bargaining position of trade unions in their demands for wage increases since higher wages are then compatible with 'reasonable profits' at the existing price levels." For Kalecki, the degree of monopoly is positively associated with corporate concentration and negatively associated with the national wage bill.

Galbraith (1952) agrees with the view that large firms no longer accept prices that are set in perfectly competitive markets and are therefore not socially optimizing, and posits that alternative institutional arrangements are needed to make modern capitalism more functional and fair. Because businesses combine with a view to administering profit-friendly prices, wage earners ought to combine in unions with a view to elevating the conditions and compensation of work. Galbraith utilizes the term 'countervailing power' to denote an institutional setting in which the power of large firms is offset by the power of labor unions and a welfare state. In the general evolution of policy, politics, and culture, labor unions act as a check on the commodified power of large firms, and this counterbalance is felt in ways as diverse as social policy, politics, and culture, not just wages.

This synopsis has furnished some examples of how the language of corporate governance may be infused with the language of institutional power. The following two sections apply these concepts to the empirical domain in order to determine their explanatory value.

The commodified power of large firms, economic growth, and income inequality

The following two sections explore the commodified power of large firms, the countervailing power of organized labor, and the effects of these counteracting forces on GDP growth and income inequality. The empirical analysis is confined to the United States of America (USA).[5] However, since the USA is the most economically significant country of the past century, standing at the center of the global capitalist system, the conclusions may well extend beyond its borders.

A key growth pathway for large firms is through mergers and acquisitions (Nitzan & Bichler 2009). The narrative around the development of mergers and acquisitions (M&A) over the past century is one of a series of 'waves,' with each wave leading to different organizational forms and market structures (McCarthy 2013; Jo & Henry 2015). At a minimum, explanations for M&A usually try to account for two things: merger motives (*causes*) and post-merger outcomes (*effects*). Growth and efficiency are two of the most commonly cited motivations for M&A activity (Gaughan 2007). But from a heterodox perspective, larger relative firm size and the attendant market power that greater size bestows is the real amalgamation prize. One way of measuring M&A is to contrast it with investment in fixed assets. A 'buy-to-build' indicator captures the basic calculation open to proprietors, which is to purchase existing industrial capacity on the market for corporate control or pay to have it built anew. The evolution of M&A activity in the USA is captured in Figure 34.1.

Three things stand out. First, the series clearly demonstrates the wave-like pattern of M&A over the past century. The second feature to note is the increasing importance of M&A relative to investment in fixed assets, especially in recent decades. Between 1895 and 1990, for every dollar spent on building new capacity, US businesses spent an average of just 18 cents on M&A. In the quarter-century since the so-called 'free trade' era began, average M&A increased to 68 percent of fixed asset investment—a fourfold increase over the previous century. The third thing to notice is the sustained nature of M&A activity in recent decades. Of the six peak merger wave values since 1895, three have come in the past 15 years. Even though 1999 represents the historic high, the period since 1990 has been unprecedented in the corporate history of the USA.[6]

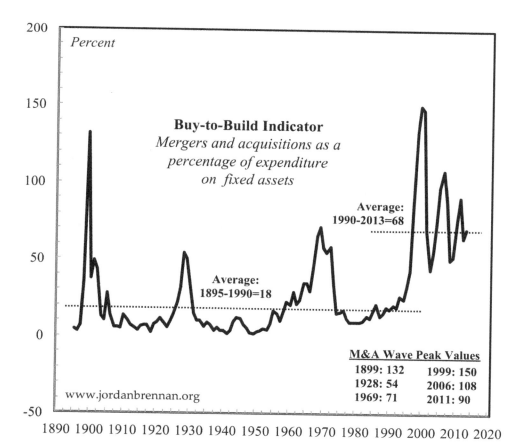

Figure 34.1 American corporate amalgamation, 1895–2013

Source: Carter *et al.* (2006); Gaughan (2007, Figure 2.7, Tables 2.3, 2.5); Kuznets (n.d.); US Bureau of Economic Analysis (Table 1.1.5); Wilmer Cutler Pickering Hale & Dorr LLP (2014).

These merger waves have restructured the US corporate sector in a growth-decelerating, inequality-exacerbating manner, and power appears to be an important causal element. By capturing the overall position of large firms in the corporate universe, aggregate concentration is one way of measuring corporate power. Figure 34.2 contrasts the buy-to-build indicator with aggregate asset concentration, the latter measured as the total assets of the top 100 US-listed firms as a percentage of total corporate assets in the USA. The two series are tightly and positively correlated over six decades, which implies that amalgamation fuels asset concentration.[7] In tandem with the 'conglomerate' merger wave, asset concentration increased by one-half between 1950 and 1970, having risen from 8 to 12 percent. With the subsiding of merger activity between 1970 and 1990, asset concentration fell by one-quarter, from 12 to 9 percent. Then, with the onset of the most sustained period of merger activity in US corporate history, asset concentration more than doubled, having risen from 9 percent in 1990 to 21 percent in 2006. There are roughly six million registered corporations in the USA, but the 100 largest account for roughly one-fifth of total assets. This is a stunning degree of concentration and it represents a post-war high.

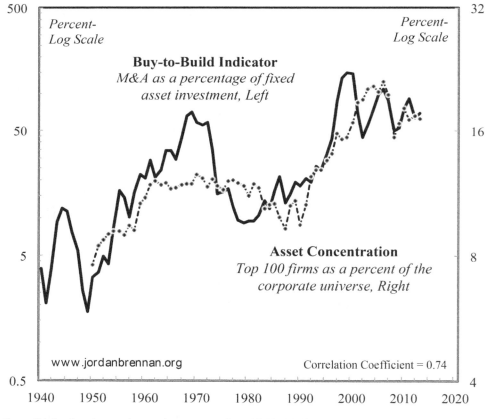

Figure 34.2 Amalgamation and concentration, 1940–2013

Note: Top 100 firms are ranked annually by equity market capitalization.

Source: Compustat database through Wharton Research Data Services; US Bureau of Economic Analysis (Table 1.1.5); US Federal Reserve (data codes: Z1/Z1/FL102000005.A and Z1/Z1/FL792000095.A).

If, as Veblen (1908a, b) posits, capital is a claim on earnings—legal title to an income stream—then the concentration of corporate assets should be associated with the redistribution of income. Figure 34.3 contrasts aggregate asset concentration with the income share of the top 100 US-listed firms, the latter measured as the percent of net income in GDP (outlaying data points, 1992 and 2002, were removed). The two series are tightly correlated over six decades. The income share of the top 100 firms is stable over the early post–war decades, having averaged 1.9 percent of GDP between 1950 and 1990. The elevated merger activity of recent decades and the associated concentration of assets have coincided with a doubling of the income share of the largest firms, peaking at 3.9 percent of GDP in 2013.

For institutional power to be a meaningful category in heterodox economics, it must include control over—*redistribution of*—income. The facts in Figures 34.2 and 34.3 are significant because they suggest that the structure of the corporate sector, which is fueled by amalgamation, leads to both asset and income concentration. Insofar as the distribution of income reflects market structure, 'power' becomes a meaningful heuristic.

How do these processes affect economic growth? Since Adam Smith's *Wealth of Nations* ([1776] 1994), economists have told a story of development that puts the capitalist at the center of

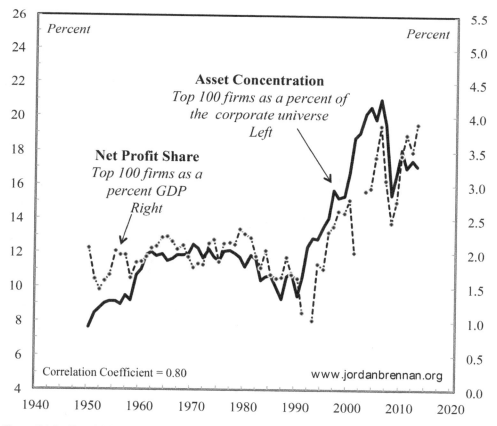

Figure 34.3 Top 100 firms: concentration and income share, 1950–2013

Note: Top 100 firms are ranked annually by equity market capitalization.

Source: Compustat database through Wharton Research Data Services; US Bureau of Economic Analysis (Table 1.1.5); US Federal Reserve (data codes: Z1/Z1/FL102000005.A and Z1/Z1/FL792000095.A).

economic progress. By converting savings into investment and by submitting to the discipline of intense price and product competition, capitalists help set the economic wheels in motion and ensure the efficient use of socio-economic resources. Part of this story is investment in fixed assets (industrial capacity), which has long been understood as a key determinant of GDP growth (De Long & Summers 1992; Jorgenson 1997, 2007). Contrasting the rate of growth of business investment in non-residential structures and equipment with the rate of growth of GDP, both adjusted for inflation and smoothed as ten-year moving averages (to capture the secular trend), yields a correlation coefficient of 0.80 from 1960 to 2013—a sufficiently strong relationship to take up nearly all of the explanatory space. In the early decades of the post-war era, the USA and other Organization for Economic Cooperation and Development (OECD) countries experienced rapid growth and in the decades since 1980 there has been a shift to comparatively sluggish growth. The inflation- and population-adjusted rate of US GDP growth averaged 2.8 percent between 1940 and 1980 and was more than halved between 1980 and 2013, falling to just 1.3 percent.

Figure 34.4 decomposes investment among the top 100 US-listed firms over the post-war era by plotting investment in fixed assets and stock repurchase (both as a percentage of revenue),

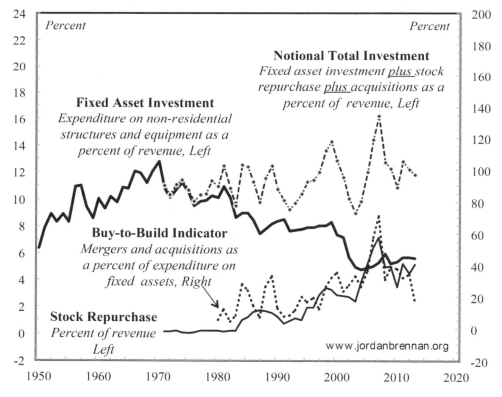

Figure 34.4 Top 100 firms: investment decomposition, 1950–2013

Note: Top 100 firms are ranked annually by equity market capitalization.

Source: Compustat database through Wharton Research Data Services; US Federal Reserve (data codes: Z1/Z1/FL102000005.A and Z1/Z1/FL792000095.A).

a buy-to-build indicator for the top 100 firms, and a metric capturing notional total investment, the latter measured as fixed asset investment plus acquisitions and stock repurchase all as a percent of revenue. Notional total investment indicates the different ways that firms can deploy available assets for the sake of growth. In the two decades between 1950 and 1970, fixed asset investment trended upward, having risen from 6 to 13 percent of revenue, only to trend downward in the decades after 1970, having fallen to a post-war low of 5 percent over the past decade. This suggests that large firms may be leading the stagnation tendencies of recent times through fixed asset under-investment.

Stock repurchase was virtually non-existent in the 1970s, but has grown in significance in each subsequent decade, having risen from less than 1 percent of revenue in the 1970s to 7 percent by 2007.[8] This means for the first time in US corporate history, large firms spent more money repurchasing their own stock than on the expansion of their industrial base. Large firms have also been on a buying spree in recent decades, plowing enormous resources into M&A. The national total investment series clearly shows that if large firms had spent all their acquisition and stock repurchase resources on fixed asset investment, the downward trend in fixed asset investment would have actually been an investment boom.

To summarize, large firms are spending comparatively less on the expansion of industrial capacity, which puts downward pressure on growth, and comparatively more on acquiring other firms and on inflating their share price via stock repurchase. Corporate amalgamation fuels asset concentration and asset concentration redistributes income. Elsewhere I have documented the strong, linear, and persistent relationship between corporate concentration and the earnings margins, profit, and cash flow of large Canadian-based firms (see Brennan 2012). Large firms merge not only to absorb their rival's income, but also to reduce competitive pressure, which thickens earnings margins. So the causal pathway runs from amalgamation through concentration toward elevated market power.

The facts portrayed in the national total investment series in Figure 34.4 demonstrate that corporate America does not suffer from a 'shortage of investment' in the general sense. Rather resource redirection within large firms, with comparatively less going towards growth-enhancing industrial expansion and comparatively more going towards asset-concentrating amalgamation and share price-inflating stock repurchase, is a key culprit in the under-investment and stagnant growth of the neoliberal era. There has been an investment boom in the USA, albeit an invisible one, because it has been hidden in amalgamation and stock option-related activities. The former upwardly redistributes corporate ownership claims between proprietors and the latter inflates share price. From the standpoint of the average US worker, this massive resource redirection has resulted in declining job opportunities and soaring inequality.

But why the frenzy for stock repurchase? Central to Berle & Means' ([1932] 1967) 'separation thesis' is the positing of a three-pronged process: an increasing concentration of corporate assets, coupled with an increasing dispersion of stock ownership, resulting in a separation of ownership from control. Putting aside the validity of the claim that control has actually detached from ownership, the idea exerts considerable influence on economic theorists and policy makers. If the large corporation is no longer under proprietary control, having fallen under managerial control, the incentive structure no longer compels those exercising corporate authority to steer the firm in a profit-maximizing direction, thus threatening the (alleged, according to neoclassical doctrine) equilibrium-seeking nature of laissez-faire capitalism. Managers might instead steer the firm in a direction that enriches themselves while sacrificing the interests of stockholders, who are too numerous and dispersed to challenge managerial authority.

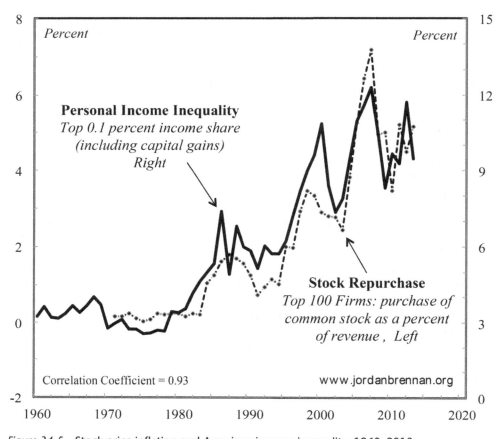

Figure 34.5 Stock price inflation and American income inequality, 1960–2013
Note: Top 100 firms are ranked annually by equity market capitalization.
Source: Compustat database through Wharton Research Data Services; US Federal Reserve (data codes: Z1/Z1/FL102000005.A and Z1/Z1/FL792000095.A); Piketty & Saez (2007); World Wealth and Income database.

The rise of stock options in the 1980s and their explosion in the 1990s may be thought of as one institutional response to the alleged separation of ownership from control (for historical overviews, see Frydman & Jenter 2010; Murphy 2012). By compensating managers with stock, their interests and attendant behavior presumably realign with those of stockholders, thus transcending the separation thesis and ensuring firms behave in a profit-maximizing manner (again, according to neoclassical assumptions). Figure 34.5 plots the value of stock repurchase (relative to revenue) among the top 100 US-listed firms with the income share of the top 0.1 percentile income group in the USA (including capital gains). The two series are almost mirror images of each other. This suggests that the redirection of resources away from fixed asset investment toward stock repurchase has not only slowed growth; it has exacerbated inequality. There is clearly more to income inequality than stock options, but insofar as top income earners drive inequality trends, and insofar as corporate executives make up a substantial proportion of the top income group, the evolution of executive compensation plays a key role in determining the overall level of income inequality.

The countervailing power of organized labor and income equality

Income within the firm is shared between workers (wages and salaries) and capitalists (profit). Kalecki (1938) argues that the degree of monopoly has a bearing on the relative share of wages, and in so doing, shapes the distribution of income between these two groups. At a national level, the total wage bill and profit share capture these proportions. When we divide aggregate corporate profit by the national wage bill for the bottom 99 percent of the workforce, excluding the richest one percent income group to approximate the class-based distribution of income, we arrive at a metric which approximates the distributive struggle between capitalists and workers over profit and wages. When this metric rises, capitalists redistribute national income from workers; when it falls, workers redistribute income from capitalists. Figure 34.6 plots the mark-up of the top 100 firms—a proxy for Kalecki's degree of monopoly and measured as the percentage of net profit in revenue—and the capital-labor redistribution metric.

The two series are tightly and positively intertwined over six decades. Between the 1940s and 1980s, the capital-labor redistribution metric trended downward, which signals that workers tended to win the distributive struggle in that period. The 1980s serves as an inflection point, with capitalists tending to win the distributive struggle after 1990. If the mark-up is a proxy for the market power of large firms, and if the capital-labor redistribution metric captures the national struggle between proprietors and workers, it is highly significant that the former moves in tandem with the latter because it suggests that Kalecki's thinking on this

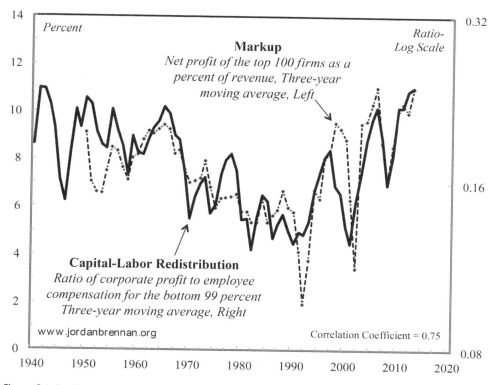

Figure 34.6   The 'degree of monopoly' and capital-labor redistribution, 1940–2013

Source: Compustat database through Wharton Research Data Services; Piketty & Saez (2007); US Bureau of Economic Analysis; US Bureau of Labor Statistics; World Wealth and Income database.

matter is empirically valid—that is, corporate power is one determinant of the distribution of income in the USA.

If amalgamation-fueled asset concentration regressively redistributes income, are there centrifugal forces that progressively redistribute income? We have already seen that, in the USA at least, the institutional-organizational structure of the corporate sector (measured through aggregate concentration) is closely shadowed by the market power of large firms (profit share of national income and the mark-up). Is there a similar set of relationships for organized labor? Galbraith (1952) would have us believe that labor unions act as a 'countervailing power' to oligopolistic corporations.

This view stands in opposition to neoclassical economics, which views the market price of labor power like other commodities: in the short-run it is determined by supply and demand and in the long-run the 'absolute' wage rate and the national wage bill reflect the proportional productive contribution of labor. For neoclassical economists, organized labor may be able to elevate labor compensation to 'artificially' high levels, but it does so at the expense of non-unionized labor and/or employment. In other words, unions can only redistribute income within a given national wage bill; they are unable to redistribute national income as such (Samuelson & Nordhaus 2010: 321). If this is true then the organizational capacity of labor institutions should have no discernable effect on the distribution of income. The facts tell a different story.

Figure 34.7 Organized American labor strength and income equality, 1880–2013
Source: Hirsch & Macpherson (2003); Mayer (2004); Carter *et al.* (2006); Piketty & Saez (2007); US Bureau of Labor Statistics; World Wealth and Income database.

Figure 34.7 contrasts union density—a proxy for the institutional power of organized labor—with the Pareto-Lorenz coefficient, a metric which captures the concentration of income among the rich (the higher the coefficient, the lower the concentration). The two series are tightly intertwined over the past century. Density increased modestly and in a non-linear fashion between 1880 and 1930. Then, with the advent of New Deal legislation and the National Labor Relations ('Wagner') Act, density increased fourfold, having risen from 7 percent in 1933 to a historic high of 29 percent in 1954, before falling to a post-war low of 11 percent by 2013. The concentration of income among the rich was significantly eroded in the decades that US labor built their unions, while in the decades that trade union power diminished, income re-concentrated among the rich.

Let us take stock. The centripetal forces of corporate amalgamation lead to the centralization of corporate ownership, manifested in asset concentration. Increased concentration reduces competitive pressure, increases the degree of monopoly, and enlarges the income share of large firms. The diversion of corporate resources away from growth-expanding industrial projects puts downward pressure on growth and leaves even more corporate income in the hands of large firms. With the rise of stock-based forms of compensation, corporate executives are given an incentive to divert corporate income into share price-inflating stock repurchase, which increases executive compensation and exacerbates inequality. It is in this way that the creation of a top-heavy corporate distribution puts downward pressure on growth and elevates inequality. On the other side of the ledger, the trade union power manifest in union density has progressively redistributed income, such that the weakened power of unions in the USA since the 1970s has contributed to heightened income inequality.

Democratizing neoliberal capitalism

In comparison with the Keynesian state-led model of capitalism that predominated between 1935 and 1980, the neoliberal corporate-led model in the USA (and elsewhere) has, since 1980, been notable for its slower growth and soaring inequality. It appears that a top-heavy market structure in conjunction with declining unionization has played a causal role in this double-sided phenomenon. A suite of policies are required to unleash growth and reduce income inequality, the combined effect of which would be to democratize, and thus transform, twenty-first century capitalism: state commitment to full employment, an amplified voice for labor, and capital controls.

Chronic unemployment (and under-employment) is one of the most socially damaging features of neoliberal capitalism. The state commitment to full employment would dramatically alter the labor market in a way that empowers workers, unleashes growth, and reduces income inequality. Recall Veblen's ([1923] 2004) claim about the 'natural right of investment': private ownership of industrial equipment grants proprietors the legal right to enforce unemployment, which is an act of institutionalized exclusion that restricts production below full socio-economic potential and alters the distribution of income in a proprietary-favoring manner. Now consider the reconfigured role of the state in the USA during World War II, the prime historic example of the state commitment to full employment. Until 1939 employment ('industry') was firmly under the control of private proprietors ('business'). World War II partially changed that insofar as the federal government oversaw the move towards a centrally planned economy. Business considerations, although not totally eliminated, were greatly diminished vis-à-vis industrial considerations and capitalists lost (some) control over employment and pricing.

The consequences for the power elite in the USA were devastating, as evidenced by a halving of the income share going to the richest 1 percent from 1939 to 1945. In terms of price formation, wage ceilings were imposed, producer and consumer prices were frozen, exchange rates were controlled, and the rate of profit was capped. As a result, unemployment shrank from 12 percent to less than 2 percent and income inequality fell by more than a third. GDP (adjusted for inflation and population) grew by 10 percent annually, on average, rising from $94 billion in 1939 to $228 billion in 1945.[9] Without exception the 1940s represents the most rapid growth period in US history and the closest it ever came to full employment.

The capitalist power manifest in unemployment was severely curtailed through the use of state power and the consequences included rapid GDP growth and a radical redistribution of income. In the contemporary milieu, pathways to full employment could include policy tools as conventional as infrastructure investment and growth-friendly monetary policy (Stiglitz 2015: 73–77) or as unconventional as the creation of a national development bank and public ownership in strategic industries like energy or advanced manufacturing.

If the state commitment to full employment would help solve the problem of stagnation, a stronger voice for labor would help ensure the gains from growth are widely distributed. But labor unions need a nurturing policy environment to grow. The Wagner Act (1935) enshrined the right to bargain collectively and compelled private sector employers to recognize the representatives of unionized workers. The National War Labor Board's 'maintenance of membership' rule (1942) automatically included new hires in the union so long as they had been recognized by the employer. It was partially because of these (and other) policies that unionization more than tripled between 1935 and 1945, rising from 8 to 25 percent. Labor unions in tandem with the exercise of the strike weapon have a demonstratively and progressively redistributive property. Anti-union legislation like the Taft-Hartley Act in 1947 and similar contemporary manifestations have aided in the demobilization of organized labor in the post-war era, with regressively redistributive consequences.

Another pathway towards the rebalancing of power between labor and capital is to have worker representation on corporate boards. This model of corporate governance—the stakeholder as opposed to shareholder model—is common in Germany (Clarke & Bostock 1997). Besides tending to flatten the compensation scheme within firms, this model reduces the proclivity of management to engage in high-risk activity that may be lucrative for shareholders in the short-run, but which threaten employment and the long-term viability of the organization. Volkswagen (VW) has worker representation on its board of directors and is 20 percent owned by the state government of Lower Saxony (the 'VW law')—an additional layer of stakeholder accountability. And while North American auto makers have been closing assembly plants for decades, because VW has labor and government representation on its board it has managed to block hostile takeovers and has not allowed a single VW assembly plant to close in Germany since 1945, despite the fact that German manufacturing workers are paid roughly one-quarter more than their North American counterparts.[10]

Another democratizing policy pertaining to labor would see the establishment of sector development councils in strategic areas, comprised of representatives from unions, employer associations, government, colleges, universities, and trade schools. These multi-stakeholder councils could undertake simple initiatives such as long-term skills training programs (to better manage innovation and emerging labor market needs) and more radical initiatives such as the setting of sectoral standards, including minimum standards pertaining to the conditions and compensation of work. Historically, unions provided workers with some degree of control over the labor process in their own workplaces. Sector development councils would provide workers with some degree of control over the evolution of entire industries.

A third transformation would constrain the size and market power of large firms through aggressive antitrust legislation. In the 40 years between 1940 and 1980, M&A activity constituted just 20 percent of investment in fixed assets. In tandem with capital controls, this period was remarkable for its elevated levels of GDP growth and reduced income inequality. In the decades since 1980, large firms have ploughed enormous resources into acquiring competitors. The resulting semi-monopolistic market structures and attendant market power concentrates income among large firms. By restricting the oligopolistic drive of M&A, the intention would be to unleash the centrifugal forces of fixed asset investment, which are associated with higher levels of GDP growth, job creation, and an inclusive prosperity.

Early merger waves in the USA tended to be followed by antitrust legislation. US legislators were fearful that centralized corporate authority would harm the public good. The drive for monopoly associated with the first merger wave, for example, led to the Sherman Antitrust Act in 1890, which was instituted to combat the power of large firms. A generation later, the US Congress passed the Clayton Act (in 1914), which also made it more difficult to merge for monopoly (Gaughan 2007: 33–38). Anti-monopolistic policies designed for the twenty-first century could help diffuse the increasingly centralized corporate power manifest in large firms, which would help accelerate growth and diminish inequality.

The state commitment to full employment, a rebuilding of the trade union movement, and increased restrictions on business consolidation are three transformative policies that would democratize neoliberal capitalism, widen economic opportunity, and create an inclusive prosperity.

Acknowledgments

The author would like to thank Joseph A. Francis for sharing his data files on the *Historical Statistics of the United States* and for forwarding a copy of Simon Kuznets' estimates on US business investment. Jim Stanford's feedback helped refine the argument and the *Handbook*'s editors deserve thanks for their manuscript-condensing recommendations.

Notes

1 Nitzan & Bichler (2009) stress the polity-economy dualism in their writing. They argue that the separation of the two domains creates numerous theoretical and empirical difficulties for the study of modern capitalism.
2 In today's globalized marketplace, where large firms in concentrated markets still face competitive pressure (and can even fail, as the North American financial and auto bailouts of 2008–2009 illustrate), the manifestation of administered prices may be more complicated than Means' original findings suggest without undermining his basic claim that large firms are subject to differences in business behavior.
3 See Downward & Lee (1999) for additional confirmation.
4 Even though the concept of the degree of monopoly was borrowed from Abba Lerner, Kalecki's modification of the concept allows him to explain the distribution of income (partially) through the market power exercised by oligopolistic corporations. See Rugitsky (2013) for an illuminating discussion.
5 Given space constraints, the description and accompanying analysis will be brief and the conclusions reached will be suggestive rather than conclusive. A more detailed explanation of the data, including sources and estimation techniques, are located in an appendix available on the author's website, http://www.jordanbrennan.org/#!publications/cee5.
6 Similar results are found for Canada in Brennan (2014, 2015).
7 All correlation coefficients are Pearsonian and are significant at 1 percent (two-tailed).
8 As Jo & Henry (2015) explain, it was only in 1982 with the adoption of Rule 10b-18 that the SEC formally permitted share buybacks (up to 25 percent of the stock's average daily trading volume).
9 GDP data from Bureau of Economic Analysis, Table 1.1.5., income inequality data from the World Wealth and Income Database and unemployment rate from Carter et al. (2006, 470–477), Table Ba.
10 Bureau of Labor Statistics' International Labor Comparisons, available at: http://www.bls.gov/fls/country.htm.

References

Berle, A.A. 1955. *The Twentieth Century Capitalist Revolution*. London: Macmillan.

Berle, A.A. & Means, G.C. [1932] 1967. *The Modern Corporation and Private Property*, Revised edn. New York: Harcourt, Brace and World.

Brennan, J. 2012. A shrinking universe: how concentrated corporate power is shaping income inequality in Canada. Canadian Centre for Policy Alternatives. Available from http://www.policyalternatives.ca/sites/default/files/uploads/publications/National%20Office/2012/11/Shrinking_Universe.pdf [Accessed February 25, 2016]

Brennan, J. 2014. The business of power: Canadian multinationals in the postwar era. PhD dissertation. Department of Political Science, York University, Toronto, Canada.

Brennan, J. 2015. Ascent of giants: NAFTA, corporate power and the growing income gap. Canadian Centre for Policy Alternatives. Available from https://www.policyalternatives.ca/sites/default/files/uploads/publications/National%20Office/2015/02/Ascent_of_Giants.pdf [Accessed February 25, 2016]

Carter, S.B., Garter, S.S., Haines, M.R., Olmstead A.L., Sutch, R., & Wright, G. (eds.) 2006. *Historical Statistics of the United States, Earliest Times to the Present*, Millennial edn. New York: Cambridge University Press.

Clarke, T. & Bostock, R. 1997. 'Governance in Germany: the foundations of corporate structure?' *in*: K. Keasey, S. Thompson, & M. Wright (eds.), *Corporate Governance: Economic, Management and Financial Issues*. New York: Oxford University Press, 233–251.

De Long, J.B. & Summers, L. 1992. 'Equipment investment and economic growth: how strong is the nexus?' *Brookings Papers on Economic Activity*, 2: 157–211.

Downward, P. & Lee, F.S. 1999. 'Post Keynesian pricing theory "reconfirmed"? A critical review of "Asking about Prices".' *Journal of Post Keynesian Economics*, 23 (3): 465–483.

Frydman, C. & Jenter, D. 2010. CEO Compensation. National Bureau of Economic Research Working Paper 16585. Available from http://www.nber.org/papers/w16585 [Accessed 12 May 2015]

Galbraith, J.K. 1952. *American Capitalism: The Concept of Countervailing Power*. Boston: Houghton Mifflin.

Gaughan, P.A. 2007. *Mergers, Acquisitions, and Corporate Restructuring*. Hoboken, NJ: John Wiley and Sons.

Gourevitch, P.A. & Shinn, J. 2005. *Political Power and Corporate Control: The New Global Politics of Corporate Governance*. Princeton, NJ: Princeton University Press.

Harper, D. 2016. *Online Etymological Dictionary*. Available from http://www.etymonline.com [Accessed December 23, 2014]

Hirsch, B.T. & Macpherson, D.A. 2003. 'Union membership and coverage database from the current population survey: note.' *Industrial and Labor Relations Review*, 56 (2): 349–354.

Jo, T.-H. & Henry, J.F. 2015. 'The business enterprise in the age of money manager capitalism.' *Journal of Economic Issues*, 49 (1): 23–46.

Jorgenson, D.W. 1997. 'There is no silver bullet: investment and growth in the G-7.' *National Institute Economic Review*, 162 (1): 57–74.

Jorgenson, D.W. 2007. 'Information technology and the G7 economies,' *in*: E.R. Berndt & C.R. Hulten (eds.), *Hard-to-Measure Goods and Services: Essays in Honor of Zvi Griliches*. Chicago: University of Chicago Press, 325–350.

Kalecki, M. [1938] 1971. 'Distribution of national income,' *in*: *Selected Essays on the Dynamics of the Capitalist Economy, 1933–1970*. Cambridge: Cambridge University Press, 62–77.

Kalecki, M. [1943] 1971. 'Costs and prices,' *in*: *Selected Essays on the Dynamics of the Capitalist Economy, 1933–1970*. Cambridge: Cambridge University Press, 43–61.

Kuznets, S. n.d. 'Annual estimates, 1869–1955: Technical tables underlying series in *Capital in the American Economy: Its Formation and Financing*.' Baltimore, MD: Johns Hopkins University. Available from http://www.nber.org/data-appendix/c1454/appendix.pdf [Accessed May 6, 2015]

Lütz, S., Eberle, D., & Lauter, D. 2011. 'Varieties of private self-regulation in European capitalism: corporate governance codes in the UK and Germany.' *Socio-Economic Review*, 9 (2): 315–338.

Mayer, G. 2004. 'Union membership trends in the United States.' Washington, DC: Congressional Research Service. Available from http://digitalcommons.ilr.cornell.edu/key_workplace/174 [Accessed May 5, 2015]

McCarthy, K.J. 2013. 'The business environment—mergers and merger waves: a century of cause and effect,' *in*: K.J. McCarthy & W. Dolfsma (eds.), *Understanding Mergers and Acquisitions in the 21st Century*. London: Palgrave Macmillan, 11–36.

Means, G.C. 1935. 'Price inflexibility and the requirements of a stabilizing monetary policy.' *Journal of the American Statistical Association*, 30 (190): 401–413.

Means, G.C. 1972. 'The administered-price thesis reconfirmed.' *American Economic Review*, 62 (3): 292–306.

Murphy, K.J. 2012. Executive compensation: where we are, and how we got there. University of Southern California Marshall School of Business Working Paper No. FBE 07.12. Available from http://dx.doi.org/10.2139/ssrn.2041679 [Accessed May 12, 2015]

Nitzan, J. & Bichler, S. 2009. *Capital as Power: A Study of Order and Creorder*. New York: Routledge.

Piketty, T. & Saez, E. 2007. 'Income and wage inequality in the United States 1913–2002,' *in*: A.B. Atkinson & T. Piketty (eds.), *Top Incomes over the Twentieth Century: A Contrast Between Continental European and English-Speaking Countries*. New York: Oxford University Press, 141–225.

Roe, M. 1993. 'Some difference in corporate structure in Germany, Japan, and the United States.' *The Yale Law Journal*, 102 (8): 1927–2003.

Rugitsky, F.M. 2013. 'Degree of monopoly and class struggle: political aspects of Kalecki's pricing and distribution theory.' *Review of Keynesian Economics*, 1 (4): 447–464.

Samuelson, P.A. & Nordhaus, W.D. 2010. *Economics*. New York: McGraw-Hill.

Smith, A. [1776] 1994. *An Inquiry into the Nature and Causes of the Wealth of Nations*. New York: Random House.

Stiglitz, J. 2015. *Re-Writing the Rules of the American Economy: An Agenda for Growth and Shared Prosperity*. New York: Roosevelt Institute.

Veblen, T. [1904] 2005. *The Theory of Business Enterprise*. New York: Cosimo Classics.

Veblen, T. 1908a. 'On the nature of capital.' *The Quarterly Journal of Economics*, 22 (4): 517–542.

Veblen, T. 1908b. 'On the nature of capital: investment, intangible assets, and the pecuniary magnate.' *The Quarterly Journal of Economics*, 23 (1): 104–136.

Veblen, T. [1908] 2003. 'Professor Clark's economics,' *in*: W.J. Samuels (ed.), *The Place of Science in Modern Civilization*. London: Transaction, 180–230.

Veblen, T. [1923] 2004. *Absentee Ownership and Business Enterprise in Recent Times: The Case of America*. London: Transaction.

Weber, M. [1919] 1946. 'Politics as a vocation,' *in*: H.H. Gerth & C.W. Mills (eds.), *Essays in Sociology*. New York: Oxford University Press, 77–128.

Wilmer Cutler Pickering Hale & Dorr LL P. 2014. 2014 M&A Report. Wilmer Hale. Available from http://www.wilmerhale.com/2014MAreport [Accessed May 5, 2015]

World Wealth and Income Database. Various years. Available from http://www.wid.world/ [Accessed on December 23, 2014]

35

Achieving full employment

History, theory, and policy

John Marsh, Timothy Sharpe, and Bruce Philp

Introduction: historical and policy context

The objective of full employment emerged as a response to periodic crises in capitalism. In the twentieth century the Great Depression (1929–1932) represented a major influence on post-Second World War policy, with economists such as John Maynard Keynes and William Beveridge exerting influence on government policies in a number of Western economies. While in the aftermath of the Great War there had been a desire to return to normality, the period from 1945 was marked by a desire to break from the disastrous economic policies and doctrine which had typified the inter-war years. The perverse nature of persistent and high levels of unemployment was articulated clearly by Keynes (1972: 90), who noted:

> The Conservative belief that there is some law of nature which prevents men from being employed, that it is 'rash' to employ men, and that it is financially 'sound' to maintain a tenth of the population in idleness for an indefinite period, is crazily improbable – the sort of thing which no man could believe who had not had his head fuddled with nonsense for years and years.

In response, between 1945 and the early 1970s, many Western governments enacted policies with the aim of ensuring full employment. In the United States (US) the *Employment Act* of 1946 tasked the President with the general goal of achieving full employment. In the period 1950–1973, US unemployment as a percentage of the total labor force fluctuated between 2.8 percent and 6.6 percent, considerably below the peaks of 24.7 percent in 1933, and somewhat below that of the 9.5 percent peak in the period 1982–1983 (see Maddison 1991: 260–265). In the United Kingdom (UK), the post-Second World War Labour governments had made a concerted effort to embrace interventionist policies, and even the Conservative administrations from 1951 had not sought to radically reverse their policy initiatives (the period of 'Butskellism'). The unemployment rate in the UK between 1950 and 1973 fluctuated between 2 and 4 percent, against an inter-war peak of 15.3 percent in 1933, and 12.4 percent during Thatcherism in 1983.

Australia made a particularly profound effort to generate full employment in the post-war period, releasing a White Paper entitled *Full Employment in Australia*. This policy stated that the people of Australia "will demand and are entitled to expect full employment" (Commonwealth of Australia 1945). In the period 1950–1973, unemployment in Australia fluctuated between 1.3 and 2.7 percent, against an inter-war peak of 19.1 percent in 1932, and 9.9 percent in the period 1974–1989. In the context of the inter-war and post-1973 period, this was a remarkable achievement.

The policy landscape has, of course, changed. However, in 2005 the objective of "full and productive employment and decent work for all" was added as a specific target associated with the United Nations (UN) Millennium Development Goal to "eradicate extreme poverty and hunger" (ILO 2015b).[1] True full employment should be a central goal of a sustainable development agenda, not only because employment is important in its own right, but because it is the foundation of sustained and growing prosperity, inclusion and social cohesion (ILO 2015b).[2]

Conceptually, unemployment can be caused by a variety of forces, motivations, and circumstances. In the familiar typology, unemployment may be frictional (as people move from job-to-job), structural (in the sense that the structure of the economy changes as industries decline), or demand-deficient (as maintained in Keynesian analyses). Heterodox approaches to unemployment are many and varied. The concept of full employment, too, is multi-faceted, with a variety of emergent policy prescriptions. The notion of full employment may, at first view, imply an absence of these various forms of unemployment. However, frictional unemployment and structural change are endemic and unavoidable in capitalism. Thus Beveridge (1945)—also famous for his influence on the provision of social security and the National Health Service in post-Second World War Britain—wrote at length on the subject of full employment. This he defined as a situation where the number of jobseekers equaled the number of job vacancies. Frictional unemployment is therefore one source of unemployment at full employment.

Two of the dominant approaches within heterodox economics are Marxian and Post Keynesian economics, with their many variants. Heterodox economics draws upon a plurality of perspectives and it may be an aspiration to integrate heterodox approaches further, where possible. Whatever the merits of this view in general, in this chapter we will illustrate some of the tensions within heterodoxy on the subject of full employment. In the next section we consider the mainstream analysis of full employment and its critics. Thereafter we explore two heterodox approaches: Marxian economics (in the context of the notion of the 'reserve army of the unemployed') and Post Keynesian aggregate demand management. The job guarantee program is then presented as a full employment policy, with particular reference to how the program accommodates issues raised by these heterodox schools of thought.

Unemployment, full employment, and orthodoxy

Mainstream approaches generally assume rational expectations and derive their outcomes from microfoundational analyses. 'Neoclassical' unemployment theory posits that government intervention and trade union activity can distort the labor market, thereby giving rise to unemployment. As Denning (2010: 85) notes:

> Neoliberal economists insisted that involuntary joblessness did not even exist; unemployment was either a choice for the marginal utility of leisure, or a temporary blockage of the labour market caused by high wages made too sticky by union monopoly and the state's minimum wage.

The relationship between unemployment and inflation has also been a consideration of the mainstream. Friedman (1968) thus argued that the notion of full employment was problematic, and that we should instead look at the natural rate of unemployment which is consistent with stable prices, and that this rate is not consistent through time. In this context, Modigliani & Papademos (1975) and Tobin (1980) introduced the notion of the non-accelerating inflation rate of unemployment (NAIRU), which is the underlying rate of unemployment in the absence of demand-deficient unemployment. The logical extension of this is that if a government is to use demand management policies to reduce the unemployment rate below the NAIRU inflation will rise, potentially giving rise to a wage-price spiral. Therefore true (Beveridge-style) full employment as a public policy objective was undermined by the so-called Phillips curve trade-off, which has informed the policy debate since the 1960s. The ostensible trade-off meant that unemployment was simply the cost of promoting macroeconomic (price and exchange rate) stability. Unemployment became a policy tool rather than a specific objective (Wray 2007).

Unemployment as a stabilization mechanism raises serious ethical and moral issues, and violates basic human rights, specifically 'the right to work' (UN 1948). Notwithstanding the economic costs (for example, lost output), the social costs of joblessness are well established: poverty, physical and psychological health effects, social isolation, crime, and a weakening of participatory democracy (see Sen 1999; Harvey 2002; Bhaduri 2005). Wray (2007) suggests that such a stabilization mechanism is particularly problematic since the costs of unemployment and poverty are not equally shared among the population. Unemployment is usually concentrated among groups that suffer other disadvantages, such as "racial and ethnic minorities, immigrants, younger and older individuals, women (especially female-heads of households with children), people with disabilities, and those with lower educational attainment" (Wray 2007: 2). Youth unemployment, especially among women, continues to be particularly concerning (ILO 2015a).

Thus, contra the neoliberalism prominent in many strands of orthodoxy, the need for specific full employment policy enacted by government is strengthened by: (i) the established interconnectedness between unemployment, poverty, and economic development and social cohesion; and, (ii) the fact that private sector employers have no desire, either on grounds of expected profitability or fears of unfavorable political economy dynamics like those identified by Kalecki (1943), to offer a job to everyone ready, willing, and able to work.

Another variant of mainstream economics, New Keynesian economics, points to a number of forms of market failure which can result in the economy failing to reach full employment. A particularly important driver of unemployment is provided by the efficiency-wage model. Shapiro & Stiglitz (1984) assume that employees derive disutility from work and such workers will shirk in the absence of pressure from surveillance (to monitor workers' effort) with the associated threat of job loss and unemployment. In the presence of full employment a worker will simply pick up a job elsewhere. In response to this, in the Shapiro-Stiglitz model, firms will pay a productivity-maximizing wage rate, which is above the market-clearing level. This increases the cost to the worker of losing their job, and creates a body of unemployed which further disincentivizes job loss, since workers will fear getting stuck in this pool of unemployed labor.

Heterodox perspectives on full employment

The reserve army of the unemployed

A reserve army of labor runs counter to the possibility of full employment in capitalism, which is why an analysis of full employment should explore this element of Marxian theory. Although often thought of as a term invented by Marx, radicals within the British labor movement had likened the emergent early-nineteenth-century factory workers to a great industrial army. Indeed, the Chartist leader Bronterre O'Brien had used the phrase 'reserve army of labor' as early as 1839, before it was picked up by Engels in 1844 (see Denning 2010: 84). In his mature work, Marx ([1867] 1976: 782–786) used various phrases—"a relatively redundant working population," an "industrial reserve army," and "a relative surplus population"—to refer to the wageless. These may include those who are involuntarily unemployed, but it also signals the possibility of under-employment among workers, and those on the fringes of, or outside of the labor market, for example people working in the 'informal sector' (Denning 2010: 89).

It is not disequilibrium, or friction, which generates the reserve army in Marxian systems. It emerges as an essential by-product of technological change, which serves the interest of the capitalist class. But, at the same time, in Marxian analyses, 'employment' is subject to critical interrogation, with focus on the negative aspects of the *extraction* of work. The creation of the labor market emerged out of a process of primitive accumulation, which rendered workers free in two senses: they were free in the sense they no longer had access to the means of production (thus could no longer self-provide), but also free in the sense they could sell their labor power (the capacity to work) on the labor market. In the early part of the industrial revolution, capital had difficulty in getting workers to accept the work routines of the modern factories. In this sense 'employment'—upon which the notion of full employment is predicated—was a qualitative facet of class conflict. So, for example, Marx's treatment of absolute surplus value looks at how long working hours are imposed upon workers, who would rather have shorter hours and reduced consumption. This essentially simultaneously creates over-employment among some workers, and under-employment among others, from which the macroeconomic notion of full employment abstracts.

The historical period from 1950 to 1973 seemed to indicate the reserve army hypothesis had little relevance in the wake of post-Second World War policies associated with the Golden Age of capitalism. However, the evidence before and after may indicate that this period was simply a temporary phase in the aftermath of the Second World War. Moreover, empirical evidence pertaining to the UK, and encompassing this period, reaffirms that the size of the reserve army of the unemployed is related to distributional struggle, for example, with regards to the rate of surplus value. Cuestas & Philp (2012) hypothesize that during periods when the magnitude of the reserve army of the unemployed is growing, employers are able to force wages down, increase the hours for those in employment (perhaps while shedding labor), and introduce new production methods, thereby increasing the rate of surplus value. For the period 1955 to 2010 they found that the traditional argument concerning the reserve army of labor accorded well with the dynamics of distribution, manifest with the rate of surplus value. In the context of the US economy, Basu (2013) also finds striking evidence in favor of Marx's analysis of capital accumulation and its impact upon workers. In particular, he finds that dynamics within the capital accumulation process "continually replenish the reserve army through the displacement of workers, destruction of subsistence farming and deskilling and discouragement of unemployed workers" (Basu 2013: 199). Thus empirical evidence in Basu (2013) indicates the reserve army of labor fluctuates with the requirement of capital accumulation, as predicted by Marx ([1867] 1976).

The 'functional' role (in explanatory terms) of the reserve army of the unemployed concurs with aspects of Kalecki's (1943: 351) thought:

> The maintenance of full employment would cause social and political changes which would give a new impetus to the opposition of the business leaders. . . . Their class instinct tells them that lasting full employment is unsound from their point of view and that unemployment is an integral part of the normal capitalist system.

John Marsh, Timothy Sharpe, Bruce Philp

This resonates with the notion of class interests, familiar from Marx, but note that there are further ills within capitalism beyond its perceived exploitative nature. And unemployment is key to understanding this. The Marxian notion of the reserve army of labor provides a rationale for why we have observed inhumane and unacceptable levels of unemployment in particular epochs of capitalism. However, as Denning (2010: 79) observes: "Under capitalism, the only thing worse than being exploited is not being exploited." The perversities of the erstwhile outcomes generated by capitalist market economies, in terms of income distribution, unemployment, and environmental threat, mean that a response should be sought. This may be a socialist alternative to capitalism, perhaps combined with a significant capitalist fringe. Yaffe (1973) argues that one of the key arguments in favor of revolutionary socialism is eradicated if capitalism can, with or without government intervention, generate continual wage growth and full employment.

Aggregate demand management

Marx, Kalecki, and Keynes all had a firm grasp on the idea of effective demand as an explanation of how and why private sector demand was chronically incapable of achieving and sustaining full employment. Keynes' analysis demonstrates that firms only hire the quantity of labor needed to produce the level of output expected to be sold at a profitable price, concluding that it is the role of government policy to "establish a closer approximation of full employment as nearly as is practicable" (Keynes [1936] 1964: 378–379).

Post Keynesian economists generally advocate aggregate demand stimulus to increase employment and, in some instances, achieve full employment using well-known income-expenditure multipliers (see, for example, Arestis & Sawyer 2012; Pollin 2012). Since Keynes had argued that private sector demand would be incapable of achieving and sustaining full employment, Post Keynesians advocate government stimulus measures (so-called 'pump-priming') to close the output gap (though distributional constraints are often acknowledged).

The aggregate demand management approach to achieve full employment can encompass policies which seek to, for example: (i) redistribute income towards individuals with higher marginal propensities to consume; (ii) reduce interest rates; and (iii) increase the expected profitability of investment via increased government spending, which partially validates previous expenditures by firms (see Tcherneva 2012).

Minsky (1986: 308) argues that "[t]he policy problem is to develop a strategy for full employment that does not lead to instability, inflation, and unemployment." When the economy is operating with excess capacity, increases in effective demand, output, and employment can coincide without generating inflationary pressures since demand increases are met through output adjustments (Hart & Kriesler 2015). In this setting, price pressures largely emerge from cost factors through a mark-up pricing mechanism, and are mediated by the bargaining process associated with conflicting claims on national income of labor and capital.

Post Keynesians recognize that as the economy approaches full capacity utilization, the bargaining power of wage earners may strengthen substantially, which can ignite an inflationary process ('wage-price spiral'). Following Kalecki, "economic, social and political power will cumulatively pass from capital to labour . . . the sack ceases to be effective, and inflationary forces tend to build up" (Harcourt & Kriesler 2015: 37). Thus, "some degree of centralisation and of coordination of wage setting is necessary if the inflationary consequences of the maintenance of full employment are to be addressed" (Hart & Kriesler 2015: 328). A permanent incomes policy is recommended to, for example, ensure that "nominal award wages are adjusted periodically for movements in the general price level and the overall level of productivity" (Hart & Kriesler 2015: 329).

A unified full employment policy

There are differences between Marxian and Post Keynesian economics regarding full employment.[3] Marxian economists see full employment as unachievable within capitalism, since technological change systematically creates a reserve army of labor. Post Keynesian economists generally argue that full employment can be achieved within a capitalist economic system via aggregate demand management. On the other hand, both Marxian and Post Keynesian economists acknowledge Kalecki's political economy concern associated with *sustaining* full employment.

It seems that a unified full employment policy must address the effective demand concern, the structural and technological change concern that has been argued by Luigi Pasinetti (1993), and Kalecki's political economy concern. The job guarantee is a policy recommendation, which can help to alleviate the economic and social effects of both types of unemployment—'Marxian technological unemployment' and 'Keynesian demand-deficient unemployment'—and is not subject to the 'Kalecki dilemma.' While both types of unemployment are inherent in capitalist economic systems, the job guarantee does not require the transformation of capitalism.

Job guarantee: general features

Drawing on the seminal contributions of Keynes, Minsky, and Abba Lerner, the job guarantee (or the employer of last resort) is a targeted policy approach to achieving sustained full employment. The job guarantee offers a job at a fixed money wage to any individual ready, willing, and able to work. The program has been developed extensively by Mosler (1997–98), Forstater (1998), Mitchell (1998), Wray (1998a), Mitchell & Muysken (2008), and Murray & Forstater (2013), among others.

The general purpose of the job guarantee is to mitigate the "indignity and insecurity of underemployment, poverty and social exclusion" (Quirk *et al.* 2006: 2), along with the "amelioration of many social ills associated with chronic unemployment (health problems, spousal abuse and family break-up, drug abuse, crime), [while enhancing] skills due to training on the job" (Wray 2012a).

The type and provision of jobs is largely at the discretion of local/regional governments but would include a range of community and environmentally based projects (for example, reforestation, sand dune stabilization, personal assistance to pensioners).[4] Job guarantee workers are paid the minimum wage, which may be set higher than the existing minimum wage (for example, at a living wage level). Advocates suggest that the job guarantee wage should be adjusted periodically, say annually, and could be supplemented with a benefits package. The total remuneration package will vary by country depending on acceptable living standards and productive capacity, but should reflect a 'living wage' (Wray 2007). Mitchell (2013) suggests that private employers who cannot 'afford' to pay the minimum/living wage should exit the economy. Thus, the job guarantee provides universal access to a basic set of guarantees of work/income security and social protection.

Traditional unemployment benefits could be maintained alongside the job guarantee, but job guarantee remuneration would be higher to promote an incentive to work. Notwithstanding this, Mitchell (2013) argues that the introduction of the program clarifies the conception of mutual obligation, so government may choose to eliminate such unemployment payments. The remuneration package, however, would not supersede the normal range of family benefits or support services to disadvantaged groups (Mitchell 2013).

While the job guarantee is operationally decentralized, it would be financed by the federal government. Here, many job guarantee advocates turn to Modern Monetary Theory which

John Marsh, Timothy Sharpe, Bruce Philp

distinguishes between a sovereign and non-sovereign currency government (see Wray 1998b, 2012b). It is often preferred, due to the associated policy freedoms, that a job guarantee is implemented by a sovereign currency government, which issues its own fiat, non-convertible currency and operates a flexible exchange rate regime (for example, Australia, the UK, and the US). A sovereign currency government establishes their own money of account (for example, the 'dollar'), imposes liabilities in that abstract unit (for example, taxes), and issues the money-thing (for example, banknotes), denominated in the same unit that are accepted to extinguish those liabilities. A sovereign currency government faces no financial constraints in its own currency; it can purchase anything available for sale in its own money of account (for example, job guarantee labor).[5] Eurozone member governments, on the other hand, face financial constraints since currency sovereignty was relinquished with the adoption of the Euro, and member governments now adhere to a strict fiscal governance framework.

Effective demand concern

Keynes' and the Keynesian approach to full employment should be distinguished. For Keynes, the issue was deficient demand for labor, not output. That is, "*any output gap that had to be plugged was measured in terms of the number of unemployed men and women who needed work*" (Tcherneva 2012: 73, original italics). Keynes specifically endorsed direct job creation policies or 'on-the-spot' employment which would be implemented irrespective of the phase of the business cycle (see Tcherneva 2012). In common with this, Minsky (1986: 308) identifies the role of government in direct job creation:

> The main instrument of such a [full employment] policy is the creation of an infinitely elastic demand for labor at a floor or minimum wage that does not depend upon long- and short-run profit expectations of business. Since only government can divorce the offering of employment from the profitability of hiring workers, the infinitely elastic demand for labor must be created by government.

Excess capacity and demand-deficient unemployment is inherent in capitalist economic systems. The job guarantee creates an 'employment buffer stock' by generating sufficient jobs to absorb workers who are unable to find employment or enough hours of work in the non-job-guarantee (traditional private and public) sector. Thus, the size of the job guarantee sector is calibrated to the state of economic flux: the buffer stock expands (declines) when non-job-guarantee sector activity declines (expands), which minimizes the economic and social costs associated with the flux of the economy, enhancing macroeconomic stability (Fullwiler 2005). Job guarantee advocates recognize that certain projects would require a critical mass (for example, tutoring of children) so it is important to distinguish between these 'continuous' projects and other 'discretionary' projects which can be quickly implemented or postponed (Wray 2007). But, since the job guarantee promotes macroeconomic stability, it is argued that the size of the core job guarantee employment would be reasonably stable.

The job guarantee and aggregate demand management policies are not mutually exclusive. Public infrastructure projects should be undertaken to achieve specific social and economic objectives which will help to reduce the degree of labor underutilization. Mitchell *et al.* (2003) argue that the job guarantee should be accompanied by increased social wage spending to increase employment in education and health care, for example.

It is well recognized that increased aggregate expenditures can encounter real constraints. Specifically, there must be enough real capacity in the economy (available resources and output space) to absorb the extra net government sector spending associated with the job guarantee and aggregate demand management policies. Job guarantee advocates, however, argue that sole reliance on aggregate demand management to achieve full employment would create considerable economic inflexibility, which is to say that full employment is unlikely to be sustained.

Aggregate demand management policies mean that the government is committed to high levels of employment at market wages so inflationary pressures can potentially emerge before full employment is reached since particular industries may already be operating near full capacity (Tcherneva 2012). Thus, it is not more demand that is required to guarantee full employment in expansions, but more appropriately distributed demand. Tight monetary policy, for example, may then induce a recession to ease the inflationary pressures which means "[e]xpansions would be curtailed long before a sufficient supply of jobs would be created to bring all out of poverty" (Wray 2007: 6). So, in a manner characteristic of the NAIRU, unemployment is still used as a 'buffer stock' to discipline the inflationary process (via contractionary fiscal and monetary policy).

With a job guarantee, "[i]f inflation does exceed the government's announced target, tighter macroeconomic policy would lead to workers being displaced from the inflating private sector to the fixed price [job guarantee] sector, which imposes a sanction, in the form of income loss" (Juniper et al. 2014–15: 299). Thus, the job guarantee's 'employment buffer stock' mechanism is used to discipline inflationary pressures. In addition, program flexibility allows the labor/capital mix of job guarantee jobs to be varied in response to looming real constraints (see Forstater 2001; Mitchell & Watts 2013). In this way, it is argued that full employment can be *sustained*, and that the indignity and insecurity of (chronic) unemployment and associated social and economic costs are avoided.

Structural and technological change concern

The employment buffer stock mechanism described above suggests that full employment can be *sustained* in the context of ongoing structural and technological change which may arise, for example, from changes in the supply of labor or natural resources, changes in the composition of final demand, or labor- or capital-displacing technical change (Forstater 2001). Ongoing threats to natural capital and the associated need for climate change mitigation and adaptation will involve inevitable and significant structural change. Advocates maintain that the job guarantee can help to alleviate the economic and social dislocations associated with the shift towards more ecologically sustainable modes of production and consumption (see Forstater 2003).

A comprehensive job guarantee program can include a training and education component to improve the productivity and flexibility of workers, and provide an opportunity to apply skills and knowledge learned (see Mitchell et al. 2003; Tymoigne 2013). In this way, the policy will: (i) help to maintain morale, work habit, and other non-job specific skills, which contrasts the current unemployed; (ii) ease the 'hysteretic inertia' embodied in the long-term unemployed, facilitating the redeployment of workers to new non-job-guarantee sector job opportunities; and, (iii) raise the skill intensity of the workforce (Mitchell 1998). More broadly, local/regional governments should be engaged in ongoing occupational planning to better align skill development, via tertiary education and on-the-job training, with future employment needs.[6]

Political economy concern

Kalecki's principal political economy concern was that the *maintenance* of full employment would lead to social and political changes which would be opposed by so-called 'business leaders.' Kalecki (1943: 351) argues that under a regime of permanent full employment, 'the sack' would cease to play its role as a disciplinary measure. The social position of the boss would be undermined and the self assurance and class consciousness of the working class would grow.

Thus, the reserve army of labor serves a functional role, ensuring that the power struggle between capital and labor remains weighted towards the former.

Kalecki's concern is more relevant to a fully employed private sector via aggregate demand management, rather than a job guarantee. The former generates 'tight' full employment where, given conflicting claims in a mark-up pricing model and a diminished effective labor supply, employees gain more influence in the wage bargain. In contrast, the job guarantee creates 'loose' full employment: the government simply purchases unwanted labor—which has no market price—at a fixed wage, so does not compete with private sector employers (see Mitchell 1998). It is argued that the job guarantee and associated training programs also lessens the depreciation of human capital, relative to the unemployed, which enhances the effective labor supply and reduces productivity-adjusted hiring costs (Wray 2007). Employers are more likely to resist inflationary wage demands in the presence of a pool of employable labor which means that, in contrast to the current unemployed, job guarantee workers are a credible threat to non-job-guarantee sector employees. Inflationary wage demands are further disciplined by the anticipated wage income loss from the transition to job guarantee sector employment (that is, 'the sack').

A related issue is that the sectoral shift within economies—manufacturing sectors in decline and service sectors in growth—coupled with an increasingly deregulated and globalized economic environment has been associated with a substantial decline in trade union membership. Mitchell (2010) notes that "[t]rade unions have traditionally found it hard to organize or cover the service sector due to its heavy reliance on casual work and gender bias towards women." In this setting, it is difficult for trade unions to impose costs on employers via the wage bargain. "Far from being a threat to employers, the Job Guarantee policy becomes essential for restoring some security in the system for workers" (Mitchell 2010).

Conclusion

This chapter has evaluated the history, theory, and policy prescriptions pertaining to full employment. Set in the context of contemporary capitalism and mainstream economics, the recommendations of both Marxian economics and Post Keynesian economics are considered. The job guarantee program is presented as a full employment policy, which accommodates issues raised by both heterodox schools of thought, but does not require the transformation of capitalism.

The job guarantee is best envisioned as a structural/permanent feature of the economic and social architecture, rather than an 'interventionist' measure *per se*. While the program can be used to implement benchmarks and effectively define the basics of social provisioning, it is not an all-encompassing strategy to satisfy all aspects of economic and social development. The job guarantee should form a core component of a broader fiscal framework to promote the 'public purpose,' which should include other strategies to address, for example, rising poverty and wage inequality, financial fragility, and threats to ecological sustainability.

The present situation is wasteful, both in terms of the environment and in terms of creative human potential. It remains to be seen whether these perspectives can be combined within a unified heterodox policy framework, but one thing that is certain is that societal development is more likely for having had the dialogue.

Notes

1 For interventionists, the Global Financial Crisis and subsequent Eurozone crisis, along with ongoing structural change, has elevated the need for job creation, which is now considered as "the most pressing global development priority" (ILO 2015b: 1).
2 'Decent work' is now classified as one of the 17 Global Goals that make up the *2030 Agenda for Sustainable Development*.
3 For example, in a paper written in 1950, Dobb criticizes Keynes for his reformist tendencies and argues that his sympathies were with the productive capitalist vis-à-vis the rentier, and not with the working class *per se* (see Dobb 1955). For Dobb, only armaments expenditure was an acceptable form of state intervention to combat depression, and full employment in capitalism was an unachievable utopian vision (see Howard & King 1992: 101–102).
4 Cook *et al.* (2008) provide an extensive (Australian) study of the projects that could be completed at the regional level if federal government financing was available.
5 The operational realities of spending and taxing by a sovereign currency government are discussed by Wray (1998b, 2012b) and Juniper *et al.* (2014–15).
6 Occupational forecasting models can be used to estimate future employment needs (for example, the Local Economy Forecasting Model used in the UK).

References

Arestis, P. & Sawyer, M. 2012. 'The 'new economics' and policies for financial stability.' *International Review of Applied Economics*, 26 (2): 147–160.
Basu, D. 2013. 'The reserve army of labor in the postwar U.S. economy.' *Science & Society*, 77 (2): 179–201.
Beveridge, W. 1945. *Full Employment in a Free Society*. New York: Norton.
Bhaduri, A. 2005. *Development with Dignity: A Case for Full Employment*. New Delhi, India: National Book Trust.
Commonwealth of Australia. 1945. Full employment in Australia. Commonwealth of Australia. Available from http://www.billmitchell.org/White_Paper_1945/index.html [Accessed November 13, 2015]
Cook, B., Mitchell, W., Quirk, V., & Watts, M. 2008. Creating effective local labour markets: a new framework for regional employment policy. Report prepared for Jobs Australia, by the Centre of Full Employment and Equity, University of Newcastle.
Cuestas, J. & Philp, B. 2012. 'Economic class and the distribution of income.' *International Review of Applied Economics*, 26 (5): 565–578.
Denning, M. 2010. 'Wageless life.' *New Left Review*, 66 (November–December): 79–97.
Dobb, M. 1955. 'Full employment and capitalism,' in: *On Economic Theory and Socialism: Collected Papers, Vol. 2*. London: Routledge, 215–225.
Forstater, M. 1998. 'Flexible full employment: structural implications of discretionary public sector employment.' *Journal of Economic Issues*, 32 (2): 557–563.
Forstater, M. 2001. Full employment policies must consider effective demand and structural and technological change. Center for Full Employment and Price Stability Working Paper 14. Available from http://www.cfeps.org/pubs/wp-pdf/WP14-Forstater.pdf [Accessed January 20, 2016]
Forstater, M. 2003. 'Public employment and environmental sustainability.' *Journal of Post Keynesian Economics*, 25 (3): 385–406.
Friedman, M. 1968. 'The role of monetary policy.' *American Economic Review*, 58 (1): 1–17.
Fullwiler, S.T. 2005. Macroeconomic stabilization through an employer of last resort. Center for Full Employment and Price Stability Working Paper 44. Available from http://www.cfeps.org/pubs/wp-pdf/WP44-Fullwiler.pdf [Accessed August 2, 2015]
Harcourt, G.C. & Kriesler, P. 2015. 'Post-Keynesian theory and policy for modern capitalism.' *Journal of Australian Political Economy*, 75 (Winter): 27–41.
Hart, N. & Kriesler, P. 2015. 'Post-Keynesian economics: a user's guide.' *The Australian Economic Review*, 48 (3): 321–332.
Harvey, P. 2002. 'Human rights and economic policy discourse: taking economic and social rights seriously.' *Columbia Human Rights Law Review*, 33 (2): 364–471.
Howard, M. & King, J. 1992. *A History of Marxian Economics: Volume 2, 1929–1990*. London: Macmillan.
ILO. 2015a. *World Employment and Social Outlook: Trends 2015*. Geneva: International Labour Organisation.
ILO. 2015b. Jobs and livelihoods at the heart of the post-2015 development agenda. International Labour Organisation concept note. Available from http://www.ilo.org/global/topics/sdg-2030/documents/WCMS_193483/lang—en/index.htm [Accessed August 4, 2015]

Juniper, J., Sharpe, T. P., & Watts, M.J. 2014–15. 'Modern monetary theory: contributions and critics.' *Journal of Post Keynesian Economics*, 37 (2): 281–307.

Kalecki, M. 1943. 'Political aspects of full employment.' *Political Quarterly*, 14 (4): 322–331.

Keynes, J.M. [1936] 1964. *The General Theory of Employment, Interest, and Money*. New York: Harcourt, Brace and World.

Keynes, J.M. 1972. 'Can Lloyd George do it?' *in*: D. Moggridge (ed.), *The Collected Writings of John Maynard Keynes, Vol. IX*. London: Macmillan, 86–125.

Maddison, A. 1991. *Dynamic Forces in Capitalist Development*. Oxford: Oxford University Press.

Marx, K. [1867] 1976. *Capital, Volume 1*. Harmondsworth, UK: Penguin.

Minsky, H. P. 1986. *Stabilizing an Unstable Economy*. New York: McGraw-Hill.

Mitchell, W.F. 1998. 'The buffer stock employment model and the NAIRU: the path to full employment.' *Journal of Economic Issues*, 32 (2): 547–555.

Mitchell, W.F. 2010. Michal Kalecki – the political aspects of full employment. Billy Blog. Available from http://bilbo.economicoutlook.net/blog/?p=11127 [Accessed January 17, 2016]

Mitchell, W.F. 2013. What is a job guarantee? Billy Blog. Available from http://bilbo.economicoutlook.net/blog/?p=23719 [Accessed August 11, 2015]

Mitchell, W.F. & Muysken, J. 2008. *Full Employment Abandoned: Shifting Sands and Policy Failures*. Cheltenham, UK: Edward Elgar.

Mitchell, W.F. & Watts, M.J. 2013. Capacity constraints and the job guarantee. Centre of Full Employment and Equity Working Paper 4. Available from http://e1.newcastle.edu.au/coffee/pubs/wp/2013/13-04.pdf [Accessed August 5, 2015]

Mitchell, W.F., Cowling, S., & Watts, M.J. 2003. A community development job guarantee. Centre of Full Employment and Equity Working Paper. Available from http://e1.newcastle.edu.au/coffee/pubs/reports/2003/CDJG.pdf [Accessed January 15, 2016]

Modigliani, F. & Papademos, L. 1975. 'Targets for monetary policy in the coming year.' *Brookings Papers on Economic Activity*, 6 (1): 141–166.

Mosler, W. 1997–98. 'Full employment and price stability.' *Journal of Post Keynesian Economics*, 20 (2): 167–182.

Murray, M.J. & Forstater, M. (eds.) 2013. *The Job Guarantee: Toward True Full Employment*. New York: Palgrave Macmillan.

Pasinetti, L. 1993. *Structural Economic Dynamics*. Cambridge: Cambridge University Press.

Pollin, R. 2012. *Back to Full Employment*. Cambridge, MA: MIT Press.

Quirk, V., Allen, E., Andresen, T., Bill, A., Cook, B., Goldsmith, B., Juniper, J., La Jeunesse, R., Mitchell, W., Myers, J., Watts, M., Welters, R., & Wrightson, G. 2006. The job guarantee in practice. Centre of Full Employment and Equity Working Paper 15. Available from http://e1.newcastle.edu.au/coffee/pubs/wp/2006/06-15.pdf [Accessed August 2, 2015]

Sen, A. 1999. *Development as Freedom*. New York: Alfred A. Knopf.

Shapiro, C. & Stiglitz, J. 1984. 'Equilibrium unemployment as a worker discipline device.' *American Economic Review*, 74 (3): 433–444.

Tcherneva, P.R. 2012. 'Permanent on-the-spot job creation—the missing Keynes plan for full employment and economic transformation.' *Review of Social Economy*, 70 (1): 57–80.

Tobin, J. 1980. 'Stabilization policy ten years after.' *Brookings Papers on Economic Activity*, 11 (1): 19–90.

Tymoigne, E. 2013. 'Job guarantee and its critiques.' *International Journal of Political Economy*, 42 (2): 63–87.

UN. 1948. United Nations universal declaration of human rights. United Nations. Available from http://www.supremecourt.ge/files/upload-file/pdf/act3.pdf [Accessed August 11, 2015]

Wray, L.R. 1998a. 'Zero unemployment and stable prices.' *Journal of Economic Issues*, 32 (2): 539–545.

Wray, L.R. 1998b. *Understanding Modern Money*. Cheltenham, UK: Edward Elgar.

Wray, L.R. 2007. The employer of last resort programme: could it work for developing countries? International Labour Office economic and labour market paper 5. Available from http://www.cfeps.org/elm07-5.pdf [Accessed August 12, 2015]

Wray, L.R. 2012a. Job guarantee basics: design and advantages. New Economic Perspectives. Available from http://neweconomicperspectives.org/2012/03/mmp-blog-43-job-guarantee-basics-design-and-advantages.html [Accessed August 11, 2015]

Wray, L.R. 2012b. *Modern Money Theory: A Primer on Macroeconomics for Sovereign Monetary Systems*. Basingstoke, UK: Palgrave Macmillan.

Yaffe, D. 1973. 'The Marxian theory of crisis, capital and the state.' *Economy and Society*, 2 (2): 186–232.

36

Social welfare and social control

Andrew Cumbers and Robert McMaster

Introduction

This chapter provides an illustration of the elements of what may be considered to be hetero-dox economic thinking on the nature of social welfare and social control, and the relationships between them. We assume that social welfare relates to a class of functions, such as education, economic security, health care, and housing, which are provided by, or associated with the welfare state in developed or high-income capitalist economies.[1] This is not to say that the state neces-sarily delivers services in those areas, but is responsible for their provisioning, implying also some varying forms of financial commitment. Our description departs from the neoclassical economic interpretation of social welfare, which is largely delineated by welfare economics, following utilitarian and/or Paretian reasoning in attempting to establish and measure well-being (Mandler 1999). Heterodox economic approaches reject the philosophical basis of this notion of social welfare (Lawson 2006). Instead, according to Lawson, heterodoxy is concerned with the analysis of the social structures and processes that influence material well-being.

Notions of social control are problematic in individualist mainstream and neoclassical eco-nomics, given the limited conceptualizations of power, which tend to center on the notion of market power. In contrast, heterodox economic schools of thought are closer to other social science disciplines in acknowledging the roles of specific institutions in establishing controlled, and to some degree predictable, patterns of behavior in society that serve the interests of certain groups or classes over others. The prominent institutions identified include markets, the legal system (including policing), religion, education, and the welfare state (Jessop 2002). It is the wel-fare state's potential function of social control in contemporary capitalist society that provides a source of controversy in some heterodox economic analyses. Studies in the Marxian tradition highlight the contradictions of the welfare state within capitalism: it represents an advance for the proletariat and the indigent in the form of protection from the inherent crises of capital-ism and an extension of opportunity, and at the same time it acts to preserve and reproduce the underlying relations of capital (O'Connor [1973] 2002; Jessop 2002). Moreover, radical political economy and feminist economics refer to the potential for overt coercion and even violence as means of social control. Indeed, such a possibility is acknowledged in Kenneth Boulding's (1973) *The Economy of Love and Fear.*

We consider that there are three fundamental propositions stemming from a heterodox economic analysis of social welfare and choice. First, the economy is a system of social provisioning. As Lee (2009: 8–9) states, social provisioning relates to "[t]he structure and use of resources, the structure and change of social wants, structure of production and the reproduction of the business enterprise, family, state, and other relevant institutions and organizations, and distribution." Lee's invocation of 'structure' and 'change' emphasizes the relationship between economies, power structures, cultural values, and hence ethical frames. Culture and power imbue social control. The economy as a social provisioning system is nested in wider society. Following this, the second proposition is of the socially embedded individual. Individuals inhabit systems of institutions that simultaneously constrain, enable, and partly constitute the individual, and *vice versa*. This implies that individuals are to some degree malleable. Third, systems and institutions are subject to evolutionary change—that is, historical processes of change and development that are partly influenced by technological innovations. Therefore, evolution embodies: the existence of variation among a species or population; heredity or continuity, whereby individual characteristics are passed on to future generations through processes of social reproduction; and selection which, for example, influences the ability of an entity to survive and reproduce within their environment, and is influential on the durability of institutions and systems at other levels of socio-economic reality (Hodgson 2008). In short, historical and geographical contingencies matter.

Amid the range of perspectives from heterodox economics, some parts of the literature privilege a particular proposition ahead of others. Some institutionalists have been critical of Marxian contributions as veering towards determinism, submerging the individual in a class analysis, and challenge Marxian interpretations of the welfare state (for example, Hodgson 2004). Nonetheless, while there are differences and areas of contestation, it is important to acknowledge that there are affinities and complementarities. This chapter identifies and illustrates some of these. The chapter demonstrates that the essential precepts of heterodox thinking generate extensive insights into the relations between the institutions of social welfare and social control. In illustrating our argument, we show how age is socially constructed and therefore possesses certain institutional properties. From a critical perspective, this is important for understanding classifications of dependency and the medicalization of what are ultimately social problems. Through the generation of particular meanings, the social construction of age helps promote and protect the interests of certain classes over others.

The remainder of the chapter is set out as follows. The second section outlines and contrasts institutionalist references to social control through Veblen's ([1914] 2000) conceptualization of habit, the 'hidden persuader' (Hodgson 2003). The third section surveys a Marxian-oriented study of the welfare state in later capitalism, noting its inherent tensions and contradictions. We draw on the important work of O'Connor ([1973] 2002), Gough (1979), and Offe (1984)—and the so-called 'O'Goffe's Tale' (Klein 1993). The fourth section turns to our examples of age and medicalization, and discusses a social economic analysis of individual dignity. The final section of the chapter outlines the institutionalist notion of the instrumental valuation principle with a view to argue for an alternative framework of social welfare. The literature in these fields is vast, and the presentation is necessarily selective, but our aim is to illustrate the breadth of heterodox analysis and the synergies within this corpus of work.

Social control

Marxian and radical contributions to understanding the nature of social control in capitalism are well known. Marxian scholars have long investigated how the state has supported the interests of capital in shaping class relations and establishing various institutions to ensure the reproduction of those relations (Jessop 2012). For instance, Marx's (1970) analysis of class established the notion of a social pyramid where the forces and relations of production were supported by a social superstructure, which through the aegis of the state, the legal system, and religion ensured the disciplinary apparatus necessary to reproduce the relations of production. Of course, subsequent scholars have developed the notion of the social superstructure as a conduit of social control. Most notably, Gramsci's ([1971] 2007) conception of hegemony intimated a nuanced exercise of power through vehicles of coercion and active consent. There have been numerous substantial contributions within this tradition, including Lukes' (2005) development of power as capacity, which is not necessarily exercised.

Such ideas of social control are predicated on a reading of the individual as socially embedded. Lukes' (2005) nuanced argument that power is capacity resonates with institutionalist thinking that institutions—as social rule systems—may simultaneously constrain and enable individuals' frame of thought and behaviors. This may be traced to Veblen's reasoning that there are feedback effects between the individual (agent) and institution (structure)—institutions have the power to partially shape an individual's aspirations, preferences, beliefs, and capacities. By doing so, they potentially change that individual. However, institutional reproduction is reliant upon individuals who through either accident or design have the capacity to change rules. Specifically, rules and norms necessarily require individuals to interpret them. Indeed, the term 'reproduction' in evolutionary thinking is suggestive of some sort of change in contrast to 'replication,' which is not.

Veblen and other institutionalists drew from American pragmatist philosophy and instinct psychology (Twomey 1998; Hodgson 2013). Instinct psychology conceives the human mind as possessing a multi-layered structure—instinct, habit, and conscious deliberation. Instinct psychology therefore emphasizes the hierarchical nature of thought in creating knowledge. Instincts are inherited propensities and drives to behave in particular ways when subject to an assortment of triggers, such as emotions, urges, and/or reflexes. As such, instincts provide the platform for higher thinking.

Habits, unlike instincts, are learned. Like instincts, habits are propensities to behave in specific ways subject to cues or triggers, such as situations in which individuals find themselves. Importantly, habit, as a propensity to behave, need not be repetitive but may lie dormant for some time, and be triggered not only by some conditioned reflex but also by 'conscious resolve' (Hodgson 2003). Critically, habits, as learned dispositions arising from repeated actions or thoughts, are formed in particular institutional settings. They are predicated on our unique experiences of such institutions. Thus, institutions are embedded within us through acquired habits and at the same time are beyond us in that they exist independently of any particular individual.

Given this, there are two important dimensions to how institutions structure individual behavior. First, because rules have an established character in the sense that they are generally enduring and well recognized, they frame people's behavior by encouraging people to act repeatedly in particular ways. Habit, then, is essential to following rules consistently; as a recurring way of acting it replaces the need to deliberate over the appropriate action each time new occasions call for some act (Twomey 1998; Hodgson 2003). In effect, as a repository of knowledge, habit possesses a powerful economizing characteristic. This is made possible by the fact that rules are typically accompanied by cues, such as 'when in X do Y,' which inform people when they apply.

Second, because rules create settled patterns of behavior, they create expectations about how individuals ought to act in various circumstances. If people do not act as expected, not only does this disrupt other individuals' habitual behaviors, but it also calls into question an institution's rules. There is the potential for an act to be perceived as illegitimate given the boundaries established by the rules. In other words, institutions establish right and wrong, good and bad. Institutions therefore possess and convey specific arrays of values, and given the central role of habit in institutionalist theory; habits facilitate the absorption of values, and act as a conduit of those values. Habits are 'the hidden persuaders' (Hodgson 2003).

Veblen ([1899] 1994, [1904] 2005) argues that the institutional framework could encourage certain instinctive behavior and suppress others and by doing so prompt particular patterns of habits of thought, and therefore value systems. The crux of his analysis was that early-twentieth-century American capitalism, through 'business enterprise', favored the accumulation of wealth and conspicuous consumption. The basic drive was predatory: instinctive behavior associated with predation was privileged by simple pecuniary gain. Investment for profit dominated investment for technical efficiency. By contrast, engineers and industrialists are driven partly by the instincts of idle curiosity and workmanship, which manifest in the industrial process as a habitual search for "mechanical efficiency" (Veblen [1904] 2005: 15). In echoes of Marx's analysis of the division of labor, values of standardization and precision came to be valued ahead of craftsmanship with the advent of mass production. There is also an interesting development of the categorization of exchange-value over use-value here. With the evolution of the business enterprise the pursuit of pecuniary rewards tends to dominate industrial concerns. With this Veblen demonstrates how institutional change reconfigures habits of thought and therefore the prevailing system of values over which way of doing things is acceptable.

More generally, some institutionalist work highlights the distinction between ceremonial and instrumental values: the so-called Veblenian dichotomy. The former represent those sets of values that are oriented in past 'tribal legends' that may encourage invidious distinctions between individuals on the basis of class, ethnicity, and gender: attitudes and conduct that may be associated with 'master–servant' relations. There is a clear affinity with Marxian accounts of social control (O'Hara 2000). In contrast to ceremonial, instrumental values are technology (in the broadest sense) and problem-solving oriented and devoid of the mendaciousness potentially engendered by overly ceremonial values.

Given this, instincts are prior to habit and habits are prior to beliefs (about right and wrong), and belief proceeds deliberation (Hodgson 2004). It is the inculcation of values through habits of thought within a particular institutional setting that is central to Veblenian institutionalist analysis. Nonetheless, institutions through habits do not completely 'brainwash': humans are not robots. Agency partially resides with the individual; control of an individual is only partial. Institutions are reproduced through individuals, and individuals are not necessarily passive vessels: they interpret, potentially resist, and through their actions and creativity have the capacity to change institutions. This sets institutionalist thought apart from more orthodox forms of Marxism, where the individual agency tends to be subsumed under the collective class interest.

The political economy of (the) social welfare (state)

An institutional arrangement that may be a source of social control and conditioning is the welfare state. This issue vexed radical political scholars in the 1970s and 1980s (O'Connor [1973] 2002; Gough 1979; Offe 1984) and has to some degree sporadically continued to generate discussion (Fine 2002; Jessop 2002; Hill 2012), and critique (Klein 1993). Indeed, it was Klein (1993) who coined the term 'O'Goffe's Tale' in his attempt to aggregate these works and offer a common line of criticism.

O'Goffe's Tale arguably provides a prescient explanation of the tensions in Western welfare state systems. For all three authors (O'Connor, Gough, and Offe), the welfare state contributes to the contradictory pressures in capitalism: the need for capital accumulation but also issues of social reproduction, and legitimization, which in the longer term undermine the foundations for accumulation. In short, capitalism is unsustainable without the welfare state, even although the latter is perceived to be the source of fiscal crisis.

O'Connor ([1973] 2002) is recognized as providing a functionalist explanation. For him, the state attempts to fulfill two contradictory functions: to create and maintain the conditions for capital accumulation, while simultaneously ensuring social harmony, that is, legitimization. Correspondingly, state welfare spending reflects those tensions. O'Connor identifies expenditure on 'social capital' and 'social expenses.' The former is directed to ensuring the generation of private profit and capital accumulation, and is composed of 'social investment' and 'social consumption.' Social investment relates to those activities aimed at increasing labor productivity, such as state financed industrial development sites and education. Social consumption consists of those projects aimed at reducing labor 'reproduction costs,' such as social insurance. 'Social expenses' refer to those expenditures required for 'social harmony,' such as welfare payments to unemployed workers. In contrast to social capital, social expenses are not directed at labor productivity improvements, but serve as a legitimizing function of the state. O'Connor acknowledges that there is a degree of ambiguity between the two categories, and that state expenditure can serve the two functions simultaneously.

In his account, O'Connor ([1973] 2002) alludes to the socialization of the costs of what he terms 'social capital' and the privatization of its benefits. This has strong resonance with Galbraith's (1967) thesis, and those of other institutionalists (for example, Kapp 1950; Dugger 1989). Again, such arguments have a remarkable prescience and relevance to the financial crisis of most Western governments and often depicted as 'socialism for the rich and capitalism for the poor' (see Cumbers 2012).

While there is agreement with much of the tenor of O'Connor's analysis, institutionalists and other radical political economists depart from his functionalism. Gough (1979), for example, explores the emergence of the welfare state in more evolutionary terms, acknowledging that it also represents a source of progressive reform that advances the entitlements of the poor through the expansion of education, social security, health care, and equal opportunities legislation. Similarly, Jessop's (2002) documenting of what he terms the post-war 'Keynesian National Welfare State' (KNWS) notes the extension in welfare rights, the emergence of a universalist narrative in state paternalism, as well as a means of demand management supporting Fordist mass production.

Since the 1980s, a 'Schumpeterian competition state' has evolved following the breakdown of the Keynesian consensus and the rise of neoliberalism. Jessop (2002) powerfully argues that this re-orientation is typified by a repertoire that: subordinates social policy to economic policy; exerts downward pressure on 'social wages'; shifts from welfarist to workfarist modes; and exhibits a propensity to move from state intervention to correct for market failure to public-private partnerships, and/or some form of self-organization. Thus, the Schumpeterian state focuses on individual innovation in the supply side, and economic policies should be tailored to promote the production of knowledge and entrepreneurship. Moreover, citizens' automatic rights to welfare benefits have been eroded (Navarro et al. 2003). For instance, welfare-to-work reforms typical in many Western countries, compel welfare benefit recipients to enroll in (re)training programs in order to qualify for benefits, while the precariousness of employment has increased (Peck & Theodore 2000; Wisman 2013). This transformation in the welfare state has also been accompanied by growing disparities in the distribution of income and wealth as the state has been 'captured' by a (neoliberal) elite (Galbraith 2008; Varoufakis 2015), as the costs of the nefarious activities of the financial sector have been socialized (Crotty 2009). Thus, in short, the socialization of costs and the privatization of benefits generate a deficit between state expenditures and revenues. Moreover, there is a tendency for this to grow as state expenditures grow more rapidly than revenues, as the state is appropriated by powerful actors, such as corporations and the finance sector, and expenditure is skewed in their favor (John K. Galbraith 1967; O'Connor [1973] 2002; Glyn 2006; James K. Galbraith 2008).

These analyses conceive of the economy as a social provisioning process subject to endogenous evolutionary change in historical time. This is clearly evident in heterodox reasoning in apprehending the evolution in social welfare, such as charting the recent transfer of risk-bearing from the state to the individual. This reflects a broader transformative movement in the globalizing 'knowledge economy,' which has converted capitalist modes of production from Fordist mass production to post-Fordist processes, where the latter is described in terms of increasing flexibility, especially of the labor force, and changes in transactions based on information and communications technologies (Harvey 2010). Accompanying this evolution in production is a segmentation of labor: some groups will experience job enrichment and multi-skilling, but for others it can entail de-skilling, low wages, and indigence resulting from the outsourcing of tasks. The capture of the state and the welfare state by the elite has arguably served to extend social control as the welfare state is more obviously aligned to the promotion of particular interests. This potentially has an impact at an individual (as well as class) level, which is arguably overlooked in some Marxian accounts where a class focus crowds out consideration of the individual (for a critique, see for example, Hodgson 2004).

Social economists have supplemented the heterodox literature in this area through an analysis of individual dignity conceiving of the economy as a social provisioning system and process. Figart (2007), for example, observes that the notion of social provisioning goes beyond the material, embodying emotional, social, and interpersonal activities. This lends itself to contemplating the individual as profoundly socially embedded (Davis 2003), and seeks to address issues of individual living standards, poverty, and dignity.

The sense of self and the social aspect of the individual contribute to an individual's sense of dignity: dignity possesses personal and social qualities embodied in feelings of self-esteem and self-respect (Davis 2006). Self-esteem, associated with the personal aspect of dignity, arises from an individual's feelings and self-opinion. Self-respect, the social aspect of dignity, is a matter of how individuals believe that they are entitled to regard themselves in virtue of their membership of social groups and other bodies. Thus, dignity is similar to pride as an articulation of self-esteem. It is also an expression of the respect individuals feel towards themselves as human beings derived from personal and moral integrity that result from being a fully accepted community member possessing equal rights to any other individual. Given this, social economists describe humiliation as the undermining of dignity. Systematic humiliation, as an outcome of a system of institutions conveyed by, for example, habits, corrodes an individual's self-respect by discriminating against them by either denying them membership or diminishing their status (Davis 2006).

We will demonstrate how social welfare conceived in a specific way as a form of social control potentially through habits of thought and narrative leads to the stigmatization of individuals and the individualization of social problems.

Age as dependency and the medicalization of social problems

Conventional economic 'wisdom' in much of the mainstream and heterodoxy represents an aging population as the demand-side source of increased expenditures on health care and social support, and therefore a source of dependency, unproductiveness, and a potential drag on the economy. As Dugger (1999) and Jackson (2001, 2007) argue, this is predicated on a simplistic association between aging and state expenditures; reality is more nuanced. Dugger and Jackson offer important insights into the social construction of age. Physical aging is a continuous process; yet the delineation between young and old is frequently founded on what can appear to be spurious and potentially insidious foundations.

Contemporary capitalism divides people's life into various stages, principally, education, work, and retirement. These stages are socially constructed. For Jackson (2001) this process of periodization creates the basis for misplaced social attitudes towards the elderly, who are frequently perceived to be dependent on younger working age groups, even when they are physically and mentally capable and not in receipt of state benefits, such as health care. This further provides the basis for the promotion of a 'depoliticized' case that the welfare state requires to be constrained as the so-called 'dependency ratio' is set to rise. Thus, by exaggerating the economic impacts of aging on state expenditures the notion of a perpetual fiscal crisis of the state is reinforced, and ideological choices disguised (Jackson 2001). In other words, through the social construction of age-related dependency the state is able to exert social control over the agenda to shape the welfare state in particular ways. Of course, similar arguments are made regarding the unemployed and working-indigent.

From the perspective advanced here the foregoing carries implications for individual dignity. Dignity is associated with individual autonomy, responsibility, and freedom from stigma. From a social economics' position all welfare state benefits and services *should* be provided in a manner that at least preserves an individual's dignity and be without stigma. Indeed, the founding ideals of the KNWS are aligned to this: citizenship of a state entitles an individual to benefits, such that a person can feel that they are receiving benefits not as charity, but as a right. Yet with the transformation to the Schumpeterian competition state (Jessop 2002), risk is passed from the state to the individual: rights are eroded and the potential for stigmatization heightened.

Dugger (1999) presents an institutionalist analysis of aging. For him, discrimination against older workers in United States (US) corporations is institutionalized through premature retirement, which conveys status loss on these individuals through commonly held perspectives of dependency. However, the aging process is complex, with a socially constructed constituent as well as a biological one. Individuals do not choose to grow old.

The twentieth-century human lifespan has steadily increased, with infectious diseases being overhauled by diseases associated with wealth, such as over-consumption. Aging may therefore be delineated between: intrinsic aging—life course as determined by an organism's internal constitution, and extrinsic aging—external influences that lead to a departure from intrinsic influences. This makes the relationship between aging and illness complex and not reducible to biological factors: the social has a considerable role (Dugger 1999; Jackson 2001). Jackson (2001) claims that there are grounds to query any simple association between age and illness. Importantly, age-related physical decline is strongly related to social factors, such as indigence. The importance of poverty and consumption patterns on health status is well recognized. With adjustments in diet, lifestyle, and preventative screening a concentrated morbidity pattern may emerge at the end of an individual's life. Hence, reduced morbidity rates would act to further attenuate the presumed impact of population aging on medical expenditure (Jackson 2001).

In his analysis of the 'consumer society,' Galbraith (1973) observes that modern illnesses are a consequence of over-consumption, and the stresses of endeavoring to increase income and wealth arising partly from the pressure of emulation and expectation and seeking economic security. Galbraith (1973) argues that with the increasing demands of working arrangements and consumption patterns, which necessitated the enlistment of women into full-time working, the emphasis in domestic life became one of convenience, given the transformation of traditional female roles. This was portrayed as the emancipation of women who were generally believed to possess greater economic autonomy, despite the wage discrimination that persists against women. The evolution of capitalist work conditions prompted the rise of the 'TV dinner,' and the agri-corporation. Agricultural production has become dominated by large corporations that attempt to increase their profit partly through the manipulation of price along the supply chain, and in the production of high fat, sugar and salt long-lived convenience products. Accordingly, the incidence of diet-related morbidity in the form of obesity-induced heart disease and diabetes, for example, has accelerated alarmingly. In spite of this knowledge, the corporate domination of food production remains largely unchecked, although recent resistance to the incursion of genetically modified food production in much of the EU and an emergent alternative sustainable food discourse (Crossan *et al.* 2016) may be indicative of some rethinking of the dominant production mode. Nonetheless, changing diets in India and China favoring the increased consumption of meat, and the persistence of mass agricultural production may suggest otherwise.

The domination of large-scale corporate production extends to medicine (Filc 2014). The Marxian-informed literature identifies three typical (but not exhaustive) modes of production in medicine: home, 'petty commodity,' and 'monopoly-capitalist' (Navarro 1983). Home production is only provided for family members. The petty commodity mode of production refers to the situation where an individual's medical skills can be sold, and hence commodified, as a means of livelihood. 'Monopoly-capitalist' refers to both the private sector employment of salaried staff and the production of commodified care as well as state provision that offers a range of services that may be subsidized through taxation and partly provided on a commodity basis. Such categories assist in identifying the commonalities across medical provision in contemporary society in that, with the exception of home production, they involve: a carer–patient relationship, which has become more distinct with the commodification of medical services engendered by a 'hegemonic struggle' in institutions leading to increased recourse to markets (Filc 2014). For some Marxians, all medical activities involve some reference to the market, whether it is the pursuit of medical training to gain employment, or the supply of pharmaceuticals and equipment, or increasing consumerism (Han 2002). In this type of analysis there is appreciation of the tendency of medical providers to medicalize disease and illness while relegating pertinent social factors (Doyal with Pennell 1979; Singer 2004).

The process of defining disease and illness is to some extent socially constructed in that it rests with a professional medical practitioner who is likely to be influenced by the biomedical paradigm. This approach assumes that illnesses and disease are only a consequence of a distortion, or malfunction of the biological process (Wade & Halligan 2004). Health is, therefore, functionally described in terms of freedom from disease. Moreover, the way the biomedical approach tends to define 'illness' is the most subjective element as it relates to how the individual feels, and therefore clearly refers to the person. 'Disease' follows from pathology and is attributed to science and objectivity. However, there are grounds for challenging the 'objectivity' of diagnosis (Wade & Halligan 2004).

Following the pioneering work of Frankenberg (1980), the process of diagnosis may be conceived as three phases: the first, 'the making of disease' is the physician's assemblage of available evidence. The operation is subject to potentially significant inaccuracies, for example, there is extensive interpretation involved, which may be subject to the underlying dispositions of particular medics (Groopman 2007). The second, 'the making individual of diseases,' refers to the influence exerted by the physician, using their position of authority, to persuade the patient to accept the biomedical reading of their condition. Finally, the third phase, 'the making social of disease,' refers to the effect of the power relations of the first two processes in ensuring the superiority of a biomedical approach to illness and disease. This for critics of the biomedical approach underpins its reductionist and exclusionist properties in, at worst, denying a social dimension to disease, or, at best, relegating it (Syme 2007). For example, if an individual experiencing job-related stress consults their physician, the symptoms may be manifest in a host of ways (Groopman 2007). The physician, following the biomedical approach, could, for example, prescribe sedatives. As opposed to addressing the causes of the individual's condition the physician's action merely masks the symptoms. In this way the physician's actions are not neutral (Doyal with Pennell 1979). For Singer (2004: 15), this "involves clinical acts of privatization, with diagnosis and intervention focused at the individual level, whatever the social origin of the disease in question." By masking the symptoms from a narrowly based diagnostic framework, a physician may inadvertently reinforce existing patterns of social relations.

Social control, then, can be seen to operate in complex and subtle ways. The configuration of aging, the corporate control of food supplies, and the medicalization of illness and disease, combine in different ways to influence habits of thought, and therefore establish what is legitimate and what is not. The social construction of age creates a notion of dependency that potentially stigmatizes a particular group, and therefore may shape the narrative around the fiscal crisis of the state. The supply and content of food has contributed to the evolution of disease, which, combined with the practice of the medicalization of social problems, acts as a further route of social control. The social is relegated in a process of shifting responsibility and risk to the individual. This is not necessarily replicated in medical provision, but here some heterodox studies signal the perhaps unintended consequence of the dominance of biomedicine in that, by relegating the social aspects of disease and illness, medical professionals (inadvertently) facilitate the enablement of the reproduction of existing power relations. Of course, the expansion of universal medical provision through many advanced industrialized·economies may be nested in the overarching evolution of the welfare state, especially the emergence of the KNWS, as a progressive development for the poor and the working class, more generally. Therefore, medicine is not immune to the tensions and contradictions highlighted in many heterodox economic analyses of social welfare. What heterodox studies indicate is that professional medicine, through its position of authority, has the potential to instill a set of relations and actions that augments an agenda of social control, thereby perpetuating a particular form of social reproduction. In doing so, it highlights the potentially significant role of specialized or expert knowledge in social welfare and social control.

An alternative framing of welfare? The instrumental valuation principle

Drawing from the pragmatist philosophy of Dewey, and Veblen's notion of progressive institutional change, Tool (1993, 1995) is among those institutionalists advocating the instrumental valuation principle (IVP) (Cumbers & McMaster 2010). Tool outlines the IVP as: "Do or choose that which provides for the *continuity* of human life and the *non-invidious* re-creation of community through the *instrumental use* of knowledge" (1995: 23, emphasis added).

In his approach, Dewey described 'instrumentalism' in terms of the continuum between means and ends; more specifically, how thought functions in influencing subsequent actions (Tool 1993). Tool further interprets this as a technological continuum—a 'tool and idea' combination in the pursuit of greater understanding. Indeed, such thinking is found in Marx and Veblen in their analysis of the shaping of production—the mode of production—by science and technology, and therefore on the social relations of production.

The IVP embodies three interrelated and mutually supporting conceptual elements: continuity, non–invidiousness, and the instrumental use of knowledge (Samuels 1995; Tool 1995; Bush & Tool 2003). The first element concerns the necessary conditions for continuity, which may include fiscal arrangements that promote and maintain human rights. Thus, given O'Goffe's Tale, and O'Connor's notion of the fiscal crisis of the state, decision-making framed by the IVP places an explicit normative emphasis on arrangements that ensure the protection of rights. Therefore, the transformation to the Schumpeterian competition state, and recent austerity may be viewed as contrary to the IVP.

The second element, non-invidious discrimination, draws from Veblen's analysis of the distinctions between classes of institutions, and Tool's invocation of a 'Veblenian dichotomy.' The latter distinguishes between instrumental judgments—those concerning the application of warranted knowledge—and ceremonial judgments—reflecting deference to custom, tradition, or established power structures. Evaluations based on a 'Veblenian dichotomy' may be invidious as they potentially discriminate individuals or classes of individual on the basis of race, ethnicity, gender, indigence, religion, age, and so forth, and therefore attach a 'value' to a person, which may not enhance that person's dignity. Accordingly, the instrumental use of knowledge avoids ceremonial evaluation criteria.

Third, the IVP is an evolving patterned *framework* for discourse and policy analysis, which embodies pluralistic values acknowledging diverse and competing forms of knowledge (Samuels 1995, 1998). It is not absolute, but it does endeavor to furnish conceptual criteria for the enhancement of just process and hence consequence in that it is disparaging of 'invidious' inequalities, and it seeks empowerment of the individual through democratic participation. It does not imply a particular pattern of ownership or governance, and, on this basis, institutionalists are resistant to those value systems that are locked into specific institutional arrangements regardless of historical and geographical contingencies. For example, Dugger (1995) is typical in asserting that 'ism-ideologies' are frequently employed to defend existing hierarchies and power structures, and detract from the potential of inquiry to address social problems. Instead, the IVP is claimed to furnish *criteria* for the selection of alternative institutional structures: regardless of ownership the promotion of individual empowerment remains central to the IVP. It demonstrates a clear association between scientific inquiry and social well-being, with institutions evaluated on the basis of the instrumental use of knowledge. For Dewey, intelligence is an instrument for the advancement of social well-being (Samuels 1995). Hence, institutional change *should* be governed by intelligent action guided by desired future consequences of that action (ends-in-view), and that this should be facilitated by widespread participation in decision-making processes that reflect the pluralism of society, and ensure the human rights and dignity of the individual (Cumbers & McMaster 2010).

Bush & Tool (2003) attempt to show the power of the IVP through differently configured exercises of authority in capital-labor relations. Employment contracts typically exhibit elements of both ceremonial and instrumental valuation. Thus, for example, if a 'superior' directs a 'subordinate' to a task, even if it is erratic, the subordinate may have little choice but to comply with the instruction, given the underlying power relation. For Bush and Tool the authority legitimizing the 'superior's' instruction is founded in a ceremonially warranted invidious distinction redolent of the 'master–servant' relation. Yet a superior may offer instruction to a subordinate, again by virtue of position, but also on the basis of the former's experience and skills, and as a means of transferring knowledge enabling the employee the opportunity to acquire additional capabilities. This latter case represents Dewey's instrumental use of knowledge, and therefore corresponds with the IVP (Bush & Tool 2003). Thus, within the archetypical capitalist production relation, there is likely to be some potential for the elements of the IVP. Yet, this is undermined by the insidious nature of ceremonial hierarchies prevalent in capitalist systems that stymie the exercise of a lack of participation in decision-making.

While the IVP may hold some appeal for heterodox economists, generally, it is ambiguous and sensitive to definitional issues. For instance, the basis of judgment is unclear. Moreover, whose judgment counts? Klein (1995) notes various judgmental criteria from Veblen's 'enhancing human life,' to Tool's Veblenian invidious–non-invidious distinction. There are ambiguities in the term 'non-invidious.' As Klein observes, for Hayek this could mean avoidance of 'serfdom,' for Marx a classless society, and for some contemporary economists the 'freeing' of the market.

It seems that some form of hierarchy is inevitable; yet this must be tempered by a toleration of pluralism in competing knowledge claims, and ensure adequate avenues for deliberation.

Perhaps such ambiguity is inevitable given that the principle refers to a process of valuation: value emerges following inquiry and discourse. Inquiry is framed by notions of 'reasonableness,' which Samuels (1995) contends are guided by Veblen's notion of progressive change. Arguably, social economists stress individual dignity may augment the IVP, and ensure the safeguarding of basic economic and social rights. Davis (2006: 81), for example, argues that "[m]aking human dignity a central value of socio-economic policy, then, means changing social institutions to eliminate humiliating institutions."[2]

Our IVP framework represents a radically challenging narrative and value frame to the power relations at work within mainstream welfare approaches which act as social control mechanisms to reproduce the status quo. The elimination of the basis of invidious distinctions suggests a rather different institutional array to that observed in many Western economies. On this basis there is a strong normative case for universal benefits as a means of social solidarity against invidious social comparisons that can engender stigmatization of individuals and certain groups. For instance, many heterodox economists have advocated a basic income funded by the state, where all citizens qualify for an income level that ensures freedom from indigence and that they receive regardless of their working income (Glyn 2006) as a tool in combating poverty and offering people greater flexibility in their working arrangements, *inter alia*. Such an approach could lead to the abolition of the state pension (and other forms of welfare payments), and hence removes the explicit economic institutions signaling dependency.

More conceptually, heterodox economic analyses of social welfare and social control highlight the importance of the socially embedded individual: we are always mutually dependent and equally deserving of dignity. This has some resonance with the likes of Sen (2009) who argues that there may be a lack of consensus about what constitutes social justice or the goals of a society, but by removing sources of injustice considerable progress may be made. For us, the framing effects of the IVP offer a powerful means of advancing this agenda. The process may involve a radical institutional reconfiguration of what may be taken to be the welfare state (especially the Schumpeterian competition state), where the last three decades have witnessed the steady transfer of risk to the individual. We do not advocate a complete return to the KNWS in the sense of its hierarchical and potentially overly paternalistic approach to social welfare. Rather, we wish to promote the universalism that featured as a key objective in the KNWS, and consider that a basic income is a means of progressing this agenda but in a way that also offers a certain liberation and empowerment of the individual. A basic income is no panacea, but it does offer the prospect of a simplified universalism, and a means of enhancing individual dignity. Moreover, as a potential approach in addressing issues associated with indigence, a basic income may also act as a counterweight to the tendency to medicalize social problems, which we alluded to above. Yet there are critical questions: what would be the geographical coverage of such a system of welfare? If the basic income is a necessary but insufficient means of promoting welfare and justice, what are its necessary conditions? In our view, heterodox economists need to investigate these issues as a matter of urgency.

Notes

1 While recognizing the welfare state also exists in lower income and less developed countries, our analysis here addresses the advanced welfare state found most extensively in the wealthier high-income capitalist economies of North America and Western Europe.
2 By humiliating we refer to those institutions that are a source of stigmatization and engender feelings of shame.

References

Boulding, K.E. 1973. *The Economy of Love and Fear: A Preface to Grants Economics*. Belmont, CA: Wadsworth.

Bush, P.D. & Tool, M.R. (eds.) 2003. *Institutional Analysis and Economic Policy*. Boston: Kluwer Academic Press.

Crossan, J., Cumbers, A., McMaster, R., & Shaw, D. 2016. 'Contesting neoliberal urbanism in Glasgow's community gardens: the practice of DIY citizenship.' *Antipode*. In press. Available from http://onlineli brary.wiley.com/doi/10.1111/anti.12220/pdf [Accessed July 27, 2016]

Crotty, J. 2009. 'Structural causes of the global financial crisis: a critical assessment of the 'New Financial Architecture'. *Cambridge Journal of Economics*, 33 (4): 563–580.

Cumbers, A. 2012. *Reclaiming Public Ownership: Making Space for Economic Democracy*. London: Zed Books.

Cumbers, A. & McMaster, R. 2010. 'Socialism, knowledge, the instrumental valuation principle, and the enhancement of individual dignity.' *Economy and Society*, 39 (2): 247–270.

Davis, J.B. 2003. *The Theory of the Individual in Economics: Identity and Value*. London: Routledge.

Davis, J.B. 2006. 'The normative significance of the individual in economics: freedom, dignity, and human rights,' *in*: B.J. Clary, W. Dolfsma, & D.M. Figart (eds.), *Ethics and the Market: Insights From Social Economics*. London: Routledge, 69–83.

Doyal, L. with Pennell, I. 1979. *The Political Economy of Health*. London: Pluto Press.

Dugger, W.M. (ed.) 1989. *Radical Institutionalism*. Westport, CT: Greenwood Press.

Dugger, W.M. 1995. 'Beyond technology to democracy: the Tool legacy,' *in*: C.M.A. Clark (ed.), *Institutional Economics and the Theory of Social Value: Essays in Honor of Marc R. Tool*. Norwell, MA: Kluwer, 195–207.

Dugger, W.M. 1999. 'Old age is an institution.' *Review of Social Economy*, 57 (1): 84–98.

Figart, D.M. 2007. 'Social responsibility for living standards.' *Review of Social Economy*, 65 (4): 391–405.

Filc, D. 2014. 'The role of civil society in health care reforms: an arena for hegemonic struggles.' *Social Science and Medicine*, 123 (December): 168–173.

Fine, B. 2002. *The World of Consumption: The Material and Cultural Revisited*, 2nd edn. London: Routledge.

Frankenberg, R. 1980. 'Medical anthropology and development: a theoretical perspective.' *Social Science and Medicine*, 14B: 197–202.

Galbraith, James K. 2008. *The Predator State: How Conservatives Abandoned the Free Market and Why Liberals Should Too*. New York: Free Press.

Galbraith, John K. 1967. *The New Industrial State*. Harmondsworth, UK: Penguin.

Galbraith, John K. 1973. *Economics and the Public Purpose*. Harmondsworth, UK: Penguin.

Glyn, A. 2006. *Capitalism Unleashed: Finance, Globalization, and Welfare*. Oxford: Oxford University Press.

Gough, I. 1979. *The Political Economy of the Welfare State*. London: Macmillan.

Gramsci, A. [1971] 2007. *Prison Notebooks*, translated and edited by A. Buttigieg. New York: Columbia University Press.

Groopman, J. 2007. *How Doctors Think*. Boston: Houghton Mifflin.

Han, G.-S. 2002. 'The myth of medical pluralism: a critical realist perspective.' *Sociological Research Online*, 6 (4). Available from http://www.socresonline.org.uk/6/4/han.html [Accessed April 14, 2016]

Harvey, D. 2010. *The Enigma of Capital and the Crises of Capitalism*. London: Profile Books.

Hill, M. 2012. 'Re-reviews: *The Political Economy of the Welfare State* by Ian Gough.' *Social Policy and Administration*, 46 (5): 582–587.

Hodgson, G.M. 2003. 'The hidden persuaders: institutions and individuals in economic theory.' *Cambridge Journal of Economics*, 27 (2): 159–175.

Hodgson, G.M. 2004. *The Evolution of Institutional Economics: Agency, Structure and Darwinism in American Institutionalism*. London: Routledge.

Hodgson, G.M. 2008. 'How Veblen generalized Darwinism.' *Journal of Economic Issues*, 42 (2): 399–405.

Hodgson, G.M. 2013. *From Pleasure Machines to Moral Communities: An Evolutionary Economics Without Homo Economicus*. Chicago: University of Chicago Press.

Jackson, W. 2001. 'Age, health and medical expenditure,' *in*: J.B. Davis (ed.), *The Social Economics of Health Care*. London: Routledge.

Jackson, W. 2007. 'On the social structure of markets.' *Cambridge Journal of Economics*, 31 (2): 235–253.

Jessop, B. 2002. *The Future of the Capitalist State*. Cambridge, UK: Polity Press.

Jessop, B. 2012. 'The state,' *in*: B. Fine, A. Saad-Filho, & M. Boffo (eds.), *The Elgar Companion to Marxist Economics*. Cheltenham, UK: Edward Elgar.

Kapp, K.W. 1950. *The Social Costs of Private Enterprise*. Cambridge, MA: Harvard University Press.

Klein, R. 1993. 'O'Goffe's tale, or, what can we learn from the success of the capitalist welfare state?' *in*: C. Jones (ed.), *New Perspectives on the Welfare State in Europe*. London: Routledge, 7–18.

510

Klein, P.A. 1995. 'Instrumental valuation in a democratic society,' in: C.M.A. Clark (ed.), *Institutional Economics and the Theory of Social Value: Essays in Honor of Marc R. Tool*. Norwell, MA: Kluwer.

Lawson, T. 2006. 'The nature of heterodox economics.' *Cambridge Journal of Economics*, 30 (4): 483–505.

Lee, F.S. 2009. *A History of Heterodox Economics: Challenging the Mainstream in the Twentieth Century*. London: Routledge.

Lukes, S. 2005. *Power: A Radical View*, 2nd edn. London: Palgrave Macmillan.

Mandler, M. 1999. *Dilemmas in Economic Theory: Persisting Foundational Problems of Microeconomics*. Oxford: Oxford University Press.

Marx, K. 1970. *A Contribution to the Critique of Political Economy*. Moscow: Progress Publishers.

Navarro, V. 1983. 'Radicalism, Marxism, and medicine.' *International Journal of Health Services*, 13 (2): 179–202.

Navarro, V., Barrell, C., Benach, J., Muntaner, C., Quirog, A., Rodriguez-Sanz, M., Vergés, N., Gumá, J., & Pasarin, M. I. 2003. 'The importance of the political and social in explaining mortality differentials among the countries of the OECD, 1950–1998.' *International Journal of Health Services*, 33 (3): 419–494.

O'Connor, J. [1973] 2002. *The Fiscal Crisis of the State*, updated edn. New Brunswick, NJ: Transaction Publishers.

O'Hara, P.A. 2000. *Marx, Veblen and Contemporary Institutional Political Economy*. Cheltenham, UK: Edward Elgar.

Offe, C. 1984. *Contradictions of the Welfare State*. London: Hutchinson.

Peck, J. & Theodore, N. 2000. "Work first': workfare and the regulation of contingent labour markets.' *Cambridge Journal of Economics*, 24 (1): 119–138.

Samuels, W.J. 1995. 'The instrumentalist value principle and its role,' in: C.M.A. Clark (ed.), *Institutional Economics and the Theory of Social Value: Essays in Honor of Marc R. Tool*. Norwell, MA: Kluwer, 97–112.

Samuels, W.J. 1998. 'The historical quest for principles of valuation,' in: S. Fayazmanesh & M.R. Tool (eds.), *Institutionalist Method and Value: Essays in Honour of Paul Dale Bush*. Cheltenham, UK: Edward Elgar, 112–129.

Sen, A. 2009. *The Idea of Justice*. Cambridge, MA: Belknap Press of Harvard University Press.

Singer, M. 2004. 'The social origins and expressions of illness.' *British Medical Bulletin*, 69 (1): 9–19.

Syme, S.L. 2007. 'The prevention of disease and promotion of health: the need for a new approach.' *European Journal of Public Health*, 17 (4): 329–333.

Tool, M.R. 1993. 'The theory of instrumental value: extensions, clarifications,' in: M.R. Tool (ed.), *Institutional Economics: Theory, Method, Policy*. Dordrecht, NL: Kluwer.

Tool, M.R. 1995. *Pricing, Valuation and Systems: Essays in Neoinstitutional Economics*. Cheltenham, UK: Edward Elgar.

Twomey, P. 1998. 'Reviving Veblenian economic psychology.' *Cambridge Journal of Economics*, 22 (4): 433–448.

Varoufakis, Y. 2015. *The Global Minotaur: America, Europe, and the Future of the Global Economy*. London: Zed Books.

Veblen, T.B. [1899] 1994. *The Theory of the Leisure Class*. London: Penguin.

Veblen, T.B. [1904] 2005. *The Theory of Business Enterprise*. New Brunswick, NJ: Transaction.

Veblen, T.B. [1914] 2000. *The Instinct of Workmanship and the State of the Industrial Arts*. Whitefish, MN: Kessinger Publishing.

Wade, D.T. & Halligan, P.W. 2004. 'Do biomedical models of illness make for good healthcare systems?' *British Medical Journal*, 329 (7479): 1398–1401.

Wisman, J. 2013. 'Wage stagnation, rising inequality and the financial crisis of 2008.' *Cambridge Journal of Economics*, 37 (4): 921–945.

Part VI

Conclusion

37

Heterodox economics as a living body of knowledge

Community, (in)commensurability, critical engagement, and pluralism

Jamie Morgan and John Embery

Introduction

The *Handbook of Heterodox Economics* contains a significant variety of contributions invited and ordered according to a number of themes. One useful way to bring final order to the whole, and by way of conclusion, is to return to the issue of what heterodox economics is, and to emphasize the characteristics that make the varieties of heterodoxy common and valuable. Heterodox economics is important irrespective of innovation within the mainstream. Its collective potential is as a critical community subject to constructive pluralism, and its further characteristics establish it as a living body of knowledge that plays an important role as social science, able to address the most important questions.

Situating heterodox economics

The purpose of the *Handbook of Heterodox Economics* has not been to criticize mainstream economics. To do so would be to shift incrementally and perhaps inadvertently from acknowledging the mainstream as a point of reference to framing heterodox economics in terms of that mainstream. This might take a variety of forms. One might overly focus on, and hence to some degree reproduce, problematic aspects of standard logics and concepts of the mainstream. One might go further and seek to reconcile these, and one might do so in ways that place the greater emphasis on these aspects. The result may then be variations within rather than alternatives to the mainstream. Of course, it is both implicit and explicit to this *Handbook* that an alternative to the mainstream is required, because the mainstream is problematic and hence a subject for reasonable critique. More than this, the mainstream is powerful and wide-ranging enough to assimilate some types of ostensibly different economics, without mainstream economics being fundamentally altered, because it has common underlying characteristics: it has, in Palley's (2013) sense, 'Gattopardo' qualities. Mere eclecticism or methodologically and philosophically naïve approaches are, therefore, unlikely to transcend the problems of the mainstream. One needs something more systematic to both critique the mainstream and offer alternatives to it.

However, one must acknowledge that there is a range of opinion regarding the nature and scope of the mainstream; and also a range of opinion regarding the status of, critical relations between, and prospects for particular aspects of, heterodox economics. Some of this is expressed within the *Handbook*. The terms of debate are important in a variety of ways and these precede this book. Fourcade *et al.* (2015) have highlighted the unusual degree of centralized organization, referencing range, publication focus, and career selection paths within mainstream economics. This sets economics apart from other social sciences because it has resulted in a relative unanimity of purpose, which translates into internal agreement, even if not consciously recognized at all times, regarding what is legitimate economics. There is on this basis great scope for a conservative disciplining of the discipline. Colander and others have explored this over several decades (see, for example, Colander 2008). Colander and others' work emphasizes both the problems of change from within the mainstream, but also the scope for change (for example, Colander *et al.* 2004; also Davis 2006; Thornton 2015). This perspective is not antithetical to difference and diversity; for example, these authors note that there is more diversity in Europe, which economists should work to preserve (Colander 2009). However, this approach differs from those that place heterodox economics at their center.

Other heterodox economists, Frederic Lee, for example, have over many years explored the systematic narrowing of the field of economics that Fourcade has recently brought to the fore from a sociology of knowledge point of view. However, his specific claim has been that the mainstream reproduces itself in ways that are antithetical to heterodox economics (see Lee 2012; Lee *et al.* 2013). Similar points have been made from within political economy, and from within the philosophy, methodology, and history of economic thought.[1] They have been conjoined with critiques of economics' role in contemporary events (for example, Hodgson 2009; Fullbrook 2010; Harcourt 2010; Sawyer 2011; Dow 2012; Boyer 2013; Fine 2013; Fukuda-Parr *et al.* 2013; Lawson 2015); and this stance has been expressed in new general texts (for example, Reardon *et al.* 2015; Van Staveren 2015; see also Birks 2015). This antithetical process of reproduction does not make projects that seek to identify positive trends or changes within mainstream economics irrelevant. It does, however, question the degree to which this can be effective, and whether it is the best way to advance a progressive economics. Not only does it return one to 'Gattopardo' issues, the terms of debate hinge also on the degree to which heterodox economics is more than simply a critique of the mainstream, and hence in some way more than simply parasitical.

With this in mind, the *raison d'être* of the *Handbook of Heterodox Economics* has been to do two things. First, it has been to clearly establish that the resources already exist for substantive alternatives to the current mainstream. There are other schools of economic thought that have been marginalized by the mainstream. The reasons for that marginalization are not a simple matter of the better argument won. Concomitantly, in many respects when the mainstream struggles to innovate it is often seeking to re-invent, create or produce insights that have already been made within existing theory and systems of thought. Second, it has been to establish that heterodox economics is a living body of knowledge. It continues to develop in a contemporary context. As such, it has something to offer both because it is a long-standing set of substantive positions, which offer important fundamental insights, and because heterodoxy writ large creates great scope for further progress in economics (see also Jo & Todorova 2015; Lee & Cronin 2016). Heterodox economics is not reducible to a critique of the mainstream and has a purpose that is important irrespective of the degree of innovation within the current mainstream.

Note that one ought not to conflate the problem of naming or semantics with other issues. The points we want to emphasize are that the different contributions within heterodox economics are important in themselves. It is not impossible that mainstream economics will change in the future in ways that may make it more like some of heterodoxy. The mainstream may even come to embrace heterodox positions. But this does not have to occur for there to be value in heterodox approaches. Moreover, as we have already stated, the current scope of the mainstream makes it unlikely that it will embrace heterodox positions and, though this is a matter of dispute as Colander's work indicates, it seems also unlikely that much of the mainstream will innovate or transform in ways that overcome its current problems.

The issue of semantics is slightly different, we have become used to defining heterodox economics as in opposition. It is conjoined in some binary fashion to the orthodox. There is a semantic sense to this, since *ortho* and *doxa* respectively refer to 'right or correct' and 'belief,' while *hetero* and *doxa* to 'other or different' and 'beliefs.' It seems then that an orthodoxy is required for heterodoxy to be named as such. In a logical sense then, changes to the nature of the mainstream may render curious the current semantic fit of positions named as heterodoxy (heterodox as a term may become semantically incongruous). However, language is malleable and if we extend the meaning frame of heterodoxy to represent what it actually is: 'many beliefs,' it requires no positioning in regard to some orthodoxy in order to be meaningful. Many subsequent strategies of naming are possible here; for example, some try to reclaim the term mainstream (see Arestis & Sawyer 2011). Putting aside issues of meaning and naming, the important points remain that heterodox economics is not reducible to a critique of the mainstream and has purpose that is important irrespective of the degree of innovation within the current mainstream.

The combination of points then leads to two initial questions: What is heterodox economics in relation to different schools of thought and theory? And, on what basis is there any commonality between these heterodox positions?

The meaning of heterodox economics: an initial minimalism

So, the purpose of the *Handbook*, implicit both in the substance of particular contributions and the *range* of those contributions, has been to provide in one place a resource, which demarcates heterodox economics from the mainstream and establishes (or confirms) heterodox economics as an alternative to it.[2] If one has read through the *Handbook* in order to get here, it should be clear that the initial definition of heterodoxy is necessarily minimalistic. In his *A History of Heterodox Economics*, Lee states that heterodox economics:

> refers to specific economic theories and a community of economists that are in various ways an alternative to neoclassical economics. Consequently, it is a multi-level term that refers to a group of economic theories—specifically Post Keynesian-Sraffian, Marxist-radical, Institutional-evolutionary, social, feminist, Austrian, and ecological economics [and] to a community of *heterodox economists* who engage with and are associated with one or more of the heterodox approaches and embrace a pluralistic attitude towards them without rejecting contestability and incommensurability among the theories.
>
> *Lee 2009: 6–7, original italics*

In theoretical terms, then, Lee's definition provides no more than a point of departure. It necessarily allows for different issues of emphasis and conceptual beginnings. Lee and others prefer to start from social provisioning (see for example, Jo 2011; also Morgan 2015a: 535–536). However, different schools of thought and different theories have different foci: the nature of an economic surplus, the problem of instability in a system, issues of exploitation and nurture (of the human and of nature), a resistance to subjectivity (in the special sense acquired in economics in regard of marginalism, rather than the general social theory sense that there are constructed subjects), and so forth.

As a definition of difference, heterodoxy takes as its point of reference the mainstream, though here there is also some disagreement regarding what exactly is the mainstream and how it should be named, that is, neoclassical or otherwise (see Morgan 2015b). However, as a definition of difference, the issue of belonging begs the question of what it means to belong. If heterodoxy was simply a definition whose point of reference was an acknowledgment that one was *not* mainstream (neoclassical or otherwise named), then in a certain sense there would be no heterodoxy, merely multiplicity beyond the mainstream. This is particularly so when one notes the different foci of different schools involve also different avenues of investigation, such as care, justice, full employment, financial stability, growth, limits to growth, or class emancipation. There are many excellent histories that have been written of theories and schools and ongoing developments of the same that place little emphasis on the position of that theory or school within heterodoxy (for example, Harcourt 1972; King 2002; Folbre 2009; Wray 2015). Equally there are many that place developments in broader frames of one kind or another (for example, Dow 1996; Davis 2003, 2011; Milonakis & Fine 2009; Stilwell 2011; Martins 2014; Keen 2015).

Relatedly, one must note that some within the schools of thought encompassed by the term do not identify as heterodox. They are content to self-identify as institutional, Post Keynesian, Marxian, feminist, and so forth (see Ranson 2007). However, one might equally note that many mainstream economists do not recognize or self-identify as mainstream (or neoclassical, see Arnsperger & Varoufakis 2006). In neither case does the relevance of the term fully reduce to acceptance as interpellation or common usage. At the same time, recognition is not irrelevant. It is here that the further aspects of Lee's initial definition become important, that is, community, (in)commensurability, critical engagement, and pluralism. Some reflection on their status and role provides grounds for what it means to meaningfully differentiate heterodox economics from the mainstream, and then provides the basis of a justification for heterodox economics as a living body of knowledge.

Heterodoxy as community, (in)commensurability, critical engagement, and pluralism

Consider first, it may be that a non-mainstream economist has not actually rejected a meaningful recognition of heterodoxy. Rather, she has simply never had occasion to engage with and reflect upon its general relevance, or she has never had occasion to use the term. She might then, given a suitable context of argument and/or further reflection, be minded or persuaded of the salience and suitability of the term. Furthermore, it may be that she rejects the term, but is rejecting something of a straw person. She may perhaps accept that there is a common cause expressed as opposition to the mainstream, but little sense of recognized commonality of approach, purpose, or content (in some sense). Embracing heterodoxy might then be perceived as conceding too much to other schools of thought, creating an onerous constraint that prevents the proper development of one's own work and the proper critique of others. Heterodoxy would then be reduced to a 'flag of convenience' that could be potentially inconvenient: the enemy of my enemy is my friend, interpreted as a somewhat superficial understanding of a common cause of some limited strategic value (strength in numbers or solidarity based on antipathy).

However, consider what this minimalism might imply: a disaggregated multiplicity where there is no substantive (rather than strategic) value in mutual recognition. A multiplicity where there is no possibility of meaningful mutual critique, and hence no potential value in that critique (in terms of different standpoints and perspectives) of and by members of other schools of thought. This would be to neglect the possibility that each provides others with insights, or the possibility that the confluence of several critiques could result ultimately in transcending the limits of one, both, or all positions that are so engaged. In turn, this would tend to close down (practically speaking) taking fallibility seriously at the broadest level of interaction (theories, schools, and so forth). It undercuts a potentially important resource for dialectics of learning and hence for progress in knowledge. By broadening one's horizons one opens up the possibility of commensuration between positions, as well as recognizing important problems emergent from *discovering* incommensurability. All of which is to say no more than that there are good reasons to recognize a broader critical community. One might then argue that, appropriately considered, heterodoxy (as a critical community) is not an onerous constraint, but rather an opportunity to be embraced. Understood in this way heterodoxy becomes productively oriented by its values, and so is more than of merely limited strategic value (strength in numbers, for instance). Concomitantly, its core value orientation becomes (and necessarily so) pluralism, a pluralism shaped by a commitment to constructive critique (see Dow 2004; Dobusch & Kapeller 2012). That is, pluralism as more than mere disinterested tolerance.

If we return, then, to Lee's initial definition of heterodox economics, recognition of schools and theories as a minimalist point of departure becomes more than just recognition. It becomes so because of the potentials of community, (in)commensurability, critique, *and* pluralism.[3] Moreover, the conjoining of these can be more than mere arrogation as juxtaposition (liable to dissolution). The latter (community, etc.) may inform the former (recognition). In a certain sense this is optimism, insofar as for heterodoxy to mean anything it must demonstrate and so *construct* its community relations. At the same time, optimism is more than mere hope (in the ephemeral sense of hoping against hope). This is so if one goes further and considers the grounds of, and for, optimism.

Commonality as real world relevant

If practice and conduct give meaning to a normative core of heterodoxy, it still remains the case that for such a community to be operative, in any significant sense, it must collectively produce adequate knowledge. The collective of schools, theories, and any developments of and from them must be in some sense similarly oriented, and in some justifiable and so appropriate way. For collective difference to be relevant to a world in which knowledge can be wrong or limited in some way then the world must exceed each position. What is meant by collective or similar is then both a central and problematic issue.

Consider again the claim that heterodox economics is not reducible to a critique of the mainstream, and has purpose irrespective of the degree of innovation within the mainstream. For heterodox economics to be more than a critique of the mainstream and for the term heterodox to have collective significance, then the question, *on what basis is there any commonality between heterodox positions*, seems to entail, and so must be answerable in a way, which goes beyond the otherwise important components of community, (in)commensurability, critique, and pluralism. It must have some basis in terms of defensible as adequate investigation of the world that is sufficiently common to each as investigations of (socio-political) economies. Without this then it seems problematic to argue that heterodox economics could actually *sustain* any viable sense of community. Moreover, it would be difficult to *justify* the claim that heterodox economics provides an alternative to the mainstream—the alternative begs the question of whether as an alternative it is both defensible and worthy of defense. In two senses, therefore, heterodox economics calls forth fundamental issues in regard of commonalities.

One might be tempted at this point to state the issue of commonalities arises and is to be recognized, and articulated, *despite* differences between schools of thought (a minimal minimalism tending to multiplicity as heterodoxy). However, it might equally follow *because of* the nature and significance of such differences. Here, another important aspect of the purpose of the *Handbook of Heterodox Economics* becomes relevant. The stated purposes of the *Handbook* include to establish that resources already exist for there to be substantive alternatives to the mainstream, and also to establish that heterodox economics is a living body of knowledge, which continues to develop in a contemporary context. As a corollary, the intent has also been to reclaim economics as a social science. The intent is premised on long-standing contrasts between different elements of heterodox economics and the mainstream, and also specific critique of the mainstream in its parts and particulars as *anti-social* science. Anti-social has been variously inflected as:

1. Problems of theory: its introverted technical focus, use of idealized assumptions, and subsequent tendency to innovate through deviations from core problematic elements, rather than through more basic repudiation of them. That is, scientism as non-science (see, for example, Fullbrook 2013).
2. Problems of method: tendency to default to (and innovate within) a narrow range of methods one is already familiar with, rather than to experiment with many and multiple methods, which may be more appropriate to the specific object of inquiry (see for example, Dow 2012: Chs. 7 & 8; however, see Starr 2014).
3. Problems of actions within the world: tendency to construct practical schematics as theoretical objects with real-world applications and then to eschew responsibility for their adverse consequences (such as financial instruments), and more broadly, a tendency to construct idealized model worlds, where one anticipates the real world can become a second best version of such theory; tendency to constantly expand the domain of relevance of an economic analysis (an imperialism that substitutes for appropriate interdisciplinarity; for example, Fine & Milonakis 2009); and tendency to eschew responsibility for policy that is positional and divisive in its consequences. That is, a persistent potential to slide from objectivity to amorality to the unethical (see, for example, DeMartino 2013; Davis & Hands 2013).

Though inflected, there are many ways the critique has been put together to emphasize different elements and generalities at the level of theory, method, and policy; for example, a technical apparatus, a set of fundamental commitments etc. However, the significant point here is that to reclaim economics as a social science is contrastive in terms of its form of referential relation to at least a significant part of the mainstream.[4] In order to be contrastive, it involves the basic claim that *particular* heterodox approaches are different from the mainstream in some fundamental way. That is, each is more than simply critique. At the same time, the point of contrast is relatively stable: the mainstream is like x and we are like y, y is non-x in its orientation. The contrast emphasizes some element of investigation as *pro-social social science*. In each case, something about the nature of inquiry allows for (though by no means guarantees) more constructive contexts for theory, method, and actions within the world. So, to be heterodox seems to imply that each *shares* some features, which are different from the mainstream in their differences. This way of thinking immediately invokes the work of Tony Lawson, and particularly his 'The Nature of Heterodox Economics' essay (see Lawson 2015).[5] This brings us to matters of philosophy and methodology as a component of heterodox economics.

The development of critique: methodology and philosophy as integral to heterodox economics

A key feature of heterodox approaches has been the development of critique; essentially a continuous methodological awareness and interplay between philosophically posed inquiry, theory building, and applications. This is quite different than much of the mainstream that has been more technically focused, where technical means narrow in terms of formalism, model building, and appropriation of experimental forms, and hence creating an abnormal version of normal science in the Kuhnian sense.[6] The development of critique has various aspects. It is intrinsic to particular positions. For example, classical-Keynesian economics began from a critique of Say's law and also of the problematic approach of Pigou and others to employment within a system. Keynes' original work was both profoundly methodological in its critique, but also contextualized by contemporary problems and concerns. It sought to bring the two together. Post Keynesian economics continues in the same way, and this bleeds into a variety of competing accounts of, for example, the nature of money, finance, and broader issues of distribution and stability. The focus is on the changing or shifting aspects of an object of concern, that is, its processes through conventions in a context of fundamental uncertainty. The whole is thus historically sensitive as socio-economically sensitive (the past weighs on the present and conditions but does not determine the future). Thereafter, the actual history and experience of Keynesian economics has also encouraged a positional argument of a historical variety, *and* the struggle to survive within economics has motivated a continuous concern to remind the world of the significance of a Keynesian tradition. As such, the history of economic thought has also become important as a component *within* Post Keynesianism (see King 2002; Cohen & Harcourt 2003; Dow 2012).

So, there are a set of characteristics here: a critical orientation that is methodologically aware and draws on philosophical resources, a contextualized drive to be real world relevant (that shifts back and forth with critique), a focus on processes in one sense or another, a sense of the historical nature of processes, and a continuous engagement with the history of economic thought, in order to promote a position and combat 'forgetting.' In a conscious sense, Post Keynesians advocate a theory that is historical, while they also promote a discourse in which they resist their theory becoming history (it is contemporarily oriented as a body of active research and historically sensitive as a body of constructed tradition). This is quite a different framing of knowledge to the stripped-down approach of much of the mainstream, which attempts to simulate the natural and biological sciences.

The important point is that one can find this combination of characteristics in *all* of the older schools of thought claimed by heterodoxy (for example, Hodgson 2001; Mayhew 2001). Moreover, one can find it (as a form of good practice) in the way each relates to the other, even as they disagree. There seems far less of a tendency to hermetic isolation within the different heterodox positions (see, for example, Pivetti (2015) on Keynes and Marx). If we refer back to the earlier point that heterodoxy involves constructed community relations, then it is significant that positions do in fact take the time to disagree. There is mutual awareness and interaction, though one must acknowledge that this does not always manifest in citations. Moreover, interaction is more than simply a periodic stocktaking of no great significance for dialectics of learning. It may involve attempts to construct significant identifiable features of particular positions (for example, O'Hara (2012) on political economy). More broadly, it may involve categorization as critique—that is, identifying limits and questioning some forms of relations as conflations or problems (for example, Mearman 2012; Chester & Schroeder 2015). What examples tend to illustrate is that critique and the pursuit of methodological qua philosophical issues is *intrinsic* to heterodox activity. There is far more of a division of labor within mainstream economics—a division that has delegated philosophy, methodology, and history to sub-disciplines with which the majority do not engage (and which some do not even consider to be 'economics'). Beyond fairly standardized survey essays in *Journal of Economic Literature*, *Journal of Economic Perspectives*, and *Journal of Economic Surveys* there is no real equivalent of this integrated activity within much of the mainstream. Sociologically speaking it remains disaggregated into parts, but also in an often non-reflexive way, collectively unitary (as Fourcade's research shows). Scholars such as Colander or McCloskey are notable precisely because they resist easy categorization.

It is also worth noting here that the combination of characteristics of heterodox positions has led periodically to greater interest in heterodox work at times when current mainstream economics has been found wanting. For example, the global financial crisis led quickly to both a repudiation of the efficient market hypothesis and a general set of claims from elite decision-makers(within the International Monetary Fund, Organization for Economic Co-operation and Development, World Bank, and major state central banks and treasuries) that fundamental changes were required, and significant and neglected insights seemed to exist within the work of Marx, Keynes, Minsky, and others. This was transmitted also through such outlets as the *Financial Times* and the *Economist* magazine. However, it was short-lived, and quickly restricted in its scope, claims, and consequences. It tended also to neglect the contemporary work of those who had come after these economic thinkers, developing such issues as the asymmetric structures of modern globalized capitalism and financialization, such as Steve Keen, Thomas Palley, Luigi Pasinetti, and many others (however, for the student context see Morgan 2014, 2015a). One might argue here that heterodox approaches become more attractive at problematic moments not simply because they are non-mainstream, but rather because of *the way in which* they are non-mainstream—that is, their core characteristics. It may be the case that the media seeks novelty in response to crisis, but the potential appeal of heterodox approaches stems from the development of knowledge in a context of critique that is process focused.

It is a focus on processes that requires heterodox approaches to be real world relevant (in a historically aware context). So, the very approach to economies lends them continual relevance. They are change sensitive and so sensitive to the underlying causes of change, and the general trajectories of the same, both of which the mainstream has demonstrated over and again that it can distort or neglect. Most importantly, the concept of change is not simply one of deviations from a given position to which the whole then reverts (an equilibrium, a normal, etc.). Change is a complex cumulative matter; things can be and do become otherwise in significant ways. Relevance and change sensitivity was also demonstrated by the recent sudden interest in wealth and income inequality. The interest was partly provoked by Piketty's work, but more broadly revealed that proponents of heterodox schools and theories have been exploring the issue for over a decade—for example, James Galbraith, Engelbert Stockhammer, and many others. Mainstream theory has typically assumed away or marginalized (no pun intended) issues of inequality, creating a very clear (and perhaps ideologically useful) divergence between theory concerns and observed reality. Piketty's work has sought to bridge that gap (though has also been critiqued for some of his use of problematic mainstream concepts, see Morgan 2015c; Pressman 2015).

What we want to suggest here is that the development of critique and its characteristics is one way to think about a family resemblance, which makes heterodox economics more than simply multiplicity. There are general aspects of each that are intrinsic (though perhaps not always pursued, or always fully expressed). Moreover, the whole actively encourages changes in knowledge forms as the world changes or critique identifies spaces in current concerns, and this is one reason why one can make the case that heterodox economics is a living body of knowledge, rather than simply the iteration of a few long-standing ideas within hidebound traditions. The old is renewed and new concerns emerge as more than mere novelty. Heterodox approaches are responsive as real world relevant. One need only think of the emergence of gender economics (see, for example, Nelson 1996; May 2002; Barker & Kuiper 2003) or ecological economics (for example, Spash 2013). Furthermore, it is through the construction of community relations within heterodox economics that many potentially difficult issues are confronted, such as the ecological challenge for Post Keynesian approaches (see Holt *et al.* 2009).

Claims regarding what is integral to heterodox economics in general create one way in which one might construct the positive case for heterodox economics as a community. At the same time, what it means for heterodox economics to be critical—to be methodologically aware and in interplay with philosophically posed questions in relation to real world relevance and theory building—is not unproblematic. What is actually shared and to what degree is a contested issue.

Important distinctions: real world relevance, social ontology, and realism

One might argue that claims of commonality lend themselves to controversy precisely because heterodox economics is methodologically aware and draws on philosophical resources, and because it encourages work in the history of economic thought—all as *integral to* rather than *additional for* an economic investigation. It is one thing to suggest that heterodox approaches tend to be concerned with critique and contemporary context. However, it is another to suggest they share matters of philosophy, methodology, theory, and policy prescriptions in anything other than the most general sense. Here, it is important to make a series of distinctions, which ultimately strengthen the standing of heterodox economics.

Insofar as different schools of thought and new approaches are critically founded, each has its own particular tradition of methodological critique and sets of philosophically posed issues that have also influenced the way in which real world relevance has been pursued. For example, Marx on vulgar political economy, his various critiques of the limits of contemporary philosophy and its ideational and reproductive effects, his work on dialectics, and his advocacy of historical materialism as a distinct approach. Clearly, there is a particularity to Marx's concerns, when compared to others, such as Keynes. This in turn raises a problem regarding generality in a heterodox context, one that may equally apply to other schools. Insofar as each can be viewed in this particularistic way, in what sense can any additional set of methodological claims or philosophical inquiries add anything to the approach?

Though not new, this issue of more generalized methodological and philosophical analysis of and across schools and theories has gained new significance over the last two decades. It has done so over the period in which the movement to articulate and build a more collective sense of heterodox economics has occurred. The most prominent source of methodological and philosophical analysis has derived from the social ontology movement centered on Cambridge, UK, and most closely associated with the work of Tony Lawson (1997, 2003, 2015). The articulation of heterodox economics and the development of social ontology are also associated, though one is not reducible to the other. One of the key contributions of social ontology has been to change the context in which issues of methodology and philosophy are considered within economics (see Fullbrook 2009; Pratten 2015), and within a broader social science context (see C. Lawson *et al.* 2007). Previously, general methodological and philosophical analysis had been dominated by quite narrow concerns drawing on philosophy of science, such as the status of laws, tests, verification, confirmation, falsification, normal science, the hard core of research programs, and so forth; based on the work of Hempel, Popper, Kuhn, Lakatos, Feyerabend, and others. While these provided important sources for the exploration of mainstream economics and its tendencies and limits (most notably by Blaug 1992; Hausman 1992; Caldwell 1994), because of the focus of the work, these did not provide adequate accounts of what was constructively different about non-mainstream approaches nor (by contrast) what remained problematically similar as things changed in mainstream approaches.

The contrast required a rather different framing of the issues. That is, one that began from what the different approaches were required to assume (implicitly or explicitly) about the nature of the aspect of reality under investigation in order for the construction of theory (and the building of schools) to proceed in the way it had. One could then consider the mismatch between basic commitments and the otherwise recognized characteristics of the aspect of reality under investigation, leading to a critical questioning regarding knowledge justification, explanatory success, and so forth (including via what it meant to focus on laws, tests, and the like, and allowing for problems regarding what may appear empiricist in such statements as 'recognized characteristics of aspects of reality'). This is the basis of ontology as philosophical inquiry. As critique, it begins from the claim that all forms of knowledge have some form of underlying ontology, and it is important to clarify what that is and whether it may be problematic.

As such, the initial context of social ontology emphasized its 'underlaboring' role. Social ontology was not positioned as a new approach to economics *per se*, nor was it positioned as a replacement for particular schools, theories, and so forth (nor could it be, given each could also articulate a basic ontology; see for example, Hodgson 2004). Rather it was conceived as an invitation to consider the consistency, coherency, similarities, and differences within and across schools and theories. It was, in this sense, a renewal or re-energizing of the methodological and philosophical concerns intrinsic to the different heterodox positions, rather than a rejection or refutation of them. From this ontological point of view, to suggest, therefore, that different schools of thought and theories share matters of philosophy and methodology in the most general sense is important rather than irrelevant. The relevant claim is that social ontology as under-laboring has provided an important resource for the articulation of heterodox economics as more than minimalistic multiplicity, and has provided a medium for community building. Ontology opens up many ways to consider and explore schools and theories, leading to possibilities of re-description, translation, and reconciliation of common concepts, as well as a tighter focus on accounting for explanatory adequacy, use of methods, and so forth.

The corollary claim is that social ontology can then be deployed within schools and theories as well as between—and so provides one (not the only) potential resource through which each can develop—including in terms of a focus on what it means to be real world relevant. Considered in this way social ontology does not create an immediate dichotomy, where the particulars of schools and theories and the internal tradition of development of critique—methodologically and philosophically situated—are opposed to generality. Rather, the general provides a domain of argument in regard of which constructive questions can be posed both within and beyond schools and theories. The general (via ontology) is a potential contribution to what is *intrinsic* or integral to heterodox approaches as critical. At the same time, insofar as it is potential, the degree to which a constructive contribution has been made depends in large part on the demonstrated productive consequences of actual social ontological investigation. This is, necessarily, both a matter of contingency and perspective, and so an open and hence disputable issue.

However, it is worth considering what dispute has occurred and what that dispute also implies. There has been a general acknowledgment within and across schools that each is focused in some sense on processes in relation to the economy; and there has been general acknowledgment that heterodox approaches are, in relation to a process approach, committed to 'open systems' as a basic concept, and that this is legitimately expressible as a matter of ontology (see Dow 2012; Morgan 2015b). On this basis, there has been a generally positive reception of social ontology within heterodox economics. Thereafter, there remains considerable disagreement regarding the nature of open systems, the degree of emphasis one places on ontology, and the degree to which different methods are compatible with basic ontological claims (see, for example, Fleetwood 1999; Brown & Fleetwood 2002; Downward 2003; Lewis 2004; Chick & Dow 2005; Fullbrook 2009).[7] This, however, might best be viewed as an important consequence of what social ontology is intended to do. It has contributed to dialogue and debate and has done so through a re-energized set of philosophical and methodological concerns. It has thus contributed to critical development within and for heterodox economics as both a source of agreement and disagreement.[8]

Several distinctions made by proponents of social ontology are relevant. Social ontology encourages economists to focus on real world relevance and adequate explanation of the world. However, what is real and what is adequate explanation (and understanding) are not reducible to a particular position based on social ontology. There is a difference between social ontology as a domain of argument (deriving varieties of philosophical ontology) and more substantive claims regarding the ontological aspects of a general or particular entity, object, phenomenon, and the like (what proponents refer to as 'scientific ontology').

'Realism' is a branch of philosophy and social theory and so should not be confused with social ontology as a general domain of argument or necessarily with the adequacy of claims about what is real. The real world may well be more adequately accounted for by differently posed positions in philosophy and social theory—this is an open issue; one that can only be explored in terms of the positions and potentials. As such, social ontology by its very orientation to critical engagement opens up spaces. This includes reaffirmation of existing approaches and interschool critique (for example, the relative positioning of Marx and Sraffa, and various combinations, such as the work of Pierangelo Garegnani). But it also opens up spaces within economics for consideration of social construction, actor network theory, systems analysis, post-structuralism, postmodernism, and so forth. It creates spaces for work that particular proponents of social ontology may actually be opposed to—that of Peter Berger & Thomas Luckmann, Pierre Bourdieu, Mario Bunge, Judith Butler, Giles Deleuze, Jacques Derrida, Michel Foucault, Jürgen Habermas, Bruno Latour & Steve Woolgar, Niklas Luhmann, John Searle, Slavoj Žižek, and many others.[9] It has, in this sense (and along with gender economics, ecological economics, and others), created greater scope for economics to become more effectively interdisciplinary in a contemporary context. This too is important because it speaks to the general sense of heterodox economics as an open set of inquiry and as a living body of knowledge.

We have suggested that heterodox economics recognizes a multiplicity of schools of thought and theories, that these are significant and important irrespective of innovation within the mainstream, although they are also in some respects referenced in terms of and contrasted with the mainstream. Insofar as these schools are different they involve also similarities of difference—that is, a critical development with integral roles for methodology and philosophically posed questions, as well as a derived sense of tradition via the history of economic thought. This, arguably, forms the basis of community and of pluralism, which take heterodoxy beyond a minimalism as multiplicity, though community must be built and pluralism demonstrated rather than merely asserted. Finally, the development of social ontology as a critical endeavor has provided an important means via which heterodox economics has been articulated over the last two decades. That articulation has included a common recognition of the importance of process or open systems within heterodox approaches, but also has extended to dispute and disagreement (which may also be considered a significant contribution given the claimed defining features of heterodoxy).

These general points help to situate what the *Handbook* has intended to achieve. What it has actually achieved can also be demonstrated by brief reference to some of the chapters and what they illustrate, based on the points we have made.

The *Handbook* as a demonstration of the best of heterodox economics

In her chapter in this volume, 'Heterodox economics and theories of interactive agency,' Mary Wrenn focuses on a particular concept within economics. Her initial point of reference is the mainstream concept of the agent. That is, the rationally calculative individual optimizer (a construct that cannot exist, and when used as a point of departure for more sophisticated versions of the agent—sub-optimal, partly rational, subject to rules, etc.—remains problematic because of the point of departure and the problems of reconciling methodological individualism). However, her substantive argument does not concern this agent instead she briefly references it as a point of contrast with heterodox concepts. The contrast is with a demonstrably more realistic concept of the agent.

Wrenn's argument is that heterodox schools (original institutional economics, Marxian economics, Post Keynesianism), despite their different foci and emphases, share a common conception of the interactive agent; specifically, an agent who is analytically distinguishable from a set of structural relations and institutions. The agent is born into a set of structures and is socialized through them. Structures are more than constraints since the nature of the agent is, in part, created by the ongoing activity that occurs within ensembles of structures (they are significant for the cognitive configurations or mental models of the agent, and these in turn help to shape the further configuration of structures and institutions as particular decisions are made—there is a process ontology).

This competent, creative person is not reducible to either unchanging inner determining regular calculative compulsion (a mainstream agent) or to external forces of social determination. She is socially situated, interactive and interdependent, but also causally significant within a complex of causes that together make the social world, including the economy, we live in. According to Wrenn, this concept of the agent is basic to the original institutionalism's concept of the evolutionary agent (and Hodgson in particular has explored this based on the work of Veblen and other institutionalists). It is basic to Marx's development of the agent-structure relation, where class identity within capitalism provides a primary socialization of agency, but one that is not reductive (insofar as this would make it impossible for agents to comprehend their structural position and to challenge it). It is also basic to the Post Keynesian rationale of the role of conventions and fundamental uncertainty; agents develop and fall back on conventions as responses to the potential for uncertainty, but then may also continue to use them even as the socio-economic contexts in which they have been developed change. At the same time, agents are both creatures of habit and impulse, but also active learners (and so, in total, for a Post Keynesian, socio-economic situations involve non-syncopated complex processes that can be profoundly non-ergodic).

In reading Wrenn's contribution one might at first sight think of it as no more than the exploration of a given concept. In this context, it has interest and importance insofar as it clearly distinguishes a heterodox usage from a mainstream position. But let us consider what it also demonstrates. It immediately demonstrates that the development of critique is integral to a heterodox approach to economic inquiry. The approach is based on a continuous methodological awareness and interplay between philosophically posed inquiry, theory building, and applications. This is not immediately clear until one considers what role agency plays in economic theory. Concepts become important points of departure for further theorizations and applications. They become part of what is assumed (or subsumed for purposes and applications). For much of the mainstream the assumed (conceived) economic agent is an idealization (an entity that cannot exist, but serves some heuristic purpose, possibly in relation to simplifications for tractability). In contrast, the heterodox agent may be one that is abstracted (isolated from other processes for the purposes of investigation in a context), but is one that has been constructed with a focus on what is realistic (a different issue than realism *per se* in terms of a position in ontology).

So, Wrenn's contribution also indicates something fundamental about the status of heterodox economic inquiry, and the basis of heterodox economic investigation as theorizations. While mainstream economics often struggles to reconcile its points of departure with more realistic accounts of those entities within theorizations (precisely because of the point of departure, which has not been relinquished merely modified), heterodox economics has far greater potential for consistency qua realistic points of departure. Heterodox approaches are distinct from mainstream approaches, and when mainstream approaches seek to innovate beyond initial restrictive assumptions, they are actually seeking to recover (such as in the case of the agent) what already has been incorporated within heterodox approaches. Moreover, those heterodox approaches, though by no means perfect or lacking in grounds for a critique of positions and of the consistency of theory, can at least claim that they are far less constrained by their initial point of departure in terms of the capacity to develop adequate concepts for further theory. As such, Wrenn's contribution also illustrates that heterodox approaches are distinct from much of the mainstream (substantively and sociologically), and can be justified or defended irrespective of developments within that mainstream. *Inter alia* her contribution demonstrates that heterodox economists have a strong sense of a critical community as a point of reference for the development of more adequate economics. Her work is a form of constructive (structured) pluralism based on the valuing of (and hence normative commitment to) broader community relations.

Of course, Wrenn's contribution, though manifestly about real world relevance (at the level of social theory as economics) is neither theory nor application in quite the way most economists expect economic theory and application to look. One might argue that it is important (as is a great deal of current work in heterodoxy as social theory and social ontology) because it is helping to change how we think about what is legitimate as economic argument, theory, and application.[10] At the same time, based on common expectations one can shift to other contributions to the *Handbook*. For example, Nuno Martins's chapter in this volume (Chapter 3, 'The social surplus approach: Historical origins and present state') demonstrates how current heterodox theory can be deeply rooted in and referenced to the history of economic thought, while also being profoundly concerned with specific contemporary problems.

Drawing on his (2014) *The Cambridge Revival of Political Economy* (see also Morgan 2016) Martins clearly sets out how a focus on the social surplus has developed over time, and involves fundamental issues for the nature of society and economic processes. For example, the Cambridge Capital Controversies were more than simply technical issues regarding the construction of production functions and so forth.[11] They provided a basic insight into the problem of capital and social reproduction in relation to distribution. For a Sraffian, distribution cannot be a matter of marginal productivities (which cannot be defined independently), but is an institutional issue, and so includes matters of power and politics. Distribution then implies quite different trajectories of socio-economic change (processes), which can be explored in terms of the quantitative aspects of qualitatively constructed contexts (multipliers, employment, growth, and so forth). However, as qualitative contexts one must consider the deep issues of the normative dynamics of economic activity: how is capitalism currently operating and what grounds exist for different institutional frameworks—extending to issues that the mainstream struggles with, such as ethics and capabilities (as well-being). Within heterodox economics these are not additional issues (to be considered after an economic problem has been defined economically, and so difficult to reconcile to an economic approach or 'economic thinking'), but are rather basic issues for an appropriately integrated understanding of economics (and here one might also consider Ajit Sinha's or Wesley Marshall's respective contributions on value and the financial system to the *Handbook*). It is for this reason that many heterodox economists take as their primary context the issue of social provisioning, irrespective of whether they consider themselves to be proponents of a particular position.

One might argue, then, based on the many *Handbook* contributions, that the problem of well-being and distribution calls forth more innovative and multiple theoretically referenced work.

That is, heterodox economics motivates progress in response to critique and a changing world through process—it is by inclination a living body of knowledge. For example, one can imagine amalgams of gender economics, ecological economics, Post Keynesian economics, and so forth without one thinking of this as mere eclecticism. An amalgam can be more than this because we live in one world, which is simultaneously a place of gendered agency, gendered distributions, ecological harms, and more. Though these may be analytically distinguishable, they are in many ways part of the same totality—that is, expansive capitalist society. The very nature of capitalism as a system in process seems to call forth historically sensitive theorization.

For example, in Chapter 24 in this volume, Fernández & Brondino explore the transitions in capitalism from the Fordist accumulation more typical of the period until the 1970s. They emphasize the way capitalism involves processes that combine inter-state and inter-capitalist competition. The two interact within a system whose characteristics emerge and evolve based on the positioning of states and corporations, and the attendant issues of class struggle, instantiated in particular institutional arrangements for labor. Tensions within the system call forth 'spatial fixes' (the extension of new spaces as sites for capital accumulation) that can alleviate but never resolve distributive conflicts. Fernández & Brondino bring together World Systems Theory, the work of Arrighi and of Harvey, in order to provide an account of underlying mechanisms, which no current mainstream economics approach could readily replicate—that is, the role of a state system, the role of specific states in that system, and the geographical extension and reconstitution of the corporation. This enables the exploration of economics as also a set of political processes within a purposive critique. That critique also extends to an account of the current work on global value chains, which, it is argued, lacks an appropriate framework to understand or explain the actual activity of corporations. Fernández & Brondino's work is real world relevant, multiple referenced within theory without being merely eclectic, and is both constructively pluralistic and interdisciplinary.

The reconstitution of the corporation and its significance for labor is a central issue within contemporary capitalism. One can explore this at the broadest possible level of a global system, but one can also productively focus on specific mechanisms and consequences. For example, in Chapter 34 in this volume Brennan explores the positioning of the modern corporation. His approach is one that seeks to explore specific mechanisms resulting in inequality, drawing on available data. However, in order to make sense of that data, he begins from Veblen's concept of capital as an immaterial legal right of control (a claim on an income stream), and differentiates industry (as production) and business (as commercial control). He does so in order to provide a way to think of the operative aspects of power occurring in processes, which he can then apply to corporations of the United States (US) and their contemporary consequences.

According to Brennan, in the twenty-first century the 100 largest US corporations account for approximately 20 percent of total assets by value. Moreover, corporations have, beginning in the late twentieth century, grown by merger and acquisition more than by organic growth related to investment in new productive capacity. That is, the transfer of ownership and thus *claims* on wealth rather than the *creation* of wealth. So, institutional power has been constructed and concentrated via this medium, and this in turn has been associated with further changes in practices within the largest corporations, including rapid increases in executive remuneration and the diversion of income into stock repurchase to maintain and augment equity prices. This has resulted in shareholder value effects, and also share-option benefits for executives, but at the expense of real total investment. The further result has been slower overall growth, as well as a reduced labor share, enabled by reduced legal rights for unions. So, over time the economy has been cumulatively shaped in ways that favor a minority (of corporations and of the populous). Historical processes have responded to and augmented power.

Brennan's work provides an excellent addition to many other accounts of the same contemporary issue—how we account for and explain ongoing processes of income and wealth inequality (notably from James Galbraith, Thomas Palley, and William Lazonick). It clearly illustrates how a heterodox approach encourages creative exploration of a problem and so a creative approach to understanding data. Brennan is interested in evidence rather than simply collecting and 'testing' data in some narrowly purposed analytical statistical model.

If one reads through from Wrenn to Martins to Fernández & Brondino and then to Brennan, it becomes clear that the combination illustrates a further characteristic of heterodox economics. Heterodox economics does not marginalize, or put aside ultimate concerns, something that a mainstream approach beginning from definitions based on the allocative problem tends to do. The positive-normative divide does not create an artificially imposed impediment within heterodoxy. Wrenn and the others illustrate an identifiable theme of ultimate concerns: social theory as a real world concern, the history of economic thought as theory development for real world concerns, and empirical exploration of real world problems as matters of urgent concern. As a final point, one might argue that a focus on processes within heterodox economics is not just a commonality expressed methodologically or philosophically, it imbues heterodox economics with, in many different ways, moral purpose.

One cannot claim that mainstream economics simply ignores ultimate concerns, but anyone familiar with welfare economics, game theory applications of rule-based activity (as ethical simulations), or the experiments of behavioral economics regarding decision situations (loss aversion, altruism as self-interest etc.) will recognize that they are very differently situated for mainstream economics. In much of the mainstream there is no systematic sense of responsibility for the social and economic system we live in, nor is there any sense that economics is founded on basic questions regarding how we want to live, and that this is a communal challenge, subject to collective deliberation (even if one chooses to be more individualized, since a society of maximally free individuals is still a society and requires construction). One might argue that this focus on ultimate concerns is basic to heterodox economics though variously focused (distributional issues, full employment, equivalence of non-pecuniary and non-remunerated work, justice, freedom, flourishing, etc.). Appropriately considered, therefore, ultimate concerns are implicit to all of the contributions that comprise this *Handbook*.

Conclusion

An edited collection inevitably confronts the challenge of how to appropriately frame what might otherwise appear to be disparate contributions. There is, however, a clear meta-theme to the *Handbook*. That is, to demarcate heterodox economics from the mainstream and establish (or confirm) it as an alternative, an alternative whose position within the world may be contrasted with much of the mainstream, but does not subsist parasitically in relation to that mainstream.

Arguably, there is more to heterodox economics than mere multiplicity beyond the mainstream. Heterodox economics recognizes a multiplicity of schools of thought and theories, but does so based on constructed community relations and a strong normative commitment to pluralism. Pluralism and community are possible because of shared elements of difference: a critical orientation within which methodological and philosophically posed inquiry are integral to theory building and applications, and where a process focus creates a continuous pressure to be real world referenced and relevant (subject sociologically also to a continuous engagement with the history of economic thought). Based on these combined characteristics heterodox economics is a living body of knowledge, it is critically aware and so continuously open to theoretical and conceptual change and interchange, and it is sensitive to the processes within the world that call forth new areas of research and theorization. It is in all these respects quite different to mainstream economics. Heterodox economics is conducive to change while the mainstream continuously resists change.

The mainstream is constrained by its social ontology, its sociology, its forms of theory, and its political positioning (not least its instrumentality). So, it is not that the mainstream does not change, it is more that it is problematically posed for change. However, it would not be appropriate to conclude the *Handbook* by dwelling on the mainstream. It is far more appropriate to emphasize what the *Handbook* has achieved—the quality and clarity of the individual contributions. Thereafter, it is most appropriate to state just why heterodox economics is needed. Heterodox economics is at core pro-social social science.[12] It does not evade but rather calls forth the most basic questions for economics: how can we meaningfully, justly, and sustainably live?

Acknowledgments

Thanks to Tony Lawson and Andrew Mearman for reading an earlier version of this chapter.

Notes

1 Political economy is a contested term. For a useful discussion of its meaning in relation to heterodox economics see Stilwell (2016).
2 Noting that this creates scope for counter-critique, which reverses the claim that the mainstream involves a relative unanimity of purpose, which translates into internal agreement, even if not consciously recognized at all times, regarding what is legitimately economics (heterodoxy operates according to the same rules). The heterodox response requires both a refusal to be a conservative disciplining of the discipline and a substantive claim to be demonstrably more adequate in knowledge terms (see later).
3 Lee's complete argument is slightly different in its enumerations than the one we pursue here and is best summarized via:

> In addition to pluralism, the identity of heterodox economists has three other components. The first is that the process of developing heterodox theory, engaging in applied work, and developing economic policies involves a critical engagement with their mainstream counterparts; the second is that the process of developing heterodox theory also involves an engagement with the history of economics; and the final component is that heterodox theory is fundamentally distinct from mainstream theory. Thus, heterodox economists value not just the right 'theory-applied work-policy' configuration but also how and why it is different from mainstream conclusions. Similarly, they value the historical understanding of how and why heterodox economics emerged and evolved; thus, the history of economics is considered indispensible to doing heterodox economics. Linked together, the two components make heterodox economists critically reflective, provide them with a sense of where they stand in the profession and why, and enable them to engage across paradigms as an important (perhaps necessary) way to develop heterodox economics. The four components of the heterodox orientation, irreducibly linked together, create an economist that is tolerant of alternative theories, open to cross-paradigm engagement, who values the history of economics, and is reflectively confident that heterodox economics is the best way to understand and affect the social provisioning process.
>
> *Lee 2012: 347*

4 'Significant part,' of course, invokes the issues of how and to what degree the mainstream is unitary and how and to what degree it changes—that is, bringing one back to the terms of debate created by Colander and others and disputed by Lee and various others.
5 But also his essay 'What is this 'School' called neoclassical economics?' which creates a different frame of reference (see Lawson 2015; Morgan 2015b).
6 This has not always been the case and this too is a matter of interest within the history of economic thought—for example, the role of Marshall explored by Neil Hart and many others.
7 Extending also to such issues as mixed methods, grounded theory, triangulation, etc. (see Lee & Cronin 2016).

8 The reverse is that at some point its over-emphasis becomes a distraction and this too has been a matter of critique (notably from Ben Fine). The point also extends to the development of alternative approaches to methodology and general underpinning social theory. For example, Geoff Hodgson, drawing on old institutionalism.

9 One finds this work in *Journal of Cultural Economy*, *Big Data & Society*, *Economy & Society*, and then in journals that publish across economic and organization issues with an interest in sociology and social theory (as well as digital economy), such as *Organization Studies*, *Human Relations*, *British Journal of Sociology*, and so forth. Julie Froud, Karel Williams, Adam Leaver, Hugh Wilmott, Ismael Al-Amoudi, John Latsis, and various others have made contributions here. Fred Lee & Bruce Cronin (2010) set out the position of various journals within economics, though not extending to all of the above.

10 Providing in some ways a recovery of the literary tradition in economics, though by no means reducible to this.

11 The technical point of departure is circularity: to determine the return on capital one requires first 'capital,' and such capital must already have aggregated what cannot really be conceived as a composite, and does so such that a return is already internal to the calculation (yet marginal productivity of capital claims to be an explanation of returns, not a simple imposed statement of what return relations are, idealized though that may be). Samuelson was to eventually acknowledge the incoherency of the basis of the position (effectively conceding defeat, though this then had no bearing on the subsequent development of mainstream economics).

12 The most appropriate way to establish this highly generalized point (and its contrast with the mainstream) is to explore the range of heterodox work, notably published in *Review of Social Economy*, *Review of Political Economy*, *Cambridge Journal of Economics*, *Journal of Economic Issues*, *Journal of Institutional Economics*, *Feminist Economics*, *Journal of Post Keynesian Economics*, *Historical Materialism*, and many more.

References

Arestis, P. & Sawyer, M. (eds.) 2011. *New Economics as Mainstream Economics*. Basingstoke, UK: Palgrave Macmillan.

Arnsperger, C. & Varoufakis, Y. 2006. 'What is neoclassical economics?' *Post-Autistic Economics Review*, 38: 1–8.

Barker, D. & Kuiper, E. (eds.) 2003. *Towards a Feminist Philosophy of Economics*. London: Routledge.

Birks, S. 2015. *40 Critical Pointers for Students of Economics*. London: WEA Books.

Blaug, M. 1992. *The Methodology of Economics or How Economists Explain*, 2nd edn. Cambridge: Cambridge University Press.

Boyer, R. 2013. 'The present crisis: a trump for a renewed political economy.' *Review of Political Economy*, 25 (1): 1–38.

Brown, A. & Fleetwood, S. (eds.) 2002. *Critical Realism and Marxism*. London: Routledge.

Caldwell, B. 1994. *Beyond Positivism: Economic Methodology in the Twentieth Century*, 2nd edn. London: Routledge.

Chester, L. & Schroeder, S. 2015. 'Conflation of IPE with heterodox economics? Intellectually negligent and damaging.' *Journal of Australian Political Economy*, 75: 153–176.

Chick, V. & Dow, S. 2005. 'The meaning of open systems.' *Journal of Economic Methodology*, 12 (3): 363–381.

Cohen, A. & Harcourt, G. 2003. 'Whatever happened to the Cambridge Capital Controversies?' *Journal of Economic Perspectives*, 17 (1): 199–214.

Colander, D. 2008. *The Making of an Economist, Redux*. Princeton, NJ: Princeton University Press.

Colander, D. 2009. *The Making of a European Economist*. Cheltenham, UK: Edward Elgar.

Colander, D., Holt, R., & Rosser Jr, B. 2004. 'The changing face of mainstream economics.' *Review of Political Economy*, 16 (4): 485–499.

Davis, J. 2003. *The Theory of the Individual in Economics*. London: Routledge.

Davis, J. 2006 'The turn in economics: neoclassical dominance to mainstream pluralism?' *Journal of Institutional Economics*, 2 (1): 1–20.

Davis, J. 2011 *Individuals and Identity in Economics*. New York: Cambridge University Press.

Davis, J. & Hands, W. 2013. 'Introduction: methodology, systemic risk and the economics profession.' *Journal of Economic Methodology*, 20 (1): 1–5.

DeMartino, G. 2013. 'Epistemic aspects of economic practice and the need for professional economic ethics.' *Review of Social Economy*, 71 (2): 166–186.

Dobusch, L. & Kapeller, J. 2012. 'Heterodox United versus Mainstream City? Sketching a framework for interested pluralism in economics.' *Journal of Economic Issues*, 46 (4): 1035–1057.

Dow, S. 1996. *The Methodology of Macroeconomic Thought: A Conceptual Analysis of Schools of Thought in Economics.* Cheltenham, UK: Edward Elgar.

Dow, S. 2004. 'Structured pluralism.' *Journal of Economic Methodology*, 11 (3): 275–290.

Dow, S. 2012. *Foundations for New Economic Thinking: A Collection of Essays.* Basingstoke, UK: Palgrave Macmillan.

Downward, P. (ed.) 2003. *Applied Economics and the Critical Realist Critique.* London: Routledge.

Fine, B. 2013. 'Economics: unfit for purpose.' *Review of Social Economy*, 71 (3): 373–389.

Fine, B. & Milonakis, D. 2009. *From Economics Imperialism to Freakonomics.* London: Routledge.

Fleetwood, S. (ed.) 1999. *Critical Realism in Economics: Development and Debate.* London: Routledge.

Folbre, N. 2009. *Greed, Lust and Gender: A History of Economic Ideas.* Oxford: Oxford University Press.

Fourcade, M., Ollion, E., & Algan, Y. 2015. 'The superiority of economists.' *Journal of Economic Perspectives*, 29 (1): 89–114.

Fukuda-Parr, S., Heintz, J., & Seguino, S. 2013. 'Critical perspectives on financial and economic crises: heterodox macroeconomics meets feminist economics.' *Feminist Economics*, 19 (3): 4–31.

Fullbrook, E. (ed.) 2009. *Ontology and Economics: Tony Lawson and His Critics.* London: Routledge.

Fullbrook, E. 2010. 'How to bring economics into the 3rd millennium by 2020.' *Real World Economics Review*, 54: 89–102.

Fullbrook, E. 2013. 'New paradigm economics.' *Real World Economics Review*, 65: 129–131.

Harcourt, G.C. 1972. *Some Cambridge Controversies in the Theory of Capital.* Cambridge: Cambridge University Press.

Harcourt, G.C. 2010. 'The crisis in mainstream economics.' *Real World Economics Review*, 53: 47–51.

Hausman, D. 1992. *The Inexact and Separate Science of Economics.* Cambridge: Cambridge University Press.

Hodgson, G. 2001. *How Economics Forgot History: The Problem of Historical Specificity in Social Science.* London: Routledge.

Hodgson, G. 2004. *The Evolution of Institutional Economics.* London: Routledge.

Hodgson, G. 2009. 'The Great Crash of 2008 and the reform of economics.' *Cambridge Journal of Economics*, 33 (6): 1205–1221.

Holt, R., Pressman, S., & Spash, C. (eds.) 2009. *Post-Keynesian and Ecological Economics: Confronting Environmental Issues.* Cheltenham, UK: Edward Elgar.

Jo, T.-H. 2011. 'Socio-provisioning process and socio-economic modeling.' *American Journal of Economics and Sociology*, 70 (5): 1094–1116.

Jo, T.-H. & Todorova, Z. (eds.) 2015. *Advancing the Frontiers of Heterodox Economics: Essays in Honor of Frederic S. Lee.* London: Routledge.

Keen, S. 2015. *Developing an Economics for the Post-Crisis World.* London: WEA Books.

King, J. 2002. *A History of Post Keynesian Economics since 1936.* Cheltenham, UK: Edward Elgar.

Lawson, C., Latsis, J., & Martins, N. (eds.) 2007. *Contributions to Social Ontology.* London: Routledge.

Lawson T. 1997. *Economics and Reality.* London: Routledge.

Lawson, T. 2003. *Reorienting Economics.* London: Routledge.

Lawson, T. 2015. *Essays on the State and Nature of Modern Economics.* London: Routledge.

Lee, F.S. 2009. *A History of Heterodox Economics: Challenging the Mainstream in the Twentieth Century.* London: Routledge.

Lee, F.S. 2012. 'Heterodox economics and its critics.' *Review of Political Economy*, 24 (2): 337–351.

Lee, F.S. & Cronin, B. 2010. 'Research quality rankings of heterodox economic journals in a contested discipline.' *American Journal of Economics and Sociology*, 69 (5): 1409–1452.

Lee, F.S. & Cronin, B. (eds.) 2016. *Handbook of Research Methods and Applications in Heterodox Economics.* Cheltenham, UK: Edward Elgar.

Lee, F.S., Pham, X., & Gu, G. 2013. 'The UK research assessment exercise and the narrowing of UK economics.' *Cambridge Journal of Economics*, 37 (4): 693–717.

Lewis, P. (ed.) 2004. *Transforming Economics.* London: Routledge.

Martins, N. 2014. *The Cambridge Revival of Political Economy.* London: Routledge.

May, A. 2002. 'The feminist challenge to economics.' *Challenge*, 45 (6): 45–69.

Mayhew, A. 2001. 'Human agency, cumulative causation, and the state.' *Journal of Economic Issues*, 35 (2): 239–250.

Mearman, A. 2012. 'Heterodox economics and the problem of classification.' *Journal of Economic Methodology*, 19 (4): 407–424.

Milonakis, D. & Fine, B. 2009. *From Political Economy to Economics*. London: Routledge.

Morgan, J. 2014. 'Necessary pluralism in the economics curriculum: the case for heterodoxy.' *Royal Economic Society Newsletter*, 167: 14–17.

Morgan, J. 2015a. 'Is economics responding to critique? What do the UK QAA subject benchmarks indicate?' *Review of Political Economy*, 27 (4): 518–538.

Morgan, J. (ed.) 2015b. *What is Neoclassical Economics? Debating the Origins, Meaning and Significance*. London: Routledge.

Morgan, J. 2015c. 'Piketty's calibration economics: inequality and the dissolution of solutions?' *Globalizations*, 12 (5): 803–823.

Morgan, J. 2016. 'The contemporary relevance of a Cambridge tradition: Economics as political economy, political economy as social theory and ethical theory.' *Cambridge Journal of Economics*, 40 (2): 663–700.

Nelson, J. 1996. *Feminism, Objectivity and Economics*. London: Routledge.

O'Hara, P. 2012. 'Core general principles of political economy.' *The Journal of Economic Analysis*, 3 (1): 1–24.

Palley, T. 2013. 'Gattopardo economics and the mainstream response of change that keeps things the same.' *European Journal of Economics and Economic Policies: Intervention*, 10 (2): 193–206.

Pivetti, M. 2015. 'Marx and the development of critical political economy.' *Review of Political Economy*, 27 (2): 134–153.

Pratten, S. (ed.) 2015. *Social Ontology and Modern Economics*. London: Routledge.

Pressman, S. 2015. *Understanding Piketty's Capital in the Twenty-First Century*. London: Routledge.

Ranson, B. 2007. 'Heterodox theoretical convergence: possibility or pipedream?' *Journal of Economic Issues*, 41 (1): 243–263.

Reardon, J., Madi, M., & Cato-Scott, M. 2015. *Introducing a New Economics: Pluralist, Sustainable and Progressive*. London: Pluto.

Sawyer, M. 2011. '"It" keeps happening: Post Keynesian views on the financial crisis and the great recession.' *History of Economic Ideas*, 19 (2): 149–164.

Spash, C. 2013. 'The shallow or the deep ecological economics movement?' *Ecological Economics*, 93: 351–362.

Starr, M. 2014. 'Qualitative and mixed-methods research in economics: surprising growth, promising future.' *Journal of Economic Surveys*, 28 (2): 238–264.

Stilwell, F. 2011. *Political Economy: The Contest of Economic Ideas*. Oxford: Oxford University Press.

Stilwell, F. 2016. 'Heterodox economics or political economy?' *World Economics Association Newsletter*, 6 (1): 2–6.

Thornton, T. 2015. 'The changing face of mainstream economics.' *Journal of Australian Political Economy*, 75: 11–26.

Van Staveren, I. 2015. *Economics After the Crisis: An Introduction to Economics from a Pluralist and Global Perspective*. London: Routledge.

Wray, R. 2015. *Modern Money Theory*. Basingstoke, UK: Palgrave Macmillan.

Index

Locators for figures are in *italics* and those for tables in **bold.**

full employment 483–4, 488; global production
335, 336; labor processes 350; large firms 474–80;
political independence 242–3
unpaid labor 121–2
Upadhyaya, Radha 259
use value: Marx 105–6; price theory 113
USSR *see* Soviet Union
Uzzi, Brian 258–9

valuation, instrumental 507–9
value chains, financialization 260; *see also* global
value chains (GVC) approach
value theory: accumulation regimes 58; ecological
economics 417; legal institutions 227–8; Marx
105–8; Ricardo 103–5; Smith 101–5, 109; social
surplus 49, 50; Sraffa 108–10; terminology
113–14; theoretical context 15, 101–11; *see also*
prices
variable capital 227–8
Veblen, Thorstein: capital 46, 51–2, 472–3, 477;
institutions 16–17, 164–5, 166, 173; interactive
agency 178, 185; legal institutions 234–5;
markets 214; political economy 32–3; price
theory 117; shadow banking 266; social control
501, 502; state 169, 170; systemism 155–6,
155–6; welfare 508
Vercelli, Alessandro 368
Verdoorn's Law: accumulation 308; trade 326
virtual money 239
voice option, heterodox research 13–14
volitional institutionalism 460–2
Volkswagen law 484
vulgar political economy 44
vulnerability: informal economy 281–3, 284; social
exclusion 295

wage employment 283, 284
wage fund 70
wages: accumulation 311, 315; accumulation
regimes 62–3; distribution 129–31, 134, 135–9;
economic fluctuations 362, 363; growth 376–7,
378–9; labor unions *481*, 481–3; minimum
wage 171, 493; social surplus 50
Washington Consensus 402–8
wealth, political economy 30
web of rules, labor processes 352–3, *353*
Weber, Max: accumulation 57; private ownership
473
welfare 22–3, 499–500; age as dependency
504–7; growth 381; informal economy 285;
instrumental valuation principle 507–9; micro-
macro link 153; neoliberalism 314–15; political
economy 502–4; social surplus 45, 47–9, 50–1;
state 467; Washington Consensus 404
Western Marxians 464
wholes (vs parts) 148–9
widow's cruse theory of profits 131
Williamson, John 402
Williamson, Oliver 163–4
Winnett, A. 422
worker ownership 466–7
World Bank: international development 410;
Washington Consensus 402, 407–8
World Overshoot Day 418
World Systems approaches 334–5
World Trade Organization (WTO) 328
World Wildlife Fund (WWF) 418
Wray, L. Randall 266, 490
Wright, Ian 138–9

zapovedniki 420–1

Taylor & Francis eBooks

Helping you to choose the right eBooks for your Library

Add Routledge titles to your library's digital collection today. Taylor and Francis ebooks contains over 50,000 titles in the Humanities, Social Sciences, Behavioural Sciences, Built Environment and Law.

Choose from a range of subject packages or create your own!

Benefits for you

» Free MARC records
» COUNTER-compliant usage statistics
» Flexible purchase and pricing options
» All titles DRM-free.

REQUEST YOUR FREE INSTITUTIONAL TRIAL TODAY

Free Trials Available
We offer free trials to qualifying academic, corporate and government customers.

Benefits for your user

» Off-site, anytime access via Athens or referring URL
» Print or copy pages or chapters
» Full content search
» Bookmark, highlight and annotate text
» Access to thousands of pages of quality research at the click of a button.

eCollections – Choose from over 30 subject eCollections, including:

Archaeology	Language Learning
Architecture	Law
Asian Studies	Literature
Business & Management	Media & Communication
Classical Studies	Middle East Studies
Construction	Music
Creative & Media Arts	Philosophy
Criminology & Criminal Justice	Planning
Economics	Politics
Education	Psychology & Mental Health
Energy	Religion
Engineering	Security
English Language & Linguistics	Social Work
Environment & Sustainability	Sociology
Geography	Sport
Health Studies	Theatre & Performance
History	Tourism, Hospitality & Events

For more information, pricing enquiries or to order a free trial, please contact your local sales team:
www.tandfebooks.com/page/sales